Instructor's Manual with Case Teaching Notes

STRATEGIC MANAGEMENT

A DYNAMIC PERSPECTIVE

Mason A. Carpenter
University of Wisconsin, Madison

Wm. Gerard Sanders
Brigham Young University

PEARSON

Prentice Hall

Upper Saddle River, New Jersey 07458

VP/Editorial Director: Jeff Shelstad
Senior Acquisitions Editor: David Parker
Assistant Editor : Denise Vaughn
Associate Director Manufacturing: Vincent Scelta
Production Editor & Buyer: Wanda Rockwell
Printer/Binder: Offset Paperback Manufacturers

10 9 8 7 6 5 4 3 2
ISBN 0-13-145653-9

CONTENTS

PREFACE

This instructor's manual (IM) provides you with suggestions and tools for teaching with Carpenter & Sanders, Strategic Management: A Dynamic Perspective, 1/e. In this preface you will find general suggestions on teaching with our text, along with sample syllabi outlines for undergraduate and MBA strategy courses (semester and quarter teaching contexts), and a syllabus that suggests how you might incorporate a simulation with the text. If you are teaching the course in an online context, paring the concepts-version of the text with a simulation is a viable model, and you might consider adapting the simulation syllabus for this purpose. The Preface is followed by specific Chapter guides that walk you through the purpose, key chapter points, case selection suggestions, possible answers to the end of chapter questions and exercises, supplemental experiential exercises, and appendices to support the chapter further when mentioned in the IM. The final sections of the IM contain case selection notes that link the strategy diamond and three text differentiators -- dynamic strategy, formulation/implementation, strategic leadership – to each case, followed by specific case teaching notes, and Part B cases, where appropriate.

GENERAL TEACHING SUGGESTIONS

Overview. Strategic management is a complex subject, but it is easy to make it seem too complex and abstract and needlessly detract from the students' learning environment. Keep in mind two teaching mantras – "frame it" and "rule of three." Used in combination in each session throughout the semester, they will help you have a stellar strategy course. The frame-it mantra means that you start each session with a road map of its learning objectives and frame the objectives in the context of the strategy formulation diamond and the implementation levers. The rule-of-three mantra simply refers to the fact that you will spell out three overarching learning objectives for the students in your session – you state these at the opening of the class, anchor them in the formulation and implementation frameworks, and close each session by showing how the students learned about those three key strategy topics. Obviously, each chapter has more than three learning objectives but you will see in the respective IM chapters that those multiple chapter objectives can be mapped to three overarching learning objectives (you can of course use your own logic to develop your rule-of-three for the chapters or follow the ones that we suggest).

Making a strong first impression. With the exception of an online course, we suggest that, regardless of class level, you start with some form of the following to set the tone and compass-heading for your strategy course.

Session 1: Use the first session to define the topic of strategy, as you plan to teach it, using an experiential exercise called Alaska Gold Mine (the case and teaching note are found at the end of this IM chapter). This short, two-part case gets the students quickly involved in your course and provides a useful reference point throughout the semester. It also allows you to avoid throwing away your first session because students have not yet read the material, beyond perhaps the course syllabus (at best!). The exercise takes about 30 minutes (though with limited time you can do it in 20 minutes and extended discussion can allow 45 or 60 minutes for the case). There is an ethical facet to the case that you can build on if that avenue is emphasized in your course. It is often useful to tie the Alaska Gold Mine to the Sears vs. Wal-Mart mini-case as the beginning of Chapter 1 – for instance, just as students group into clusters for the Alaska Gold Mine case, so too do firms cluster in something called strategic groups…Sears, JC Penney, and Macy's and Wal-Mart, K-Mart, and Target are examples of two groups in the retailing industry. The remainder of the class can be devoted to foreshadowing the topics that you intend to cover and your expectations about the students' performance in the class.

Session 2: This session can be built around a case to introduce the students further to the topics you will cover throughout the course of your class. For that reason, we recommend that you use any case that lets you touch on the broad array of concepts which strategy addresses. By the end of the session it will be very useful for the students if they can walk out of the classroom having completed the five elements of strategy and introduced the implementation framework we use in Chapter 11. By starting or finishing each session with some reference to one of these frameworks, always the five elements and others as appropriate, you provide continuity in your course and let the students see how much they have learned and are learning as the course progresses. The frameworks are also helpful summary or punctuation points throughout the semester where you can take 15 minutes at the start of a class to review what the students have learned and foreshadow what you will cover next.

At this point we note that the five elements and implementation framework provide students with two powerful tools for understanding a firm's strategy and the relationships between formulation and implementation. For single business firms and firms who have relatively little diversification the five elements model provides a concise way of viewing and talking about strategy. However, when firms become more diversified or are contemplating diversification moves that seem to test the parsimony of the five-elements model, we have found it useful to ask the students to think about the Arenas more broadly, as if they were Strategic Business Units for example, and the economic logic that allowed to operate within one firm – this is also a point where you can later show how implementation is a key part of realizing the economic logic of the diversified firm, and we treat both product and international market diversification as aspects of diversification. You will also see that the all the models, the five elements and implementation, map nicely to the notion of strategic coherence developed in Chapter 2.

SAMPLE SYLLABI

In this section, we provide the basic framework for a course syllabus and include schedules that accommodate both semester and quarter length courses.

Classroom-based courses. For courses where you will be working in a classroom setting, there are two significant differences in the balance between lecture and discussion, and topic breadth and depth between an undergraduate and graduate-level teaching environment. Your actions and grading should reflect these differences.

1. There is an adage that undergraduates are learning the strategic management vocabulary and that graduate students are mastering it. Therefore, when not discussing a case as the classroom activity, the balance between lecture and class discussion varies based on the audience. Undergraduate courses will generally entail more lecture time to present and review material than graduate courses. Many instructors find this split to approximate 60/40. In graduate courses this split is generally reversed as graduate students should be able to talk more in a strategy class since they should be bringing a greater level of outside experience to the course. Likewise, many instructors find that the debrief and review following a case discussion may entail more detail when teaching undergraduates. For these reasons the differences in the undergraduate and MBA course calendars are subtle, but intended to reinforce the different pedagogical needs of those respective audiences. But, these choices are a matter of style and preference.

2. Since undergraduates will be learning the subject matter, you should also find yourself covering more breadth in both your lectures and case discussions, and probably not exploring the interesting depths and nuances of most topics. This means that you will touch on more strategy vocabulary items to expose and let students exercise their meaning. In a graduate course, in contrast, you can expect that students to be more prepared and to have greater experiential context to relate the

material to, which will allow you to dig deeply into several key subjects that are relevant to the chapter(s) and the case, if a case is used.

Simulation-Based Courses: Simulations are popular with many strategy professors. This is because students, like all people, learn best when they use multiple learning approaches. And learning by doing, a key element of the simulation, helps most people learn in ways that lectures and case discussions do not. However, incorporating a simulation in your course entails significant tradeoffs (think of Porter's strategy tradeoffs). Consequently, if you use a simulation you will most likely not do as many cases, and you may elect not to cover some content. There are several ways to incorporate a simulation. The attached schedule only outlines one such option (a schedule that happens to work well for us). This schedule follows the logic of introducing course material before starting the simulation, then moving to a combination of chapter content, cases, and simulation in the latter two thirds of the semester. If you are on a quarter system then you will either need to drop a few years of the simulation, drop a few additional cases, or both.

Given that the broader subject matter is the same across undergraduate and graduate strategy course, the wording in syllabus introduction to these courses follows a common flow.

COURSE SYLLABUS

Sample Introductory Material For a Course Syllabus

Course Description: This is a learning-by-doing course. Through the combination of lectures, readings, experiential exercises, case studies, and class participation, this course introduces you to the tools and vocabulary prerequisite to critical and effective strategic analysis, thinking, and communication. *Strategy* is the central, integrated, externally oriented concept of how a firm will achieve its objectives. A strategy encompasses the pattern of organizational actions taken in pursuit of an advantage over its competitors. Or put another way, a strategy outlines how a firm will create unique value. The concepts in Strategic Management integrate the knowledge and skills you acquired in earlier courses so that you may apply them using the same multi-disciplinary perspective demanded of a general manager -- irrespective of the industry or position you are targeting for employment or advancement.

Course Objectives: In *Strategic Management* you will exercise and improve (1) your ability to think strategically, (2) your knowledge of, and ability to apply strategy tools and strategy vocabulary, (3) and your written and verbal communication skills. You can accomplish these objectives through careful reading of the syllabus and assignments, detailed case analyses, regular attendance and attentiveness to class lectures, and active participation in class discussions.

[If you are using a simulation, you will want a section like the following as well. How much weight you place on the simulation is debatable. We generally allocate enough points so that students take it seriously, but spread those points across several aspects of the simulation experience.]

Simulation-Based Courses: People learn best by doing. You will be assigned to a group that will compete against other groups in a computer-based strategy simulation. No matter how well your group does on the simulation, you will have a much better appreciation for the demands of running a business by the time the simulation is complete. Do not underestimate the simulation, neither its time demands nor its impact on your grade. The simulation is time consuming and difficult. It requires teamwork and rigorous analysis. If you take the simulation seriously, you will learn a great deal and you will have fun in the process. The simulation will allow you to experiment with strategic concepts, as well as basic business skills that you should have acquired in your other classes (e.g., finance, marketing, operations).

The simulation is worth 40% of your grade. You will be graded on four aspects of the simulation: (1) your written objectives and intended strategy (5%), (2) your score on a pre-test that covers the instructions in the student manual (5%), (3) how well your "firm" performs over the course of the simulation (15%), (4) your individual participation on the team as judged by your peers and as reflected in the simulation logs (5%), and (5) a written (and for a few lucky teams, an oral) presentation to your "board of directors" which demonstrates your learning and justifies your further existence and job security (10%). More details on each aspect will be delivered in class. Please note that the 15% of your grade that is based on your team's performance is enough weight to be a significant carrot, but it is not so great that the simulation determines your overall grade. It is possible to be on the worst performing simulation team and still receive an "A"s in the course. However, it is much easier to get an A if your team performs fairly well in the simulation.

Because the simulation is time consuming and requires group work, I allocate a significant amount of class time to group work. This time is noted on the attached calendar as Simulation Lab time. I have provided these days to help facilitate group meetings. [n.b. During lab time, I will always show up in class for team consultation.] It is unlikely that you will be successful in the simulation if you only use the time I provide; you will need some time devoted to the simulation outside of class (certainly for individual work, but perhaps for team work as well). More information on the simulation will be provided in class.

As long as each team demonstrates concerted effort to compete and succeed, the grade distribution for the performance part of the simulation grade will be A, A-, B+, B, B-. (i.e., if you manage to go bankrupt, you will not receive the real world equivalent grade). Instructions for how to register for the simulation will be provided in class.

CALENDARS

[No simulation]

16-Week Undergraduate Strategic Management (Semester – two 75-minute sessions per week)

Session	Assignment
1	Alaska Gold Mine Case (distributed in class) and Syllabus
2	Chapter 1
3	Case: Kmart: Fall of a retailing giant
	Chapter 2
4	Case: Trilogy Farm OR Charlotte Beers
5	Chapter 3
6	Case: The Formula One Constructors OR Prince Edward Island Preserve
7	Chapter 4
8	Case: Carrefour vs. WalMart OR Chinese Fireworks Industry
9	Chapter 5
10	Case: Home Depot's Strategy Under Robert Nardelli OR Ryan Air
11	Chapter 6
12	Case: Advanced Micro Devices OR Airbus: From Challenger to Leaders
13	Review of What We Learned from Chapters 1-6
14	Midterm – Individual
15	Chapter 7
16	Case: McDonald's McCafe Initiative OR Moving TATA Consultancy Services into the Global Top 10
17	Chapter 8
18	Case: Coca-Cola's Reentry and Growth Strategies in China OR revisiting Carrefour vs. WalMart
19	Chapter 9
20	Case: Neilson International in Mexico (A) OR Fuji Xerox
21	Chapter 10
22	Case: Cisco Systems OR The HP-Compaq Merger
23	Chapter 11
24	Case: Porsche OR Holsim
25	Chapter 12
26	Case: Blue Whale Moving OR Reviving Iridium
27	Chapter 13
28	Case: Trouble in the Magic Kingdom OR Daimler Chrysler Corporate Governance in a Global Company
29	Review of What We Know About Strategic Management
30	Group Case Presentations*
31	Group Case Presentations
32	Cumulative Final - Individual

*You can determine if teams present their strategic assessment and recommendations for the same company or different firms.

10-Week Undergraduate Strategic Management (Quarter or module – two 75-minute sessions per week)

Session	Assignment
1	Alaska Gold Mine Case (distributed in class) and Syllabus
2	Chapters 1 & 2
3	Case: Trilogy Farm OR Charlotte Beers
4	Chapter 3
5	Case: The Formula One Constructors OR Prince Edward Island Preserve
6	Chapter 4
7	Case: Carrefour vs. WalMart OR Chinese Fireworks Industry
8	Chapter 5
9	Case: Home Depot's Strategy Under Robert Nardelli OR Ryan Air
10	Midterm – Individual
11	Chapter 6
12	Case: Advanced Micro Devices OR Airbus: From Challenger to Leaders
13	Chapters 7 & 8
14	Case: McDonald's McCafe Initiative; Moving TATA Consultancy Services into the Global Top 10; OR revisiting Carrefour vs. WalMart
15	Chapter 9
16	Case: Neilson International in Mexico (A) OR Fuji Xerox
17	Chapters 10 & 11
18	Case: Cisco Systems
19	Review of What We Know About Strategic Management
20	Cumulative Final - Individual

MBA Strategic Management (Semester)

Session	Assignment
1	Alaska Gold Mine Case (distributed in class) and Syllabus
2	Chapter 1
3	Chapter 2
4	Case: Trilogy Farm OR Charlotte Beers at Ogilvy and Mather
5	Chapters 3 & 4
6	Case: The Formula One Constructors OR Prince Edward Island Preserve
7	Case: Carrefour vs. WalMart OR Chinese Fireworks Industry
8	Chapter 5 and Carrfour vs. WalMart OR Chinese Fireworks Industry
9	Case: Home Depot OR Ryan Air: The Southwest of European Airlines
10	Chapter 6
11	Case: Advance Micro Devises OR Airbus: From Challenger to Leader
12	Midterm – Individual (Typically a case analysis)
13	Review of What We Learned from Chapters 1-6
14	Chapter 7
15	Case: McDonald's McCafe Initiative OR Moving TATA Consultancy
16	Chapter 8
17	Case: Revisting Carrefour vs. WalMart OR other earlier global firm case
18	Chapter 9
19	Case: Fuji Xerox OR Neilson International in Mexico (A)
20	Chapter 10
21	Case: H-P Compaq OR Cisco Systems
22	Chapter 11
23	Case: Cisco Systems OR Blue Whale Moving OR Holcim OR Porsche
24	Chapter 12
25	Case: Blue Whale Moving OR Reviving Iridium
26	Chapter 13
27	Case: Daimler Chrysler OR Trouble in the Magic Kingdom
28	Review of What We Know About Strategic Management
29	Group Case Presentations*
30	Group Case Presentations
31	Group Case Presentations
32	Cumulative Final – Individual (Typically a case)

*You can determine if teams present their strategic assessment and recommendations for the same company or different firms.

MBA Strategic Management (Quarter)

Session	Assignment
1	Alaska Gold Mine Case (distributed in class) and Syllabus
2	Chapters 1 & 2
3	Case: Trilogy Farm OR Charlotte Beers
4	Chapter 3
5	Case: The Formula One Constructors OR Prince Edward Island Preserve
6	Chapter 4
7	Case: Carrefour vs. WalMart OR Chinese Fireworks Industry
8	Chapter 5
9	Case: Home Depot OR Ryan Air: The Southwest of European Airlines
10	Chapter 6
11	Case: Advanced Micro Devices OR Airbus: From Challenger to Leader
12	Midterm – Individual
13	Chapter 7 and Case: McDonald's McCafe Initiative OR Moving TATA Consultancy
14	Chapter 8 and prior global firm case
15	Case: Carrefour vs. WalMart OR Coca Cola's Reentry and Growth in China
16	Chapter 9
17	Case: Fuji Xerox OR Neilson International in Mexico (A)
18	Chapters 10 & 11
19	Case: Cisco Systems OR prior case involving M&A
20	Cumulative Final - Individual

Undergraduate or MBA Strategic Management (Semester)

[with a simulation]

Session	Assignment
1	Alaska Gold Mine
2	Chapter 1
3	Chapter 2
4	Introduction to simulation
5	Case: Trilogy Farm OR Charlotte Beers
6	Chapter 3
7	Lab time Simulation practice round 1 due
8	Case: The Formula One Constructors OR Prince Edward Island Preserve
9	Lab time Simulation practice round 2 due
10	Chapter 4
11	Lab time Simulation practice round 3 due
12	Case: Carrefour vs. WalMart OR Chinese Fireworks Industry
13	Chapter 5
14	Home Depot's Strategy Under Robert Nardelli OR Ryan Air
15	Lab time Simulation competition round 1 due
16	Chapter 6
17	Midterm – Individual
18	Lab time Simulation competition round 2 due
19	Chapter 7
20	Lab time Simulation competition round 3 due
21	Chapter 8
22	Lab time Simulation competition round 4 due
23	Chapter 9
24	Lab time Simulation competition round 5 due
25	Chapter 10
26	Lab time Simulation competition round 6 due
27	Chapter 12
28	Case: Blue Whale Moving OR Reviving Iridium
29	Simulation Board meetings
30	Chapter 13 Case: Trouble in the Magic Kingdom OR Daimler Chrysler Corporate Governance in a Global Company
31	Review of What We Know About Strategic Management
32	Cumulative Final - Individual

PART ONE
STRATEGY AND STRATEGIC
LEADERSHIP IN DYNAMIC TIMES

CHAPTER 1 – INTRODUCING
STRATEGIC MANAGEMENT

I. PURPOSE OF THE CHAPTER

After studying this chapter, students should be able to:

1. Understand what a *strategy* is and identify the difference between business-level and corporate-level strategy.
2. Understand the relationship between *strategy formulation* and *strategy implementation*.
3. Describe the determinants of *competitive advantage*.
4. Recognize the difference between a *temporary* and a *dynamic competitive advantage*.
5. Understand why we study *strategic management*.

The opening chapter identifies the components of strategy that we will work through in this text; you can use it to set the stage for your course plan. The text is organized to deliver an integrated perspective of strategy—(1) positional and dynamic advantages, (2) formulation and implementation, and (3) strategic leadership.

If you have 75-minute sessions, you will probably find it useful to spend the first two class sessions working around Chapter 1 or an integration of Chapters 1 and 2. The first session introduce students to the broader topic, whereas the second lets you use a regular case to walk through the different dimensions that you will touch on. Your two teaching objectives should be (1) to have the students gain some general familiarity with the "What is strategy" question and (2) be able to clearly answer the "Why we study strategy" question.

In this chapter, the three differentiators are introduced on page 7. The differentiators, and hence your teaching approach for the chapter, are manifested in the following ways:

- **Dynamic strategy.** Starting with the opening vignette on Sears versus Wal-Mart, students are made aware of how dynamic competitive environments can be. Three facets of dynamism are introduced in Chapter 1: (1) change may be rapid and incessant, (2) change may be slow and punctuated (as shown in the opening vignette), and (3) change is inevitable. Also, early in the chapter the students are introduced to the staging facet of the strategy diamond (see Exhibit 1.4 and "How Would You Do That? 1.1" on the strategy diamond at JetBlue), which again reinforces that good strategies inherently anticipate and foster change. With this foundation in place, students are well prepared to understand that they will need to learn about snapshot and dynamic perspectives of strategic management. The chapter closes with a section on recognizing the difference between the fundamental (snapshot) and dynamic views of competitive advantage.
- **Formulation and implementation interdependency.** The opening vignette also gives students some sense of this interdependency. Students see that Wal-Mart's initial strategy led it to put particular implementation levers and capabilities into place, which in turn fueled the dynamo

1

strategy we see today. This interdependence in Wal-Mart's strategy is reiterated on page 10, at the start of the section "Strategy Formulation and Implementation." In the section "Strategy Implementation Levers," students further see this interdependency when they are introduced to the intended versus realized and emergent strategy contexts (summarized in Exhibit 1.6).

- **Strategic leadership.** Again, strategic leadership is introduced on page 7 as one of the three differentiating features of the text, and the students see the imprint of leadership on the strategies of Sears and Wal-Mart through the opening vignette. The chapter quickly moves into strategy from the strategic leader's perspective, which further reinforces this role. The specific roles of strategic leadership in formulation and implementation are then spelled out in the "Strategy Formulation and Implementation" section, and summarized in Exhibit 1.6.

Additional Readings:

Andrews, K. (1987). *The concept of corporate strategy*. New York: Dow Jones-Irwin.

Hambrick, D. C., and A. Cannella. (1989). Strategy implementation as substance and selling. *Academy of Management Executive 3*(4), 278–285.

Hambrick, D. C., and J. W. Fredrickson. (2001). Are you sure you have a strategy? *Academy of Management Executive, 15*(4), 48–59.

II.   BRIEF CHAPTER OUTLINE

pp. 2–7, PPT #1–5	**Chapter 1 Introduction** The purpose is to introduce the strategy diamond and the five elements framework and present the three major themes of this text: (1) the dynamic nature of firms and industries, (2) strategy formulation and implementation inextricable connection; , and (3) strategic leadership. **Opening Vignette:** A Tale of Two Stores, pp. 3–6 Ex. 1.1 Two Retailers at a Glance; Ex. 1.2 Sears & Wal-Mart: A Financial Comparison	
pp. 7–10, PPT #6–14	**WHAT IS STRATEGIC MANAGEMENT?** • The process by which a firm manages the formulation and implementation of strategy. **Why Study Strategy?** • Better employee understanding of a firm's strategy means better implementation of strategic initiatives. **What Is Strategy?** • Encompasses the pattern of organizational actions taken to pursue an advantage over its competitors. **Business and Corporate Strategy** Firms focus business activities in one or very few industries to many unrelated industries; various levels of diversification span the spectrum from these extremes. p. 8, e.g., Rolls Royce versus GE in the aircraft engine industry **Business Strategy** refers to how a firm will compete with current and future rivals within an industry. Two critical questions are (1) how it will achieve its objectives *today* when competitors may be present and (2) how it plans to compete *in the future*. **Corporate Strategy** addresses three questions:	p. 9, Ex. 1.3 The Strategic Management Process

2

	1. What business will we compete in? 2. How can a corporate parent add value to our businesses? 3. How will diversification help a firm compete in its other industries?	
pp. 10–11, PPT #15–19 pp. 11–15	**Strategy Formulation and Implementation** • Strategy formulation is deciding what to do; strategy implementation is performing the activities to carry out the strategy. Strategy formulation and implementation are iterative and interdependent; need consistent and coherent set of elements between the two. Strategy solves problems external and internal to the firm. **Strategy Formulation** can be the result of a rational and methodical planning process or emerge over time. p. 10, e.g., Emergence of Intel's DRAM chips in the 1970s and 1980s **The Strategy Diamond and The Five Elements of Strategy** A strategy consists of an integrated set of choices that can be categorized into five related elements: **1. Arenas: Where will we be active?** Arenas encompass products, channels, market segments, geographic areas, technologies, and stages in the value-creation process. p. 12, e.g., outsourcing of production by Pacific Cycle and Nike **2. Vehicles: How will we get there?** Vehicles provide the means for participating in the targeted arenas (acquisitions, internal development, joint ventures, etc.). **3. Differentiators: How will we win the marketplace?** Differentiators are features and attributes of a company's product or service that help it beat its competitors in the marketplace. The best strategies combine several differentiators. Critical factors in selecting differentiators are (1) making decisions early and (2) identifying and executing successful differentiators means making tough choices. **4. Staging: What will be our speed and sequence of moves?** *Staging* refers to the timing and pacing of strategic moves, which depends on resources, including cash, human capital, and knowledge, or other considerations, such as urgency, credibility, and need for early wins. p. 14, e.g., Salt Lake City Olympics turnaround to establish credibility **5. Economic logic: how will we obtain our returns?** Economic logic reflects the fact that the four other elements must be aligned for the firm to generate positive returns above its cost of capital. **Strategy Implementation Levers** Strategy implementation is taking the actions that put the strategy into effect and ensuring that organizational decisions are consistent with it. It encompasses the refinement, or change, of a strategy as the amount of information increases. The goal of implementation is twofold: 1. To ensure that strategy formulation is comprehensive and well informed 2. To translate good ideas into actions that can be executed	*p. 11, *Fig. 1.1 Rolls Royce Jet Engines* p. 9, Ex. 1.3 The Strategic Management Process p. 12, Ex. 1.4 The Business Strategy Diamond *p. 13, *Fig. 1.2 Pacific Cycles' Arenas* pp. 16–17, *1.1 How Would You Do That? The Five Elements of Strategy at Jet Blue,* p. 16, Ex. 1.5 JetBlue and Its Industry
pp. 17–19		p. 18, Ex. 1.6 Implementation Framework

	The processes of strategy formulation and strategy implementation are linked inextricably. The five elements of strategy are related to both formulation and implementation. Organization leaders use levers from three broad categories to implement strategies: 1. Organization structure 2. Systems and processes 3. People and rewards	
p. 19, PPT #18	**STRATEGIC LEADERSHIP** Strategic leadership plays two critical roles: 1. Making substantive resource allocation decisions 2. Developing support for the strategy from key stakeholders	
p. 19, PPT #21	**WHAT IS COMPETITIVE ADVANTAGE?** • Defined as a firm being able to create value in a way that its rivals can't. Firm performance is not a competitive advantage, but a result of it.	
pp. 19–22, PPT #22	**DETERMINANTS OF COMPETITIVE ADVANTAGE** Two primary perspectives: 1. The *internal perspective* focuses on firms and potential internal sources of uniqueness. 2. The *external perspective* focuses on the structure of industries and the ways in which firms can position themselves within them for competitive advantage. *Dynamic strategy*, a third view, bridges the two perspectives by seeking to explain why competitive advantage does not typically last over long periods of time. **Internal Perspective** The resource-based view of the firm suggests that firms are heterogeneous bundles of resources and capabilities; superior resources and capabilities provide a competitive advantage relative to other firms. **External Perspective** Based on industrial/organizational (I/O) economics; the external perspective views competitive advantage as resulting from positioning in the business environment. Firms should (1) compete in attractive industries or (2) adopt strategies to increase the attractiveness of current industries. **Fundamental Versus Dynamic Perspectives** Competitive advantage is more likely to endure in stable markets, but it can be brief in unstable ones. p. 20, e.g., Global chocolate industry with M&M/Mars, Nestle, and Hershey is relatively stable. **The Dynamic Perspective** suggests that current market position is not an accurate predictor of future performance because market position is an outcome of past activities. The past has clues to explain a firm's current position and support efforts to predict the future competitive landscape.	

	The External Dimension of the Dynamic Perspective is useful in analyzing "high-velocity" markets and multimarket competition; changing technology and globalization contribute to these competitive dynamics. **The Internal Dimension of the Dynamic Perspective** focuses on resources and capabilities, especially ones leading to a flow of advantages in resources or market position and those that strengthen continuous and sometimes disruptive change.	

*Figure or Exhibit **NOT** enumerated in the PDF file.

III.   SUGGESTED CASES TO ACCOMPANY TEXT

Regardless of whether you have the concepts-with-cases or concepts-only version of the text, we suggest you use the "Alaska Gold Mine" case (Parts A and B) in your first or second session. This case and teaching note points can be found in the appendix of this IM chapter. PowerPoint slides to support the case are also provided. The second case provided in the concepts-with-cases version is "Kmart: Fall of a Retailing Giant." The students will already be familiar with retailing from the opening chapter vignette on Sears versus Wal-Mart.

Beyond this short case, we recommend cases that get students thinking about the three themes they will see throughout the book. Retailing cases are good because they provide a nice tie-in with the opening vignette about Sears and Wal-Mart, and you can frame the retailing-case company in that context. An objective of any case is to have the students try to summarize the firm's strategy using the strategy diamond. Any formal case you use can be employed in a similar manner. We have also found it can be useful to use the same case for Chapter 1 that we use for Chapter 4 (external environment), to show the students how much they have learned about strategy (the Carrefour versus Wal-Mart case is provided for Chapter 4, for instance). This latter approach allows them to contrast the strategy diamond they develop from Chapter 1 with one they develop after being exposed to vision and mission (Chapter 2), the internal environment (Chapter 3), and the external environment (Chapter 4).

Need help selecting cases? Pearson Prentice Hall and Pearson Custom Publishing are pleased to present the ultimate resource for creating and customizing case books.

- Start with a CaseMap correlated to your text or start from scratch; do it yourself using our easy-to-use interface or collaborate with a developmental editor.
- Cases can be selected from a variety of sources, including Harvard Business School Publishing, Darden, Ivey, Thunderbird, and NACRA.
- We clear permissions for you on cases and content not in the database.
- You can also create custom course packs by adding articles, original material, and textbook chapters.
- Pearson Custom case books can be delivered in print or online.
- Additionally, we supply you, the instructor, with a free evaluation copy delivered 7 to 10 days after you create your book, free access to teaching notes, and case-method teaching resources.

We're here to help: Looking for a case on a specific topic, company, country, or scenario? Or looking for a new case to substitute for one you've used in the past? We will help you find the right cases for your course and help you create a casebook that meets all your teaching needs. For guidance on building a casebook to reflect your course needs, e-mail our editorial consultant at: customcases@prenhall.com.

Visit www.prenhall.com/custombusiness for more information and to see which Prentice Hall titles are available for short-run customization and to view suggested cases. To start your own straightforward search for material:

Step 1: Select "search content and create your book" and log in.
Step 2: Search by case number or keyword or browse by discipline to find suggested cases based on the book you use or course you teach.
Step 3: Browse, preview, and select the cases, articles, or chapters you wish to include (you will see that price and page count of the book in the top right-hand corner of the screen as you "build" the book).
Step 4: Finalize your selections, get them in the order you want, package your customized book with any Prentice Hall title for a discount (if you wish), click "confirm book," and you have the option to request a free evaluation copy.
Step 5: The Web site immediately gives you the ISBN of your custom book. You should give this ISBN to your bookstore; they will use it to place their order with us.

Beyond our cases and Pearson Custom Publishing, if you choose to compile your own casebook you will have an opportunity to draw from a variety of sources. These sources include going direct to Hartwick Leadership Cases, IVEY Case Publishing, European Case Clearing House (ECCH), Harvard Business School (HBS), Darden, and others.

Given the popularity of Harvard cases, we have selected these additional cases for use with this chapter:

		ID#	Pages	TN
Yahoo!: Business on Internet Time	HBSP	9-700-013	27	Y
Executive Decision Making at General Motors	HBSP	9-305-026	21	N

Yahoo!: Business on Internet Time In the wake of major competitive moves, CEO Tim Koogle and his senior team at Yahoo!, an Internet portal, must decide whether and how to adjust their strategy. Following deals between AOL and Netscape, Excite and @Home, Infoseek and Disney, and Snap and NBS, Yahoo! faces the prospect of being the last portal without a significant partner. Students must grapple with the benefits and costs of integration in the rapidly changing world of the Internet. Teaching Purpose: Examines how a company organizes itself to formulate strategy in the midst of rapid environmental change. Reveals how external turbulence puts new pressures on a firm's strategy, its organizational structure, and its managers. Considers how one successful company has structured itself to cope with severe environmental uncertainty. Special emphasis is given to the interactions among Yahoo!'s functions and the effects of those interactions on firm flexibility. Also permits students to examine the structural attractiveness of the portal industry and the strength of Yahoo!'s position in the industry.

Executive Decision Making at General Motors Describes the evolution of General Motors' strategy, organizational structure, and management processes from its founding to the present day. Focuses on the role of GM's management committee—the senior-most decision-making body at the company, now called the Automotive Strategy Board (ASB)—and how it operates under Rick Wagoner, its current CEO. In October 2004, Wagoner and the ASB were wrestling with recent changes in GM's planning and budgeting processes and how they would affect the balance between global and local needs. Teaching Purpose: Students explore issues of executive decision making in a complex, global, matrixed organization. Case focuses on the role of the management committee and discusses the range of decisions senior teams must manage, the mechanics that make such teams effective, and the challenges of working within a matrixed organization. It also explores the relationship among strategy, structure, and management processes.

IV.   LINKING THE CHAPTER TO A COMPUTER SIMULATION

Because of the integrated nature of the text, you have ample opportunity to tie in a strategy simulation such as CapSim (www.capsim.com) or Mikes Bikes (www.smartsims.com). A number of other simulations are referenced at:

http://instruction.bus.wisc.edu/mcarpenter/PROFESSIONAL/Toolkit/bpstools.htm.

Many instructors that we have surveyed report that they start the simulation only after working through the business strategy chapters of the text, sometimes with and sometimes without cases. An example of a syllabus for a course incorporating the simulation is provided in the sample syllabus section.

V.   END OF CHAPTER ANSWER GUIDE

Discussion Questions

1.   What is strategic management?

Guide: Strategic management is the process by which a firm manages the formulation and implementation of its strategy. The word *strategy* is derived from the Greek word *strategos*, which roughly translated means "the general's view." In a business context, strategy is likewise about the general's view, the general's plan, and the general's ability to marshal the successful deployment of resources and capabilities in a competitive environment in a manner that leads to success. Just as a military general is responsible for all strategic and tactical decisions, so, too, a business general manager is charged with taking an overall view of the firm.

2.   What are the key components of the strategic management process?

Guide: This is where you want the students to be able to map out the components of Exhibit 1.3 and have a general understanding of how the pieces fit together. The components are vision and mission, goals and objectives, strategy, strategic analysis, and implementation.

3.   How does business strategy differ from corporate strategy?

Guide: Business strategy deals with questions about how a firm will compete against its present and future rivals within an industry or within one or more particular segments of an industry. Corporate strategy addresses the set of issues related to three fundamental questions: (1) In what businesses will we compete? (2) How does the corporate parent add value to its various lines of business? (3) How does diversification or our entry into this industry or business help us compete better in our other businesses?

4.   What is the relationship between strategy formulation and strategy implementation?

Guide: Strategy formulation is *deciding what to do,* whereas strategy implementation is all that goes into *doing what has been planned.* Neither formulation nor implementation can succeed without the other. For this reason, the processes of formulation and implementation are iterative and interdependent, with the objective being a consistent and coherent set of elements.

5. What five elements comprise the strategy formulation diamond?

Guide: The five elements managers use to formulate their strategy are those regarding arenas, vehicles, differentiators, staging, and economic logic. Answers to the questions about each of these elements will help managers determine whether a strategy is an integrated whole and identify areas in which a strategy may need to be amended or overhauled.

6. What are the internal and external perspectives of competitive advantage?

Guide: The internal perspective of competitive advantage—usually referred to as the resource-based view of the firm—postulates that firms are heterogeneous bundles of resources and capabilities. That is, firms are not clones of each other in terms of what resources they own or have access to and they have varying degrees of capability to do different economic tasks. As a result, firms with superior resources and capabilities are in a position of competitive advantage relative to other firms. The external perspective of competitive advantage asserts that variations in firm competitive advantage and performance are primarily a function of industry attractiveness. That is, industries have different structural features that determine the ease with which firms earn high levels of performance or are confined to lackluster performance. In addition, various segments of an industry may be more attractive than other segments, which accounts for variation in profits within industries.

7. What are the fundamental and dynamic perspectives of competitive advantage?

Guide: The fundamental perspective considers strategy in relatively stable environments. From this perspective, managers can take a snapshot of the firm and its environment and develop and implement strategy based on that snapshot. The dynamic perspective assumes that a firm's current market position is not an accurate predictor of future performance, because position itself is not a competitive advantage. Instead, the dynamic perspective looks to the both the past for clues about how the firm arrived at its present position and to the future to divine what the new competitive landscape might look like or what the firm wants it to look like. The dynamic strategy perspective has external and internal facets as well.

8. Why should you study strategic management?

Guide: It is important to study strategy because firm performance is affected directly by strategy and the firm's ability to implement it. Given its relationship to firm performance, strategy development and implementation preoccupies the attention of top executives. Through the firm's strategy, the goal of the executives is to make sure that overall firm performance is more than simply the sum of the firm's parts. By addressing all parts of the firm, strategy is an integrative topic. A good strategy will inform and touch on all functional areas in a firm, such as marketing, finance, accounting, and operations.

How Would You Do That?

9. Go to Warren Buffet's Letter to Shareholder's page at www.berkshirehathaway.com/letters/letters.html and read the most recent letter. How many of the strategy topics covered in this chapter can you find references to in the letter? Pick one of the businesses owned by Berkshire Hathaway and draft a strategy formulation diamond model for it similar to the one outlined in the JetBlue example in "How Would You Do That? 1.1."

Guide: This exercise in intended to help students develop a better hands-on understanding of the diamond model and how the pieces fit together. Because Berkshire is so diversified, you can pick a firm in an industry you are familiar with and develop a detailed diamond model based on it. Buffet tends to provide the most emphasis to the element of economic logic. This is particularly helpful because this element is often the most difficult for students to comprehend.

10. Go back to the discussion of JetBlue example in "How Would You Do That? 1.1." Use the strategy implementation model in Exhibit 1.6 to identify what would be necessary to successfully implement JetBlue's strategy. How would the implementation levers be different in JetBlue than in some of the major airlines?

Guide: As with the prior "How Would You Do That?" this exercise lets the students try their hand at implementation. A highly desirable outcome is being able to point out how implementation and formulation are interdependent and interrelated. This exercise also lets you show them how they, as future business leaders, fit into strategy implementation.

Group Activities

11. Identify the characteristics of a firm that the members of your group would like to work for and try to identify an example of this type of firm. What's the difference between business and corporate strategy at this firm? How might that affect your experiences and opportunities in that organization? Use your knowledge of the firm's strategy to construct a high-impact job application cover letter to apply for a job with this firm.

Guide: This simple exercise is effective at helping students see the differences and relationships between business and corporate strategy. You can link this question to an end of the semester closing dialogue in which you ask students to describe the business and corporate strategies of a firm they identified in the first session and then show them how much they have learned since that time.

12. How is international expansion related to business and corporate strategy? Identify a firm that may be thinking of expanding into new international markets. Apply the staging element of the strategy diamond to the firm's international expansion opportunities or plans. Which markets should it target first and why?

Guide: This question further drills the definition of business and corporate strategy so that students see that international expansion, even for a single business firm, can be considered part of the corporate strategy because it addresses "what businesses and markets we compete in." You can also tie geographic locations to the arenas, staging, and economic logic elements of strategy. You might ask the students how much geographic diversification limits the "differentiators" in how well they can be extended from one country to another. Finally, you can also show how implementation is key to connecting the dots when arenas are separated by great geographic and cultural distance, as well as the difficulty of identifying ideal nondomestic markets.

VI. SUPPLEMENTAL EXPERIENTIAL EXERCISES

These exercises are drawn with permission from the Strategy Teaching Tool-kit found at:

http://instruction.bus.wisc.edu/mcarpenter/PROFESSIONAL/Toolkit/bpstools.htm

1. In the appendix, we provide a copy of the Tolerance for Ambiguity Scale that students will find in Chapter 2. Instructors have found that they can use the results of this scale to tell students why and how they may respond in situations defined as strategic; that is, situations characterized by high uncertainty and lack of information. You can also use these results to help students understand their

response to the case-study method, because individuals with a high-tolerance for ambiguity tend to be comfortable making decisions with less or little information (typical of a case), whereas intolerant individuals always want more information. You can also point out the benefits of teams composed of individuals with differing tolerances, because a heterogeneous team will be less likely to rush to judgment (i.e., take unreasonable risks) or suffer from paralysis of analysis. After all, strategy is about reasoned risk taking and taking action in the face of uncertainty.

2. The "Alaska Gold Mine" case is provided in the appendix along with a teaching note for this case. As explained there, this is an ideal and easy-to-run case that requires no preparation but frames the course context well.

VII. APPENDICES

Tolerance of Ambiguity Scale

Please respond to the following statements by indicating the extent to which you agree or disagree with them. Fill in the blanks with the number from the rating scale that best represents your evaluation of the item. The scoring key is attached.

1	Strongly disagree	5	Slightly agree
2	Moderately disagree	6	Moderately agree
3	Slightly disagree	7	Strongly agree
4	Neither agree or disagree		

_____ 1. An expert who doesn't come up with a definite answer probably doesn't know too much.

_____ 2. I would like to live in a foreign country for a while.

_____ 3. There is really no such thing as a problem that can't be solved.

_____ 4. People who fit their lives to a schedule probably miss most of the joy of living.

_____ 5. A good job is one where what is to be done and how it is to be done are always clear.

_____ 6. It is more fun to tackle a complicated problem than to solve a simple one.

_____ 7. In the long run, it is possible to get more done by tackling small, simple problems rather than large and complicated ones.

_____ 8. Often the most interesting and stimulating people are those who don't mind being different and original.

_____ 9. What we are used to is always preferable to what is unfamiliar.

_____ 10. People who insist upon a yes or no answer just don't know how complicated things really are.

_____ 11. A person who leads an even, regular life in which few surprises or unexpected happenings arise really has a lot to be grateful for.

_____ 12. Many of our most important decisions are based upon insufficient information.

_____ 13. I like parties where I know most of the people more than ones where all or most of the people are complete strangers.

_____ 14. Teachers or supervisors who hand out vague assignments give one a chance to show initiative and originality.

_____ 15. The sooner we all acquire similar values and ideals the better.

_____ 16. A good teacher is one who makes you wonder about your way of looking at things.

Source: Budner, 1962

Tolerance of Ambiguity Scale Scoring Key

To score the instrument, the **even-numbered items must be reverse scored**. That is, the 7s become 1s, 6s become 2s, 5s become 3s, and 4s remain the same. After reversing the even-numbered items, sum the scores for all 16 items to get your total score. High scores indicate a greater *intolerance* for ambiguity. Use the comparison scores provided to benchmark your own score and read the following paragraphs to interpret such results.

Total Score ☐

Subscores (follow same even/odd reverse scoring)

(N) Novelty score (sum 2, 9, 11, 13)   _____

(C) Complexity score (sum 4, 5, 6, 7, 8, 10, 14, 15, 16)   _____

(I) Insolubility score (sum 1, 3, 12)   _____

Comparison total scores: Senior executives 44–48; MBAs 55–60

Interpreting Your Score

In order to capitalize fully on your own personal strengths, you should be aware of your attitude toward change. Your **tolerance of ambiguity** is a critical indicator of your attitude toward change and a good predictor of your behaviors in the face of ambiguity. This is important, because as the environment in which managers operate continues to become more chaotic, more temporary, more complex, and more overloaded with information, your ability to process information is at least partly constrained by your fundamental attitude about change.

Ambiguity, the information state that clouds cause-effect relationships, is considered a critical dimension and consequence of change. Your **tolerance of ambiguity** refers to the extent to which you are threatened by or have difficulty coping with situations that are ambiguous, where change occurs rapidly or unpredictably, where information is inadequate, or where complexity exists. Stimulus-rich and information-overloaded environments (e.g., air traffic control towers) are examples of such situations.

People differ in the extent to which they can cope with ambiguous, incomplete, unstructured, dynamic situations. Individuals who have a high tolerance for ambiguity also tend to be more cognitively complex (however, note that cognitive complexity *is not* an evaluation of how smart a person is). Such individuals tend to pay attention to more information, interpret more cues, and possess more sense-making categories than less complex individuals do. Research has found that cognitively complex and tolerant individuals are better transmitters of information, more sensitive to the internal (nonsuperficial) characteristics of others when evaluating their performance at work, and more behaviorally adaptive and flexible under ambiguous and overloaded conditions than less tolerant and less cognitively complex individuals.

Managers with higher tolerance-of-ambiguity scores are more likely to be entrepreneurial in their actions, to screen out less information in a complex environment, and to choose specialties in their occupations that possess less-structured tasks. It also should be pointed out, however, that individuals who are more tolerant of ambiguity have more difficulty focusing on a single important element of information—they are inclined to pay attention to a variety of items—and they may have somewhat less ability to concentrate without being distracted by interruptions. However, for the most part, in an information-rich environment, tolerance of ambiguity and cognitive complexity are more adaptive than the opposite characteristics.

In scoring your **tolerance for ambiguity**, three different subscores are assessed. One is the **Novelty** score, which indicates the extent to which you are tolerant of new, unfamiliar information or situations. The second subscale is the **Complexity** score, which indicates the extent to which you are tolerant of multiple, distinctive, or unrelated information. The third subscale is the **Insolubility** score, which indicates the extent to which you are tolerant of problems that are very difficult to solve because, for example, alternative solutions are not evident, information is unavailable, or the problem's components seem unrelated to each other. In general, the more tolerant people are of novelty, complexity, and insolubility, the more likely they are to succeed as managers in information-rich, ambiguous environments. They are less overwhelmed by ambiguous circumstances.

As noted earlier, it is important to recognize that cognitive complexity and tolerance for ambiguity are not related to intelligence, and your score on the **Tolerance of Ambiguity Scale** is not an evaluation of how smart you are. Most important, individuals can learn to tolerate more complexity and more flexibility in their information-processing abilities. The first step toward increasing tolerance is becoming aware of where you are now by completing and scoring the scale. Then, exercises in problem-solving and creativity can be drawn upon to improve your cognitive complexity and tolerance for ambiguity.

References for problem-solving and creativity development:

Adams, J. (1990). *Conceptual blockbusting: A guide to better ideas*. New York: Perseus Press.

DeBono, E. (1994). *Serious creativity*. New York: Harper-Collins.

DeBono, E. (1996). *Teach yourself to think*. New York: Penguin Books.

Gryskiewicz, S. (1999). *Positive turbulence: Developing climates for creativity, innovation, and renewal*. New York: Jossey-Bass.

Jones, G. (1997). *Imaginization: New mindsets for seeing, organizing, and managing*. New York: Sage.

THE ALASKAN GOLD MINE[1]

PART [A]

You have taken a three-month option on a possible gold mine in Alaska. It took you two months of dangerous journey to get there. In two weeks of exploration (and recuperation) you have regained your health, except for your injured left hand, which sometimes can become suddenly quite weak. In the last 24 hours, you have finally discovered gold in what appears to be good quantity. You have exactly two weeks to get to the claims office. If you arrive late, and attempt to secure the property (with the owners knowing you have visited it), there will probably be an auction at which you could be easily out-bid, given your limited resources. Here are your alternatives:

Wait 3–4 weeks until the weather warms up and enjoy a safe trip home.

Go over the mountains. This is dangerous. It is sometimes impassable. It is quick, if you can make it without harm: 7–10 days. If you encounter storms or injury, you will probably have to turn back or perish, as the longest part of the journey is on the way over the top.

Go through the valley passes. This is less dangerous and is usually passable. It is slow and tiring. You can probably make it in 2 to 3 weeks.

The weather is only moderately favorable, with what may be a mountain storm brewing. You will know if it is a storm within 48 hours, and whether the mountain is passable (if the storm comes) about one day later.

Wait 2–3 days, take #2 weather permitting; if not, take #3. (There is no advantage to waiting if you prefer #3 anyway, and waiting to take #1 = #1.)

What do you do? (Circle your answer)   #1   #2   #3   #4

---

[1] Authored and copyrighted by Jeffrey Barach, Graduate School of Business, Tulane University, New Orleans, LA. 1977.

THE ALASKAN GOLD MINE

PART [B]

Assume you chose the valley passes (#3). Five days later you are halfway there. You have pushed too hard and sprained your ankle. Pat, an old friend on a trapping expedition, comes along and takes you to a cabin. Pat could get to the claims office town, and offers to take you. Traveling together, it might take 10 to 14 more days to get there.

If you tell Pat and make a deal, Pat alone could get there in about 8 to 9 days. If you were well, you could do it easily in 7 days, but you presently cannot make it without a few days rest and then 10 days to 2 weeks of travel.

You are not sure whether Pat can exercise the option and file the claim correctly, because Pat is not too bright, tends to drink to excess, and is not the single-minded hustler that you are. Pat is a simple, decent old friend who likes trapping, but would, you suspect, both need and desire financial independence. You think you can trust Pat if you offer to split 50:50, since your expertise and help would be needed to capitalize on the discovery.

What is your decision? Go with Pat _____

Go it alone _____

Send Pat _____

Explain and detail your best strategy for success and how you plan to do it.

_____

_____

_____

_____

Alaska Gold Mine—Teaching Note

This case is a great kickoff to a course or particular session about strategy. Part A showcases issues of strategy formulation; Part B shows how formulation and implementation are linked.

Part A

Hand out Part A and give students 5 to 7 minutes to make a choice about options 1 through 4. Write the four alternatives on the board. After the students have had time to read the case, analyze the situation, and commit to a course of action (have them write it down on the case), take a poll of what the students chose. To keep them engaged, sprinkle a little humor in as you count their votes. After counting those that chose the second alternative (going over the mountain), note that "We apparently have X number of entrepreneurs in the class." Or, after counting those who voted for the fourth alternative (waiting to see what happens to the weather), comment that "X people already qualify for an honorary MBA," and quip that many MBAs constantly comment that there isn't enough data yet to make a choice. Talk through each option, asking students to voice their opinions as to why or why not they chose a particular option. You want to be playful here, so try to get students to disagree and state the basis for their disagreement.

The common elements for the decision maker are that (1) they must recognize a goal (money, life, other), but that their goal may have been implicit; (2) they must understand the environment, and all of them assessed it differently though given identical information; (3) same with the internal situation; (4) they acted as filters in interpreting the external environment and the internal environment; (5) based on this they needed to assess strategic alternatives and choose a course of action; (6) each choice is a strategic choice, and it mimics the types of strategic choices firms make with respect to resource allocation choices; (7) there was tremendous uncertainty, as in all strategy situations, and how they treated the "facts" varied according to how liberally or strictly they held themselves to the constraints presented in the case.

This is where you use the Strategy Formulation PowerPoint slide to walk through what they chose.

To conclude this part, you can link the exercise to strategy, where you must recognize a goal, resources, and life issues. You must determine what constitutes external threats and opportunities and internal strengths and weaknesses. Your own values and attitudes toward risk flavor your interpretation of the issues—there is not much data, and this uncertainty and ambiguity characterize strategic choices. You also had to assess strategic alternatives and the fact that there were clusters of choices (usually more than one vote for each alternative), which suggests that you interpreted and responded to the data in patterned ways, a characteristic of strategic groups. Finally, even if you don't think you had a strategy, you actually did. I usually contrast intended versus emergent strategies here. It is also fun to point out how some groups explicitly target the gold as their goal, whereas others have longer-term interests, such as preserving their lives. Like firms, some are betting the company, whereas others are taking a more patient, incremental approach.

Again, have the students read Part B and instruct them to mark down a decision.

Part B

At this point, you need to introduce Part B, which requires that you assume that the second alternative was chosen. You can either simply say, "Let's assume that you chose alternative 2; let's see what happened." Alternatively, you can foreshadow a linkage to corporate life and take the approach that the board of directors told you to choose the second alternative.

Again, hand out the case and allow students about 7 minutes to make a choice and think about the agreement they would come to with Pat. About 5 minutes into this I interrupt and ask them to also think of how much and what kind of information and communication they would provide Pat. After they have silently committed to their choice, have the students team up in groups of two to four and compare their choices. If they differ, tell them that they must come to a consensus before moving on to plotting their implementation strategy. If their responses are the same, have them immediately begin plotting their implementation strategy. Take a poll and again post the numbers—stress that the second part of the case demonstrates how the eventual strategy problem is getting something done through people. It may be useful to also spend some time asking groups that started with a disagreement on how to proceed to disclose what their initial votes were, who changed their mind, and why.

The debriefing allows you to discuss the issue of group-level strategic decision making. The situation is now complicated by the need to work through people, and focus your debriefing on the alternatives on many of the people issues. Although Part A is pretty open ended in terms of preferable strategies (though most people don't choose the first option and instead choose one of the remaining three strategies, usually the fourth because it has embedded options), Part B sets them up with the reality that implementing strategy usually requires you to get things done through others, and often those others are out of your direct control.

Do you trust Pat? Is he competent? Honest?

What kind of deal do you strike? A case of booze, a new gun, and a truck or 50:50 split?

This is where you put up the Strategy Formulation/Implementation PowerPoint slide to walk through the implementation model they chose, as well as the interdependence of formulation and implementation. You can point out that your prior relationship with Pat is what allowed you to consider this revised strategy in the first place!

The point of Part B is that the goal is lost unless you can work with and depend on Pat. This means there must be some level of trust; you must make a fair deal that incentivizes him but that also allows some form of control and give him a pep talk to avoid the personal problems. Specifically, you need Pat to try harder, extend himself, and believe in the partnership with you.

The options are all risky no matter what you do.

Tying in the strategy diamond, implementation framework, and differentiators:

The PowerPoint slides present you an opportunity to foreshadow the strategy diamond and implementation frameworks that are used in the text. You may want to talk about the three differentiators up front. We typically talk through the diamond after debriefing Part A and then walk through the implementation framework after debriefing Part B. If you will use another implementation framework, then you can apply it here instead, because our model integrates well with others.

CHAPTER 2 – LEADING STRATEGICALLY THROUGH EFFECTIVE VISION & MISSION

I.   PURPOSE OF THE CHAPTER

After studying this chapter, students should be able to:

1.   Explain how strategic leadership is essential to strategy formulation and implementation.
2.   Understand the relationships among vision, mission, values, and strategy.
3.   Understand the roles of vision and mission in determining strategic purpose and strategic coherence.
4.   Identify a firm's stakeholders and explain why such identification is critical to effective strategy formulation and implementation.
5.   Explain how ethics and biases may affect strategic decision making.

This chapter introduces students to strategic leadership and how leadership affects strategy and competitive advantage. Two specific enabling mechanisms that are highlighted are organizational vision and mission. Although vision and mission can take on a superficial air in annual reports and the business press, this chapter strives to give them substance by linking them to strategy implementation via stakeholder analysis and by clearly differentiating vision and mission from strategy.

The concept of strategic leadership is crucial to effective strategy formulation and implementation. However, because this chapter reviews some of the "softer" sides of strategic management, some students (and instructors!) may dread having to discuss such concepts as vision and mission. One way to hit this resistance head on and diffuse the issue through humor is to use one of the experiential exercises included in the appendix to this chapter's Instructor's Manual. We find that using the "Vision-Craft-O-Meter" early in the discussion can work as a nice hook to get students' interest and allows for the instructor to then use the exercise as a bridge to discuss why leadership does matter, how leaders help steer the organization, and how things such as vision and mission assist or detract from effective strategy formulation and implementation.

In this chapter, the three differentiators—and hence your teaching strategy for the chapter—are manifested in the following ways:

- **Dynamic strategy.** Students encounter the dynamics of strategy in the opening vignette, where Xerox CEO Anne Mulcahy successfully turns around the flagging company's fortunes. Although dynamism is not the central focus of this chapter, students are shown how vision and mission, and the strategic leadership that fosters or stewards them, help firms survive in both stable and dynamic contexts.
- **Formulation and implementation interdependency.** Staffing is normally considered part of strategy implementation, but in this case we happen to start with the CEO and other top executives who are collectively the strategic leadership of the firm. The student is shown early in the chapter how such leadership flows through vision and mission to the effective formulation and execution of the strategy. This is further reinforced in "How Would You Do That? 2.1," which stresses the interdependence between the strategic needs of the firm and choosing a new CEO. The treatment of stakeholder analysis later in the chapter, and the application of it in "How Would You Do That? 2.2," reinforces the interdependence message by showing students that engagement with stakeholders prior to and during formulation will help or undermine effective strategy implementation.

- **Strategic leadership.** The opening vignette shows how the strategic leadership of CEO Anne Mulcahy contributed to the turnaround of Xerox. It is only appropriate that the introductory section in the chapter is "Strategic Leadership," which walks students through the roles that strategic leadership plays (these are summarized in Exhibit 2.1). Students are also shown how the firm's vision and mission are the imprint of effective (and ineffective) strategic leadership. Because we often associate strategic leadership with CEOs, the first "How Would You Do That?" (2.1) in the chapter, walks through the CEO succession process. The second "How Would You Do That?" (2.2) shows you how strategic leadership makes a difference through effective stakeholder analysis. Finally, the chapter closes with the treatment of ethics and biases and how certain factors may negatively affect strategic leaders' decision-making processes.

Additional Readings:

Bossidy, L., R. Charan, and C. Burck. (2002). *Execution: The discipline of getting things done.* New York: Crown Business.

Collins, J. (2001), Level 5 Leadership. *Harvard Business Review,* Jan. 2001: 66–76.

Collins, J., and J. I. Porras. (2002). *Built to last: Successful habits of visionary companies.* New York: Harper Business Essentials.

Rosener, J. (1990). Ways women lead. *Harvard Business Review,* November-December, 1990: 119–125.

Slater, R. (1998). *Jack Welch & the G.E. way: Management insights and leadership secrets of the legendary CEO.* New York: McGraw-Hill.

Watkins, M. (2003). *The first 90 days.* Boston, MA: Harvard Business School Press.

II.   BRIEF CHAPTER OUTLINE

pp. 26–29, PPT #1–2	**Chapter 2 Leading Strategically** The purpose of this chapter is to explain strategic leadership in strategy formulation and implementation by addressing (1) vision, mission, values, and strategy; (2) the shaping of purpose and coherence; (3) the role of stakeholders; and (4) ethics and biases. **Opening Vignette:** How to Pull a $15 Billion Dollar Cow Out of A Ditch, pp. 27–28	
pp. 30–32, PPT #3–5	**STRATEGIC LEADERSHIP** Strategic leadership involves the following: • Managing an overall enterprise and influencing key outcomes (e.g., firm performance, competitive superiority, innovation, strategic change, and survival) • Modeling and communicating the firm's vision and mission • Making decisions and exhibiting behaviors that have a symbolic and substantive impact on outcomes **The Roles Leaders Fill** Mintzberg's typology: interpersonal roles, informational roles, and decisional roles: • **Interpersonal roles:** Figurehead (ceremonial), liaison (with stakeholders), and leader (authority to motivate and direct) • **Informational roles:** Monitor, disseminator, and spokesperson	p. 30, Ex. 2.1 The Roles That Leaders Play

	• **Decision roles:** Entrepreneur (designs firm strategy), disturbance handler, resource allocator, and negotiator (nonroutine transactions with other organizations) **The Surprised CEO** The complex role offers many surprises.	
pp. 32–34, PPT #6-7	**The Skill Set of the Effective Strategic Leader** Levels of leaders: 1. Capable individual 2. Contributing team member 3. Competent managers 4. Effective leaders 5. Executives Level 5 leaders have an unusual paradoxical set of skills: • **Professional will.** They have the professional will to carry out bold strategy by translating strategic intent into the resolve to pursue a strategy. p. 33, e.g., Charles Walgreen III, CEO phasing out soda/food service operations to transform Walgreen into a drugstore chain • **Professional modesty.** They tend to be modest people—a fairly rare trait among people with upward career trajectories. **What does it take to be CEO?** No single answer to this question. **Personality Differences** Some answers involve charisma and emotional intelligence, others point to demographic variables and psychological profiles. (See exercises for students to gauge their profile compared to the skill set that may be needed to run a complex organization.) **Background and Demographic Differences** Work experience, education, gender, nationality, race, religion, network ties, etc. Profile of typical *Fortune 500* top executive: 45- to 60-year-old white male with a law, finance, or accounting degree from an Ivy League school; legal and social influences slowly starting to diversify management ranks. In 2005, there were 9 female CEOs among the largest 500 U.S. companies (1.8%), double from 1994. Sixteen percent of the corporate officers of these same companies were female.	p. 33, Ex. 2.2 Level 5 Leaders: A Hierarchy of Capabilities
pp. 34–39,	**The Virtues of Diversity** Besides the fact that it is unethical (and, in many countries, illegal) to discriminate, explanations for increasing diversity include: (1) requirements for an advanced degree for promotion, and college education is available to more people, regardless of race, gender, or religion; (2) heterogeneous groups tend to make better decisions, especially in turbulent or uncertain environments; (3) companies need top managers with strong international skills; (4) firms increasingly seek competitive advantage through high-quality human capital. **Competence and Actions** A "talent for strategic thinking" added to "toughness"; a willingness and ability to change an organization's strategic course even when change represents departure from traditional business practices. *See self-assessment exercises in Ex. 2.3 & 2.4.* **What Makes an Effective Executive Team?** A mark of great leadership is knowing when and how to follow the lead of others; a division of labor in teams.	p. 35, Ex. 2.3 Can You Tolerate Ambiguity? p. 37, Ex. 2.4 Are You a Strategist?

PPT #8–9	**Teamwork and Diversity** Three criteria: (1) responds to complex, changing environment; (2) manages the needs of interdependent and diverse units; (3) develops a plan for executive succession. **How to Find a Quality CEO** From 1980 to 2000, external candidates selected for new CEO positions soared from 7 to 50 percent. However, external selection is not always the cure-all, and more boards are trying to promote from within rather go outside the firm. Careful selection involves: • Assessing a candidate's passion, convictions, and ability to lead. • Mapping the firm's strategy to its operating needs to understand how a CEO can affect the firm's success. Due to gaps in understanding the firm's value-creation process, the board should "map" the firm's strategy at a high level to visualize why and how activities help to achieve objectives and goals along critical dimensions. • Conducting background checks. Personal conversations often yield unexpected insights into a candidate's personality. • Having a shared view of leadership among board members. • Having a smooth transition to foster positive outcomes for the company and its stakeholders.	p. 40, *2.1 How Would You Do That? The Strategy for Finding the Right CEO?*
pp. 39–44, PPT #10–16	**THE IMPRINT OF STRATEGIC LEADERSHIP: VISION AND MISSION** The firm's vision and mission provide the context for strategy formulation and implementation. **Defining *Vision* and *Mission*.** *Vision* is a simple statement or understanding of what the firm will be in the future; it identifies the firm's desired long-term status. *Mission* is a declaration of what a firm is and stands for—its values and purpose. Vision and mission reinforce and support strategy; conversely, strategy provides a coherent plan for realizing vision and mission. **What Should Vision and Mission Statements Encompass?** • Provide direction but not strategies in and of themselves • Convey organizational identity and purpose to stakeholders **Vision: The Uses of Ambition and Ambiguity** Expresses the firm's long-term horizons in ambitious and ambiguous terms. **Mission: The Uses of Core Values** Identifies core concepts (e.g., purpose or raison d'être, values and beliefs, standards of behavior) or corporate-level aims. **Why Vision and Mission Statements Are Not Substitutes for Strategy** Vision and mission can be powerful tools, but they must be realized through carefully crafted and executed strategy. **Goals and Objectives** Strategic actions require specific quantitative or qualitative goals and objectives; a superordinate goal serves as an overarching reference point.	p. 39, Ex. 2.5 Vision, Mission, and Strategy p. 43, Ex. 2.6 Key Elements of Gerstner's 1993 Vision for IBM
pp. 44–46,	**STRATEGIC PURPOSE AND COHERENCE** Two important aspects of vision and mission are strategic purpose and coherence. **Strategic Purpose** The firm's strategic purpose guides executives in making difficult corporate decisions and provides employees with a widely shared mental model or picture of the organization and its future, including anticipated environmental changes.	p. 45, Ex. 2.7 Creating a Strategic Purpose at Matsushita

PPT #17–20	**Tradeoffs, Options, and Other Decisions** Selecting a course of action may eliminate other options; it may satisfy the needs of some stakeholders, but adversely affect others. **The Challenge of Closing the Gap** The gap lies between a firm's aspirations and its current capabilities and market positions; strategies must address the tradeoff between efficiency and effectiveness. **Strategic Coherence** This is the symmetrical co-alignment of the five elements of the firm's strategy and the overarching fit of various businesses under the corporate umbrella. **Applying the Strategy Diamond** The strategy diamond is applied to achieve strategic coherence with shared organizational vision and values and to test the coherence of a strategy. **The Clear and Compelling Vision Statement** The vision statement functions as a guideline for the development of clear and compelling strategies.	
pp. 46–49, PPT #21–23	**STAKEHOLDERS AND STAKEHOLDER ANALYSIS** Stakeholders are individuals or groups with interest in an organization's quantitative and qualitative outcomes. **Stakeholders and Strategy** Stakeholder analysis is used to determine who may influence firm performance. Vision and mission should meet or exceed needs of key stakeholders. **Identifying Stakeholders** Step 1 in stakeholder analysis is identifying the major stakeholders. Major stakeholders may be *external* (e.g., governmental bodies, community organizations, social and political action groups, trade unions and guilds, and even journalists) or *internal* (e.g., shareholders, business units, employees, and managers). **Steps in Identifying Stakeholders** Stakeholders fall into one of four categories: *organizational, capital market, product market,* and *social*. **Step 1:** Determine influences on strategy formulation; identify who should be consulted as strategy is developed or who has a role in strategy implementation. **Step 2:** Determine the effects of strategic decisions on stakeholders. **Final step:** Determine stakeholders' degree of power and influence on the firm's decisions.	p. 47, Ex. 2.8 Some Financial and Nonfinancial Performance Metrics p. 49, Ex. 2.9 Mapping Stakeholder Influence and Importance pp. 50–51, *2.2 How Would You Do That? Driving Stakeholder Analysis at Tritec Motors* p. 51, Ex. 2.A Stakeholder-Analysis Grid
pp. 49–56, PPT #24–25	**ETHICS, BIASES, AND STRATEGIC DECISION MAKING** Two factors affect the soundness of strategic decisions: Is the decision ethical? Are biases clouding the decision-making process? **Ethics and Strategy** Questionable strategies can be disastrous for shareholders, clients, and even decision makers themselves (e.g., a number of Enron, Adelphia, and Tyco executives have been indicted—and some convicted—for diverting firm resources for private use). **Why Organizations Are Vulnerable to Ethics Violations** Important conditions—*authority structures* and *incentive systems*—may show how avoiding certain pitfalls can reduce a firm's risk of executives violating legal and ethical standards.	*p. 52, *Fig. 2004, Enron CEO, Jeffery Skilling, in Handcuffs*

Authority Structures The structure of authority at a firm may foster opportunities for exploiting the system and/or discourage potential whistle-blowers; when responsibility is distributed, people tend to assume that someone else will blow the whistle on suspicious activity.

Incentive Systems When people are faced with the prospect of large potential rewards, they are more likely to compromise standards. Research shows that managers are more likely to defer income to the subsequent accounting period when earnings target are of their bonus plans won't be met or when they have already reached the maximum payout.

The Role of Corporate Governance Good corporate governance can reduce the risk of unethical and illegal activities; *poor* corporate governance provides a breeding ground for *un*ethical behavior.

Threats to Rational Decision Making Threats occur when biases influence managerial judgment and strategic decision making.

Theories About Ourselves People are confident in their ability to make judgments. **Confidence** may include the illusion of **favorability,** whereby people take credit for successes but not for failures. The illusion of **optimism** leads to underestimating a negative future while overestimating positive outcomes. The illusion of **control** is people's belief that they have greater control of a situation than rational analysis would support.

Escalation of Commitment The three illusions may lead to the allocation of additional resources to a failing course of action.

Self-Serving Fairness Bias This occurs when executives do a better job of tracking their own contributions and tend to take more credit for good outcomes than they give.

Overconfidence Bias This is the tendency of people to place erroneously high levels of confidence in their own knowledge or abilities; they seek confirmatory evidence of their beliefs while discounting contradictory evidence.

The Consequences of Bias Bias may lead executives to think that they can get away with unethical or even felonious behavior because they believe that they won't be caught or that, if they are, their status will protect them from the consequences.

Theories About Other People Biases about others can be tied to such far-reaching negative outcomes as industry overexpansion, which often occurs because each industry incumbent assumes that the others won't take competitive action, when in fact every firm almost certainly will.

Ethnocentrism and Stereotyping

Ethnocentrism is a belief in the superiority of one's own ethnic group; a conviction that one's own national, group, or cultural characteristics are "normal" and ordinary. **Stereotyping** relies on a conventional or formulaic conception of another group based on some common characteristic.

The Consequences of Ethnocentrism and Stereotyping

Stereotyping increases the risk of unethical, unfair, and sometimes illegal decisions because evaluations are limited to group affiliation,

	ignoring individual qualities. Ethnocentrism may lead to rationally and ethically unsound decisions because it exaggerates the differences between us and them. **Theories About the World** It is important to know what you don't know; it is impossible to foresee all possible consequences of a strategic choice. **Risk and Cause-and-Effect Assessment** Research shows that people tend to be *risk seeking* when a positive outcome is perceived but *risk averse* when a negative outcome is perceived—even when rational analysis shows an equal probability of the outcomes.	

* Figure or Exhibit **NOT** enumerated in the PDF file.

III. SUGGESTED CASES TO ACCOMPANY TEXT

The cases you choose for this chapter should generally look at how a company develops a vision and mission and how they are connected or disconnected from the firm's actual strategy and its implementation. Two types of cases seem to fit: The first type looking at vision and mission, then at implementation more generally; the second type showing how vision is developed or stewarded (or ruined) by strategic leadership. For the concepts-with-cases version, we have chosen Charlotte Beers (A) and Trilogy Farms. The first case shows how a new CEO brings a fresh vision to the firm and must adjust the strategy and implementation levers accordingly. The second is an entrepreneurial firm case that shows the linkages among strategic leadership, vision, strategy, and implementation. In both cases, the leaders are women, and an instructor can bring out this dimension if they choose.

Need help selecting cases? Pearson Prentice Hall and Pearson Custom Publishing are pleased to present the ultimate resource for creating and customizing casebooks.

- Start with a CaseMap correlated to your text or start from scratch; do it yourself using our easy-to-use interface or collaborate with a developmental editor.
- Cases can be selected from a variety of sources, including Harvard Business School Publishing, Darden, Ivey, Thunderbird, and NACRA.
- We clear permissions for you on cases and content not in the database.
- You can also create custom course packs by adding articles, original material, and textbook chapters.
- Pearson Custom casebooks can be delivered in print or online.
- Additionally, we supply you, the instructor, with a free evaluation copy delivered 7 to 10 days after you create your book, free access to teaching notes, and case-method teaching resources.

We're here to help: Looking for a case on a specific topic, company, country, or scenario? Or, looking for a new case to substitute for one you've used in the past? We will help you find the right cases for your course and help you create a casebook that meets all your teaching needs. For guidance on building a casebook to reflect your course needs, e-mail our editorial consultant at customcases@prenhall.com.

Visit www.prenhall.com/custombusiness for more information and to see which Prentice Hall titles are available for short-run customization and to view suggested cases. To start your own straightforward search for material:

Step 1: Select "search content and create your book" and log in.
Step 2: Search by case number or keyword or browse by discipline to find suggested cases based on the book you use or course you teach.

Step 3: Browse, preview, and select the cases, articles, or chapters you wish to include (you will see that price and page count of the book in the top right-hand corner of the screen as you "build" the book).

Step 4: Finalize your selections, get them in the order you want, package your customized book with any Prentice Hall title for a discount (if you wish), click "confirm book," and you have the option to request a free evaluation copy.

Step 5: The Web site immediately gives you the ISBN of your custom book. You should give this ISBN to your bookstore; they will use it to place their order with us.

Beyond our cases and Pearson Custom Publishing, if you choose to compile your own casebook you will have an opportunity to draw from a variety of sources. These sources include going direct to Hartwick Leadership Cases, IVEY Case Publishing, European Case Clearing House (ECCH), Harvard Business School (HBS), Darden, and others.

Given the popularity of Harvard cases, we have selected these additional cases for use with this chapter:

		ID#	Pages	TN
Jack Welch: General Electric's Revolutionary	HBSP	9-394-065	22	Y
Apple Computer—2002	HBSP	9-702-469	22	Y

Jack Welch: General Electric's Revolutionary Describes the work of Jack Welch, CEO of General Electric from 1981 to 1992, focusing on his transformation of the company's portfolio through extensive dispositions and acquisitions and the company's culture through a mandated process called "work out." To a considerable extent, the case tells the story in Welch's own words, drawing on earlier cases on Welch prepared by Richard Hammermesh and Frank Aguilar, as well as a 1991 interview with Welch from the *Harvard Business Review* and an article in *Fortune,* "GE Keeps Those Ideas Coming."

Apple Computer—2002 In 1980, Apple was the leader of the personal computer industry, but by 2002 it had suffered heavy losses at the hands of the Wintel camp. This case examines Apple's strategic moves as the PC industry evolves in the twenty-first century and poses the question: Can Steve Jobs make Apple "insanely great" again?

IV. LINKING THE CHAPTER TO A COMPUTER SIMULATION

If you are planning to use a simulation (CapSim or other computer simulation), this chapter marks a nice tie-in and starting point for that process. You can have students hand in as their first sim-related assignment a statement of vision and mission and the goals and objectives of their strategy. It's up to you whether you grade this initial effort or use it as a way to frame later discussions about strategy formulation and implementation, emergent versus intended strategy, and the degree to which the vision and mission and underlying strategy were later changed as a consequence of environmental forces (i.e., what other companies were doing in the sim).

V. END OF CHAPTER QUESTION ANSWER GUIDE

Review Questions

1. Why is strategic leadership important for effective strategy formulation and implementation?

Guide: Strategic leadership is concerned with the management of the overall enterprise. Executives, through their decisions and actions, affect key organizational outcomes. Executives affect these outcomes through the various roles they fill (e.g., figurehead, leader, liaison, monitor, disseminator, spokesperson, entrepreneur, disturbance handler, allocator of resources, and negotiator). How executives fill these roles has a large bearing on the effectiveness of strategic management processes.

2.   How do the characteristics of strategic leadership differ between individuals and teams?

Guide: No one person can single-handedly manage a large complex organization. Teams have advantages over individuals because they can divide responsibilities and tap into a diverse portfolio of skills and capabilities. However, management teams can present their own unique problems…

3.   What is a vision? A mission?

Guide: We define *vision* as a simple statement or understanding of what the firm will be in the future. A statement of vision is forward-looking and anticipates the desired long-term status of the company. In contrast, a mission is a declaration of what a firm is and what it stands for—its fundamental values and purpose. Together, mission and vision statements describe the identity and work of a firm as well as the mental picture of where the firm is going.

4.   How are vision and mission related to strategy? What roles does strategic leadership play in realizing vision and mission?

Guide: Executing strategies often require making tradeoffs—a firm cannot do all things. Vision and mission statements can help guide important decisions on these tradeoff issues by identifying the core values that should guide long-term decisions. Top executives provide the organizational context for strategy formulation and implementation, and vision and mission statements can help establish that context. Executives sometimes draft the vision and mission statements, more often they are the stewards of the values espoused in vision and mission statements long ago established.

5.   How does strategy differ from vision and mission?

Guide: Vision and mission statements do not address how the company will achieve its objectives. Rather, they provide direction and a moral compass to guide decision making and actions. Strategies are more concrete plans about how objectives will be achieved. Thus, vision and mission statements may seem a bit ambiguous, whereas a high-quality strategy will provide more definitive direction.

6.   What is strategic purpose?

Guide: Strategic purpose is a simplified and widely shared mental model or picture of the organization and its future. Vision and mission statements may help with the diffusion of strategic purpose throughout the organization. Strategic purpose is also concerned with the desired leadership position aspired to in the future. It is an aspirational bridge between vision and specific goals and objectives.

7.   What is strategic coherence?

Guide: Strategic coherence is the symmetrical co-alignment of the five elements of strategy, the congruence of functional area policies, and the overarching fit of the various businesses within the corporate umbrella. The opposite of strategic coherence would be incoherence, or strategic fragmentation.

8. Who are a firm's stakeholders? Why are they important?

Guide: Stakeholders are individuals or groups who have a vested interest in the formulation and implementation of a firm's strategy and have some influence on firm performance. Externally, these groups will include representative governmental bodies, community-based organizations, social and political action groups, trade unions and guilds, journalists, and academics. Internally, these groups will include business units, employees, and managers. Because vision and mission are long-term in orientation, the identification of important stakeholder groups helps managers understand which constituencies stand the most to gain or lose from their realization. Stakeholders can both complement and clash with the firm in its efforts to execute its strategy.

9. What tools can you use to identify the impact of various stakeholders on the firm and the impact of the firm on various stakeholders?

Guide: A stakeholder map can be used to identify important constituents of the firm. These stakeholders can then be analyzed to determine the importance and influence of each party.

10. Why are ethics and biases relevant to strategic decision making and strategic leadership?

Guide: The stakes are very high when strategic decisions are made; some strategic decisions can literally determine whether the firm will be viable in the future or end in ruin. Ethical lapses and decision-making biases are two processes that can interfere with effective and rational decision making. Unethical decisions can literally bring the firm down and result in the dissolution of the enterprise; they can also result in time behind bars for those orchestrating such activities. Decision-making biases are more subtle, but they can have equally dramatic effects. For instance, executives with excessive overconfidence may irrationally think that they will be able to extract more synergy from an acquisition than anyone else, and thus afford to pay an excessive premium. Excessive premiums can result in losses of hundreds of millions of dollars.

How Would You Do That?

11. Building on the CEO-successor selection process described in "How Would You Do That? 2.1," devise a succession plan for the dean of your business school. Be sure to include the following in your succession-planning process: (a) Translate your school's strategy into actual operating needs and key activities; (b) identify the skills needed for these operating needs and activities; (c) outline an internal and external candidate search process; and (d) develop a list of goals and milestones and a compensation structure that ties actions to the strategic drivers of success at your school.

Guide: Although students will likely not have nearly enough information about the governance of your institution, with a short primer they should be able to have a basic understanding. And, understanding the governance realities is less important to this exercise than going through the steps identified. Completing these steps facilitates a strong linkage between strategy formulation and implementation. In this case, the strategy is taken as a given, and the goal is to find a leader to implement it in a manner consistent with the vision and objectives of the organization. Use the following bullet points to organize their recommendations and observations:

- Translate your school's strategy into its actual operating needs and key activities.
- Identify the skills needed to fulfill these operating needs and activities.
- Outline the internal and external candidate search processes.
- Develop a list of goals and milestones and describe a compensation structure that ties actions to the strategic drivers of success at your school.

12. Based on the framework applied in "How Would You Do That? 2.2" on Tritec Motors, use the opening vignette on Anne Mulcahy at Xerox to map out the key stakeholders in her turnaround effort. Which stakeholders would you expect to be most resistant? Most supportive? Write up a 90-day action plan for Mulcahy following the example laid out by Bob Harbin in "How Would You Do That? 2.2."

Guide: Here the goal is to have students gain an appreciation for identifying key stakeholders, prioritizing their importance in the early stages of assuming leadership, and committing to an early action plan. Many students will have tendency to be able to develop long lists of things that need to get done but have more trouble prioritizing what must be done immediately. Like most strategic decisions, such prioritization requires making tradeoffs. By choosing to do something first, you are necessarily choosing to neglect another item. Which prioritization students make at this point is much less important than developing a plan and justifying it.

Group Activities

13. (a) Craft a vision and mission statement for your business school and then for the college or university as a whole. How are these statements related? How are they similar? How do they differ? How are they similar or different from those that you might draw up for a for profit organization? (b) Using the vision and mission you crafted, develop a list of key stakeholders for your school and their relative power and stake in the school. Which of these stakeholders for your school and their relative power and stake in the school. Which of these stakeholder groups is accounted for in your vision and mission statement, and which ones are left out? Did you identify any stakeholder groups that could negatively affect your realization of this vision and mission?

Guide: The first underlying objective of this exercise is to have students compare a vision and mission for a nonprofit organization with any hypothetical for-profit firm. The second objective is for them to see how such statements may vary when the stakeholder group is very diverse—as it will likely be when you move from the business school to the university level of discussion. As a closing example, you can also show how a vision and strategy are most likely to be tightly coupled when the organization has a narrow range of activities—have them look at the Tuck School of Business at Dartmouth. This school only has a general MBA and no other activities, such as undergraduate or executive education, which allows it to be extremely focused. Sometimes ethical issues will come up naturally in the course of the discussion, which you can then draw out in the debriefing. One objective would be to make students aware of the fact that ethics and social responsibility usually need to be explicit in the firm's vision and mission for people to act upon them, or at least understand that they are a part of the firm's overall strategy and strategic decision making. You can also create a debate around whether ethics should be an explicit part of a business school curriculum. Avoid red-herring questions such as, "Is it fair to assume that business students are unethical" or "Why should there be required ethics courses for business students but not physics majors?" Again, the goal is to stimulate a healthy discussion and come back to the point that business leaders will have a tremendous impact on their communities and society, and therefore cannot escape questions of ethics and social responsibility.

14. What roles should strategic leadership play in the realization of the vision and mission statements that you articulated in the previous question? Whom have you identified as strategic leaders?

Guide: Here you'll want students to recall the implementation framework from Chapter 1 and to then integrate it with the roles of the strategic leader outlined in this chapter. Doing so will help them appreciate the various roles that leaders play (without an exercise like this, the discussion of roles may appear to simply be a laundry list). You'll want students to debate the roles and skills that may be necessary to develop support among stakeholders compared to very distinct roles and skills, such as those necessary to designing the structure and recruiting the people necessary to implement a strategy. This also allows for a discussion of how in some organizations, the division of strategic leadership roles may be necessary to effectively fulfill all the roles that are encompassed in realizing a implementation of an organizational vision and mission.

You can find more group activities at:

http://instruction.bus.wisc.edu/mcarpenter/PROFESSIONAL/Toolkit/bpstools.htm.

VI. SUPPLEMENTAL EXPERIENTIAL EXERCISES

These exercises are drawn with permission from the Strategy Teaching Tool-kit found at http://instruction.bus.wisc.edu/mcarpenter/PROFESSIONAL/Toolkit/bpstools.htm.

1.   For the first exercise, we like to refer students to Ben & Jerry's mission statement. You can track it down on the Ben & Jerry's Web site (www.benjerry.com/our_company/our_mission/) or use the version we repeat below. It is helpful to put it on the board or an overhead slide. It reads:

Our Mission Statement—Ben & Jerry's is founded on and dedicated to a sustainable corporate concept of linked prosperity. Our mission consists of three interrelated parts:		
Product Mission	**Economic Mission**	**Social Mission**
To make, distribute, and sell the finest quality all natural ice cream and euphoric concoctions with a continued commitment to incorporating wholesome, natural ingredients and promoting business practices that respect the Earth and the Environment.	To operate the Company on a sustainable financial basis of profitable growth, increasing value for our stakeholders and expanding opportunities for development and career growth for our employees.	To operate the company in a way that actively recognizes the central role that business plays in society by initiating innovative ways to improve the quality of life locally, nationally and internationally.
Central To The Mission Of Ben & Jerry's is the belief that all three parts must thrive equally in a manner that commands deep respect for individuals in and outside the company and supports the communities of which they are a part.		

You may have to provide students with some background on Ben & Jerry's if they aren't familiar with its egalitarian and socially responsible roots. Its fun to paint a picture of a company that put profits second to its ethical and social beliefs. You can read this background at:

www.benjerry.com/our_company/about_us/our_history/timeline/index.cfm.

This exercise is particularly effective if the students are not aware that Unilever, one of the world's largest consumer products companies, acquired Ben & Jerry's in April 2000. We ask students what they think about the mission statement and what, based on the statement, they think it might be like to work at Ben & Jerry's. What would a typical day be like? We then tell them of Unilever's acquisition of Ben & Jerry's and ask them if their perspective of the company has changed—we also ask them what the company would have to do to convince you that it was still true to its mission. Is it enough that, under the terms of the agreement, that Ben & Jerry's operates separately from Unilever's current U.S. ice cream business, with an independent board of directors to provide leadership for Ben & Jerry's social mission and brand integrity? Students typically associate Ben & Jerry's with a fun-loving atmosphere where profits come second to socially responsible behavior. They have a different perception of the company after they hear about the acquisition, and this is a great opportunity to show that a mission must be more than words for it to be effective with key stakeholders, such as employees and customers.

2. A second exercise involves the application of stakeholder analysis to Wal-Mart. This is a good exercise if you will use the Wal-Mart case with Chapter 4 or later with Chapter 8. Have the students identify potential threats as part of their preparation of the case. Then at the end of that class tell them that part of their preparation for Chapter 4 discussion will be to evaluate the following sites and determine if they pose a threat. (Note: You can also raise this topic when discussing ethical and strategic decision making in Chapter 2.) Ask them how they would rank these groups in a stakeholder analysis map:

www.walmartwatch.com
www.sprawl-busters.com
www.sierraclub.org/sprawl/factsheet.asp
www.uffdawalmart.org/default.htm

VII. APPENDIX

Vision-Craft-O-Meter[1]

Use this easy and humorous class opener to craft a vision statement for any organization. The point here is that its easy to come up with some blather of a vision statement, but it is meaningless if it not backed up by executives actions and widely shared and understood by all members the organization and its external stakeholders.

OUR VISION IS TO BE A

(A) growing; leading; worldclass; premier; benchmark; first-mover

ORGANIZATION THAT PROVIDES

(B) dynamic; innovative; creative; breathtaking; cost-effective; diverse; high-quality

(C) products; services; people; products and services; people and services

TO

(D) thrill our shareholders; delight our customers; enrich our stakeholders' lives

IN THE

(E) hypercompetitive; emerging; growing; attractive; thriving

(F) business-solutions; health-solutions; consumer-solutions; financial-solutions; environmental-solutions

MARKETPLACE.

---

[1] Adapted from Stewart, T. (1996). A refreshing change: Vision statements that make sense. *Fortune, 134*(6), 195–197.

PART TWO
THE INTERNAL AND EXTERNAL ENVIRONMENT OF STRATEGY

CHAPTER 3 – EXAMINING THE INTERNAL ENVIRONMENT

I.   PURPOSE OF THE CHAPTER

After studying this chapter, students should be able to:

1. Explain what is meant by the *internal context of strategy*.
2. Identify a firm's resources and capabilities and explain their role in its performance.
3. Define *dynamic capabilities* and explain their role in both strategic change and a firm's performance.
4. Understand how value-chain activities are related to firm performance and competitive advantage.
5. Explain the role of managers with respect to resources, capabilities, and value-chain activities.

Chapters 3 and 4 are interdependent, and they are treated as such throughout the text. Timing constraints and taste will determine whether you teach them collectively, individually, and in what order. Students and managers tend to gravitate to the firm level of analysis easily, and many instructors start with some form of internal analysis. If you have a strong finance or accounting dimension to your course, you can complement the text content with treatment of DuPont analysis or other financially oriented indicators of a firm's resources and capabilities.

You have three objectives with this chapter. First, students should leave the chapter with fluency in the workings of the VRINE framework. The benefit here is that the students learn how to work with a specific strategy tool and are reminded that the external environment still figures into internal analysis (value, rarity, and inimitability are all functions that require external analysis). Second, they should also leave the chapter with fluency in the terminology and application of the value chain, because it is a fundamental tool in strategy more generally and is applied throughout the chapters of this text. Finally, they should understand that this constellation of resources and capabilities doesn't just come about, but instead results from the choices and stewardship of strategic leadership and the resource-base strategy that leadership has crafted to keep the firm competitive.

In this chapter, the three differentiators—and hence your teaching strategy of the chapter—are manifested in the following ways:

- **Dynamic strategy.** The opening vignette is on Intel, and this mini-case itself is about the intersection of the resource-based perspective and dynamic strategy. The VRINE model lets you show that dynamism is contingent on several firm-specific factors as well as a how long the external environment, vis-à-vis competitors and other changes, allows VRINE resources and capabilities to lead to competitive advantage. The VRINE discussion in the chapter is followed immediately by a discussion of dynamic capabilities, and the chapter closes with a section on the roles of leaders, who are presented as a possible specific case of dynamic capabilities.
- **Formulation and implementation interdependency.** This interdependency can be highlighted in the opening vignette, where you can show that Intel's top leaders made choices about implementation

and resource allocation that allowed the firm to morph from one set of core arenas to another. You can also note that the "E" part of the VRINE framework summarized in Exhibit 3.4 and applied in "How Would You Do That 3.1" should have students thinking about if and how the firm is able to implement a strategy around these VRINE resources and capabilities. This and other aspects of the formulation/implementation interdependency are brought full circle in the closing section on "Strategic Leadership."

- **Strategic leadership**. As discussed earlier and shown in Exhibit 3.2, leadership is a common thread to the dynamic strategy and interdependence differentiators of this chapter. The critical role played by leaders is first mentioned in the opening vignette, then reinforced in the closing section on "Strategic Leadership: Linking Resources and Capabilities to Strategy."

Additional Readings:

Barney, J. B. (1995). Looking inside for competitive advantage. *Academy of Management Executive, 9*, 49–61.

Dierickx, I., and K. Cool. (1989). Asset stock accumulation and sustainability of competitive advantage. *Management Science, 35*, 1,504–1,511.

Eisenhardt, K. M., and J. A. Martin. (2000). Dynamic capabilities: What are they? *Strategic Management Journal, 21*, 1,105–1,121.

Porter, M. E. (1985). *Competitive advantage*. New York: Simon & Schuster. (See Chapter 2.)

Porter, M. E. (1996). What is strategy? *Harvard Business Review, 74*(6), 61–78.

Teece, D. J., G. Pisano, & A. Shuen. (1997). Dynamic capabilities and strategic management. *Strategic Management Journal, 18*, 509–529.

II.   BRIEF CHAPTER OUTLINE

pp. 60–63, PPT #1-3	**Chapter 3 Examining the Internal Context of Strategy** The purpose of the chapter is to develop an internal perspective by focusing on (1) resources and capabilities with the VRINE model; (2) dynamic capabilities; (3) value chains; and (4) strategic leadership. **Opening Vignette:** Intel	
pp. 63–65, PPT #4	**INTERNAL DRIVERS OF STRATEGY AND COMPETITIVE ADVANTAGE** Examination of internal drivers focuses on differences in resource portfolios. **Models of competitive advantage:** 1) What firms own and what they can do; how these differences evolve over time. 2) Use the value chain to select activities and may gain advantages by configuring value chain. Management decides how and what resources to acquire, allocate, and discard and organizes value-chain activities. Managers are both resources and capabilities.	p. 65, Ex. 3.1 Firms in U.S. Semiconductor Industry, Global Auto Industry, and U.S. Grocery Stores
	RESOURCES AND CAPABILITIES Resources and capabilities are the fundamental building blocks of a firm's strategy:	p. 66, Ex. 3.2 Resources, Capabilities, and

pp. 66–68, PPT #5–8	• **Resources. Tangible** resources include land, plants, equipment, financial capital, goods in inventory, etc. **Intangible** resources include knowledge, organizational culture, location, patents, trademarks, and reputation. p. 67, e.g., Wal-Mart's rural locations; Union Pacific Railroad's key rail property; McDonalds' brand name • **Capabilities.** These include the firm's skill in creating goods and services; similar to competences. **Distinctive capability** (or distinctive competence) sets a firm apart from other firms. **Core capabilities** (or core competencies) are central to the main business operations and help generate new products and services. p. 68, e.g., the "Intel Inside" marketing campaign; in the oil industry, BP, Chevron, Texaco, Exxon Mobil, and Royal Dutch/Shell are vertically integrated and Valero Energy and Sunoco are refiners and distributors; McDonalds' site location capability.	Managerial Decisions p. 67, Ex. 3.3 Extraordinary Capabilities in WalMart, Vanguard's, 3M's. p. 70, Ex. 3.5 Union Pacific p. 71, Ex. 3.6, Monsanto's NutraSweet
pp. 68–74, PPT #9–16	**The VRINE Model** Five basic characteristics can be used to analyze and test a resource or capability: 1. **Value** 2. **Rarity,** p. 71, e.g., Pfizer's patent for Viagra and later Levitra and Cialis; Toyota and Honda cars 3. **Inimitable** 4. **Nonsubstitutability,** p. 72, e.g., Barnes & Noble and Borders volume capability substituted by Amazon.com; Cisco purchased Cerent for $6.9B; Mickey Mouse trademark; government building support for Coca-Cola's 64 bottling plants during World War II 5. **Exploitable,** p. 74, e.g., Novell and Xerox's inability to rapidly move innovations to market	p. 73, Ex. 3.7, 3M's Innovativeness
pp. 74–77, PPT #17–19	**DYNAMIC CAPABILITIES** The process of developing, accumulating, and losing resources and capabilities is inherently dynamic: 1. **Stocks** are resources and capabilities a firm possesses. 2. **Flow** is the creation of resources and capabilities over time. 3. **Dynamic capabilities** are firm processes that integrate, reconfigure, acquire, or divest resources to achieve new configurations of resources and capabilities, especially important in fast-paced competition. Evidence of dynamic capabilities can be found in a firm's organizational culture, knowledge base, and ability to learn. Dynamic capabilities result in an ability to integrate different resources and capabilities to create new revenue-producing products and services or rebundle of resources and capabilities through alliances and acquisitions. Resources and capabilities can both be acquired and lost through these vehicles. p. 76, e.g., Disney's "Princess Line," Mail Boxes Etc.'s "templates" for franchising, Cisco's ability to integrate acquisitions	
	THE VALUE CHAIN 1. **Primary activities** 2. **Support activities**	p. 78, Ex. 3.8, The Value Chain for an Internet Startup

pp. 77–80, PPT #20–25	**Using Value Chains to Gain Competitive Advantage** 1. Finding better ways to perform activities; short-lived due to ease of imitation 2. Finding different ways to perform activities **Tradeoff Protection** Organizing differently involves complex systems and makes imitation more difficult because rivals may have made investments in their systems of activities that may be irreversible. **Innovation and Integration in the Value Chain** • Develop value-chain activities that differ from those of rivals. • Configure activities so that they are integrally related and can't be imitated without significant tradeoffs, thus locking out competitors. p. 80, e.g., IKEA's and Dell's reconfigured value chain **Outsourcing and the Value Chain** p. 80, e.g., Nike and Pacific Cycle (Schwinn)	p. 79, Ex. 3.9 Southwest's Value Chain p. 79, Ex. 3.10 Cost of U.S. Airlines
pp. 80–83, PPT #26–29	**STRATEGIC LEADERSHIP: LINKING RESOURCES AND CAPABILITIES TO STRATEGY** • **Senior managers** decide how resources and capabilities will be used, configure a firm's value-chain activities, and set the context. They see the organization as a portfolio of processes—specifically, entrepreneurial, capability-building, and renewal processes. • **Middle managers** have key roles in what the firm is currently doing and what it may do in the future; contribute as entrepreneurs, communicators, psychoanalysts, and tightrope walkers. Aligning leadership-development programs with long-term aspirations is strategically important. The central role of upper and middle management distinguishes the internal perspective on strategy from the external perspective (Chapter 4).	p. 82, Ex. 3.11 Herb Kelleher, CEO Southwest Airlines

III.   SUGGESTED CASES TO ACCOMPANY TEXT

This chapter pairs up well with an introductory case that showcases a firm's resources, capabilities, and dynamic capabilities. This is why we have chosen the "Formula One Constructors" and "Prince Island Preserves Co." cases to accompany the concepts-with-cases version of our text. Ideally, the case will have enough information for you to show the application of the VRINE and value-chain frameworks. Sometimes, particularly if you try to use financial analyses, such as the DuPont framework, you may need to collect additional financial information for the industry comparison aspects, but this is a relatively easy task given the ready access to such data on such financial sites as Yahoo! and The Motley Fool (www.fool.com). The best cases are descriptive ones that allow you to catalogue a given firm's resources, capabilities, and dynamic capabilities using the suggested tools. It is important that the case also lets you highlight and distinguish between tangible and intangible assets.

Need help selecting cases? Pearson Prentice Hall and Pearson Custom Publishing are pleased to present the ultimate resource for creating and customizing casebooks.

• Start with a CaseMap correlated to your text or start from scratch; do it yourself using our easy-to-use interface or collaborate with a developmental editor.

- Cases can be selected from a variety of sources, including Harvard Business School Publishing, Darden, Ivey, Thunderbird, and NACRA.
- We clear permissions for you on cases and content not in the database.
- You can also create custom course packs by adding articles, original material, and textbook chapters.
- Pearson Custom casebooks can be delivered in print or online.
- Additionally, we supply you, the instructor, with a free evaluation copy delivered 7 to 10 days after you create your book, free access to teaching notes, and case-method teaching resources.

We're here to help: Looking for a case on a specific topic, company, country, or scenario? Or, looking for a new case to substitute for one you've used in the past? We will help you find the right cases for your course and help you create a casebook that meets all your teaching needs. For guidance on building a casebook to reflect your course needs, e-mail our editorial consultant at customcases@prenhall.com.

Visit www.prenhall.com/custombusiness for more information and to see which Prentice Hall titles are available for short-run customization and to view suggested cases. To start your own straightforward search for material:

Step 1: Select "search content and create your book" and log in.
Step 2: Search by case number or keyword or browse by discipline to find suggested cases based on the book you use or course you teach.
Step 3: Browse, preview, and select the cases, articles, or chapters you wish to include (you will see that price and page count of the book in the top right-hand corner of the screen as you "build" the book).
Step 4: Finalize your selections, get them in the order you want, package your customized book with any Prentice Hall title for a discount (if you wish), click "confirm book," and you have the option to request a free evaluation copy.
Step 5: The Web site immediately gives you the ISBN of your custom book. You should give this ISBN to your bookstore; they will use it to place their order with us.

Beyond our cases and Pearson Custom Publishing, if you choose to compile your own casebook you will have an opportunity to draw from a variety of sources. These sources include going direct to Hartwick Leadership Cases, IVEY Case Publishing, European Case Clearing House (ECCH), Harvard Business School (HBS), Darden, and others.

Given the popularity of Harvard cases, we have selected these additional cases for use with this chapter:

		ID#	Pages	TN
JetBlue Airways: Starting from Scratch	HBSP	9-801-354	20	Y
Matching Dell	HBSP	9-799-158	31	Y

JetBlue Airways: Starting from Scratch JetBlue Airways shows how an entrepreneurial venture can use human resource management, specifically a values-centered approach to managing people, as a source of competitive advantage. The major challenge faced by Ann Rhoades is to grow this people-centered organization at a rapid rate, while retaining high standards for employee selection and a small company culture. Teaching Purpose: To consider the role of human resource management, leadership, and values in a start-up venture and to address the tension between a strong organizational culture and rapid growth.

Matching Dell After years of success with its vaunted "direct model" for computer manufacturing, marketing, and distribution, Dell faces efforts by competitors to match its strategy. This case describes the evolution of the personal computer industry, Dell's strategy, and efforts by Compaq, IBM, Hewlett-Packard, and Gateway 2000 to capture the benefits of Dell's approach. Students are called on to formulate strategic plans of action for Dell and its various rivals.

IV.   LINKING THE CHAPTER TO A COMPUTER SIMULATION

If you are planning to use a simulation (StratSim, MikesBikes, or other computer simulation), this chapter can be linked to the bases on which students formulated their strategies. Ask students what they considered to be their resources and capabilities. Later you can ask them to comment on how those resources and capabilities evolved over time and whether they thought their organization possessed any dynamic capabilities. It is easy to apply the DuPont formula and other financial analytics here to compare firms as well as to compare each firm to its own intended strategy.

Again, examples of simulations are found under the simulations heading at:

http://instruction.bus.wisc.edu/mcarpenter/PROFESSIONAL/Toolkit/bpstools.htm.

V.   END OF CHAPTER QUESTION ANSWER GUIDE

Review Questions

1.   What are resources? How do different types of resources differ?

Guide: Resources are the tangible and intangible inputs used by firms to create products or services. Tangible resources are rather easy to identify; they include land, plants, equipment, financial capital, goods in inventory, and so on. Alternatively, intangible resources are more difficult to handle and quantify, but are very much involved in the value-creation process. Intangible resources refer to property owned or controlled by a firm that is not physical in nature.

2.   What is a capability?

Guide: Capabilities refer to the firm's skill at utilizing it resources (tangible and intangible) to create products and services. In essence, capabilities are the procedures and expertise manifest in the way the firm produces its products and services.

3.   What are the five components of the VRINE model?

Guide: The characteristics are: **value**—a resource or capability is said to be valuable if it allows the firm to exploit opportunities or negate threats in the environment; **rarity**—a firm that possesses valuable resources that are not rare is not in a position of advantage relative to competitors; **imitability**—this concept includes any form of *acquiring* the lacking resource or *substituting* a similar resource that provides equivalent benefits; **nonsubstitutability**—meaning that there are no ready market substitutes; and **exploitability**—this element essentially addresses whether the firm is able to capture any value that the resource or capability may generate.

4.   How do time and causal ambiguity relate to the value, rarity, and inimitability of a resource or capability?

Guide: Time and causal ambiguity make a resource or capability more difficult to imitate. Further, when resources or capabilities are difficult to imitate it also means that they are rare. However, in order for a resource or capability to lead to competitive advantage it must also be valuable. Therefore, those conditions can contribute to the importance of a resource, but only if the resource is valuable.

5. What is the difference between a stock of resources and capabilities and a flow of resources and capabilities?

Guide: Some researchers have used a bathtub metaphor to illustrate the distinction between stocks and flows of resources and capabilities. At a given point in time, a firm's stock of resources is symbolized by the level of water in a tub, and the flow of water into the tub represents the rate of investment a firm is making. Just as the level of water is the cumulative result of the flow of water into the tub through the faucet (and the possible leakage of water through the drain or splashing), a firm's level of resources is a function of investment in resource accumulation over time and leakage or depreciation.

6. What are dynamic capabilities and how do they differ from general capabilities?

Guide: The term *dynamic* refers to a firm's ability to modify and revise its resources and capabilities in order to fit with an ever-changing environment. Dynamic capabilities are processes that integrate, reconfigure, acquire, or divest resources in order to use the firms' stocks of resources and capabilities in new ways.

7. What is a firm's value chain? How does it figure into a firm's competitive advantage?

Guide: Firms can use value-chain activities to create value by either finding better ways to perform the same activities or by finding different ways to perform them. Configuring value-chain activities in different ways than competitors makes it difficult for rivals to imitate them. This is due to what is known as tradeoff protection.

8. What is your role as a manager in linking resources and capabilities to strategy and competitive advantage?

Guide: It is important to not lose sight of the fact that it is a firm's managers who scan the external and internal environment and consequently decide how to use resources and capabilities and how to configure value-chain activities based on their assessment of those sometimes rapidly changing environments. The role of managers is so critical that some experts include managerial human capital among a firm's resources; others include management among a company's dynamic capabilities.

How Would You Do That?

9. In "How Would You Do That? 3.1," we walked through how to apply the VRINE model to evaluate the value of Pfizer's patents. Later in the chapter, we walked you through the concept of the value chain. Identify the value chain for another organization. Are there activities that this organization performs differently than its rivals? Start by looking at the firm's products, services, or target markets. Likewise, examine the programs of a few leading rivals. Do any of the rival firms' value-chain activities give them a competitive advantage? If so, why don't others imitate these activities?

10. What resources and capabilities does your focal organization possess? What are the resources and capabilities possessed by rivals? How do your focal organization's resources and capabilities fare relative to those of the rivals' when you apply the VRINE model to them?

Guide to 1 and 2: Here you want to see your students map out the VRINE model for another focal firm, based on the example provided in the "How Would You Do That?" A worksheet is provided in this chapter's Instructor's Manual that you can copy and distribute or you can develop your own based on the particular aspects of the framework you would like to emphasize. The important part of this exercise is that the students develop a short list and not an extensive laundry list of resources and capabilities for their firm. You want to press them to be very specific. For instance, if they pick Disney and say that Disney is very good at movie production, then press them to specify whether they are talking about animated or live-action films. With regard to Disney, for instance, analysis shows that it beats industry averages in terms of animated feature performance but only do as well as the industry in the case of live-action films. A second area to press is if and how a firm's resources and capabilities operate in an interrelated fashion. The point here is that it is harder for firms to replicate a competitor's bundle of resources than it is to copy any single one.

Group Activities

11. What is the role of luck in gaining possession of a particular resource or capability? Can a firm manage luck? Give an example of a resource or capability that a firm garnered through luck and determine whether it was subsequently well managed.

Guide: The idea here is to get the students to think about how firms are able to capitalize or manage chance to their advantage. Strategy, particularly dynamic strategy, is all about putting the firm in a position where it has the opportunity and capability to capitalize on changes on a regular basis.

12. Some firms' products are so well known that the entire category of products offered in the industry (including rivals' products) are often referred to by the leading firm's brand name (which is called an *eponym*). Identify one such product and discuss whether its brand recognition gives the leading firm a competitive advantage. Why or why not?

Guide: This lets you talk about brand names as intangible resources and what it means when they become eponyms.

Proprietary Eponyms Proprietary eponyms are general words that are, or were at one time, proprietary brand names or service marks. Kleenex, for example, is a brand of facial tissues, yet today the word is used to refer to facial tissues of any brand. Xerox is a brand of photocopy machine; that word, too, has been since been adopted to refer to any brand of photocopy machine and, moreover, is also employed as a verb to describe the act of photocopying. The following are some other examples of eponyms:

- Band Aid
- Chapstick (Chap Stick)
- Cool-Aid (Kool-Aid)
- Jello (Jell-O)
- Kleenex
- Levi's
- Q-Tips
- Rollerblade
- Wite-Out
- Xerox

You can read more about eponyms at http://rinkworks.com/words/eponyms.shtml.

VI.   SUPPLEMENTAL EXPERIENTIAL EXERCISES

These exercises are drawn with permission from the Strategy Teaching Tool-kit found at:

http://instruction.bus.wisc.edu/mcarpenter/PROFESSIONAL/Toolkit/bpstools.htm.

1.   **The Tower Building Exercise.** This experiential exercise presents the opportunity to talk about the VRINE framework in dynamic contexts. This exercise requires that you have a set of building toys, such as tinker toys, Builderifics, or Zome (www.zometool.com). You have probably heard of this exercise before, but regardless you will find the outline and debrief provided by Coff and Hatfield immensely valuable.[1] Coff and Hatfield suggest that this exercise can be used to teach students about the concepts of first-mover advantages (or lack thereof) and the resource-based view.

The exercise requires the class to be broken up into teams. Each team is then assigned the task of building the tallest tinker toy tower they can in a short amount of time (we use a limit of 2 or 3 minutes). We generally allow the teams to take about 15 minutes to experiment with the building set to help come up with a design. Each team is then allowed to sequentially attempt to build a tall tower. The class then discusses why later teams tended to do better than earlier teams at accomplishing this task, though this is not always the case. When early teams build a large tower, later teams tend to adjust their designs on the fly, which tends to lead to failure.

An interesting level of complexity can be added to the exercise by requiring that the structures support a golf ball, and the winning height is the height of the top of the golf ball.

Discussion should revolve around the resource-based view concepts of rarity, imitability, and substitutability and first-mover advantages (technological leadership, preemption, switching costs, and buyer uncertainty) and disadvantages (free-rider effects, resolution of technological or market uncertainty, shifts in technological or customer needs, and incumbent inertia).

2.   Following the pharmaceutical examples provided in the text, use the VRINE model to develop an argument about whether Java provides Sun Microsystems with an advantage over other firms in its industry.

The objective here is to have the students gain a hand-on understanding of the use of the VRINE framework and to develop an understanding of Sun Microsystems resource-based advantages using the framework. You can use the following information, which comes from public sources. You can remind students that a simple Web search led you to the information and that the difficulty lies less in finding the information than applying it in the context of the VRINE framework.

Resources and Capabilities: Leadership and Human Capital

Java is the preeminent language of the Internet. Responding to the rise of the online environment, Java is designed to offer features that streamline programming for a highly distributed architecture. Java is a platform-independent language that produces code on a variety of CPUs under differing environments.

---

[1] Coff, R., and D. Hatfield. (2003). Tinkering in class. *Journal of Strategic Management Education, 1*(1), 289–304. This article can be also be found at:
http://instruction.bus.wisc.edu/mcarpenter/PROFESSIONAL/Toolkit/bpstools.htm#Group.

The Internet is a diverse, distributed universe populated with many types of computers, operating systems, and CPUs. A portable language is necessary for the Internet to function; Java is that language.

Java allows applications to be transmitted over the Internet and executed by a Web browser. Java gives the user the ability to download information from the many types of computers and operating systems on the Internet with confidence that no harm will be done to the user's computer.

A variety of resources and capabilities were needed to develop Java at Sun Microsystems. Java was not originally designed for the Internet. In fact, the primary motivation for Java was the need for a platform-independent language that could be used to create software to be embedded in various consumer electronic devices, such as toasters, microwave ovens, and remote controls. The senior managers at Sun and the members of the Java design team needed vision to realize that the problems encountered by creating code for embedded controllers are also found when attempting to create code for the Internet. Had Sun Microsystems not made the switch from consumer electronics to Internet programming, Java may have ended up an obscure language for programming consumer electronics. Sun also required the financial resources to engage in the research and development to design the language of the Internet.

The impact of Java on the Internet cannot be understated. It transformed the Web into the highly interactive environment it is today.

Valuable?

Were these resources and capabilities valuable? Yes. Sun introduced the first universal software platform designed from the ground up for the Internet and corporate intranets. Java technology enables developers to write applications once to run on any computer. Without Java, different versions of the same program would have to exist for each type of CPU connected to the Internet. Sun established a history of innovation and leadership that began from the protocols that propelled the Internet to our widely adopted Java technology.

http://www.sun.com/aboutsun/coinfo/history.html

Rare?

Were Sun's resources and capabilities rare? Apparently, other firms in the computer networking industry were committing their time and energy to the original programming language architectures of the World Wide Web and were less willing to commit to the development of an entirely separate computer language.

Costly to Imitate?

Were Sun's resources and capabilities costly to imitate? It would have been reasonable to expect Sun's competitors to have tried to imitate Java's platform-independent computer language, but this was not the case. Java is very difficult to imitate because it is designed to run on independent of platforms. Microsoft tried to displace Java by designing Internet Explorer to not be compatible with Java. The U.S. courts found Microsoft to be in violation of antitrust laws and forced Microsoft to make Internet Explorer compatible with Java.

Exploitability?

Was Java exploited by the organization? In 1996, Sun licensed Java technology to all major hardware and software companies. Today, Java is the preeminent language of the Internet.

http://www.sun.com/aboutsun/coinfo/history.html

Java2: A Beginner's Guide. Herbert Schildt.

VII.   APPENDICES

VRINE Framework

Resource	Valuable?	Rare?	Inimitable and Nonsubstitutable?	Exploitable by Organization?	Performance Implication	If Imitable or Substitutable, Why? (Briefly!)

CHAPTER 4 – EXPLORING THE EXTERNAL ENVIRONMENT

I. PURPOSE OF THE CHAPTER

After studying this chapter, students should be able to:

1. Explain the importance of the external context for strategy and firm performance.
2. Use PESTEL analysis to identify the macro characteristics of the external context.
3. Identify the major features of an industry and the forces that affect industry profitability.
4. Understand the dynamic characteristics of the external context.
5. Show how industry dynamics may redefine industries.
6. Use scenario planning to predict the future structure of the external context.

This chapter introduces the theories and models and tool that, from an external perspective, help explain why some industries outperform others and the potential dynamics that an industry may experience now or in the future. Chapters 3 and 4 are interdependent, and they are treated as such throughout the text. Timing constraints and taste will determine whether you teach them collectively, individually, and in what order. Regardless, after finishing this chapter students should have achieved three dominant goals.

The first dominant goal will be that industry analysis is focused on an industry or industry segment, not on a particular firm. That is why you are talking about industry analysis, not Wal-Mart–industry analysis. From the one or two leading firms' perspective, any industry can look attractive, but that misses the point of the exercise of industry analysis. The students need to identify characteristics of the industry and perhaps identify subgroups, strategic groups, or segments in an industry if their initial definition of an industry is too broad. This distinction has to be drilled into students, otherwise they are likely to miss the various dimensions that truly characterize an industry (including its strategic groups). The second objective is that the students should thoroughly understand the application of the five-forces model plus complementors analysis in stable and dynamic contexts. At a fundamental level, the vocabulary surrounding industry analysis is the vocabulary of most top executives, and fluency in these tools will help your students gain an equal footing with their competitors (and potential partners) at other schools. The third objective, which is foreshadowed a bit by the second objective, is that students should leave the session understanding that changes in industry structure, whether gradual or dramatic, are inevitable. Therefore, an understanding of the larger macro issues through the application of dynamic five forces, PESTAL, and scenario planning is critical.

In this chapter, the three differentiators—and hence your teaching strategy of the chapter—are manifested in the following ways:

- **Dynamic strategy.** The opening vignette chronicling the Cola Wars introduces students to one dimension of industry dynamism—competitive rivalry. Another driver of dynamism—globalization—is introduced and summarized in Exhibit 4.4. A later section of the chapter, the "Dynamic Characteristics of the External Content," explicitly outlines several additional drivers of industry change. The chapter concludes with an introduction of scenario planning as a tool for drawing on PESTAL and industry analysis to anticipate and integrate dynamism into industry analysis.
- **Formulation and implementation interdependency.** Because this chapter deals primarily with external analysis and the tools that students can employ to make that analysis, the

formulation/implementation relationship is less apparent. Nonetheless, a common theme carried through the chapter, starting with the opening vignette, is that change is inevitable, that firms need to anticipate change in some shape or form through the various implementation and leadership factors they have in place, and that students can build change into their strategy formulation process through the staging facet of the strategy diamond. This theme is heavily leveraged in the later chapters of the text that deal with strategy formulation and implementation and the various vehicles for achieving competitive advantage (and sometimes survival).

- **Strategic leadership.** Although the chapter focuses on external analysis, the opening vignette opens the door to the critical role played by strategic leadership as students see the Cola Wars unravel as a reflection of the perspectives and personalities of the respective leaders of Coke and Pepsi over time. To foreshadow material to come in later chapters, you might ask students to think about how industry structure defines or is defined by the mindset of the executives leading particular firms in industries or strategic groups. As an instructor, you add value to this chapter by showing students that they need to connect the dots, so to speak, between Chapters 3 and 4; between the information revealed by their industry and macro analyses and how firms' resources and capabilities and the outlook of their executives serve to filter and frame their assessment of the competitive environment (i.e., stable, dynamic, need for change, no need for change, etc.). The question—"What industry are you in?"—is a useful starting point for this framing, and you can show how it matters through the dialogue on industry determination in the chapter.

Additional Readings:

Brandenburger, A., and B. Nalebuff. (1996). *Co-opetition*. New York: Currency Doubleday.

Christensen, C. (2000). *The innovator's dilemma*. Cambrige, MA: Harvard Business Press.

Gordon, M. E., and G. R. Milne. (1999). Selecting the dimensions that define strategic groups: A novel market-driven approach. *Journal of Managerial Issues, 11*(2), 213–233.

Porter, M. (1980). *Competitive strategy: Techniques for analyzing industries and competitors*. New York: Free Press.

Schoemaker, P. J. H. (1991). When and how to use scenario planning. *Journal of Forecasting, 10*, 549–564.

II. BRIEF CHAPTER OUTLINE

pp. 86–118, PPT #1–4	**Chapter 4 Exploring the External Environment: Macro and Industry Dynamics** The purpose of the chapter is to explain the impact of external factors, the macro and industry environment, on firm strategy and what managers can do to address them; how industry dynamics redefine competition; and the use of scenario planning to address external dynamics. **Opening Vignette:** A Chronicle of the Cola War, pp. 87–89	
pp. 89–90, PPT #5–6	**THE EXTERNAL CONTEXT OF STRATEGY** The external context provides opportunities and poses threats to firms' profitability. **Industry-wide versus Firm-Specific Factors** These factors can be used to understand the competitive position of firms and determine viable strategies; firm managers can influence these factors to their advantage.	p. 90, Ex. 4.1 Comparative Industry-wide Levels of Profitability, 1995–2004

	FUNDAMENTAL CHARACTERISTICS OF THE EXTERNAL CONTEXT	
pp. 90–91, PPT #7–8	The external context has two major components: (1) the macro environment and (2) the industry environment, which includes strategic groups. **Key Questions:** What macro environmental conditions will impact implementation of a firm's strategy? What industry am I in? What are the industry characteristics? How stable are these characteristics?	p. 91, Ex. 4.2 The External Environment of the Organization
pp. 91–94, PPT #9–10	**MACRO ENVIRONMENT** **PESTEL analysis** involves an examination of the Political, Economic, Sociocultural, Technological, Environmental, and Legal contexts of a firm. It is used to help align strategy with changes in the business landscape; avoid strategies that may fail; and provide an entry point into a new country or region. PESTEL analysis consists of three steps: 1. Determine the relevance of each of the PESTEL factors to the firm's context. 2. Identify and categorize the information for each factor. 3. Analyze the data and draw conclusions. **Political factors** involve the stability of the political environment. **Economic factors** may have short- and long-term effects and include factors such as inflation rates, interest rates, tariffs, the growth of the local and foreign national economies, exchange rates, unemployment, and the availability of critical labor. **Sociocultural factors** vary from country to country; such factors include local languages, dominant religions, leisure time, age and lifespan demographics and attitudes toward consumerism, environmentalism, and the roles of men and women. **Technological factors** may lower production costs and/or improve quality, create product and service innovations, reduce communications costs and increase remote working, and alter distribution. **Environmental factors** relate to access to raw materials, which is best viewed as a direct and indirect cost for the firm, and the firm's footprint on its respective environments. **Legal factors** reflect laws and regulations, as well as whether the rule of law is well-established or not, how laws change, and costs of regulatory compliance.	p. 93, Ex. 4.3 The Dimensions of PESTEL Analysis
	Globalization spans both PESTEL analysis and industry analysis; it is characterized by the evolution of distinct geographic product markets to global interdependence of product markets. Four categories	p. 95, Ex. 4.4 Factors in Globalization

pp. 94–95	globalizing process: *market*, *cost*, *government*, and *competition*. **1. Markets.** The more similar markets in different regions are, the greater the pressure for an industry to globalize. **2. Costs.** Costs favor globalization to realize economies of scope/scale. **3. Governments.** Governments can provide favorable trade policies for globalization in the critical role of determining and regulating technological standards. **4. Competition**	
pp. 95–105, PPT #11–12 pp. 97–98, PPT #13–14	**INDUSTRY ANALYSIS** When firms earn above normal profits, competition will increase, usually with the entry of new firms, driving profits back to normal levels. If profits fall *below* normal levels, some firms will exit, and profits will rise to normal levels. But some industries have long-run average profits far exceeding "normal" levels; others have profits way below such levels. **The Ramifications of Imperfect Competition** Above-normal returns are possible due to imperfect competition, which is characterized by relatively few competitors, numerous suppliers and buyers, asymmetric information, heterogeneous products, and barriers to entry. Industry analysis helps determine the nature of competition, possible sources of imperfect competition, and the possibility of firms earning above-normal returns. **I/O Economics and Key Success Factors** Firms perform best with a strategy that fits the industry environment. Firms need skills and resources—key success factors (KSFs). The appropriate strategy, key assets, and requisite skills are dictated by *industry* characteristics. KSFs are easily transferred between firms. **What Is an Industry?** Defined as a firm or group of firms that produce or sell the same or similar products to the same market. **Fragmentation and Concentration** In a *duopoly* or *oligopoly*, the market is dominated by only two or a few large firms—high industry concentration versus industries without clear leader—fragmentation or low concentration. **The Concentration Ratio** This calculates the combined revenues of the largest industry participants as a ratio of total industry sales. Concentration affects the intensity of competition; fragmented markets tend to be more competitive than concentrated markets. **Defining Industry Boundaries** The question "What industry am I in?" is difficult to answer because of	*p. 95, *Fig. 4.1 Government Setting Industry Trade Standards* p. 98, Ex. 4.5 Concentration in Selected U.S. Industries

	many segments with different industry structural characteristics.	
pp. 98–104,	**A Model of Industry Structure** The industry five-forces model, coined by Michael Porter, can be used to determine the basic structure of an industry. These "forces" act as countervailing sources of power vying for the industry's total profits. Porter's five forces are:	p. 99, Ex. 4.6 The Five Forces of Industry Structure
	1. **Rivalry.** This is the intensity of competition: Who are the competitors? How do rival firms compete?	
PPT #15–21	2. **Threat of entry (and exit barriers)**. Industries with consistently high average profitability tend to be the most difficult to enter. Conditions that make it hard to enter an industry are called *barriers to entry*. Conversely, firms may face high *exit barriers* that typically force them to compete aggressively.	*p. 102, Ex. 4.2 DeBeer's Control of Half the World's Diamonds
	3. **Power of suppliers**. The ability of suppliers in an industry to dictate favorable terms to contracts and extract profit is referred to as *supplier power*; it is high when supplier firms forward integrate or when there are high switching costs for changing suppliers.	pp. 106–107, *How Would You Do That? A Five-Forces-Plus-Complementors Analysis of the U.S. Airline Industry*
	4. **Buyer power.** This is the degree to which firms in the buyer's industry are able to dictate favorable terms on purchase agreements that extract profit from the focal industry. Buyer power is greater when the product is important to sellers; when the product has little value for the buyer group; and when the buyer has numerous choices.	
	5. **Threat of substitutes.** This occurs when products in other industries can satisfy the same demand as the focal industry.	
	Complementors are players who provide complementary rather than competing products and services; they make it more attractive for suppliers to supply an industry or make it more attractive for a buyer to buy products or services at prices higher than they would pay absent the complementor. Strong complementors can *increase* profits by increasing demand for an industry's products.	
pp. 104–105	**Applying the Industry-Structure Model** The model can be used to determine the general attractiveness of an industry as well as opportunities and threats facing firms; the five forces are not static.	
pp. 105–109,	**Assessing Competitor Behavior** Managers analyze an industry to understand who the competitors are and what their behaviors are likely to be.	
PPT #22	**Strategic Group Analysis** This analysis involves identifying a distinguishable subset of competitors	p. 108, Ex. 4.7 A Strategic Group Map of the U.S. Bicycle Industry

	within an industry with similar strategies, resources, and capabilities that compete against each other more intensely than with other firms in the industry. **Mapping Strategic Groups** Determine the dimensions that most clearly differentiate firms (similar to segmenting a market) and then identify *direct competitors* characterized by the most intense *internal competition*. Analyzing strategic groups helps managers identify growth opportunities because it focuses on potential competitive positions that are compatible with a firm's unique set of resources and capabilities. **Predicting Competitor's Behaviors** This helps managers gain a better understanding of competitors' future behavior. Porter suggests a four-step approach for making predictions about competitors: 1. Understand their objectives; public firms provide this information in disclosure documents. 2. Determine their current strategies by using the strategy diamond to identify competitors' arenas, vehicles, differentiators, staging, and economic logic. 3. Determine their assumptions about rivalry and about themselves. 4. Determine their resources and capabilities.	
pp. 109–115, PPT #24–27	**DYNAMIC CHARACTERISTICS OF THE EXTERNAL CONTEXT** **Drivers of Change: Making the Five-forces Model Dynamic** When any of the five forces change significantly, the industry's structure and balance of power will probably be upset. **Industry Life Cycle** At the industry level, the competitive dynamics often follow an evolution similar to the product life cycle—a powerful driver of industry dynamics. **Evolution and Commoditization** A common result of industry evolution is price competition, because many or most of its incumbents acquire similar resources and capabilities and thus offer fairly similar products. Commoditization is the process by which sales shift from unique product features more to price. **Evolution and Reinvigoration** Certain industry segments may emerge to reinvigorate it, restoring it to a growth industry. **Evolution and Information** The effects of learning, information, and competition may enable newer entrants to replace industry leaders, especially in later stages of industry change. **Evolution and Tactics** In the early stages, industry incumbents are a source of education and a form of	p. 111, Ex. 4.8 Dynamics of Industry Structure p. 112, Ex. 4.9 Industry Life Cycle Curve

	"insurance" with product support. From introduction to growth, incumbents often add extra services to retain sales momentum. **Technological Discontinuities** These are a special, intensive case of changes in action; the two major forms are process and product discontinuities. **Disruptive Product-related Change** Most technological changes are gradual, incremental, and evolutionary. Episodic changes punctuate industry evolution as discontinuous change with breakthrough technologies. Competency-sustaining technologies are typically introduced by incumbents; disruptive technologies destroy incumbents' competencies. **Disruptive Process-related Change** May involve process-related as well as product-related technologies. **When Industries Divide** This occurs when one industry becomes two or more distinct, but often related, industries; happens when a firm divests a core business that is separated from the original core. **When Industries Collide** New industry definitions can arise from the consolidation of two or more separate industries into one; results in fewer industries. Industry division and convergence provide opportunities to create value for firms, which lead the charge in convergence and division of industries.	
pp. 115–118, PPT #28–30	**USING SCENARIOS TO PREDICT THE FUTURE** SWOT analysis generally deals best with one situation or scenario; scenario planning helps with uncertainty about how features of the scenario might change over time. **Scenario Planning** Leaders can use scenario planning to develop detailed, internally consistent pictures of a range of plausible outcomes as an industry evolves over time; provides a bigger picture. The steps of scenario planning are: 1. Define the target issue, time frame, and scope for the scenarios. 2. Brainstorm key drivers, decision factors, and possible scenario points; distinguish between **trends**, the direction of change, and **uncertainties** in the direction and pace of change. 3. Develop the framework by defining two specific axes. 4. Flesh out the pictures that detail the four worlds. 5. Specify indicators that can signal which scenario is unfolding. 6. Assess the strategic implications of each scenario.	p. 116, Ex. 4.10 Six Steps in Scenario Planning p. 118, *4.2 How Would You Do That? Developing Scenarios for Credit Unions*

* Figure or Exhibit **NOT** enumerated in the PDF file.

III. SUGGESTED CASES TO ACCOMPANY TEXT

In our concepts-with-cases version of the text, we have chosen the "Carrefour versus Wal-Mart" (secondarily mapped to the global strategy chapter) and the "Chinese Fireworks Industry" cases. With the latter case, it is relatively easy to reinforce the objective that industry analysis should be from an industry-level perspective. With the Carrefour case, you have the opportunity to remind students that external analysis starts with the landscape, and only after that is understood can you begin to talk in terms of firm-specific opportunities and threats. Again, any case you use should provide industry-level data and some special reports provided by stock analysts; *The Economist* or *BusinessWeek* could provide "live" data for all the external analytics identified in the chapter. The availability of such a report may flavor your choice of firm/industry for the internal analysis conducted in conjunction with Chapter 3.

Need help selecting cases? Pearson Prentice Hall and Pearson Custom Publishing are pleased to present the ultimate resource for creating and customizing casebooks.

- Start with a CaseMap correlated to your text or start from scratch; do it yourself using our easy-to-use interface or collaborate with a developmental editor.
- Cases can be selected from a variety of sources, including Harvard Business School Publishing, Darden, Ivey, Thunderbird, and NACRA.
- We clear permissions for you on cases and content not in the database.
- You can also create custom course packs by adding articles, original material, and textbook chapters.
- Pearson Custom casebooks can be delivered in print or online.
- Additionally, we supply you, the instructor, with a free evaluation copy delivered 7 to 10 days after you create your book, free access to teaching notes, and case-method teaching resources.

We're here to help: Looking for a case on a specific topic, company, country, or scenario? Or, looking for a new case to substitute for one you've used in the past? We will help you find the right cases for your course and help you create a casebook that meets all your teaching needs. For guidance on building a casebook to reflect your course needs, e-mail our editorial consultant at customcases@prenhall.com.

Visit www.prenhall.com/custombusiness for more information and to see which Prentice Hall titles are available for short-run customization and to view suggested cases. To start your own straightforward search for material:

Step 1: Select "search content and create your book" and log in.
Step 2: Search by case number or keyword or browse by discipline to find suggested cases based on the book you use or course you teach.
Step 3: Browse, preview, and select the cases, articles, or chapters you wish to include (you will see that price and page count of the book in the top right-hand corner of the screen as you "build" the book).
Step 4: Finalize your selections, get them in the order you want, package your customized book with any Prentice Hall title for a discount (if you wish), click "confirm book," and you have the option to request a free evaluation copy.
Step 5: The Web site immediately gives you the ISBN of your custom book. You should give this ISBN to your bookstore; they will use it to place their order with us.

Beyond our cases and Pearson Custom Publishing, if you choose to compile your own casebook you will have an opportunity to draw from a variety of sources. These sources include going direct to Hartwick Leadership Cases, IVEY Case Publishing, European Case Clearing House (ECCH), Harvard Business School (HBS), Darden, and others.

Given the popularity of Harvard cases, we have selected these additional cases for use with this chapter:

		ID#	Pages	TN
Southwest Airlines—2002: An Industry Under Siege	HBSP	9-803-133	24	Y
Delta Air Lines (A): The Low-Cost Carrier Threat	HBSP	9-704-403	15	N

Southwest Airlines—2002: An Industry Under Siege The company's management is faced with long-term questions regarding the rate and manner of growth in the wake of the 9/11 attacks and general industry malaise. Teaching Purpose: To understand ways of achieving and maintaining both a differentiated and a low-cost service offering.

Delta Air Lines (A): The Low-Cost Carrier Threat The top management of Delta Air Lines must decide how to respond to the threat posed by low-cost carriers such as Southwest and JetBlue. Among the options considered is the launch of a low-cost subsidiary by Delta itself. Prior efforts by Delta and by other full-service airlines to launch a low-cost subsidiary have failed. Can Delta devise a better response? Teaching Purpose: To examine why it is difficult for one company to pursue multiple targets or strategies within a single organization.

IV. LINKING THE CHAPTER TO A COMPUTER SIMULATION

Again, if you are already using a simulation then it is appropriate to tie in this chapter by having students talk about the characteristics of their "industry" and the external context more generally. If your simulation is pretty well underway by now, you will likely see that firms are grouped around particular strategies, and you can point out to students that these are realistic strategic groups. You can also ask them to identify environmental KSFs and to determine whether any firm seems to be gaining a competitive advantage simply by possessing one or more KSFs or through the better execution of one or more. Finally, because simulations always have constraints, ask the students to point out what the simulation does well in terms of capturing the external context and what it does relatively poorly here. Sometimes this is a place for you to offer your own ideas about the strengths and weaknesses of the sim in this regard. It is important to teach students about the advantages and disadvantages of sims, with the overriding advantage being that it is nice to be able to learn from possible mistakes in a simulated environment!

V. END OF CHAPTER QUESTION ANSWER GUIDE

Review Questions

1. What constitutes the external context of strategy?

Guide: A firm's external context is composed of both its industry and the larger sociopolitical environment. An industry is a firm or group of firms that produce or sell the same or similar products or services to the same market.

2. What are the five forces affecting industry structure?

Guide: The five dimensions are industry rivalry (how competing firms compete), threat of entry (from new competitors), power of suppliers, buyer power, and threat of substitutes.

3.   What are complementors?

Guide: Complementors are firms in other industries that provide products or services that tend to increase the value and sale of products or services in the focal industry. It is important for students to see that firms can fill more than one role. For instance, a firm may be a complementor in one relationship but a competitor in another business interaction. (Airlines are competitors when trying to sell airline seats to travelers but complementors when purchasing new planes).

4.   What is a key success factor (KSF)?

Guide: KSFs are the requisite skills and resources that all firms in an industry or industry segment must possess simply to be viable. They are like table stakes in a poker game—you need to have them to simply enter the game.

5.   What are strategic groups?

Guide: Strategic groups are distinguishable clusters of competitors within an industry. A strategic group is a subset of firms that compete against each other more intensely than with other firms in the industry because they share similar strategies, resources, and capabilities.

6.   What factors increase industry dynamics?

Guide: Here it is useful to employ the dynamic five forces plus complementors model – an overarching framework to better understand and analyze the external context from a dynamic strategy perspective. This model provides a general framework for understanding change.

7.   What is the industry life cycle?

Guide: In other courses, such as marketing, students will have probably seen industry evolution portrayed at the product level by the familiar S-curve. At an industry level, this evolution similarly starts with industry emergence and ends with maturity, or perhaps even stagnation and abandonment. One common consequence of this evolutionary process is that the industry tends to become characterized by price competition, partly because many or most of the industry incumbents acquire similar resources and capabilities and product and service offerings become fairly similar.

8.   What is a technological discontinuity?

Guide: Breakthrough technologies, or discontinuous technological change, sometimes enhance the competencies of incumbent firms and at other times appear to be competence destroying. Competence destroying technologies are referred to as disruptive technologies. Disruptive technologies are generally introduced by new firms, while competency enhancing technologies are typically introduced by incumbent firms.

9.   How does globalization affect the external context of strategy?

Guide: Industries that are not defined as global can have purely domestic players competing alongside firms with operations in many foreign countries, with both sets of firms doing equally well. In contrast, a truly global industry is one in which the core product or service is standardized across geographic markets, the marketing approach is relatively uniform, and firms integrate their competitive moves across countries. In these industries, competitive advantage, let alone firm survival, clearly accrues to the cluster of firms with global competitive capabilities.

10. What is industry redefinition?

Guide: Industry redefinition is a potential consequence of the drivers of change that affect industry structure. At some point, the accumulation of changes will result in a redefinition of the industry entirely. The new definition is a subset of the old definition or the new definition is the agglomeration of several old definitions.

11. What is scenario planning and when would you use it?

Guide: Scenario analysis helps managers to develop detailed and internally consistent pictures of a range of plausible futures as a foundation for strategy formulation and implementation; it provides a big picture to determine the significance of any single underlying uncertainty or trend. Unlike forecasting, scenarios are not straight-line, one-factor projections from the present, but rather are complex, dynamic, and interactive stories from a future perspective.

How Would You Do That?

12. "How Would You Do That? 4.1" illustrates the five-forces model for the airline industry. Use that analysis as an example and perform a five-forces analysis for one of the following industries: soft drinks, cable television, or cell-phone service providers. What are the one or two most important issues that arise in your analysis that managers in that industry must take into account when they revisit their strategies?

Guide: We use an exercise like this to remind students to analyze the industry from the perspective of the industry. This may sound simple, but too often students will apply industry analysis tools from the perspective of one firm, instead of providing an analysis of the industry overall. You want them to understand the industry characteristics first, and then be able to relate a specific firm to that industry context. If they are finding that their focal firm does not seem to fit the larger industry they have analyzed, then you can suggest that their firm may occupy a segment of the industry with different characteristics or that their firm is exploiting resources and capabilities that allow it to overcome the normally undesirable characteristics of that industry. Finally, we ask students to make managerial recommendations, because industry analysis, in and of itself, does not have a strategic action orientation. Because you are teaching students about strategy and how to take relevant actions, it is useful to have them talk about how they would transition from analysis to action.

13. Using the scenario-planning example in "How Would You Do That? 4.2" as a model, create a scenario that predicts the future of the airline industry. What are reasonable best-case scenarios? What does a pessimistic view look like? Are some competitors better prepared for the range of outcomes than others?

Guide: This exercise can be done with any industry, but it is often richer if you conduct it using the context of a case you are studying or an industry that you are very familiar with. Because we provided some information on the airline industry, and there is a later case in the concepts-with-cases version about this industry, we suggest it here. When done well, this exercise gives students a better grasp of how strategies need to be developed in a way that gives them both focus and flexibility. If you search on

"Credit Unions 2005: An executive report," using Google, you will find a fully fleshed out example that also provides you with a great how-to guide to conduct a scenario analysis exercise in your class (and the basis for "How Would You Do That? 4.2"). http://www.cues.org/repository/2005scenario.pdf

Group Activities

14. Pick two of the industries listed in Exhibit 4.1, one on the high end of profitability and one on the low end. What are the boundaries of these industries? What are their market and geographic segments? Who are the key players? Draw up a five-forces model of each industry and compare and contrast their industry structure. Now shift your analysis to the dynamic five-forces model. What dimensions of the five forces model are most likely to change in the near future? Which are most likely to stay relatively stable? Answer these questions for both 5- and 10-year windows.

Guide: This set of questions lets you help students follow a logic whereby static industry analysis cascades into a more dynamic view of that industry. Such an analysis is done irrespective of a focal firm's characteristics, other than its industry membership. Remind the students that they are conducting an industry analysis, not an analysis of a particular firm's situation. The objective is to show students how the analyses are undertaken, how each perspective gained is valuable, and how they can gain a more dimensional understanding of an industry while still having static and dynamic perspectives, respectively. Once students have mastered the five-forces model, the next level of complexity is the addition of the sixth force, complements. In many ways this provides a nice pathway to the dynamic six-forces model in general.

Students often gloss over how difficult it can sometimes be to identify an industry and its boundaries, and at the very least this exercise gives you an opportunity to do that. The cola companies and the discussion of bottled water from this chapter provide a case in point. Beyond this, the exercise lets the students work through a five-forces model, and we typically encourage them to also identify the complementors. With regard to industry dynamics, savvy students will refer to the scenario-planning tool to begin this or to communicate what they have concluded. If you choose, you can recommend that they use the tool for this part of the exercise. One way to forestall the use of that tool until Group Activity 2 is to ask them to use the stakeholder analysis tool, in conjunction with the dynamic five forces, to map out possible changes.

15. Develop a simple scenario for one of the industries you selected for Group Activity 1. What were the key dimensions of uncertainty (pick only two)? Did your findings in this exercise influence your responses to the questions in Group Activity 1? If so, in what ways? If you examined more than one segment within your focal industry, how did your scenarios differ from segment to segment?

Guide: If you have not already done this with the previous activity, this final step lets students flesh out a scenario plan for their chosen industry. If they have done a good job with question #3, then they will simply need to evaluate those items to determine the two that present the industry with the greatest amount of uncertainty. Often the biggest challenge is identifying and agreeing upon (if in groups) those two dimensions. You should push the students to come up with catchy names for each of the quadrants, similar to the example with the credit unions presented in the chapter. Finally, have them identify which quadrant offers the most likely scenario and why and which offers the least likely scenario and why. Have them identify the type of firm (resources, capabilities, etc.) that would be most likely to benefit from the most likely scenario. Then ask them what changes would need to be made to the firm, and how hard these might be, if the least likely scenario actually prevailed. Point out to them that the continued dominance of the global auto industry by the Japanese was in fact the least likely scenario predicted by most (and many now-defunct) U.S. and European auto manufacturers.

VI. SUPPLEMENTAL EXPERIENTIAL EXERCISES

These exercises are drawn with permission from the Strategy Teaching Tool-kit found at

http://instruction.bus.wisc.edu/mcarpenter/PROFESSIONAL/Toolkit/bpstools.htm.

1. **The Paper Chase**. The paper chase, or paper fight, is an exercise that simulates hypercompetition—the situation where industry members rapidly erode each others temporary competitive advantages. Strategies emerge but are perfectly imitable. As a result, a strategy will not create an advantage beyond one period. Each round might also be used to simulate different stages of the industry life cycle.

Preparation:

1. Place two uneven piles of paper on each side of the room (uneven piles allows you to talk about different resource endowments).
2. Invite two groups to the front (on each side).
3. With no warning or explanation, say "We are going to have a paper fight. Ready, go!"
4. Let them go for a short period of time (until you see a strategy of any kind).
5. Have a discussion about what happened.
6. Invite two other groups (or another group to challenge the winner) to do it again. Possibly repeat a third time.

What happens the first round: The first time, the groups will hesitate. There are no rules—this is an undefined landscape (embryonic industry). Sometimes, it will not even be clear that they should "organize" as two "firms," and they will fight amongst themselves. Generally, they will attack the other team after a short hesitation. However, they will often hold their position more than chase the other team around the room (no flanking maneuvers or more complex strategies). The organization will either have the same people crumpling and throwing or people will specialize in crumpling or throwing.

Discussion questions:

- Why did you fight? Why did you hesitate?
- Who won? Why do you say so? (Criteria for success/organizational performance: Number of paper wads on the other side versus number of hits scored.)
- What were the internal structures of the "firms"?
- Were the teams on equal footing with regard to resources? What resources mattered (not the amount of paper)?
- What strategies emerged? Did it matter? How did the other side respond?

What happens the second round: The second time we tend to see more complex strategies and organizations. The landscape is changed, and they can now throw back the crumpled wads from the last bout. Strategies include: (1) everyone throws back wads and no one crumples, (2) flanking maneuvers, (3) steal the other team's paper, (4) movement around the room.

Discussion questions:

- What was different this time? How did the rules change?
- What does it take to win now? Would the same strategy work again?
- What were the internal structures of the "firms"?
- What would happen if we ran it again? And after that? How long is a strategy useful? (Note that for each strategy, there is a response that neutralizes it.)

2. **Key success factors!** Remind students that key success factors are typically defined by industry characteristics (consider these as table stakes in a poker game—all viable players need to possess them). Have groups pick an industry and each identify 5 to 10 KSFs. Then have them map the industry using a grid where the KSFs are dimensions of the base and the vertical axis represents high and low levels of competence or investment in each KSF. How different or similar are the companies based on this grid? Next, from the four scenario quadrants you identify through scenario analysis, how will key success factors change? What are the implications of these changes for the five-diamond strategy model?

Many of the learning benefits of the end-of-chapter questions are reinforced here as well, albeit in a more condensed fashion and with a slightly different emphasis—here the emphasis is on KSFs. One additional point you can make here is that a firm can have many of the KSF's requisite to effective competition in an industry, but this does not give them a competitive advantage, unless they are executing one or perhaps all the KSFs better (more efficiently and/or effectively, depending on the need to differentiate based on uniqueness or low cost or both) than the competition. For instance, all major retailers need to excel at supply chain management, but perhaps only for Wal-Mart is this a competitive advantage, due to the coupling of its supply chain sophistication and sheer size. This is where you can help students see the difference between table-stake's competencies, things that are complicated and expensive to do but just keep a firm in the game, and true differentiating competencies, those that give a firm some near, and perhaps long-term, competitive advantage.

VII.   APPENDIX

Industry concentration is a topic that students usually understand better when they try to see the C2, C4, C8, etc., concentration ratios themselves across many industries. For this exercise, send them to:

www.census.gov/epcd/www/concentration.html

This government site uses business census data to detail concentration across just about every industry. Ask the students to pick two industries, have them look at the concentration data, and ask them to paint a picture which, using the concentration information alone, suggests whether the industry would be attractive or not. Then you shift gears in the discussion by asking them, based on the opposite of the industry characterization that they have offered, what kind of firm resources and capabilities might be most valued in this industry or leased valued, again based on its concentration characteristics.

PART THREE
BUSINESS, CORPORATE, AND GLOBAL STRATEGIES

CHAPTER 5 – CRAFTING BUSINESS STRATEGY

I.   PURPOSE OF THE CHAPTER

After studying this chapter, students should be able to:

1.   Define *generic strategies* and show how they relate to a firm's strategic position.
2.   Describe the drivers of low-cost, differentiation, and focus strategic positions
3.   Identify and explain the risks associated with each generic strategic position.
4.   Show how different strategic positions fit with various stages of the industry life cycle.
5.   Evaluate the quality of a firm's strategy.

This chapter builds on Chapters 3 and 4 to help students understand how firms formulate business strategies that utilize their resources and capabilities to exploit opportunities in their competitive environment. The chapter also outlines how successful positioning strategies take into account the impact of rivalry and competitive retaliation and the life cycle of an industry and provide a step-by-step process for testing the quality of the strategy.

You might target three primary takeaways from this chapter. First, students should be fluent in the terminology of the generic strategies shown in Exhibit 5.1 and how they map to differences in the five elements of strategy model. Second, even though this chapter is about strategy in relatively stable environments, strategies must also take into account the learning curve (Exhibit 4.4 and "How Would You Do That 5.1") and the industry life cycle (Exhibit 5.9), which means that even firms in relatively stable environments need to think about changes in strategy. This allows you to again tie in the staging facet of the strategy diamond. Third, and as reinforced in the last section of the chapter, a strategy is not good if it is not feasible, and this includes taking into account a firm's VRINE-based resources and managerial capabilities. If your students can recite the criteria in Exhibit 5.10 by heart, then you will have fully achieved this third objective.

In this chapter, the three differentiators—and hence your teaching strategy of the chapter—are manifested in the following ways:

- **Dynamic strategy.** Although this chapter focuses mostly on a relatively static view of industry contexts (as Chapter 6 is about business strategy in dynamic contexts), the dynamic perspective nonetheless is touched on in this chapter. For example, the opening vignette on three different players in the bicycle industry shows students how various firms have approached the changes in that industry context. Treatment of the learning curve, as shown in "How Would You Do That 5.1," also reinforces the notion of change in the way that learning relates to organizational performance. Finally, the second-to-last section of the chapter shows students how strategic positions may vary by stages in the industry life cycle.
- **Formulation and implementation interdependency.** This interdependence is part of the subtext of the first part of the chapter, and perhaps becomes the most obvious in "How Would You Do That 5.1," which applies the learning curve to the bicycle industry. This feature shows that "how" a firm executes its strategy will influence "what" the strategy can be in the first place. To bring this point

full circle, the final chapter section, summarized in Exhibit 5.10, provides students with a way to evaluate the quality of their strategy, and the final check-list item is "Can your strategy be implemented?"

- **Strategic leadership.** The first parts of the chapter deal with the different strategies a firm can adopt, and we word this in a way that students can see that these are the result of choices made by a firm's leaders. In the section and checklist mentioned previously (Exhibit 5.10), one of the key implementation questions is: "Is the management team able and willing to lead the required changes?" This last point reinforces both the importance of strategic leadership and its role in strategy formulation and implementation, but also again foreshadows the dynamic nature of strategy.

Additional Readings:

Liao, S. S. (1988). The learning curve: Wright's model vs. Crawford's model. *Issues in Accounting Education, 3,* 302–315.

Porter, M. E. (1980). *Competitive strategy.* New York: Free Press.

Prahalad, C. K., and G. Hamel. (1990). The core competence of the corporation. *Harvard Business Review, 68*(3), 79–91.

Teece, D. (1980). Economies of scope and the scope of the enterprise. *Journal of Economic Behavior and Organization, 1,* 223–247.

II.   BRIEF CHAPTER OUTLINE

pp. 122–124, PPT #1	**Chapter 5 Creating Business Strategies** The purpose of this chapter is to discuss how different generic business strategies relate to strategic positions, explain the risks of each generic strategy position, relate the strategy positions to the industry life cycle, and evaluate the quality of a firm's strategy. **Opening Vignette:** A Tale of Three Wheels in the Bicycle Industry, pp. 123–124	
pp. 125–126, PPT #2–4	**AN INTRODUCTION TO BUSINESS STRATEGIES** Remember from Chapter 1 that *business strategy* refers to choices about a firm's competitive posture; it is summarized by the *strategy diamond* and its *five elements of strategy.* For diversified firms, business strategy is typically applied at the level of an individual business or a strategic business unit (SBU). Alternative strategic positions are compatible with different industry life cycle stages. To assess a strategy, the criterion is consistency between a firm's resources and its environment.	*p. 125, Fig. 5.1 Pacific Cycles Positions Differently From Trek*
pp. 126–132, PPT #5–6	**TYPES OF STRATEGIES—FINDING A POSITION THAT WORKS** **Strategic positioning** refers a firm's location on competitive dimensions relative to its rivals (e.g., Michael Porter's generic strategy model). The purpose of strategic positioning is to *reduce the effects of intense rivalry on profitability.* **Strategic Positioning and the Generic Strategy Model** Strategic positioning relates to the strategy diamond's *arenas* (geographic breadth and product scope), *differentiators*, and *economic logic.* Two important factors that affect strategic positioning are (1) the firm's resources and capabilities and (2) industry structure.	p. 127, Ex. 5.1 The Strategic Positioning Model *p. 130, Fig. 5.2 Harley Davidsons' Focus on High-End Motorcycles* p. 131, Ex. 5.2 Integrated Positions: Low-Cost,

	Generic Strategies Porter's generic strategies identify four positions: *low-cost, differentiation, focused-cost leadership, and focused differentiation.*	Differentiation, Stuck-in-the-Middle
	Cost and Differentiation Occurs in two dimensions: the potential source of strategic advantage and the breadth of the target market.	p. 132, Ex. 5.3 The Interplay Between Cost and Differentiation
	A firm can gain an advantage over rivals in one of two ways:	
	1. Produce a similar product at a lower cost than its rivals.	
	2. Produce a differentiated (unique) product and charge a higher price to more than offset the added costs of differentiation.	
	Strategic positions are configurations of elements in a firm's strategy. Along the horizontal dimension of Exhibit 5.1, firms choose the underlying economic logic of whether to compete on differentiation or cost.	
	Scope of Involvement This refers to how broadly firms compete.	
	Low-Cost Leadership A firm strives to produce goods or services at a lower total cost than competitors; produces substantially similar products to its rivals but at a lower cost; some features or services are sacrificed.	
	Differentiation The firm provides products or services of higher quality, reliability, and/or prestige than rivals. Successful differentiation allows the firm to (1) set prices at the industry averages (and gain market share because consumers will choose higher quality at the same price) or (2) raise prices over those of competitors (and reap the benefits of higher margins).	
	Focused Low-cost Leadership The firm is a low-cost leader in a narrow segment of the market.	
	Focused Differentiation The firm targets relatively small segments; the greater its differentiation, the smaller market segment, because fewer customers can afford the higher prices.	
	Integrated Positions Such positions are achieved when elements of one position support a strong standing in the other. Elements of a differentiating position can be adopted by low-cost competitors. Firms whose products don't seem to be low cost or differentiated are often stuck in the middle between strategic positions.	
	Generic Strategy and Firm Resources Successful positions are predicated on the effective implementation of the drivers of cost or differentiation advantage, or both.	
pp. 132–139, PPT #7–20	**Economic Drivers of Strategic Positioning** Choices in strategic positioning are influenced by economic logic.	p. 134, Ex. 5.4 Scale and Cost
	Drivers of low-cost advantages include economies of scale, learning, production technology, product design, and location advantages for sourcing inputs.	
	Economies of scale result when fixed costs are spread over greater levels of output (e.g., specializing in a specific production process, practicing superior inventory management, exercising purchasing power, spending more effectively on advertising or R&D).	p. 136, 5.1 *How Would You Do That? How To Take the Learning Curve on Two Wheels*
	Diseconomies of scale can result from bureaucracy, high labor costs, inefficient operations, and inflexibility.	
	Minimum efficient scale (MES) is the output level that delivers the lowest possible costs; operating below or above MES leads to	p. 136, Ex. 5.5 The Time Value of

	cost disadvantage. MES is the smallest scale necessary to achieve maximum economies of scale. **MES & Technology** MES is a function of technology. With some technologies, MES is reached only at relatively low levels of production, and although there's no scale advantage at higher levels, neither is there any disadvantage. **The Learning Curve** The basic principle holds that incremental production costs decline at a constant rate as production experience is gained. Two firms of the same scale may have significantly different operating costs due to the **learning curve**. Economies of scale reflect the scale of the operation during any given period of time—the volume of current production. Cost decreases attributable to the learning curve reflect the cumulative level of production since the production of the first unit. **Putting the Learning Curve to Use** The learning curve can be used to improve total-cost forecasts, which can enable more aggressive pricing decisions. **Multiunit Organizations and the Learning Curve** When learning is transferred from one unit to another, the organization achieves positive gain. Franchise systems, for instance, can codify their knowledge without each new franchise starting from scratch. **Other Sources of Cost Advantage** **Economies of Scope** Refers to the potential cost savings associated with multiproduct production; a firm can share a resource among one or more of its products, thus lowering the cost of each product. **Production Technology** Different production technologies entail different costs. **Product Design** The design of a product can sometimes be altered to lower a firm's production costs (e.g., Canon redesigned the photocopier so that it required fewer parts and allowed for simpler assembly compared with Xerox). **Drivers of Differentiation Advantages** Firms must use *market segmentation* to identify subgroups of buyers with distinguishable needs, select one or more of these unique buyer needs, and satisfy them in ways that competitors don't or can't. **Creating Value and Promoting Willingness to Pay** Firms must price products or services to (1) recoup added costs of delivering the value-added feature and (2) generate enough profit to make the strategy worthwhile. The point is to drive up the customer's willingness to pay.	Learning at East Side Bikes p. 137, Ex. 5.6 The Learning Curve at East Side Bikes p. 137, Ex. 5.7 Spreadsheet for East Side Bikes
pp. 139–141, PPT #21	**Threats to Successful Competitive Positioning** A successful strategic position must satisfy two requirements: 1. It must be based on the firm's resources and capabilities. 2. It must achieve some level of consistency with industry conditions. **Threats to Low-Cost Positions** The following are threats to low-cost positions: certain technologies can be imitated; failure to offer sufficient quality to satisfy buyers' basic needs; a serious threat in labor-intensive industries is increased public awareness of questionable labor practices in developing countries.	p. 139, Ex. 5.8 Low Cost and Differentiation: Drivers and Threats

	Threats to Differentiation Positions The following are threats to differentiation positions: a differentiating feature that buyers don't care about; failing to understand the total costs entailed by differentiation; overfulfillment; ease of imitation; competitors emulate differentiation element quickly or cheaply. **Threats to Focused Positions** Focused positions may be out-focused by competitors when they more uniquely satisfy the needs of that segment. **Threats to Integrated Positions** Firms that try to differentiate and achieve a low-cost position end up straddling two inconsistent positions. **The Importance of Understanding Tradeoffs** Few firms can succeed in being all things to all customers; firms need to know exactly what opportunities they're forgoing, what tradeoffs to make.	
pp. 141–145, PPT #22	**STRATEGY AND FIT WITH INDUSTRY CONDITIONS** Generic competitive positions requires choosing *objectives* related to elements of the strategy diamond—differentiators, economic logic, and certain aspects of arenas. **Strategies for Different Industry Conditions** Strategies tend to vary across different phases of the industry life cycle. **Embryonic Stage** In the embryonic stage, business models are unproven, the technology has not been standardized, capital needs generally outstrip the resources and capabilities of startups, and uncertainty is high. Early movers create a strong position for later phases. **Growth Stage** During the growth stage, the speed of the learning curve increases, providing firms the opportunity to establish low-cost positions that are difficult to imitate. However, technologies can change as new entrants learn from and improve on the work of early movers. **Maturity Stage** During this stage, the products are more familiar to the majority of customers. Product information is more widely available, and quality becomes more important in consumer choices. This increases the potential for premium prices from differentiation strategies, and mature industries often undergo *consolidation.* **Decline Stage** During this stage, products have attributes of quasi-commodities. Price competition can be intense; cost containment is critical. Firms with low-cost positions have an advantage, and the industry may suffer from overcapacity.	p. 143, Ex. 5.9 Life-Cycle Strategies *p. 145, *Fig. 5.3 General Dynamics Faced Declining Defense Industry After the Cold War*
pp. 145–147, PPT #23–24	**TESTING THE QUALITY OF A STRATEGY** A simple five-step process makes use of all of the relevant tools and models to evaluate the quality of a firm's strategy. **Does Your Strategy Exploit Your Firm's Resources and Capabilities?** Low-cost strategic positions require manufacturing resources and capabilities that can contribute to a cost advantage. **Does Your Strategy Fit with Current Industry Conditions?** Is the environment hostile, benign, or somewhere in between; determine whether strategy aligns with the key success factors favored by the firm's competitive environment.	p. 146, Ex. 5.10 Testing the Quality of Your Strategy

			ID#	Pages	TN
Are Your Differentiators Sustainable? If competitors can imitate the firm's differentiators, can you protect your current relationship with your customers? **Are the Elements of Your Strategy Consistent and Aligned with Your Strategic Position?** Ensure that arenas, vehicles, differentiators, staging, and economic logic are mutually reinforcing and consistent with objectives. **Can Your Strategy Be Implemented?** Make sure that the strategy is aligned with the appropriate implementation levers.					

* Figure or Exhibit **NOT** enumerated in the PDF file.

III. SUGGESTED CASES TO ACCOMPANY TEXT

At this point, you will want to look for cases where the firm is in a fairly focused set of businesses. Single-business firms are the best, because you can really drill down the fundamental aspects of business strategy. If you are using a case where the focus is on the SBU of a larger corporation, it will be useful to have the students contemplate the advantages and disadvantages of being a subsidiary as opposed to a stand-alone firm. For instance, what are the advantages and disadvantages for Coke being a firm concentrated in one industry versus Pepsi being in a firm that also has snack food (Frito Lay) and restaurants (Taco Bell, Kentucky Fried Chicken, and Pizza Hut)?

Given the popularity of Harvard cases, we have selected these additional cases for use with this chapter:

		ID#	Pages	TN
Airborne Express (A)	HBSP	9-798-070	23	N
Cat Fight in the Pet Food Industry (A)	HBSP	9-391-189	13	Y

Airborne Express (A) In the wake of a highly successful quarter, senior managers of Airborne Express, the third largest player in the express mail industry, review the firm's competitive position. Airborne has survived, and recently prospered, in an industry with significant economies of scale, even though it is much smaller than industry giants FedEx and UPS. The case challenges students to understand Airborne's unusual position. Detailed data allow students to analyze Airborne's relative cost position, the fit among its activities, the differences between Airborne and its rivals, and the evolution of its industry. Using these analyses, students make recommendations concerning the firm's pricing policy, its globalization efforts, and a partnership with a related company. Designed to be taught in a course on business-unit strategy.

Cat Fight in the Pet Food Industry (A) Describes the pet food industry in the mid-1980s, prior to the breakout of a major competitive battle. Illustrates that when there are benefits to playing in multiple markets, competitors will take action in one market to preserve their position in others. Case provides an example of multimarket competitive interaction. Covers competitor analysis and prediction and economies of scope.

IV. LINKING THE CHAPTER TO A COMPUTER SIMULATION

Business strategy is the focus of most computer simulations, and this will be readily evident from their support material. In the Preface, we included selections from syllabi from two courses that used simulations along with cases and text material. The first example was of a class that utilized Mike's Bikes, and the second example was from a course that used Capstone. As mentioned in the Instructor's Manual text for Chapter 1, it is usually best to start the sim after you have worked through at least one of the business strategy chapters. Almost any business simulation can be used in conjunction with a course in strategic management, but the key will be to tie the experiential exercise into the content and flow of the course. We have found that a simple quiz on the rules helps to ensure that the students actually read them. As you can probably imagine, when something goes wrong with the sim, the students will blame the instructor (you J), but it is usually a failure on their part to adequately understand the system.

V. END OF CHAPTER ANSWER GUIDE

Review Questions

1. What do we mean by generic strategies?

Guide: The two generic strategies defined by Porter are low cost and differentiation. The term *differentiation* is used to represent a general state of uniqueness for which customers are willing to pay a premium price. Alternatively, firms can make decisions to generate superior returns and a competitive advantage by trying to beat competitors through having lower costs.

2. What criteria must be met in order for differentiators or low-cost leaders to be successful?

Guide: A firm with products or services of discernibly high quality can either price at industry averages, in which case it will gain market share because consumers will choose the higher quality product for a given price, or it can raise its prices over that set by competitors and again reap higher margins. In order to be successful, this differentiation must produce a general state of uniqueness for which customers are willing to pay a premium price. Firms attempting to compete by being low-cost leaders strive to produce a good or offer a service at a lower total cost than it takes competitors to offer the same good or service. A firm that can produce substantially similar products as its rivals but do so at a lower cost has a substantial competitive advantage.

3. What's the relationship between economies of scale and minimum efficient scale?

Guide: Economies of scale exist if the average total cost for a unit of production is lower at higher levels of output during a given period of time. Economies of scale flow primarily from spreading fixed costs over a greater level of output. Other possible sources of economies of scale include possible efficiencies related to higher volumes of production, spreading fixed costs over more volume, specialization in the production process, superior inventory management, purchasing power, advertising, and R&D. With regard to minimum efficient scale, costs may decline over some range of production but increase over others. This suggests that total average cost has a "U" shaped relationship and that the average total cost function has a minimum point. The output level that delivers the lowest possible costs is referred to as minimum efficient scale (MES). Another way to think of MES is that it is the smallest scale necessary to achieve maximum economies of scale.

4. What are economies of scope?

Guide: Economies of scope are conceptually similar to economies of scale but relate to potential cost savings associated with multiproduct production. When a firm producing two or more products or services (i.e., greater scope in operations) is able to share a resource and thereby lower the costs of one or more of these units, it experiences economies of scope.

5.   How does the learning curve work?

Guide: The basic intuition for the learning curve is that the incremental costs of production decline at a constant rate as experience is gained. The learning curve phenomenon has been found to exist in most production situations, though the rate of cost decline varies by situation, industry, and technology. The steeper the learning curve, the more rapidly costs decline.

6.   What is market segmentation? What role does it play in strategic positioning?

Guide: Differentiation strategy, in practice. requires that executives properly perceive market segmentation—identifying specific subgroups of buyers who have distinguishable needs. Market segmentation involves selecting one or more of these unique needs that are valued by the buyer and satisfying them in ways that competitors do not, much in the same way that strategic positioning involves selecting the competitive dimensions on which firms will compete.

7.   What is meant by *willingness to pay*? How does it relate to strategic positioning?

Guide: Successful differentiation occurs only when customers are willing to pay a premium price, a premium that exceeds the cost of delivering the added benefit of the differentiation. The point of differentiation is to drive up customers' willingness to pay. The goal of differentiation is to expand the margin between customers' willingness to pay and (supplier opportunity) cost.

8.   How does the industry life cycle affect the business strategy?

Guide: Industry conditions have an important effect on the formulation of firm strategy. That is, industry analysis gives us a snapshot view of an industry at one particular point in its industry life cycle, and we now examine how alternative strategies fit those conditions. As industries move through different stages of the life cycle, the types of strategies will succeed, fail, or change.

9.   What are the steps in testing the quality of a strategy?

Guide: The first step in evaluating a firm's strategy is to determine whether the strategy and competitive position exploits the firm's resources and capabilities. The second step in evaluating a firm's strategy starts with asking whether the current strategy fits with current conditions in the firm's competitive environment. The third step is to determine whether the firm's differentiators are sustainable. The fourth step is to determine whether all the elements of the strategy diamond are internally consistent and aligned with the firm's current or foreseen strategic position. The final step, but by no means the least, is determining whether the strategy can be implemented.

How Would You Do That?

10. Let's revisit the learning curve and change some of the assumptions that we made for the scenario in "How Would You Do That? 5.1." Assume that the first bike took 100 hours, the second 85, and the fourth 72.25. What would be the incremental "cost" in hours for the 16th bike? For the 124th? For the 1,000th? Try to find these numbers using both the formula explained in the box and the learning curve calculator located at www.jsc.nasa.gov/bu2/learn.html.

11. Based on the information in "How Would You Do That? 5.1," assume that you have determined that established leaders have such an experience advantage that you'll never catch their cost position. Devise a realistic strategy for entering and competing against an established player that has a significant low-cost leadership position.

Guide to 1 and 2: In the example provided, each time the units doubled—from 1 to 2 and 2 to 4—a 15-percent efficiency improvement was realized. This means that the learning percent for this sample is 85 percent. To calculate the costs for the 16th, 124th, and 1,000th bikes using the learning curve calculator, simply enter 100 hours for the first unit, the number of units, and 85 into the learning percent. Using Crawford's method for each quantity results in 52.20 hours for the 16th unit, 32.30 for the 124th, and 19.80 for the 1,000th. Using the formula of $y = ax^{-b}$, the resulting forecasted costs are 65.98 for the 16th, 48.53 for the 124th, and 35.48 for the 1,000th.

This exercise gives the students a chance to try to apply the learning curve on their own. Variations on this exercise include using data, such as passenger miles, from the airline industry. The airline industry typically shows that the most profitable players also benefit from a learning curve. Astute students will point out, with regard to the airline industry, that perhaps it is not just passenger miles but gate turns (i.e., how quickly and airline can turn planes at the gate) that is the factor that should be accounted for in the learning curve calculation. This, for instance, would explain why a player like Southwest Airlines is consistently profitable. In discussing the tool conceptually, students may gain a deeper understanding that it is not just any learning that matters, but rather learning related to the core drivers of profitability in an industry; these are often industry key success factors.

Group Activities

12. Review our opening case about the three bicycle manufacturers. Use the strategy diamond and the generic strategy model to describe the positioning strategy of each firm. With what you know about the bicycle industry, can you identify any underserved (or overserved) segments?

Guide: Pacific Cycle: arenas, all product categories, distributed through mass retailers; vehicles, internal growth with some acquisitions, differentiators, vary by product line; staging, fast growth; economic logic, low cost mixed with branding. Trek: arenas, high-end segment; vehicles, distributes through specialty shops; differentiators, innovative styles and design; staging, growth through acquisitions; economic logic, design and manufacture high-quality, innovative bikes. Montague: arenas, high-end segment, travel-friendly bikes; vehicles, not discussed; differentiators, portability of a high-performance bike; staging, not discussed; economic logic, design and manufacture high-quality, portable bikes. This discussion should lead nicely into under- or overserved markets.

13. Go back to Exhibit 4.1 in Chapter 4. Identify low-cost leaders from two of these industries. What seem to be the drivers of their cost-leadership positioning strategies? Are they the same? If not, why?

Guide: The idea here it to get students thinking about how much firms follow similar or different competitive repertoires. This exercise tends to flow better if you suggest two low-cost competitors in industries that are relatively familiar to the students, for instance, Southwest Airlines from the airline industry and Dell from the computer industry. Generally, students will see that while the economic logic (low-cost leadership) is being followed by both firms, the other elements of their strategies may be quite different. Indeed, the cost drivers of their low-cost position will also likely vary.

VI. SUPPLEMENTAL EXPERIENTIAL EXERCISES

These exercises are drawn with permission from the Strategy Teaching Tool-kit found at:

http://instruction.bus.wisc.edu/mcarpenter/PROFESSIONAL/Toolkit/bpstools.htm.

1. One useful exercise is to have students pick a company and then discern whether it is pursuing a low-cost or differentiation strategy. Once they have "guestimated" the overarching strategy, ask them to summarize the value-chain activities that the firm is exploiting to realize the strategy. Also ask them to identify those activities that appear to be working against the strategy. Finally, have the students map the strategy with the strategy diamond.

This staged learning approach has two benefits. First, students will gain a better understanding of the generic strategies, how generic strategies can be reflected in value-chain activities, and how generic strategies are mapped using the strategy diamond model. The second benefit is that you can point out how other firms may use different combinations of activities and elements to achieve the same strategy.

2. Have students examine segmentation in the auto industry. How many real segments can they identify? Are there equal numbers of firms in each segment? What criteria led the students to see the various strategic positions they have identified? One potential breakdown could include compact, mid-sized, luxury, SUVs, trucks, vans, and sports cars. However, letting the students decide on segments will be instructive. It is always useful to also suggest that students consider geographic and price segments. Walking through the number of firms in each segment as well as outlining how these companies compete will help to highlight key issues from this chapter.

CHAPTER 6 – CRAFTING DYNAMIC BUSINESS STRATEGIES

I.   PURPOSE OF THE CHAPTER

After studying this chapter, students should be able to:

1.   Identify the challenges to sustainable competitive advantage in dynamic contexts.
2.   Understand the fundamental dynamics of competition.
3.   Evaluate the advantages and disadvantages of choosing a first-mover strategy.
4.   Analyze and develop strategies for managing industry evolution.
5.   Analyze and develop strategies for technological discontinuities.
6.   Analyze and develop strategies for high-speed environmental change.
7.   Explain the implications of a dynamic strategy for the strategy diamond and of strategy implementation.

The purpose of this chapter is to highlight the dynamic contexts in which firms compete. Dynamic contexts challenge firms to continuously improve their game and perhaps even strive to rewrite the rules of competition. This is what differentiates the fundamental context of strategy, even strategies that address one stage of the industry-product life cycle, from the dynamic context of strategy. The term *strategic intent* implies that firms not only respond to changes in their environment, but also try to manage the environment in ways that favor them over their competitors and force other firms to follow them. Moreover, successful dynamic strategies increasingly require the nearly seamless integration of strategy formulation and implementation combined with an appetite for experimentation and risk taking.

Your goal with this chapter is to hammer home the three themes about dynamic contexts that we introduced in the first chapter: (1) Change may be gradual, (2) change may be rapid, and (3) change is inevitable. In doing so, you create an additional opportunity to reinforce the roles of staging and the interdependence of strategy formulation and implementation in a firm's success.

In this chapter, the three differentiators—and hence your teaching strategy of the chapter—are manifested in the following ways:

- **Dynamic strategy.** The chapter is true to its title and deals with many aspects of dynamic strategy formulation and implementation, from the opening vignette on Napster through the closing section on using the staging facet of the strategy diamond to formulate and implement strategies for dynamic contexts.
- **Formulation and implementation interdependency.** Although this interdependence is true in all contexts, it is particularly salient in dynamic ones, where how a firm executes its strategy quickly reveals what its next options are. You see this cascading effect through the opening vignette on Napster; Exhibits 6.2 and 6.3 on competitive interaction and first-mover choices, respectively; through the description of improvisation and simple rules in dynamic strategy; and the closing section of the chapter, "Formulating and Implementing Dynamic Strategies." These latter concepts are reinforced in "How Would You Do That? 6.2."
- **Strategic leadership.** Strategic leadership is central to crafting and executing strategies in dynamic contexts due to dynamic capabilities represented in a firm's executives and managers. Although the opening vignette on Napster does not delve much into the characteristics of the reborn firm's CEO, Chris Gorog, strategy researchers would say that it's no coincidence that his background in the music

industry is now reflected in Napsters present state and strategy (see the bio of Chris Gorog in the appendix). The chapter's final sentences reiterate that "both the strategic leadership of senior management and the culture of the organization that they foster should reflect a commitment to reasoned risk taking, learning, and responding to change. Indeed, it's hard to promote core values that support the strategy implementation in dynamic contexts if top management doesn't practice and champion them."

Additional Readings:

Brown, S., and K. Eisenhardt. (1998). *Competing on the edge: Strategy as structured chaos.* Boston: Harvard Business School Press.

Chan, W. K., and R. Mauborgne. (1997). Creating new market space. *Harvard Business Review, 77*(1), 83–93.

Chan, W. K., and R. Mauborgne. (2005). *Blue ocean strategy.* Boston, MA: Harvard Business School Press.

Christensen, C., and M. Raynor. (2003). *The innovator's solution.* Boston: Harvard Business School Press.

Eisenhardt, K., and D. Sull. (2001). Strategy as simple rules. *Harvard Business Review,* January 2001: 106–116.

Smith, K. G., W. J. Ferrier, and C. M. Grimm. (2001). King of the hill: Dethroning the industry leader. *Academy of Management Executive, 15*(2), 59–70.

II.   BRIEF CHAPTER OUTLINE

	Chapter 6 Crafting Business Strategy for Dynamic Contexts	
pp. 150–153, PPT #1–3	The purpose of this chapter is to examine the necessity for seamless integration between formulation and implementation of strategy in a dynamic context; to compare and contrast the advantages and disadvantages of first mover advantage; and to analyze strategies for managing industry evolution, technological discontinuities, and high-speed environmental change. Opening Vignette: Roxio and the Resurrection of Napster, pp. 151–153.	
p. 153, PPT #4	**Dimensions of Dynamic Contexts** Dynamic competition needs dynamic strategies to improve and possibly alter the rules of competition.	
pp. 153–155, PPT #4	**THE CHALLENGES TO SUSTAINABLE COMPETITIVE ADVANTAGE** Three interrelated dimensions that cause dynamic contexts are competitive interactions, industry evolution, and technological disruptions. Speed of change complicates strategy. **Competitive interaction** is the interactions between incumbents and the interactions of new entrants and incumbents' responses. New entrants often use a strategy that varies from incumbents. **Industry evolution** creates change from firms with obsolete resources and capabilities to those favored by industry conditions. **Technological change** is risky when it primarily affects business	*p. 155, Fig. 6.1 Sony's Digital Technological Advantage over Kodak*

	processes. Discontinuities that affect product technology often favor differentiation strategies. **Speed of change** is a critical factor in competition. Reacting to change means detecting and responding quickly; anticipating change means foreseeing global markets, new market segments, and complementary or conflicting technologies. **Scenario planning** helps to anticipate change.	
pp. 155–163, PPT #5–15	**BUSINESS STRATEGY AND COMPETITIVE INTERACTION** **Strategy and Strategic-Positioning in the Face of Competition** The strategy diamond, the VRINE model, and industry-structure analysis support strategy formulation for a strategic position. Strategic-positioning decisions are supported by tactical decisions to implement strategy. **Competitive Interaction Theory** A firm's managers should predict reactions to its actions and determine the best course of action given competitors' likely reactions. Four ways to initiate competitive action are aggressiveness, complexity of the competitive action repertoire, unpredictability, and tactics to delay reaction. New competitors with new business models create disruptive change—strategies that are both different from and in conflict with those of incumbents. Disruptions often have the following characteristics: emphasize different product attributes; start as rather low-margin businesses and grow into significant companies; and new firms' business models cannot be imitated easily. **Competitive Dynamics and Incumbent Positioning** Incumbent firms' respond to industry dynamism through (1) containment, (2) neutralization, (3) shaping, (4) absorption, or (5) annulment. **The Pitfalls of the Retaliatory Mindset** Defensive strategies. **First Movers, Second Movers, and Fast Followers** First movers are firms that initiate a strategic action such as introduction of a new product or service or development of a new process that improves quality, lowers price, or both. **First-Mover Strategy and the Industry Life Cycle** Many effective second movers can be characterized as fast followers. **The Pros and Cons of First-Mover Positioning** A first-mover advantage is valuable under certain conditions: 1. When it achieves an absolute cost advantage in terms of scale or scope 2. When image and reputation advantages are hard to imitate later 3. When first-time customers are locked into a firm's products or services because of preferences or design characteristics 4. When the scale of a firm's first move makes imitation unlikely First movers also bear risks, including the costs of designing, producing, and distributing new products and educating	p. 156, Ex. 6.1 Phases of Competitive Interaction p. 158, Ex. 6.2 The Spectrum of Competitive Response Strategies *p. 160, *Fig. 6.2 Ralston Purina's Defensive Strategy* p. 162, Ex. 6.3 A Gallery of First Movers and Fast Followers p. 163, Ex. 6.4 Evaluating a Firm's First-Mover Dependencies on

	customers. First-mover advantages diminish—and fast-follower advantages increase—under conditions such as: 1　Technological advances allow a second mover to leapfrog. 2.　The first mover's product or service strikes a positive chord but is flawed. 3.　The first mover lacks a complement that a follower possesses. 4.　The first mover's costs outweigh the benefits. **First Movers and Industry Complementors** A first-mover strategy should consider the inimitability of the new product, the switching costs of customer relationships, and the *strength* of complementary assets.	Industry Complements
pp. 163–166, PPT #16	**STRATEGIES FOR MANAGING INDUSTRY EVOLUTION** **Approaches to the Pressure of Commoditization** Two alternatives can be used to deal with the pressures of commoditization: **Anticipating Commoditization** 1.　**Value-in-use Approach** occurs when the first approach with a value-added or "bundling" as a firm increases service benefits while simultaneously either raising or holding prices. 2.　**Process-Innovation Approach** is a second approach to anticipating commoditization to lower its cost position so that it can further cut prices (or to remain the low-price leader). **Responding to Commoditization** 1.　**Market focus** is a focused-differentiation strategy. 2.　**Service innovation** is a tactic for achieving a cost advantage by eliminating services that were once bundled. The best response to industry commoditization is usually: 1.　Improve services and raise prices to serve a more narrowly defined market. 2.　Serve a larger market but lower costs and prices through process improvements.	*p. 165, *Fig. 6.3 Badger Meters, Inc. Bundling of Products in Response to Low-Priced Competitors*
pp. 166–169, PPT #17–19	**STRATEGIES FOR TECHNOLGICAL CHANGES** A double-S curve is based on interlocking industry life cycles. Industries do not fall into decline when technology propels the industry into another growth phase. A technological discontinuity has innovation that dramatically advances an industry's price versus performance frontier, triggering a period of ferment that is closed by the emergence of a dominant design. This is followed by incremental technical change, which is, in turn, broken by the next shift. New entrants can change the business landscape with disruptive technologies. Incumbent firms may be marginalized or eliminated unless they create new opportunities or react defensively. **Creating New Markets—The Value Curve** A strategy for anticipating industry evolution or creating technological	p. 166, Ex. 6.5 The Effect of Technological Disruption

	discontinuities involves creating new market segments and value curves. The value curve graphs a company's relative performance across its industry's factors of competition. **The Dimensions of New-Market Creation** Four questions can be used to discover the keys to a new-market space: 1. What product or service attributes that rivals take for granted should be reduced well below the industry standard? 2. What taken-for-granted industry factors should be eliminated? 3. What product or service attributes should be raised above the industry standard? 4. Are there any factors that the industry has never offered that should be created? Three categories of new value curves are high-end disruptions, low-end disruptions, and hybrid disruptions: 1. High-end disruption is a new-market disruption, which changes the industry value curve by disrupting customer expectations with vastly improved product performance. Often results in huge new markets where new players unseat the largest incumbents. 2. Low-end disruption is at the low end of industry offerings. Entrants often target the least valuable of incumbents' customers as platforms to later migrate to higher-value space. **The Value Curve** The value curve is a tool that can be used to plot how major groups of firms are competing currently and reveal underlying assumptions firms make about the market and customers. 1. Determine the existing KSFs as perceived by incumbents. The major strategic groups lead to some KSFs. 2. Plot the performance of each group on the KSFs identified. 3. For each strategic group, draw the line that connects the points plotted on the graph—this is that group's value curve. It visually represents how they present their products to customers along key buying criteria. **A Shift in the Focus of Strategic Thinking** Shifting from head-to-head rivalry to a new-market-space mindset requires emphasizing actions and capabilities that eclipse the competition.	p. 167, Ex. 6.6 The Four-Actions Framework: The Key to the Value Curve
pp. 169–177, PPT #20–28	**STRATEGIES FOR TURBULENT AND HYPERCOMPETITIVE MARKETS** "Turbulence" leads to firms perceiving disruptions to be more traumatic than they are because root causes are surfacing that have festered unheeded for years. **Turbulence and Hypercompetition** Strategy that depends on rapid change needs organizational flexibility and responsiveness. **A Model for Competing in the Face of Hypercompetition** Competing in turbulent environments requires adept finesse of the staging element of the strategy diamond with regular deployment and testing of options of new growth initiatives,	pp. 170–171, *6.1 How Would You Do That? [yellow tail] Creates a New Value Curve in the Wine Industry* p. 171, Ex. 6.7 A

	businesses, and ways of doing business. Dynamic context is typically anchored in so-called systems, chaos, or complexity theories. They share a basic premise—firms need some degree of "chaos" to survive. **Improvisation and Simple Rules** Managerial practices that contribute to a culture of frequent change are moderated by a few simple rules. Complexities in turbulent environments require a simplified strategy with a few cast-iron rules that define direction. **Sequencing Past and Future** The bridge between past activities and future conditions is built on experimentation and learning. Managers' knowledge of the competitive environment guide their selection and reconfiguration of business practices. **Tactical Probing** Low-cost "probes" can be used to test a strategy and suggest future changes. Tactics can be both tools for competing today and experiments in new ways of competing tomorrow. **Setting Pace and Rhythm** Many managers fail to appreciate the role played by time and timing in formulating and executing strategy. **Putting a Value on Staging and Pacing** Real-options analysis is used to evaluate the substantive financial aspects of the firm's dynamic strategies. The idea behind real options is to preserve flexibility to be well positioned in the future when the competitive environment shifts. A real option is the opportunity (though by no means the obligation) to take action that will either maximize the upside or limit the downside of a capital investment. The purpose of real-options analysis is to uncover and quantify an initiative's embedded options or critical decision points. The greater the projects uncertainty and flexibility, the greater the potential value of having options in managing it. **Five categories of real options**: 1. Waiting-to-invest options 2. Growth options 3. Flexibility options 4. Exit (or abandonment) options 5. Learning options	Value Curve for the U.S. Wine Industry p. 172, Ex. 6.8 Conventional Versus New-Market-Creation Strategic Mind-Sets p. 173, Ex. 6.9 Creating Options for Future Competitive Advantage and Profitability p. 175, Ex. 6.10 Staging and Pacing in the Real World p. 177, Ex. 6.11 The Value of Real Options
pp. 177–180, PPT #29	**FORMULATING AND IMPLEMENTING DYNAMIC STRATEGIES** **Focusing on Arenas and Staging** **The Role of Arenas** The choice of customers and products varies according to environmental dynamics. **Industry Evolution** Arenas must fit with a firm's resources, capabilities, and dynamic capabilities. **Technological Discontinuities** Arenas overlap with their role in low-end disruption strategies, was broadened to include noncustomers, particularly when strategy is designed to create new markets. **Globalization** Apply lessons about competing in one geographic arena to competing in others.	pp. 178–179, 6.2 *How Would You Do That? Integrating Formulation and Implementation in Dynamic Contexts: The Case of R.R. Donnelly*

| | **Turbulent and Hypercompetitive Markets** Use arenas as laboratories to conduct experiments or to launch probes into the possible future of the firm and its strategy.
The Role of Implementation Levers Managers should seek balance among the elements of the model—reflected in organizational structures, systems, and processes that accommodate the strategic needs of firms in turbulent and hypercompetitive environments. Staging can serve to bridge formulation and implementation.
Due to forecasting difficulties in dynamic contexts, apply scenario planning and real-options analysis. Strategic leadership and organization culture should foster a commitment to reasoned risk taking, learning, and responding to change. | |

* Figure or Exhibit NOT enumerated in the PDF file.

III. SUGGESTED CASES TO ACCOMPANY TEXT

Fortunately, more and more cases are being written that deal with dynamic strategy. The concepts-with-cases version of the text includes cases on Advanced Micro Devices ("Life Beyond Intel") and Airbus ("From Challenger to Leader").

Historically, texts treated competitive dynamics as the sole facet of dynamic strategy, which meant that you might use a case like the "Cat Fight in the Pet Food Industry" (Harvard Case 9-391-189) or the "China Beer Wars" series (INSEAD 398-090-1). However, although rivalry is important, as is multimarket competition, you may find greater value by delving into cases on basic technological shifts and globalization. Cases such as "NUCOR" or "NUCLEON" are good examples, and various versions are on the market from some of the providers noted below. Other useful cases include "EMI and CT scanner (Part A)" (HBS); electric cars (in Clayton Christensen's, *The Innovator's Dilemma,* Chapter 9; esp. 191–199); "Delta and Pine Land" (HBS); "Boston.com" (HBS); "World VCR" (HBS); and "The Honda Effect," excerpted from "Perspectives on Strategy: The Real Story. Behind Honda's Success," Richard T. Pascale, *California Management Review.*

Need help selecting cases? Pearson Prentice Hall and Pearson Custom Publishing are pleased to present the ultimate resource for creating and customizing casebooks.

- Start with a CaseMap correlated to your text or start from scratch; do it yourself using our easy-to-use interface or collaborate with a developmental editor.
- Cases can be selected from a variety of sources, including Harvard Business School Publishing, Darden, Ivey, Thunderbird, and NACRA.
- We clear permissions for you on cases and content not in the database.
- You can also create custom course packs by adding articles, original material, and textbook chapters.
- Pearson Custom casebooks can be delivered in print or online.
- Additionally, we supply you, the instructor, with a free evaluation copy delivered 7 to 10 days after you create your book, free access to teaching notes, and case-method teaching resources.

We're here to help: Looking for a case on a specific topic, company, country, or scenario? Or, looking for a new case to substitute for one you've used in the past? We will help you find the right cases for your course and help you create a casebook that meets all your teaching needs. For guidance on building a casebook to reflect your course needs, e-mail our editorial consultant at customcases@prenhall.com.

Visit www.prenhall.com/custombusiness for more information and to see which Prentice Hall titles are available for short-run customization and to view suggested cases. To start your own straightforward search for material:

Step 1: Select "search content and create your book" and log in.
Step 2: Search by case number or keyword or browse by discipline to find suggested cases based on the book you use or course you teach.
Step 3: Browse, preview, and select the cases, articles, or chapters you wish to include (you will see that price and page count of the book in the top right-hand corner of the screen as you "build" the book).
Step 4: Finalize your selections, get them in the order you want, package your customized book with any Prentice Hall title for a discount (if you wish), click "confirm book," and you have the option to request a free evaluation copy.
Step 5: The Web site immediately gives you the ISBN of your custom book. You should give this ISBN to your bookstore; they will use it to place their order with us.

Beyond our cases and Pearson Custom Publishing, if you choose to compile your own casebook you will have an opportunity to draw from a variety of sources. These sources include going direct to Hartwick Leadership Cases, IVEY Case Publishing, European Case Clearing House (ECCH), Harvard Business School (HBS), Darden, and others.

Given the popularity of Harvard cases we have selected these additional cases for use with this chapter:

		ID#	Pages	TN
Apple Computer--2002	HBSP	9-702-469	22	Y
Amgen Inc.: Planning the Unplannable	HBSP	9-492-052	18	Y

Apple Computer—2002 In 1980, Apple was the leader of the personal computer industry, but by 2002 it had suffered heavy losses at the hands of the Wintel camp. This case examines Apple's strategic moves as the PC industry evolves in the twenty-first century and poses the question: Can Steve Jobs make Apple "insanely great" again?

Amgen Inc.: Planning the Unplannable By the early 1990s, Amgen—a pharmaceutical company started little over a decade ago as Applied Molecular Genetics—was within range of becoming a billion-dollar company. With two extremely successful biotechnology drugs on the market, Amgen stood as the largest and most powerful independent company of its type in the world. Top executives in the company viewed long-range planning as an important ingredient in the firm's success; many others—including some of the firm's scientists—were less sure. With Amgen's sales expected to continue to grow rapidly, the firm's long-range planning process would be put to the test. Shows the different, sometimes paradoxical perspectives held within a single, dynamically changing company toward the issue of long-range planning. Students are challenged to synthesize these views into a coherent picture of a firm's growth amid great uncertainty.

IV.   LINKING THE CHAPTER TO A COMPUTER SIMULATION

Few simulations have much dynamism to them beyond competitive interaction, but some do allow you to introduce certain "shocks" to the system—in that sense you should feel free to improvise but be careful not to be too critical of student's performance if they happen to be on the losing end of the technological shift. Some sims let you give certain teams cost a performance advantages, and you can attribute these to technology shifts.

V.   END OF CHAPTER ANSWER GUIDE

Review Questions

1.   What are four sets of challenges to sustained competitive advantage outlined in this chapter?

Guide: Industry evolution often changes the basis of competition from differentiation to cost or price. Technological discontinuities may foster a similar path, particularly when the discontinuities are primarily in the area of business processes. Globalization, too, will change the basis for competition. Finally, over and above the particular driver or source of change, the speed of change itself is a critical factor. Examples: Industry evolution, PC's when the product became commoditized; technological discontinuity, photo industry moving from film to digital; globalization, clothing or shoe manufacturing; speed, auto industry, cars are now designed in a fraction of time it used to take.

2.   What is the relationship between first and second movers?

Guide: First movers are firms that choose to initiate a strategic action. This action can be the introduction of a new product or service. Second movers are simply those firms that are not first, but the actions that they take and timing of their entry are nonetheless important. Second mover is not synonymous with late mover, and for that reason many effective second movers are characterized as fast followers, even if the elapsed time between first and second mover is several years or more. Why might a firm prefer a second-mover strategy? Because a first mover also bears significant risks and costs, including the costs of educating customers about the new product or service and the costs of design, production, distribution, and marketing missteps. Second movers typically evaluate new product or process innovations and only adopt them once they begin to gain traction in the market, which will be around the market takeoff stage.

3.   What is industry commoditization? What are two strategies a firm may undertake to combat commoditization?

Guide: Firms can typically pursue one of two strategies prior to the onset of industry commoditization. The first approach can be considered a sort of value-added or bundling strategy, where the firm increases the service benefits while at the same time raising prices or at least holding them firm. A second approach that anticipates industry commoditization is called a *process-innovation strategy*. This approach is different from the value-added strategy from the standpoint that the firm seeks to decrease price, or remain the low-price leader, through reductions in operating costs and costs to serve. After commoditization, one approach is referred to as a *market-focus strategy*. This approach is very similar to the focused-differentiation strategy, but requires that the firm further narrow, or focus, its customer base. In many ways, these firms are saying that some market segments or customer groupings, in conjunction with the firm's geographic location and customer relationships, are more attractive than are others. The service innovation strategy is the second approach that firms can pursue in response to industry commoditization. This is perhaps one of the most challenging strategies, because it requires a firm to strip away those services which used to be included with the product so that the firm can be price competitive.

4.   What is a new-market-creation or high-end disruption strategy?

Guide: First movers can use this strategy to set the direction of industry change, whereas fast followers can use it to help shape the change. An important characteristic of a market creation strategy is that it shifts strategic focus from head-to-head competition to the creation of new markets. Essentially, the creation of a new market requires the introduction of new things *and* the elimination of things that are considered necessary by incumbent firms.

New market disruption is essentially a new-market-creation strategy. The difference, however, is that new market disruptions eventually result in huge new markets where the new players unseat and overwhelm the largest of traditional industry incumbents. In contrast, new-market-creation strategies may or may not result in huge new markets. Like new-market-disruption strategies, they shift a firm's competitive focus from head-to-head competition to the redefinition of the business model for some proportion of the existing market.

5.   What is a low-end-disruption strategy?

Guide: Some disruptive technologies appear at the low end of industry offerings. Low-end-disruption strategies cause problems for incumbents because they are easy to ignore. Incumbents are rationally focused on serving their best customers—those who are demanding high margin products at the leading edge of the industry. Low-end entrants who target lower-margin business are often able to use their entry (which is often unopposed) to build a platform from which to migrate into more attractive market space. And as their products or services improve, they often end up satisfying the needs of the center of the market better than incumbents, largely because incumbents have been busy making incremental improvements to satisfy their best clients' demands—improvements that cause them to overshoot the needs of the middle market.

6.   What are the three layers of activity that underlie strategies for turbulent and hypercompetitive markets?

Guide: The three interrelated horizons of activity are (1) defend and extend current business, (2) drive growth in emerging new businesses and, (3) seed options for future growth businesses.

7.   What is the role of timing and pacing in strategies for handling turbulent and hypercompetitive markets?

Guide: Firms that manage this aspect of their strategy well will actually have an understanding of their internal rhythm for introducing new products or services. This rhythm will typically be synchronized with internal resources and capabilities and the needs and characteristics of key suppliers and customers. Moreover, this rhythm will typically be reflected in the dynamic capability of transitioning from old product and service markets to new ones, including the ability to exit the old ones quickly. Indeed, it is often harder for firms to drop a product than launch a new one.

8.   How might you apply real-options analysis, financially and conceptually, in the context of strategies for turbulent and hypercompetitive markets?

Guide: The key here is for students to recognize that conventional uses of NPV and DCF analysis can systematically bias decision making against potentially valuable real options. A real-options analysis (the technical specifications of which are beyond the scope of this course) recognizes that managers can and do obtain valuable information after a project is launched. Thus, a real option seeks to uncover and quantify a project's embedded options, or critical decision points. The greater the uncertainty and flexibility, the greater the value of real options.

9. What five defensive strategies might industry incumbents pursue in turbulent and hypercompetitive markets?

Guide: Incumbents are those who are defensive in nature. The chapter discusses five responses that incumbents can use to in dynamic markets: containment, neutralization, shaping, absorption, and annulment.

10. What are the implications of dynamic strategies for strategy formulation and implementation?

Guide: Although all five elements of strategy are important and must be managed in concert, the arenas and staging diamonds are perhaps the most important here. In addition to the need for dynamic capabilities, it is your relative attention to these facets that will typically differentiate a dynamic strategy from strategies developed for more stable contexts. In terms of strategy implementation, you must seek a balance among the implementation levers.

How Would You Do That?

11. Pick an industry and use "How Would You Do That? 6.1" as a template to map out its value curve. What are the key success factors that define industry participation? Does there appear to be more than one strategic group in this industry with different value curves? Can you come up with a new value curve that would change the industry?

Guide: Students love this tool when they see it because it is so intuitive. That said, these maps are easier to present than they are to create, and this exercise can prove rather challenging. Kim and Mauborgne's book (*Blue Ocean Strategy*) has lots of examples.

12. Identify an industry that you believe is very dynamic and identify the drivers of that dynamism. Now pick a firm in that industry and formulate a strategy and basic implementation scheme to exploit its dynamic context. Use the R. R. Donnelley example presented in "How Would You Do That? 6.2" as a template for your recommendations.

Guide: Your goal here should be to let students see how formulation and implementation are related in dynamic contexts. The Brown and Eisenhardt book (*Competing on the Edge*) provides numerous examples as well as surveys at the end of each chapter that you can have students apply to focal companies. Eisenhardt's articles in *Harvard Business Review* on patching, stitching, and so on are useful as well for anecdotes and examples.

Group Activities

13. If you were the CEO of Napster (which started out as Roxio in the opening vignette), what material from this chapter would be most relevant to you? How would this material help you to formulate a strategy? What might key components of that strategy be? Now put yourself in Microsoft's shoes, would you see either Sonic Solutions or Napster a threat? If so, what strategy would you formulate in response?

Guide: Of the three dimensions of industry evolution, technological discontinuity, and globalization, strong arguments could be made for either industry evolution of technological discontinuity. Industry evolution may favor a model that is incompatible with Roxio's current capabilities or a technological discontinuity may render Roxio's software obsolete.

The outcome of the Microsoft discussion should be to differentiate these two approaches in the minds of students and to highlight the differences and potential overlap between these two strategic directions.

14. Review the list of first- and second-mover firms in Exhibit 6.3. What specific resources and capabilities do you think successful first movers must possess? What specific resources and capabilities do you think successful second movers and fast followers must possess? Do you think that a firm could be both a first mover and fast follower if it wanted to be?

Guide: First movers typically have large investments in R&D and/or a history of innovation. Also, they are very often, although not exclusively, new entrants into the market. Typically, established firms tend to make improvements to current products while new entrants to the market more commonly introduce a new product or service. Second movers and fast followers typically invest fewer resources in R&D and innovation. These types of firms invest heavily in bringing products to the market quickly. The ability to identify potentially successful new products early is also important.

VI. SUPPLEMENTAL EXPERIENTIAL EXERCISES

These exercises are drawn with permission from the Strategy Teaching Tool-kit found at:

http://instruction.bus.wisc.edu/mcarpenter/PROFESSIONAL/Toolkit/bpstools.htm.

1. Take a firm you discussed in the context of Chapter 5. How might you change the five elements of strategy to account for a more dynamic environment? What implementation levers would you need to pay particular attention to help the firm make the transition from competing with a relatively static strategy to a dynamic one?

The idea of this exercise is to take a previous discussion that was rooted in a static model of strategy and translate that discussion into a more dynamic context. Important ideas in this discussion could include keeping an element of flexibility when designing structures or staffing arrangements or keeping an eye on potential future conditions rather than focusing on past or current conditions.

2. Pick a giant firm like Microsoft or Coca-Cola and based only on your first-hand knowledge, and perhaps information from its Web site, map out its five elements of strategy. One aspect of the dynamic defensive strategies pursued by industry titans is the emergence of industries that are characterized as oligopolistic by some stakeholder groups. At least one nongovernmental group, www.oligopolywatch.com, espouses this view. You will know whether you picked a mega-firm based on whether it is discussed on this site. Now revisit your strategy summary and modify it to reflect the write-up by oligopolywatch. How did your perspective on the strategy change in this process? What general strategies from the last section of Chapter 6 do you see in play here?

The idea behind this exercise is to stress to students that the nature of competition for some firms changes when they are one of the large firms in a concentrated industry. Very often, students only consider how firms try to get to the top; this exercise will highlight how firms try to stay at the top through defensive maneuvers.

VII. APPENDICES

1. Biography—Chris Gorog (as of January 1, 2006), Napster Chairman and Chief Executive Officer

Chris Gorog's career spans virtually all aspects of the media and entertainment industry and its convergence with technology. In 2002, Gorog led the acquisition of Napster, relaunched the game-changing music service in 2003 as a legal digital music provider, and took the company public in 2005 (NASDAQ: NAPS). Today, Napster (www.napster.com) is acknowledged as the leading innovator in digital music, has established relationships with all of the top music labels in the industry with a catalog of over 1 million tracks, and is the pacesetting pioneer of the music subscription model.

Before the acquisition of Napster, Gorog was Chairman and CEO of Roxio, the leader in CD recording and digital media software, which he took public in 2001. Prior to joining Roxio, Gorog served as President of New Business Development and Executive Vice President of Group Operations for Universal Studios Recreations Group. Prior to Universal, Gorog was President and CEO of ITC Entertainment Group, a leading motion picture and television producer, and led a management buy-out of the group's global business. Before joining ITC, Gorog served as Vice President of Business Affairs for Motion Pictures and Television at The Walt Disney Company.

In addition to serving as Chairman of Napster's Board, Gorog is a director of House of Blues, a leading North American concert producer and The Guitar Center, the nation's largest musical instrument retailer.

2. LEK Real Options Model for Pharmaceutical Firm's Calculation (see newsletter at www.lek.com to view more examples and a more-detailed walk-through of the analyses.

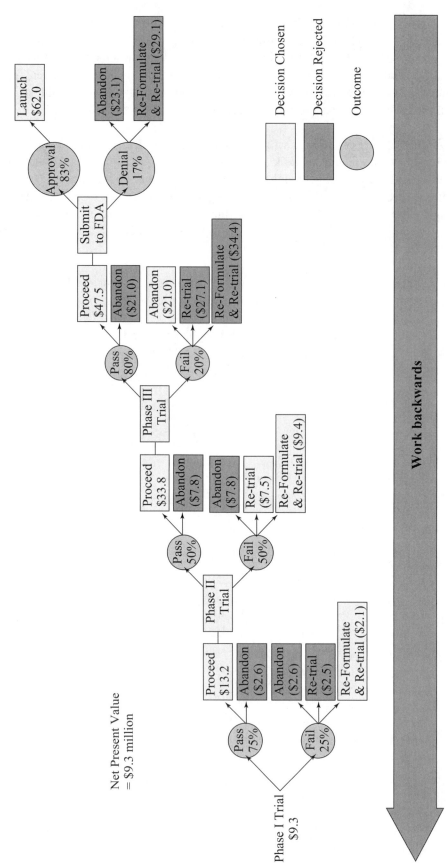

Net Present Value
= $9.3 million

Phase I Trial
$9.3

Work backwards

Pass 75%
Proceed $13.2
Abandon ($2.6)

Fail 25%
Abandon ($2.6)
Re-trial ($2.5)
Re-Formulate & Re-trial ($2.1)

Phase II Trial

Pass 50%
Proceed $33.8
Abandon ($7.8)

Fail 50%
Abandon ($7.8)
Re-trial ($7.5)
Re-Formulate & Re-trial ($9.4)

Phase III Trial

Pass 80%
Proceed $47.5
Abandon ($21.0)

Fail 20%
Abandon ($21.0)
Re-trial ($27.1)
Re-Formulate & Re-trial ($34.4)

Submit to FDA

Approval 83%
Launch $62.0

Denial 17%
Abandon ($23.1)
Re-Formulate & Re-trial ($29.1)

Decision Chosen

Decision Rejected

Outcome

Source: www.lek.com/ideas/publications/sva16.pdf.

CHAPTER 7 – DEVELOPING CORPORATE STRATEGY

I.   PURPOSE OF THE CHAPTER

After studying this chapter, students should be able to:

1.   Define corporate strategy.
2.   Understand when it makes sense for a firm to own a particular business.
3.   Outline the different forms of diversification.
4.   Understand the roles of economies of scope and scale in corporate strategy
5.   Describe the relationship between corporate strategy and competitive advantage.
6.   Outline the corporate strategy implications of the static and dynamic perspectives

Corporate strategy is a difficult concept for students, undergraduate and graduate students alike (and sometimes faculty), to get their arms around. They can readily identify with business strategy, because it addresses how a firm competes with one or more related products or services. Corporate strategy, however, has to be able to answer three questions: (1) Why these businesses? (2) how does corporate ownership add value to these businesses? and (3) how does ownership of one business contribute to the competitive advantage of other businesses that the corporation owns?

Too often, students will argue that diversification helps reduce a firm's risk because it reduces the firm's dependency on any one business or market. At this point you can note that investors can do this themselves—quickly, cheaply, and efficiently—simply by buying a basket of single business stocks or a mutual fund. In fact, by donning the risk-reduction hat, you can point out that the students are taking a managerial position of reducing their unemployment risk, not necessarily increasing the competitive advantage of the corporation and its underlying business.

Boiling this all down then, you will want your students to leave a session on corporate strategy with two key concepts under their belt: (1) a good corporate strategy provides clear, coherent, and compelling answers to the three questions just mentioned and (2) why corporate diversification is different from investor diversification. Simply ask them what the difference is between the two. They need to understand that as an investor, you can buy and sell your investments with very low transaction costs, whereas corporate ownership means that the firm not only owns the investment, but it must run it as well, and if things go badly, then exit is costly, and sometimes impossible.

Although the mutual fund/investor comparison to corporate diversification is a practical starting point, other instructors have found it useful to lead students into the topic of corporate strategy by noting that firms diversify simply by launching a new product. New products typically have different requirements, markets, life cycles, and so on. This way you can use a single business case as a way of moving into the topic of corporate strategy. Students also like this approach because they can apply the diamond model, starting with the arenas, and then contemplate the importance of common resources and also links in implementation issues by design (and you can bring in the staging element here). Highly diversified firms are different from two-product firms simply in terms of degree. You can then jump to highly diversified firms such as GE or others with lesser degrees of diversification. Disney is always a good corporate strategy case, because you can show how it's much easier to realize synergies when the firm is sharing a cartoon character across different business units as opposed to some very complex technology. The students will also find you to be brilliant if you point out that a firm has diversified when it converts a cost center to a profit center. For instance, when SAP started charging for the advising services that it used to bundle for free with its ERP software, it actually had diversified into a new industry (consulting), where it competed with all the other big consulting firms in the world.

The concept of synergy is central to corporate strategy; therefore, you should ask students to think about how synergies are possible (exploited and unexploited) in the targeted arenas and where arenas pose potential conflicts in terms of strategy formulation and implementation.

In this chapter, the three differentiators—and hence a teaching strategy for the chapter—are manifested in the following ways:

- **Strategic leadership.** Strategic leadership is implicitly relevant to corporate strategy for the simple reason that top managers only have so many hours in the day and the more diversified the corporation, the less they can pay explicit attention to any single arena or subarena. Your students see strategic leadership starting with the opening vignette, which includes Jack Welch at GE. In that vignette, they will also see the culture of innovation at 3M, which you should point out is a consequence of the culture fostered by 3M's leadership (and reinforced by the internal reward structure, including 10% of each employee's time dedicated to identifying new products). Strategic leadership, both the light and dark sides, is next explicitly addressed in the subheadings of "Dominant Logic" and "Ulterior Motives for Diversification." Although dominant logic pervades the firm, it is also the notion that the top management team is able to create value through its corporate strategy because of an overarching and compelling strategic logic. The dark side of diversification, something you may have brought up earlier in the session, is that diversification can reduce top management's employment risk by decreasing the variation in overall firm performance—this is self-serving and does not necessarily benefit shareholders. Moreover, because CEO and other top-executive compensation are often a reflection of firm size, diversification that fosters growth at the expense of profitability can be motivated purely by executive greed. In the "Implementation" subheading of the "Competitive Advantage and Corporate Strategy" section, students then see how leaders make choices about the levers to execute the strategy well. Exhibit 7.6 further contrasts the different strategic choices that leaders must make, though in comparing stable to dynamic contexts. These choices are implicit in the "How Would You Do That?" on Disney that closes the chapter.
- **Formulation and implementation interdependency.** You can choose when and how you bring out this interdependency, but students will (should) clearly see that how the firm is going about implementing its current strategy has implications for its diversification moves, and vice versa. As mentioned earlier, this can be brought in at the simple level of simply introducing a new product in what is perceived to be the same arena. After all, Dell nearly went out of business when it first tried to sell laptops in addition to its desktop computers. Ostensibly, both products are in the same industry, but Dell found that the competences that allowed it to excel in the desktop market provided it little advantage in the laptop market because of differing design constraints and customer demands. Exhibit 7.2 presents another way that the formulation/implementation relationship is manifested. There, the students see the genealogy of the conglomerate ITT. The various snippets on Disney throughout the chapter, including "How Would You Do That 7.1," provide perhaps the most dramatic example of this interdependence—unless a new Disney film is a big hit, or at least viewed as successful, the entire power of the Disney corporate strategy is undermined. A new film drives licensing revenues, new spin-off products, follow-on movies, and character draw at Disney's theme parks around the world.
- **Dynamic strategy.** Dynamism is part and parcel of corporate strategy. This is apparent in two ways. First, a firm's entry into and exit from new arenas creates an internal dynamic. Your students will see this in the three examples of diversified firms (GE, 3M, and MITY) provided in the opening vignette and in Exhibit 7.2 on the evolution of ITT. The second way students see this dynamism is under the subheading of "Corporate Strategy in Dynamic Contexts" found in the final section of the chapter.

One example they are presented with is Palm, where the evolution of the PDA industry resulted in the emergence of a PDA hardware and software industry, which were previously incorporated simply in the relatively newly emerged PDA industry (you can remind students of the section from Chapter 4 on the external environment about how industries collide and divide). In this last section, students are introduced to the notion of coevolution, and the difference between corporate strategy in static versus dynamic contexts is crystallized in Exhibit 7.6.

Additional Readings:

Collis, D., and C. Montgomery. (1998). Creating corporate advantage. *Harvard Business Review,* May-June: 71–83.

Eisenhardt, K., and C. Galunic. (2000). Coevolving: At last a way to make synergies work. *Harvard Business Review,* January-February: 91–101.

Gadiesh, O., and J. Gilbert. (1998). Profit pools: A fresh look at strategy. *Harvard Business Review,* 76(3), 139–148.

Goold, M., and A. Campbell. (1998). Desperately seeking synergy. *Harvard Business Review,* September-October: 131–143.

Prahalad, C. K., & G. Hamel. (1990). The core competence of the corporation. *Harvard Business Review,* May-June: 79–91.

II.   BRIEF CHAPTER OUTLINE

pp. 184–187, PPT #1–3	**Chapter 7 Developing Corporate Strategy** The purpose of this chapter is to explain the development of corporate strategy based on economies of scale and scope, different forms of diversification, and implications of static and dynamic contexts for implementing corporate strategies. **Opening Vignette:** Diversification at GE, 3M, and MITY Enterprises, pp. 185–187	
pp. 187–191, PPT #4–8	**CORPORATE STRATEGY** Corporate strategy is related to entering or exiting an industry and the management of a multibusiness enterprise to achieve synergies. Three issues are: 1. In which business *arenas* should a company compete? 2. Which *vehicles* should it use to enter or exit a business? 3. What underlying *economic logic* makes it sensible to compete in multiple businesses? **The Evolution of Diversification in the United States** The first form of diversification was **vertical integration**. By the 1960s, many large firms grew with unrelated diversification to address antitrust concerns. The **conglomerate** model raised new issues. The portfolio-planning model identified "dogs"—businesses without a strong competitive position in bad industries that should be sold. Businesses with strong competitive positions in slow-growth industries were referred to as "cash cows." These should be maintained because the cash could support promising high-growth businesses ("stars"). This model led to questionable diversification	p. 188, Ex. 7.1 Diversification Profiles p. 198, Ex. 7.2 A Brief History and Genealogy of a Conglomerate

	(e.g., telecommunications firms entered the hotel industry). Diversification doesn't necessarily create shareholder value and may dissipate it.	
pp. 191–196, PPT #9–16	**ECONOMIC LOGIC OF DIVERSIFICATION: ECONOMIES OF SCOPE AND SYNERGY** Two concepts for evaluating diversification and value creation are *economies of scope* and *synergy*. **Economies of Scope** are reductions in average costs that result from producing two or more products jointly instead of separately; possible when the company can leverage a resource across more than one product or service. **Revenue-Enhancement Synergies** create more value than independent ownership; may result from bundling products, sharing complementary knowledge, or increasing shared distribution. A *parenting advantage* exists when the joint cash flows exceed the sum of their independent cash flows. **Sources of Economies of Scope** stem from common resources across business units. **Sources of Revenue-Enhancement Synergies** arise from bundling and joint-selling opportunities (e.g., financial-services industry bundling products in different sectors). **How and When to Seek Economies of Scope and Synergy** Two processes can generate economies of scope: 1. Sharing resources 2. Transferring capabilities **Limits of Diversification Benefits** A harmful side effect of diversification is increasing complexity. Complex firms are more difficult to manage than simple, focused firms due the fact that higher compensation is required to attract and retain top management personnel and fewer top executives are capable of managing complex firms. **Resource Relatedness and Competitive Similarity** **Related diversification** is when business units are highly related. Unrelated diversification is when business units are dissimilar (e.g., GE). Extreme unrelated diversification leads to *conglomerates*. Related diversification is more likely to create value. **Dominant Logic** refers to how managers view the firm's competitive activities and allocate resources. Managers need to assess the fit of resources to compete. Similarity in dominant logic means a firm's managers can respond more quickly and effectively. Maximizing economies of scope and synergies lie at the intersection of two dimension: (1) fit among parent–subsidiary resources and (2) fit of parent–subsidiary dominant logic. **Ulterior Motives for Diversification** Managers motives for diversification are not necessarily in shareholders' best interests. Three motives are *risk reduction*, *empire building*, and *compensation*.	p. 194, Ex. 7.3 Diversification and Performance in S&P 500 and S&P Midcap Firms (1992–2000)
pp. 196–200,	**FORMS OF SCOPE AND DIVERSIFICATION** A firm can expand with *vertical*, *horizontal*, and *geographic* diversification.	*p. 197, *Fig. 7.1 Pulte and D.R.*

PPT #17–19	**Vertical Scope** may result from the firm's need to protect critical input, suppliers' inability to satisfy the firm's needs, and from the firm's desire to take advantage of growth opportunities. Vertical expansion is a logical growth option because a firm is familiar with the arena. **The Pitfalls of Increased Vertical Scope** may be due to fundamentally different structural features. **Horizontal Scope** may result in one of two ways: 1. Move from an industry market segment into a related segment. 2. Move from one industry into another. The desirability of horizontal expansion depends on relatedness to a firm's home industry in terms of similarity of human capital in value-chain activities or similarity in customer needs. **Economies of Scope and Synergies** Increased horizontal scope is attractive because it 1. Exploits possible economies of scope 2. Enhances revenue through synergies Closely related industries often use similar assets and resources to enable cost savings by sharing resources among businesses. *Profit pools* is a tool that incorporates key complementary businesses near the point at which a firm is directly involved in customer transactions. It identifies the size of value-chain segments and the attractiveness of each segment. *Profit* concentration in an industry rarely occurs in the same place as *revenue* concentration. A basic managerial mistake stems from focusing on growth and market share by assuming that profits will follow automatically. **Geographic Scope** increases when the firm moves into new geographic arenas without altering its business model—*internationalization*—entering new markets in other parts of the world. Relatedness is assessed on differences in national markets, including laws, customs, cultures, consumer preferences, distances, common borders, language, socioeconomic development, and other factors. **Economies of Scale and Scope** R&D, a relatively fixed cost, can be amortized over a larger market; for example, high R&D expenditures in pharmaceuticals and computer-related products can be spread over a global market. **Strategy and the Local Environment** Firms must adapt parts of their strategies to accommodate local environments. Different countries have different models of competition, which means strategies must vary across markets.	*Horton Moving Down the Value Chain* p. 198, Ex. 7.4 The U.S. Auto Industry's Profit Pool *p. 200, *Fig. 7.2 Dell's Strategy in the United States versus Asia*
pp. 200–202, PPT #20–21	**WHO SHOULD OWN THE BUSINESS?** This decision should be based on creating shareholder value: 1. Does the business unit add value to the corporation? 2. Does the corporation owning the business unit add more value than alternative ways of linking a business to the corporation? **Determining Comparative Value** Managers must determine whether owning a business creates shareholder value and how to create the most value. **How to Create Value** Managers must ask whether the firm's financial or market performance is better because its businesses are	

	bundled instead of being separately owned. If yes, then the benefits of ownership versus alliance and the mode of entry of must evaluated. **Alternatives to Direct Ownership** A firm may create value by entering into alliance or joint venture. **Alternative Modes of Entry** Two common modes of entry are (1) internal development and (2) acquisition of new businesses. Acquisitions allow for quick entry but entail significant upfront capital costs. Internal development has lower upfront costs, but the risks are high and it takes a long time to build a business.	
pp. 202–204, PPT #22–23	**COMPETITIVE ADVANTAGE AND CORPORATE STRATEGY** A goal is to identify the conditions under which owning a corporate portfolio of businesses creates value for shareholders. **Arenas, Resources, and Competitive Advantage** Corporate strategy has operations in more than one arena. The combination of arenas, resources, and implementation determines competitive advantage. **Arenas** Firms tend to select arenas that are connected—similar in markets, use of resources, and comparable dominant logic. **Resources** The usefulness of a resource in creating a competitive advantage depends on four factors: (1) is it valuable, (2) rare, (3) costly to imitate, and (4) exploitable. At the corporate level, the VRINE framework must include how specialized or general firm's resources are: • **Specialized resources** have a narrow range of applicability. • **General resources** can be exploited over a wide range of activities. Implementation levers include organizational structure, systems, and processes. Some of the more important levers to achieve successful diversification include coordination mechanisms, rewards, and corporate oversight.	
pp. 204–208, PPT #24–27	**CORPORATE STRATEGY IN STABLE AND DYNAMIC CONTEXTS** Vehicles for business and corporate strategy tend to play different roles in stable versus dynamic contexts. Even if a strategy is similar in both stable in dynamic contexts, the context will influence its implementation. **Corporate Strategy in Stable Contexts** Many ideas of the relationship between diversification and corporate strategy are based on the firm being in relatively stable contexts. **Static Arenas and Formal Structures** Synergies are often conceived as functions of static business-unit arenas and the formal structural links among them. The main corporate objective is ensuring that the firm operates as a tightly interwoven whole. **Corporate Strategy in Dynamic Contexts** **Diversification in Dynamic Contexts** Firms diversifying in dynamic contexts usually need strong resources and capabilities in learning, knowledge transfer, and rapid responsiveness.	p. 206, Ex. 7.5 Masco: A Holding Company at a Glance p. 207, Ex. 7.6 Comparison of Corporate Strategies in Stable and Dynamic Contexts

	Coevolution is a process of shifting linkages among evolving businesses; from biology, it describes successive changes between ecologically interdependent species that adapt to their environment and to each other. Cross-business synergies are usually temporary. Managers must deal with the tension from the agility of fewer linkages and the efficiency of more. Corporate strategy may be temporary networks among businesses. Divestitures and corporate spin-offs can be an effective vehicle for dealing with disruptive innovations.	p. 208, *7.1 How Would You Do That? Diversification in a Dynamic Context at Disney*

* Figure or Exhibit **NOT** enumerated in the PDF file.

III. SUGGESTED CASES TO ACCOMPANY TEXT

In the concepts-with-cases version of the text, we have supplied "McDonald's and the McCafe Coffee Initiative" and "Moving Tata Consultancy Services into the Global Top 10." The first case showcases the challenges of product diversification and tries to inform students about when such diversification can lead to sustainable competitive advantage. The second case examines if and how Tata should diversify its consulting business and introduces the question as to whether it should do so through organic growth or via acquisition and domestically versus internationally.

Beyond these cases, if you choose to compile your own casebook you will have an opportunity to draw from a variety of sources. These sources include Pearson Custom Publishing, Hartwick Leadership Cases, IVEY Case Publishing, European Case Clearing House (ECCH), Harvard Business School (HBS), Darden, and others.

Need help selecting cases? Pearson Prentice Hall and Pearson Custom Publishing are pleased to present the ultimate resource for creating and customizing casebooks.

- Start with a CaseMap correlated to your text or start from scratch; do it yourself using our easy-to-use interface or collaborate with a developmental editor.
- Cases can be selected from a variety of sources, including Harvard Business School Publishing, Darden, Ivey, Thunderbird, and NACRA.
- We clear permissions for you on cases and content not in the database.
- You can also create custom course packs by adding articles, original material, and textbook chapters.
- Pearson Custom casebooks can be delivered in print or online.
- Additionally, we supply you, the instructor, with a free evaluation copy delivered 7 to 10 days after you create your book, free access to teaching notes, and case-method teaching resources.

We're here to help: Looking for a case on a specific topic, company, country, or scenario? Or, looking for a new case to substitute for one you've used in the past? We will help you find the right cases for your course and help you create a casebook that meets all your teaching needs. For guidance on building a casebook to reflect your course needs, e-mail our editorial consultant at customcases@prenhall.com.

Visit www.prenhall.com/custombusiness for more information and to see which Prentice Hall titles are available for short-run customization and to view suggested cases. To start your own straightforward search for material:

Step 1: Select "search content and create your book" and log in.
Step 2: Search by case number or keyword or browse by discipline to find suggested cases based on the book you use or course you teach.

Step 3: Browse, preview, and select the cases, articles, or chapters you wish to include (you will see that price and page count of the book in the top right-hand corner of the screen as you "build" the book).
Step 4: Finalize your selections, get them in the order you want, package your customized book with any Prentice Hall title for a discount (if you wish), click "confirm book," and you have the option to request a free evaluation copy.
Step 5: The Web site immediately gives you the ISBN of your custom book. You should give this ISBN to your bookstore; they will use it to place their order with us.

Beyond our cases and Pearson Custom Publishing, if you choose to compile your own casebook you will have an opportunity to draw from a variety of sources. These sources include going direct to Hartwick Leadership Cases, IVEY Case Publishing, European Case Clearing House (ECCH), Harvard Business School (HBS), Darden, and others.

Given the popularity of Harvard cases we have selected these additional cases for use with this chapter:

		ID#	Pages	TN
The Walt Disney Co.: The Entertainment King	HBSP	9-701-035	27	N
Agora SA	HBSP	9-706-425	23	N

The Walt Disney Co.: The Entertainment King The first 10 pages of this case describe the company's history from 1923 to 2001. The Walt years are described, as is the company's decline after his death and its resurgence under Eisner. The last five pages are devoted to Eisner's strategic challenges in 2001: managing synergy, managing the brand, and managing creativity. Students are asked to think about the keys to Disney's mid-1980s turnaround, about the proper boundaries of the firm, and about what Disney's strategy should be beyond 2001.

Agora SA Tells the story of Agora, the largest media company in Poland, describing its corporate strategy of diversification since its founding in 1989 by entrepreneurial journalists closely linked to the anticommunist movement Solidarity. Describes in detail *Gazeta Wyborcza,* the country's best-selling daily newspaper and Agora's main revenue contributor. In late 2003, *Fakt,* the new daily owned by a German publishing house, took the lead in the Polish newspaper market, harming *Gazeta Wyborcza*'s sales and advertising revenues. The case places students in the position of Wanda Rapaczynski, Agora's CEO, who, in mid-2005, explores ways to improve Agora's position in an increasingly competitive environment.

IV.   LINKING THE CHAPTER TO A COMPUTER SIMULATION

Again, if you are using a simulation that has a single-industry focus (such as shoes or bikes) then you will need to frame the corporate strategy question as one of market segments, channels, and customers. Once students start to see how market demands and product characteristics differ across segments, they can more readily understand why diversification, even in its simplest form, puts pressures on management that they may be unable to cope with. You can show students that firms with many products ultimately are only able to add or leverage general management and finance skills across the segments, because they lack the time and resources to gain in-depth insights into each segment's needs and characteristics.

V. END OF CHAPTER QUESTION ANSWER GUIDE

Review Questions

1. How does corporate strategy differ from business strategy?

Guide: Corporate strategy encompasses issues related to decisions about entering and exiting businesses. A fundamental part of corporate strategy is the decision about what business *arenas* to enter and exit. However, corporate strategy also encompasses the overall management of the multibusiness enterprise, such as corporate headquarters' efforts to orchestrate the cross-business-unit synergies. It is corporate-level strategy that should provide the logic or strategic coherence across business units and facilitate the inter-business-unit cooperation or competition necessary to create value for shareholders. Thus, although they are fundamentally related to each other through the common goal of achieving competitive advantage, business strategy and corporate strategy have different objectives.

2. How has the practice of corporate strategy evolved over time?

Guide: Perhaps the first form of diversification observed in modern business history was vertical integration. Firms often moved upstream (i.e., closer to the source of raw materials) in the industry value chain in order to secure valuable inputs and because other firms were unwilling to make the investments necessary to completely handle the contingencies facing large firms. Later, in the late nineteenth century, the booming U.S. economy entered a period of rapid consolidation. Holding companies, called *trusts*, were created to consolidate firms in certain industries (e.g., sugar, tobacco, steel, oil). Owing to antitrust policies that were much more strictly defined and enforced than they are today, firms in the 1960s had a difficult time growing into some profitable businesses that were related to their core business. As a result, many large firms chose to use their free cash flow and excess financial resources to fund growth in new businesses that were unrelated to their core business, and thus generally exempt from antitrust considerations.

3. What is a conglomerate?

Guide: Conglomerates are firms that have a great deal of unrelated diversification. These firms grew as a result of antitrust policy, because many large firms chose to use their free cash flow and excess financial resources to fund growth into new businesses that were unrelated to their core business, and thus generally exempt from antitrust considerations.

4. How can managers decide whether they should diversify into a new business?

Guide: Which businesses a firm should own should depend less on industry attractiveness and relative market share than on value creation. Who should own a particular business should be driven by two related questions related to the value added: Does the business unit add value to the corporation (or vice versa)? And does ownership add more value than alternative ways to link the business to the corporation?

5. What are the types of diversification and how is value created in each type?

Guide: The three types are vertical, horizontal, and geographic (global). Sometimes vertical expansion is pursued due to economic necessity, such as preserving the supply of critical inputs or because the investments necessary in the supply industry to meet the firm's specific needs are so specific to the firm that suppliers are hesitant to make these investments. Vertical scope can be a logical growth option because managers and employees will be very familiar with the context of expansion. Horizontal scope is increased by moving from one market segment within the same industry to another related segment and by moving from one industry to another (more typically simply called *diversification*). The degree to which horizontal expansion is desirable is a function of how related the new industry is to the home industry. Increasing geographic scope simply entails moving into new geographic arenas with the same business model. Early in a firm's growth, this may simply mean moving into new locations within the same country.

6. What is the difference between economies of scope and synergies?

Guide: Economies of scope are reductions in average costs for producing two or more products and services jointly than the total average costs associated with producing the products and services separately. Alternatively, synergy is revenue enhancement through joint ownership. That is, if two business units are able to generate more revenue by being collectively owned by the same corporate parent, their common ownership is synergistic.

7. What is the relationship between diversification and firm performance?

Guide: Because diversified firms are more difficult to manage, it stands to reason that there must be limits to the benefits of diversification. Indeed, research demonstrates that the positive benefits of diversification are only valued by the market to a point, after which firm performance actually starts to decline. Our analysis of the data for S&P 500 and S&P madcap firms finds an inverted-U-shaped ($\cap$) association between the level of firm diversification and firm performance. Thus, on average, diversification seems to benefit shareholders to a point, but becomes value destroying the more the portfolio of businesses is unrelated.

8. What factors tend to limit the attractiveness of diversification?

Guide: One of the side effects of diversification is a significant increase in the complexity of the firm. Complex firms are more difficult to manage than simple, focused firms. Indeed, research demonstrates that the positive benefits of diversification are only valued by the market to a point, after which firm performance actually starts to decline. Similarity in dominant logic allows managers to be able to respond quicker and in more appropriate manners to strategic issues. Conversely, when the dominant logic between disparate industries within a corporation's portfolio differs significantly, senior managers will generally take longer to respond.

9. How does a dynamic industry context affect the possible benefits of diversification?

Guide: Diversification can be a viable strategy for firms in dynamic contexts as well. However, firms in dynamic contexts must usually have strong resources and capabilities in the areas of learning, knowledge transfer, and rapid responsiveness for diversification to yield benefits. Otherwise, the nimbleness and responsiveness required of business units in dynamic contexts is dampened as a consequence of corporate ownership being more of an encumbrance than an advantage.

How Would You Do That?

10. What are the specific resources and capabilities that Disney might be able to share across the traditional family-oriented businesses and this new one? Internally, Disney executives view one of their dynamic capabilities as that of being the best at creating world-class entertainment within financial constraints. What are your thoughts on this view? As you think about Disney, and what you

view as its resources and capabilities, what arenas should it consider for future diversification or diversification moves?

Guide: Your goal in this first part of the "How Would You Do That?" might be to get students to note that, at least historically, Disney's successes have all spun off its animated feature films, and therefore the bundle of resources and capabilities that allow it to create "timeless entertainment."

If you can get a hold of a Mickey's classic video or DVD, just play the first film *Steamboat Willie* (a 7-minute silent cartoon) to make this point. Some students may also note that Disney is known for its exceptional customer service, as well as the fact that once at its theme parks, you are a relatively captive customer.

So, with live-action and adult film, Disney would seem to be stretching its creativity gained through animated films and knowledge of film production and distribution. However, you should point out that live-action movies involve actors who (a) have varying degrees of talent and name recognition (and therefore bargaining power) and (b) actors can do things outside the cinema in their own lives that may reflect positively or negatively on the film itself (whereas Disney has total control over Mickey Mouse's image). Your students may also observe that Disney owns a major network and several cable channels that it can use to leverage these new films, and possibly television series that spin off of them. And to the extent that older children and adult entertainment is incorporated into Disney theme parks, then these live-action characters may be able to be leveraged there as well.

The closing question is meant to have students think about what Disney can and cannot enter, based on its resources and capabilities. It has done well in Broadway musicals, the *Lion King,* for instance. Should it go into the movie theater business? Etc. Again, here you can reinforce that what Disney is doing, in terms of its corporate strategy, business strategies, and their implementation, all affect the businesses that it can or should diversify into (and you might raise the question about which businesses it should exit; for instance, was it good to get out of retail? Should it be in the book publishing business? Etc.

Group Activities

11. Choose two firms well known to your group members—perhaps firms that you've done in-depth case analyses on in the past. For each of these firms, identify their vertical, horizontal, and geographic scope. Having done that, evaluate the resources that are necessary for each business arena. How similar are the resource requirements?

Guide: The key to this activity is to gain experience recognizing that most firms operate in a set of diverse businesses and that vertical and geographic scope varies significantly. More importantly, these differences have significant implications for firm performance. Consistent with the course material learned to date, one of the key reasons scope matters is likely to be found in evaluating the resources required for success in each business. Several of the chapter models will help groups come to grips with these issues, but the corporate strategy triangle and the concepts of resource similarity and general versus specific resources are particularly pertinent.

12. Try to apply the profit pool tool to another industry. Where would you turn for data to do this? How "friendly" is that data for the purposes of using this tool? If you are having trouble being precise, make informed estimations for what you are missing. You will likely find some profit pools that are deeper than others. Why are there big differences between segments? Which firms in the value chain are best able to enter these attractive segments?

Guide: Like many models, the profit pools model is intuitively pleasing, but executing an analysis with the model can prove rather difficult. The originators of this model published an accompanying "users guide" in *Harvard Business Review*,[1] which accompanies the conceptual article "Profit pools: A fresh look at strategy."[2] The "how to" article provides helpful suggestions for estimating the size of industry segments and the profits within those segments. The conceptual article contains a completed profit pool for the PC industry, which may be helpful for students to understand the mechanics of the tool.

VI. SUPPLEMENTAL EXPERIENTIAL EXERCISES

These exercises are drawn with permission from the Strategy Teaching Tool-kit found at:

http://instruction.bus.wisc.edu/mcarpenter/PROFESSIONAL/Toolkit/bpstools.htm.

1. **Portfolio Management Jeopardy** Effective portfolio management is at the center of corporate-level strategy. Because of their "tidiness" and clever terminology, various analytical tools, such as the BCG and McKinsey matrices, have achieved popularity in teaching corporate portfolio management. These matrices, though, have some inherently concerning qualities that can be easily overlooked. The Portfolio Management Test is designed to bring these issues to the forefront.

During the class discussion on corporate portfolio management, I tell my students that they are going to take a test on the material. The test, though, will be a group effort. Instruct the students to form four groups and sit together in the classroom. While the students are organizing, create a scoreboard on the chalkboard. On this scoreboard, write names (of your own choosing) for each group. Use names such as "The A Team," "Fast Trackers," "Lost Souls," and "Dead Enders." (These names respectively correspond to Cash Cow, Star, Problem Child, and Dog. Of course, don't explicitly communicate this to your students.)

The reason for the scoreboard is that you conduct the test with a twist; the test is designed like a television game show. Begin by reading a question to group 1 (could be any of the four groups). Group 1 gives an answer that is either correct or incorrect. Then, read a question to group 2, and so on. When a correct answer is given, the group receives the number of points that that question is worth. When an incorrect answer is given, the group loses the number of points the question is worth. However, the "game" isn't exactly "on the level."

Each group's performance is predestined. For example, the Dead Enders (Dogs) will continue to answer questions incorrectly, getting deeper into negative numbers. The Lost Souls (Problem Children) also continually answer questions incorrectly; however, persistently take points away from The A Team (Cash Cows), which continually answers questions correctly. The Fast Trackers (Stars) answer some questions correctly and some incorrectly, producing a net effect of breakeven.

You need to do three things to ensure this distribution of points. First, prior to class, "stack the deck" of questions. Questions for the Dead Enders and the Lost Souls are very high in level of difficulty. Questions for The A Team are very low in level of difficulty. Questions for the Fast Trackers are mixed in level of difficulty. Second, be strict in acceptance of correct answers from the Dead Enders and the Lost Souls. Be lenient in acceptance of correct answers from The A Team. And be sometimes strict and sometimes lenient in accepting correct answers from the Fast Trackers. Third, if your above efforts don't ensure the desired balance of points, you will just move points from one group to another for whatever reason.

---

[1] Gadiesh, O., and J. L. Gilbert. (1998). How to map your industry's profit pool. *Harvard Business Review, 76*(3), 149–158.

[2] Gadiesh, O., and J. L. Gilbert. (1998). Profit pools: A fresh look at strategy. *Harvard Business Review, 76*(3), 139–148.

By the end of the "test," students will have a broad mixture of feelings and issues that they want to discuss (usually in a good-natured way). The most obvious issue is "fairness." Why should some teams receive points when they weren't answering questions correctly? Why are the needs of one group for a good grade more important than the needs of other groups that were able to correctly answer questions? These issues lead to a discussion about "synergy" and the need to forsake personal gain for the greater good of the whole. Further, the exercise raises issues about "rights." Who has the right to make decisions that move resources from one division of an organization to another? To what extent does this form of resource reallocation affect motivation? Finally, raise the issue of the affect of labels. How did you feel about the group name with which you were labeled? To what extent did this label impact your perceived self-efficacy?

2. It's a Dog's Life Students are presented with abbreviated information about Sears in the 1980s. Each group uses the information to analyze their line of business and plot it on the McKinsey matrix. You can simulate politics in the process by urging them to identify with their business unit (rewards, etc.).

Inevitably, they conclude that the retail division is a cash cow (borderline dog) and they should sell several of the other divisions. When they hear its Sears several things come to light:

- The analysis ignored that retail is the corporate identity and what they know.
- The analysis ignored ties between businesses or strategies that cut across businesses.

Line of Business Information

	Retail	Credit Card	Insurance	Stock Brokerage	Real Estate
Competitive Position					
Market share (rank)	1 (big share)	2	4	5 (small share)	3
Profitability (ROS)	1.2%	11.7%	4.9%	4.3%	8.8%
Industry Attractiveness					
Industry growth rate	4.01%	4.34%	12.09%	13.90%	4.15%
Competitive rivalry (rank)	5 (high rivalry)	4	3	2	1 (low rivalry)
Portion of business					
Share of revenue	52.0%	5.1%	35.0%	4.9%	3.0%
Share of profit	18.0%	17.8%	50.2%	6.2%	7.8%

Analyzing the Portfolio							
COMPETITIVE POSITION				**INDUSTRY ATTRACTIVENESS**			
Key Success Factors	Weight	Rating	Score	Criteria	Weight	Rating	Score
Market share	0.50			Industry growth rate	0.60		
Profitability (ROS)	0.50			Competitive rivalry	0.40		
Totals	1.00				1.00		
Rating: 4 = "Best"; 3 = "Near the top"; 2 = "Average"; 1 = "Poor"							

McKinsey Matrix Portfolio Analysis Worksheet

		Competitive Position					
		4	High	3	3 Medium	2	2 Low	1

<table>
<tr><td rowspan="6">Attractiveness</td><td rowspan="2">4
High
3</td><td></td><td></td><td>Problem child?</td></tr>
<tr></tr>
<tr><td>3
Medium
2</td><td></td><td>Average</td><td></td></tr>
<tr></tr>
<tr><td>2
Low
1</td><td></td><td></td><td></td></tr>
</table>

It's a Dog's Life

Use the information in the "Line of Business Information" chart to analyze the company's portfolio. Use your analysis to plot the firm's businesses and to determine a strategy for the portfolio. Will you keep all businesses or should you sell some of them?

Line of Business Information

	Retail	Credit Card	Insurance	Stock Brokerage	Real Estate
Competitive Position					
Market share (rank)	1 (big share—good)	2	4	5 (small share—bad)	3
Profitability (ROS)	1.2%	11.7%	4.9%	4.3%	8.8%
Industry Attractiveness					
Industry growth rate	4.01%	4.34%	12.09%	13.90%	4.15%
Competitive rivalry (rank)	5 (high rivalry—bad)	4	3	2	1 (low rivalry—good)
Portion of business					
Share of revenue	52.0%	5.1%	35.0%	4.9%	3.0%
Share of profit	18.0%	17.8%	50.2%	6.2%	7.8%

Analyzing the Portfolio							
COMPETITIVE POSITION				**INDUSTRY ATTRACTIVENESS**			
Key Success Factors	**Weight**	**Rating**	**Score**	**Criteria**	**Weight**	**Rating**	**Score**
Market share	0.50			Industry growth rate	0.60		
Profitability (ROS)	0.50			Competitive rivalry	0.40		
Totals	1.00				1.00		
Rating: 4 = "Best"; 3 = "Near the top"; 2 = "Average"; 1 = "Poor"							

McKinsey Matrix Portfolio Analysis Worksheet

		Competitive Position					
		4 High 3	3 Medium 2	2 Low 1
Attractiveness	**4** High **3**			Problem child?
	3 Medium **2**		Average	
	2 Low **1**			

McKinsey Matrix Portfolio Analysis Worksheet
MAP YOUR RANKINGS AND RECOMMEND ACTION

		Competitive Position					
		4 High 3	3 Medium 2	2 Low 1
Attractiveness	4 High 3			Problem child?
	3 Medium 2		Average	
	2 Low 1			

Use this page to calculate each business' position and then chart them in the McKinsey Matrix.

Retail

COMPETITIVE POSITION				INDUSTRY ATTRACTIVENESS			
Key Success Factors	Weight	Rating	Score	Criteria	Weight	Rating	Score
Market share	0.50			Industry growth rate	0.60		
Profitability (ROS)	0.50			Competitive rivalry	0.40		
Totals	1.00				1.00		
Rating: 4 = "Best"; 3 = "Near the top"; 2 = "Average"; 1 = "Poor"							

Credit Card

COMPETITIVE POSITION				INDUSTRY ATTRACTIVENESS			
Key Success Factors	Weight	Rating	Score	Criteria	Weight	Rating	Score
Market share	0.50			Industry growth rate	0.60		
Profitability (ROS)	0.50			Competitive rivalry	0.40		
Totals	1.00				1.00		
Rating: 4 = "Best"; 3 = "Near the top"; 2 = "Average"; 1 = "Poor"							

Insurance

COMPETITIVE POSITION				INDUSTRY ATTRACTIVENESS			
Key Success Factors	Weight	Rating	Score	Criteria	Weight	Rating	Score
Market share	0.50			Industry growth rate	0.60		
Profitability (ROS)	0.50			Competitive rivalry	0.40		
Totals	1.00				1.00		
Rating: 4 = "Best"; 3 = "Near the top"; 2 = "Average"; 1 = "Poor"							

Stock Brokerage

COMPETITIVE POSITION				INDUSTRY ATTRACTIVENESS			
Key Success Factors	Weight	Rating	Score	Criteria	Weight	Rating	Score
Market share	0.50			Industry growth rate	0.60		
Profitability (ROS)	0.50			Competitive rivalry	0.40		
Totals	1.00				1.00		
Rating: 4 = "Best"; 3 = "Near the top"; 2 = "Average"; 1 = "Poor"							

Real Estate

COMPETITIVE POSITION				INDUSTRY ATTRACTIVENESS			
Key Success Factors	Weight	Rating	Score	Criteria	Weight	Rating	Score
Market share	0.50			Industry growth rate	0.60		
Profitability (ROS)	0.50			Competitive rivalry	0.40		
Totals	1.00				1.00		
Rating: 4 = "Best"; 3 = "Near the top"; 2 = "Average"; 1 = "Poor"							

KEY

Retail

COMPETITIVE POSITION				INDUSTRY ATTRACTIVENESS			
Key Success Factors	Weight	Rating	Score	Criteria	Weight	Rating	Score
Market share	0.50	5	2.50	Industry growth rate	0.60	1	.60
Profitability (ROS)	0.50	1	.50	Competitive rivalry	0.40	1	.40
Totals	1.00		3.00		1.00		1.00
Rating: 4 = "Best"; 3 = "Near the top"; 2 = "Average"; 1="Poor"							

Credit Card

COMPETITIVE POSITION				INDUSTRY ATTRACTIVENESS			
Key Success Factors	Weight	Rating	Score	Criteria	Weight	Rating	Score
Market share	0.50	4	2.00	Industry growth rate	0.60	2	1.20
Profitability (ROS)	0.50	4	2.00	Competitive rivalry	0.40	2	.80
Totals	1.00		4.00		1.00		2.00
Rating: 4 = "Best"; 3 = "Near the top"; 2 = "Average"; 1 = "Poor"							

Insurance

COMPETITIVE POSITION				INDUSTRY ATTRACTIVENESS			
Key Success Factors	Weight	Rating	Score	Criteria	Weight	Rating	Score
Market share	0.50	2	1.00	Industry growth rate	0.60	3	1.80
Profitability (ROS)	0.50	2	1.00	Competitive rivalry	0.40	2	.80
Totals	1.00		2.00		1.00		2.60
Rating: 4 = "Best"; 3="Near the top", 2="Average", 1="Poor"							

Stock Brokerage

COMPETITIVE POSITION				INDUSTRY ATTRACTIVENESS			
Key Success Factors	Weight	Rating	Score	Criteria	Weight	Rating	Score
Market share	0.50	1	.50	Industry growth rate	0.60	4	2.40
Profitability (ROS)	0.50	2	1.00	Competitive rivalry	0.40	3	1.20
Totals	1.00		1.50		1.00		3.60
Rating: 4 = "Best"; 3 = "Near the top"; 2 = "Average"; 1 = "Poor"							

Real Estate

COMPETITIVE POSITION				INDUSTRY ATTRACTIVENESS			
Key Success Factors	Weight	Rating	Score	Criteria	Weight	Rating	Score
Market share	0.50	2	1.00	Industry growth rate	0.60	1	.60
Profitability (ROS)	0.50	3	1.50	Competitive rivalry	0.40	4	1.60
Totals	1.00		2.50		1.00		2.20
Rating: 4 = "Best"; 3 = "Near the top"; 2 = "Average"; 1 = "Poor"							

CHAPTER 8 – LOOKING AT INTERNATIONAL STRATEGIES

I. PURPOSE OF THE CHAPTER

After studying this chapter, students should be able to:

1. Define international strategy and its implications for the strategy diamond.
2. Understand why a firm would want to expand internationally and the relationship between international strategy and competitive advantage.
3. Describe different vehicles for international expansion.
4. Apply different international strategy configurations.
5. Outline the international strategy implications of the static and dynamic perspectives.

Like corporate strategy (Chapter 7), international strategy is one of the more difficult topics for students to understand, because their comprehension of the topic is often a function of their previous work and international experience. Therefore, it is sometimes helpful to preface or supplement the chapter with an experiential exercise like "BaFa BaFa" or "Barnga" (both identified in Section VI of this chapter of the Instructor's Manual) to give students an understanding of how cultural and geographic differences make strategy formulation and implementation more complex than that typically experienced by purely domestic firms. If your students learn only two fundamental things from this chapter, they should (1) know how to use the strategy diamond to evaluate and design international strategies (see Exhibit 8.3) and (2) understand how international strategy affects the implementation side of the equation (here is where you develop the four international strategy configurations and explore "How Would You Do That? 8.2" and its relevant chapter section).

In this chapter, the three differentiators—and hence your teaching strategy of the chapter—are manifested in the following ways:

*   **Dynamic strategy.** Again, the opening vignette on Dell is an example of dynamic strategy in action. In an earlier chapter, students were introduced at a macro level to the drivers of globalization, so you can refer back to that as a context for dynamism or at least the need for considering internationalization. This chapter emphasizes the role of staging, and its link with implementation, to exploit and manage the opportunities and challenges of internationalization. The final section of the chapter is devoted to contrasting international strategy in relatively static versus dynamic contexts.
*   **Formulation and implementation interdependency.** The opening vignette on Dell's entry into China should show how its China strategy (the five elements of the strategy diamond) was predicated on how it was already implementing its current strategy elsewhere in the world, its international strategy implementation capabilities, and how it leveraged the staging component of the diamond model in entering and building both a production and distribution base in China. You can again draw in Exhibit 8.3 to ask students to think about how staging applies to international strategy, and if a firm does want to increase its international footprint, what it must do on the implementation side to support this (which also circles back to strategic leadership and international management capabilities). You can further develop the formulation/ implementation relationship by referring and developing the CAGE framework, summarized in Exhibit 8.5. For instance, "distance" will be a function of what the firm is already implementing as a strategy and any further internationalization that relates to distance will again require adjustments on the implementation side. The final chapter

section, which explores international strategy in dynamic contexts, emphasizes how formulation informs implementation, and vice versa, on a continuous basis, akin to organizational learning.

- **Strategic leadership.** This dimension is first introduced through an example of Lincoln Electric in the "Learning and Knowledge Sharing" subheading and then developed further in Exhibit 8.6 in the section on "International Strategy and Competitive Advantage." The students learn there that one of the reasons for Lincoln Electric's early international stumbles was its lack of managers with international experience. Although "How Would You Do That 8.1" does not talk much about strategic leadership, you can point out that many business people foster successful international alliances when they have a personal counterpart who understands and trusts them, and given the increasing number of non–U.S. students who have gone to school in the United States, these are natural soul-mates because they will already have an understanding of what U.S. culture is like (for better and for worse). You might also ask students to think about what type of managerial skills would be needed in each of the international strategy configurations, which are summarized in Exhibit 8.9. Finally, the strategic leadership dimension is developed explicitly the last part of the section "International Strategy in Static and Dynamic Contexts," at the end of the chapter, and concludes with "How Would You Do That? 8.2" on developing your students' global strategy mindset.

Additional Readings:

Adler, G. (1995). The floundering expatriate. *Harvard Business Review*, July–August, 4–15.

Ghoshal, S., and N. Nohria. (1993). Horses for courses: International strategies for multinational corporations. *Sloan Management Review,* Winter, 23–35.

Hastings, D. (1999). Lincoln Electric's harsh lessons from international expansion. *Harvard Business Review,* May–June, 3–11.

Trompenaars, F., and C. Hampden-Turner. (1998). *Riding the waves of culture* (2d ed.). New York: McGraw-Hill.

Weiss, S. (1994). Negotiating with Romans: Parts 1 and 2. *Sloan Management Review*, Winter, 51–61; Spring, 85–95.

II.   BRIEF CHAPTER OUTLINE

	Chapter 8 Looking at International Strategies	
pp. 212–215, PPT #1–2	The purpose of this chapter is to relate international strategy to the strategy diamond, discuss how international expansion contributes to a competitive advantage, and explain the vehicles and international strategy configurations in static and dynamic contexts. **Opening Vignette:** Dell Goes to China, pp. 213–215; p. 215, Ex. 8.1 China: A Black Hole or a Diamond Mine	
pp. 216–217, PPT #3–6	International expansion is a form of diversification. A firm's international strategy is how it approaches the cross-border activities of its own firm and competitors and how it contemplates doing so in the future. International strategy reflects the choices about sourcing and selling its goods in foreign markets.	p. 216, Ex. 8.2 The International Presence of Selected MNCs p. 217, Ex. 8.3 International Strategy and the

pp. 217–226, PPT #7–11	**INTERNATIONAL STRATEGY AND COMPETITIVE ADVANTAGE** Global expansion is necessary for firms because (1) capital markets and employees favor fast-growing firms and many domestic markets in developed countries are becoming saturated; (2) efficiencies in all value-chain activities are linked across borders and pressures for efficiency continue to escalate; (3) knowledge is not uniformly distributed and increasingly new ideas are coming from emerging economies; (4) customers are becoming global; and, finally, (5) competitors are globalizing. International strategy can support a firm's competitive advantage. The four most important aspects of international strategy are economies of scale and scope, location, multipoint competition, and learning. The costs of geographic diversification include the liabilities of newness and foreignness and governance and coordination costs. Liability of newness poses disadvantages related to being a new player in the market. Liability of foreignness is the disadvantages of not being a local player; these include lack of local market knowledge and the costs of starting a new foreign division relative to local or more established competitors. These disadvantages may dissipate with gains in local experience. Although disadvantages of newness and foreignness may decline, governance and coordination costs tend to increase with international diversification (e.g., information distortion across divisions, coordination difficulties, and possible misalignment between headquarters and international divisional managers). Economic benefits of internationalization are modest at first, and then become quite significant before leveling off. Bureaucratic and management costs can spike at extreme levels of internationalization, which leads to diseconomies of scale. **Global Economies of Scale and Scope** Given the strategy diamond, international strategy affects a firm's economic logic with economies of scale and scope. High R&D costs require firms to seek a larger revenue base, typically outside of their home countries. Large scale from global expansion creates competitive advantage if the firm has operating efficiency. The firm should focus on scale-sensitive resources and activities; resources must be concentrated in just a few locations. A specialized form of scope economies is available to global firms (e.g., MITY used excess capacity by sharing resources to produce tables and chairs). Economies of scope face numerous hazards. Strategy must still be	p. 219, Ex. 8.4 The Benefits and Costs of Internationalization *p. 221, *Fig. 8.1 McDonald's Economies of Scope*

	executed at the national level, and this can easily lead to a tension between the need to identify and satisfy the local client contact with the goal of lowering costs by sharing resources and coordinating actions across markets. **Location** National and regional geographic location impacts competitive advantage and its input costs, competitors, demand conditions, and complements. A five-forces industry analysis that includes related and supporting industries and true complements can be used to determine the importance of a location. Location differences present the opportunity for arbitrage. Firms can improve performance and potentially build competitive advantage by optimizing the value-chain location activities with cost differences. Generally, the greater the distance covered and the greater the value differences between the disconnected markets, the greater the profit potential arising from arbitrage. However, greater distance also tends to be accompanied by greater entry costs and risks. CAGE-related risks would be most relevant where language or cultural identity are important, the government views related products as staples or essential to national security, or income or input costs are key determinants of product demand or cost. To apply the CAGE framework, identify attractive locations based on raw material costs, access to markets or consumers, or other key decision criteria. **Multipoint Competition** This occurs when firms compete in multiple international markets. *Stronghold assault* refers to the competitive actions a firm takes in another firm's key markets that are most important to a competitor's profitability and cash flow, particularly when the attacking firm has little presence in that market. To employ this tactic, firms should have strategies in the staging component to determine when and how to shift from price to more sustainable bases of competition. **Learning and Knowledge Sharing** This refers to the need for firms to learn how to cope with different institutional, legal, and cultural environments. The benefits of being international must outweigh the added costs necessary to support the firm's nondomestic operations. The strategically most important markets will be those where intrinsic market attractiveness is high and learning from that market improves the firm's operations, products, and services. Finally, firms can exploit opportunities for inter-business-unit collaboration that result in valuable knowledge sharing.	p. 222, Ex. 8.5 The Cage Distance Framework: Opportunities for Global Arbitrage p. 225, Ex. 8.6 How Lincoln Electric (Eventually) Achieved Global Success
	FOREIGN COUNTRY ENTRY VEHICLES The various foreign country entry mechanisms are referred to as *vehicles of strategy*. There are essentially three ways to view foreign country entry vehicles—exporting, alliances, and foreign direct investment (FDI), either through the acquisition of a company or simply starting one from scratch.	p. 227, Ex. 8.7 Choices of Entry Modes

pp. 226–233, PPT #12–18	Foreign country entry is usually seen as a staged process: Import, then export, and then end with partial or full ownership. In practice, the process varies. Different entry vehicles have differing degrees of risk and control. **Exporting** is the sale of products and services abroad. The main costs are transportation, packaging, and ingredient requirements of the target country. Exporting is common when competitors and substitutes for the firm's products are not readily available in the target market. **Licensing and franchising** transfer the risk of implementing market entry to another firm that pays the licensor a fee for the right to use its name in the local country. Franchising in a foreign country works similarly to franchising in the domestic market. **Alliances** are used for foreign entry because of government regulations. **Foreign direct investment (FDI)** is when the firm makes a financial investment in a foreign market to facilitate the startup of a new venture. FDI is the most extensively used form of international entry tactic because it requires the greatest commitment of a firm's time and resources (e.g., acquisition or start-up of a greenfield investment). Acquisitions provide the firm with rapid entry. **Importing and International Strategy** Importing requires firms to be knowledgeable of customs requirements, customs regulations, entry of goods, invoices, classification and value, special requirements, fraud, marking, trade finance and insurance, and foreign trade zones. Importing takes many forms, from the sourcing of components, machinery, and raw materials, to the purchase of finished goods for domestic resale, to outsourcing production or services to nondomestic providers. IT is the impetus for international outsourced services and production. Foreign outsourcing locations tend to be defined by how automated a production process or service can be made and the transportation costs involved. When transportation costs and automation are both high, then the knowledge worker component of the location calculation becomes less important.	p. 228, Ex. 8.8 Vehicles for Entering Foreign Markets pp. 230–231, *8.1 How Would You Do That? Finding a Global Partner to Deliver the Goods* *p. 232, Fig. 8.2 South African Breweries entered the United States by Acquiring Miller Brewing Co.*
pp. 233–237,	**INTERNATIONAL STRATEGY CONFIGURATIONS** International strategy must deal with tradeoffs between customizing for local needs and achieving cost efficiencies in the firm's value chain. Each of the configurations identified in Exhibit 8.8 presents tradeoffs between global efficiency and local responsiveness. **Multinational Configuration** The firm has a portfolio of geographical units that maximize local responsiveness and uniqueness. **International Configuration** The firm leverages a global brand and distribution capabilities, but each unit is defined based on the country or region in which it operates; allows economies of scale and scope to create and exploit innovations on a global basis.	

PPT #19–21	**Global Configuration** The firm focuses on global efficiency and sacrifices local responsiveness for lower costs to achieve economies of scale; sacrifices higher prices of customization. **Transnational Configuration** The firm capitalizes on both local responsiveness and global efficiency, allowing it to achieve global economies of scale, cross-subsidization across markets, and the ability to engage in retaliatory and responsive competition across markets. It is difficult to find the balance between cost-efficiencies and the ability to customize to local tastes and standards. **Born Global Firms** These are firms that have operations that span the globe early in their existence. Their offerings complement the products or capabilities of other global players, take advantage of global IT infrastructure, or tap into a product or service that is somewhat uniform across national geographic markets. Global startups need to pass through two phases: **Phase 1: Should my firm be a global startup?** 1. Do I need human resources from other countries for success? 2. Do I need financial capital from other countries for success? 3. Will my target customers prefer the services of my company over competitors if I am global? 4. Can I establish a global system faster than domestic competitors? 5. Do I need global scale and scope to justify the financial and human capital investment in the venture? 6. Will a domestic focus now make it harder to go global later? **Phase 2: Committed to going global, the following needs are:** 1. A strong management team with international experience 2. A global network of suppliers, customers, and complements 3. Preemptive marketing or technology 4. Strong intangible assets. 5. Lock in customers with innovating of products and services 6. Close worldwide coordination and communication among business units, suppliers, complements, and customers	p. 235, Ex. 8.9 International Strategy Configurations, Global Efficiency, and Resource Requirements
pp. 237–242, PPT #22–24	**INTERNATIONAL STRATEGY IN STATIC AND DYNAMIC CONTEXTS** Firms in emerging economies that produce inexpensive yet high-quality products will compel incumbents to do the same and lead to dynamic global competition. International implications evolve with the industry life cycle as competitive dynamics change from introduction to decline. The resource-based perspective addresses staging and geographic arenas from the diamond strategy model for effective international strategies. Staging is necessary because the firm's global resources and capabilities do not materialize overnight. The most successful firms at internationalizing combine both greenfield investments with acquisitions and alliances. When a firm decides to enter a new foreign market, it must also develop resources necessary for market entry success. **Developing a Mindset for Global Dynamic Competitiveness** The effectiveness of a firm's international strategy is contingent on	pp. 240–241, 8.2 *How Would You Do That? Tactics for Developing Globally Minded Executives* *p. 242, Fig. 8.3 Lincoln Electric's*

106

	the internationally related capabilities and global mindset of the firm's executives. A global mindset has two distinct but related dimensions. The first, *a global perspective,* is an executive's appreciation that countries and their peoples differ culturally, socioeconomically, and sociopolitically. The second, *capacity to learn,* results from participation in geographic markets and the transfer of that knowledge to benefit other parts of the firm.	*International Strategy Investment with Acquisitions, Greenfield, and Alliances*

* Figure or Exhibit **NOT** enumerated in the PDF file.

III. SUGGESTED CASES TO ACCOMPANY TEXT

In the concepts-with-cases version of the text, we have supplied "Coca-Cola's Re-entry and Growth Strategies in China" and "Carrefour vs. Wal-Mart." The Coke case let's you explore aspects of international expansion, particularly entry into an emerging market. Even though its mapped primarily to Chapter 4 (external analysis), the Carrefour case presents students with an opportunity to see global competition in an arena where they assume that Wal-Mart is always going to be the leader, when in fact it is not the leader in many non–U.S. markets.

Need help selecting cases? Pearson Prentice Hall and Pearson Custom Publishing are pleased to present the ultimate resource for creating and customizing casebooks.

- Start with a CaseMap correlated to your text or start from scratch; do it yourself using our easy-to-use interface or collaborate with a developmental editor.
- Cases can be selected from a variety of sources, including Harvard Business School Publishing, Darden, Ivey, Thunderbird, and NACRA.
- We clear permissions for you on cases and content not in the database.
- You can also create custom course packs by adding articles, original material, and textbook chapters.
- Pearson Custom casebooks can be delivered in print or online.
- Additionally, we supply you, the instructor, with a free evaluation copy delivered 7 to 10 days after you create your book, free access to teaching notes, and case-method teaching resources.

We're here to help: Looking for a case on a specific topic, company, country, or scenario? Or, looking for a new case to substitute for one you've used in the past? We will help you find the right cases for your course and help you create a casebook that meets all your teaching needs. For guidance on building a casebook to reflect your course needs, e-mail our editorial consultant at customcases@prenhall.com.

Visit www.prenhall.com/custombusiness for more information and to see which Prentice Hall titles are available for short-run customization and to view suggested cases. To start your own straightforward search for material:

Step 1: Select "search content and create your book" and log in.
Step 2: Search by case number or keyword or browse by discipline to find suggested cases based on the book you use or course you teach.
Step 3: Browse, preview, and select the cases, articles, or chapters you wish to include (you will see that price and page count of the book in the top right-hand corner of the screen as you "build" the book).
Step 4: Finalize your selections, get them in the order you want, package your customized book with any Prentice Hall title for a discount (if you wish), click "confirm book," and you have the option to request a free evaluation copy.
Step 5: The Web site immediately gives you the ISBN of your custom book. You should give this ISBN to your bookstore; they will use it to place their order with us.

Beyond our cases and Pearson Custom Publishing, if you choose to compile your own casebook you will have an opportunity to draw from a variety of sources. These sources include going direct to Hartwick Leadership Cases, IVEY Case Publishing, European Case Clearing House (ECCH), Harvard Business School (HBS), Darden, and others.

Given the popularity of Harvard cases we have selected these additional cases for use with this chapter:

		ID#	Pages	TN
The DaimlerChrysler Merger (A): Gaining Global Competitiveness	HBSP	IMD130	20	Y
KTM—Ready to Race	HBSP	905M36	29	Y

The DaimlerChrysler Merger (A): Gaining Global Competitiveness Provides an overview of current trends in the global automotive industry and a description of Daimler-Benz AG and Chrysler Corp. prior to their merger. Describes this first transatlantic merger, raising the issues of strategic positioning, potential tradeoffs, and competitive moves. Teaching Purpose: To discuss and evaluate the challenges companies face in this hypercompetitive market.

KTM—Ready to Race KTM is a successful European off-road motorcycle manufacturer that sells in 72 countries. KTM has been experiencing impressive growth in both its top and bottom lines over the past several years, but it is facing significant growth pressure from its venture capitalist investor. The chief financial officer must determine how the company could achieve its growth objectives. Options include geographic expansion (increase U.S. emphasis or expansion to new European Union countries) or product expansion. Implementation options include a merger, acquisition, or internal growth. Several opportunities for geographic expansion and product diversification exist, and implementation options include make, buy, or ally decisions.

IV. LINKING THE CHAPTER TO A COMPUTER SIMULATION

The degree to which you can tie your computer simulation to this strategy is largely a function of whether any international or geographic conditions have been incorporated into the simulation. If not, then you can engage in some "what-if" dialogues with your class. For example, how might your business strategy have to be modified if you wanted to expand into Canada, Brazil, or China? What additional capabilities might be required? What are the implications for implementation, and how would you address this international expansion objective through the staging piece of the diamond model? Encourage students to incorporate the CAGE framework into their explanations. If the simulation is global or has geographic dimensions, then these issues should be easy to integrate.

Again, examples of simulations are found under the simulations heading at:

http://instruction.bus.wisc.edu/mcarpenter/PROFESSIONAL/Toolkit/bpstools.htm.

V. END OF CHAPTER ANSWER GUIDE

Review Questions

1. What is meant by international strategy?

Guide: International strategy essentially reflects the choices a firm's executives make with respect to sourcing and selling its goods in foreign markets. In the narrowest sense, a firm's managers need only think about international strategy when they conduct some aspect of their business across national borders. Some forms of international activities are designed to augment a firm's business strategy, such as when sourcing key factors of production in cheaper labor markets (i.e., attempts to be more competitive within a core business). Other international activities represent key elements of the firm's corporate strategy (i.e., entering new businesses or new markets).

2. Which aspects of the strategy diamond are related to international strategy?

Guide: International strategy must be reflected in all facets of the strategy diamond.

3. What are the four most important ways a firm's international strategy can be related to its competitive advantage?

Guide: International strategy, particularly in the form of international expansion, can figure into a firm's competitive advantage in a number of interrelated ways. The four most important aspects are economies of scale and scope, location, multipoint competition, and learning. Firms must understand the specific benefits in one or more of these areas if they are to say yes to international expansion plans.

4. What three foreign country entry vehicles are emphasized in this chapter?

Guide: The three foreign country entry vehicles emphasized in this chapter are exporting, alliances, and foreign direct investment (FDI), either through the acquisition of a company or simply starting one from scratch.

5. What is typically the most cost- and time-intensive entry vehicle?

Guide: Foreign direct investment (FDI). As the term implies, FDI is an international entry strategy whereby the firm makes a financial investment in a foreign market to facilitate the startup of a new venture. FDI tends to be the most extensive form of international entry tactic because it requires the greatest commitment of a firm's time and resources. FDI can be implemented in several ways, such as through an acquisition or through the startup of a foreign entity from scratch. This latter form of FDI is called a *greenfield investment*.

6. What are the four international strategy configurations discussed in this chapter?

Guide: How a firm becomes involved in international markets, which appears to be increasingly important if not obligatory for many if not all firms, differs from how it configures the interactions between headquarters and country operations. The four international strategy configurations discussed in this chapter are multinational, transnational, international, and global.

7. On what two dimensions do these four configurations differ?

Guide: Each of the configurations involves (1) tradeoffs between global efficiency and local responsiveness and (2) the firm's internal resources and capabilities to support a particular international strategy configuration.

8.   What does the external perspective tell you about international strategy in dynamic contexts?

Guide: The external view draws attention to how firms need to adapt to or modify their competitive position and strategy to the external environment in order to position the firm in a manner conducive to superior returns. Taking the external perspective, for instance, typically draws managerial attention to the dynamic nature of the firm's product life cycle and how that drives decisions to internationalize. Specifically, as products mature, the international implications of industry structure, and therefore strategic choices and firm behavior, should change in fundamental ways. Similarly, when you are discussing international strategy from an external perspective, you are also taking into account the fact that geographic markets differ in many legal, cultural, and institutional ways, which in turn are likely to have implications for product demand.

9.   What does the resource and capabilities-based perspective tell you about international strategy in dynamic contexts?

Guide: One of the fundamental ideas of having a dynamic view of strategy is to continuously build and renew firm capabilities. By continuously evolving the firm's stock of resources and capabilities, the chances for adaptation to changing environmental conditions are maximized. Thus, when a firm decides to enter a particular new foreign market, it must also embark on developing the resources necessary to make that market-entry decision a success. At the same time, what it learns in those new geographic markets should be evaluated for application or adaptation to existing market positions. In addition, as a firm internationalizes and becomes more dependent on a particular foreign location, the need for high-level capabilities to perform the local activities increases commensurately.

10.   What role do managers play in effective international strategies, particularly in dynamic contexts?

Guide: Given our emphasis on the importance of leadership skills throughout this text, it should come as little surprise that what may make or break the effectiveness of a firm's international strategy is the internationally related capabilities and global mindset of the firm's executives, particularly in dynamic markets. Moreover, such capabilities and mindset may allow one firm to change a once relatively stable competitive context into a dynamic and vibrant one. Global mindset has two distinct but related dimensions. The first dimension is something that strategy researchers have referred to simply as a *global perspective*. It also refers to the leadership skills necessary for managing a culturally diverse managerial team and a worldwide workforce. The end result of this combination of knowledge and skills is that the firm is able to build strong relationships within the organization across geographies and with customers in different geographic locations.

How Would You Do That?

11.   What sources of information can management draw upon to identify the ideal international alliance partner? What risks does Laura Ashley taking when it becomes so dependent on one firm, such as FedEx? What can Laura Ashley do to reduce its dependence on FedEx?

Guide: One way to approach this is to ask the students who a potential partner could be – the answer is any company that you could identify in a five-forces model and identification of complementors, and in the extreme case any stakeholder. The second two questions foreshadow some of the content of the chapter on alliances and other cooperative strategies, because by definition a strategic alliance puts at least one of the partners at risk. If delivery is delayed or if other things could affect Laura Ashley's reputation, then these are risks. Also, if FedEx raises its prices and Laura Ashley has no alternatives, then it suffers financially. One way for Laura Ashley to reduce its risk would be to develop partnerships with more than one logistics company. This way, Laura Ashley is not dependent on any single firm and can also have a basis for comparison in terms of price and service.

12. Many experts argue that business students must have a global mindset if they are to be competitive in the human capital marketplace. Your assignment is to design a learning program for yourself that would advance your global mindset through an internship. What is the learning purpose of your internship? What are your specific global learning objectives? What experiences would contribute to those objectives? What firms would you target for this mission, and what resources would you engage to approach them? Now, approach a firm and take action on your global mindset agenda!

Guide: We pose this question to encourage students to think about (1) the fact that they need to be knowledgeable about global markets and (2) that any experience they gain related to international business will be valuable. You should point out that this does not mean that they should learn 10 languages or live in another country for 5 years. However, they could seek an assignment with a local firm to help them with their import or export operations as a starting point. Moreover, most schools have some form of international education or work experience program, and this question forces them to explore those options (if that is how you set up the assignment, you may want to bring in your international programs person to talk about these opportunities).

Group Activities

13. Why have firms typically followed an international strategy path that started with importing or exporting, followed by alliances, then foreign direct investment? What risks do born-global firms run in trying to do both at once? What resources and capabilities must they possess to do both effectively at once?

Guide: For the first part of this question, you can show how the students' intuition serves them well. Firms typically internationalize incrementally, so they are learning as they go along, gradually expanding into more familiar adjacent territory, whether it be from importing, exporting, investing abroad, or moving from one geographic area to another (you can invoke the CAGE framework here). For the second part of the question, on born-global firms, it is best to point to examples like SKYPE or Logitech so that you can show how the product characteristics lent themselves to globally present at an early stage. However, you also need to emphasize that the firm needed the managerial capabilities and the structures, systems, and processes to support it.

14. Are all Internet firms global by definition? What opportunities and barriers does the Internet present to firm internationalization?

Guide: You can adopt various strategies to answer this question. One is to focus on the product characteristics, as with born-global firms. Another is to talk about whether language or culture or laws allow or prevent an Internet firm to grow its business globally *and* profitably. This is another example where the CAGE framework can also be used, as well as specific reference to how the students would configure the strategy diamond and answer the relevant questions about how internationalization adds value to each of the five components and the completed diamond.

VI. SUPPLEMENTAL EXPERIENTIAL EXERCISES

These exercises are drawn with permission from the Strategy Teaching Tool-kit found at:

http://instruction.bus.wisc.edu/mcarpenter/PROFESSIONAL/Toolkit/bpstools.htm.

1. Two fun but extremely educational international exercises are "BARNGA" (can be done in an hour) and "BaFa BaFa" (can be done in two to three hours). Both simulations are self-contained and introduce students to the managerial challenges presented by cultural differences. References to both can be found under cultural simulations on the BPS teaching toolkit site at

   http://instruction.bus.wisc.edu/mcarpenter/PROFESSIONAL/Toolkit/bpstools.htm.

2. The Ivey Case 9A95G001, "Where have you been: An exercise to assess your exposure to the rest of the world's people," is a fun way to show participants both how populous and diverse the world is in terms of population along with how little exposure they've actually had to the rest of the world's people. The case can be obtained from www.ivey.uwo.ca/cases/. We sometimes modify the case to use GDP instead of population. A variation of this is to print out a blank map of the world from the Web or some other resource and have teams try to fill in the names of the countries they can either name or have visited or both. Then you can show them what percentage of the world's population or cumulative GDP they have encountered. All of these exercises drive home the fact that the world is a big place and that we often view the United States as the center of the world.

PART FOUR
STRATEGY VEHICLES FOR NEW DIRECTIONS

CHAPTER 9 – UNDERSTANDING ALLIANCES AND COOPERATIVE STRATEGIES

I.   PURPOSE OF THE CHAPTER

After studying this chapter, students should be able to:

1.   Describe why strategic alliances are important strategy vehicles.
2.   Explain the various forms and structures of strategic alliances.
3.   Describe the motivations behind alliances and show how they've changed over time.
4.   Explain alliances as both business-level and corporate-level strategy vehicles.
5.   Understand the characteristics of alliances in stable and dynamic competitive contexts.
6.   Summarize the criteria for successful alliances.

Alliances are fun to teach about because they are so common and many students can easily cite examples of them in action. We often start by noting the similarities between personal relationships and alliances—there are reputations, exploration of common interests to determine compatibility, some dating, surprises (good and bad) once a more formal relationship is established, and then some eventual closure to the relationship (dissolution or merger. . . marriage). By setting up the topic this way, you can lay out the many dimensions of alliances that students should be familiar with: How do you find partners? What types of individuals or firms make the best partners? How do you set up alliances? What makes a good alliance? How do you manage the alliance? What do you do when one of the partner's circumstances changes? How do you dissolve alliances?

The most important take-away from this chapter for students is that alliances are not substitutes for strategy; instead, they are a vehicle for realizing a strategy, and a firm needs to possess particular resources and capabilities to execute an alliance-based strategy well. This is stated in the first section of the chapter, where the students are reminded that alliances map mainly to the vehicle and economic logic facets of the strategy diamond in Exhibit 9.1. Another very important take-away from the chapter is the notion of alliance evolution (discussed later in the chapter), because this reinforces that even vehicles introduce a degree of dynamism into strategy. Finally, a third objective you might set for yourself is that students understand what an alliance is, and is not. You may have your own particular perspective here that can be reinforced, but at the most extreme an alliance is a relationship between one or more parties that does not end with one transaction (like a sale), but instead anticipates a relationship that continues over some period of time. Exhibit 9.3 provides you with a spectrum of such continuous, cooperative arrangements.

In this chapter, the three differentiators—and hence your teaching strategy of the chapter—are manifested in the following ways:

*   **Strategic leadership.** The students see the importance of strategic leadership right away through the opening vignette on White Wave – Dean Foods experienced a change in leadership, and this new leadership opted to acquire its partner, White Wave, sooner than later. In contrast, Dean's new management knew it did not understand the soy business well enough to run it itself, so it retained

White Wave's founder, Steve Demos, with a 10-year retention contract. You can also remind students that executives and other managers are often distracted by the demands of managing alliances, and top executives in particular are seduced by the alliance-deal-making process, but then pass off the execution to lower-level managers. Finally, the section "What Makes an Alliance Successful" should be used to emphasize that trust (Exhibit 9.9), knowledge, and learning involves people, particularly strategic leaders. Managers also need to stay on top of the evolution of the alliance relationship and put in place alliance performance management metrics and some form of dedicated alliance function, as summarized in Exhibit 9.11.

- **Formulation and implementation interdependency.** It should be clear from the start for students reading this chapter and the next ("Mergers and Acquisitions") that using an alliance vehicle and making it work are requisite for making an economic impact. You can use the analogy of borrowing a friend's car (since they trust you). If you wreck your friend's car because you don't know how to drive it, it will likely have negative financial repercussions for you and damage your relationship with your friend. It will also decrease the probability of other friends lending you their cars in the future. "How Would You Do That? 9.1" further dramatizes this interdependence, but in a different way. It shows how choices about implementing the alliance influenced its ultimate success, as well as the ability of the partners to upgrade their respective resources and capabilities, and hence their strategy. You can bring this interdependency full circle with the Experiential Exercise 2 (see Section VI), which asks students to relate Millennium's use of alliances as a strategy vehicle.

- **Dynamic strategy.** You can bring out three aspects of dynamic strategy in this chapter. First, alliances introduce a degree of dynamism in and of themselves. Relationships evolve over time (trust, learning, and relative dependence or need for the alliance), and you can talk the students through this evolution. A quick skim of the *Harvard Business Review* alliance article by Bleeke and Ernst (1994) noted in the Additional Readings gives you plenty of fodder to talk about this type of evolution, and we refer to it briefly at the end of the chapter. The second aspect of dynamism is with respect to corporate strategy and how alliances facilitate diversification and corporate strategy in general. This topic is treated under the "Corporate and International Strategic Alliances" heading of the chapter. If you delved into the concept of real options in Chapter 6, and regardless of whether you are emphasizing alliances in the context of business or corporate strategy, you can also show students how alliances often present an option on a future action, and therefore again brings them back to the staging facet of the strategy diamond. Finally, alliances may serve different functions and play different roles in stable versus dynamic contexts, and the contrast between the two settings is developed under the heading "Alliances in Stable and Dynamic Contexts" found toward the end of the chapter.

Additional Readings:

Bleeke, J., and D. Ernst. (1995). Is your strategic alliance really a sale? *Harvard Business Review,* January-February: 97–105.

Brandenburger, A., and B. Nalebuff. (1996). *Co-opetition.* New York: Currency-Doubleday.

Dyer, J. (2000). *Collaborative advantage.* New York: Oxford University Press.

Harbison, J., and P. Pekar. (1998). *Smart alliances.* San Francisco: Jossey-Bass.

Reuer, J. (2004). *Strategic alliances.* New York: Oxford University Press.

II. BRIEF CHAPTER OUTLINE

pp. 246–248, PPT #1–6	**Chapter 9 Understanding Alliances and Cooperative Strategies** The purpose of this chapter is to explain the importance of alliances as strategy vehicles at the business and corporate levels; describe the different forms and structures of alliances; and identify the characteristics and criteria of successful alliances in stable and dynamic contexts. **Opening Vignette:** The Alliance Life Cycle at White Wave, pp. 247–248	
pp. 249–251, PPT #7–11	**STRATEGIC ALLIANCES** Alliances enable partners to share investments and rewards while reducing the risk and uncertainty that each firm would otherwise face on its own. Each firm can focus its resources on what it does best. Alliances foster economies of scale and scope that companies wouldn't otherwise be unable to achieve in the same cost-effective manner. Firms that are most active in alliances outperform the least-active firms by 5 to 7 percent. An alliance is one vehicle for realizing a strategy. A strategic alliance is a partnership between two or more firms in which the performance or competitive advantage achieved by one or more of the parties results from the alliance. As a percentage of revenues, alliances grew from 2 to nearly 16 percent from 1980 to 1995. The failure rate for alliances is about 50 percent (and nearly 70% in some cases). An alliance is a failure when it does not achieve the objectives of one or more of the partners. Alliances can be high risk as well as high return. The failure rate is explained by economic theories of behaving in one's own *self-interest*. The success of alliances depends on one's willingness to subordinate one's own interests to those of the alliance. Changes over time may compromise the best intentions.	p. 249, Ex. 9.1 The Place of Alliances in the Five Elements Model p. 250, Ex. 9.2 Possible Alliance Linkages
pp. 251–253, PPT #12–15	**FORM AND STRUCTURE OF ALLIANCES** Cooperative arrangements can take different forms. The two primary dimensions are the nature of the commitment (e.g., time frame and resources) and respective ownership of the alliance and inputs (from cash to people to technology). **Joint Ventures and Other Equity Alliances** The form of an alliance depends on such factors as legal structure, the number of objectives, and so on. In a **joint venture**, two companies form equity investments to create an independent third entity. Many joint venture are 50/50 in ownership and control, but this is not always the case. Many **equity strategic alliances** involve unequal partners. **Nonequity Alliances** The most common form of strategic alliance involves neither equity interest nor separate organizations. *Sole-sourcing*, *just-in-time supply*, *licensing*, *cobranding*, and *franchising* are different forms of **nonequity alliances**. They are usually contracts to supply, produce, market, or distribute over an extended period of time. **Multiparty Alliances** *Consortia* involve many participants. The primary contribution is information and maybe cost sharing.	p. 251, Ex. 9.3 Examples of Cooperative Arrangements in the Continuum of Organizational Forms *p. 252, Fig. 9.1 Dow Corning as a Joint Venture Between Dow Chemicals and Owens Corning* p. 253, Ex. 9.4 Starbucks Coffee: Creating Value Through a Set of Alliances

pp. 253–256, PPT #16–19	**WHY ALLIANCES? KNOWLEDGE AND COMPETITIVE ADVANTAGE** Alliances can spread risk and reduce competitive uncertainty in four ways: *joint investment*, *knowledge sharing*, *complementary resources*, and *effective management*. **Joint Investment** Alliances can increase returns by motivating firms to make investments that they'd be unwilling to make alone. **Knowledge Sharing** Partners can learn from another. This means partners must cooperate in transferring knowledge, which requires mutual trust and familiarity, and implement consistent information-sharing routines. **Complementary Resources** An alliance may be able to create resources that are not available to other competitors. If resources complement, the alliance may generate a shared advantage. If the combination is valuable and rare, the alliance may generate greater profits than the sum of the partners' profits. **Effective Management** An alliance may be more cost-effective to manage than either an arm's-length transaction or vertical or horizontal integration. Alliances lie between the *buy* or *make* decision. Formal protection mechanisms to minimize risk include equity investments and formal contracts. True cost savings come from less formal control and depend on self-enforcement and informal agreements that are based on trust. Alliances may build a competitive advantage if: • Rivals cannot ascertain generation of returns because of causal ambiguity surrounding the alliance. • Rivals cannot quickly replicate the resources owing to time decompression diseconomies. • Rivals cannot imitate practices or investments because they are missing complementary resources. • Rivals cannot find partner with the complementary resources. • Rivals cannot access potential partners' resources because the resources and capabilities are indivisible. • Rivals cannot replicate a distinctive and socially complex institutional environment that makes the alliance possible. **Alliance Motivation over Time** In the late 1980s, Booz-Allen began studying the alliance practices of 1,000 U.S. firms. **Product Performance** Alliances formed during the 1970s emphasized product and service performance. **Market Position** In the 1980s, firms tended to stress the building and reinforcing of market position. **Resources and Capabilities** Recently, firms are emphasizing more complex benefits, such as organizational learning and the development and accumulation of valuable resources and capabilities. These drivers represent *cumulative* needs.	p. 256, Ex. 9.5 Changing Motivation for Alliances
	ALLIANCES AS STRATEGY VEHICLES Selecting alliance partners is a matter of a firm's business and corporate strategies. **Alliances and Business Strategy** Potential alliance partners include rivals, new entrants, suppliers, substitutes, and	

pp. 256–262, PPT #20–26	complementors. Business-strategy alliances tend to fall into three categories: *vertical alliances, horizontal alliances,* or *complementary alliances* **Vertical Alliances** Firms involved in a vertical alliance leverage partners' resources and capabilities to (1) create more value for the end customer and (2) lower total production costs along the value chain. **Value Net Model and Coopetition** The **value-net model** in Exhibit 9.6 can be used to identify opportunities for cooperative relationships among exchange partners and even competitors—a principle known as *coopetition.* This model helps managers find potential parties to alliances. J.H. Dyer found that vertical alliances can create lean value chains by reducing total supply-chain costs in four areas: transaction, quality, logistics, and product-development costs. Also, alliances can increase speed to market, improve quality, introduce newer technologies, and enable firms to respond quickly to market changes. **Applying the Value Net to Horizontal Alliances** Horizontal alliances enable a firm to have a presence in multiple industry segments. As a component of a firm's value net, a horizontal alliance can create value by reducing risks, achieving greater efficiency, and fostering learning to develop and innovate new products. **What Makes Horizontal Ventures Work?** Horizontal ventures are potentially beneficial when partners' strategic goals converge and competitive goals diverge. All partners acknowledge that each must be willing to share knowledge as well as each can and protect proprietary skills. **Corporate and International Strategic Alliances** These are vehicles for corporate strategy. 1. Determine the right mix of businesses in the corporate portfolio; and 2. Ensuring that this mix creates shareholder value. Alliances are vehicles to explore and implement diversification options. It allows a firm to create more value in a portfolio of businesses than it could create by allowing them to be independent. **Alliances and International Strategy** As discussed in the Laura Ashley and FedEx example in Chapter 8, an international strategy should be based on the firm's business- and corporate-strategy objectives. In cross-border alliances, governments, public policies, and national cultures have significant roles; differences in workplace regulation and socioeconomic conditions also lead to much more complexities than domestic contexts. **Alliance Networks** The use of an alliance network has two implications: (1) the strategy discussion shifts from particular alliances as a vehicle to networks of alliances as a vehicle and (2) as networks take on characteristics of organization, competition among networks should arise both within and across industries.	p. 257, Ex. 9.6 The Value Net p. 259, Ex. 9.7 The Coopetition Value Chain at Timken p. 261, Ex. 9.8 Networks of Alliances

	Risks Arising from Alliances Cooperative ventures can be risky. These risks include: • Poor contract development • Misrepresentation of resources and capabilities • Misappropriation of resources and capabilities • Failure to make complementary resources available • Being held hostage through specific investments • Misunderstanding a partner's strategic intent	
pp. 262–263, PPT #27–28	**ALLIANCES IN STABLE AND DYNAMIC CONTEXTS** The suitability of an alliance as a strategic vehicle depends on the level of stability or dynamism in a firm's context. Relative dynamism may affect an alliance in two ways: 1. Stable environments are more forgiving of mistakes, such as poor choices in partners or alliance structures. 2. Stable environments allow firms to engage in more alliances and offer the luxury of learning from mistakes and regrouping. **Relative Stability and Alliance Motivation** Stability affects alliance objectives and influences the evolution of alliance motivation. In stable environments, partners tend to seek access to production technologies or markets. Objectives are to consolidate market positions and generate economies of scope and scale. **Relative Stability and the Coevolution Model of Corporate Strategy** Alliances enable firms to develop their specific dynamic capabilities in concert with the best resources and capabilities available. Alliances can sustain a specific focused strategy.	*p. 263, *Fig. 9.2 Nestle and Mars Alliance of M&M in Ice Cream*
pp. 263–270, PPT #29–37	**WHAT MAKES AN ALLIANCE SUCCESSFUL?** **Understanding the Determinants of Trust** A network of trustworthy partners and a reputation for trustworthiness are essential to the success of an alliance. Formal mechanisms such as long-term contracts, stock ownership, and collateral bonds can signal credible long-term commitments. Benefits of mutual trust include a greater willingness to make investments in assets customized to the alliance; increased learning with greater information sharing; reduced costs in monitoring and maintaining an alliance; foregoing new legal agreements; and relying on a simple management structure. **Relational Quality** Four elements are key to establishing and maintaining interorganizational trust: *initial conditions* refers to mutual attitudes before negotiations; *the negotiation process* determines whether any promise held by the initial conditions is realized; *reciprocal experiences* measure stock and flow in the partners' experiences; and *outside behavior* is a function of the reputation the firm develops with other firms outside the alliance. **Managing Knowledge and Learning** Management of knowledge and learning is enhanced if a firm develops specific processes. **Learning and Supplier Support at Toyota** One of the most successful firms at managing learning through alliance networks is Toyota. Efficiency gains resulted from concentrated efforts to ensure that learning flowed both ways and suppliers learned from each other.	p. 264, Ex. 9.9 Benefits of Trust p. 267, *9.1 How Would You Do That? Managing Coevolution at Fuji Xerox* p. 268, Ex. 9.10 Components of a

	Understanding Alliance Evolution Almost 80 percent of equity joint ventures end in the sale of one partner to another.	Dedicated Alliance Function
	Measuring Alliance Performance Few firms have effective systems for monitoring alliance performance. The following are three barriers to monitoring: 1. Partners have different information and reporting systems. 2. Inputs that the alliance receives from its corporate parents may be difficult to track and account for. 3. Hard to put a precise value on alliance outputs.	*p. 269, *Fig. 9.3 GM, Suzuki, and Isuzu Strategic Alliance*
	Dedicated Alliance Function A dedicated alliance function increases the likelihood of alliance success; it provides a structural solution to manage trust, learning, evolution, and performance. **When Do Partners Fit?** The following questions can be used to assess whether partners are a good fit: • Strategic fit between partners' objectives? For how long? • Resource and financial fit—willing to contribute? • Cultural fit for understanding each other? • Structure, systems, and processes fit—aligned decision-making and control mechanisms? • Additional fit criteria?	*p. 270, 9.2 How Would You Do That? Assessing Alliance Fit at Millennium Pharmaceuticals*

* Figure or Exhibit **NOT** enumerated in the PDF file.

III.   SUGGESTED CASES TO ACCOMPANY TEXT

Literally hundreds of alliance cases are available. For our concepts-with-cases version, we have incorporated the "Fuji-Xerox" and the "Xerox Corp and Neilson International in Mexico" cases. The Fuji-Xerox case gives students an idea of how the relationships between parties in large alliances can evolve, along with the necessary resources and capabilities required to execute them. The Neilson case provides students with the example of a smaller firm evaluating using the alliance vehicle in the context of international business.

Alliance cases also provide you with an opportunity to bring in cross-cultural and international dimensions of strategy to the class, because many of them involve cross-border partnerships. "Mondavi's Caliterra" case (IVEY) and "Bejing Jeep" (written by multiple sources) are two nice ones in this area. "Millennium Pharmaceuticals" (HBS) is a great case from the standpoint that it deals with a dynamic context, demonstrates how strategy and alliances intersect, and then shows Millennium walking away from a lucrative alliance. There is also a B case that allows students to consider an alliance and an acquisition; you can use the B case in conjunction with the next chapter on mergers and acquisitions.

Need help selecting cases? Pearson Prentice Hall and Pearson Custom Publishing are pleased to present the ultimate resource for creating and customizing casebooks.

• Start with a CaseMap correlated to your text or start from scratch; do it yourself using our easy-to-use interface or collaborate with a developmental editor.
• Cases can be selected from a variety of sources, including Harvard Business School Publishing, Darden, Ivey, Thunderbird, and NACRA.
• We clear permissions for you on cases and content not in the database.
• You can also create custom course packs by adding articles, original material, and textbook chapters.
• Pearson Custom casebooks can be delivered in print or online.

- Additionally, we supply you, the instructor, with a free evaluation copy delivered 7 to 10 days after you create your book, free access to teaching notes, and case-method teaching resources.

We're here to help: Looking for a case on a specific topic, company, country, or scenario? Or, looking for a new case to substitute for one you've used in the past? We will help you find the right cases for your course and help you create a casebook that meets all your teaching needs. For guidance on building a casebook to reflect your course needs, e-mail our editorial consultant at customcases@prenhall.com.

Visit www.prenhall.com/custombusiness for more information and to see which Prentice Hall titles are available for short-run customization and to view suggested cases. To start your own straightforward search for material:

Step 1: Select "search content and create your book" and log in.
Step 2: Search by case number or keyword or browse by discipline to find suggested cases based on the book you use or course you teach.
Step 3: Browse, preview, and select the cases, articles, or chapters you wish to include (you will see that price and page count of the book in the top right-hand corner of the screen as you "build" the book).
Step 4: Finalize your selections, get them in the order you want, package your customized book with any Prentice Hall title for a discount (if you wish), click "confirm book," and you have the option to request a free evaluation copy.
Step 5: The Web site immediately gives you the ISBN of your custom book. You should give this ISBN to your bookstore; they will use it to place their order with us.

Beyond our cases and Pearson Custom Publishing, if you choose to compile your own casebook you will have an opportunity to draw from a variety of sources. These sources include going direct to Hartwick Leadership Cases, IVEY Case Publishing, European Case Clearing House (ECCH), Harvard Business School (HBS), Darden, and others.

Given the popularity of Harvard cases, we have selected these additional cases for use with this chapter:

		ID#	Pages	TN
OXO International	HBSP	9-697-007	19	N
Amazon.com: Evolution of the e-Tailer	HBSP	SM83	20	N

OXO International OXO, a kitchen tools and gadgets company, was started by a businessman who had 30 years of experience in the housewares industry. With his wife and son as founders, he created a new niche in the gadgets industry for high-end gourmet stores. The company has headquarters in New York City, but it has outsourced product design to a New York City industrial design firm, manufacturing to Asia, and warehousing to a site in Connecticut in order to manage startup costs and growth. Because of the veteran businessman's reputation and industry sense, the company grew very quickly. and in 1992 is sold for $6.2 million to a large housewares distributor, General Housewares.

Amazon.com: Evolution of the E-Tailer Describes the evolution of Amazon.com from its inception in 1996 as an online bookseller to its position in 2001 as a globally recognized e-commerce brand. Reviews the evolution of the company's business model through an interview with Amazon.com's founder and CEO, Jeff Bezos. At its founding, Amazon.com mostly brokered book purchases through its Web site. After 5 years of phenomenal growth, the company expanded into international markets and added many categories, partners, and physical infrastructure. This case examines Amazon.com's growth, fueled by the Internet bubble, and looks at how the company coped with increased scrutiny on profitability. Teaching Purpose: Reviews the evolution of Amazon.com's business model from online book order broker to include many new categories of products, greater fulfillment, and new avenues of service.

IV.   COMPUTER SIMULATION

Most of the popular computer simulations that we are aware of (e.g., CapSim, MikesBikes, The Business Strategy Game, Glo-Bus) do not allow for the formation of alliances between student firms. One that does is StratSim (www.interpretive.com), which allows teams to engage in sourcing/licensing agreements.

V. END OF CHAPTER QUESTION ANSWER GUIDE

Review Questions

1.   What is a strategic alliance?

Guide: Alliances are not strategies in and of themselves. Instead, they are one of the vehicles for a strategy's realization. A strategic alliance represents a partnership between two or more organizations where the performance or competitive advantage of one or more of the parties to the agreement is believed to be a consequence of the alliance. Alliances may involve sharing resources related to only one key value-chain activity, such as R&D.

2.   Do most strategic alliances succeed?

Guide: The failure rate for alliances is about 50 percent, though it approaches 70 percent in some cases, which in turn suggests that they are a high-risk, high-return vehicle for realizing a firm's strategy.

3.   What forms can strategic alliances take?

Guide: Alliances can take on various forms depending on such factors as the objectives, legal structure, and number of participants. The types of alliances considered in this chapter include joint ventures, legal agreements, nonequity alliances, and multiparty alliances.

4.   What is the difference between equity and nonequity strategic alliances?

Guide: An equity alliance occurs when companies make equity investments in the creation of a third, independent legal entity. There is no requirement that an alliance have a separate legal structure or that ownership be equal, and in many cases equity strategic alliances involve partners with unequal shares. A nonequity alliance occurs when companies, usually in the form of a contract, agree to supply, produce, market, or distribute a firm's goods or services without investing any equity.

5.   What is an example of a nonequity strategic alliance?

Guide: A good example involves Starbucks. Starbucks has extended the presence of its brand into a myriad number of customer-contact locations through alliances with companies such as Barnes & Noble (bookstore cafes), United Airlines (inflight coffee service), Ben & Jerry's (ice cream flavors), Pepsi (Frappacino® ready-to-drink coffee), and Kraft (ground and whole coffee beans distributed nationwide through grocery stores).

6. Why do firms enter into alliances?

Guide: Firms with effective alliances may be able to improve their competitive position and gain a competitive advantage through their network of alliances. Alliances can help firms generate competitive advantage and spread risk and reduce competitive uncertainty in four ways: joint investments, knowledge sharing, complementary resources, and effective management.

7. What are the three forms of alliance that support business strategy?

Guide: Alliances can figure into most aspects of business strategy but generally provide a means to manage competitive pressures, uncertainty, or both. As a result, business strategy alliances tend to fall into three categories: vertical alliances, horizontal alliances and complementary alliances.

8. What do the value net and six-forces model tell you about potential alliance partners?

Guide: The value net helps managers break down conventional win-lose competitive mindsets as well as the need for vertical integration by identifying opportunities for cooperative relationships among exchange partners and even competitors. Recall that the purpose was to find ways to increase the total value created by parties in the value net, rather than just identifying how to compete for industry profits. Thus, the value net helps managers find potential parties to alliances. The value net also shows that value can be created through horizontal and complementary alliances. Horizontal alliances allow competitors or potential competitors to have a presence in multiple segments of an industry.

9. How do alliances serve as a vehicle for corporate strategy?

Guide: Alliances are typically a vehicle for business strategy, though they can also be vehicles for corporate strategy as well. Alliances can also be used by the corporation to create more value across individual business than might be otherwise created had they been independent. In terms of business mix, alliances provide vehicles for exploring and implementing diversification options.

10. What risks do alliances pose to partner firms?

Guide: Although alliances are usually viewed as a strategy vehicle that reduces uncertainty, such cooperative approaches can be risky in and of themselves for six reasons: (1) poor contract development, (2) misrepresentation by the partner, (3) misappropriation, (4) failure of a partner to make complementary resources or capabilities available, (5) one partner holding the other hostage, and (6) misunderstanding a partner's strategic intent.

11. How do stable and dynamic context alliances differ?

Guide: They differ to the extent to which they make the alliance more or less risky. First, from a very practical standpoint relatively stable environments are much more forgiving in terms of mistakes, such as those relating to partner choice or structure of an alliance. Stable environments also allow firms to participate in more alliances because their ongoing maintenance and management attention are typically less taxing. Also, although wasted time, effort, and resources are undesirable in any situation, relatively stable contexts provide firms with the luxury of learning from their mistakes and eventually regrouping.

12. What are the five criteria for successful alliances?

Guide: Four of these—understanding the determinants of trust, being able to manage knowledge and learning, understanding alliance evolution, and measuring alliance performance—apply readily to firms of all size and domestic and international alliances alike. The last criterion—the creation of a dedicated alliance function—is a step usually undertaken by larger firms and those that otherwise use alliances as a key vehicle for strategy execution. Taken together, these five criteria will put you in a better position to design alliances in a way that contributes to firms' competitive advantage.

How Would You Do That?

13. Use the VRINE framework to map out the resources and capabilities that you believe evolved at Xerox as a result of the Fuji-Xerox alliance. Why might these resources and capabilities be valuable in a dynamic competitive environment?

Guide: Your objectives here are twofold. First, remind the students that alliances are designed to gain access to resources and capabilities external to the firm, but that in the end the collection of the firm and its alliances must still satisfy the VRINE framework to create competitive advantage. You can also use this first objective as a segue to the questions of whether the firm, the alliance, or the alliance partner has most of the control over the VRINE resources and capabilities and how constant this control will likely be in the future. Second, you can also note that the ability to manage alliances effectively is a scarce and valuable resource, and it, too, then is subject to VRINE analysis. In most instance, the bottom-line question will be the "E": Is the firm *exploiting* the value from the alliance that it should be able to?

14. Apply the Millennium alliance framework to the alliances of another firm you are familiar with. Do these appear to be "good" alliances? Do any of the alliances suggest that your focal firm is on a pathway to acquire its partner or be acquired by it?

Guide: As demonstrated by the opening vignette on White Wave, many alliances lead to the acquisition of one partner by the other. The important point for the students to note is that this should be by design, and not default. A table titled "Seller Beware" in the *Harvard Business Review* alliance article by Bleeke and Ernst (1994) quickly summarizes the disadvantages of selling a company after it has already entered into an alliance, and you can use it to guide your talking points.

Group Activities

15. Increasingly, firms such as Corning (www.corning.com) and Millennium Pharmaceuticals (www.millennium.com) claim to have a core competency and competitive advantage based on their ability to manage alliances. Develop statements that both defend and critique this proposition. Identify risks that firms run when their strategy is essentially a network of alliances.

Guide: This question mirrors the critical thinking question posed above. You again want students to get to the point where they see that the content of the alliance and its effective implementation are the key determinants of its effectiveness, not the simple matter of having alliances with prestigious partners. This dialogue also gives you the opportunity to remind students that alliance management takes time and that often the alliance may evolve in ways that are inconsistent with the partners' strategies. Indeed, the alliance can be financially successful independent of the benefits it provides to the partners. However, if a focal firm is involved in many alliances that have evolved away from its core strategy then it is at risk of becoming a conglomerate and losing its strategic focus; that is, the alliances may become a substitute for strategy. Corning is a good example of a firm that has run this risk over the years. Involved in many alliances that stretched the firm in different directions, Corning lost focus on its core glass-based technological prowess. Only by divesting itself of many of the unrelated alliances (commodity, low-growth, and unrelated businesses) was management able to return Corning to its core focus.

16. Identify a firm and document its alliance activity over the past 5 to 10 years (this is usually easy to do with public firm's Web sites and their "history" pages). From your experiences with the cases we have covered thus far and what you have learned from this chapter, how many firms would have to make minimal changes if they were to follow the recommendations on implementation levers necessary to achieve an effective dedicated alliance function? What would be the costs and benefits of such a change?

Guide: One option with this question would be to add it to the dialogue on a case discussion where you are assessing different issues related to alliances. You can take the case company and ask the students to sketch out a rough estimate of the firm's alliance capabilities and then ask them to estimate what it would take for the firm to develop a dedicated alliance function. You can push the usefulness of the dialogue further by asking students to map out a transition path from the current state to the desired state and ask them how long this transition should take and in what order changes should be made. On the cost–benefit question, you want to encourage students to think out of the box. For instance, in a small firm all these functions could reside within one person, and in fact many smaller firms have an individual responsible for managing partner relations and developing new ones. Larger firms obviously have the resources to develop a more highly staffed dedicated alliance unit. However, the question for both small and large firms is whether they have the capabilities to extract values from an alliance vehicle.

VI. SUPPLEMENTAL EXPERIENTIAL EXERCISES

These exercises are drawn with permission from the Strategy Teaching Tool-kit found at:

http://instruction.bus.wisc.edu/mcarpenter/PROFESSIONAL/Toolkit/bpstools.htm.

1. **The Blue Chip Game** The objective of this exercise is to introduce students to the concepts of game theory, cooperation, collusion, and opportunism and to reinforce learning about framing and boundaries. While we don't employ game theory extensively in this chapter you can also use to explore it as well.

Time: Approximately 15 minutes

Materials needed: Eight index cards (four blue and four of another color—in this exercise we use yellow ones) and four envelopes (preferably thick enough to conceal the content of the cards). If you prefer, you can use poker chips.

Game overview: Each team submits one card each round (we like four rounds, but it isn't a sacred number). Each team earns or loses points depending on what the other teams do. If everyone submits a yellow card, then everyone wins. If only one group "defects," then it does best of all. But if everyone defects, everyone loses points.

Prior to class: Each class has four teams. Each team gets an envelope and one card of each color. I number the cards and envelopes, so we can keep track of the game more easily. You'll also want to make up a viewgraph (or a class handout) that shows how the game is scored.

Cards turned in	Blue is worth	Yellow is worth
0 Blue & 4 Yellow	0	25
1 Blue & 3 Yellow	75	-25
2 Blue & 2 Yellow	50	-50
3 Blue & 1 Yellow	25	-75
4 Blue & 0 Yellow	-75	0

In class: Divide the class into four teams and have the team members sit together. Announce the following: "This game has four rounds. In each round you'll have 60 seconds to turn in one card, either a blue card or a yellow card. Your score is determined partially by what you choose and partially by what the other teams choose. Your objective is to score as many points as possible. There is one rule: You must turn in, using the envelopes provided, one card each round. (Note: This rule is optional.) Turning in two or turning in zero will cost you 100 points. Good luck."

After each round, the current scores are posted, as well as the cumulative scores for each team. You may want to remind students of the rules and the objective and banter jokes with the teams. After each round, you announce there is a secret for winning. Roughly half the time the groups will figure out they can collude with other groups. For the times when they don't, you should ask students what the rules are; after some prodding, they acknowledge that collusion is not illegal in this game. About half of the time the groups collude successfully, and half the time they don't.

Sample discussion questions:

1. How do you win at this game?
2. At what point did you realize you could cooperate with other teams?
3. What rules did you assume existed that didn't?
4. For the "industry," which scenario is most lucrative? How about for individual teams?
5. What steps could you have taken to ensure cooperation?
6. What made cooperation more difficult?
7. Are any teams "untrustworthy" or are they rational?
8. How might you address "defections"?
9. What were the more interesting strategies?
10. Can you think of any situations where this situation exists (e.g., cartels such as OPEC)?
11. Can cartels succeed?
12. How would you play the game differently now? (Sometimes I repeat this game a week or so later).

When you announce that there is a "trick to winning," you'll get some really creative efforts:

- One instructor had a football player, a lineman, in class; he was polite but physically intimidating. None of the teams would cooperate, and he got frustrated. During the fourth round he went to the other three groups and told them to submit the #$^$^* (expletive) yellow card. Each group, feeling coerced, did so. Afterwards, they complained of being pressured. The instructor gave them the quip, "Coercion is just cooperation by other means" (okay, we guess you had to be there).
- One instructor had a group cut its cards in half and taped the mismatched pairs together—that way they could claim it was yellow (provided everyone else was yellow) or blue (in case it was a split decision).

125

2. What role does implementation play in the five success criteria of strategic alliances—the ability to develop trusting relationships, the ability to learn and transfer knowledge, an understanding of alliance evolution, an ability to monitor alliance performance, and understanding of the factors that comprise a dedicated alliance function?

Guide: This exercise can be fun because it usually gives rise to a number of varied and competing perspectives on alliance management. A great reference here is Dyer, Kale, and Singh's article "How to make alliances work."[1] A quick read of the paper and your students will think that you are an expert on the intricacies of alliance implementation. Pages 42–43 of the article, reproduced here, give you enough ammunition to structure this experiential exercise. One byproduct of this discussion should be the acknowledgement that diversifying alliances may be harder to manage in this fashion than business strategy alliances, because there will be fewer lower-level linkages—the last part of the following material helps clarify the issues of alliance management with regard to corporate strategy.

How To Organize an Effective Strategic-Alliance Function

One of the major challenges of creating an alliance function is knowing how to organize it. It is possible to organize the function around key partners, industries, business units, geographic areas or a combination of all four. How an alliance function is organized influences its strategy and effectiveness. For instance, if the alliance function is organized by business unit, then the function will reflect the idiosyncrasies of each business unit and the industry in which it operates. If the alliance function is organized geographically, then knowledge about partners and coordination mechanisms, for example, will be accumulated primarily with a geographic focus.

Identify Key Strategic Parameters and Organize Around Them

Organizing around key strategic parameters enhances the probability of alliance success. For example, a company with a large number of alliances and a few central players may identify partner-specific knowledge and partner-specific strategic priorities as critical. As a result, it may decide to organize the dedicated alliance function around central alliance partners.

Hewlett-Packard is a good example of a company that created processes to share knowledge on how to work with a specific alliance partner. (See "Hewlett-Packard Alliance Structure for Key Alliance Partners.") It identified a few key strategic partners with which it had numerous alliances, such as Microsoft, Cisco, Oracle and America Online and Netscape (now part of AOL Time Warner) among others. HP created a partner-level alliance-manager position to oversee all its alliances with each partner. The strategic-partner-level alliance managers had the responsibility of working with the managers and teams of the individual alliances to ensure that each of the partner's alliances would be as successful as possible. Because HP had numerous marketing and technical alliances with partners such as Microsoft, it also assigned some marketing and technical program managers to the alliance function. The managers supported the individual alliance managers and teams on specific marketing and technical issues relevant to their respective alliances. Thus HP became good at sharing partner-specific experiences and developing partner-specific priorities.

Citicorp developed a different approach. Rather than organize around key partners, the company organized its alliance function around business units and geographic areas. In some divisions, the company also used an alliance board—similar to a board of directors—to oversee many alliances. The corporate alliance function was assigned a research-and-development and coordinating role for the

[1] Dyer, J., P. Kale, and H. Singh. (2001). How to make alliances work. *Sloan Management Review*, *42*(4), 37–44.

alliance functions that resided in each division. For instance, the e-business-solutions division engaged in alliances that were typically different from those of the retail banking division; therefore, the alliance function needed to create alliance-management knowledge relevant to that specific division. Furthermore, to respond to differences among geographic regions, each of Citicorp's divisions created an alliance function within each region. For example, the e-business-solutions alliance group in Latin America would oversee all Citicorp's Latin American alliances in the e-business sector. The e-business division's Latin American alliance board would review potential Latin American alliances—and approve or reject them.

Organize To Facilitate the Exchange of Knowledge on Specific Topics

The strategic-alliance function should be organized to make it easy for individuals throughout the organization to locate codified or tacit knowledge on a particular issue, type of alliance or phase of the alliance life cycle. In other words, in addition to developing partner-specific, business-specific or geography-specific knowledge, companies should charge certain individuals with responsibility for developing topic-specific knowledge.

For example, when people within the organization want to know the best way to negotiate a strategic-alliance agreement, what contractual provisions and governance arrangements are most appropriate, which metrics should be used, or the most effective way to resolve disagreements with partners, they should be able to access that information easily through the strategic-alliance function. In most cases, someone within the alliance function acts as the internal expert and is assigned the responsibility of developing and acquiring knowledge on a particular element of the alliance life cycle. For some companies, it may be important to develop expertise on specific types of alliances—for example, those tied to research and development, marketing and co-branding, manufacturing, standard setting, consolidation joint ventures or new joint ventures. The issues involved in setting up such alliances can be very different. For example, whenever the success of an alliance depends on the exchange of knowledge—as is the case in R&D alliances equity-sharing governance arrangements are preferable because they give both parties the incentives necessary for them to bring all relevant knowledge to the table. But when each party brings to the alliance an "easy to value" resource—as with most marketing and cobranding alliances—contractual governance arrangements tend to be more suitable.

Locate the Function at an Appropriate Level of the Organization

When done properly, dedicated alliance functions offer internal legitimacy to alliances, assist in setting strategic priorities and draw on resources across the company. That is why the function cannot be buried within a particular division or be relegated to low-level support within business development. It is critical that the director or vice president of the strategic-alliance function report to the COO or president of the company. Because alliances play an increasingly important role in overall corporate strategy, the person in charge of alliances should participate in the strategy-making processes at the highest level of the company. Moreover, if the alliance function's director reports to the company president or COO, the function will have the visibility and reach to cut across boundaries and draw on the company's resources in support of its alliance initiatives.

CHAPTER 10 – STUDYING MERGERS AND ACQUISITIONS

I.   PURPOSE OF THE CHAPTER

After studying this chapter, students should be able to:

1.   Explain the motivations behind acquisitions and show how they've has changed over time.
2.   Explain why mergers and acquisitions are important strategy vehicles.
3.   Understand the various types of acquisitions.
4.   Understand how the pricing of acquisitions affects the realization of synergies.
5.   Describe the alternatives for acquisition integration and the implementation process.
6.   Understand the characteristics of acquisitions in different industry contexts.
7.   Summarize the criteria for acquisition success

Like Chapter 8 on alliances, the purpose of this chapter is to familiarize students with an important, but complex, strategy vehicle. Acquisitions are one of the most common vehicles, and for a variety of reasons their use is likely to remain a regular element of strategy. Some professors we know shy away from teaching about mergers and acquisitions because they think that this is an activity that students are unlikely to participate in during the early stages of their careers. We disagree, and our personal experience is that most students will be part of an acquisition early in their careers. The more they understand about why they are used and how they work the better chance they have of not being a casualty of an acquisition.

If you used the dating analogy in the alliances chapter, then you can use marriage here for acquisitions. Acquisitions allow firms to quickly move into new strategic arenas, renew corporate resources and capabilities, and change their competitive position. Not all mergers and acquisitions are the same, and each type of deal has a specific aim for how synergies will be derived. This chapter was meant to introduce common sources of problems associated with mergers and acquisitions, in particular, pricing. The pricing of an acquisition, specifically the premium paid for a target, has serious implications for required performance improvements and the potential success of a transaction. Finally, this chapter was intended to introduce the idea that the acquisition process is also critical in relation to the success of the acquisition itself. Although most of the excitement and managerial attention on doing mergers and acquisitions is on the front end, the process of how acquisitions are consummated and integrated is one of the key determinants of whether the transaction will succeed in achieving its aims. Consequently, successful acquirers make the acquisition-integration process a full-time activity.

If you can have students leave this chapter having learned three basic objectives then you will have done a good job. The first objective is to have students understand that mergers and acquisitions are not a substitute for strategy, but a vehicle for it. So if profitable growth is the firm's goal, then the employment of this vehicle must be complemented by the other facets of a firm's business and corporate strategy, its VRINE resources and capabilities, and its implementation and strategic leadership. A second teaching objective could be that mergers and acquisitions are a natural outcome of many alliances, and in fact many alliances are intentional (at least on one party's part) precursors to acquisition. For this reason, you can show students how mergers and acquisitions, via alliances, fit into the staging facet of the strategy diamond. Finally, students need to leave this chapter understanding that the successful use of mergers and acquisitions in business and corporate strategy requires significant resources and capabilities related to target identification, negotiation, and integration (to the degree that there is integration). This is treated in depth in the section on "Integrating and Implementing an Acquisition."

In this chapter, the three differentiators—and hence your teaching strategy of the chapter—are manifested in the following ways:

- **Strategic leadership.** Students see strategic leadership in the opening vignette, which poses the challenge to eBay CEO Meg Whitman of making the PayPal acquisition work. In the introductory section of the chapter, it is made pretty clear that one of the reasons for so many merger and acquisition failures is, ironically, a lack of strategic leadership, as demonstrated in the section titled "Managerial Self-Interest" and later in the chapter in the sections "Reaching a Walk-away Price" and "Escalation of Commitment." A theme running through the entire chapter is that top executives must have a deep understanding of the complexities of mergers and acquisitions to be good at them and make the choice to involve lower-level managers in the due diligence and integration process.
- **Formulation and implementation interdependency.** You can make this linkage most apparent when you note how many alliances lead to mergers and acquisitions, which maps directly onto the staging facet of the strategy diamond. This interdependency should also be readily apparent from the fact that mergers and acquisitions are not a strategy, but rather simply another vehicle. Therefore, what the firm does before, during, and after an acquisition—which involves all the factors of strategy implementation—will determine whether the activity created or squandered shareholder and other stakeholder value.
- **Dynamic strategy.** Like alliances, mergers and acquisitions have several levels of dynamism. Mergers and acquisitions introduce dynamism simply because, to be successful, the firm must do something better with what it has acquired to cover the costs of the acquisition and/or integrate the firms in such a way that business and corporate strategy are more effective after the acquisition than before it, including financially covering the costs of the acquisition. The section titled "Synergy Trap" and the related "How Would You Do That? 10.1" should drive this last point home. Moreover, in the beginning of the chapter the students are shown how mergers and acquisitions relate to the facets of the strategy diamond, and one of those facets is staging (i.e., suggesting change is anticipated and required). Mergers and acquisitions typically allow firms to enter (and exit) businesses more rapidly than if they were to do so from scratch. Although this is relevant in stable and dynamic contexts alike due to the industry life cycle, we talk specifically about mergers and acquisitions in dynamic contexts in the latter parts of the chapter. If you explored real options in Chapter 6 with your students, this is a good chapter to reinforce this concept, because some firms use relatively small acquisitions to stake out options on future growth opportunities in uncertain and dynamic contexts.

Additional Readings:

Child, J., D. Faulkner, and R. Pitkethly. (2001). *The management of international acquisitions*. New York: Oxford University Press.

Devine, M. (2002). *Successful mergers: Getting the people issues right*. London: Economist Books.

Harvard Business Review on mergers and acquisitions (compilation of various HBR M&A articles). (2001). Boston: Harvard Business School Press.

Haspeslagh, P., and D. Jemison. (1991). *Managing acquisitions*. New York: Free Press. (This is one of our favorite resources, and Appendix C has a nice checklist for mergers and acquisitions.)

Hitt, M., J. Harrison, and R. Ireland. (2001). *Mergers and acquisitions*. New York: Oxford University Press.

Sirower, M. (1997). *The synergy trap*. New York: Free Press.

II.   BRIEF CHAPTER OUTLINE

pp. 274–276, PPT #1–4	**Chapter 10 Studying Mergers and Acquisitions** The purpose of this chapter is to explain motivations for acquisitions and their use as strategy vehicles, identify types of acquisitions, outline the impact of M&A pricing on implementation, and describe the integration approaches and impact of industry contexts. **Opening Vignette:** eBay + PayPal: How to Acquire Customers, pp. 275–276	
pp. 276– 280, PPT #5	**MOTIVES FOR MERGERS AND ACQUISITIONS** **Differences Between Acquisitions and Mergers** Acquisition means a transfer of ownership—one firm buys another. A merger is a procedure for an acquisition, and one firm disappears when two firms combine. Three categories of motives for mergers and acquisitions are synergy, manager self-interest, and hubris. **Synergy** is when the value of two firms combined can be greater than the sum of the two firms independently. Synergy may be derived from: • Reducing threats • Increasing market power • Realizing cost savings • Generating revenue enhancement • Increasing financial strength • Sharing and leveraging capabilities **Managerial Self-Interest** This is exhibited when decisions are based on personal self-interest rather than shareholders' best interests, because executive compensation tends to be linked to firm size. **Hubris** Richard Roll posed the hubris hypothesis to explain why acquisitions premiums are so large and why acquisitions are so common. Managers make valuation mistakes and have unwarranted confidence both in their valuations and in their ability to create value. **Changing Motivations for M&As** The ways in which mergers and acquisitions contribute to competitive advantage have changed. **Financial Synergies** In the 1960s and early 1970s, mergers and acquisitions were motivated by financial synergies, and diversification was the vehicle. *Unrelated diversification* violated the interests of shareholders, who were better off simply diversifying individual stock portfolios. This led to deconglomeration during the 1980s. **Focused Growth** Threat of hostile takeover motivated many CEOs to start refocusing on core activities.	p. 277, Ex. 10.1 eBay and PayPal Business Model *p. 279, Fig. 10.1 Pepsico Purchased Carts of Colorado in 1992*
	MERGERS, ACQUISITIONS, and STRATEGY **The Vehicle and Its Economic Logic** Acquisitions allow firms to enter new businesses quickly; reduce the time and risks; and rapidly reach minimum efficient scale. Mergers and acquisitions are a *vehicle* for realizing a strategy to enter or exit a business.	p. 280, Ex. 10.2 The Place of Acquisitions in the Five-Elements Model

pp. 280–283, PPT #6–9	Acquisition activity tends to occur in waves. Some mergers and acquisitions were notable "mistakes" (e.g., AT&T's acquisition of NCR, Quaker's acquisition of Snapple, and AOL's merger with Time Warner). **The Flipside: Divestiture** The flipside of acquisition, divestiture, is the selling off of a business. It is also a key strategy vehicle. **Benefits of Acquisition over Internal Development** One of the primary advantages of an acquisition is *speed*. The following are other advantages of acquisitions: <ul><li>The firm is able to quickly establish a new business.</li><li>The firm is able to enter a new business with sufficient size.</li><li>The firm is able to achieve viable competitive strength.</li><li>The firm is assured of entering at minimum efficient scale for cost purposes.</li><li>The firm gains access to complementary assets and resources.</li></ul>**Drawbacks of Acquisition over Internal Development** The drawbacks of acquisitions are as follows: <ul><li>They are often expensive.</li><li>They are unlikely to generate sufficient return on capital to justify the premium cost.</li><li>The firm may inherit several unnecessary adjunct businesses.</li><li>Potential problem of organizational conflict—eruption of cultural clashes that can impede integration of two firms.</li></ul>	p. 281, Ex. 10.3 U.S. Acquisition Activity, 1995–2004 p. 282, Ex. 10.4 Ups and Downs at Snapple
pp. 283–287, PPT #10–11	**TYPES OF MERGERS AND ACQUISITIONS** Each type of merger and acquisition has a purpose for creating synergies: **Types of Acquisitions** Business-strategy acquisitions tend to be related to the firm's core business through *vertical, horizontal,* or *complementary relationships.* **A More Complex Classification of Types of Acquisitions** The following is a typology on the strategic logic of more complex acquisitions: <ul><li>*Product/market extension* expands the firm's product line into a geographic market in which it has no presence.</li><li>*Geographic roll-up* is when a firm buys another firm in the same industry segment, but in many different geographic arenas.</li><li>*M&A as R&D* occurs when the firm uses an acquisition in lieu of or in addition to internal research and development (R&D) to gain technology.</li><li>*Overcapacity M&As* reduce the number of competitors in a mature industry in which capacity exceeds decreasing demand.</li><li>*Industry Convergence M&As* occur due to overlap of complementary industries as they begin to *converge.*</li><li>*Investor/Holding Company M&As* occur when independent investors or holding companies purchase existing firms or engage in a leveraged buyout and the buyer brings management, operating, and financial discipline to the company, intending to sell it later at a profit.</li></ul>**International acquisitions** may fall into any of the categories described.	*p. 284, *Fig. 10.2 Best Buy's 1992 Acquisition of the Geek Squad* p. 285, Ex. 10.5 Bower's Classification of Acquisitions p. 286, Ex. 10.6 M&As as R&D

pp. 287–290, PPT #12–16	**PRICING AND PREMIUMS** **Pricing** No single correct price for an acquisition or merger. Price depends on the target's intrinsic value, current market value, and the value from potential synergies between target and buyer. **Intrinsic and Market Value** Intrinsic value is the present value of a company's future cash flows from existing assets and businesses. Market value is the current market capitalization of a firm (typically calculated by multiplying the number of shares outstanding time their market price). The purchase price is the value actually paid to target shareholders. **Synergy Value** This is the difference between the combined values of the target and the acquiring firm after the transaction and the sum of the values of the two firms taken independently. Intrinsic synergy value is the sum of cost savings, revenue enhancements, financial-engineering activities, and tax benefits generated by the transaction. Market-based synergy value is the financial market's expectation of management's ability to extract intrinsic value. **Premium** This is the difference between current market value and the purchase price. In the United States, the average acquisition premium has ranged between 30 to 45 percent over the past 15 years. **The "Synergy Trap"** Mark Sirower of Boston Consulting Group (BCG) identified two problems with premiums: (1) they increase the required returns from the combined businesses and (2) delays raise the ante on required performance improvements. **Reaching a Walk-away Price** Buffet opposed Coke's CEO Daft's purchase of Quaker Oats to add Gatorade because of the high premium and advised that Coke should walk away from negotiations. **Escalation of Commitment and the "Winner's Curse"** Executives escalate the commitment to their initiative as they proceed through the transaction. This results in bidders making questionable decisions. They win the "prize" but face consequences of paying too much; this phenomenon is called the **winner's curse**.	*p. 289, *10.1 How Would You Do That? The Impact of Premiums on Required Synergies* p. 289, Ex. 10.7 Synergy Required to Justify $10 Million Premium *p. 290, Fig. 10.3 1982 Warren Buffett*
pp. 290–293, PPT #17–19	**THE ACQUISTION PROCESS** **Stages of the Acquisition Process** Exhibit 10.9 offers a four-stage model for acquisition: idea generation, justification (including due diligence and negotiation), integration, and result. This model identifies two types of problems: decision-making problems and implementation or integration problems. **Idea** is the impetus for acquisition. **Justification, due diligence, and negotiation** is the major analytical stage with internal and external logic. Critical decisions include strategic assessment, purpose and strategic logic; identification of possible benefits and problems. • **Understand the Conditions for Creating Synergies** • **Control the Timing of Implementation and Integration** • **Establish a Walkaway Price** **Integration** means understanding interactions between target and acquiring firms.	p. 291, Ex. 10.8 Acquisition Process Stages p. 292, Ex. 10.9 Organizational Fit Acquisition Screening by Cisco Systems

pp. 293–296, PPT #20–24	**INTEGRATING AND IMPLEMENTING AN ACQUISITION** **Strategic interdependence** depends on the types of resource sharing and skill transfers that the two firms anticipate. **Need for autonomy** depends on whether it is needed to create value. **Types of Integration** With regard to interdependence and autonomy, there are four types of M&A transactions: *absorption*, *preservation*, *holding*, and *symbiosis*. **Absorption** requires extensive interdependence and little autonomy; the integration requires complete consolidation of the target firm with the acquiring company. **Preservation** requires a high need for autonomy and a low need for interdependence—the transfer of financial and general management expertise. **Holding** calls for low degrees of both autonomy and interdependence; relatively rare. **Symbiosis** calls for both high levels of autonomy and interdependence; it is probably the most difficult to implement. **The Process of Implementing the Acquisition** **Serial acquirers** Firms that engage in frequent acquisitions. **It's a Continual Process, Not an Event** The best serial acquirers start the integration process during initial screening interviews and negotiations—**due diligence**. **Integration Management Is a Full-Time Job** Ideally, firms are integrated by someone from the due-diligence team who understands both companies. **Key Decisions Should Be Made Swiftly** Decisions about management structure, key roles, reporting relationships, layoffs, restructuring, cost cutting, and other career-affecting aspects of the acquisition should be made within days of the acquisition announcement. **Integration Should Address Technical and Cultural Issues** Managers tend to focus on technical issues, but corporate culture should also be addressed immediately.	p. 294, Ex. 10.10 Types of Acquisition Integration
pp. 296–298, PPT #25–26	**ACQUISITIONS IN DIFFERENT INDUSTRY CONTEXTS** **M&As and Industry Life Cycle** Different types of acquisitions play different roles in corporate strategy. **Introduction.** This stage tends to involve the purchase of startup firms by well-established firms in related but more mature industry segments. Usually R&D and product/market-extension acquisitions. **Growth.** Firms from one industry segment enter other segments with proven and growing targets. Geographic roll-up becomes more common; in high-velocity industries, industry-convergence acquisitions continue into the maturity stage. **Maturity.** This stage has overcapacity acquisitions; consolidation occurs to rationalize the industry and continues throughout the decline stage of the cycle. **M&As in Dynamic Contexts** In dynamic contexts, firms engage in acquisitions at a frantic pace with discontinuities and globalization. Factors affecting the attractiveness of acquisitions include the following:	

	<ul><li>**Technological changes.** Some firms respond with aggressive acquisition campaigns to ensure that innovation doesn't erode strong competitive positions.</li><li>**Demographic changes.** Changes in demographics, such as aging of the population and mass emigration, may alter customer profiles.</li><li>**Geopolitical changes.** Geopolitical changes, such as the fall of the Iron Curtain, the creation of EU, the opening of China, and conflict in the Middle East, have effects on global companies.</li><li>**Trade liberalization.** Liberal trade policies generate opportunities for doing business.</li><li>**Deregulation.** Loosening of regulations impacts M&A activities in banking and telecommunications industries.</li></ul>**M&As and Coevolution** Firms choose to develop more formal, hierarchical linkages among businesses, whether along vertical, horizontal, or complementary lines; allow firms to absorb capabilities of its targets to develop specific dynamic capabilities.	
pp. , PPT #27	**Please note the following section is NOT in the PDF text file:** **CRITERIA FOR ACQUISITION SUCCESS** Several factors can help to increase the probability of creating wealth through acquisitions. **Learning Through Acquisitions** is conducive to learning economies; firms that develop experience by making acquisitions perform better in subsequent acquisitions than do firms with little experience. Firms that combine acquisitions with internal development tend to broaden their knowledge base and avoid inertia, thus enhancing the chances of success in later ventures. **Acquiring Firms in Similar Businesses** tends to create more wealth; allows learning from each other. If firms are too closely related, learning is diminished and performance declines. There is an inverse "U"-shaped relationship between relatedness and patent activity. Firms should focus on acquisitions different enough for learning to create value from shared knowledge. **Retaining and Transferring Resources, Capabilities, and Dynamic Capabilities** can create value when top managers orchestrate resource transfers between the acquiring firm and target. **Avoiding Bidding Wars and Excessive Premiums** The probability of a success is inversely related to the premium paid. Try to avoid or neutralize situations that inflate premiums. **Effectively Managing the Implementation Process** The following are lessons from successful acquirers:<ul><li>Integration is a continual process that begins during the negotiation and due-diligence stages.</li><li>Dedicate key personnel to the job of implementation.</li><li>Make key decisions swiftly and don't delay painful news.</li><li>Address both technical and cultural issues; unsuccessful integration results from focusing myopically on the technical side of the acquisition.</li></ul>	p. , Ex. p. , Ex. p.

* Figure or Exhibit **NOT** enumerated in the PDF file.

III.   SUGGESTED CASES TO ACCOMPANY TEXT

The "HP–Compaq Merger" is the first case we include in the concepts-with-cases version, because it documents well the challenges facing such mega mergers. You can also draw out the strategic leadership role played by CEO Carly Fiorina and how her personality may have played into the merger. If you can introduce more recent *Fortune*-type coverage of her dismissal, then you can bring the dialogue full circle. Our second case is "Cisco." Despite its performance ups and downs, Cisco is still one of the most phenomenal growth-through-acquisition firms and should be used as a benchmark for discussions of what best acquisition practices might look like.

Mergers and acquisitions cases are many and varied. It is usually a good strategy to identify cases where you can give attention both to the fit between the two firms and the implementation issues that may arise. Another good tactic would be to use the "Millennium B" case (HBS) following up from your use of the "Millennium A" case with Chapter 8 on alliances. The combination of the HBS "Masco" case and its partner, "The Household Furniture Industry," case is also a classic and has several learning gems.

Need help selecting cases? Pearson Prentice Hall and Pearson Custom Publishing are pleased to present the ultimate resource for creating and customizing casebooks.

- Start with a CaseMap correlated to your text or start from scratch; do it yourself using our easy-to-use interface or collaborate with a developmental editor.
- Cases can be selected from a variety of sources, including Harvard Business School Publishing, Darden, Ivey, Thunderbird, and NACRA.
- We clear permissions for you on cases and content not in the database.
- You can also create custom course packs by adding articles, original material, and textbook chapters.
- Pearson Custom casebooks can be delivered in print or online.
- Additionally, we supply you, the instructor, with a free evaluation copy delivered 7 to 10 days after you create your book, free access to teaching notes, and case-method teaching resources.

We're here to help: Looking for a case on a specific topic, company, country, or scenario? Or, looking for a new case to substitute for one you've used in the past? We will help you find the right cases for your course and help you create a casebook that meets all your teaching needs. For guidance on building a casebook to reflect your course needs, e-mail our editorial consultant at customcases@prenhall.com.

Visit www.prenhall.com/custombusiness for more information and to see which Prentice Hall titles are available for short-run customization and to view suggested cases. To start your own straightforward search for material:

Step 1: Select "search content and create your book" and log in.
Step 2: Search by case number or keyword or browse by discipline to find suggested cases based on the book you use or course you teach.
Step 3: Browse, preview, and select the cases, articles, or chapters you wish to include (you will see that price and page count of the book in the top right-hand corner of the screen as you "build" the book).
Step 4: Finalize your selections, get them in the order you want, package your customized book with any Prentice Hall title for a discount (if you wish), click "confirm book," and you have the option to request a free evaluation copy.
Step 5: The Web site immediately gives you the ISBN of your custom book. You should give this ISBN to your bookstore; they will use it to place their order with us.

Beyond our cases and Pearson Custom Publishing, if you choose to compile your own casebook you will have an opportunity to draw from a variety of sources. These sources include going direct to Hartwick Leadership Cases, IVEY Case Publishing, European Case Clearing House (ECCH), Harvard Business School (HBS), Darden, and others.

Given the popularity of Harvard cases, we have selected these additional cases for use with this chapter:

		ID#	Pages	TN
The DaimlerChrysler Merger (A): Gaining Global Competitiveness	HBSP	IMD130	20	Y
Newell Co.: Acquisition Strategy	HBSP	9-794-0660	22	N

The DaimlerChrysler Merger (A): Gaining Global Competitiveness Provides an overview of current trends in the global automotive industry and a description of Daimler-Benz AG and Chrysler Corp. prior to the merger. Describes this first transatlantic merger, raising the issues of strategic positioning, potential trade-offs, and competitive moves. Teaching Purpose: To discuss and evaluate the challenges companies face in this hypercompetitive market.

Newell Co.: Acquisition Strategy Newell is a $1.5 billion manufacturer and distributor of low-tech home and hardware products, geared to serve volume purchasers. In 1992, Newell is considering two approaches to expand its current product line with the acquisitions of Sanford Corp., a $140 million manufacturer and marketer of writing instruments and office supplies, and Levolor, a $180 million manufacturer of window blinds. The case focuses on Newell's enduring corporate strategy as a guide for selecting appropriate acquisitions to grow the company.

IV.   LINKING THE CHAPTER TO A COMPUTER SIMULATION

A few simulations allow you to engage in mergers and acquisitions, but they are pretty rough. Mike's Bikes, for instance, has this option, and it is one that you might want to explore. More often we use mergers and acquisitions as a discussion around strategy and ask students to answer what-if questions in terms of whether this vehicle was available to them and if, when, and how they would have used it.

V.   END OF CHAPTER ANSWER GUIDE

Review Questions

1.   What is an acquisition?

Guide: An acquisition is the purchase of one firm's assets or stock by another firm. The terms *mergers* and *acquisitions* are often used rather interchangeably in practice, but typically a merger is used to describe two firms of similar size being combined into one enterprise. An acquisition is usually used to describe the event when one firm takes over another. Legally, a merger is a distinct legal procedure that is sometimes used in the transaction.

2.   Why would firms use acquisitions instead of creating a new business internally?

Guide: Acquisitions allow firms to quickly enter new businesses, reduce the time and risks associated with starting new businesses internally, and reach minimum efficient scale rapidly. An acquisition quickly establishes a platform in a new business, while developing a new business internally can take years. A corollary benefit to speed is critical mass. Through an acquisition, a firm can ensure that it enters a business with sufficient size to not be at a serious disadvantage to competitors. Another benefit of acquisitions over internal development is that acquisitions provide access to complementary assets and resources. When developing a new business internally, the firm uses its existing stock of resources and capabilities. By acquiring another firm, new resources and capabilities can be grafted into the firm, potentially improving its competitive position in other businesses over time. Finally, by acquiring a firm in a new business, the firm removes a potential competitor.

3.   What are the possible motives for acquisitions?

Guide: The three primary motives for acquisitions are synergy (in all its varieties), managerialism, and hubris. Synergy is the potential that the value of two firms combined might be greater than the sum of the value of the two firms independently. When managers pursue mergers and acquisitions to serve their own personal self-interest rather than the best interests of shareholders, it is a reflection of managerialism. For instance, mergers and acquisitions for the purpose getting larger might benefit managers through higher wages. Hubris is exaggerated self-confidence. Hubris can lead to doing more mergers and acquisitions than should be done and paying more for acquisitions than should be paid.

4.   What are the ways in which synergies can be created in acquisitions?

Guide: Synergy can be derived from cost savings and revenue-enhancement opportunities. Examples of these include reducing threats from suppliers by internalizing the supply chain, increased market power, operational efficiency, superior financial strength, economies of scope and scale, and the sharing and leveraging of capabilities.

5.   How easy or difficult are the alternative types of synergies to achieve?

Guide: Cost-savings synergies tend to be easier to implement than revenue-enhancement synergies. There is less ambiguity about how to cut costs than there is about how to generate new revenue. Consequently, the market tends to discount potential revenue synergies more than cost-savings synergies.

6.   What types of acquisitions are there?

Guide: Bower's typology includes six distinct types of mergers and acquisitions: product/market extension, geographic roll-ups, R&D, overcapacity, industry convergence, and investor or holding company acquisitions.

7.   What is the difference between a market extension acquisition and a geographic roll-up?

Guide: A market extension acquisition is incremental movement into new geographic areas. A geographic roll-up is a systematic process of acquiring a presence across most geographic markets in the industry sector.

8.   Give examples of product extension, overcapacity, and R&D acquisitions.

Guide: The purpose of a product extension acquisition is to extend the product line of the company. Quaker's purchase of Snapple is the example used in the text. Yum!'s acquisition of new fast-food lines in another example. The purpose of an overcapacity acquisition is to reduce the number of competitors and rationalize industry capacity. Daimler-Benz's acquisition of Chrysler is an illustration. Some acquisitions are used to acquire technology (R&D acquisitions). Cisco, Microsoft, Intel, and others have all supplemented internal R&D with acquisitions used to acquire key technologies.

9. What is an acquisition premium?

Guide: An acquisition premium is the price paid for a target that is in excess of its market value before the acquisition process began.

10. How can you calculate the synergies that must be extracted from an acquisition with a given premium?

Guide: Using Sirower's formula for required performance improvement, one can easily calculate the performance gains that must be achieved in order to justify a premium of a given amount. The formula allows for sensitivity analysis on the number of years estimated before improvements would kick in.

11. How do acquisitions tend to be used in different stages of industry life cycle?

Guide: Whether an acquisition is a suitable vehicle for a firm's business or corporate strategy, and the type of acquisition that is viable, are partially a function of the competitive context. During introduction stages, acquisitions tend to be M&A as R&D and product-market extension acquisitions. During the growth phase of industry life cycle, we see product/market extensions, R&D, and geographic roll-up (during the latter stages). In high-velocity industries, industry convergence acquisitions begin to appear at this point as well and continue into the maturity stage. During the maturity stage of an industry life cycle, overcapacity acquisition begins to emerge.

12. What are the alternative ways in which acquisitions can be integrated into the purchasing firm and what determines which method to use?

Guide: Absorption, preservation, holding, and symbiosis are the four types of integration. The choice of which method to use is a function of the need for autonomy and strategic interdependence of the acquirer and the target.

How Would You Do That?

13. Pick a company that has recently announced an acquisition. Study the terms of the deal and identify, to the extent possible, the intrinsic value of the target, its market value, and the acquisition price. What was the acquisition premium? Using the synergy required formula presented in "How Would You Do That? 10.1," determine the performance improvements required to justify this acquisition premium. Calculate these required performance improvements with different assumptions for how long it takes to implement them, say 1 year, 3 years, and 5 years. What is the difference in these required performance improvements if the acquisition premium were 50 percent lower and higher that was paid?

Guide: The purpose of this exercise is to have students play with the synergy trap model so they can see how premiums affect what a firm must do with a merger or acquisition, once culminated. Not only does this exercise let them try out a specific tool, but it also reinforces the interdependence between formulation and implementation. For instance, the higher the premium paid, the more critical and drastic are the implementation levers for recovering the premium.

Group Activities

14. Pick a firm of interest to your group. Identify potential acquisition candidates. Explain why these companies would make sense as an acquisition target. Evaluate and describe possible implementation barriers to this acquisition.

Guide: There are three parts to this question, which really lets you show students the subtle facets of the mergers and acquisitions' realm. To be good at mergers and acquisitions, firms must be able to (1) identify candidates, (2) negotiate terms that make the deal good, and (3) have the internal capabilities to integrate the acquisition as it needs to be given the firm's strategy. If it has no internal expertise with mergers and acquisitions, the firm might hire an outsider or an advisor with significant experience in the process. Given the problems of overpayment and poor implementation, patience, determination, and caution are in order. Finally, although not actually part of the question, you can raise the issue of how competitors will bid for the firm, too, raising the price, and therefore challenging the firm to revise its implementation plans or abandon the merger and acquisition attempt.

15. Many firms consider themselves to be very good at acquisitions. Given that firms typically pay premiums far in excess of the acquired firm's market value, can acquisitions truly be a source of competitive advantage?

Guide: Evidence does suggest that some firms do quite well using acquisitions, but most firms also make some mistakes. However, the same can be said of internal development. How do firms overcome the penalty of paying premiums? The only rational explanation is that they must be creating synergies, either through cost savings or revenue enhancement, to a greater extent than non-acquirers are doing so through internal means. In the short term, a firm may be able to "fool" the market (depending on your belief of market efficiency), but in the long term the firms that are generating value are overcoming the premium penalty. It should be recalled that acquisitions are an alternative strategy vehicle. Other strategy vehicles also face significant risks. Thus, when a firm uses acquisitions and surpasses rivals in performance it suggests that the cost of the premium they paid was less than the costs of internal development at rivals, all else being equal.

VI.   SUPPLEMENTAL EXPERIENTIAL EXERCISES

These exercises are drawn with permission from the Strategy Teaching Tool-kit found at:

http://instruction.bus.wisc.edu/mcarpenter/PROFESSIONAL/Toolkit/bpstools.htm.

1. **Two Winner's Curse Exercises** One good behavioral take-away from this chapter and these exercises is how winner's curse functions. If students find these exercises to be interesting, you can refer them to a game that further demonstrates the winner's curse at:

www.gametheory.net/Mike/applets/WinnerCurse/

Dollar Auction. For the auction, we mention that if anyone wants to make money they'll have the opportunity to do so at the start of the next class session. You can vary the amount at stake; we use the winnings to buy a treat for the next class session. The rules are important, but you'll see that you'll quickly make more than the $20 you auction off, because the second-highest bidder also has to pay. This generates a real escalation of bidding to minimize losses. Quite often, the winning bid will be greater than the $20 prize. As students learned in this chapter, escalation of commitment is what happens when the level of resources that have been expended to-date is so significant that it—when coupled with excessive fear of failure—causes irrational decision making.

Put up an overhead that summarizes the rules as follows:

Auction Rules

- No talking.
- Last bidder pays their bid to me and gets my $20 (vary this to your tastes).
- Second to the last bidder pays their bid to me and gets nothing.
- First bid must be more than $2 but less than $5 (if you change the upper limit, then you need to adjust this as well).
- Anyone can enter at any time.
- Please raise your hand if you wish to bid.
- The bidding is over when 1 minute has passed with no one offering additional bids.

Gourmet Adventures. This exercise is also designed to demonstrate the winner's curse, though it is a bit more elaborate than the dollar auction. Teams are faced with a situation with a risk and cost of overbidding. How do they adjust their bids to avoid being cursed?

Instructions to Students

Your investment firm wants to buy a restaurant group called Gourmet Adventures, which is represented by the jar of coins you see at the front of the room. They have three business units that serve different markets that you must value. In addition, you are concerned that there are competing bidders. You want to buy Gourmet Adventures, but only at the right price.

About the Target

Gourmet Adventures consists of three restaurant chains:

- **Quarters Fine Dining.** Quarters is a chain of upscale steak houses in major cities across the United States.
- **Nickels Family Feast.** Nickels is a chain of moderately priced sit-down family restaurants.
- **Pennies Pizza.** Pennies is a chain of take-out pizza restaurants primarily serving college campuses.

Valuing the Target

Your first task is to develop a methodology for valuing the target. You have information about the relative profitability of the three restaurant chains, and you know the revenue of the firm as a whole. You can use this information to develop a valuation model/methodology.

- The firm (jar), as a whole, is 500 milliliters in size (revenue).
- Quarters: 9 milliliters of quarters generates $2.00 of net present value.
- Nickels: 14 milliliters of nickels generates 50¢ of net present value.
- Pennies: 20 milliliters of pennies generates 25¢ of net present value.

Develop a Bid

Given your estimated value, what are you willing to bid for the target? If you win the bidding contest and get it at a bargain, I will pay you the difference plus a prize. If you overbid, you will pay the shareholders of Gourmet Adventures (your Professor) the difference.

1. Circle your team:

    1.   NY Life/Grp Health Divestiture   2.   Cooper Industries
    3.   Cintas Corporation   4.   McBoeing
    5.   Danimal Corporation   6.   Monsanto/Solutia
    7.   Gillette/Duracell

2. Describe your valuation methodology.

3. What is the estimated value of Gourmet Adventures according to your methodology? Note: Although I need this information to run the exercise, it will have no bearing on your firm's returns, so please be honest (only your actual bid counts).

    Estimated Value $_____

4. What is your bid for Gourmet Adventures?

    Actual Bid $_____

2. **Acquire** Acquire is a box game that is easy to learn and can be played in about an hour by four players. We break the class up into teams and link the game to cases on rivalry, competition, and acquisitions. It does a great job of putting students in the position to see how serendipity and strategy interact and how wins are a function of others' actions, intentions, and hubris. The following Web site has a couple of free and simple DOS versions of the game that students can use for practice and familiarization: www.webnoir.com/bob/sid/acquire.htm.

PART FIVE
IMPLEMENTATION, NEW VENTURES, AND GOVERNANCE IN DYNAMIC CONTEXTS

CHAPTER 11 – EMPLOYING STRATEGY IMPLEMENTATION LEVERS

I. PURPOSE OF THE CHAPTER

After studying this chapter, students should be able to:

1. Understand the interdependence between strategy formulation and implementation.
2. Show how to use structure as a strategy implementation lever.
3. Design systems and processes as strategy implementation levers.
4. Understand the roles of people and rewards as implementation levers.
5. Show the dual roles that strategic leadership plays in strategy implementation.
6. Understand how global and dynamic contexts affect your use of implementation levers.

This chapter elaborates on the relationship between strategy formulation and strategy implementation by delineating some of the key underlying dimensions of implementation. If you are used to using other implementation frameworks (such as the 7-S), you will find that they map easily to ours, so you can either adapt your teaching to our framework or superimpose yours over ours. Also, we talk about the balanced scorecard; we have found that some instructors like to use that framework as a way to talk about a firm's goals and objectives. If that is your practice as well, you might think about framing the goals and objectives component of the strategy process model introduced in Chapter 1 (Exhibit 1.3) using the balanced scorecard or whatever version of it you prefer (dashboard, etc.).

Although formulation–implementation interdependence has been a constant theme throughout the text, this chapter presents you an opportunity to remind students that many managers tend to erroneously treat strategy formulation and implementation as separate topics, when in reality implementation affects formulation (relationships, feasibility, etc.) and often leads to the reformulation of a firm's strategy. In fact, some of the most productive and successful firms are those whose implementation efforts can be considered a core competency, and it is up to management to identify markets where those capabilities can be deployed the most effectively and profitability while at the same time making sure that they are periodically renewed and upgraded.

Implementation is probably one of the tougher subjects to teach, and some schools actually have separate courses devoted to strategy formulation and strategy implementation. Oftentimes, implementation is equated with organizational structure, and we have employed an overarching model so students can see that structure is but one of the dimensions of implementation. You may choose to focus entirely on formulation with this text and simply ask students to consider implementation issues with each strategy they recommend. A more balanced approach would involve asking students to give equal treatment to formulation and implementation in their case discussions, perhaps asking them to revisit a proposed new strategy once you have more thoroughly evaluated implementation issues. Other options are to have students read this chapter along with Chapters 1 and 2 or have them use it as a reference for their case analyses in the earlier chapters. As you know, implementation is not something treated in isolation from strategy so, in that way, it dovetails nicely with all the earlier chapters on strategy.

Ideally, students will leave this chapter with three key observations. First, as we have said from the beginning, strategy formulation and implementation are interdependent. Exhibit 11.1 summarizes the formulation–implementation relationship. This chapter helps them see in more detail how this interdependence comes about and how it can be managed. Second, students should leave this chapter understanding that implementation is a consequence and reflection of strategic leadership. Executives choose when and how to employ the implementation levers; they also make choices about what the firm does and does not do by virtue of their resource-allocation choices. These relationships are summarized in Exhibit 11.2. Finally, students should understand that, as strategies change and external threats and opportunities change, so too should implementation adapt to and facilitate these changes. This again brings you back to the staging facet of the strategy diamond.

In this chapter, the three differentiators—and hence your teaching strategy of the chapter—are manifested in the following ways:

- **Strategic leadership.** The importance of strategic leadership in this chapter is evident from the tone and culture set in place by Gore's founders and its current leaders and the implementation framework that guides the organization of the chapter (see Exhibits 11.1 and 11.2). Specifically, students are shown how leadership figures into implementation as a consequence of the firm's lever and resource-allocation choices and the communication of the strategy to stakeholders.
- **Formulation and implementation interdependency.** Because this has been the theme of the entire text, this chapter serves to put further meat on the details of strategy implementation. The components summarized in Exhibit 11.2 are fleshed out in succeeding chapters. "How Would You Do That? 11.1," which features SAP, and "How Would You Do That? 11.2," which features NUWC, reinforce the nature and depth of this interdependence.
- **Dynamic strategy.** Dynamism is introduced through the "How Would You Do That?" feature on SAP (11.1) as well as early initial commentary on the dynamic environment the firm faced, internally and externally. Depending on your preferences, you can also show dynamism by linking the balanced scorecard to the goals and objectives portion of the strategy process, summarized in Exhibit 1.3 in Chapter 1. The balanced scorecard section of the chapter has the heading "Making Strategy a Continuous and Dynamic Process." Following that, the section "Implementation Levers in Global Firms and Dynamic Contexts" spells out different contexts that implementation must be adapted to—this further reinforces the dynamic nature of strategy and the interdependence of formulation and implementation. Finally, dynamism is also echoed and institutionalized by the fact that you can tie implementation to the staging facet of the strategy diamond, as reiterated in the closing section of the chapter.

Additional Readings:

Fulmer, R., and J. Conger. (2004). *Growing your company's leaders*. New York: AMACOM.

Kravetz, D. (2004). *Measuring human capital*. Mesa, AZ: KAP.

Liker, J. (2004). *The Toyota way*. New York: McGraw-Hill.

Pfeffer, J. (1992). *Managing with power*. Boston: Harvard Business School Press.

Pfeffer, J., and R. Sutton. (2000). *The knowing-doing gap*. Boston: Harvard Business School Press.

Watkins, M. (2003). *The first 90 days*. Boston: Harvard Business School Press.

II. BRIEF CHAPTER OUTLINE

pp. 302–305, PPT #1–3	**Chapter 11 Employing Strategy Implementation Levers** The purpose of this chapter is to explain the relationship between strategy formulation and implementation with organizational structure, systems, processes, people, rewards, and strategic leadership in a dynamic global context. **Opening Vignette:** W. L. Gore & Associates: Weaving the Fabric of Organizational Culture, pp. 303–305	
pp. 305–309, PPT #4–10	**INTERDEPENDENCE OF STRATEGY FORMULATION AND IMPLEMENTATION** Strategy formulation and implementation can be successful when they are iterative and interdependent and the strategy elements and implementation levers are consistent and coherent. When a firm experiences difficulties, ask three questions: 1. Is its strategy flawed? 2. Is the implementation of its strategy flawed? 3. Are both strategy and implementation flawed? **A Model Company** W. L. Gore integrates all the key elements. **The Knowing-Doing Gap** This occurs when firms have more difficulty implementing good ideas than creating new ideas and knowledge. **What Causes the Knowing-Doing Gap?** The gap occurs when the firm does not share the strategy formulation process with stakeholders; when the firm fails to determine implementation levers; when it fails to take appropriate strategic-leadership actions; and/or when it fails to assess implementation obstacles. *The Impact of Culture* Firms with strong shared values are better at implementing strategy and achieving higher performance than firms with weaker values. Organizations with a strong shared culture give meaning, identity, and purpose to its members. Mismatches between strategy and implementation levers or strategic-leadership actions may stem from executives; they may be overly optimistic and downplay obstacles to execution.	p. 305, Ex. 11.1 Formulation and Implementation p. 308, *11.1 How Would You Do That? Picking Up the Pieces at SAP* p. 309, Ex. 11.2 Key Facets of Strategy Implementation
pp. 309–315,	**IMPLEMENTATION LEVERS** **Structure** is the relatively stable arrangement of responsibilities, tasks, and people; it is the framework that divides tasks, deploys resources, and coordinates departments. **Control and Coordination** Structure has two key functions: • Ensuring control • Coordinating information, decisions, and the activities of employees at all levels With more complexity, firms modify their structure accordingly. Structure should be consistent with the firm's strategy. Firm structure includes the functional, multidivisional, matrix, and network forms. Traditionally, structure is determined by a firm's strategy. But the firm's existing structure provides information to revise its existing strategy. **Functional Structure** With this structure, the firm organizes activities according to specific functions. If the focus of a functional unit is too narrow, it loses sight of other functional	p. 311, Ex. 11.3 The Functional Structure *p. 312, *Fig. 11.1 Platypus, Inc.—A Functional Structure*

| PPT
#11–18 | activities, customer needs, and corporate objectives; it may become sluggish in responding to customer demands.
Multidivisional Structure As shown in Exhibit 11.4, the multidivisional structure is organized around geographic markets, products, or business groups, with division heads responsible for strategy. With this structure, firms can implement division incentives and performance standards, foster speedier reactions, and coordinate diverse economic activities. Headquarters plans, coordinates, and evaluates operating divisions.
Matrix Structure This is a hybrid of the functional and multidivisional structures. Its utility increases when pressures are unpredictable and require high degrees of control and extensive coordination. Implementing a matrix structure is difficult because of the need to share resources across divisions. It is feasible only when strong culture and shared values support cross-division collaboration.
Network Structure This firm structure consists of small, semiautonomous, temporary groups that focus on specific purposes (e.g., a new products team). Authority is based on control of resources, knowledge, and expertise; highly flexible to alter staff and resources. Drawbacks include potential confusion and ambiguity.
Partnerships and Franchises These are legal forms of ownership and organization structures. **Professional partnership** is a common structure in some industries (e.g., law, accounting, consulting, advertising, and real estate). Partners own shares or units and vote in a managing partner to supervise and serve at their pleasure. The managing partner has authority and prestige, but not nearly the power of a CEO.
Franchise Structure With the franchise structure, the firm transfers ownership of local facilities to a franchisee. This shifts local management responsibility to the franchisee and allows for rapid growth. | p. 312, Ex. 11.4 Typical Multidivisional Organization

p. 313, Ex. 11.5 Matrix Structure at GM |
| | **Performance Measurement and Management Systems** These systems enable firms to balance the need to report short-term financial returns with the pursuit of longer-term, and often intangible, objectives. The *balanced scorecard* evolved into a *strategy scorecard* to help managers measure vision and strategy against business- and operating-unit-level performance. Three fundamental lessons:
1. Translate strategy into tangible and intangible performance metrics (re: financial and nonfinancial measures in Exhibit 2.8).
2. Use a *strategy map* to align metrics with strategy.
3. Make strategy a continuous and dynamic process.
Relying on a Range of Metrics Four perspectives are:
• *Financial perspective*: Growth, profitability, and risk
• *External relations:* Creating value and differentiation
• *Internal-business process:* Priorities among processes according to their contributions to customer and shareholder
• *Learning and growth:* Change, innovation, and growth | p. 316, Ex. 11.6 Translating Vision and Strategy in Action Through the Balanced Scorecard System

p. 317, Ex. 11.7 The Balanced Scorecard in the Context of a Strategy Map |

pp. 315–322, PPT #19–23	**Developing a Strategy Map** A strategy map can be used to diagram activities across the four perspectives (e.g., what must be done in terms of people and product and process development) from the external relations and financial objectives that reflect the desired firm outcomes. **Making Strategy Continuous and Dynamic Process** This requires managers to succeed at two tasks: 1. Disseminating the key features of a strategy and stipulating responsibilities for executing it throughout the firm 2. Linking the strategy with the financial budget The balanced scorecard also serves as a tool for communicating the firm's vision, mission, and strategy. **People and Rewards** can be used to align their energies and actions with the organization's objectives. **People** The firm needs the right people with the right experience and competencies; recruitment, selection, and training are critical to strategy implementation. **Rewards** What gets done is that which is rewarded. ***The Components of the Reward System*** • Performance evaluation and feedback • Compensation: Salary, bonuses, stock, promotions, etc. ***Rewards as a Form of Control*** Rewards requires performance and behavior targets. The control function has one of two forms: outcome controls or behavior controls. **Outcome Controls** These are preferable when one or two performance measures (e.g., ROI or ROA) are good gauges of a firm's health. **Behavior Controls** These are direct evaluations of managerial decision making; appropriate when there are many external and internal factors that affect a manager's decisions and organizational performance. **Compensation in the Diversified Firm** Compensation should link managers' rewards to actual decisions and other balanced-scorecard criteria to generate synergies.	p. 318, *11.2 How Would You Do That? Developing a Balanced Scorecard for the NUWC* p. 318, Ex. 11.8 Balanced Scorecard Development at the Naval Undersea Warfare Centre (NUWC) *p. 320, Fig. 11.2 Staffing Cuts and Performance Decline in the Long Term*
pp. 322–326, PPT #24–27	**STRATEGIC LEADERSHIP AND STRATEGY IMPLEMENTATION** Strategic leadership plays two roles in strategy implementation: 1. Making substantive implementation lever and resource-allocation decisions 2. Communicating the strategy to key stakeholders **Decisions About Levers** Decisions involve tradeoffs. **Decisions About Resource Allocation** These decisions must be consistent with the firm's strategy. Internal interests—political, self-serving, or misguided—can sabotage effective resource-allocation decisions. **Communicating with Key Stakeholders About Strategy** This begins in the strategy-formulation process; it is a strategic leadership function. Managers must evaluate both the need and the necessary tactics for communicating strategy in four directions: *upward, downward, outward,* and *across.*	p. 323, Ex. 11.9 Resource-Allocation Decisions in the Airline Industry *p. 325, Fig. 11.3 IBM's Thinkpad Rapid Success Growth*

	The Three C's of Strategy Communication The three C's are contacts, cultural understanding, and credibility.	
pp. 326–331, PPT #28–32	**IMPLEMENTATION LEVERS IN GLOBAL FIRMS AND DYNAMIC CONTEXTS** **Implementation Solutions for Global Firms** Four structural forms address the need for efficiency versus local responsiveness. **Structure for Multinational Configurations** This configuration resembles a decentralized federation. Control and coordination are managed through the interactions of home-office corporate executives and overseas executives, who are usually home-country managers. **Structure for International Configurations** This structure is a coordinated group of federations with administrative control exerted by headquarters. Resources, assets, and responsibilities are delegated to foreign offices; additional control is central. Uniform services can be provided to global clients in terms of quality and price. **Structure for Global Configurations** This configuration is based on centralization of assets, resources, and responsibilities. Demand is filled by centralized production. Top management views foreign operations as a global homogeneous marketplace. **Structure for Transnational Configurations** This structure was designed to achieve efficiency, local responsiveness, and innovation; key functions are *dispersion*, *specialization*, and *interdependence*. **People and Rewards Solutions in Global Firms** Local managers can enhance a firm's understanding local markets. Home-country managers strengthen the relationship between the foreign subsidiary and the parent company. When MNCs have subsidiaries in culturally distant locations (not just geographically distant), costs and risks increase because of an *information-asymmetry* problem: Information is not readily available to the parent company. Parent-country managers improve subsidiary performance because it's easier to culturally control and it enhances transfer of firm-specific resources from the parent to the subsidiary. **Implementation Levers in Dynamic Contexts** Competitive pressures are compounded in dynamic, "high-velocity" industries, thus firm strategies become more complex. Two of the most effective adaptations are the ambidextrous organization and patching. **The Ambidextrous Organization** *Incremental Change Versus Radical Innovation: Revisiting the Innovator's Dilemma* One division may pioneer a disruptive technology but the rest of the organization may resist. Strong organizational norms may favor continued influence of large established divisions. To sustain long-term competitiveness in a dynamic context, a firm must integrate both incremental changes and radical innovations.	p. 330, Ex. 11.10 The Ambidextrous Organization

<table>
<tr><td></td><td>

Four Structures for Handling Innovation

- A functional structure with innovation integrated into structure.
- A cross-functional or matrix-style structure with groups of people from established divisions working outside the functional hierarchy.
- Teams or units, nominally independent and working outside the established hierarchy, are limited in their independence and relatively unsupported by the organizational hierarchy.
- An "ambidextrous" form, with project teams focusing on radical improvements in structurally independent units. In Exhibit 11.10, these semiautonomous units may be integrated into the hierarchy at the top management level.

The ambidextrous structure is effective in integrating radical innovations; 93 percent of radical innovations were launched by ambidextrous firms. Corporate hierarchy often stymies radical innovations. Ambidextrous forms allow for the maintenance of the status quo and proactive industry-wide alterations.

Diversified Firms in Dynamic Markets: Patching This is the process of regularly remapping businesses with changing market conditions and restitching them into new business structures. Structure is altered to maintain focus on core and growth businesses while seeding and protecting new opportunities; resulting in relatively incremental changes. Firms adjust internal systems so that when a business is detached from one division and restitched elsewhere, company-wide systems do not require extensive modification.

The Intersection of Chaos and Complexity Dynamic markets are rather chaotic. Complexity theory explains that systems survive chaotic environments when elements of the system, though connected, are loosely coupled rather than rigidly linked.

Patching helps diversified firms operate in multiple product or geographic markets. It leverages either existing businesses or new, but related, businesses. The ambidextrous organization allows the radically new businesses to develop unencumbered by existing structures and processes.

Linking Strategy Implementation to Staging In the five-diamond model, staging refers to the timing and pacing of strategic moves. A firm needs structure, systems, human capital, expertise, and culture to support its evolution into a global competitor.

</td><td></td></tr>
</table>

* Figure or Exhibit **NOT** enumerated in the PDF file.

III. SUGGESTED CASES TO ACCOMPANY TEXT

In the concepts-with-cases version of the text, we have supplied the cases "Multiplication of Best Practices at Holcim" and "Implementation of the Balanced Scorecard at Porsche." The Holcim case lets you talk about implementation practices more generally and how difficult they are to apply from one part of the firm to another. The Porsche case lets you introduce students to the notion of a balanced scorecard, and a detailed example of one for the furniture industry is provided in the Appendix. Both of these cases dive deeply into specific implementation levers, and if you are interested in looking more broadly at the relationship between strategy and implementation then you might choose one of the other cases that is secondarily mapped to this chapter. For instance, the Charlotte Beers case explicitly deals with changes in levers and leadership as a consequence of changes in strategy. The Cisco case is a best practices case of sorts with regards to the implementation of mergers and acquisitions integration.

Although the conceptual material (other than this text) on implementation is often pretty dense and scant, there is no dearth of cases on implementation issues. Simply go to the ECCH or Harvard case Web sites and search for "strategy implementation," and you will find more choices than you can probably sift through. The best cases will be those that involve dramatic changes in strategy, such as turnarounds or major diversification efforts. These situations will typically require leadership changes and/or changes in many of the implementation levers. Three cases in this vein are "Bishay Industries" (HBS), "Laura Ashley" (HBS), and "Peter Browning" (HBS).

Need help selecting cases? Pearson Prentice Hall and Pearson Custom Publishing are pleased to present the ultimate resource for creating and customizing casebooks.

- Start with a CaseMap correlated to your text or start from scratch; do it yourself using our easy-to-use interface or collaborate with a developmental editor.
- Cases can be selected from a variety of sources, including Harvard Business School Publishing, Darden, Ivey, Thunderbird, and NACRA.
- We clear permissions for you on cases and content not in the database.
- You can also create custom course packs by adding articles, original material, and textbook chapters.
- Pearson Custom casebooks can be delivered in print or online.
- Additionally, we supply you, the instructor, with a free evaluation copy delivered 7 to 10 days after you create your book, free access to teaching notes, and case-method teaching resources.

We're here to help: Looking for a case on a specific topic, company, country, or scenario? Or, looking for a new case to substitute for one you've used in the past? We will help you find the right cases for your course and help you create a casebook that meets all your teaching needs. For guidance on building a casebook to reflect your course needs, e-mail our editorial consultant at customcases@prenhall.com.

Visit www.prenhall.com/custombusiness for more information and to see which Prentice Hall titles are available for short-run customization and to view suggested cases. To start your own straightforward search for material:

Step 1: Select "search content and create your book" and log in.
Step 2: Search by case number or keyword or browse by discipline to find suggested cases based on the book you use or course you teach.
Step 3: Browse, preview, and select the cases, articles, or chapters you wish to include (you will see that price and page count of the book in the top right-hand corner of the screen as you "build" the book).
Step 4: Finalize your selections, get them in the order you want, package your customized book with any Prentice Hall title for a discount (if you wish), click "confirm book," and you have the option to request a free evaluation copy.
Step 5: The Web site immediately gives you the ISBN of your custom book. You should give this ISBN to your bookstore; they will use it to place their order with us.

Beyond our cases and Pearson Custom Publishing, if you choose to compile your own casebook you will have an opportunity to draw from a variety of sources. These sources include going direct to Hartwick Leadership Cases, IVEY Case Publishing, European Case Clearing House (ECCH), Harvard Business School (HBS), Darden, and others.

Given the popularity of Harvard cases, we have selected these additional cases for use with this chapter:

		ID#	Pages	TN
IDEO Product Development	HBSP	9-600-143	21	Y
World Bank (A): Under Siege	HBSP	9-797-022	28	N

IDEO Product Development Describes IDEO, the world's leading product design firm, and its innovation culture and process. Emphasis is placed on the important role of prototyping and experimentation in general, and in the design of the very successful Palm V handheld computer in particular. A studio leader is asked by a business startup (Handspring) to develop a novel handheld computer (Visor) in less than half the time it took to develop the Palm V, requiring several shortcuts to IDEO's legendary innovation process. The case focuses on (1) prototyping and experimentation practices at a leading product developer; (2) the role of playfulness, discipline, and structure in innovation processes; and (3) the managerial challenges of creating and managing an unusually creative and innovative company culture. Includes color exhibits.

World Bank (A): Under Siege Describes the issues that James Wolfensohn faced when he took over the World Bank as president in June 1995. Presents several lines of criticism of the bank's strategy, structure, and relevance. Teaching Purpose: Students are asked to evaluate Wolfensohn's situation and options and recommend a response.

IV. LINKING THE CHAPTER TO A COMPUTER SIMULATION

Computer simulations seem to be devised to work best around formulation issues, so you will need to improvise in order to tie in a formulation perspective into aspects of implementation. At the very least, you should be able to point out how structure may have played a role in the firm's strategy, particularly if it is a simulation that has options for diversification. Additionally, you can have the students talk about the choices they made with regard to the structure of their organizational team, and how they think this organization affected their performance. We have found that simply asking students to interpret their implementation using our framework model actually leads to them identifying all of the components, even when the simulation is purely a strategy-formulation one.

V. END OF CHAPTER ANSWER GUIDE

Review Questions

1. What is strategy implementation?

Guide: Strategy implementation is the execution of the firm's strategy—taking the actions that bring into effect the strategy and ensuring that organizational decisions are consistent with that strategy. The goals of implementation are to see that strategy formulation is comprehensive and well informed and to translate good ideas into execution.

2. How are formulation and implementation related?

Guide: This is an overarching question that is answered in detail through a number of the questions that follow. At the very least, your students should identify the components shown in Exhibits 11.1 and 11.2 that summarize the formulation–implementation relationship. Finally, students should understand that as strategies change, and external threats and opportunities change, so, too, should implementation adapt to and facilitate these changes. This again brings students back to the staging facet of the strategy diamond.

3. What are the basic forms of organizational structure and when is each appropriate?

Guide: There are four basic forms of organization structure: functional, multidivisional, matrix, and network. A functional structure tends to work best in smaller firms and in firms with few products or services. The multidivisional structure is appropriate for multiproduct, multimarket firms. The utility of a matrix structure increases when the pressures facing the firm are unpredictable and require both high degrees of control and the ability to coordinate extensively. A network structure is most appropriate where flexibility and ability to reconfigure staff and resources rapidly is needed to exploit opportunities.

4. What are some common systems and processes that are relevant to strategy implementation?

Guide: People most often think of information systems in this regard, but in reality this is just one of several relevant systems. Management control, performance and rewards, budgeting, quality, planning, distribution, and resource allocation are all managed by systems.

5. How are people relevant to strategy formulation and implementation?

Guide: For a strategy to succeed, a firm needs the right people with the right experiences and competencies. Thus, recruitment, selection, and training are critical to strategy implementation because successful strategy formulation and implementation are dependent on having the right people and developing and training them in ways that support the firm's strategy.

6. How can rewards affect strategy?

Guide: Here you will want students to differentiate between different types of incentives, outcome and behavioral controls, and so on. You essentially want to remind them of the adage that it is folly to "hope for A, while rewarding B." Firms must align their reward systems with their strategies, and rewards include pay in addition to promotion and retention.

7. What are the roles of strategic leadership in successful strategy implementation?

Guide: A narrow answer to this question is the summary of executive roles shown in Exhibit 11.2—executives make choices about levers and resource allocation and also communicate the strategy to important stakeholders. A broader answer should refer to culture. When executives foster a firm that has widely held shared values (a strong culture), it increases the behavioral consistency across individuals in a firm. Firms with strong shared values may or may not be better at strategy formulation; however, a strong corporate culture should improve strategy implementation. This is because widespread consensus and endorsement of corporate values allows for the detection and correction of inappropriate behaviors; enhances goal alignment; and enhances employees' motivation and performance, because they perceive that their actions are freely chosen. For a strategy to be implemented successfully, it should be consistent with the organization's shared values. Thus, it is important to understand what is really important to members of the organization.

8. How does globalization affect organization structure?

Guide: Firms that are deeply involved in international business adopt one of four organizational structural forms in an attempt to manage the tension between the need for efficiency and the need for local responsiveness. Most of these structural forms place more emphasis on one or the other of these two competing forces—efficiency and local responsiveness.

9. What are organizational solutions to the problems caused by dynamic environments?

Guide: Two effective responses that help firms implement strategies in dynamic contexts are the ambidextrous organization and the use of patching in the context of diversified firms. The ambidextrous organization structure is one in which projects involving radical improvements are organized as structurally independent units that are allowed and encouraged to develop their implementation approaches and integrated into the organization only at the level of senior management. Conversely, patching is a process of regularly remapping businesses in accordance with changing market conditions and restitching them into new business structures within the firm.

10. What component of the strategy diamond maps most closely to issues related to strategy implementation?

Guide: Staging. This is the point where the firm is moving forward and changing, and because strategy formulation and implementation are interdependent, staging should take implementation into account and drive needed changes.

How Would You Do That?

11. In "How Would You Do That? 11.1," you were introduced to how SAP America responded to performance problems primarily through changes in strategy implementation and only minor changes in its actual strategy. Find one or two firms that were once high-flyers but have recently fallen on hard times. Are these hard times primarily a function of a flawed strategy, flawed implementation, or both? Using SAP as an example, what changes would you suggest in terms of implementation?

Guide: Here your goal is have the students walk through how they would apply the implementation factors to the strategic needs of the firm. This brings them full circle to the opening questions in the chapter:

When a firm is experiencing difficulties, it's always good to ask three questions:

1. Is its strategy flawed?

2. Is the implementation of its strategy flawed?

3. Are both strategy and implementation flawed?

12. The example of the NUWC in "How Would You Do That? 11.2" starts you on the process of strategy mapping and developing a balanced scorecard for that organization. Review Exhibits 11.7 and 11.8 and come up with suggestions for specific objectives, measures, targets, and initiatives that would complete the scorecard. If you prefer using the scorecard with a for-profit firm, then apply the framework from scratch to a firm of your choosing.

Guide: The goal here is to have students exercise the balanced scorecard concept. A narrowly scoped version of this assignment is to draw out the linkages among the scorecard, implementation, and formulation. Here you can point to the fact that the scorecard is one way to think about the goals and objectives set out in the strategic management process in Chapter 1 (Exhibit 1.3). A broad version of this assignment is to have them learn the scorecard approach to the point where they can apply it fluidly. Although the tool is fairly intuitive, it is also challenging to apply in practice. This can be a learning point in and of itself.

Group Activities

13. Apply the concepts of strategy formulation and strategy implementation to your college experience. What was your objective in going to college? When did your strategy for achieving this objective emerge? Has it ever changed? How would you adapt the 7-S model to evaluate how well you have implemented your strategy? What is your overall personal evaluation?

Guide: This is a self-reflection exercise that you might suggest students keep in mind throughout their careers. The implementation framework is obviously a model with firms in mind, but it is easily adapted to students' personal lives. The key in this conversion is not how many factors they settle on, but the concept of alignment. For instance, factors that might be widely applicable to a diverse set of students would be strategy, values, family, work, recreation, and learning. You might have to work at it to get a nice alliteration out of these factors, but students can easily see how the quality of their lives is enhanced when they achieve balance across these areas and that all areas are in alignment.

14. Refer to the Gore opening case. Assume that for reasons of family estate planning, the Gore family (75% owners of the company) decided finally to take the company public through an IPO. What would the effect on the firm's strategy and implementation practices be if this were to happen? What, if anything, would need to change?

Guide: Whether this is likely in the near future isn't material to the exercise. They key is to identify what would change as a result of going public. The most obvious answer is that the stakeholders change, from family ownership to a significant stake owned by institutional and individual investors. Some students will raise the point that these buyers know what they are getting themselves into and that the firm should not change any of its core attributes (e.g., strategy, shared values). Practically speaking, over time external owners seem to come to the opinion that it doesn't matter if they knew the nature of the beast when they bought in, what matters is that the firm attempt to maximize their wealth. External owners tend to be less patient than family owners. Consequently, there will likely be increased pressure to perform consistently from quarter to quarter. Some students will argue that this would spell doom for the company as we know it today. Others will point out that some public companies do quite well with similar innovation strategies (e.g., 3M). The biggest threat of such an event might well be to shared values. Similar strategies and structures can be found (though the lattice structure is indeed a bit extreme in comparison to most firms the size of Gore).

VI. SUPPLEMENTAL EXPERIENTIAL EXERCISES

These exercises are drawn with permission from the Strategy Teaching Tool-kit found at:

http://instruction.bus.wisc.edu/mcarpenter/PROFESSIONAL/Toolkit/bpstools.htm.

1. **The Beer Game** This exercise ties into the section on best practices and represents a way to field test a new best practice. The BeerGame is a logistics game that was originally developed by MIT in the 1960s and has since been played all over the world by people at all levels, from students to presidents of big multinational groups. It is played online at www.masystem.com/beergame.

2. **Builderific: Razing the Ivory Tower** Use sound planning skills to design and build the tallest possible free-standing structure with one Builderific construction set in 3 minutes. Use Legos, tinker toys, wood scraps, or any other material you think that someone may be able to use to construct a structure.

Instructions: This exercise is divided up into two periods: a planning period and a building period.

Planning: 15 minutes

You will have 15 minutes to plan how your team will reach its objective of building the tallest structure during the building period.

- During this time, you may remove the pieces from the box, but you cannot assemble any pieces. You may lay out the pieces, take an inventory, draw diagrams, or use any other planning tool that does not require assembling the pieces.
- Your team should set a goal of how high they intend the structure to be (from the base to the top). You should be realistic in what you expect to accomplish—most employees are evaluated based on the extent to which they accomplish the goals they have planned.
- Write down the goal (in inches) on a note card and turn it in to the instructor.
- Put all of the pieces back in the box.

Building: 3 minutes

You will have 3 minutes to execute your plan. At the end of this time, you will be asked to step back so we can measure the height of your free-standing structure.

Debrief

- Type of task: nonprogrammable, uncertain resources, time constraint, teams
- Why did the winner win? Why did the loser lose?
- How did the team resources differ? Did it matter?
- What was the business definition?
- What was the mission? Did you achieve it?
- What factors prevented you from achieving it?
- What were the key success factors or resources? Objectives?
- Were people responsible for the key success factors or resources? What roles emerged?
- Which of the implementation factors played the most important roles?

Debrief II (if you run it again)

- Differentiate between learning by imitating/observing and learning by doing
- Compare Builderific to the papchase exercise
- What resources did you have the second time that you didn't have the first?
- Which of the implementation factors played the most important roles? How did your implementation differ between the two rounds?

VII. APPENDICES

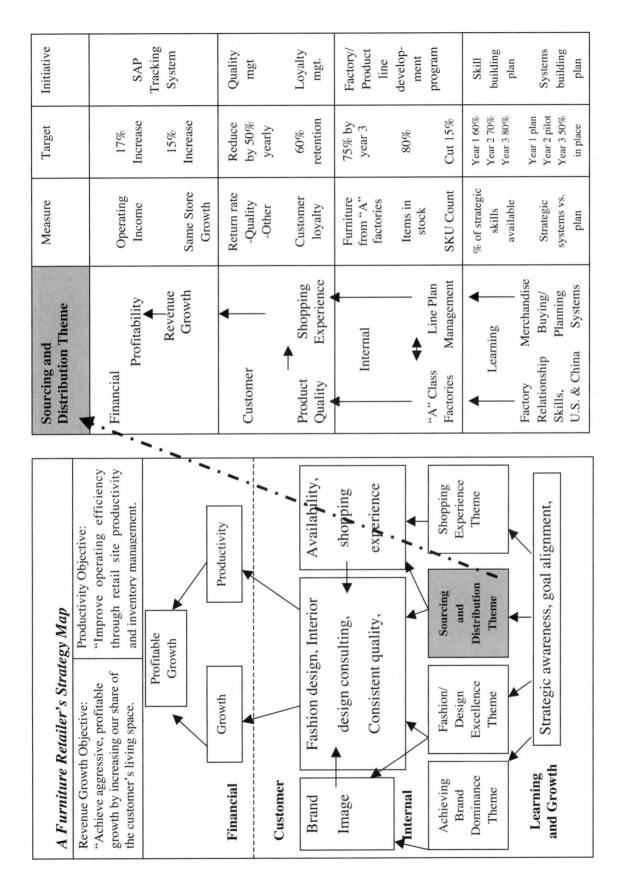

A Furniture Retailer's Strategy Map

		Measure	Target	Initiative
Sourcing and Distribution Theme	Financial Profitability → Revenue Growth	Operating Income Same Store Growth	17% Increase 15% Increase	SAP Tracking System
	Customer Product Quality — Shopping Experience	Return rate -Quality -Other Customer loyalty	Reduce by 50% yearly 60% retention	Quality mgt Loyalty mgt.
	Internal "A" Class Factories — Line Plan Management	Furniture from "A" factories Items in stock SKU Count	75% by year 3 80% Cut 15%	Factory/Product line development program
	Learning Factory Relationship Skills, U.S. & China — Merchandise Buying/Planning — Systems	% of strategic skills available Strategic systems vs. plan	Year 1 60% Year 2 70% Year 3 80% Year 1 plan Year 2 pilot Year 3 50% in place	Skill building plan Systems building plan

Revenue Growth Objective: "Achieve aggressive, profitable growth by increasing our share of the customer's living space.

Productivity Objective: "Improve operating efficiency through retail site productivity and inventory management.

Financial

Profitable Growth

Productivity

Growth

Customer

Availability, shopping experience

Fashion design, Interior design consulting, Consistent quality,

Brand Image

Shopping Experience Theme

Sourcing and Distribution Theme

Fashion/ Design Excellence Theme

Internal

Achieving Brand Dominance Theme

Strategic awareness, goal alignment,

Learning and Growth

Seven Common Causes of Balanced Scorecard Implementation Failure[2]

1.   Lack of support from the top. The board of directors, CEO, and members of the top management team have little understanding of or commitment to the scorecard approach.

2.   Narrow employee involvement. The firm has not engaged a significant proportion of its people in the strategy process.

3.   Scorecard stays at the top. Only senior executives are involved in the strategy process.

4.   Delays in implementation. Firms have the tendency to treat the balanced scorecard as a single event, not an ongoing process, and delay learning through doing until the plan is "perfect."

5.   Considering the scorecard a "project." Sometimes the scorecard is put into place along with extensive computerized information systems and once the installation is "complete," the organization loses regular touch with the scorecard.

6.   Cookie-cutter scorecard. Because the scorecard approach has tremendous managerial appeal, the organization may rush into an arrangement with advisors who are ill-informed about the organization's strategy or unique characteristics and instead put into place a scorecard developed for another organization with different internal and external stakeholder issues.

7.   Using the scorecard only to link compensation to performance. Although compensation should ideally be tied to the performance dimensions of a business unit's scorecard, individuals differ with respect to their role in strategy implementation—like a sales manager versus a production manager—and these differences should be reflected in the dimensions on which they are evaluated.

---

[1] Adapted from Kaplan & Norton, 2001, ibid.
[2] Adapted from Kaplan & Norton, 2001, ibid.

CHAPTER 12 – NEW VENTURES

I.   PURPOSE OF THE CHAPTER

After studying this chapter, students should be able to:

1. Define new ventures, initial public offerings, and corporate renewal, and their relationship with strategic management.
2. Understand entrepreneurship and the entrepreneurial process.
3. Describe the steps involved in new venture creation and corporate new venturing.
4. Map out the stages leading up to an initial public offering (IPO).
5. Understand the external and internal causes of organizational failure.
6. Outline a plan of action for strategic change and corporate renewal.

This chapter is focuses on the birth of new ventures, the transition to a larger company through initial public offerings (IPO) or other growth strategy, and the rescue of established ventures when they hit the skids. Ironically, the managers of startups have to learn firsthand what it takes to develop, grow, and run a business, whereas the managers of distressed firms have to be reminded about the entrepreneurial orientation that gave rise to their firm in the first place. One additional benefit of considering such seemingly disparate contexts is that you will quickly find out that what you have learned about strategy is equally applicable to small and large, new and old, and stellar and failing firms alike. In the process, your students will gain a better understanding of the common process linking them altogether. This common link is the entrepreneurial process. At the same time, they will develop a tool-kit that allows them to understand firms at each respective stage and perhaps even develop a new venture themselves.

You might set three teaching objectives for yourself with regard to this chapter. First, students should leave the chapter understanding that the entrepreneurial process is relevant to all stages of a firm's evolution. This also reinforces the importance of the dynamic perspective you are providing them with. Second, the students should be able differentiate between the three different stages of firm evolution that are developed in the chapter, as well as the respective tools they might employ for strategy formulation and implementation during these stages. Finally, it is ironic that entrepreneurship classes often neglect some fundamental aspects of strategy and the management of growth (i.e., they might emphasize the business plan and its feasibility, not the "how" of executing the plan if it is actually funded), and this chapter gives you an opportunity to make that tie explicit.

In this chapter, the three differentiators—and hence your teaching strategy of the chapter—are manifested in the following ways:

- **Dynamic strategy.** Like Chapter 6, which includes the word *dynamic* in its title, Chapter 12 is steeped in dynamic strategy, albeit using three categories of firms: (1) entrepreneurial startups, (2) smaller firms seeking to grow into larger firms, and (3) firms under financial duress that are in need of revitalization. In many ways, firms in the first two categories represent opportunistic responses to (and sometimes drivers of) dynamic environments, whereas those in the third category represent the consequences of inaction or inappropriate action in the face of change. Students are presented with a useful framework, summarized in Exhibit 12.8, for identifying and diagnosing pathways for strategic change.
- **Formulation and implementation interdependency.** Entrepreneurial firms typically provide the clearest example for students of this interdependence, and you can remind them of how their strategy unfolded in the "Alaska Gold Mine" case if you used it as an introduction to the course. Most

successful entrepreneurial firms represent a rapid iteration of planning–doing–planning–doing, and indeed, sometimes the doing part precedes the planning part! The importance of this interdependence is brought out more fully in the section "Forms of Corporate New Venturing," and you can ask students to identify the formulation–implementation overlaps in Professor Garvin's inventory of successful new corporate venture characteristics. Although the strategic change section that closes the chapter points to many external causes of organizational decline, the failure to execute a strategy well is the overarching theme.

- **Strategic leadership.** The opening vignette on Jones Soda highlights founder Peter van Stolk's important role in the fledgling firm's emergence and success in the face of competitors such as Pepsi and Coca-Cola. This is fitting given that one of the three components of the entrepreneurial process, summarized in Exhibit 12.3, is the entrepreneur and the entrepreneurial team. This theme is carried through the new-venturing section, though taking the form of implementation-lever and resource-allocation choices made by strategic leaders. Finally, leadership failure is identified as both a cause of organizational decline and a source of renewal. The starting domino in the strategic change framework summarized in Exhibit 12.8 is the communication of strategic vision by the leader, and oftentimes this happens to be new leadership, as demonstrated in "How Would You Do That? 12.2."

Additional Readings:

Bibeault, D. (1998). *Corporate turnaround*. New York: Beard Books.

Finkelstein, S. (2003). *Why smart executives fail*. New York: Portfolio Press.

Moore, G. (2002). *Crossing the chasm*. New York: Harper Business Essentials.

Roth, C. (2000). *From alchemy to IPO*. New York: Perseus Publishing.

Sahlman, W., H. Stevenson, M. Roberts, and A. Bhide (Eds.). (1999). *The entrepreneurial venture*. Boston: Harvard Business School Press.

II.   BRIEF CHAPTER OUTLINE

pp. 336–365, PPT #1–3	**Chapter 12 Considering New Ventures and Corporate Renewal** The purpose of this chapter is to examine entrepreneurship, the entrepreneurial process, and new-venture creation; map stages to an IPO process; and identify the external and internal causes of organizational failure with plans for strategic change and corporate renewal. **Opening Vignette:** Entrepreneurship at Jones Soda Company, pp. 337–339, p. 339, Ex. 12.1, Jones Soda at a Glance
pp. 339–340, PPT #4	**FROM NEW VENTURE CREATION TO CORPORATE RENEWAL** *Strategies provide solutions to problems.* **New Venture Creation Versus Corporate Renewal** *New venture creation* refers to entrepreneurship and the creation of a new business. *Corporate renewal* refers to successful strategic change. Initial public offerings (IPOs) often occur in the early stages in a firm's life cycle.
	ENTREPRENEURSHIP AND THE ENTREPRENEURIAL PROCESS Success depends on the entrepreneurial team and the lead entrepreneur.

pp. 340–343, PPT #5–6	**What Is Entrepreneurship?** It is the consequence of actions based on the identification and exploration of opportunity in the absence of obviously available resources. The entrepreneurial process is the set of activities leading up to and driving the entrepreneurial venture. **The Entrepreneurial Process** The process has three elements: an opportunity, key resources and capabilities, and the entrepreneur and the entrepreneurial team. **Taking the Opportunity** This is the starting point for new ventures. Existing firms start with an assessment of the firm's resources and capabilities. *How Do People Find Opportunities?* An entrepreneur identifies an opportunity and seeks to assemble resources to exploit it. Opportunities can be identified through close contact with scientific breakthroughs. Also need to complement with specific technical knowledge and the experience of the people who created it. (See also discussion in Chapter 6 on new-market-creation, low-end-disruption, and new-market-disruption strategies.)	p. 341, Ex. 12.2 Orthodoxies That Have Created Entrepreneurial Blind Spots p. 341, Ex. 12.3 The Entrepreneurial Process *p. 342, Fig. 12.1 Google, Inc.'s Growth to IPO*
pp. 343–347, PPT #7–12	**NEW VENTURE CREATION AND CORPORATE NEW VENTURING** The first step in new venture creation is identifying an opportunity. **New Venture Scenarios** With traditional new venture creation, an entrepreneur exploits an opportunity by creating a business plan, obtaining financing, and launching a product. In practice, entrepreneurs use their own resources to launch a product and seek financing to stay in the game. **Financing the New Venture** Too much money, too early, produces more damage than good because the entrepreneur's flexibility is reduced. Ample funding can obscure problems and shelter the need to innovate in all aspects of the business. **Bootstrapping** This is a means of exploiting a new business opportunity with limited funds. **The Business Plan** A business plan must be devised that brings the elements of the new venture together to ensure a well-considered strategy and managerial acumen. The five elements of strategy, implementation levers, and frameworks for analyzing external organizational context can be used to prepare a business plan. **Corporate New Venturing** Coopetition and coevolution reveal challenges and opportunities in corporate new venturing. **The Forms of Corporate New Venturing** A firm may develop a new business based on a valuable process or technological breakthrough. Firms face three obstacles in corporate new venturing: • False starts and failures versus the desire for firm efficiency. • Resistance may occur as established practices are challenged. • Commitment of too many resources; large firms must be patient and tolerant of risk on the one hand and stingy on the other. *The Structural Approach* With this approach, the firm sets up an internal new venture division. It acts like a venture capitalist or business incubator to provide expertise and resources and impart	p. 343, Ex. 12.4 Activities in New Venture Creation p. 345, Ex. 12.5 Table of Contents of a Typical Business Plan

	structure and process to develop new opportunities. This approach has two possible objectives: • To create a high-growth new venture for sale in an IPO • To create and retain internally a new business for growth and, possibly, corporate renewal A new venture division is a form of diversification. Firms must balance the requirements of entrepreneurial ventures. Corporate new ventures are more likely to succeed when they: • Are developed and validated with supportive climates • Have senior executive sponsorship • Are based on related products and services • Appeal to an emerging subset or current set of customers • Employ market-experienced personnel • Test concepts and business models with potential users • Experiment, probe, and prototype in early development • Balance demands for profitability with realistic time lines • Introduce required systems and processes in time, but not earlier, than the new venture's evolution required • Combine disciplined oversight and stinginess with entrepreneurial autonomy	
pp. 347–350, PPT #13–15	**INITIAL PUBLIC OFFERINGS** An IPO is a pivotal point in a firm's transition. **How Does an IPO Work?** The company establishes a market value in the private sector. It is estimated by an investment- banking institution, which sells the firm's shares to public investors. The company files an **S-1 statement**, which states its value proposition and financial prospects, with the Securities and Exchange Commission (SEC) and various state securities commissions. Finally, the company and its brokerage firm "time" the offering to get maximum value from the sale of its stock. **Selected Sections of the S-1 Statement** Risk factors refer to the challenges facing management, including comparing financial performance and market valuation against competitors. The **dilution** section of an S-1 calculates the impact of the IPO on current shareholders. **Management's discussion and analysis** has an "overview" of the firm. The **business** and **management** sections sell the firm to investors. **What Does an IPO Entail?** The IPO process will cost $400,000 in professional fees alone, and the underwriter's commission on a $25-million share offering will be 6.5 percent—$1,625,000. **Financial and Legal Requirements** A SEC-approved CPA firm must audit financial statements for the previous 3 years. **Presenting Your Business Plan** The firm needs to define its vision, mission, business initiatives, and objectives; staging is important. **The "Road Show"** In the pre-IPO period, the CEO and top-management team give a series of presentations to promote the company to interested investors and analysts.	p. 349, Ex. 12.6 Minimum Costs of Going Public to Raise $25 Million
	WHY DO ORGANIZATIONS FAIL? A set of common factors underlies business failures.	

pp. 350–355, PPT #16–18	**External Causes of Organizational Failure** These are trends and events that strike at the firm's core. Four types of external change are economic, competitive, social, and technological. **Economic Change** These changes include (but are not limited to) slackening overall demand, devaluation of currencies, international monetary crises, interest rate hikes, and credit squeezes. About 9 percent of firm failures are caused chiefly by economic factors. **Competitive Change** The appearance of new companies in an industry, or the merger of two competitors, can drastically change the competitive landscape. Thirty-five percent of business failures are related to competitive change. More sudden and less predictable competition comes from either foreign countries or new technology. **Social Change** Such changes are often less abrupt and less obvious than the other types of changes discussed. **Technological Change** These changes are reflected in the increasing effectiveness of IT and transportation technology. The growing number of advanced communications technologies will greatly increase the availability of knowledge that is produced. Transportation technology has increased the number of markets. The amount of information regarding markets and the number of markets has increased. **Internal Causes of Organizational Failure** The percentage of business failures from internal causes is between 65 and 100 percent. Bad luck and sudden change have little effect on business failure. **Management Problems** These generally result from poor executive judgment and financial management—both contribute to the faulty strategy formulation and ineffective implementation. *Management Failure* When the CEO or entire top-management team come across as dictators or insulated, ignore input from others, lack depth, or offer unbalanced leadership in one product or function area, problems will likely result. Dishonesty and fraud are not common causes of business failure, even though such cases are highly visible (e.g., Enron, WorldCom, and Tyco). However, dishonesty and fraud still cause financial harm to businesses. A weak financial function emerges during economic downturns—*creative accounting*. A weak accounting function is likely to show up in one of four areas: *poor working capital controls* (accounts receivable, accounts payable, and inventories), *excessive fixed assets*, *excessive debt*, and *inadequate capital*. **Warning Signals of Organizational Decline** Unexpected decreases in earnings or revenues are always a red flag for organizational decline. Sometimes deterioration is revealed through a closer look at financial ratios in comparison to historical numbers and industry averages. Declining customer satisfaction scores should also be considered a red flag.	p. 351, Ex. 12.7 Business Risks of Jones Soda p. 354, *Fig. 12.2 Economic Change with Rising Gas and Oil Prices*
	STRATEGIC CHANGE AND ORGANIZATONAL RENEWAL Strategic management in dynamic contexts is a process for dealing with strategic change and organizational renewal.	

pp. 355–363, PPT #19–25	**Stages of the Turnaround Process** The following are five caveats about turnaround stages: 1. Each turnaround is unique, and each stage is not necessarily distinguishable. 2. The number of stages depends on the seriousness of the financial crisis: The more dire the trouble, the more stages involved. 3. The importance of each stage varies. 4. The firm may be involved in more than one stage at a time; overlap and some tasks may affect more than one stage. 5. The length of time in each stage is fluid and varies greatly based on the firm size and severity of its financial straits. Addressing every stage may take 12 to 36 months. **Stages in the Turnaround Process** A stage-by-stage process provides a template for designing a change-management program. **Stage 1: Changing management.** Either management changes the way it thinks or, more often, there is a change in top personnel. The board of directors selects and hires turnaround specialists. **Stage 2: Analyzing the situation.** Executives determine the chances of the business's survival, identify appropriate strategies, and develop a preliminary action plan; includes fact-finding and diagnosing the scope and severity of the company's ills. Three requirements for viability are analyzed: one or more viable core businesses, adequate bridge financing, and adequate firm resources. **Stage 3: Implementing an emergency action plan.** Management implements an emergency action plan when the company's condition is critical. Such plans are drastic and simple. Emergency surgery is performed to stop the bleeding and enable the organization to survive; employees are laid off or entire departments eliminated. In a turnaround, the firm emerges as a smaller organization, but is no longer losing cash. **Stage 4: Restructuring the business.** Management should try to increase profits and return on assets and equity. Eliminating losses is one thing, but achieving an acceptable return on the firm's investment is another. The team must concentrate on sustained profitability and the smooth operation of its existing facilities. **Stage 5: Returning to normal.** This occurs when the firm returns to profitability. This stage focuses on institutionalizing profitability, generating return on equity, and enhancing economic value added. Rebuilding momentum and morale is almost as important as rebuilding the ROI. Corporate culture must be renewed; negative attitudes must be transformed into positive ones. **Judging the Success or Failure of a Turnaround** A company may succeed in blocking disastrous losses without attaining acceptable ROI. Management may sell the business. ***Turnaround Management as a Function of Culture*** is the best indicator; it routinely practices turnaround management. The causes, cures, and prevention of turnarounds are closely related. ***The "Cash Is King" Attitude*** Management will put systems and processes in place that get and keep getting the most cash possible out of accounts receivable, inventory, and accounts payable.	p. 355, Ex. 12.8 A Pathway for Strategic Change p. 356–357, *12.1 How Would You Do That? Are Jones Soda's Numbers Fizzy or Flat?* p. 359, Ex. 12.9 Stages in the Turnaround Process p. 360–361, *12.2 How Would You Do That? A Successful Turnaround at ISH* *p. 362, *Fig. 12.3 Krispy Kreme's Restructuring*

| | *The Value of Information* A cash-oriented management team is more likely to invest time and energy in gathering firsthand operating information from employees, middle managers, customers, and creditors. Top executives at troubled firms often complain that they didn't know about fundamental problems until it was too late.

The value of good internal and external intelligence suggests that firms benefit information flows freely; successful reorganizations encourage managers to stay in touch with employees and diverse parts of the organization. | |

* Figure or Exhibit **NOT** enumerated in the PDF file

III. SUGGESTED CASES TO ACCOMPANY TEXT

In many ways, this chapter is a nice pairing with Chapter 11 on implementation, because startups, high-growth firms (including IPOs), and turnarounds are essentially major strategic-change efforts. For our concepts-with-cases version of the text, we have provided "Blue Whale Moving" (a small but growing venture) and "Reviving Iridium" (a turnaround case). Blue Whale is particularly rich in letting you flesh out the implementation and leadership issues that arise in growing firms, whereas Iridium gives you an opportunity to exercise the turnaround framework.

Need help selecting cases? Pearson Prentice Hall and Pearson Custom Publishing are pleased to present the ultimate resource for creating and customizing casebooks.

- Start with a CaseMap correlated to your text or start from scratch; do it yourself using our easy-to-use interface or collaborate with a developmental editor.
- Cases can be selected from a variety of sources, including Harvard Business School Publishing, Darden, Ivey, Thunderbird, and NACRA.
- We clear permissions for you on cases and content not in the database.
- You can also create custom course packs by adding articles, original material, and textbook chapters.
- Pearson Custom casebooks can be delivered in print or online.
- Additionally, we supply you, the instructor, with a free evaluation copy delivered 7 to 10 days after you create your book, free access to teaching notes, and case-method teaching resources.

We're here to help: Looking for a case on a specific topic, company, country, or scenario? Or, looking for a new case to substitute for one you've used in the past? We will help you find the right cases for your course and help you create a casebook that meets all your teaching needs. For guidance on building a casebook to reflect your course needs, e-mail our editorial consultant at customcases@prenhall.com.

Visit www.prenhall.com/custombusiness for more information and to see which Prentice Hall titles are available for short-run customization and to view suggested cases. To start your own straightforward search for material:

Step 1: Select "search content and create your book" and log in.
Step 2: Search by case number or keyword or browse by discipline to find suggested cases based on the book you use or course you teach.
Step 3: Browse, preview, and select the cases, articles, or chapters you wish to include (you will see that price and page count of the book in the top right-hand corner of the screen as you "build" the book).

Step 4: Finalize your selections, get them in the order you want, package your customized book with any Prentice Hall title for a discount (if you wish), click "confirm book," and you have the option to request a free evaluation copy.

Step 5: The Web site immediately gives you the ISBN of your custom book. You should give this ISBN to your bookstore; they will use it to place their order with us.

Beyond our cases and Pearson Custom Publishing, if you choose to compile your own casebook you will have an opportunity to draw from a variety of sources. These sources include going direct to Hartwick Leadership Cases, IVEY Case Publishing, European Case Clearing House (ECCH), Harvard Business School (HBS), Darden, and others.

Given the popularity of Harvard cases, we have selected these additional cases for use with this chapter:

		ID#	Pages	TN
OXO International	HBSP	9-697-007	19	N
Acer in 2001: The Reorganization	HBSP	HKU171	29	Y

OXO International OXO, a kitchen tools and gadgets company, was started by a businessman who had 30 years of experience in the housewares industry. With his wife and son as founders, he created a new niche in the gadgets industry for high-end gourmet stores. The company has headquarters in New York City, but it has outsourced product design to a New York City industrial design firm, manufacturing to Asia, and warehousing to a site in Connecticut in order to manage startup costs and growth. Because of the veteran businessman's reputation and industry sense, the company grew very quickly. In 1992, he sold OXO for $6.2 million to a large housewares distributor, General Housewares.

Acer in 2001: The Reorganization In July 2001, Acer, Taiwan's best-known company, was in the midst of an ambitious reorganization. The goal was to reverse flagging sales in Acer's branded computer and peripherals businesses and to address the concerns of major clients of its contract manufacturing business. The reorganization would involve splitting the company into three parts, massive layoffs, a shift in geographic focus, and a complete change in business philosophy. Acer's chairman and cofounder Stan Shih had personally taken charge of the reorganization, signaling the seriousness of Acer's position and his commitment. However, questions remained as to whether the reorganization would be effective in meeting Acer's challenges and turning the company's fortunes around. This case can be used to teach strategy development in volatile environments, the challenges of creating a successful brand, and the links between company strategy and location advantages and disadvantages.

IV. LINKING THE CHAPTER TO A COMPUTER SIMULATION

A few simulations set firms up for an IPO, but only a few. However, most simulations provide a nice context for turnaround management, because inevitably one or more sim firms will get into financial difficulties. Students will find that the information provided in this chapter will begin to bail them out of their dire predicament.

V.   END OF CHAPTER ANSWER GUIDE

Review Questions

1.   What is entrepreneurship?

Guide: Specifically, entrepreneurship is the consequence of actions taken based on the perception and exploration of opportunity in the absence of obviously available resources.

2.   What is the entrepreneurial process?

Guide: The entrepreneurial process is the set of activities leading up to and accompanying entrepreneurship. The entrepreneurial process consists of the integration and coordination of (1) opportunity, (2) key resources and capabilities, and (3) the entrepreneur and the entrepreneurial team.

3.   How is the entrepreneurial process related to strategy?

Guide: Perhaps the biggest difference between strategy in existing firms and new ventures is the starting point. Indeed, most entrepreneurship researchers agree that the starting point for new ventures is opportunity, whereas strategy for existing firms typically starts with some assessment of the firm's underlying resources and capabilities.

4.   What steps are involved in new venture creation?

Guide: Once the idea passes the acid tests, there is no systematic way to select the second step. Entrepreneurs often begin a process of experimentation that involves the confluence of several activities over time. Very often, entrepreneurs launch a product or service using their own resources and then find they need financing to stay in the game. A business plan is drafted to obtain financing or generate additional market interest (e.g., either additional financing or sale of the business).

5.   What is a business plan?

Guide: A business plan provides a vehicle for sharing goals and objectives and the implementation plans for them with members of the entrepreneurial team. The staging component of the five elements of strategy can be used to set milestones, time lines, and otherwise manage the scale and pace of the business' growth. When it does come time for seeking external support, the plan provides a coherent basis for engaging outside professionals who can assist in securing financing or strategic supplier and customer relationships.

6.   How do entrepreneurial new venture and corporate new venture creation differ?

Guide: What distinguishes corporate new venturing from the normal entrepreneurial context are the resources, capabilities, and corporate environment that come with large established firms. Ironically, most of these kill new ventures before they even start, or at least result in performance below what the firm might have achieved in other investments or simply through buying a portfolio of market stocks.

7.   What must organizations do to prepare for an IPO?

Guide: In order to execute an IPO, the company must first prepare itself for a securities offering. Then, it establishes a market value in the private sector. To do this, it must find an investment banker who will estimate a value for the firm and sell its shares to investors. During this process, the company files a registration statement called an S-1 statement with the SEC and various state securities commissions. Finally, the company and its broker "time" the offering to achieve maximum value.

8.   What are some of the external causes of organizational failure?

Guide: When discussing external reasons for decline and failure, the causes being considered are not minor changes in everyday business life, but rather the relatively few trends and events that strike at the core of a company's business. The four main type of external change are economic change, competitive change, social change, and technological change.

9.   What are some of the internal causes of organizational failure?

Guide: Pinning down an exact percentage of business failures that are the result of internal causes is nearly impossible, but most experts agree that it is somewhere between 65 and 100 percent. Some of the main internal causes of failure are management problems and a weak finance function.

10.   What are the stages of a turnaround plan?

Guide: Although the aim of this chapter is to outline the distinct stages of a turnaround, due to the fact that all turnarounds are unique, each stage may not be distinguishable in every turnaround. Further, the number of stages each company encounters will depend on how serious the financial trouble is at a given company. Keeping in mind these caveats, the five major stages of a turnaround are: changing management, analyzing the situation, implementing an emergency action plan, restructuring the business, and returning to normal.

11.   How do you know that a turnaround is successful?

Guide: If, as in many cases, the firm does remain independent and its operations have returned to normal, then perhaps one of the best indicators of turnaround success is the establishment of a corporate culture that lives and practices turnaround management every day. Indeed, research on turnarounds suggests that the cause, cure, and prevention of turnarounds are closely related.

How Would You Do That?

12.   "How Would You Do That? 12.1" introduces you, through the example of Jones Soda, to a number of financial tools for predicting a firm's financial troubles. Pick a public company that has recently announced financial woes and run the "How Would You Do That? 12.1" analyses on the last 3 years of that company's financial results. Does one of these indicators seem to detect looming problems? What might be the limits of these financial tools?

Guide: One approach to this exercise is to provide students with an Excel spreadsheet with the data required to compile these ratios. With that starting point, all the students will be working with the same information, and you can move on to explore the questions. One subtext objective is to remind students that they will usually need to connect the strategy and its implementation to outcomes seen in balance sheets and income statements, and here they will see the different levers that the firm's strategic choices have affected. In terms of the limits of these tools, you can talk about the limits of static measures in general (i.e., that they tend to lag the data that management may have internally) as well as the effect of choices they make. Moreover, many accounting figures represent timing choices that managers have made, so this is both a fact and a caveat. Finally, and this may be obvious, but it should be made clear that many of these tools do not work well with firms that have negative profitability; many startups run in the negative for some period of time, which may not be a true reflection of the organization's potential (take Amazon.com for example).

13. You get a pretty good view of a successful turnaround through ISH GmbH in "How Would You Do That? 12.2." Identify another company in the business press that you believe to be in the process of turnaround. From Exhibit 12.8, which stages has it entered and what have managers chosen to do in those stages? What stages remain? What do you think are the key challenges facing management in returning this firm to the normalcy stage?

Guide: This framework is fairly intuitive, so students should find it easy to apply. One objective you could set for any dialogue around this exercise is to have the students flesh out the strategy diamond, as well as the implementation pieces, using the guide that we provide. A second approach is to assign teams to find and describe companies at particular stages of the turnaround process so the end result is a set of companies that provide examples of the continuum.

Group Activities

14. Entrepreneurship starts with an idea. Without being critical or judgmental, brainstorm a set of 10 ideas that could lead to the start up of a new business. Now screen these ideas and select those that might enjoy the greatest market demand, most attractive market structure and size, and best profit margins. Which of these screens caused most of the ideas to be discarded? What additional information would you need to seek out to answer all the screening questions?

Guide: This exercise is useful in that it helps students understand how specific an idea must be in the first place just to distinguish it as a potential opportunity. It also usually screens out many, if not all, of the ideas that are brought to the table. Typically, the ideas that seem like they make it through the screen will be very specific and linked to some unique resource or capability that the student has access to or is aware of. The four screens that typically scuttle ideas are (1) 20 percent share, 20 percent growth market size, and 40 percent gross profit margins. Your own patterns may emerge, and this provides useful dialogue. In terms of additional information needed, this question usually leads to discussions around the need for better operating information (costs, etc.) and market information (demand).

15. For the opportunities that your team generated, which ones would be better pursued in an entrepreneurial setting and which ones in a corporate new ventures setting? What was the basis for this distinction? Would the entrepreneurial or corporate setting have influenced your assessment of the opportunity? Why?

Guide: This question provides you an opportunity to link up with material covered in Chapter 6. In particular, you can reinforce the new-market-creation, new-market-disruption, and low-end disruption frameworks to show how they really do work as nice tools for identifying opportunities and explaining the persistence of businesses set up to exploit those opportunities. You can also tie in the first-mover table, in terms of first-mover advantages and complementary assets (Table 6.4). This provides you with a nice segue to the screens question, because the availability of complementary assets and the strength of protection from imitation should mean that the entrepreneur or corporate setting provides different starting points. You can then draw on the alliances chapter to talk about how an entrepreneur could use an alliance to start the business, grow it, or generate a pathway to both grow and eventually sell the business.

VI. SUPPLEMENTAL EXPERIENTIAL EXERCISES

These exercises are drawn with permission from the Strategy Teaching Tool-kit found at:

http://instruction.bus.wisc.edu/mcarpenter/PROFESSIONAL/Toolkit/bpstools.htm.

1. **The Lego Game** This "game" provides a nice context to communicate the inputs into entrepreneurship and the entrepreneurial process.

Materials

1. Six Lego car kits, all the same if possible.
2. A pool of Legos from which students can draw at a cost.
3. Duplo blocks to construct two tunnels so that the tunnels can be altered, if necessary.
4. Tupperware containers to hold parts.
5. Colored markers to mark tunnel (one color mark for each team).
6. Masking tape to put on tunnel to store marks.
7. 10 chips per team = 50 chips

Procedure

Before-Class Preparations

• Instructor should assemble two tunnels of different heights prior to class and keep the tunnels from view in a box until ready.
• Assign reading Eckhardt & Shane, 2003.

Introduction

We are going to play a game to understand the role entrepreneurs play in the economy. The team with the most points at the end of the game will be given $10. Break into 5 teams.

> **Do not mention that we will play multiple rounds!**
> **We want them to go all or nothing at each event.**

Each team will have:

1. One representative at the Lego exchange
2. One runner to convey information and pieces between the exchange and the assembly group
3. One assembly group
4. An initial endowment of Legos (the car kits)
5. An initial endowment of 50 points (ten 5-point chips)

For each round, the team is awarded points for satisfying the goals of the round. The following costs will be assessed:

1. One point is charged for each piece utilized in the vehicle.
2. Ten points are charged for each piece drawn from the resource pool.
3. No transactions costs are charged for pieces exchanged between groups.
4. Groups are free to exchange pieces for points or pieces for pieces between groups at the exchange only.

Round 1: Team-Building Exercise (Means, Ends Given)

The first team to correctly assemble the car according to plan will gain 100 points, less construction costs. Note that construction costs will be the same for each team at this point (number of pieces in the car kit).

Each team is given one Lego kit that consists of:

1. Plastic container
2. One Lego car kit
3. The plan on how to build the car in the kit

Round 2: Reaction to Opportunity (10 minutes) (Ends Given, Means Unknown)

The team that builds the car that comes closest to touching the top of the tunnel without actually touching it will receive 100 points, less construction costs. Teams may make adjustments to the car at no cost (e.g., operate a door), but no piece may be added or removed from the vehicle once the tunnel trial begins.

Before the start of the round, provide the exchange with a resource endowment of new pieces that can be drawn from to modify the vehicle (this will be discussed later as exogenous growth in resource endowment). Pool should have big pieces and lots of little pieces. The idea here is that big pieces will become scarce, while the little pieces won't be needed.

Round 3: Change in the Market (5 minutes) (Ends Given, Means Unknown)

During this round, provide the exchange with a new technology (some new key pieces).

The team that builds the car that comes closest to touching the top of the original tunnel without actually touching it will receive 50 points, less construction costs. Teams may make adjustments to the car at no cost, but no piece may be added or removed from the vehicle.

The team that builds the car that comes closest to touching the top of the niche tunnel without actually coming into contact with it will receive 100 points, less construction costs.

A new small market niche has opened up. A team may try to serve either market or both. One piece can be repositioned on the vehicle or between tunnels, at a cost of 50 points.

Teams may be capital constrained. Ability to use smaller pieces instead of large ones will be hampered for teams that used chips to purchase big pieces in the first round to meet tall-tunnel criteria.

Round 4: Means and Ends Unknown (5 minutes or fewer)

The group that builds the car that I like the most gets 50 points, less construction costs. Give students sufficient time to debate what the criteria should be. Encourage students not to waste time.

Teaching Points

Things to look for in the game:

- Define and discuss the role of each of the following:
  a. Opportunity
  b. Entrepreneur
  c. Resources

- Lead discussion of risks faced by the teams (entrepreneurs):
  a. Don't know what will work until tried (market acceptance)
  b. Don't know what will work until tried (technology)
  c. Several different strategies possible, but ultimate success unclear
  d. Risk of new technology undermining the validity of the plan

- Current plans don't take into account future markets.
- Prices:
  a. Current prices don't take into account future markets (the niche tunnel will lead to exchange)
  b. Prices in all markets through efforts to service the niche market
  c. Failure and:
  i. not "recorded in prices"—how pieces configured not reflected in prices and if failed configuration not made aware to market participants
  ii. individuals attempting to implement "failing" strategies can constrain actions and options of other market participants

- Does anyone discover the third opportunity? Be sure to construct points so it is possible to win the game via trading.
  a. Could a team win the game via trading pieces in the market?
  b. Is such a "trader" an entrepreneur? How would you describe this person?

- Path dependence:
  a. Satisfying the requirements of the first tunnel constrains how you can satisfy the requirements of the second tunnel.

- Entrepreneurs update the plans of all:
  a. Try to detect how the strategy of one group flowed through the market and impacted other groups.
  b. Ideally, groups should select pieces based on exchange prices.

- Identify means-ends-given decision making (building the car from a plan).
- Types of decision making:
  a. Means and ends from entrepreneur.
  b. Ends given, means from entrepreneur.
  c. In round one, no major shifts in the plan are possible.

- Entrepreneurship as discovery, evaluation, exploitation process:
  a. This will work really well if someone discovers the trading-to-win strategy.

172

2. **Business Turnaround** Have students, typically in teams, find a company in the business press that has recently experienced financial difficulty or even gone into bankruptcy. What is the nature and extent of the business problem? What are the respective internal and external causes of the decline? Does your assessment differ from or confirm that of the business press? How and when were the problems identified? Who is currently in charge? Have any recent changes been made in the composition of the top management team? What appears to be the turnaround plan? Which turnaround stages are applicable and which have been undertaken already? Which key stakeholders are involved and how are they related to the causes and solutions to the crisis? What is your assessment of the results so far and prospects for a successful turnaround?

This exercise is one that is used by the Turnaround Management Association (TMA) in its continuing education series for its members. Students love this exercise because it lets them bring all their knowledge of strategy to bear in the context of a troubled firm. It also lets them second guess the turnaround process, and you can ask students to give updates on their chosen firms at the end of the semester, which again lets them show off all they have learned about strategy. We often provide these questions along with a TMA summary table that small groups are asked to complete out of class. They provide a narrative to the rest of the class on the situation and the key changes that have been made in response to those changes. The table also asks them to identify key stakeholders, which you can also use to help them see if there are gaps in the turnaround plan.

TMA Turnaround Summary Company Name:	
Causes: External Internal	Turnaround: Applicable stages: Current stage: Strategic changes: Operational changes:
Key external stakeholders:	Key internal stakeholders

CHAPTER 13 – GOVERNANCE

I.   PURPOSE OF THE CHAPTER

After studying this chapter, students should be able to:

1.   Explain what is meant by corporate governance.
2.   Describe how corporate governance can relate to competitive advantage and understand its basic principles and practices.
3.   Identify the roles of owners and different types of ownership profiles in corporate governance.
4.   Describe how boards of directors are structured and the roles they play in corporate governance.
5.   Explain and design executive incentives as a corporate-governance device.
6.   Describe how the market for corporate control is related to corporate governance.
7.   Compare and contrast corporate governance practices around the world.

Your students will have a good overview of corporate governance once they have read the chapter. It is important that student's leave this chapter with three areas of understanding. First, they should understand that governance covers a specific but broad area that includes the market for corporate control, boards of directors, and executive compensation. Second, students should be able to explain that governance serves three distinct needs: monitoring management, advising management, and advocating the interests of the firm and its shareholders. Third, although all firms have these needs, students should understand that different firms, due to nationality, public ownership, or size, may approach corporate governance differently.

In this chapter, the three differentiators—and hence your teaching strategy of the chapter—are manifested in the following ways:

- **Dynamic strategy.** Dynamism is an implicit part of this chapter, because executive incentives, the board of directors, and ultimately the market for corporate control will help to determine whether the strategic leadership of the firm keeps the strategy and its implementation in sync with changes in the competitive environment. The opening vignette on Sunbeam shows, for instance, how the board removed a CEO for improper (and illegal) behavior and helped turn the firm's fortunes around.
- **Formulation and implementation interdependency.** Governance, at least in the form of the board of directors and executive compensation, can be considered to be critical inputs into the implementation of a strategy. In most public companies, the board determines who the CEO is and how he or she is paid, and as your students learned earlier in the text, the CEO and members of their top-management team are responsible for fostering and stewarding a firm's strategic vision and ultimately crafting and making further choices about the execution of its strategy. "How Would You Do That? 13.1" helps students to see what it takes to put an executive compensation program into place, so that they ostensibly make formulation and implementation choices consistent with shareholders' interests. "How Would You Do That 13.2?" gives students the opportunity to suggest the broad-stroke components of a CEO's pay.
- **Strategic leadership.** The preceding discussion should indicate to you that governance and strategic leadership are related, and you will see this in two ways in the chapter. First, boards monitor and advise the firm's strategic leadership. So at one level, you will see strategic leadership in the form of the people put in place and incentivized to create value for shareholders. Second, board members themselves form a strategic leadership group, and this can be seen in their roles in succession

planning, choosing successor CEOs, monitoring and mentoring them, and the advocacy role they play with external stakeholders.

Additional Readings:

Ellig, B. (2001). *The complete guide to executive compensation*. New York: McGraw-Hill.

Lechem, B. (2002). *Chairman of the board*. Hoboken, NJ: Wiley.

Lorsch, J., and E. Maciver. (1989). *Pawns or potentates*: *The reality of America's corporate boards*. Boston: Harvard Business School Press.

Millstein, I., and P. MacAvoy. (2004). *The recurrent crisis in corporate governance*. Palo Alto, CA: Stanford Press.

Monks, R., and N. Minow. (2003). *Corporate governance*. London: Blackwell.

II.   BRIEF CHAPTER OUTLINE

pp. 366–369, PPT #1–2	**Chapter 13 Corporate Governance in the Twenty-First Century** The purpose of this chapter is to examine the relationship between corporate governance and competitive advantage with different ownership structures and explain different governance mechanisms, such as boards of directors, executive compensation, and the market for corporate control, in a global context. **Opening Vignette:** Corporate Governance in Action at Sunbeam, pp. 367–369	
pp. 369–370, PPT #3–4	**WHAT IS CORPORATE GOVERNANCE?** Separation of the ownership of the firm's capital from the management of the business results in the agency problem. Separation of ownership seeks to ensure that corporate resources and profits will not be squandered and that investors will receive a positive return on their investment. Corporate governance is the system by which organizations are directed and controlled by their owners. Corporate governance addresses the rights and responsibilities of the board, managers, shareholders, and other stakeholders and spells out the rules and procedures for making decisions on corporate affairs.	
pp. 370–376, PPT #5–8	**CORPORATE GOVERNANCE AND COMPETITIVE ADVANTAGE** Good governance can help firms outperform those with poor governance characteristics. Market valuations of Internet-based firms were tightly linked to firms' corporate governance characteristics (e.g., executive and director stock-based incentives, institutional and large block stock ownership, board structure, and venture capital participation). The governance factors were stronger predictors of firm valuation and survival than firm sales and profits. Effective governance may not prevent executive fraud, but it enables faster recovery for the firm in the event it does occur. Corporate governance impacts firms' ability to create a competitive advantage and exploit it to benefit shareholders.	*p. 371, *Fig. 13.1 Italian Companies Listing on STAR* p. 372, Ex. 13.1 Early Warning Signals of Problems with Krispy Kreme from GMI

The Case of Krispy Kreme Analysis of Krispy Kreme's stock price performance suggests that good governance has a positive impact on firm performance. Morningstar, a respected investment advisory firm, grades firms on an A to F scale based on the degree to which the companies align their corporate governance practices with shareholders' interests.

Principles of Corporate Governance Corporate governance involves controls and incentives to ensure that the firm's vision and mission are reflected in its strategy, the way it is executed, and the career and financial consequences in cases of failure or success.

A number of corporate governance mechanisms help shareholders avoid losing control of the corporation to unscrupulous on incompetent management.

The Major Parties in the Corporate Governance An agency relationship exists when one party, the agent, acts on behalf of another party, the principal. Both shareholders and executives are self-interested decision makers in that they make decisions in their own best interests. The interests of principals and agents do not naturally overlap.

When owners also manage the firm, there are no conflicts between the interests of owners and managers, because the principals are also the agents. By early in the twentieth century, most modern corporations had taken advantage of these capital markets and sold a majority of their shares in the open market, resulting in significant changes in ownership structure.

Codes of Governance Such codes target four main issues: (1) shareholder equality—upholding shareholder rights; (2) accountability by the board and management; (3) disclosure and transparency through accurate and timely financial and nonfinancial reporting; and (4) independence (audits and oversight, directors).

The most far-reaching governance reform in the United States has been the Sarbanes-Oxley Act of 2002, which was signed on July 30, 2002, in response to corporate scandals. The essential components of Sarbanes-Oxley deal with accounting oversight, auditor independence, disclosure, analysts' conflicts of interests, accountability for fraud, and attorneys' responsibilities.

Sarbanes-Oxley created the Public Company Accounting Oversight Board to oversee the audit of public companies and set standards and rules for audit reports.

Sarbanes-Oxley dictates that auditors cannot perform certain nonaudit services during an audit. The Act imposes a 1-year waiting period for audit firm employees who leave an accounting firm to become an executive for a former client.

Conflict-of-interest disclosures need to be made by research analysts who make public appearances or offer research reports. Analysts must report whether they hold any securities in the company or have received corporate compensation. Brokers and dealers must disclose if the public company is a client.

*p. 374, *Fig. 13.2 Sir Adrian Cadbury for Corporate Governance Reform*

p. 375, Ex. 13.2 Examples of Codes of Governance

	All governance guidelines have four control mechanisms in common: (1) ownership concentration and power, (2) boards of directors, (3) incentive compensation, and (4) the market for corporate control.	
pp. 376–377, PPT #9	**OWNERSHIP AND THE ROLES OF OWNERS** The ownership of for-profit firms is either public or private. Problems arise when a powerful owner extracts private benefits at the expense of other, less powerful owners. Investors such as Vanguard are known as **institutional investors**. Sometimes they own large blocks of individual companies and have voting power, in which case they are known as blockholders. Such investors can be quite active. Managers of public pension funds prefer firms with strategies for internal innovation, whereas professional investment funds' managers prefer firms that acquire innovations.	p. 377, Ex. 13.3 Ownership Structure Comparison
pp. 377– 382, PPT #10–12	**THE BOARD OF DIRECTORS** Boards of directors should ensure that executives are acting in shareholders' best interests. Public U.S. firms are required to have a board of directors that formally represents shareholders and oversees top executives. Boards have a number of informal roles, including serving as conduits of external information, providing leads for acquisition and alliance partners, influencing important external parties, and providing advice and counsel for the CEO and other top executives. Executives of the firm who serve on the board are insiders; those on the board who are not employed by the firm are outsiders. Outsiders can be more independent in fulfilling their board responsibilities, but this does not necessarily make a director independent. In 70 percent of U.S. firms, the CEO serves as the chair of the board. In Germany, such duality is prohibited. Boards have several committees (e.g., an audit committee, compensation committees for setting executive compensation). **Monitoring** is the process of the board acting in its legal and fiduciary responsibility to oversee executives' behaviors and performance and to take action when necessary to replace management. **Advising Managers** CEOs with social ties and friendships to board members could put shareholders at risk because they may make the board less likely to monitor the CEO effectively. Social ties typically improve the ability of the CEO to tap board members for advice and counsel on strategic issues. Social ties between CEOs and board members may increase board involvement. When the firm is in an unstable environment, board involvement is most effective when outside board members are from strategically dissimilar firms. **Using the Board as a Lever of Power and Influence** Boards provide access to external resources.	p. 379, Ex. 13.4 Board Roles and Actions p. 379, Ex. 13.5 CEO Firing *p. 381, *Fig. 13.3 Home Depot's CEO, Robert Nardelli Sits on Multiple Boards*
	EXECUTIVE COMPENSATION When professional managers, rather than owners themselves, run the operations of a firm, situations can arise where there may be	

pp. 382–388, PPT #13–18	conflicts of interests—where what is best for shareholders is not necessarily what is best for management. Incentives are sometimes used to motivate managers to formulate and implement strategies that will improve shareholder value. Of course, it is also true that sometimes incentives motivate bad strategies that harm shareholders. That's why it is important to understand how incentives work, including how people tend to respond to different types of incentives. The use of rewards to solve the agency problem is the process of incentive alignment. In practice, structuring executive compensation to completely overcome all possible conflicts of interests is impossible. **Executive Ownership** The most direct way to align incentives is to require that executives own stock in the firm. However, the ownership requirement may backfire. Executives cannot diversify their risk exposure as well as large shareholders. Consequently, executives are very exposed to firm-specific risk. This type of risk exposure could lead some executives to become very risk averse. **Incentive Compensation** This type of compensation is used to reward executives and align the interests of their top-management team with those of shareholders; common incentives are annual bonus plans and stock options. **Annual Bonus Plans** The board can subjectively evaluate executives' performance on multiple dimensions and allocate a year-end cash award. This has two principle drawbacks: (1) executives may make accounting decisions to maximize their bonus payout and (2) it may have unintended consequence of short-term bias and inattention to long-term strategic needs. **Stock options** These are used to align incentives by simulating the effects of executive stock ownership. Most firms grant stock options with a strike price equal to the firm's share price on the date the option was granted. Most option packages use a 10-year option period. There is no real downside to options, other than an opportunity cost. **Other Long-term Incentives** Restricted stocks and long-term incentive plans (LTIPs) are more recent compensation initiatives that have been designed to avoid the problems associated with annual bonus plans and stock options. LTIPs are long-term bonuses that tie payouts to accounting returns over a 3- to 5-year period. Proper use of incentives tied to long-term performance metrics (as opposed to the current stock price) increases the likelihood that executives will make necessary capital investments. Options pay should be balanced with other forms of incentives, such as annual bonus plans and stock ownership. The best-performing firms tend to compensate their second-level managers (i.e., CFO, COO, etc.) at levels close to the pay of the CEO.	p. 383, *13.1 How Would You Do That?* *Establishing Executive Ownership Requirements at Dendrite International* p. 384, Ex. 13.6 Executive Stock Ownership in 2004 p. 385, Ex. 13.7 CEO Pay Comparison p. 386, Ex. 13.8 Highest Paid CEOs p. 387, Ex. 13.9 U.S. Executive Pay Trends
pp. 388–389,	**THE MARKET FOR CORPORATE CONTROL** Corporate control is the right to choose the board of directors and control major firm decisions. One of the principle mechanisms of corporate control is mergers and acquisitions. Corporate raiders,	

PPT #19	competitors, and leveraged buyout firms are investors who buy underperforming firms, restructure them, and sell out for a profit. In the United States, the market for corporate control was spurred by hostile takeover activity and leveraged buyouts in the 1980s, and hostile takeover activities have been around ever since.	
pp. 389–392, PPT #20–24	**THE FACES OF CORPORATE GOVERNANCE AROUND THE WORLD** Ownership is very dispersed in the United States; it is much more concentrated in Canada, Germany, Japan, and China. In the latter three countries, the national government is often a major shareholder. The government has negligible ownership in countries such as the United States, the United Kingdom, and Canada. High ownership concentration relates to a high level of influence over a firm. Board composition differs greatly where owners and workers typically sit on the board, such as in France, Germany, Japan, and China, whereas outsiders and managers occupy those seats in firms based in the United States, the United Kingdom, and Canada. The effects of particular governance mechanisms are somewhat dependent on the national context. Managers and shareholders in Japan are often members of the same keiretsu. Because of the varying ownership structures, boards of directors are very different across countries. In U.S. firms, an average board is split with about 75 percent outsiders and 25 percent insiders. China is perhaps the newest market to face corporate governance issues. The majority of firms listed on the Chinese exchanges started off as state-owned enterprises. The Chinese public firms are controlled by state-owned or state-controlled shareholders.	p. 390, *13.2 How Would You Do That? How to Hire and Compensate the Big Banana* p. 391, Ex. 13.10 Executive Compensation Among Competitors

* Figure or Exhibit **NOT** enumerated in the PDF file.

III. SUGGESTED CASES TO ACCOMPANY TEXT

Prior to the recent Enron and Tyco scandals, it was difficult to find cases that focused on corporate governance. Now, along with substantial regulatory reform in the United States, you will find many governance cases from which to choose. For our concepts-with-cases version of the text, we have included "Daimler-Chrysler" and "Trouble in the Magic Kingdom." The first case addresses the governance challenges following the mega-merger between Daimler, a German firm, and Chrysler, an American company. The second case looks at governance reforms undertaken by the Walt Disney Company in response to investor and other stakeholder criticism.

Need help selecting cases? Pearson Prentice Hall and Pearson Custom Publishing are pleased to present the ultimate resource for creating and customizing casebooks.

- Start with a CaseMap correlated to your text or start from scratch; do it yourself using our easy-to-use interface or collaborate with a developmental editor.
- Cases can be selected from a variety of sources, including Harvard Business School Publishing, Darden, Ivey, Thunderbird, and NACRA.
- We clear permissions for you on cases and content not in the database.
- You can also create custom course packs by adding articles, original material, and textbook chapters.

- Pearson Custom casebooks can be delivered in print or online.
- Additionally, we supply you, the instructor, with a free evaluation copy delivered 7 to 10 days after you create your book, free access to teaching notes, and case-method teaching resources.

We're here to help: Looking for a case on a specific topic, company, country, or scenario? Or, looking for a new case to substitute for one you've used in the past? We will help you find the right cases for your course and help you create a casebook that meets all your teaching needs. For guidance on building a casebook to reflect your course needs, e-mail our editorial consultant at customcases@prenhall.com.

Visit www.prenhall.com/custombusiness for more information and to see which Prentice Hall titles are available for short-run customization and to view suggested cases. To start your own straightforward search for material:

Step 1: Select "search content and create your book" and log in.
Step 2: Search by case number or keyword or browse by discipline to find suggested cases based on the book you use or course you teach.
Step 3: Browse, preview, and select the cases, articles, or chapters you wish to include (you will see that price and page count of the book in the top right-hand corner of the screen as you "build" the book).
Step 4: Finalize your selections, get them in the order you want, package your customized book with any Prentice Hall title for a discount (if you wish), click "confirm book," and you have the option to request a free evaluation copy.
Step 5: The Web site immediately gives you the ISBN of your custom book. You should give this ISBN to your bookstore; they will use it to place their order with us.

Beyond our cases and Pearson Custom Publishing, if you choose to compile your own casebook you will have an opportunity to draw from a variety of sources. These sources include going direct to Hartwick Leadership Cases, IVEY Case Publishing, European Case Clearing House (ECCH), Harvard Business School (HBS), Darden, and others.

Given the popularity of Harvard cases, we have selected these additional cases for use with this chapter:

		ID#	Pages	TN
The General Mills Board and Strategic Planning	HBSP	9-491-117	11	Y
Lukens Inc.: The Melters' Committee (A)	HBSP	9-493-070	12	N

The General Mills Board and Strategic Planning Examines the General Mills Board of Directors' role in the General Mills joint venture with Nestle S.A. to sell cereals outside of North America. It raises the more general question of the appropriate role for the board of directors in strategy formulation.

Lukens Inc.: The Melters' Committee Discusses the Lukens board's involvement in strategic planning.

IV.   LINKING THE CHAPTER TO A COMPUTER SIMULATION

Corporate governance is typically not a central feature of strategy simulations, so you will need to be creative if you want to tie in governance with a simulation that you are using. One effective approach, and this works best if the simulation allows you to put several teams in different "worlds," is to assign one team to serve as the board for another. You can even make part of the team's grade be based on the performance of the team it advised. At the very least, you can ask why one team did better than the other (advisor versus advisee).

V.   GUIDE TO END-OF-CHAPTER MATERIALS

Review Questions

1.   Explain what is meant by corporate governance.

Guide: Corporate governance is the system by which organizations, particularly business corporations, are directed and controlled by their owners. Corporate governance addresses the distribution of rights and responsibilities among different participants in the organization, such as the board, managers, shareholders, and other stakeholders, and spells out the rules and procedures for making decisions on corporate affairs. By doing this, governance also provides the structure through which the company's objectives are set, attainted, and monitored.

2.   Who are principals and agents in the modern corporation and how do their interests differ?

Guide: An agency relationship exists when one party, the agent, acts on behalf of another party, the principal. In corporations, shareholders are viewed as principals and executives are viewed as agents. Most theoretical treatments of the agency relationship in a modern corporation assume that both shareholders and executives are self-interested decision makers. However, in most situations, the interests of principals and agents do not naturally overlap completely, and some things that would be in shareholders' best interests may be detrimental to executives, and vice versa. For example, high executive salaries come at the expense corporate profits, which may be reflected in lower relative earnings per share if the pay has not lead to higher firm performance in the first place. Thus, the key for shareholders then is to either find a way to align the interests of executives with their own or to closely monitor and control what executives do so that shareholders' interests are protected.

3.   How does governance affect firm performance and competitive advantage?

Guide: Although the answer to this question is actually very complex, and the governance mechanisms themselves required by regulators and peer pressure are very costly to implement and maintain, strong evidence suggests that good governance is favored by shareholders and that it can help firms outperform those with poor governance characteristics. Sometimes effective governance may not prevent executive fraud, but it does allow the firm to recover more quickly from its consequences. In summary, in many instances corporate governance has a strong bearing on the ability of firms to create a competitive advantage and exploit that advantage for the benefit of shareholders.

4.   How can large, powerful owners reduce the agency problem? How can they exacerbate the problem?

Guide: Some firms have a few select owners that control significant stakes in the firm. Consequently, these parties have so much voting power that they can have significant influence and control over the firm's strategy and governance. They can then use that influence to determine who stays in power as CEO or chair of the board. However, the presence of a powerful owner does not remove all agency problems. One specific type of problem arises when a single powerful owner uses that power to extract private benefits from the company at the expense of other less powerful owners.

5. When are inside directors beneficial to the functioning of the board of directors?

Guide: Research reveals that in some circumstances increasing the number of insiders (i.e., executives) on the board can increase the effectiveness of the board of directors. For instance, when the firm operates in highly technical areas, more insiders help provide information to the board that independent outsiders may not have access to or expertise to understand absent knowledgeable insiders who can serve as expert advisors.

6. What are the three primary roles played by boards? How do boards carry out these roles?

Guide: The primary roles played by boards are monitoring, advising, and advocacy. Monitoring is the process of the board acting in its legal and fiduciary responsibility to oversee executives' behaviors and performance and taking action when necessary to replace management. Advising involves tapping into the expertise and contacts of the board and using members as confidants and information sources. Advocacy involves boards providing access to external resources.

7. What is the difference between stock options and restricted stock? What are the advantages and disadvantages of each?

Guide: A stock option gives an employee the right to buy a share of company stock at a later date for a predetermined price. That predetermined price is called the *strike price*. In practice, most companies grant stock options with a strike price equal to the firm's share price on the date the option was granted. The option will specify the period of time for which the employee has the right to exercise, and most option packages use a 10-year option period. Restricted stock represents a special kind of stock grant. These grants have restrictions built in to ensure that managers do not sell the stock to convert it to cash (and thus lose the incentive power of stock ownership). The restrictions usually entail vesting over a period of 3 to 5 years and prohibitions on the sale of the stock for some extended period of time.

8. What is the market for corporate control and what role does it play in solving or exacerbating the agency problem?

Guide: Several types of battles for the control of large corporations may occur. Collectively, this phenomenon is referred to as the *market for corporate control*. When a firm is the target of a raider or a fight for the control of a board, it is a potential signal that the firm's board and its management have been ineffective, or at the very least that the board and management see no way to combat the competition without merging with or being acquired by another entity. Therefore, although the market for corporate control may serve to discipline management, eventually it is a very costly and time-consuming remedy to implement, and its benefits to the buyer will always be of concern.

9. What are some primary differences and similarities in governance practices between the United States and other countries?

Guide: Governance problems are not unique to the United States, even though they may seem most visible to you. For example, the Netherlands Ahold Group (grocery stores), Italy's Parmalat (dairy and food products), and France's Vivendi (entertainment), and French–Belgian firm Elf (petroleum) are all very recent examples of scandal-ridden non–U.S. multinationals. Most of these firms' problems can be traced to faulty governance, and, in the end, fraudulent accounting and executive excesses such as that that eventually brought down Enron, MCI, and Tyco. Some of these differences are illustrated by recent cross-national comparisons of corporate governance practices, which differ considerably around the globe. For instance, ownership is very dispersed in the United States, but much more concentrated in Canada, Germany, Japan, and China. In the latter three countries, the national government is often a major shareholder. In countries such as the United States, the United Kingdom, and Canada, the government has negligible ownership. Where ownership is very concentrated, owners typically have a corresponding high level of influence over corporate affairs. Finally, board composition differs greatly where owners and workers typically sit on the board, such as in France, Germany, Japan, and China, whereas outsiders and managers occupy those seats in firms based in the United States, the United Kingdom, and Canada.

How Would You Do That?

10. Refer back to "How Would You Do That? 13.1," the case of establishing executive stock ownership requirements at Dendrite International. Many business press outlets, such as *BusinessWeek* and *Fortune,* publish articles that are critical of the governance practices, particularly with regard to executive compensation, of one firm or another. Using these outlets, identify a recent example as well as whether executive or director stock ownership was a factor. What action plan for remedying this situation would you propose?

Guide: This exercise gives students an opportunity to look at one aspect of executive compensation, look to public data to make comparisons, and then provide action-oriented recommendations. One benefit of this exercise is that it forces students to identify "peer" firms, and justify why they chose these peers (growth rate, industry, relative performance, size, etc.). To leverage the students' information base, exercises can be tied to a case company if it happens to be public.

11. Identify a firm that is looking for a new CEO (or pick one whose CEO you think should be replaced!). Using "How Would You Do That? 13.2" as a model, imagine that the firm is turning toward a compensation model that requires the CEO to own stock. What, specifically, do you think that compensation package should look like? How different will your company be from the competition in terms of the compensation package you are offering your new CEO? (Hint: Pull up competitors' 10-K statements on the Web.) What are the implications of the differences?

Guide: This is a variation on "How Would You Do That? 13.1" that gives your students license to look at the entire compensation package. Some instructors like to link these two so that students are already familiar with the firm, and they can try to evaluate its overall CEO package. To leverage the students' information base, both exercises can be tied to a case company if it happens to be public.

Group Activities

12. Prior to class, either individually or as a team, visit the Web site www.theyrule.net. This Web site allows you to conveniently map out the interlocking board of directors of U.S. firms. Develop or pick from the various interlock arrangements, print out your example, and bring it to class for discussion. What are the implications of the interlocks you identified for strategy formulation and implementation? What is provocative about your network structure? How might it affect the formulation and implementation of strategy?

Guide: The purpose of this exercise is to introduce students to board interlocks, which is when one director might connect two or more firms by sitting on their respective boards. Part of this activity is one of learning in a fun setting—students can look at a range of firms, directors, and their respective ties. On a more serious note, you can ask students whether we can generalize about the negative or positive aspects of interlocks. Do they provide firms with strategic information that betters their shareholders and other stakeholder interests? Or, do they represent a source of collusion? What more should they know in order to make this evaluation, generally or regarding a specific director or firm.

13. Talk about the dynamics that might be involved in a hostile takeover, where the market for corporate control is ultimately manifested by an acquisition or merger. Who are the key stakeholders? Who do you see benefiting and losing from this drastic governance mechanism? Do hostile takeovers create value? Why might this aspect of the market for corporate control vary by country?

Guide: One way to kick off this activity is to play the "greed is good" speech made by Michael Douglas in the movie *Wall Street*. This snippet, and the movie, actually paint a broad palette in terms of stakeholder groups—management, employees, stockholders, neighborhoods, suppliers, customers, and so on. See the first supplemental experiential exercise for more on this movie and how you might link this activity with the exercise. On one level, you can treat the variance-by-country question simply as a function of local laws and customs—the example in the chapter of T. Boone Pickens in Japan makes a nice case-in-point. If you want to get more technical, you can point to the fact that some markets are more financially efficient than others. And only public companies, in typically efficient financial markets, give rise to the hostile takeovers we see in *Wall Street*. You can also mention deterrents, such as the poison pill and others, and who they may serve (executives or shareholders?).

VI. SUPPLEMENTAL EXPERIENTIAL EXERCISES

1. **Market for Corporate Control Structured Debate** For this exercise, you will need to track down a copy of the movie *Wall Street*, starring Michael Douglas and directed by Oliver Stone. Ask individuals to vote either in favor of or against hostile takeovers as a tool for creating value. Divide the class into teams. Assign one-half of the class to make arguments in favor of the value created by hostile takeovers and the other half to make arguments against such takeovers. Have them present their competing perspectives and then ask if anyone is reconsidering their vote. Show the snippet from the movie and then ask the question again. At the end, you should ask who benefits from hostile takeovers.

If the movie is new to you, its story involves a young stockbroker, Bud Fox (played by Charlie Sheen), who is desperate to get to "the top". He settles on a plan to become involved with his hero, the extremely successful corporate raider Gordon Gekko (Douglas).

After succeeding in meeting Gekko, Fox gives him a stock tip based on insider information he happened to come across while talking to his father, Carl (Martin Sheen, Charlie's real-life father). Carl is a maintenance chief at a small airline, Bluestar, and learns that it will soon be cleared of a safety concern from a previous crash.

Gekko uses the information Bud reveals to him about Bluestar to make a small profit when the stock jumps after the verdict on the crash is released. Fox quickly learns that this is the "secret" to Gekko's success—insider information—but the illegalities and ethical conflict involved bother him only slightly as he is quickly admitted into Gekko's "inner circle." Fox quickly becomes very wealthy and gets all the perks—the fancy apartment, the trophy blonde interior decorator Darien (Darryl Hannah), and the cars.

This diffidence changes when Gekko decides to do a corporate raid on Fox's father's company. At this point he must choose between the rich insider's lifestyle offered by working outside the law and his father's more traditional blue-collar values of fair play and hard work. He chooses to try to preserve the latter by utilizing what he has learned from Gekko. To achieve this, Bud uses a business rival to break the deal, getting indicted for insider trading in the process. He gets his last revenge by turning state's evidence against Gekko, going to jail himself in the process.

The movie is significant in terms of reflecting the public's general malaise with the current state of affairs in the "big business" world both in the late 1980s and in the wake of the late-1990s post-Internet bubble scandals.

Carl's character represents the working class in the movie, he is the union leader for the maintenance workers at Bluestar. The conflict between Gekko's relentless pursuit of wealth and Carl Fox's leftward leanings form the basis of the film's subtext. This subtext could be described as the concept of the "two fathers," one good and one evil, battling for control over the morals of the "son," a conceit Stone had also used in Platoon.

In *Wall Street,* the hard-working Carl Fox and the cutthroat businessman Gordon Gekko represent the fathers. The producers of the film use Carl as their voice in the film, a voice of reason amid the destructive actions brought about by Gekko's unrestrained greed.

Gekko clearly represents the stereotypical corporate raider of the 1980s, whose dealings were being reported on daily. Stone was not trying to point out illegal dealings, but to illustrate the corrupt lifestyle of some involved in the financial system, legal or not. The system values "The Deal" more than what the deal represents, people and goods—a system Stone apparently believes is without value.

The most remembered scene in the movie is a speech by Gekko to a shareholders' meeting of Teldar Paper, a company he is planning to take over. Stone uses this scene to give Gekko, and by extension, the Wall Street raiders he personifies, the chance to justify their actions, which he memorably does, pointing out the slothfulness and waste that corporate America accumulated through the postwar years and from which he sees himself as a "liberator":

The point is, ladies and gentlemen: Greed, for lack of a better word, is good. Greed works, greed is right. Greed clarifies, cuts through, and captures the essence of the evolutionary spirit. Greed in all its forms, greed for life, money, love, knowledge has marked the upward surge in mankind—and greed, you mark my words—will save not only Teldar Paper but that other malfunctioning corporation called the USA.

His catchphrase from the speech, "greed is good," came to symbolize what some simplistically describe as the ruthless, profit-obsessed, short-term corporate culture of the 1980s and 1990s, and by extension became associated with so-called unrestrained free-market economic policies. It remains prevalent to the present day in the investment banking industry, with a highly popular Greed Is Good silicone wristband launched in 2005.

The inspiration for the "greed is good" speech seems to have come from two sources. The first part, where Gekko complains that the company's management owns less than 3 percent of its stock and that it has too many vice presidents, is taken from similar speeches and comments made by Carl Icahn about companies he was trying to take over. The defense of greed is a paraphrase of a 1985 commencement address at UC Berkeley delivered by arbitrageur Ivan Boesky (who himself was later convicted of insider-trading charges) in which he said, "Greed is all right, by the way. I want you to know that. I think greed is healthy. You can be greedy and still feel good about yourself."

Ultimately the "greed is good" speech is a mischaracterization of what Adam Smith concluded about human nature. He believed that in general honest people freed to pursue their own interest would fare better than they would under a system that dictated what was "good." In the process, persons pursuing their own interests would eliminate inefficiencies and allocate commodities where they would benefit the greater society.

CASE SELECTION AND TEACHING NOTES

Kmart—Fall of a Retailing Giant

Charlotte Beers at Ogilvy & Mather Worldwide (A)

Trilogy Farm (A)

The Formula One Constructors

Prince Edward Island Preserve Co.

Carrefour vs.Wal-Mart: The Battle for Global Retail Dominance

The Chinese Fireworks Industry

Home Depot's Strategy Under Bob Nardelli

Ryanair—The "Southwest" of European Airlines

Advanced Micro Devices—Life Beyond Intel

Airbus—From Challenger to Leader

Moving Tata Consultancy Services into the "Global Top 10"

McDonald's and the McCafé Coffee Initiative

Coca-Cola's Re-Entry and Growth Strategies in China

Fuji Xerox and the Xerox Corp.: Turning Tables?

Neilson International in Mexico (A)

The HP-Compaq Merger Story

Cisco Systems, Inc.: Acquisition Integration for Manufacturing (A)

Multiplication of the Best Practices at Holcim: A History of Firsts

Implementation of the Balanced Scorecard as a Means of Corporate Learning: The Porsche Case

Blue Whale Moving Company, Inc. (A)

Reviving Iridium

DaimlerChrysler: Corporate Governance Dynamics in a Global Company

Trouble in the "Magic Kingdom"—Governance Problems at Disney

Case	Industry/ Case Date	Industry Type			Country	Firm Size	Central Themes							Ethics	Chapters Primary / Secondary
		Mfg. Firms	Service Firms	High Tech Firms			Strategic Leadership	Implementation	E-ship	Joint Ventures	International Expansion	Resource-Based View	Industry Change		
Kmart: Fall of a retailing Giant	Retailing, 2003		X		U.S.A.	Large	X	X				X			1 / 4, 5, & 12
Charlotte Beers at Ogilvy & Mather Worldwide	Advertising, 1999		X		Global	Medium	X	X			X	X		X	2 / 6, 10, & 11
Trilogy Farm	Riding Horses, 2004		X		U.S.A.	Small	X		X			X		X	2 / 5, 11 & 12
The Formula One Constructors: Combined	Racing, 2005			X	Global	Medium	X		X		X	X			3 / 4, 6 & 12
Prince Edward Island Preserve	Specialty Foods, 1991	X			Canada & Japan	Medium	X	X		X	X	X			3 / 4, 5 & 12
Carrefour vs. Wal-Mart	Retailing, 2000		X		Global	Large		X			X	X	X		4 / 3, 6, & 8
Chinese Fireworks Industry	Fireworks, 1999	X			China & U.S.A.	Small			X		X		X	X	4 / 6, 8 & 12
Home Depot's Strategy Under Bob Nardelli	Home Improvement Stores, 2004		X		U.S.A.	Large	X	X				X	X		5 / 3, 4, & 12
Ryan Air: The Southwest of European Airlines	Airlines, 2003		X		U.K & Europe	Medium	X		X			X			5 / 3, 4, & 12
Advanced Micro Devices: Life Beyond Intel	Computers, 2003	X		X	Global	Large				X	X	X	X		6 / 3, 4, & 8
Airbus: From Challenger to Leader	Airframes, 2003	X		X	Global	Large		X				X	X		6 / 3, 4, & 8
Moving TATA Consultancy Services into the Global Top 10	Consulting, 2004		X		Global	Large	X				X	X	X	X	7 / 6, 8, & 10

Case	Industry	Mfg. Firms	Service Firms	High Tech Firms	Country	Firm Size	Strategic Leadership	Implementation	E-ship	Joint Ventures	International Expansion	Resource-Based View	Industry Change	Ethics	Chapters Primary / Secondary
McDonalds and the McCafe Initiative	Fast Food, 2002		X		U.S.A.	Large		X	X	X		X			7 / 3, 4, & 12
Coca-cola's Reentry and Growth Strategies in China	Beverage, 2004	X			U.S.A. & China	Large		X		X	X	X		X	8 / 3, 4, & 6
Fuji Xerox and the Xerox Corp: Turning Tables?	Imaging, 2003	X		X	Global	Large		X	X	X	X	X			9 / 6, 7, & 11
Neilson International in Mexico (A)/(B)	Candy, 1995	X			Canada & Mexico	Medium		X	X	X	X	X			9 / 5, 8, & 11
The HP-Compaq Merger	Computers, 2004	X		X	Global	Large	X				X	X	X	X	10 / 6, 7, & 12
Cisco Systems	Communications, 1999	X			Global	Large		X	X			X			10 / 3, 6, & 12
Holsim	Cement, 2003	X			Global	Large	X	X			X	X			11 / 3, 6, & 8
Porsche	Auto, 2003	X		X	Global	Medium		X			X	X	X		11 / 3, 4, & 6
Blue Whale Moving	Relocation, 1997		X		U.S.A.	Small	X	X	X			X		X	12 / 3, 5, & 11
Reviving Iridium	Communications, 2002			X	Global	Medium	X	X	X		X			X	12 / 3, 6, & 11
Daimler Chrysler: Corporate Governance Dynamics in a Global Company	Auto, 2003	X		X	Global	Large	X	X			X			X	13 / 8, 10, & 11
Trouble in the Magic Kingdom: Governance Problems at Disney	Entertainment, 2004		X		Global	Large	X	X						X	13 / 2, 3, & 11

1 – Kmart – The case details the journey of US-based retailing company Kmart from being an integral successful part of the country's corporate history, to bankruptcy in 2002. The company's origins and its evolution into a retailing giant over the decades have been traced. The reasons for its poor performance vis-à-vis rivals Wal-Mart and Target have also been explored. The case takes a look at the restructuring moves taken during CEO Conaway's tenure and examines the reasons for the failure. The case also takes a look at Kmart's reorganization plans and its efforts to emerge from bankruptcy during 2002-2003. Finally, the case discusses Kmart's future prospects in light of its changed strategic game plan and the various problems that still persist. The case is structured to enable students to: (1) understand the major causes that contributed to the failure and bankruptcy of Kmart; (2) appreciate how remote and operating environments impact a company's performance over a period of time if they are not factored into the strategic framework; (3) understand how competition, operational efficiencies and positioning strategies can significantly alter market shares, leadership position and financial success; (4) understand how and why blindly following the market leader's strategies can create a crisis situation for the concerned company; (5) understand the importance of developing an IT infrastructure and an efficient supply chain for a retailer; and (6) analyze how a bankrupt company can cope with bankruptcy by overhauling its strategies.

2 – Charlotte Beers at Ogilvy and Mather – Examines Beer's actions on assuming leadership of Ogilvy & Mather Worldwide, the world's sixth largest advertising agency, during a period of rapid industry change and organizational crisis. Focuses on how Beers, the first outsider CEO, engages and leads a senior team through a vision formulation process. Chronicles closely the debates among senior executives struggling to reconcile creative, strategic, and global vs. local priorities. Sixteen months later, with a vision statement agreed upon, Beers faces a series of implementation problems. Turnaround has begun, but organizational structures and systems are not yet aligned with the firm's new direction. Concludes as Beers must decide how to work best with her senior team to achieve alignment.

2 – Trilogy Farm – Trilogy Farm illustrated the entrepreneurial struggles of a three-year old business in the hunter jumper barn business. Michelle Heine, the new business owner, had assumptions and expectations that were confronted by numerous unexpected challenges from inside and outside the organization. The central strategic issue focused on aligning internal resources and capabilities with trends in a competitive environment that was generally based upon 'gentlemanly agreement'. Multiple conflicts among employees concerning the strategic direction required management attention such as the tension between providing costly high quality service versus keeping tight control over costs. The success of the hunter jumper business was closely tied to the success of the customers' ability to win equestrian competitions. A clear vision was established for the strategic direction of the business. But significant challenges confronted the implementation process of trying to achieve what appeared to be contradictory features such as being fun and serious.

3 – The Formula One Constructors – This case is used to address the issues of achieving competitive advantage in a highly competitive, technological and international context. The introduction outlines the competitive nature of Formula One and the fact that this is an industry of sophisticated multi-million pound organizations competing at the highest international level. The case then focuses on a constructor who achieved sustained competitive advantage in a particular period. The case is used to illustrate a number of principles relating to the resource based view of strategy, such as defining sources of competitive advantage; the problems of imitation and appropriation of key resources; and the idiosyncratic and path-dependent nature of sources of advantage.

3 – Prince Edward – Prince Edward Island Preserve Co is a producer and marketer of specialty food products. The case opens with the company president contemplating future expansion. Two cities were of particular interest: Toronto and Tokyo. At issue was whether consumers in both markets should be pursued, and if so, how. The choices available for achieving further growth included mail order, distributors, and company controlled stores. The case helps students watch existing resources and capabilities with potential growth opportunities.

4 – Carrefour vs. Wal-Mart – In the Carrefour vs. Wal-mart case there are three main ideas to get across. First, the case presents an opportunity to discuss how the styles of operation adopted by companies that compete internationally are a consequence of the environment in which they have historically dealt. This leads to a nice discussion on path dependence. Secondly, the case gives the reader an opportunity to discuss the need to build transnational capabilities in an increasingly competitive world, and how companies are constrained by their "administrative heritage" or "managerial orientation" in developing this transnational capability. Finally, the case illustrates the threats global competition creates for governments and companies and the way they align their strategies in order to compete in an increasing global and interdependent world.

4 – Chinese Fireworks Industry – The Chinese Fireworks Industry case illustrates an industry that is experiencing intensifying competition and regulation. The Chinese fireworks industry thrived after China adopted the 'open door policy' in the late 1970s, and grew to make up 90 per cent of the world's fireworks export sales. However, starting from the mid-

1990s, safety concerns led governments both in China and abroad to set up stricter regulations. At the same time, there was rapid growth in the number of small family-run fireworks workshops, whose relentless price-cutting drove down profit margins. Students are asked to undertake an industry analysis, estimate the industry attractiveness, and propose possible ways to improve the industry attractiveness from an individual investor's point of view.

5 – Home Depot's Strategy Under Bob Nardelli – Home Depot was the biggest home improvement retailer in the world in 2004. Set up in the late 1970s, to provide low price, warehouse-like products, Home Depot grew rapidly over the 1980s and early 1990s, adding stores at the average annual rate of 20 percent. However, in the late 1990s, the company's comparable store growth rate began declining. It was also experiencing operational difficulties due to its tardiness in developing systems to manage its rapid growth. In this situation, the board brought in Bob Nardelli as the CEO (Chief Executive Officer) of company in 2000. Nardelli was responsible for implementing new initiatives that changed Home Depot's culture and strategic direction. The case discusses the changes implemented by Nardelli at Home Depot in the early 2000s. It discusses the measures he took to eliminate inefficiencies from the company and to streamline its processes. The case also talks about the difficulties that Nardelli, who was the first outside CEO of Home Depot, faced in implementing these changes. The case concludes with an analysis of how Home Depot compared with Lowe, its nearest competitor, in the early 2000s and an analysis of the reasons why the company's share price had fallen. The teaching objectives of the case are: (1) to analyze the growth strategy followed by a large home improvement retailer in the US; (2) to study the retailer's attempt to revive growth in the face of market saturation and the steps it took to offset saturation; (3) to understand the impact on a company's strategy of the passing on of leadership from founders to an outsider and first timer in the industry; (4) to examine the difficulties faced by an outsider in bringing about changes in a company; (5) to understand the competitive position between the two top companies in the home improvement market in the US; and (6) to examine the reasons for a company's comparatively low share price despite its improved financial performance.

5 – Ryan Air: The Southwest of European Airlines – Ryanair is one of the oldest and most successful low cost airlines in Europe. Started in 1985 as an independent Irish airline, Ryanair expanded to become the biggest carrier on the London-Ireland route. By the late 1990s, it was the biggest low cost airline in Europe. However, in 2002, rival easyJet overtook it to the top position. Ryanair's operations were based on the operational model of the most successful discounter of all time – the Dallas-based Southwest Airlines. Ryanair adopted most of the operational policies which made Southwest Airlines so successful. Along with an operational model to support its strategy of cost focus, the airline also made use of extensive, sometimes cheeky publicity, to make its brand more popular. By early 2003 the low cost airlines segment in Europe showed signs of consolidation. Ryanair and easyJet had emerged as the major players in the market. The positioning of the two airlines vis-à-vis each other also forms a part of the case. The teaching objectives of this case are: (1) to analyze the business model and operating strategies adopted by a successful low cost airline in order to emerge as the leader in a highly competitive market; (2) to examine the role of publicity as adopted by the airline and analyze its efficacy in creating higher brand awareness; (3) to analyze the positioning of the airline vis-à-vis competitors operating in the same market segment, and understand the competitive advantages enjoyed by the airline against rivals; and (4) to study the sustainability of the airline's competitive and operational advantages in the long-run in the light of new competition and the stage of evolution of the industry in which it operates.

6 – Advanced Micro Devices: Life Beyond Intel – The case discusses the competition between Intel and Advanced Micro Devices Inc (AMD), the number one and two players respectively, in the global semiconductor industry. The war between the two companies in terms of product superiority, technology transfer issues, pricing strategies, marketing campaigns have been explored in detail. The case provides information on AMD's evolution over the years and traces the events that led to the two companies becoming bitter rivals from business partners. The launches of various microprocessor chips by the two companies, and their competitive moves have also been detailed. The case also briefly discusses the future prospects of the two companies, the industry as well as the consumers in the light of this intense competition. The case is developed to enable students to: (1) examine the nature and dynamics of the global semiconductor industry and the role of the leading players Intel and AMD; (2) learn about the strategies adopted by companies to survive in an industry that is primarily controlled by high technological obsolescence, economy of scale, price competition, and intense rivalry; (3) analyze how original equipment manufacturers and end users play an important role in determining the market share of a company functioning in the semiconductor industry; (4) understand the marketing strategies adopted by a challenger to garner market share in a highly competitive market with several players with good brands; and (5) evaluate the direction in which the industry and the two companies are heading and analyze the pros and cons of the competitive moves for all the parties concerned.

6 – Airbus: From Challenger to Leader – The case study focuses on the growth of Airbus and it also covers extensively the competition in the aerospace industry. The case provides a detailed account of the structure of the aerospace industry and the nature of competition in the industry. It explains how Airbus achieved a leadership position with market share increasing from 13% in 1995 to 57% in 2002. The case also provides information about the Airbus's A-380 aircraft and how the success of this model could provide a competitive

190

advantage for Airbus. The case is structured so as to enable students to: (1) understand the structure and nature of competition in the aerospace industry; (2) understand how innovative product development can lead to competitive advantage, catapulting a company to the No 1 position; (3) understand the strategies adopted by a challenger to take on the established and entrenched market leader in a highly regulated industry; (4) understand the impact of operational efficiencies on the success of a company; and (5) evaluate the impact of the external environment on the performance of the aerospace industry.

7 – Moving TATA Consultancy Services into the Global Top 10 – This case study examines three strategic questions that India's largest software services firm, Tata Consultancy Services (TCS), faced in 2003. TCS had pioneered the industry and remained the market leader; of late, its lead over domestic rivals had been slipping, even while much larger multinational rivals were establishing large Indian operations. TCS needed a strategy to move up the software value chain. Meanwhile, a new industry was emerging, namely business process outsourcing (BPO), growing at 50 percent per year. There seemed to be synergies between BPO and software services, but also differences. TCS's Indian rivals had made major investments in BPO, while TCS had only a small presence. TCS had to quickly settle on its BPO strategy. The questions are: (1) how may TCS move up the software value chain?; (2) should TCS enter the BPO business?; and, if so (3) should it make a major acquisition or grow organically?

7 – McDonalds and the McCafe Initiative – While McDonald's breakfast and snack sales have been increasing, they have not kept pace with industry growth. The primary barrier to this sales growth in the Canadian market, according to a franchise owner, is the quality of the coffee. McDonald's in Canada has been attempting to build its coffee brand equity for many years. They had switched to the Higgins and Burke coffee but had little success changing customers' negative perceptions. To truly change customer perceptions, McDonald's needed to revolutionize their coffee program. McCafe was introduced in response to this coffee issue. McCafe was full service coffee bar, located in a McDonald's restaurant as an extension to the front counter or located as a stand-alone restaurant. Over 300 McCafes existed worldwide. While McDonald's would like to get a piece of the lucrative coffee market, McCafe's main objective was to eliminate coffee as a barrier to breakfast and snack sales. The question for one franchise owner is whether McCafe's strong initial sales can be sustained.

8 – Coca-cola's Reentry and Growth Strategies in China – Coca-Cola has a presence in over 200 countries worldwide and is acknowledged as the most recognised brand in the world. This case explains Coca-Cola's entry and growth strategies in China and the reasons for its success in this market. The case discusses its strategy for re-entry into the Chinese market and its long-term localisation strategy. The case also looks at how Coke co-operated with the Chinese government in order to soften the impact of the restrictive policies regarding foreign direct investment in China, and how it designed its marketing and promotion strategies to suit the Chinese market. The teaching objectives of the case are to: (1) understand the re-entry strategy of a multinational beverage company; (2) understand how a multinational company can work with the government in a situation where policies are restrictive of foreign direct investment; (3) understand the long-term localisation strategy of a multinational company; and (4) understand how a multinational company adapts its distribution, marketing and promotion to the new market that it enters.

9 – Fuji Xerox and the Xerox Corp: Turning Tables? – In the early 1960s Fuji-Xerox is formed as a joint venture of two leading US and Japanese firms. Over time the venture acquires increasing autonomy, as its strategic vision, quality improvement expertise, and innovative capabilities render its most active parent, Xerox, increasingly dependent on its success. The case can be used to illustrate issues relating to corporate control of alliances and joint ventures, and in particular when, whether and to what extent to tight or loosen control is appropriate. It also allows a discussion of the success conditions for local entrepreneurship in multinational companies. The evolution of alliances and joint ventures over time, and the means by which parties on either and both sides may resolve or exacerbate conflicts according to circumstances, may also be probed.

9 – Neilson International in Mexico (A)/(B) – This case examines a proposed marketing joint venture which would introduce Neilson brand chocolate bars to Mexican consumers. Pepsico Foods' Mexican subsidiary — already servicing 450,000 retail stores — has suggested a joint branding agreement. Alternative distribution arrangements are available which would allow Neilson to maintain greater control over its name, at the cost of slower market access.

10 – The HP-Compaq Merger – HP-Compaq merger, one of the largest mergers of the IT industry attracted widespread attention and criticism right from the day the $20 billion merger was announced. Shareholders and members of the founding family opposed the merger as it was planned during the economic slump and integrating such large companies would take at least two years, which would dampen HP's competitive position. But Carleton S Fiorina, HP's CEO, could successfully overcome the opponents and close the deal. Even

after closure of the deal, critics and analysts were skeptical about Fiorina's ability to integrate the two companies. However, Fiorina could successfully integrate both the companies. Now, one year after, the merger has started yielding profits for the IT-mammoth.

10 – Cisco (A) – Describes the procedures and processes used by Cisco Systems in its acquisition of high-technology firms. Its goal is to retain key engineering talent and to leverage existing product development efforts, but to quickly merge acquired companies its own systems and procedures. In addition to describing the general approach used by Cisco, this case describes some of the specifics involving its acquisition of Summa Four, a designer/manufacturer of a related product line, whose major activities are located in New England.

11 – Holcim – Looking for a case study demonstrating concrete knowledge management? Or an example of how to become a learning organization? Looking for a case that entails both of the above as well as teaching the difficulties and key success factors of the multiplication of a best practice, that focuses on issues such as defining a best practice, making it explicit and transferring it to other companies in other countries with other cultures? The Holcim case does all of this and more. This fascinating case, relating the efforts that allowed the world's largest cement producer to successfully transfer its new sales tool, webSALES, from Thailand - where it was first implemented - to Vietnam and other Asian countries and back again, was successfully used in executive training and MBA courses. By highlighting the roles played by specific key personalities across the spectrum of the company hierarchy, on the culture-specific training and modification required, the Holcim case cannot but be a useful teaching material. Since the purpose of this case is to teach the difficulties and key success factors of the multiplication of a best practice, it is suitable as part of an organizational behavior, knowledge management or strategy course.

11 – Porsche – Porsche was able to regain its position as one of the world's most successful sports car manufacturers after a long crisis had been overcome. In order to maintain this top position and to stay ahead of competitors, it was crucial for the small and independent company not to stagnate, but to continuously improve every single element of its business. Striving to find new ways to secure its future, decisions were taken in 2000 to implement a balanced scorecard in the international dealer network to turn it into a learning organization. Knowledge had to be collected from dealerships around the world and turned into a profit for the entire enterprise. The management instrument, here called Porsche Key Performance Indicators, was designed with the assistance of an experienced automotive IT consultancy as well as all levels of the distribution network. In addition, ways had to be found to ensure that it would be used efficiently. By following the idea of the balanced scorecard from the initial decision to its design phase and implementation, this case focuses on its use as a source of corporate learning rather than as a controlling tool.

12 – Blue Whale Moving – Case follows the start-up and evolution of a new venture based in Austin, TX. The two founders had tried a variety of management structures and controls over the preceding years, yet they remained unsure about which was the most effective. While they liked the idea of having a vice-president in charge of day-to-day operations, they wondered whether their direct involvement was essential to the functioning of the firm and were concerned that a vice-president might impede this contact. Everything seemed to go so smoothly when the business was smaller and people were guided solely by the Blue Whale vision of customer service. Now the business was more complicated and control of the business and its employees was much more difficult. Despite the "growing pains," Brad Armstrong and Blake Miller were as excited as ever about the possibilities that lay ahead of them, but they knew one thing for sure, the journey would not be easy. They had to not only get control of their business, but also reach the goal of expansion they set forth in their mission statement. As they planned their discussions regarding the actions to be taken on some of the specific labor issues, they each thought individually about what needed to be done to get the entire business moving in the right direction again. It was important to Blake and Brad that Blue Whale expand in its current markets, as well as in new markets. In the Blue Whale Vision Statement, they established an aggressive goal of opening 100 Blue Affiliates in different cities by the year 2000. As a first step along this path, they made a concerted effort to expand by opening offices in other Texas cities. Although they were optimistic about their plans, they questioned the timing and implementation of their expansion efforts. They also wondered if they could continue to use the management approach that had made their initial efforts so successful.

12 – Reviving Iridium – The case discusses the problems faced by Iridium after the launch of its mobile satellite services. These problems landed the company in deep financial trouble, which led Iridium to file for Chapter 11-bankruptcy protection in the US Bankruptcy Court. The case also talks about Dan Colussy's turnaround strategies that resurrected the company and made it a success. The case is developed to enable students to: (1) examine the consequences and implications of assumptions associated with launching a new product, service and its impact on the survival and success of such ventures; (2) identify the critical success factors in the mobile satellite services industry; (3) apply SWOT analysis as a means to appreciate its impact on the success of a strategy with respect to a new large project with considerable resource commitment; and (4) understand the strategy adopted to revive a bankrupt company and ensure its survival and possible success.

13 – Daimler Chrysler: Corporate Governance Dynamics in a Global Company – The development of the corporate governance system of DaimlerChrysler is of special interest, because few companies made such an organisational leap to globalisation in such a short period of time. At the time of the merger in 1998, Daimler-Benz AG was an export-oriented, predominantly German company, whereas Chrysler Corporation focused almost exclusively on the US market. The $36 billion merger to form DaimlerChrysler AG (DC) was massive by any standard. But what happened afterwards? This case gives a detailed overview of what took place in the five years after the announcement of the deal in 1998. The main purpose of this case is to outline the intricacies DC encountered in the process of merging American and European corporate governance features. DC had to design a governance system, which overcame national differences, regulatory divergence and reflected business developments. Although DC was based in Germany, it was operating globally and had to comply with many rules and regulations. How could DC set up a governance system, which offered on the one hand transparency and accountability while allowing top managers enough time to properly do their day-to-day job?

13 – Trouble in the Magic Kingdom: Governance Problems at Disney – The case discusses the governance problems at Disney. In late 2003, Roy Disney and Stanley Gold, both of whom were directors at the company resigned from the board in protest against the bad governance practices at Disney. They alleged that CEO Michael Eisner ran the company like a 'personal fiefdom' and that the board was only a rubber stamp to his decisions. The case looks into this allegation and studies a few instances which support the fact that Disney did not conform to the principles of good corporate governance. It also discusses the future of Disney in the context of the allegations of bad governance and the bid by Roy and Gold to oust Eisner from the company and install a new board. The teaching objectives of the case are: (1) to understand corporate governance practices at a major media conglomerate; (2) to appreciate the importance of good governance to maximize shareholder benefit, especially in large companies; (3) to analyse the implementation of new governance norms at a large media company and the credibility of these norms; (4) to examine the importance of critical issues like succession planning and board independence in large public companies; and (5) to study some of the important elements of good governance and the problems arising out of bad governance.

Case: Kmart: Fall of a Retailing Giant
Primary Chapter: Chapter 1
Secondary Chapters: Chapters 4, 5, & 12

Introduction: The case details the journey of US-based retailing company Kmart from being an integral successful part of the country's corporate history, to bankruptcy in 2002. The company's origins and its evolution into a retailing giant over the decades have been traced. The reasons for its poor performance vis-à-vis rivals Wal-Mart and Target have also been explored. The case takes a look at the restructuring moves taken during CEO Conaway's tenure and examines the reasons for the failure. The case also takes a look at Kmart's reorganization plans and its efforts to emerge from bankruptcy during 2002-2003. Finally, the case discusses Kmart's future prospects in light of its changed strategic game plan and the various problems that still persist. The case is structured to enable students to: (1) understand the major causes that contributed to the failure and bankruptcy of Kmart; (2) appreciate how remote and operating environments impact a company's performance over a period of time if they are not factored into the strategic framework; (3) understand how competition, operational efficiencies and positioning strategies can significantly alter market shares, leadership position and financial success; (4) understand how and why blindly following the market leader's strategies can create a crisis situation for the concerned company; (5) understand the importance of developing an IT infrastructure and an efficient supply chain for a retailer; and (6) analyze how a bankrupt company can cope with bankruptcy by overhauling its strategies.

Strategy Diamond: The case provides insight into Kmart's decisions in all areas of the strategic diamond, especially the effects of staging and economic logic.

The Dynamic Nature of Strategy: The retail industry is not known for its highly dynamic context, however because Kmart failed to adapt its strategy to the changing operating environment for so many years it finds itself technologically backwards and significantly behind retail powers Wal-Mart and Target. The case does a nice job of showing Kmart's decision processes as it tries to adapt and catch up to a modernizing industry.

Formulation/Implementation: A key point in the case is the difficulty in formulating an effective strategy in a business under stress. The details of the case also provide an excellent opportunity for discussion and analysis on the speed and timing of implementing a strategy. Discussion can also be focused on whether or not the restructuring strategies developed were flawed, or if the timing of the implementation led to their demise.

Strategic Leadership:

The decisions made by Conaway are outlined in more detail than his predecessors. However, students can discuss whether Conaway's decisions led to Kmart filing chapter 11 bankruptcy or whether he inherited a company inevitably headed in that direction.

Kmart: Fall of a Retailing Giant is a great case for active discussion in any of the areas described above giving the professor the opportunity to focus on any particular one, or simply to use it as an introductory case addressing all the issues.

KMART:
FALL OF A RETAILING GIANT
TEACHING NOTE

SUMMARY

The case details the journey of US-based retailing company Kmart from being an integral, successful part of the country's corporate history to bankruptcy in 2002. The company's origins and its evolution into a retailing giant over the decades have been traced. The reasons for its poor performance vis-à-vis rivals Wal-Mart and Target have also been explored. The case takes a look at the restructuring moves taken during CEO Conaway's tenure and examines the reasons for the failure of the same. The case also takes a look at Kmart's reorganization plans and its efforts to emerge from bankruptcy during 2002–03. Finally, the case discusses Kmart's future prospects in light of its changed strategic game plan and the various problems that still persist.

TEACHING OBJECTIVES & TARGET AUDIENCE

The case is structured to enable students to:

- Understand the major causes that contributed to the failure and bankruptcy of Kmart.
- Appreciate how remote and operating environments impact a company's performance over a period of time if they are not factored into the strategic framework.
- Understand how competition, operational efficiencies and positioning strategies can significantly alter market shares, leadership position and financial success.
- Understand how and why blindly following the market leader's strategies can create a crisis situation for the concerned company.
- Understand the importance of developing an IT infrastructure and an efficient supply chain for a retailer.
- Analyze how a bankrupt company can cope with bankruptcy by overhauling its strategies.

The case is aimed at MBA/PGDBA students, and is intended to be a part of the Business Strategy curriculum.

TEACHING APPROACH & STRATEGY

The case can be used effectively in classroom discussions as well as in distance learning programs. The moderator could initiate the discussion by asking the following questions:

- Would you agree that Conaway was the single largest cause for Kmart's demise?
- Is Kmart fighting a losing battle? Wouldn't Wal-Mart and Target ensure that it does not get back on track?

The moderator can provide information on the following topics:

- Updates on the performance of Kmart as and when the case is being discussed.
- The dynamics of the US discount retailing industry and the nature of the competition.
- Brief profiles of competitors Wal-Mart and Target and their strategies.

- The controversy surrounding Kmart's key private label, Martha Stewart, and its possible impact on Kmart's future prospects.
- The corporate scams occurring in the US since the 1990s and the reasons for the same.

ADDITIONAL READINGS & REFERENCES

1. Muller Joann & Brady Diane, **A Kmart Special: Better Service,** www.businessweek.com, September 4, 2000.
2. **Kmart Files Chapter 11,** www.money.cnn.com, January 22, 2002.
3. Yue Lorene & Angel Cecil, **Shipment of Food Grinding to a Halt,** www.freep.com, January 22, 2002.
4. Russell Nancy, **Retailing Giant Kmart Files for Bankruptcy,** www.wsws.org, January 26, 2002.
5. Hayes Frank, **Lessons From Kmart,** Computerworld, January 28, 2002.
6. Patsuris Penelope, **For Kmart, Bankruptcy May Be Best,** www.forbes.com, March 01, 2002.
7. Isaac Jerry, **US Retailer Kmart Cuts 22,000 Jobs,** www.wsws.org, March 09, 2002.
8. **Insights on Strategy,** www.ratoffconsulting.com, April 2002.
9. Ferraro Cathleen, **Kmart to Fire 35,000,** www.sacbee.com, January 15, 2003.
10. Walsh David, **Mass Job Destruction at US Retailer Kmart,** www.wsws.org, January 18, 2003.
11. Dybis Karen, **Kmart Gets New CEO,** The Detroit News, January 20, 2003.
12. Dybis Karen, **Will Kmart Battle Plan Work?,** The Detroit News, January 24, 2003.
13. Hudson Mike, **Kmart Pins Comeback on 'Neighborhood' Plan,** The Detroit News, January 26, 2003.
14. Dixon Jennifer, **Judge OKs Closing 318 More Kmarts,** www.freep.com, January 29, 2003.
15. Bott Jennifer, **Bankruptcy Blues: Kmart Workers Face Job Loss, Tough Search,** www.freep.com, March 17, 2003.
16. Bosak Pete, **Deep Discounts Lure Shoppers to Kmart,** www.tribune-democrat.com, March 18, 2003.
17. Coons Ken, **Kmart Fights $1.4 Billion Claim by Fleming,** www.seafood.com, March 18, 2003.
18. Dybis Karen, **Kmart Settles Claim for $ 400 Million,** The Detroit News, March 21, 2003.
19. Runk David, **Kmart: Strategy Working,** www.lenconnect.com, March 25, 2003.
20. Ahlberg Erik, **Judge Approves Claim Settlement Between Kmart & Fleming,** http://biz.yahoo.com, March 25, 2003.
21. Kaiser Emily, **Kmart Braces for Reorganization Hearing,** www.reuters.com, April 14, 2003.
22. Kaiser Emily, **Kmart Vows to Become a Leaner Operation,** www.reuters.com, April 15, 2003.
23. **Objections Jeopardize Kmart Plan,** www.usatoday.com, April 16, 2003.
24. Robinson Mike, **Kmart Officials 'Jubilant' as Bankruptcy Court OK's Reorganization Plan,** www.nola.com, April 23, 2003.
25. Walsh Tom, **Kmart a Little Wobbly from its Experience,** www.freep.com, April 24, 2003.
26. Krotz L. Joanna, **Kmart's 5 Big Blunders,** www.bcentral.com
27. The Detroit Press.
28. www.freep.com
29. www.bankrupt.com
30. www.bigcharts.com
31. www.kmartcorp.com
32. Company Annual Reports.

RELATED CASE STUDIES

1. Fiat Auto: The Italian Giant in Trouble, Reference No. 303-085-1.
2. Yahoo! In Trouble, Reference No. 302-084-1.
3. Reviving Iridium, Reference No. 302-157-1.

Case: Charlotte Beers at Ogilvy & Mather
Primary Chapter: Chapter 2
Secondary Chapters: Chapters 6, 10 & 11

Introduction: Examines Beer's actions on assuming leadership of Ogilvy & Mather Worldwide, the world's sixth largest advertising agency, during a period of rapid industry change and organizational crisis. Focuses on how Beers, the first outsider CEO, engages and leads a senior team through a vision formulation process. The case chronicles closely the debates among senior executives struggling to reconcile creative, strategic, and global vs. local priorities. Sixteen months later, with a vision statement agreed upon, Beers faces a series of implementation problems. Turnaround has begun, but organizational structures and systems are not yet aligned with the firm's new direction. Concludes as Beers must decide how to work best with her senior team to achieve alignment. A supplementary video is available through HBS.

Strategy Diamond: The strategy diamond is not the specific focus of this case. However, issues associated with the establishment of differentiators (specifically image and styling) and staging of an overall strategy are addressed in the story of this turnaround.

The Dynamic Nature of Strategy: Adapting Ogilvy & Mather's strategy becomes a central issue in this case. Successful for so long, the company was slow to adapt to the changing industry environment and finds that aspects of its former strategy are beginning to retard the company's future progress. Adapting the strategy to the changing landscape is an issue at hand.

Formulation/Implementation: The case highlights the complexities of formulating a vision and implementing that vision across a large, multinational organization. Company culture and outside leadership also become issues in the formulation and implementation.

Strategic Leadership: The paramount focus of the case is the strategic leadership of Charlotte Beers. The firm faced a leadership vacuum for many years and finally found hope in Beers. The case outlines in considerable detail the problems she faced in the company along with her moves to counter those problems. Examples of interpersonal roles (specifically personal characteristics), informational roles and decisional roles are provided in abundance. The case provides opportunity for discussion on the dilemmas she faced regulating and reconciling the concerns and priorities of management and other relevant stakeholders.

CHARLOTTE BEERS AT OGILVY & MATHER WORLDWIDE (A) AND (B) TEACHING NOTE

CASE SUMMARY

This two-part case examines Beers' actions on assuming leadership of O&M worldwide—the world's sixth largest advertising agency—during a period of rapid industry change and organizational crisis. The case focuses on how Beers, O&M's first outsider CEO, engages and leads a senior team through a vision formulation process. It chronicles closely the debates among senior executives as they struggle to reconcile creative, strategic, global, and local priorities. Sixteen months later, with a vision statement agreed upon, Beers faces a series of implementation problems. Turn-around has begun, but internal constituencies remain confused about or skeptical of the vision. As well, organizational structures and systems are not yet aligned with the firm's new direction. The (A) case concludes as Beers must decide how to work best with her senior team to achieve alignment in 1994. The (B) case, designed for in-class distribution, presents key business successes and organization changes in 1994.

LEARNING OBJECTIVES

Both cases are designed for a unit on leadership or managing organizational change. They focus on the:

- Complex, often chaotic, process of formulating a vision or new direction
- Need for massive communication to align constituencies to the new direction
- Need to align structures and systems to the new direction

*This note was prepared by Research Associate Nicole Sackley under the supervision of Professor Herminia Ibarra for the sole purpose of aiding classroom instructors in the use of "**Charlotte Beers at Ogilvy & Mather Worldwide (A) and (B),**" HBS Nos. 495-031 and 495-032 respectively. It provides analysis and questions that are intended to present alternative approaches to deepening students' comprehension of business issues and energizing classroom discussion.*

This teaching note provides tools to assess how Beers guided her senior management team through the process of formulating a new direction for Ogilvy & Mather. The note is organized into five segments. The first describes the dramatic environmental changes that shook the advertising industry in the 1980s and challenged traditional modes of operating. Ogilvy's weaknesses vis-à-vis its environment, at the time of Beers's taking charge, are identified. The second segment assesses Beers's early actions as the new CEO of a beleaguered firm. The crux of the case is examined in the third segment, which provides tools for evaluating both the vision itself and the process of formulating the vision. Fourth, we consider the challenges of aligning diverse constituencies and organizational systems to the new direction. We conclude the discussion by considering issues pertaining to women in leadership.

CASE ANALYSIS

1. INDUSTRY AND COMPANY CONTEXT

The mid-1970s to mid-1980s are widely considered the "golden age" of advertising. While industrial firms faced reduced growth,[1] rapid technological innovation, standardization in consumer preferences, and increasing global competition, the advertising industry remained largely buffered from these changes.[2] Clients competed for market share with large budgets, and advertising revenues soared —on average between 10% and 15% per annum. By the mid-1980s, however, five industry forces affected agencies profoundly, creating a strong need for change and adaptation. They were: declining **media expenditures,** increasing technological capabilities of **alternative marketing channels,** changes in **agency compensation,** increased agency **mergers and acquisitions,** and client **globalization.**

High annual growth rates were fueled by the growth of media, since an advertising firm's billings consisted traditionally of a fixed 15% commission on **media expenditures.**[3] Advances in information technology, however, began to shift expenditures away from mass media to **targeted channels** capable of reaching more selective and fragmented markets. As demand for media advertising stagnated, revenues fell and profit margins declined. Firms responded by bundling their array of services—media advertising, marketing strategy consulting and direct marketing—selling themselves as providers of "integrated marketing communications."[4] Ogilvy attempted such a strategy in the 1980s but, in the words of one executive, "failed to provide clients with a rationale for why **they** benefitted from 'one-stop-shopping.'" Industry-wide, clients increasingly rejected the bundling concept in favor of relationships with a portfolio of agencies selected for specialized expertise and reputation in each discipline.

In the new competitive environment, clients also began to demand services on a reduced commission or fee basis. By 1992, an *Association of National Advertisers* survey of **compensation practices** reported that traditional 15% commissions were used by 34% of large advertisers—down from a 1983 level of 52%; use of fees reached 38% in 1992, relative to 29% in 1983.[5] These trends in compensation challenged the agencies' management practices and control systems. The fixed commission compensation structure had focused attention on revenues and away from costs, which were merely passed along to the client. In many cases, firms found themselves grossly inefficient in their internal operations.

During the mid-1980s, advertising agencies grew by **merger and acquisition,** with many firms—such as Interpublic, WPP, and Saatchi & Saatchi—consolidating into mega-agencies. Mergers and acquisitions allowed agencies to better serve multinational clients, broaden their service mix to include "non-traditional" disciplines such as direct response, and realize economies of scale and scope, which play a major role in determining agency costs.[6] Traditional client conflict policies further encouraged the rise of

---

[1] Uninflated GNP in the United States grew at an annual average of 3.43% between 1950 and 1973, and 2.44% between 1973 and 1994. *Statistical Abstract of the United States.*

[2] Theodore Levitt, "The Globalization of Markets," *Harvard Business Review,* May-June 1983: 92-102.

[3] A.J. Silk, "Restructuring in the Advertising Industry," Harvard Business School presentation, May 1993.

[4] A.J. Silk and E.R. Berndt, "Costs, Institutional Mobility Barriers, and Market Structure: Advertising Agencies as Multi-product Firms," *Journal of Economics and Management Strategy,* Fall 1994: 437-480.

[5] A.J. Silk, "Restructuring in the Advertising Industry," Harvard Business School presentation, May1993.

[6] A.J. Silk and E.R. Berndt, "Costs, Institutional Mobility Barriers, and Market Structure: Advertising Agencies as Multi-product Firms," *Journal of Economics and Management Strategy,* Fall 1994: 437–480.

the mega-agency: they had constrained expansion by prohibiting firms from serving competing accounts.[7] By agglomerating, the mega-agency allowed competitive accounts to coexist under one roof.

The **globalization** of business fostered explosive growth opportunities for those agencies which had developed substantial international presence. But as clients expanded internationally, they began to expect greater coordination across regions and advertising disciplines. Ogilvy's tradition of local autonomy and strong individualism had spawned a form of multinational organization termed *multi-local* by Bartlett and Ghoshal.[8] The strengths of this type are strong local presence and sensitivity to national differences; a key weakness is integration. Many of Ogilvy's clients were developing *transnational* structures and demanding concomitant capacities from their advertising agencies. As defined by Bartlett and Ghoshal, transnational firms combine local presence with global efficiencies and rapid innovation. Ogilvy's worldwide client organization lacked the clout and flexibility to organize horizontally to meet clients' needs. Worldwide management supervisors held no formal authority over the office presidents. O&M Direct's position as an independent subsidiary hampered coordination between media advertising and direct marketing.

Ogilvy & Mather, successful for so long, was slow to adapt to the changing industry environment. Following the pattern identified by Kotter and Heskett: success bred a strong, arrogant culture; managers became internally focused; and bureaucracy stifled initiative and innovation.[9] The firm faced a leadership vacuum, unfilled since founder David Ogilvy's retirement in 1975. The agency's next four chairmen were not considered inspirational leaders and proved incapable of curbing costs and integrating the firm's resources across national borders. Kotter distinguishes between **management** which produces predictability and order, and **leadership** which creates new direction and organizational change (see **Exhibit 1**). Ogilvy, lacking in both, especially needed strong leadership to break the "victim of its own success" cycle and establish a new strategic focus.

Amidst the turmoil, the 1989 takeover of Ogilvy & Mather by WPP, ltd. profoundly shook the firm. WPP, which purchased the agency for $864 million (25 times 1988 Ogilvy's net income), required strong financial and managerial discipline to recover its investment. This focus shocked top creative and account executives, accustomed to independence and few constraints. Many resigned, morale plummeted, and critical account losses followed the talent diaspora. Labeled "beleaguered" by the press, the agency was unable to initiate turnaround. CEO Graham Phillips stepped down in 1992, and Beers was chosen to lead the company.

II. BEERS' TAKING CHARGE

Gabarro argues that five steps characterize successful turnarounds:

- Moving quickly to **diagnose underlying causes** of performance problems
- **Taking initial corrective actions** that deal with obvious problems even before their diagnosis or strategy is complete
- **Creative a sense of urgency** which highlights the organization's problems and communicate this sense of urgency throughout the entire organization
- **Articulating a mission** and a shared purpose which mobilizes the sense of urgency they have created.
- **Creating measurable and visible successes** as early in the turn- around process as possible.[10]

---

[7] Ibid.

[8] Christopher A. Bartlett and Sumantra Ghoshal, *Managing across Borders: the Transnational Solution* (Boston: HBS Press, 1991).

[9] John P. Kotter and James Heskett, *Corporate Culture and Performance* (New York: Free Press, 1992).

[10] John J. Gabarro, *The Dynamics of Taking Charge* (Boston: HBS Press, 1987).

Beers early actions, i.e., her first six months, parallel closely Gabarro's model. She spent most of her time talking with dozens of clients, then applied their insights and her past expertise to **diagnose a flagging confidence and lack of direction.** O&M was removed from clients, and insufficiently focused on clients' brands, both locally and globally. She **created a sense of urgency** by asking for and communicating client feedback directly and bluntly within the organization. Beers spoke of change incessantly and clearly signaled her conviction by firing a top executive who resisted efforts. This indicated a radical departure from the status quo given Ogilvy's culture of politeness and civility. The 1993 Strategy (the "Chewton Glen Declaration") addressed immediate concerns: winning back lost clients—particularly multinationals, producing consistent, higher quality work, and tightening management of financial resources. These goals produced **initial corrective actions** and **measurable and visible successes** within a year of her taking charge. Although WPP prohibits publicly releasing net income, the case does show that operating margins in 1993 jumped to 7.6%, from 4.9% the previous year. Major client wins from Jaguar and American Express were important, early, and visible successes. While typically impressed by these results, students will also point out that the focus on shorter-term goals may create confusion with regard to the future direction.

Students will also note that Beers' status as an outsider CEO was both an asset and a challenge. Kotter and Heskett report that few leaders of major cultural change efforts are true insiders. Most take charge with "outsider" perspectives, characterized by broader views, greater emotional detachment, and significant experiences in other firms. Gabarro found that outsider CEOs were more effective when they could couple their outsider perspective with industry expertise.[11] Valuable assets for Beers were her industry reputation (e.g., past president of AAAA), turnaround experience, and network of relationships with senior management in client and potential client firms. Her ability to inspire also stood out in contrast to her predecessors.

As noted by Gabbarro, however, outsider CEOs generally experience longer "taking charge" processes, as they must first learn the firm's culture, discern potential allies and foes, and gain credibility with internal constituencies. The case reports that Ogilvy is "intolerant of outsiders" and Beers was viewed as coming from a significantly smaller agency and lacking in international experience. Building internal credibility quickly was key. She did so by bringing clients on board, projecting her charismatic personality, and creating alliances with key executives. She is described as "delightfully informal but you know she means business." Also important is her choice of framing the need for change as consistent with, rather than in opposition to, traditional Ogilvy values. One of her early actions was to find "kindred spirits" to begin the process of forming a guiding coalition. Her initial selection criteria were individuals who demonstrated urgency for change and willingness to take risks. Not until two years later, did she announce the formation of an executive committee.

III. DEVELOPMENT OF THE BRAND STEWARDSHIP VISION

Generating urgency and achieving short-term wins were critical, but Beers concluded quickly that Ogilvy needed major cultural and organizational change to succeed in the new business environment. **Exhibit 2** describes a sequential model of organizational transformation. Once a transformation process is initiated, significant and enduring change required direction. Returning to Kotter's distinction between leadership and management, setting direction and aligning the appropriate constituencies are at the heart of leadership. **Direction setting** helps produce changes needed to cope with a dynamic business environment, while **alignment** brings people behind a vision so as to help produce those changes (see **Exhibit 1** for more detail on the two activities). The discussion below focuses on direction setting, examining both Ogilvy's new direction—Brand Stewardship, as well as the direction setting process.

---

[11] Ibid.

Alignment issues, however, also play a critical role at this stage. Part of what makes a vision formulation process effective is whether it aligns key internal constituencies.

A. Evaluating the Vision

A good vision provides both a strategic and a motivational focus: it is a clear statement of purpose as well as a source of inspiration and commitment. Kotter argues that a effective visions have three characteristics. A vision must be **clear** and specific enough to provide guidance, yet also vague enough to encourage initiative and remain relevant under varied conditions. A good vision is also **desirable** in that it meets the needs of all key stakeholders (e.g., clients, shareholders, employees). Finally, it should be **feasible**, implying that a reasonable strategy exists for getting there, one that accounts for competition, organizational strengths and weaknesses, and business trends.[12]

The Brand Stewardship vision was encapsulated in the statement: "To be the agency most valued by those who most value brands." The case suggests, however, that considerable confusion existed internally over the meaning and implications of this statement, raising questions about the vision's **clarity**. Brand Stewardship is based on two tenets. The first is that companies can only compete over the long-term by building strong brands. The second is that the role and value of advertising is to build brands by uncovering the rational and emotional significance of a product in a user's life. During 1993, a step-by-step process was developed:

- **Brand Probe:** Formal research designed to unveil how consumers really feel about a brand.
- **Brand Audit:** An effort to set down the intangible cluster of feelings, impressions, and opinions that blend together to form the consumer's perceptions of the brand. Together, the brand team and client attempt to answer a series of questions from consumer's point of view.
- **BrandPrint™:** A succinctly written articulation of the relationship between the consumer and the brand. The BrandPrint becomes the basis for all Ogilvy's future work for the brand—positioning, communication and creative strategies.

Students will want to consider the extent to which these definitions offer sufficient guidelines for action. Many tend to judge the vision as vague. Does its vagueness, then, encourage initiative and company-wide relevance? Or is the vision too vague to provide guidance in daily behavior?

The **desirability** of a vision is evaluated by the extent to which it reflects the legitimate interests and values of stakeholders. The Brand Stewardship vision resonated best with clients. Account services recognized this appeal and valued its ability to win business for Ogilvy. Top creative executives saw a tool for guiding the creative process, but initially, creatives in local offices found Brand Stewardship unoriginal and constraining. Brand Stewardship also appeared to have less to offer to O&M Direct, a successful independent subsidiary that had maintained market dominance throughout the late 1980s.

Students will want to consider whether the new direction fits current business demands, environmental pressures, and Ogilvy's organizational strengths. Evidence suggests that Brand Stewardship does provide clients with a convincing rationale for integrated services, something agencies had been trying to promote for years. Recent marketing studies have shown that strong brands—built through the consistent, complementary efforts of media advertising and direct marketing—are **the** basis for enduring, profitable growth. Price promotions, coupons, and similar mechanisms alone may produce short peaks in sales, but fail to sustain loyalty over time.[13] Further, as compensation structures tighten and clients demand global

---

[12] John Kotter, *A Force for Change* (New York: Free Press, 1990).

[13] A.S.C. Ehrenberg, "The After-effects of Price-related Consumer Promotions," *Journal of Advertising Research*. July-August 1994.

economies of scale, Brand Stewardship focuses Ogilvy on promoting efficiency by knitting the local "fiefdoms" together and reigning in costs. Concentrating on multi-national clients also appears advantageous in light of multi-national's strong revenue growth potential and their interest in building brands worldwide. As well, this strategy seems to complement Ogilvy's strong combination of global network with local talent. (**Exhibit 3** provides more information on relevant stakeholder groups, their representatives and perspectives).

Kotter's final criteria for a sound vision is **feasibility**. Based on the information provided in the (A) case, this may be difficult to evaluate. By the end of 1993, Beers and top executives have only begun to shape an implementation strategy.

Along with Kotter's criteria, students will likely debate the **originality** of the new direction. Is it distinctive, and can other firms copy Ogilvy? Nanus has argued that a vision should reflect the uniqueness of the organization, its distinctive competence."[14] Yet, during the 1990s, most of the large, multi-national advertising firms claimed a brand focus. Others, pointing to the explosion of multi-media and information technology, will wonder whether Brand Stewardship is sufficiently innovative and future-focused. Kotter, however, notes that, although effective visions may be highly creative or innovative, most are not. The key to their effectiveness, he argues, are effective communication and follow-through. Remarks by an industry observer in the (B) case suggested Beers had succeeded in this regard:

All the major agencies focus on brands. What is amazing is that no one had staked out this territory before. Beers came up with the term and put all the muscle of the organization behind it. She preempted other agencies by stating the obvious . . . in a way that resonates well with clients.

B. Evaluating the Vision Formulation Process

The case illustrates the messy, non-linear nature of vision formulation. Two popular notions about visions are that they can be developed from several days of strategic brainstorming or that they are sheer inspiration. Instead, Conger argues, the process of formulating a vision is generally "opportunistic, fragmented, and intuitive" but also requires systematic work.[15] Beers began with a conviction that the power of advertising is its ability to build sustainable brand loyalty. She then invited others to debate, focus, and articulate this idea. The group she asked to begin the vision formulation process was small, diverse, and most significantly, informal. Several "painful" off-site meetings were held. Much progress occurred "off-line" when Putter and Bassat, and Wright and O'Dea worked from opposite sides of the globe to refine one another's ideas. Throughout, Beers spoke to internal groups about the power of brands long before the vision was fully developed. This early communication allowed her to try out and refine her message. As the need arose, Beers added a separate ad-hoc group to develop Brand Stewardship "tools" and a new organization, WCS, to take responsibility for the global implications of a brand focus.

Classroom discussion of the effectiveness of the process can also focus on Beers' management of dual demands for leading in directive fashion to impose order over a potentially chaotic situation while also responding to the high need for involvement, open communication and debate. In guiding the vision formulation, Beers appeared to alternate between directive and participative leadership. At Vienna, a first attempt was made to organize and analyze Ogilvy's problems and goals using a business model framework and a high degree of participation. At Chewton Glen, Beers sensed the process was derailing and chose to take control by announcing her own short-term strategy. Participation and involvement was

---

[14] Burt Nanus, *Visionary Leadership: Creating a Compelling Sense of Direction for your Organization* (San Francisco: Jossey-Bass, 1992).

[15] Jay Conger, *The Charismatic Leader* (San Francisco: Josssey-Bass, 1989).

203

broadened again at Arrowwood, yet, when a lack of consensus threatened progress, Beers stated: "In any change effort, a are supporters, a are resisters, and a are apathetic. I'm in the first group. Where are you?"

Beers' challenge throughout the vision formulation process was to keep a highly diverse team moving in the same direction. Class discussion focuses on the dilemmas she faced managing and reconciling the concerns and priorities of relevant stakeholders. During the formulation process, debates tended to emerge along group lines. Creative executives pushed for an improved creative product, while several account executives urged financial restraint. Direct executives emphasized integrated communications over traditional media advertising. Executives from the beleaguered U.S. region felt the urgency of generating client "wins", while European and Asian representatives pressed for structural changes (see **Exhibit 3**). More broadly, Beers' team seemed to disagree about what a vision was: some saw it as an inspirational statement, while others demanded something that clearly guided business strategy.

Some students may question the importance of these debates, arguing that Beers had her vision all along and simply persuaded others to buy in without seriously considering their issues. Others will see a more participative process. Debate tends to converge around Beers' approach of gaining client buy-in for Brand Stewardship long before she had established the vision internally. Speaking with clients about the new direction at this stage had two advantages: their buy-in indicated that the process was on course; and client enthusiasm helped sustain internal momentum and energy. The downside was less input from internal constituencies before "going public" and Ogilvy's unpreparedness to satisfy early requests by clients for Brand Audits.

IV. VISION IMPLEMENTATION

A. Communicating the Vision

Once direction is established—and even while it is being established, a critical leadership challenge is aligning relevant constituencies. Alignment is a communications challenge—getting people to both comprehend and buy into the new direction.[16] Undercommunicating is a key reason why transformation efforts fail. In successful communication: the message is repeated over and over again; every conceivable communication channel is employed, especially those generally squandered on non-essential information; and leaders of the change effort become living symbols of the new corporate culture, acting in ways consistent with the new vision.[17]

For Beers and her senior team, making the vision real, actionable, and motivating for internal constituencies proved the greatest communication challenge. Kotter and Schlesinger have outlined several reasons for why various stakeholders resist change and how communication efforts may counteract that resistance. People resist because of:

- **Misunderstanding & Lack of Trust.** The implications of the new direction are poorly understood, leading to perceptions that the new vision is irrelevant or damaging. Ogilvy's creatives believed initially that the BrandPrint™ process either failed to enhance their work or actively forced formulaic results. Employees of O&M Direct wondered about the relevance of a brand-focused vision to direct marketing.
- **Parochial Self-interest.** Employees may believe they will lose something of value if they follow the new direction. This often results when what is in best interests of one group not in best interests of

---

[16] John P. Kotter, *A Force for Change* (New York: Free Press, 1990).

[17] John P. Kotter, "Leading Change: Why Transformation Efforts Fail," *Harvard Business Review,* March-April 1995.

whole organization. Ogilvy's local office presidents, particularly those in charge of small offices, had always been the firm's "feudal chieftains." Focusing on global brands clearly changed their status. Beers, however, hoped to transcend parochial interests by aligning O&M's diverse sub-units in service of the brand.

- **Differing Assessment.** Stakeholders may interpret information differently than the leaders of the change effort. For example, members O&M Direct, who did not experience a "beleaguered" period, were less likely to feel urgency.
- **Low Tolerance for Change.**   Certain stakeholders may worry that to go along with the change would be an admission that some of their previous decisions or beliefs were wrong. As one Ogilvy [executive] noted in the (A) case: "Doing a Brand Audit on existing business can be seen as an indictment of what we have been doing."

Kotter and Schlesinger explain further that several options are available to leaders attempting to align people to a new direction. **Education and communication** diffuses misunderstanding, but can be very time consuming if many people are involved. **Participation** and involvement leads to commitment—not merely compliance—but can also take considerable time. **Negotiation** combats self-interest by offering incentives to potential or actual resistors. **Explicit and implicit coercion** forces change with punitive threats. A potent tactic when speed is essential, it may leave resistors angered at initiators.

Beers and senior executives approached the communication challenge in several ways. Beers herself acted as the principal missionary for the new direction, while senior executives focused on education tactics. By the end of 1993, conferences, handbooks, and training programs had been planned. With regard to the local office presidents, Beers communicated forcefully that they must accept some centrally managed campaigns and give priority to global accounts. She also, however, reminds WCS about the importance of maintaining and cultivating local talent and creativity. At several key moments, she took stronger measures, firing a top executive early on, and later, at Arrowwood challenging directly the "skeptics" and resistors to the vision.

B. Aligning Structures and Systems

Once a turnaround gains momentum, the key challenge faced by the leaders of change is how to align structures and systems to fit the transforming vision (see **Exhibit 2**). Nadler and Tushman's congruence model of organizations describes how organizational design supports the implementation of strategy.[18] In particular, alignment or congruence is needed between strategy and formal organization, and among the elements of the formal organization, including the structure of reporting relationships, the staffing of jobs, incentive and compensation systems, and financial control systems. At Ogilvy, the key areas of misalignment may be categorized into **structure, staffing,** and **systems.**

At the end of the (A) case, the **structure** of reporting relationships between WCS and local offices remains ambiguous. The intended role of WCS is to coordinate the design and implementation of multi-national campaigns in order to best serve global brands and achieve the global efficiencies sought by multi-national clients. Beers and her senior team weigh the advantages of high control by WCS with a more flexible relationship. The advantages of tight WCS control include uniformity in creative product, clear priority given to global accounts, and fewer inefficiencies caused by duplicate work. Potential drawbacks are diminished creative input by local offices, morale issues at smaller offices without major multi-national accounts, and resources drained from large, local accounts. In the case, Beers states that

---

[18] David A. Nadler and Michael L. Tushman. "Designing Organizations that have Good Fit: A Framework for Understanding New Architectures" in *Organizational Architecture: Designs for Changing Organizations*. David Nadler (ed.) (San Francisco: Jossey-Bass, 1992).

she wants "to continue to cultivate the tension between local and center," in the service of a better creative product. This flexible approach, however, is reflected in the lack of financial control systems and concomitant conflicts over how to split fees and allocate costs between WCS and local offices. Should conflicts be handled on a per-case basis, or should Beers and her team institute formal guidelines? If they continue with a more flexible strategy, how can they encourage collaboration despite ambiguity of pay-offs?

Tensions in the balance of power lead, in some cases, to **staffing** concerns. Beers must weigh how strengthening the WCS role will affect the retention of top talent at smaller offices. The information provided by the (B) case about the IBM win heightens the dilemma. Staffing is also an issue with regard to creative talent. An important implication of the new vision is having people who understand the new way of operating and can deliver a consistently superior, brand-focused product. The (B) case reports that Beers hired a Worldwide Brand Director for IBM, but was still searching for creative leaders. Staffing top leadership positions presents a further challenge. Beers operated throughout the vision formulation process with an informal coalition and forms no formal executive committee until the end of the (B) case. Students may consider whether Beers should formalize roles and procedures or continue to leave things vague—as is her style?

Beers must also contend with decisions about incentive and compensation **systems.** People are working in new roles toward the new vision, but incentives—titles, promotions, and seats on the Worldwide Board of Directors—remain unchanged. Students learn at the end of the (B) case that a decision is made by the executive committee to link executive compensation more closely to performance, and more important, to favor WCS in allocating a fixed bonus pool.

At the end of the (A) case, Beers and her senior team face a management challenge: aligning staff, structures, and systems requires strong coordination and control (see **Exhibit 1**). Management, however, is neither Beers' strength nor her preference. She is client-focused, driven by creative ideas, and disinterested by "financial minutia." Students will want to consider how Beers should approach this challenge. What role should she play as the transformation effort enters its next stage? The (B) case reveals that Beers has appointed a COO, whose intended focus will be administration and operations.

V. WOMEN AND LEADERSHIP

This case can also be used to discuss whether men and women exhibit different leadership styles. In a recent *Harvard Business Review* article, Rosener suggests that women tend to practice "transformational" leadership. She argues that women leaders place priority on getting subordinates energized and aligned to a broader group goal; they rely often on personal sources of power such as charisma, hard work, or personal contacts to gain cooperation; and they tend to encourage greater levels of involvement, participation and information sharing than their male counterparts. She argues that men, by contrast, are more likely to practice "transactional" leadership. Exhibiting "command and control" influence styles, they tend to view their relationships with subordinates as exchanges of rewards for services rendered and rely more heavily on formal authority and their ability to reward and punish.[19]

Beers' focus on communicating an inspirational vision, her ability to motivate through passion and personal charisma, and her candid demeanor suggests she is indeed a "transformational" leader. Yet, these

---

[19] Judy B. Rosener, "Ways Women Lead" in *Managing People in Organizations,* John J. Gabarro (ed.) (Boston: HBS Press, 1992). Transactional and transformational leadership were first conceptualized by James McGregor Burns in *Leadership* (New York: Harper & Row, 1978) and later developed by Bernard Bass in *Leadership and Performance Beyond Expectations* (New York: Free Press, 1985).

are also qualities that distinguish leaders from managers (see **Exhibit 1**) and charismatic leaders from non-charismatic ones.[20] While some students will argue that Beers exhibits a "high commitment, female" style, other will state that women "leaders" have more in common with male "leaders" than with female "managers." Further, those arguing for a distinctive female leadership style will tend to view Beers' intuition, passion, and inspiration as "female traits," overlooking her toughness and decisiveness, which have been traditionally regarded as "male traits." Unlike Rosener's women, Beers was not always willing to share power and information, and on several occasions in the case we witness her acting rather unilaterally. Her Chewton Glen declaration, her early decision to take Brand Stewardship to clients first, and her hesitancy to expand the Arrowwood meeting to include a larger group are all key examples.

A productive discussion might contrast the role of gender with situational requirements—in this case, the demands of turnaround for a new CEO. Like many successful managers, Beers is "versatile and inconsistent," viewing strategies and operating styles as flexible and adjusting them to changing circumstances.[21] Greater detail on research on gender differences in managerial styles is provided in *Gender Differences in Managerial Behavior* which may be used by the instructor as background lecture material or, may be assigned to the students as a reading along with the case.[22]

Assignment Questions

1. What is Beers trying to accomplish as CEO of Ogilvy & Mather Worldwide?
2. What is your assessment of the vision?
3. What is your assessment of the process Beers and her team went through to create the vision?
4. What are the key challenges facing Beers at the end of the case?

Teaching Plan

The teaching plan outlined below is designed for an 80-minute class session.

I. INTRODUCTION (5 MINUTES)

This case chronicles Charlotte Beers' actions on assuming leadership of O&M worldwide—the world's sixth largest advertising agency—during a period of rapid industry change and organizational crisis. We will use the case to focus on the role of a leader in setting a direction and getting relevant constituencies aligned to that direction. We'll also consider the variety of challenges Beers faces at the end of the case to sustain momentum towards the new direction.

II. WHAT IS BEERS TRYING TO ACCOMPLISH AS CEO OF O&M? (15 MINUTES)

A. Why was Ogilvy & Mather having problems when she took over?

- Industry Context
- Internal organization

---

[20] Jay Conger, *The Charismatic Leader* (San Francisco: Jossey-Bass, 1989).

[21] C.W. Skinner and W.E. Sasser, "Managers with Impact: Versatile and Inconsistent" *Harvard Business Review* November 1977.

[22] Herminia Ibarra, "Gender Differences in Managerial Behavior: The Ongoing Debate," HBS Case No. 495-038, 1995.

B. How do you evaluate Beers' first few months?

- What were the biggest challenges that she faced?
- What was her "taking charge" strategy?
- How effective has she been so far? Why or why not?

III. WHAT IS YOUR ASSESSMENT OF THE VISION? (15 MINUTES)

- What exactly is the vision?
- Is it a "good vision?" What makes for a "good vision?"
- Is it clear?
- Is it original? Is it just stating the obvious? How important is originality?
- Does it make sense strategically?
- Does it meet the needs of internal and external constituencies? Who are they?
- Why are most company vision statements so uncompelling?

IV. WHAT IS YOUR ASSESSMENT OF THE PROCESS BEERS AND HER TEAM WENT THROUGH TO CREATE THE VISION? (15 MINUTES)

- Was it a high involvement process or did she formulate the vision largely on her own?
- Did she involve the right people?
- Why not involve a larger group earlier?
- Were all those meetings necessary? Why or why not?
- How did she get buy-in?
- How effectively did she deal with resistance to the vision?
- What is her leadership style? How effective is it in this situation?

V. OPTIONAL: A DISCUSSION OF MEN'S AND WOMEN'S LEADERSHIP STYLES MIGHT BE PLACED HERE IN THE SEQUENCE. (10 MINUTES)

VI. WHAT ARE THE KEY CHALLENGES FACING BEERS AT THE END OF THE CASE? (10 MINUTES)

- Which are most urgent? Most important?
- What if anything should she do differently?
- What are the trade-offs?

VII. WRAP-UP (10 MINUTES)

A. Distribute "B" case and elicit reactions

(if pressed for time, describe what happened)

B. Conclusion

I typically end the discussion by referring back to either Exhibit 1 or 2, emphasizing the importance of leadership in creating change. I close with a few remarks on direction setting and gaining alignment:

- Effective leaders are master communicators. They need not propose an original or innovative vision as long as the direction is clear and aligned with the needs of relevant constituencies.
- Gaining alignment is not simply about communication; it is also a political challenge. Outsiders with big knowledge gaps must leverage strengths and power sources to build credibility quickly. As Beers demonstrated by taking Brand Stewardship first to clients, external buy-in can drive internal alignment. Leaders must also achieve short-term successes to gain the credibility needed to affect longer term change. Sequencing is key (see **Exhibit 2**).

Exhibit 1   Comparing Management and Leadership

	Management	**Leadership**
Creating an agenda	Planning and Budgeting–establishing detailed steps and timetables for achieving needed results, and then allocating the resources necessary to make that happen	Establishing Direction–developing a vision of the future, often the distant future, and strategies for producing the changes needed to achieve that vision
Developing a human network for achieving the agenda	Organizing and Staffing–establishing some structure for accomplishing plan requirements, staffing that structure with individuals, delegating responsibility and authority for carrying out the plan, providing policies and procedures to help guide people, and creating methods or systems to monitor implementation	Aligning People–communicating the direction by words and deeds to all those whose cooperation may be needed so as to influence the creation of teams and coalitions that understand the vision and strategies, and accept their validity
Execution	Controlling and Problem Solving–monitoring results vs. plan in some detail, identifying deviations, and then planning and organizing to solve these problems	Motivating and Inspiring–energizing people to overcome major political, bureaucratic, and resource barriers to change by satisfying very basic, but often unfulfilled, human needs
Outcomes	Produces a degree of predictability and order, and has the potential of consistently producing key results expected by various stakeholders (e.g., for customers, always being on time; for stockholders, being on budget)	Produces change, often to a dramatic degree, and has the potential of producing extremely useful change (e.g., new products that customers want, new approaches to labor relations that help make a firm more competitive)

Source: John P. Kotter, *A Force for Change: How Leadership Differs from Management,* New York: Free Press, 1990: p. 6.

Exhibit 2 The Process of Renewing and Transforming Organizations

1	**Establishing a Greater Sense of Urgency**
•	Getting people to examine seriously the competitive realities
•	Identifying crises, potential crises, or major opportunities

2	**Creating the Guiding Coalition**
•	Putting together a group with enough power to lead the change
•	Getting the group to work together like a team

3	**Establishing a Transformational Vision and Strategy**
•	Creating a vision to help direct the change effort
•	Developing strategies for achieving that vision

4	**Communicating the Change Vision**
•	Using every vehicle possible to constantly communicate the new vision and strategies
•	Role modeling needed behavior by the guiding coalition

5	**Empowering Others to Act**
•	Getting rid of blockers
•	Changing systems or structures that seriously undermine the change vision
•	Encouraging risk taking and nontraditional ideas, activities, and actions

6	**Creating Short-Term Wins**
•	Planning for some visible performance improvements
•	Creating those wins
•	Visibly recognizing and rewarding people who made the wins possible

7	**Consolidating Gains and Producing Even More Change**
•	Using increased credibility to change all systems, structures, and policies that don't fit together and don't fit the transformation vision
•	Hiring, promoting, and developing people who can implement the change vision
•	Reinvigorating the process with new projects, themes, and change agents

8	**Institutionalizing New Approaches into the Culture**
•	Creating better performance through customer and productivity oriented behavior, more and better leadership, and more effective management
•	Articulating the connections between new behaviors and firm success
•	Developing means to ensure leadership development and succession

Source: John P. Kotter, *Leading Change: Why Transformation Efforts Fail,* HBR March-April 1995: p. 61.

Exhibit 3 Stakeholder Analysis

Function *Account services,* responsible for winning and keeping clients, placed a strong priority on a vision that would sell well to them. This perspective was represented most clearly in the point of view of Lazarus and Walsh. *Creatives* who develop the art and copy for brand campaigns saw instead an opportunity for a better, more innovative creative product. Bassat, Hamilton, and Putter were strong advocates for this perspective. *Media, Information Services, Planning, et al.* are the functions that support account services and creatives in planning and producing campaigns. During debates, questions arose about what a brand focused vision implied for their work. O'Dea, Wright, and Reid showed particular concern for how the new direction would affect all internal functions.

Discipline *Advertising* focused on traditional mass marketing and had suffered the most damaging losses between 1989-1992. Producing consistently better media campaigns and winning back large accounts were strong priorities, championed in debates by Beers, Lazarus, Walsh, and Hamilton. *Direct Marketing,* which created targeted advertising (e.g., catalogues, coupons, infomercials), had performed well prior to Beers' takeover. Direct's priority, articulated by Wright and Thedens, was establishing a long-term commitment to brandbuilding through a wider range of communication services. As initially articulated, Brand Stewardship seemed to better reflect the interests of advertising.

Region The *U.S.* offices, particularly corporate headquarters in New York, were Ogilvy's traditional center. Highly autonomous, with large U.S.-based accounts, and flagging performance, priorities centered around restoring confidence and aggressively regaining accounts for each office. Beers and Lazarus articulated the U.S. position. The *Europe* and *Asia/Pacific* regions had each outperformed most U.S. offices in 1989-1992. Top priorities included meeting client demands for efficiencies and coordinated services across the region. Compared to the U.S. view of Brand Stewardship as a creative philosophy, these regions saw a structural solution. Representatives were Reid, Thedens, Wright, Walsh, and O'Dea.

Global vs. Local *Worldwide Client Service directors,* responsible for international account coordination, sought to direct Ogilvy away from geographic fragmentation and toward a more flexible organizational design. O'Dea was their strongest advocate. *Local office and country presidents,* emphasized Ogilvy's position as "the most local of the internationals, the most international of the locals." Reid and Lazarus articulated this position.

Parent Company *WPP,* concerned about declines in net income and low operating margins, pushed for a focus on financial results. Reid was a consistent voice for financial discipline. *Ogilvy & Mather* emphasized that a long-term commitment to a brand focus (and all its implications) required sufficient resources.

Case: Trilogy Farm
Primary Chapter: Chapter 2
Secondary Chapters: Chapters 5, 11 & 12

Introduction: Trilogy Farm illustrates the entrepreneurial struggles of a three-year old business in the hunter jumper barn business. Michelle Heine, the new business owner, had assumptions and expectations that were confronted by numerous unexpected challenges from inside and outside the organization. The central strategic issue focused on aligning internal resources and capabilities with trends in a competitive environment that was generally based upon 'gentlemanly agreement'. Multiple conflicts among employees concerning the strategic direction required management attention such as the tension between providing costly high quality service versus keeping tight control over costs. The success of the hunter jumper business was closely tied to the success of the customers' ability to win equestrian competitions. A clear vision was established for the strategic direction of the business. But significant challenges confronted the implementation process of trying to achieve what appeared to be contradictory features such as being fun and serious.

Strategy Diamond: Trilogy Farms deals with a differentiating strategy that is centered on integrated differentiation *and* cost leadership which bogs them down into a 'stuck-in-the-middle' strategy. While easily discernible in hindsight, it illustrates the need for a precise upfront differentiating objective including the potential risks and benefits to the image of the company and ultimately its economic feasibility.

The Dynamic Nature of Strategy: The case offers insight into the complexities of implementing even the simplest of strategic moves on changing fronts such as customer relations, supplier's cost and availability, and competition.

Formulation/Implementation: The main points of discussion in the case are the challenges associated with the transferring of a strategy, that in the mind of the individual is clear and succinct but which becomes ambiguous and elusive when it is implemented. The link between formulation and implementation is poignant here. The internal conflicts Michelle is dealing with illustrate the difficulty of implementing a strategy that attempts to encapsulate conflicting directions.

Strategic Leadership: Michelle's relationship with her partners and her employees gives an opportunity to examine leadership roles in partnerships and roles in disturbance handling.

TRILOGY FARM
TEACHING NOTE

by
Diana J. Wong-MingJi, Eastern Michigan University
Phone: (734) 487-6823
Email: Diana.Wong@emich.edu

Michelle Lane, Bowling Green State University
Phone: (419) 372-9512
Email: mlheine@cba.bgsu.edu

1.   CASE SYNOPSIS

Trilogy Farm illustrated the entrepreneurial struggles of a three-year old business in the hunter jumper barn business. Michelle Heine, the new business owner, had assumptions and expectations that were confronted by numerous unexpected challenges from inside and outside the organization. The central strategic issue focused on aligning internal resources and capabilities with trends in a competitive environment that was generally based upon 'gentlemanly agreement'. Multiple conflicts among employees concerning the strategic direction required management attention such as the tension between providing costly high quality service versus keeping tight control over costs. The success of the hunter jumper business was closely tied to the success of the customers' ability to win equestrian competitions.

The case is suitable for undergraduate or graduate courses in strategic management, entrepreneurship, and small business. A clear vision was established for the strategic direction of the business. But significant challenges confronted the strategy implementation to achieve what appeared to be contradictory features such as being a hunter jumper barn that was serious about riding and a fun place to be.

2.   OBJECTIVES

Students will be able to use the case study of Trilogy Farm to
- apply strategic management concepts to analyze internal and external dynamics;
- evaluate an entrepreneur's opportunities, resources, and capabilities for future viability to be profitable;
- analyze the complexities of making managerial decisions under conditions of significant pressures of limited resources, increasing losses, internal conflicts, and potential new opportunities.

3.   COURSE TARGETS

a. Business Policy and Strategy – suggested position of this case at the start of a course to stimulate discussion and thinking about the strategic complexities of a seemingly simple small business or in the middle of the course to conduct a thorough application of different strategy concepts. Trilogy Farm is a case that illustrates how things appear obvious in hindsight but much more difficult to see when one is actually in the situation. Students with little experience can relate to

213

the unique situation of a hunter jumper barn because the business does not have a high level complexity. But the challenges of running a small business become quite real. The case of Trilogy Farm is suitable for class discussions, a group written assignment, and a comprehensive exam.

b. Entrepreneurship – suggested position of this case at the beginning of the course to stimulate thinking about the multiple challenges of starting a business, even one in a competitive environment that is based on 'gentlemanly agreement'. Some students may consider starting a business with a compatible partner but the case illustrates the need for more careful considerations of basic issues in forming a business partnership. Many businesses are challenged by intense rivalry but the low level competition in the environment sets this case apart. This case can be use as a pre-test for students who have taken a strategy course and entering into an entrepreneurship course. Within an entrepreneurship course, Trilogy Farm would also be suitable for class discussion, written case assignment, and a case exam.

4.   AUDIENCE

a. Undergraduate Students for case discussion, written assignment or take home exam

b. Executive Students for case discussion in the middle of a course.

5.   CONCEPTS AND TOPICS

a. **Porter's Five Forces for industry analysis** addressed a competitive environment that was based on 'gentlemanly agreement' (this is the term used in the industry). The competitive environment had a relatively stable and cushioned from business cycle fluctuations due to the high socioeconomic status of the customer base. The hunter jumper barn business has three dimensions that range from local to state to national horse competition circuits. The case provided information on the competitive forces of buyers (low bargaining power), suppliers (low to moderate bargaining power), and intensity of rivalry (low intensity of rivalry) while the competitive forces of new entrants (moderate barriers to entry) and substitutes (high threat from other potential recreational activities) have to be extrapolated from reading the case and the reader's general knowledge.

b. **Competitive dynamics** directly focused on the immediate competitors of Trilogy Farms. Descriptions of the four immediate competitors and Trilogy Farm allowed students to rank order their relative importance to one another and the close relationships among the competitors. Particular quotes emphasized the coexistence of the barns engaging in 'gentle*manly*' (sic) competition for customers, which was quite unique from the fierce intense competitive pressures of many industries in the business media.

c. **Generic business level strategies** at Trilogy Farm centered on an integrated differentiation and cost leadership or 'stuck-in-the-middle' strategy. The internal conflicts illustrated the difficulty of implementing a strategic direction that attempted to encapsulate conflicting directions.

d. **Strategic Vision** was clearly articulated to provide the organization with a direction for future development. But there was a lack of policy and coherent unity among the organizational stakeholders to move the firm towards fulfilling the vision. The internal employee conflicts and possibly, the late diversification efforts created difficulties in achieving necessary results for future survival. The importing and selling of German horses may be a distraction from successfully implementing the current vision.

e. **Internal analysis of firm resources and value chain activities** in a service business were also relevant. The strengths and weaknesses of Trilogy Farm allowed for various options to be considered. Important decisions needed to be made about how to allocate the resources and energies of the management and employees.

f. **International business strategy** can be considered as global differentiation for a small business to engage in diversification activities.

6. LEARNING OBJECTIVES

The students will be able to

a. Evaluate the numerous assumptions of a new business that is entering into the hunter jumper barn business;

b. Develop insights into important elements of forming business partnerships to start a business;

c. Analyze the strengths and weaknesses of a small company's internal resources;

d. Examine the multiple difficulties of implementing an integrated strategic vision that attempts to fulfill seemingly contradictory directions of being 'serious' and 'fun';

e. Discuss diversification opportunities in a global context for a small business;

f. Use Trilogy Farm as an example of competitive dynamics that are based on 'gentlemanly agreement' as compared to other class discussions related to more competitive environments.

7. RELATED READINGS

Related to strategic mission and visions:
a. Duncan, W.J. 1999. *Management: Ideas and Action*. New York, Oxford University Press, p. 122-125.
b. Ireland, R.D. & Hitt, M.A. 1992. Mission statements: Importance, challenge, and recommendations for development, *Business Horizons*, 35(3): 34-42.
c. Baum, J.R., Locke, E.A., & Kirkpatrick, S.A. 1998. A longitudinal study of the relation of vision and vision communication to venture growth in entrepreneurial firms, *Journal of Applied Psychology*, 83(1): 43-54.

Starting a business with a partner:
d. Lussier, R. N. 1995. Startup business advice from business owners to would-be entrepreneurs. *S.A.M. Advanced Management Journal*. 60(1): 10-13.
e. Timmons, J. A. 1977. The team: key to venture success. *Executive*. (4)1: 22-25.

Related to Internal Resources and Value Chain:
f. Hall, R. 1991. The contribution of intangible resources to business success. *Journal of General Management*, 16(4): 41-52.

g. Barney, J.B. 1991. Firm resources and sustained competitive advantage. *Journal of Management*, 17(1): 99-120.

h. Dess, G.G., Gupta, A., Hennart, J.F. & Hill, C.W.L. 1995 Conducting and integrating strategy research at the international, corporate and business levels: Issues and directions. *Journal of Management*, 21(3): 357-393.

Related to Conducting SWOT Analysis

i. Smith, Julia A 1999. The behaviour and performance of young micro firms: Evidence from businesses in Scotland. *Small Business Economics*. (13): 185-200.

j. Hill, T. & Westbrook, R. 1997. SWOT analysis: It's time for a product recall. *Long Range Planning*. 30(1): 46-52.

k. Valentin, E K. 2001. SWOT analysis from a resource-based view. *Journal of Marketing Theory & Practice*. 9(2): 54-69.

Related to Diversification in Small Business:

l. Robson, G., Gallagher, C., Daly, M. 1993. Diversification strategy and practice in small firms. International Small Business Journal. 11(2): 37-53.

m. Sandvig, J. C. & Coakley, L. 1998. Best practices in small firm diversification. Business Horizons. 41(3):33-40.

n. Farjoun, M. 1998. The independent and joint effects of the skill and physical bases of relatedness in diversification. *Strategic Management Journal*. 19: 611-630.

o. Lesaux, P. B. 1993. Atlantic Canada poised to benefit from new world markets. *Canadian Business Review*. 20(2): 40-41.

Related to Competitive Dynamics:

p. Grimm, C.M. & Smith, K.G. 1997. *Strategy as action: Industry rivalry and coordination*. Cincinnati, OH, South-Western Publishers.

q. Fehr, E. & Schmidt, K. M. 1999. A theory of fairness, competition, and cooperation. *The Quarterly Journal of Economics*. 114(3): 817-868.

r. Lant, T. K., Milliken, F. J. & Batra, B. 1992. The Role of Managerial Learning and Interpretation in Strategy. *Strategic Management Journal*. 13(8): 585-608.

8. TEACHING OUTLINE AND ASSIGNMENT QUESTIONS

Problem Statement

a. What was the essential strategic issue that Michelle Heine faced at Trilogy Farm?

The strategic problem was the need to fulfill the strategic vision by creating the alignment between internal resources in Trilogy Farm and external opportunities. Trilogy Farm needed to compete effectively in a low rivalry environment of the hunter jumper barn industry.

Internal Analysis

b. How did Michelle's assumptions influence some of the organizational outcomes and firm performance?

The partnership between Michelle and Pamela appeared to be a mutually compatible relationship where they contributed complementary resources to the business. Michelle provided the capital while Pamela contributed the horse training and barn management expertise. Michelle assumed that her partner Pamela Wallace had all the requisite capabilities to fulfill the responsibilities of running a hunter jumper barn and providing a comprehensive lesson program. Michelle relied on Pamela's report of qualifications and business forecasts without conducting a reference check, completing an operating agreement, or verifying costs through research to create the pro forma projections. The minimal amount of experience and knowledge Michelle had in running a hunter jumper barn contributed to the subsequent development of difficulties and the ending of the partnership. As a result, Michelle became the sole owner with a series of financial losses.

c. What was the SWOT analysis of Trilogy Farm?

Strengths – clear vision; pleasant clubhouse facilities; upgraded facilities and physical assets; enthusiastic talented head trainer; large lesson program to provide a range of times for group lessons; Michelle's ability to rebuild damaged relationships with customers; participation in horse showing the B and C circuits; and convenient geographical location to the target market. Michelle ability to rebuild customer relationship was an indicator of her interpersonal skills to develop a customer base for Trilogy Farm. The proximity to Toledo made the location attractive to potential riders who want to serious train for competitions. The lesson program was supported with a talented trainer in small group lessons that allowed for more individualized attention.

Weaknesses – increasing debt load due to under estimated costs; excessive financial commitments at the start of the business; unsubstantiated assumptions that lowered the organizational performance from the beginning; unresolved conflicts between the property manager and the head trainer; gossiping and rumor mills among the customers are creating unpleasant group dynamics; weak development of central business focus in the hunter jumper barn to support diversification activities; management's lack of experience in the business. Michelle had many conflicting distractions because she was frustrated by many of the people issues among the employees and customers. She seemed to have minimal expertise apart from loving horses to run a hunter jumper barn business and a similar set of dynamics was repeated with importing the German horses. Michelle does have the enthusiasm for running the business even when things are not working out. She was also learning fast from her mistakes.

Opportunities – community organizations willing to engage in partnerships in lesson programs, which provided the potential to expand the target market; international opportunities for diversification to provide an additional source of cash flow; and low level of competition that allows time for business development. The external environment was relatively stable where the competitors appeared to be somewhat supportive of one another because of the community proximity and relationships they have amongst themselves. There seemed to be an outstanding unmet demand for German horses that may provide Trilogy Farm with a source of cash flow. The current resources can be leveraged to engage in this business.

Threats – poor results from horse show competitions may lead customers to leave Trilogy Farm for another hunter jumper barn to obtain more consistent training; creditors may become impatient with delayed payments and refuse supplies in the future. Trilogy Farm faced few competitive threats from competitors but suppliers and creditors may not continue to extend their support if Trilogy Farm does not turn the business around.

d. What was the relationship between the vision for Trilogy Farm and the implementation of the business strategy?

The vision at Trilogy Farm was "to provide a riding facility that was serious about training and horse care but casual, relaxed and a fun place to be." The generic business level strategy was focus differentiation because Trilogy allocated resources for higher than above average quality in terms of the horse care, lesson programs with smaller groups than competitors, and a new clubhouse. However, the competitive pricing did not reflect a differentiation approach to cover all the related costs of implementing a differentiation strategy. As a result, the emerging business strategy was an integrated focus differentiation and cost leadership or also referred to as 'stuck-in-the-middle' when poorly implemented. The poor implementation was also reflected in the relationship between the property manager and the head trainer who had a conflict over the strategic direction by focusing on different directions for the business. Michelle's assumptions about managing a hunter jumper barn business were based more on her interests and passions than on an objective analysis of all the inputs for starting an entrepreneurial venture. She did not have enough substantiated research to support a more successful start into the business. But she learnt lessons quickly enough to make a tough decision to dissolve the partnership.

e. How did the international diversification activities fit with the vision of the business?

German horses had a desirable reputation in the US market because of their numerous desirable qualities for riders competing in horse shows. The training and caring for German horses allowed Trilogy Farm to leverage some of the business's capabilities. But managing the purchasing and selling functions required different capabilities that were not currently in existing portfolio of internal resources. The development of the additional marketing on a national basis and managing logistics for international purchases demanded more management attention than what was currently available. The primary business focus was not sufficiently developed for expansion by diversification. Some of the internal issues required management attention to resolve before extending itself further. However, if the sales of German horses occurred quickly, the business strategy may evolve in a substantially different direction.

This question allows for significant debate and application of motivations for diversification.

External Analysis

f. Discuss the nature of the competitive environment by applying Porter's five forces of competition.
Intensity of rivalry was low because the hunter jumper barns were geographically clustered around the buyers of the geographical location in the Toledo market and there were close and frequent interactions among the barn owners. The established competitive dynamics were based on 'gentlemanly agreement' where one barn needed to treat the other with respect, especially in the situation where customers were switching barns. Michelle used the analogy of customers switching teams and being considered a defector.
Bargaining Power of Buyers was low and can be separated into two groups – boarders and competitive riders. The two groups may overlap. But both groups had low bargaining power because once someone owned a horse, they had little option about paying for caring expenses. Competitive riders tended to stay with a barn to develop increasing skills for horse show competition. Most of the buyers were families of girls between the ages 7-18 years old from middle to upper income socioeconomic levels. Most buyers lived within a convenient distance to the barns.
Bargaining Power of Suppliers was low because the inputs are basic commodities. A significant issue was the consistency in quality and delivery of supplies for the individual barns. But for the hunter jumper barn industry, there were numerous suppliers and the supplies are basic commodity products that are easily available from local sources. However, the suppliers could be segmented between hay, grain, and bedding for a finer grain analysis where the suppliers of hay

probably had a relatively a little more bargaining power because of consistency in service that was important.

Threat of Substitutes was low. The hunter jumper barn industry provided space and care for horses as well as lesson programs for equestrian competitions. A potential substitute for the outputs of this industry was if an individual had the capabilities to do all this for his/herself. An example would be a farmer who provides lesson programs for his children. Otherwise, there is no other feasible substitute for boarding and caring of horses. If industry boundaries were defined more broadly as the animal sporting industry, the threat of substitute could be higher because alternative sports with animals can be substituted at lower costs.

Threat of New Entrants was somewhat low for the hunter jumper barn industry. The barriers to entry were increased by the limited specialized knowledge required to provide lesson programs. Existing incumbent hunter jumper barns that already had trainers and barns with excellent reputations tended to retain their status by keeping the valuable personnel and knowledge in house. The amount of capital required is not too substantial for someone with moderate means to afford buying a business. Thus, capital requirements are relatively low. Also competitive responses of incumbents to new entrants were not significant because industry competition was based on 'gentlemanly agreement' and somewhat fragmented within geographical clusters.

Therefore, the hunter jumper barn industry has an attractive industry environment for making profitable returns.

g. What is the relationship between the different horse show competition circuits and the hunter jumper barns?

The horse show competition circuits segmented the industry among the different grades of competitors - the better the performance of the riders, the higher the reputation of the hunter jumper barn. Thus, the quality of the lesson program had a critical component in defining the business level strategy for hunter jumper barns. The knowledge and skill level of the trainers played an important role in the intellectual capital of a barn. Also, success in the different circuits exposed the barns at the state and national level to further attract additional customers.

h. What were the competitive dynamics between Trilogy Farm and its direct competitors?

The competitive dynamics of Trilogy Farms resulted in a standard market cycle and possibly a slow market cycle. The industry was in an established stage of end growth and maturity. All the barns operated close to capacity but there may still be potential for further market development if a barn targeted a broader market at lower socioeconomic levels. There was a low level of innovation and competitive action-response dynamics. In fact, as customers attempted to leave Trilogy Farm for another barn, the barn owner approached Michelle to advise her to investigate the matter rather than just taking off with all the customers. The quality of the riding facilities provided an important element in attracting customers but not necessarily in retaining them. For example, Riverdale was a hunter jumper barn but did not necessarily compete for the same customer base as the other three barns. Hence, the most important strategic actions laid in attracting and retaining the critical knowledge and skills for a successful comprehensive lesson program while tactical actions laid in the pricing or décor of the facilities.

8.   Teaching Plan

Introduce the case with a summary of important highlights that include running a relatively young hunter jumper barn business for horse show competitions, increasing financial pressures from negative earnings, and the increasing pressure to make a decision about the future of the business viability.

a. What is the essential strategic problem facing Michelle Heine at Trilogy Farm?
Students may identify various symptoms as the strategic problem such as increasing debt, employee conflict or morale, departing customers, and possibly, erroneously competition by 'gentlemanly agreement'. The question should be related back to strategic concepts concerning alignment of internal resources with external environmental conditions. In this situation, the external environment presents few difficulties to the business. Thus, the focus is on how to create a more coherent and consistent portfolio of internal resources that create the necessary capabilities for success in the hunter jumper barn business.

Internal Analysis

The questions that focus primarily on the internal resources and value chain of Trilogy Farm related to b-f with the answers for discussion as above. An important point is determining which of the generic business level strategy was intended, emergent, and realized. A corporate strategy discussion can address issues of relatedness to the diversification activities and international strategies for a small business. This is an excellent case that illustrates the potential for international expansion with very small business firms.

The discussion order of the external environment can be switched with the internal analysis. The related questions for an internal analysis are listed below with related discussion comments while the answers are found in the previous section. :

b. What were some of Michelle assumptions in starting the hunter jumper barn business?
Students need to examine the case for related evidence and decisions that will help to reconstruct some of the assumptions. But some are clearly stated in the case. An important assumption to emphasize is how people form partnership with people they think they know and the lack of investigations into the background. Hence, the role of trust for starting a business together and the assumption of the 'goodness' in others merit some consideration.

Students will have to build assumptions about Michelle's capabilities to run a hunter jumper barn apart from being able to provide the capital resources. A follow up question on this point can be 'what do her actions say about her management and leadership style?' A starting place for this question lies in the vision of the organization and adding the subsequent developments of the organization with it.

c. How did Michelle's assumptions influence some of the organizational outcomes and firm performance?
Students need to relate how assumptions drive some of the business decisions and outcome among the employees and customers. Without checking on the financial projects, one of the outcomes was the unexpected high cost even though the revenue projects were close to the forecasted numbers. However, revenue earnings projection was disrupted by the assumptions concerning the partnership and the related problems that resulted.

d. What is the SWOT analysis of Trilogy Farm?
See comments in the above section.

e. What is the relationship between the vision for Trilogy Farm and the business strategy implemented?
Trilogy Farm was consistent in supporting its vision with the allocation of resources. However, the implementation process with the employees was not effective due to their dysfunctional conflicts of myopic purposes. Each one, the property manager and the head trainer, was primarily

concerned with their functions without broader consideration for the organization or for the necessity of teamwork.

f. How do the international diversification activities fit with the vision of the business?
There are potential synergies with the existing students with the buying, training, and selling of German horses. But students need to assess the existing capabilities to support the exciting opportunity of international diversification as decision for this business. The current weaknesses may prevent the Trilogy Farm from achieving the necessary integration to achieve synergy between the two business activities. This is a good point for debate because the situation is simple and tangible enough for students to relate to at an undergraduate level.

External Analysis

g. Discuss the nature of the competitive environment by applying Porter's five forces of competition.
Most undergraduate business students are confronted with many businesses facing intense competition. They tend to be quite exciting. However, by having a more stable and attractive competitive environment, that may even be mundane, students have an opportunity to focus on the development business strategy within the firm.

h. What is the relationship between the different horse show competition circuits and the hunter jumper barns?
Students have an opportunity to consider the horse show competitions at the different levels as a way to segment the industry. More importantly, it provides an external measure of firm performance with customers apart from the financial measures. The achievement of customers becomes explicit in this case and can be related to supplier-buyer relationships in a supply chain discussion.
Also, an important stakeholder analysis can be integrated into this discussion.

i. What are the competitive dynamics between Trilogy Farm and its direct competitors?
Students can access the competitive dynamics as being somewhat slow because strategic action on the part of one competitor does not necessarily result in an action from another competitor. This is the result of the nature of the 'team' orientations of the barns and the various segmentations in the industry. Also, the other four competing barns are operating at close to capacity with little need to be aggressive about attracting more customers. Their extensive experience and reputation in the area attracts customers. Trilogy Farm needs to expand their lesson program in order to attract customers. Trilogy Farm may need to reconsider the size of the group lessons compared to the other barns in the area.

9. RESEARCH DISCLOSURE

Almost all the data gathered for the case came from interviews with Michelle Heine with informed consent to have the information used for research and teaching. Additional documents concerning Trilogy Farms, the hunter jumper barn industry, and horse showing competition came from library research and internet websites.

Reference Sources:
Kursinski, A. & Lorraine, M. *Anne Kursinski's Riding and Jumping Clinic: AStep by Step Course for Winning in the Hunter and Jumper Rings*, Doubleday, 1995.
Website for the National Hunter/Jumper Council of USA Equestrian www.nhjc.org

Website for the USA Equestrian, Inc. www.equestrian.org.
American Horse Council Foundation,
1700 K St. NW, Suite 300, Washington DC 20006
American Horse Council Foundation, *The Economic Impact of the Horse Industry in the United States*, 1999..

10. EPILOGUE

As of May 2004, Michelle Heine continued to stay in business with Trilogy Farm. She developed more knowledge about German horses and created connections on the east coast for selling a couple of German horses. Michelle closed down the lesson program but a trainer asked to lease some barn stalls and the use of the farm to put on a lesson program. Michelle agreed to the business deal for a temporary period of about ten months and found the arrangement to be quite viable. She did not have to deal with the conflicts among the employees nor the gossiping among the customers in this lease arrangement. The trainer left in April, 2004 and another trainer approached Michelle for a similar leasing arrangement. Michelle agreed because she found the new business model of leasing stall and pasture spaces allowed her to have her hunter jumper barn with less stress, financial stability, and excess managerial capacity and attention to work on the importing of German horses which appeared to be quite lucrative.

Case: Formula One Constructors
Primary Chapter: Chapter 3 (resources)
Secondary Chapter: Chapter 6 (dynamic strategy)

Introduction: The Formula Constructors case focuses on the nature of competitive advantage in a highly competitive context; a context in which the nature and source of competitive advantage seems to change every few years. This case focuses on a unique situation—the pursuit of the constructors cup in formula racing. It is ideal for studying resources and capabilities and their effect on competitive advantage because all the "firms" have the same goal in mind and the appropriate performance metric is easy to identify. It is also relatively easy to isolate the resources and capabilities possessed by the several racing teams.

Strategy Diamond: As this is a specialized context, not all of the strategy diamond will be utilized in this case. Arenas: some teams do make different choices about which value chain activities they will pursue internally and which they will contract for from suppliers. Vehicles: As not all teams are vertically integrated, there is an opportunity to examine how some use contracts and some use alliances (indeed, alliances with engine manufacturers are critical for at least two teams and the effect of the dissolution of such an alliance is key for one team). Differentiators: not particularly applicable in this case. Staging: there is some opportunity to discuss the building of capabilities over time. Economic Logic: not as applicable in this case, as rather than pursuing profits the teams are pursuing the goal of winning the constructors cup.

Strategic Leadership: The case illustrates the effects of different leadership styles by contrasting the leaderships of three different teams. In some teams there appears to be stronger leadership effects than others.

Formulation/Implementation: Formula One racing is by its nature a team effort. The distinct strategies the various teams pursue are rather easy to identify and this leaves some opportunity to discuss the implementation levers that are utilized by the various teams and see the impact of how the change in a lever has a significant effect for one strategy but less so for others (e.g., recruiting the best drivers is critical for one team but less important for another with superior technology).

The Dynamic Nature of Strategy: The case is ideal to facilitate the dynamic nature of competition and the evolution of competitive advantage. The case begins with Ferrari having an advantage based on a strategy of vertical integration and the technology of powerful engines being key. Ferrari's advantage is eventually eroded by a team which uses an innovation in chassis design to allow it to overcome the disadvantage of power (creating superior aerodynamics). This advantage is then trumped later by the assemblage of an overall superior total package of technology, which is facilitated by alliances with key independent suppliers.

THE FORMULA ONE CONSTRUCTORS: FERRARI 1975–1979; MCLAREN 1988–1991; WILLIAMS 1992–1994; FERRARI 1999–2002 TEACHING NOTE

INTRODUCTION

This teaching note covers a series of mini-cases which are designed to focus on the nature of advantage in a highly competitive context. The resource based view of strategic management is providing both academics and practitioners with new and distinctive approach to strategy. Concepts such as core competence and distinctive capabilities have set an agenda for strategy which has moved the emphasis from industry dynamics to understanding the unique and idiosyncratic capabilities of every organisation. One problem with using and teaching these ideas is finding situations where advantage can be clearly demonstrated and explored from a resource based perspective. The Formula One constructors provides such a unique situation. Here the strategic goal is common to all (to consistently win races) and it is clear to all as to which teams are succeeding and which are not. The purpose of the cases are for the students to explore why particular teams succeeded in particular periods, and how the basis of this advantage was eventually lost.

OVERVIEW OF THE CASES

1. Formula One Constructors (2 pages + table)

    This case provides an overview to the industry and an introduction to the following cases which relate to specific constructors. Formula One has been the premier level of motorsport across the world since the 1950s. Originally an opportunity for car manufacturers to show their prowess and test out their ideas, it has evolved into a highly specialised industry of high technology players who operate with multi-million pound budgets.

    The rationale for using the Formula One constructors to explore strategy from a resource based perspective is introduced here. In short, it is one of the few situations where we can accurately compare the performance of organizations who hold the same goal in a changing environment over time.

    Since the Formula One series started in the 1950s, the competitive nature of the sport is illustrated by the fact that only three teams have ever [won] the constructors' championship for three or more consecutive years. These three occaisions provide the focus for the subsequent manufacturers cases.

2. Ferrari: 1975–1977 (4 pages)

    This is the oldest of the three cases and relates to a period where Formula One is moving from enthusiastic one-man bands to highly professional organizations with multi-million pound budgets. Ferrari have a distinctive pedigree, as the oldest and uniquely Italian team Ferrari were notably different to the rest. The autocratic approach of Enzo Ferrari created many problems, but there is little doubt of the spectacular talent and resource held by the Maranello team. The combination of three individuals: Mauro Forghieri, Luca Montezemolo and Niki Lauda are the focus of this successful period. Between them they succeeded in creating a car which was different and successful. Because of Ferrari's unique approach others could not imitate their approach. However changes in technology, Montezemolo's promotion and Lauda's accident all contributed to this highly complex network breaking down. Despite some success in the early eighties Ferrari have been unable to translate their wealth of talent and resource into sustained success.

Key Words:

Wealthy; Passionate; Unique Image, Clear and distinctive philosophy to car design and technology, hard work.

3. McLaren International: 1988–1991 (4 pages)

McLaren are distinctive in Formula One because of the 22 year relationship they enjoyed with Philip Morris, promoting their Marlboro brand. The professional management style of Ron Dennis also set a new standard in the industry. McLaren's initial success was through the design talents of John Barnard who developed the first carbon based race-car chassis. In 1988 the McLaren success was spectacular. The marriage of Honda engines, the driving skills of Prost and Senna and the MP4 chassis were unbeatable. However the success ended dramatically when Honda pulled out and Senna, believing McLaren to be no longer competitive decided to move to Williams.

Key Words:

Professional, Leadership (Ron Dennis), Sponsor involvement, Honda engines, Drivers (Senna & Prost), the best of everything.

4. Williams Grand Prix Engineering: 1992–1994 (4 Pages)

The success of WGPE can be attributed to a pragmatic 'engineering' based approach, this is personified through the long standing partnership between Frank Williams and Patrick Head. They placed great emphasis on developing their relationship with engine supplier Renault (having disastorously lost Honda in 1987). This was coupled with an [incremental] and evolutionary approach to design with other teams; innovations being applied in a practical and more reliable fashion.

In marked contrast to other teams the Williams philosophy tended to see the driver as a secondary factor, with many big names being ignominiously sacked by FW at the end of the season. This disregard for driver talent and their failure to persuade Renault not to supply their engine to the Benetton team, led to the combination of Benetton and driver Michael Schumacher ending the Williams domination.

Key Words:

Engineering, Williams/Head partnership, taking others ideas and making them work, relationship with Renault, team and cars more important than drivers.

5. Ferrari: 1999–2002 (4 pages)

This case focuses on Ferrari's transition into a modern F1 team following the death of Enzo Ferrari in 1988. It illustrates the company's attempts to absorb the new aerodynamic and composite technologies which had emerged from Britain's 'Motorsport Valley'. The fact that Italian icon Ferrari actually located their design and manufacturing operation in the UK was both a well-kept secret and indicative of the highly 'sticky' nature of technological knowledge. It also illustrates how transplanting a working team (Michael Schumacher and the technical from Benetton) can speed up the process of team development in this highly competitive context. Ferrari's success is a testimony to some bold recruiting decisions by Montezemolo and also the skills and motivational effects of a driver such as Michael Schumacher.

Key Words:

Technological change, organizational change, dynamic capability, team development, integration of commercial partnerships.

Where to use the cases

These cases are designed to be used on a MBA programme where students consider the application of the resource based view in order to understand competitive advantage. They would be located in a module which is concerned with competitive or business level strategy. They also provide a useful bridge between competitive strategy issues and the internal workings of organizations, for example, whilst the cases are relatively brief the students are still able to understand the distinctive cultures which exist.

The cases support much of the academic work on resource based view. Some of the following papers can be used to stimulate discussion: Wernerfeldt (1984); Dierickx & Cool (1989); Barney (1991); Amit & Schoemaker (1993).

In addition to a graduate level course, these cases can be used effectively in a management development programme to encourage delegates to consider sources of competitive advantage, the cases could be used to illustrate the principals which the delegates could then go on to apply to their own organizations. The cases could also be used to illustrate the resource based view on a undergraduate programme.

LEARNING OBJECTIVES

The overall learning objectives can be summarised as follows:

1. To understand that whilst strategy can be seen as generic at a high level, it will always be idiosyncratic at the organisational level, even where organizations are in the same industry and all have the same goal. Therefore strategic *management* has to focus on the idiosyncratic characteristics of every organisation in order to develop a strategy which will work in this context.
2. Strategies which are based on highly mobile resources (e.g. individual drivers, designers or engine suppliers) need to focus on either finding ways of locking in these resources, or in building competence to allow them to continually find and acquire new ones.
3. Whilst highly complex and idiosyncratic resources are particularly difficult to imitate (e.g. Ferrari) they are also difficult to manage and vulnerable to changes in the environment or a loss in any of the elements.
4. Sustained advantage is often achieved through the linkages between resources rather than the resource themselves (e.g. the way the drivers links in to the design engineers).
5. A shift in the environment can suddenly change the value of particular resources, an external view is therefore fundamental to sustaining advantage.
6. It can also raise the point that advantage can be created by luck: a fortuitous combination of resources or a luck event in the environment. This can be used to develop the debate about whether managers influence strategy or just postrationalise their luck in strategic terms.

TEACHING THE CASES

There are a number of different ways in which the cases can be used. It works particularly well in situations where the participants spend sometime in groupwork before discussing the cases, such as on a MBA programme.

Here the overview case would be provided to all the students (The Formula One Constructors) with separate syndicate groups being given one of the individual constructor cases to consider. A series of questions are used to guide the way in which the students approach the case:

1. What do you need in order to succeed in Formula One?
2. Why you think your team were successful during this period?
3. Why were they unable to sustain this success? or What could they have done to sustain their success further?

What do you need in order to succeed in Formula One?

This question is intended to get the students to identify the generic model which you need to succeed in this industry. At a very simplistic level this can be described as having the best driver, the best car (achieved by bringing together the chassis design and engine technology) and the best supporting team which provides race tactics, pit stops etc. All of this is supported by finance which comes from the ability to attract and retain sponsors (this is less important for Ferrari who are owned by Fiat). This discussion can be developed by discussed as to what 'best' means and how this is created. It raises issues about separating the causes for success from the effects of success: ie is Ron Dennis the cause of success for McLaren? or is this a perception created by the fact that he happens to manage a successful team?

[Why do you] think your team were successful during this period?

We now move from the generic level of success to consider the specifics of each team. The issues raised will be attributed to personalities, but will also be about the ways in which different teams approached the task of winning the championship:

Ferrari (1)

Ferrari were successful because everything worked together. Whilst they have always had a huge wealth of technical expertise and resources, the problem has been getting this to work together, in the past this had been excacerbated by the 'divide and rule' style to Enzo Ferrari. This working together was exemplified in the relationship between three key individuals: Driver Niki Lauda, Designer Mauro Forghieri and Team Manager Luca Montezemolo.

The other reason for Ferrari's success was that because they had their own unique approach (e.g. they built their own engines and gearboxes) it was very difficult for other competitors to imitate them as they did not have access to the same technology as Ferrari.

McLaren International

McLaren were successful because they were able to put together the best of everything. They secured exclusive use of the Honda engine at a time when it was the most powerful and reliable; they were also able to secure the services of the best drivers around (Senna and Prost). This was due to the high level of funds made available by sponsor Philip Morris. Another issue which often comes up is the commercial and leadership skills of Ron Dennis.

Williams Grand Prix Engineering

Williams' success was due to their engineering focus which enabled them to take many of innovations developed by other teams and to turn these into a car which was both fast and very reliable. This engineering focus can be attributed to the long standing partnership between Frank Williams and Patrick Head. Williams were notable in their disregard for drivers and their attention to building a wide ranging relationship with their engine supplier Renault.

Ferrari (2)

Ferrari were successful because they recognized the need for radical change and were not afraid to take the decisions necessary to achieve this. Their use of the expertise located in motorsport valley and the recruitment of Michael Schumacher and the technical team who supported him were central to this. However it is also important to note that Montezemolo was able to separate out Ferrari from the politics at Fiat and also used Jean Todt to bring in the management discipline which he himself had been responsible for in the mid-seventies.

Why were they unable to sustain this success? or What could they have done to sustain their success further?

Here the students will focus on the reason as to why the advantage was removed. This also allows them to consider whether or not anything could have been done to prevent this loss of advantage.

Ferrari (1)

The reason for Ferrari's loss of advantage can be isolated into two factors: First, the discontinuity created by the promotion of Montezemolo to head up the whole of Fiat's motorsport operation and Lauda's accident which took him out of racing for around six months. Second, Ferrari's unique approach constrained them in terms of responding to new innovations, most notably the introduction of ground-effect which required a slim 'V' configuration engine rather than Ferrari's traditional flat 12. This raises the point about whether an organisation which does all its activity in house can keep pace with the combined efforts of the many 'generic' suppliers used by the other teams.

McLaren International

The reasons for McLaren's demise were very simple. Honda pulled out of Formula One. This in turn broke the virtuous circle which attracted the best drivers and Ayrton Senna moved to Williams. This raised the question in terms of what value McLaren themselves generated as the key to success seemed to clearly reside in Honda engines and the skills of Ayrton Senna both of which were relatively mobile resources.

In terms of what they could have done, there is certainly evidence to suggest that McLaren chief Ron Dennis should have considered the possibility of a Honda withdrawal more seriously. It illustrates how phenomenal success can blind management to the possibility of change.

Williams Grand Prix Engineering

In the case of Williams, their advantage was eroded through a series of events. First Renault decided to provide engines to the Benetton team, this coupled with the loss of some of their know-how through their junior designers moving to other teams and the recruitment of superior drivers (specifically Michael Schumacher to Benetton) led to the advantage of the Williams car being eroded.

However it could also be argued that Williams were still in a position to dominate. When Michael Schumacher left Benetton to join Ferrari the Benetton team failed to sustain their advantage and Williams once again became dominant.

Ferrari (2)

The jury is still out on this one and it is a question of seeing what the current issues are. I suspect that the relaxing of tyre regulations will allow the Michelin teams to close the gap. [Ferrari] is also in danger of losing motivation simply because of the high level of success they have currently enjoyed. How to keep motivation going when you are constantly successful is an interesting area for discussion.

The recommended approach is to start with each syndicate presenting their responses to the case questions. At the end of each syndicate the instructor would summarise the key points on the board, these would include the key words outlined in the synopsis. As each group presents the instructor will finish up with the three constructors as headings but with a quite distinctive set of key words under each. This enables the session to move onto the learning points. The way this is handled will depend on learning maturity, but it is best to simply ask the plenary session what conclusions they would draw from the different presentations they have heard. This will take the discussion into the notion that whilst at a high level strategy might be generic at a management level it is highly idiosyncratic and context specific.

DATA COLLECTION

These cases have all been written from archival data. The BP library of motoring located at the National Motor Museum, Beaulieu, United Kingdom holds the largest archive of data on the motorsport industry. The data has been gathered from weekly, monthly and annual publications such as Autosport, Autocar, Motorsport etc. For each of the teams a scan was undertaken for any data in the period of focus with the preceding and following years also evaluated.

SOME USEFUL WEBSITES FOR UPDATING

www.autosport.com
www.grandprix.com
www.ity-fl.com
http://news.bbc.co.ulc/sportl/hi/motorsport/formula_one

This teaching note was written by Professor Mark Jenkins, Cranfield University School of Management. It was prepared to accompany the case series 'The Formula One Constructors' (reference numbers 399–001–1 to 399–004–1, 301–056–1 and 303–094–1). The cases were compiled from published sources. © 1997, 2003 & 2005, Cranfield University School of Management. No part of this publication may be copied, stored, transmitted, reproduced or distributed in any form or medium whatsoever without the permission of the copyright owner.

Case Synopsis
Case: Prince Edward Island Preserve Co.
Primary Chapter: Chapter 3
Secondary Chapters: Chapters 4, 5 & 12

Introduction: Prince Edward Island Preserve Co. is a producer and marketer of specialty food products. The case opens with the company president contemplating future expansion. Two cities were of particular interest: Toronto and Tokyo. At issue was whether consumers in both markets should be pursued, and if so, how. The owner, Bruce McNaughton is faced with the choices available for achieving further growth including mail order, distributors, and company controlled stores. The case helps students watch existing resources and capabilities with potential growth opportunities.

Strategy Diamond: Prince Edward Island Preserve Co. offers substantial detail for a broad discussion on all aspects of the strategic diamond. Staging is addressed in McNaughton's timing and speed of potential expansion into Toronto or Tokyo. Arenas are detailed in the channels and segments that the company could use and emphasize in their growth. The strategic vehicles become an issue in analyzing the company's potential move into new markets by examining possible joint ventures and licensing/franchising options. Differentiating is emphasized by the Prince Edward Island Preserve Co. commitment to quality and image, solidifying a niche market strategy. Economic logic can be discussed to determine whether profitability can be maintained using this strategy considering the barriers the company would face in international expansion.

The Dynamic Nature of Strategy: The case illustrates the need for reevaluation when a company outgrows the original domestic strategy and begins an era of evolving into an international company.

Formulation/Implementation: The case provides sufficient data for students to do an analysis of the financial viability for each major growth alternative (mail order, distributors, and company controlled stores), and then discuss the possible benefits, risks and challenges of implementing each one.

Strategic Leadership: Human resource problems are arising and Bruce McNaughton will soon face some tough decisions on placing the right people in the right positions and making correct leadership decisions to keep the people he already has.

PRINCE EDWARD ISLAND PRESERVE CO.
TEACHING NOTE

SYNOPSIS

The president of P.E.I. Preserves is contemplating expansion to Toronto and/or Tokyo. The choices available for achieving growth include mail order, distributors and company controlled stores.

CASE OBJECTIVES

1. To illustrate the importance of focus — both in terms of scope of potential activities, and on the tightening up of existing activities.
2. To provide an example of the typical growth problems confronted by owner-managers when their business moves from Stage 1 (entrepreneurially dominated) to Stage 2 (need for professional management).
3. To show that firms can begin to internationalize without leaving their home country. In this instance the company can best reach Japanese consumers visiting *in Canada*, rather than prematurely going after Japanese consumers in Japan.

POSITION IN THE COURSE

This case is intended for use in an International Business course or Strategic Management course. If used in International Business, it would best be positioned at the very beginning as a lead off case on Internationalization. If used in a two-term Strategic Management course, it serves as a useful review case on Strategy Formulation, and would be positioned at the end of the first term.

TEACHING APPROACH

We spend nearly all of the class time on the preserves part of the business, only looking at the (problems of managing an unrelated) restaurant in our closing summary on the need for focus.

Our first objective in class is to move the discussion beyond the more narrow issue of store/mail order/distributor in Toronto/Tokyo to the more general question of how McNaughton should grow his business. Where we want to ultimately land up is with the recognition that McNaughton has unrealized potential with relatively accessible Canadian and Japanese consumers in the rest of Canada. While McNaughton should definitely be targeting Toronto area consumers, there are other Canadian markets he should also be pursuing. Further, he should not be entertaining thoughts of major penetration of the market *in Japan* until he has maximized his more profitable domestic opportunities.

In order to move the discussion beyond the narrow issue, we start by putting up the headings for the major growth alternatives available to McNaughton. These are: stores (either in Tokyo or Toronto), mail order, discount distributors (i.e. Danamar, or the Japanese distributor that would have to be located to effectively target the Japanese consumer at the ¥2,000 price point), and standard distributors (i.e., those currently in place).

We then proceed through a quick financial analysis of each alternative. Our objective is to demonstrate that a legitimate argument could be made for the financial viability of each.

We now turn to the single largest part of the class, a comparison of the pros and cons of each of the major alternatives. (Certainly the financial conclusions previously reached are part of this.) During this comparison, we try to simultaneously establish the criteria that we should use for this comparison. The better students will point out that the relative importance of each criterion will change depending on the financial and managerial health of the company.

Once a detailed assessment of the various alternatives has been completed, we move to a discussion of recommendations. As part of this, an implementation schedule is required. We wrap up class by summarizing the case objectives already noted.

CASE RESEARCH METHODOLOGY EMPLOYED

This case is based on field interviews in Canada and Japan, as well as archival study in both countries. Personal interviews were conducted in P.E.I. in July 1991 and July 1992 and in Japan in August 1991. The primary source of information in P.E.I. was company president Bruce McNaughton. At Canadian World in Japan, interviews were held with Kenneth Tallack, Market Research Manager, and Makoto Hatakeyama, Managing Director. Mr. Shige Makino assisted with the latter interviews. The teaching note has been regularly updated during annual visit to P.E.I.

ASSIGNMENT QUESTIONS

1. Can an argument be made in support of the financial viability of each of the major growth alternatives McNaughton is considering?
2. What are the pros and cons of each of the four alternatives: stores, mail order, high volume-low margin distributors (i.e., Danamar) and standard distributors? What criteria should be used for this comparison?
3. What should McNaughton do? Provide an implementation schedule as part of your recommendations.

ANALYSIS

1. The financial viability of each major growth alternative

An argument in support of each of the major growth alternatives can in fact be made. No more than 15 minutes of class time should be spent on this question.

(a) *Sales Volume Required to Break Even with Company Controlled Store in Toronto*

Retail Space (from case)	$30,360	Selling Price/Unit	$5.89
Wages ($8.00/hr × 72 hrs/week)	29,952	-Variable Cost/Unit	1.25
Fixed Costs	$60,312	Contribution Margin/Unit	$4.64

$$\text{Break even} = \frac{\text{Fixed Cost}}{\text{Contribution Margin} / \text{Unit}} \qquad \frac{\$60.312}{4.64} = 13{,}000 \text{ units}$$

Is a 13,000-unit break even achievable? Equals 250 bottles a week or 42 bottles a day (on a six-day work week).

13,000 units @ $5.89 = $76,570 total sales which is just slightly more than the $75,000 expected sales in the outlet at the Prince Edward Hotel in Charlottetown. Traffic volume in Toronto should be dramatically higher than in P.E.I. However, no advertising or other expenses have been included in the calculation.

232

(b)   *Mail Order*

Retail Prices	$5.89
Variable Costs	–1.25 (from case)
Other Variable Costs	–0.15 (i.e., shipping boxes)
Contribution	$4.49 per 250 ml. bottle

Next to retail sales in New Glasgow, this is the highest contribution possible.

(c)   *High Volume/Low Margin Distributors*

There are two examples of this: (a) Danamar, and (b) the price reduction required for high volume sales in Japan.

For Danamar:

Current Wholesale	=	$3.50
less 30% discount of		1.05
Discount Wholesale Price		2.45
Versus Variable cost		1.40
Contribution per 250 ml bottle		$1.05

To achieve high volume sales in Japan, see calculation in column 2 in Table 1 below. It shows that financially this is the least attractive alternative—yet even here there is a positive contribution. Here the wholesale price is half the current wholesale price, and exceeds variable production cost by $0.43 per bottle.

Table 1

	Current Markup on Sales in Japan (from case)	Price Reduction Required for High Volume Sales in Japan	Price Required for Sales to Japanese Consumers in Rest of Canada	
Wholesale price in P.E.I.	$3.50	$1.83*	Wholesale Price	3.16
Freight ($4.20/kilo, P.E.I. to Hokkaido)	0.80	0.80	Freight (estimate)	0.40
Duty (28% of wholesale price + freight)	1.20	0.74	Duty	–
Landed cost in Japan	5.50	3.37	Landed cost in Vancouver	3.56
Importer's Margin (15%)	0.83	0.51		
Price to Primary Wholesaler	6.33	3.88		
Wholesaler Margin (10%)	0.63	0.39	Wholesaler Margin (20%)	0.71
Price to Retailer	6.96	4.27	Price to Retailer	4.27
Canadian World mark up (30%)	2.09	1.28	Markup 30%	1.28
Expected retail price	$9.05	$5.55	Retail Price 3 @ $5.55 =	$16.65
Exchange (Cdn$1.00 = 120 yen)	¥1,086	¥666	3 @ ¥666 =	¥1,998

Calculated by deduction.

233

Column 3 in Table 1 calculates the price required to reach large numbers of Japanese consumers in the rest of Canada. At a distributor price of $3.16 minus variable costs of $1.40, it still leaves a healthy contribution of $1.76 per bottle.

Returns are sensitive to exchange rate. A five per cent appreciation of the Yen would permit P.E.I. Preserves to increase wholesale price by $0.16/bottle. A question which instructors may wish to return to later in class is: "What are the implications then, three years later in June 1995, by which time the yen has undergone a *100 per cent* appreciation?" As Table 2 below suggests, they are enormous.

Table 2

	1995 Mark-ups on Potential Sales to Japan: Current Wholesale	1995 Mark-ups on Potential Sales to Japan Using ¥666/Bottle Gift Price-Point
Wholesale Price in P.E.I.	$3.50	$4.47*
Freight ($4.20/kilo, P.E.I. to Tokyo)	0.80	0.80
Duty (28% of wholesale price & freight)	1.20	1.48
Landed Cost in Japan	5.50	6.75
Importer's Margin (15%)	0.83	1.01
Price to Primary Wholesaler	6.33	7.76
Wholesaler Margin (10%)	0.63	0.78
Price to Retailer	6.96	8.54
Retailer Mark-up (30%)	2.09	2.56
Expected retail Price	$9.05	$11.10
Exchange (Cdn$1.00 = 60 yen)	¥543	¥666

by deduction

The company would be able to increase its wholesale price far beyond what it obtains now. Alternately, they would strive for volume sales by maintaining their existing margins. The margins in fact are so large that in 1995 it was eminently reasonable for students to be recommending that McNaughton visit Japan and actively seek out a new distribution arrangement. Even if McNaughton knows *nothing* about Japan, through assistance from the Canadian Embassy in Tokyo, contacts can be arranged with potential distributors. Foreign manufacturers of premium quality goods should be beating down the door of the Japanese market.

(d)   *Standard Distributors*
      Distributor Price $3.50
      Less variable costs   −1.25 (from case)
      Less additional variable costs   −0.15 (cardboard packaging)
      Contribution/250 ml bottle $2.10

2.   Pros and Cons of the Major Alternatives

Table 3 below details some of the major points which should come out of this 40-minute discussion. To put even more structure to this discussion, we try to simultaneously develop the criteria for choosing between the alternatives. These criteria will include: management resources required, control possible,

234

financial resources required; total return possible; ROI; etc. This analysis provides much of the necessary background for the final section.

Table 3

	Pro	Con
Mail order	<ul><li>high margins maintained</li><li>easy to control/manage</li><li>customer pays freight (postage)</li><li>highest ROI</li><li>reduces seasonality of the business</li></ul>	<ul><li>low response rate/not large volume</li><li>postage is extra expense for consumer</li><li>can't taste it</li><li>list limited to those who have visited P.E.I.</li><li>printing cost of $0.50/unit</li></ul>
Standard Distributor (Medium Margin/Medium Volume)	<ul><li>provides market coverage</li><li>little investment required</li></ul>	<ul><li>need high volume to make money</li><li>may lose control over promotion</li><li>distributor may not give it the push you desire</li><li>variable costs understated (exclude boxes, energy for cooking, etc.)</li></ul>
Low Margin/High Volume Distributors	<ul><li>spreads fixed costs</li><li>exposes company to largest number of consumers</li><li>fast growth</li></ul>	<ul><li>fruit price increases cannot be passed on/absorbed easily</li><li>production efficiencies more importance than ever</li><li>vulnerable to exchange rate fluctuations</li></ul>
Company Stores	<ul><li>high margins if break even exceeded</li><li>selling effort focused on company's products</li><li>allows you to reach more consumers (product loyalty may result)</li><li>can put store where customers are</li></ul>	<ul><li>failure puts whole company at risk</li><li>large incremental capital investment ($60,000+) required</li><li>company pays freight</li><li>heavy competition in Toronto—very little in P.E.I.</li><li>will it require a lot of McNaughton's time?</li></ul>

3. Recommendations

Focus on Preserves Business

(1) Divest Perfect Cup Restaurant in Charlottetown (it is physically and strategically unrelated to the preserves business, as well as a financial and time drain. Proceeds of sale will help put rest of business on a more stable financial footing).

(2) Consider reverting back to tea room status for New Glasgow Restaurant.

Target Japanese Consumers in Canada

(3) Establish relationship with duty free shop distributor for (especially) Vancouver and Toronto airports.

(4) Visit Japan to learn about Japanese consumers. (Canadian government provides assistance through Program for Export Market Development to make such a trip.)

(5) Visit Banff shops and set up distribution.

(6) Consider developing a Japanese language catalogue.

Expand Mail Order Effort

(7)   Ensure catalogue printed very early.

(8)   Provide catalogue to all product purchasers.

(9)   Consider purchasing a mailing list(s).

Increase Distributor Network in Rest of Canada

(10) Conduct detailed analysis of distributor locations and sales.

(11) Ensure a presence is established in all major urban centres and tourism centres (i.e., Niagara Falls).

(12) Participate in more gift shows across Canada.

All of the recommendations to this point can be implemented starting immediately. Taking the easier business first is the underlying philosophy of these choices. In the medium term (after one year), McNaughton can re-examine the possibility of opening a store in Toronto or some other locale.

WHAT HAPPENED

In the years following the case, the following changes took place:

(1)   The Perfect Cup Restaurant in Charlottetown was sold (albeit at a loss).

(2)   The meal offerings were *expanded* in the New Glasgow location. (Combined with the retail operation, this meant that in 1992 there were now 43 full-time people working in this location. For the three summer months, this meant a payroll of nearly $8,000 per week.)

(3)   Sales in the Charlottetown retail location were averaging only about $450 per day. This was raising concerns about its long-term viability.

(4)   McNaughton was investigating the possibility of opening a store in Halifax, but continued to be concerned that he didn't have the personal time to make a success of it.

(5)   In 1992, for the first time, the 30-page Japanese-language Canada Restaurant Guide contained an ad for P.E.I. Preserves (cost: about $1,000).

(6)   No real progress was made in selling preserves in the Toronto/Vancouver airports. The only location which sold P.E.I. Preserves was Caviar House in Terminal 3 in Toronto. They discontinued it (and eight other competing products) in order to sell a house brand only.

(7)   Tea sales were increasing dramatically, under a name registered by McNaughton: New Glasgow Tea Merchants. (Five people were employed in the bulk breaking operation for re-packaging; and in 1994 a quarter million tea bags were sold—usually in packages of 10.)

(8)   Since 80 per cent of P.E.I. Preserves were sold as gifts (20 per cent as gourmet foods), McNaughton was trying to determine how to increase the gift purchase level of his products *by Prince Edward Islanders,* a market he had not pushed to this point.

(9)   In 1994, McNaughton purchased a small local wooden box company in order to assure his supply of packaging for the gift market.

(10) Overall sales hit $1.2 million in 1994 and McNaughton was moving to the establishment of profit centres. By the summer of 1996, gross revenues exceeded $2 million, due primarily to the establishment of a gift shop and restaurant (Piece of Cake) in Charlottetown. The restaurant, like many in this highly competitive industry, was losing money. McNaughton planned to sell it, and stay out of the restaurant business.

(11) By November 1997, there were 87 Yen to the Canadian dollar (a 45 per cent appreciation since the time of the case). McNaughton had not visited Japan. Nonetheless, a number of Canadian jam/preserves companies were successfully selling in Japan.

Case: Carrefour vs. Wal-Mart
Primary Chapter: Chapter 4 (External Context)
Secondary Chapters: Chapters 2 (Strategic Leadership), 6 (Dynamic Strategy), and 8

Introduction: Even though this case is primarily mapped to Chapter 4, it is also a good fit with Chapter 8, and you might choose to revisit it and focus on the international dimensions alone. The most basic question posed by this case is which retailer was better prepared to win in an increasingly global marketplace. In the process of discovering each chain's relative standing, several important learning outcomes can be achieved. First, contrasting strategies and styles are observed and the causes of these different positions are revealed. Second, the two firms' attempts to develop transnational capabilities are discovered, as well as constraints in executing these transformations. Finally, the dynamics of global competition retailing industry are revealed. The case provides an opportunity to discuss the tension between local responsiveness and global integration (the two chains are at very different places in this matrix and each is trying to incorporate the benefits of the other's position).

This case has so much rich data that some instructors may find it a good case to use for a written case analysis project.

Strategy Diamond: This case provides excellent detail on the differing economic logics of these two giant retailers. Wal-Mart is attempting to leverage its cost advantages while expanding internationally. Carrefour has concentrated on localizing operations, thereby differentiating themselves from stores like Wal-Mart. Each position has potential advantages, but both firms engage in a number of dynamic shifts over time in an attempt to capture benefits of a transnational position. Because the case is so rich in both qualitative and financial data, all other elements of the strategy diamond are also discussed and instructors will have great flexibility to adapt this case to their particular teaching interests.

The Dynamic Nature of Strategy: This is a wonderful case to discuss the dynamics of strategy over time in a globalizing marketplace. In addition, the data in the case, both descriptive and quantitative, are more than sufficient to analyze the dynamics rather than just speculate about them.

Formulation/Implementation: As students begin to discuss proposed changes in strategy for either firm, they will often deal with changes such as localizing Wal-Mart's approach in new and different markets, or centralizing and rationalizing some of Carrefour's systems so as to reduce the cost disadvantage with Wal-Mart. However, such changes are difficult to implement. There is ripe opportunity to get into specifics such as which structures and systems will need to be altered to pull off the recommended changes? What can the leader do to increase the probability of success given that these changes seem to go against a strategic heritage opposite the intended strategy?

Strategic Leadership: This case provides some information on the current leaders as well as the leadership heritage of the companies. As the case ends by posing the question about which is better prepared to compete globally, it also implies questions about what each would have to do to better position themselves for the future. Consequently, instructors wanting to emphasize leadership issues could do so through the strategy implementation model.

CARREFOUR VS. WAL-MART: TEACHING NOTE

TEACHING ISSUES

In the Carrefour vs. Wal-mart case there are three main ideas to get across. First, the case presents an opportunity to discuss how the styles of operation adopted by companies that compete internationally are a consequence of the environment in which they have historically dealt. This leads to a nice discussion on path dependence. Secondly, the case gives the reader an opportunity to discuss the need to build transnational capabilities in an increasingly competitive world, and how companies are constrained by their "administrative heritage" or "managerial orientation" in developing this transnational capability. Finally, the case illustrates the threats global competition creates for governments and companies and the way they align their strategies in order to compete in an increasing global and interdependent world.

STUDY QUESTION

Wal-mart has historically moved from one success to another in an environment where it is the standard setter. With the merger of Carrefour and Promodes, Wal-mart is facing its first truly international competitor and is doing so on unfamiliar territory.

1. What are the historical circumstances that have created the structures of the main players in the global retail game?
2. What are the various competitive advantages and disadvantages the individual retailer's possess? How might they evolve?
3. What sort of game is being played out? How might we categorize the participants?
4. What strategies would you recommend to Wal-mart and Carrefour as they go forward?

SUGGESTED READINGS

Devinney, Timothy, Midgley, David and Sunil Venaik, "The Optimal Performance of the Global Firm," *Organization Science*, 11, 2000.

Ghoshal, Sumantra, "Global Strategy: An Organising Framework," *Strategic Management Journal*, 8, 1987.

Bartlett, Christopher, and Sumantra Ghoshal, "Managing Across Borders: New Strategic Requirements," and "...: New Organizational Responses," *Sloan Management Review*, Summer and Fall, 1987.

INTERNATIONAL STYLES OF OPERATION: A CONSEQUENCE OF HISTORICAL ENVIRONMENT

In their internationalization both Wal-mart and Carrefour have adopted very different styles of operations.

Wal-mart, is a giant that grew in the biggest and most uniform market in the world. [With] little need to adapt its concepts to local markets, it (perhaps arrogantly) adopted a global approach when going international. This approach has allowed Wal-mart to profit from economies of scale and scope through a higher concentration of assortment and logistical economies.

Carrefour, on the other hand, initially developed in a market where tastes and purchase patterns varied considerably even when considering distances as short as 50 miles. Carrefour was locally responsive even before it became a multinational! Carrefour also developed in an underdeveloped capital market causing it to rely on joint ventures with local partners as a way of securing capital. Carrefour expanded but it also shared control, which shaped the multinational posture of its international expansion. This approach had the advantage of developing the skills necessary for responding effectively to local needs but at a cost of greater coordination costs and fewer benefits from economies of scale at the corporate level.

A very good example of the different styles of operation of each company is the way they are organized internally. Carrefour, with nearly half of its turnover generated abroad, is organized by geographical regions and has transferred its top officers to these regions. Wal-mart, with one tenth of its sales coming from outside the US, still focuses very much on efficiency, being organized by concepts with its international operation aggregated in one division.

BUILDING TRANSNATIONAL CAPABILITIES: CONSTRAINTS OF A COMPANY'S HERITAGE

As both Wal-mart and Carrefour begin to compete on an international level they quickly come to understand that their rival has some distinctive advantages. Wal-mart is learning that no two markets are the same and, therefore, assuming that the same format is ideal for all the markets is a major mistake. Carrefour, while responding successfully to local needs, has understood—first in the US and now in Europe—that not capturing scale economies can be an expensive gaffe when facing a competitor like Wal-mart with twice its margins. As these two champions face each other around the globe they are seeking global efficiency while responding to national needs but doing so from different starting points. The ability to manage across borders requires that the companies link their diverse organizational perspectives and resources in ways that allow them to leverage their capabilities to achieve these ends simultaneously. The key to the case is whether such an outcome—the transnational firm—is a reality or an unachievable foolish goal?

One cannot forget that a company's ability to make transformative change will be constrained by their existing configuration of assets, their traditional distribution of responsibilities, and their historical norms, values, and management styles. This internal organization is something that cannot be changed overnight or by decree. At this point, it is useful to break this problem down and address where the change should be first for each company. That is, should this be a structural asset change with managerial beliefs and cultural norms following or a managerial belief change with the assets following? Given their orientations, it is likely that Carrefour needs a dose of structural reality and Wal-mart a change in managerial beliefs but it is not that easy. Carrefour managers have been rewarded and bred on their ability to be responsive. Just giving them systems that allow for great logistics efficiency may not work. Similarly, just educating Wal-mart managers about the needs of local responsiveness will do little if the distribution system is driving margins.

Merger Issues

To date Carrefour has been a hypermarket operator, with the organization configured to serve a single format concept. With the merger, Carrefour has to manage a multi-format retail chain. Although it can profit from increased bargaining power with suppliers and from the ability to test different concepts in different markets, the merger also creates a further integration need. Time needs to be spent on inward looking reorganization of the portfolio of businesses being operated on a global scale, most noticeably across Europe. The merger has led to duplication in management positions and there will, no doubt, be tensions between the two companies' potential candidates. These tensions will force out of some top executives that, in the long run, can become a threat as Wal-mart hires them to manage their expanding operations in Europe.

With the merger, Carrefour is following something of a GE strategy—be the first or second player in all the markets it operates. This will guarantee an edge both with suppliers and customers, as consumer goods suppliers and customers still operate very much on a national basis.

Concept and Structure Issues

Having local joint venture partners gave Carrefour a competitive edge in terms of adaptation to local needs; however, it also cost it in shared control and loss of its individual strategic imperative. Unlike Wal-mart, Carrefour's structure creates difficulties in the coordination and control of its worldwide operations. For Wal-mart the implementation of internal policies is a question of sending a global memo and having a couple of meetings. For Carrefour partners have to be 'convinced' to implement company policies, which obviously increases the level of management complexity and strategic conflict. Also, because of Carrefour's decentralized structure, much of this is also played out with the local subsidiaries even when there is no JV partner.

Carrefour lags behind Wal-mart in matters such as logistics and IT, as the locus of power is centered in the stores. Store managers are more interested in dealing with every-day in-store issues than with shared functions, such as IT and logistics. This creates a highly adaptable store concept but also a concept with costly, inefficient and short-term focused support functions.

One area where Carrefour seems to have a definite competitive edge is in HR. Its European, South American and Asian experience has shown it to be successful in integrating different languages and different cultures into its organization. This cultural assimilation allows Carrefour to have a superior understanding of local needs, a better relationship with partners, and a better acceptance of the company by the local community.

Given this discussion, it is clear that, organizationally, both firms can be expected to change in the future. Each will no doubt creep towards the other's structure as competitive pressures bite, but their natural tendency is to continue to move where their strengths and managerial preferences dictate. Carrefour, due to the portfolio of businesses it holds today and because of the need to increase control over its operations, will have to take an organizational focus on developing control systems that work but don't threaten. The question is whether a move to greater GI will be met with a reduction in LR? In the same fashion, Wal-mart, as its international portfolio increases, will have to have a more geographical focus in order to respond quickly to local needs but will need to do so within the context of its tendency to control operations from America. The question is whether the move to greater LR will be at a cost in terms of GI?

Hence the big question is not that these firms will change but what the path of change will be? The figure below outlines a number of possible scenarios. Some of these paths will no doubt be superior in the sense of greater performance (e.g., increasing both LR and GI). However, a performance impact of some of paths are not at all clear since they imply a reduction on one dimension for an increase on the other.

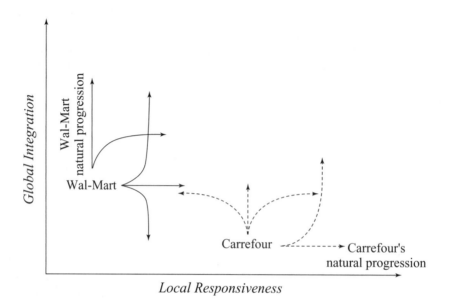

Financial Issues

Financially, Wal-mart's position is more solid than Carrefour's, giving it an edge in either handling difficulties or fuelling expansion. Additionally, Carrefour's weaker position could worsen as it is expected to increase its debt to exercise its joint venture control options in an attempt to tighten control over its JV operations.

Wal-mart, despite its superior profitability (Wal-mart's margins, ROE and ROA are nearly double of that of Carrefour), is likely to suffer some set-backs as it enters markets that are not has large as the US, where road systems are not as effective and local responsiveness is a must. Although Wal-mart can succeed commercially, these new markets will make it difficult to capture the same sorts of economies of scale that the company has achieved in the US. For example, in Europe, customers are more demanding in terms of service and food assortment. These are areas where Wal-mart supercenters are inferior to Carrefour hypermarkets. Catching up will most likely lead to a, perhaps temporary, shrinkage of operational margins, as food assortments operate at lower margins then non-food assortments. Further, as Wal-mart learns to adapt its store concept to better compete locally it will need to transfer further powers down to store managers—how to do this without increasing monitoring costs is a big question.

Wal-mart's superior ROE can also become a constraint as Carrefour can strategically leverage its lower ROE to its advantage. If Carrefour decides to enter the US, it can acquire a retailer with a lower

ROE than that of Wal-mart without hurting its own shareholder return. Wal-mart's investor community is US centric and has become used to P/E in the range of 40+ and maintaining this level puts unique strains on the strategic latitude of the company's top management team.

The State-State Competition: An Added Perspective

It is very interesting to observe that before the threat of Wal-mart's entry and dominance in Europe, a merger like that between Carrefour and Promodes would have been unlikely to be approved by the EU. Wal-mart's aura was sufficient to transform European retailers' perception of their own market as global rather than pan-European. As the retail market situation changed from one based on firm-to-firm competition (i.e., Carrefour vs. Promodes) to a one of state-to-state based competition (US vs. EU: with Wal-mart as the US flagship) the EU decided to clear the merger in spite of the consequences for intra-European concentration.

This teaching note was written by Alexandre Holtreman, MBA, and Professor Timothy Devinney for the purpose of facilitating class discussion and not for the purpose of illustrating either the good or bad handling of a specific management situation. © 2000 by the Australian Graduate School of Management.

Case: The Chinese Fireworks Industry
Primary Chapter: Chapter 4
Secondary Chapters: Chapters 6, 8 & 12

Introduction: The Chinese Fireworks Industry case illustrates an industry that is experiencing intensifying competition and regulation. The Chinese fireworks industry thrived after China adopted the 'open door policy' in the late 1970s, and grew to make up 90 per cent of the world's fireworks export sales. However, starting from the mid-1990s, safety concerns led governments both in China and abroad to set up stricter regulations. At the same time, there was rapid growth in the number of small family-run fireworks workshops, whose relentless price-cutting drove down profit margins. Jerry Yu is asked by relatives to invest in a fireworks factory that was owned by a village in China. Students are asked to undertake an industry analysis, estimate the industry attractiveness, and propose possible ways to improve the industry attractiveness from an individual investor's point of view.

Strategy Diamond: The strategy diamond is a core issue in this case. As students contemplate Jerry Yu's opportunity to enter this industry, there is the obvious connection to how he would enter. Specifically, which arenas should he enter, should he purchase an existing facility, and what would be different about his company? Most students focus on entering through the purchase of a factory and miss entirely the option of entering at a different stage of the value chain, such as an intermediary between the Chinese manufacturers and the North American display companies. The Chinese fireworks industry offers an opportunity for thorough analysis of each aspect of the strategic diamond as a potential entrant in the market.

The Dynamic Nature of Strategy: The Chinese fireworks industry is changing relatively quickly. Safety and environmental regulations along with a high volume of new entrants have created an ambiguous atmosphere for existing companies and for those thinking of entering. Some see the industry as destined for death, while others see it as a high potential for growth. Such a dynamic environment and broad range of future outlook provide interesting analysis for potential strategies and strategic moves.

Formulation/Implementation: The intent of the case is not to explore the link between formulation and implementation; however, the implications of this tension should be obvious as students develop alternative plans for entering the industry.

Strategic Leadership: The leadership positions, though not entirely irrelevant, are not core to the case. It is possible however to discuss the benefits Jerry might have by being a North American-born-Chinese relative to other potential entrants to this market.

THE CHINESE FIREWORKS INDUSTRY
TEACHING NOTE

SYNOPSIS

This case illustrates an industry that is experiencing increasing competition and regulation. Liuyang had thrived on its expertise and reputation for making first-class fireworks. Export sales had been profitable and growing for almost two decades since China had opened its door to the outside world in 1979. China-made fireworks comprised close to 90 per cent of the world's export sales.

However, in the mid-1990s, safety concerns led governments, both in China and abroad, to set stricter regulations regarding the consumption of these "entertaining explosives." At the same time, the market economy reform gave rise to the mushrooming of numerous small family-run fireworks workshops. Their relentless price-cutting drove down profit margins, and reduced much of the industry's appeal.

With the above scenario as background, the Chinese fireworks industry is analysed for its attractiveness. Students must discuss the dynamics of the industry, assess its attractiveness, and propose possible strategies Jerry Yu could adopt to succeed in the industry should he decide to invest.

POSITION IN THE COURSE

This case is suitable for an early section of the strategy (General Management, Business Policy, Competitive Strategy or International Strategy) or marketing course, which introduces the topic of industry analysis. Students are to apply Porter's Five Forces Model using the information provided in the case. The industry analysis will enable the students to understand the dynamic forces impacting the industry, evaluate the attractiveness of the industry, and find out how different industry structures could affect a firm's strategic choices. The China background poses an extra complexity in the industry analysis, because some of the market dynamics tend to be specific to China as a traditional economy.

The instructor should make sure that the students are familiar with Porter's Five Forces Model. Otherwise, the following reading could be assigned a week before the class:

Porter, Michael E. 1979. "How competitive forces shape strategy," *Harvard Business Review,* 57 (March/April): 137–145.

ASSIGNMENT QUESTIONS

1. If you were Jerry Yu, would you invest in a Liuyang fireworks factory? Why?
2. Apply Porter's Five Forces Model; evaluate the attractiveness of the Chinese fireworks industry. Use the worksheet attached.
3. Is the fireworks industry a "sunset" industry or an industry still worth being in for the long run?
4. If you were Jerry Yu, and you decided to make the investment, what would you do to win out in the competition?
5. If you were asked to provide advice to Liuyang Firecrackers and Fireworks Industry Department, as Jerry Yu, what would you say?

RESOURCES: INTERNET WEB SITES

There are a number of Web sites that provide useful and current information on the fireworks industry. The following two sites are fun to visit and have links to other sites related to fireworks and the industry.

- www.pyropage.com
- www.fireworksland.com

SUGGESTED TEACHING PROCESS (ASSUMING 80-MINUTE CLASS)

1. Size up and discuss assignment question 1   15 minutes
2. Assignment 2: Industry analysis (group presentations)   30 minutes
3. Assignment 3: The special features of the Chinese market that impact the industry   10 minutes
4. Assignment question 4: Individual choices   10 minutes
5. Assignment question 5: Government's role   10 minutes
6. Wrap-up   5 minutes

CASE ANALYSIS

1. Size up and discuss assignment question 1 (Whether to invest in a fireworks factory).

The instructor can start by putting on the board a diagram of the Five Forces Model, and briefly introducing it. As the students start to answer assignment question 1, their responses can be noted under the headings of "Pros" and "Cons."

The intent of starting with a list of pros/cons from a personal perspective is to reinforce for students the need for a more structured way of accessing industry attractiveness.

Pros

- The cost of entering will be low.
- Could capitalize on Liuyang's name recognition, in the domestic (but likely less in the export) market.
- Government incentives are available in the form of tax refunds, up to 20 per cent, for export sales.
- The market is becoming less brand-conscious, therefore, could compete on price, if efficiently managed.
- Low switching cost for the customer, therefore, easy-to-win market shares, if marketing is done well.
- As a village-owned business, no historical burdens like health care and retirement pay.
- Easily available skilled and flexible laborers.
- No close substitutes.

Cons

- Low barriers to entry imply high competition.
- Price competition will drive down the profit margin continuously.
- Regulations could get stricter both at home and abroad, driving down the demand for consumer fireworks.
- Future technological advancement could produce safer and cleaner substitutes for the functions now performed by fireworks.
- Working in fireworks industry always has an element of danger.

246

2. Industry analysis (Group Presentations)

During class, the students should be organized into five groups with each asked to prepare an analysis of how one of the five forces impacts the particular industry. Then a representative of each group will be called to do a very brief presentation. Each will take only a few minutes. The presentations should be guided by the worksheets shown in Exhibit TN-1.

Buyer Power is very high. There is very little switching cost. The buyers are well informed and assisted with knowledgeable local representatives. They can play one supplier against the other. The only switching cost exists in the case when the buyer provides product design and outsources production. In that case, commercial secret can become a binding power.

Supplier Power is very low. Standard raw materials are used. However, long-term relationship provides extra stability in quality and price.

Entry Barriers are very low. The capital cost is low. Labor force is easy to access, flexible and cheap. The fixed cost is low. Technology requirement is low. Skilled workers may be a scarce resource elsewhere, yet abundant in Liuyang.

Competitive Rivalry is very intense because of the low entry barriers. It often boils down to cutthroat price competition.

Substitute threat is mixed. If fireworks are viewed as a special traditional way of celebrating national holidays, no close substitutes are available. However, if fireworks are viewed as a promotional tool or entertaining amusement, then many alternatives exist.

3. PEST Analysis and Industry Outlook

If there are students from China in the class, the instructor can ask them to do an individual or group presentation on the special features of the China market. The presentation can cover the trends in the political, economic, social and technological (P-E-S-T) environments.

Political

China is a transitional economy turning from command economy to market economy. Government can change laws and policies easily. Export incentives, for instance, can be reduced or taken away anytime. Government can also set price floors, or tightening export permit control to protect the few state-owned factories in the industry. It is mostly under the "rule for man." A city mayor alone can basically decide on banning or lifting a ban on fireworks.

Economic

After more than a decade of double-digit growth, China's economy started to slow down after 1997. Deflation has set in; the consumer confidence is low.

Social

There are mixed trends going on in China. There is a strong trend of westernization, where people—especially the young generation—admire and adopt the western lifestyle. At the same time, there is a nostalgic trend, where people look to tradition as their guide. This is nowhere clearer than in the ways people choose to get married. There are those who prefer to get married in church, dressed in suits and white gowns. There are also those who want to take old-style bridal sedan chair, dressed in traditional long robes and red Qi-pao.

Technological

There are new patents filed on fireworks everywhere. For instance, scientists in the famous Los Alamos lab in New Mexico, U.S. found a new compound that could replace the current black powder to make safer and brighter fireworks. Research and development barely exists in the Chinese fireworks industry. Most of the work is being done manually.

Based on the information provided in the case, and the PEST analysis, ask students to debate whether the industry is declining. Remind the students to make separate analyses for consumer fireworks and display fireworks.

For the consumer fireworks, unless new technology changes the raw materials that the product is made from, pollution and safety concerns tend to foretell only more stringent regulations in the future.

For the display fireworks, there are more alternative positionings available, such as display shows as public entertainment or promotional events. Encourage the students to list possible usages.

4. Individual Investor's Strategic Choices

Jerry Yu could have a look at the value chain structure of a fireworks manufacturer to see if he could do something to improve the attractiveness of the industry.

Cost Leadership versus Differentiation Strategy

Jerry could choose to become the low-cost manufacturer by organizing the production in a more efficient way. For instance, he could improve the process technology, cutting down on scraps and improving the workers' productivity. However, the fact that fireworks-making is a low-technology, labor-intensive, and largely a manual process suggests that the small workshops would probably win out in a cost war due to their low expenses in labor, administration and technology.

Jerry could also go the differentiation route by establishing a reputation as a quality manufacturer. In fact, a few factories in Dongguan had done that with reasonable success. This would imply more initial investment in building up the research and development (R & D) and design facilities, management capabilities, marketing strength and corporate culture that are required. The return probably will be slow in coming. Since quality and reputation will be more salient purchase factors for display fireworks end users than the consumer fireworks market, differentiation will probably work better in the display fireworks market.

Forward Integration into Distribution in Export Market

Since the overseas distributors enjoy a larger share of the profit in fireworks sales, Jerry might consider establishing his own distribution company in North America. His experience running gift stores and his MBA background in North America may put him in an advantageous position, compared to most of the Chinese manufacturers. If done successfully, forward integration into distribution may help to secure profit from his investment.

5. Suggestions to Liuyang Firecrackers and Fireworks Industry Department

Looking at Liuyang fireworks industry as a whole, we see that the municipal government should and could play a bigger role in enhancing the competitiveness of Liuyang fireworks.

For instance, the government:

- Can support large factories in enhancing their R & D capabilities.
- Can encourage large factories to develop display fireworks.
- Can continue and strengthen its promotion campaign in the provinces.
- Can differentiate those small workshops from the larger, more resourceful factories. Make them adopt different strategies: for instance, cost leadership versus differentiation strategy, consumer fireworks versus display fireworks.
- Lobby the central government for better co-ordination, even price floor for fireworks (ask the students why that is advantageous to Liuyang), and more export incentives.
- Can consider opening wholesale companies overseas, pooling the resources of the government and industry, so as to bypass the middlemen and retain more profit from export sales.

KEY LESSONS

Porter's Five Forces Model can be effectively used in assessing the attractiveness of the Chinese fireworks industry. However, we can see that the special characteristics of China's transition from a command to a market economy had impact on the evolution of the industry structure. Reform made possible the emergence of private-owned enterprises, which changed the competitive landscape of the industry. Small workshops were squeezing out the more established manufacturers. The somewhat chaotic competition had brought problems. The Chinese fireworks industry entered the world market with good reputation and considerable cost advantage in late 1970s. Today, in spite of having close to 90 per cent share of the world's fireworks export sales, it had lost most of its brand equity and enjoyed little pricing power. Should the government have played a larger role in industrial policy co-ordination, the industry might have evolved in a different way. Therefore, in analysing an industry in a transitional country like China, government might have to be incorporated as the sixth force.

Exhibit TN-1
WORKSHEET ON INDUSTRY STRUCTURE

1. **Threat of entrants:**

	YES (+)		NO (–)	REMARKS
1. Do large firms have a cost or performance advantage in your segment of the industry?			X	No economies of scale in consumer fireworks. Some in the display fireworks.
2. Are there any proprietary product differences in your industry?		X		Liuyang fireworks used to have brand equity. However, price competition and imitations had eroded the brand equity.
3. Are there any established brand identities in your industry?	X			Yes. "Red Lantern" and other domestic and international brands.
4. Do your customers incur any significant costs in switching suppliers?			X	Switching is relatively easy and costless.

	Yes (+)		No (−)	REMARKS
5. Is a lot of capital needed to enter your industry?			X	
6. Is serviceable used equipment expensive?			X	
7. Does the newcomer to your industry face difficulty in accessing distribution channels?		X		It's hard to get into government-controlled channels and export sales. It's easy to get to wholesaling centers.
8. Does experience help you to continuously lower costs?			X	
9. Does the newcomer have any problems in obtaining the necessary skilled people, materials or supplies?			X	Skilled workers are scarce elsewhere, but abundant in Liuyang.
10. Does your product or service have any proprietary features that give you lower costs?			X	
11. Are there any licences, insurance or qualifications that are difficult to obtain?			X	
12. Can the newcomer expect strong retaliation on entering the market?			X	Retaliation is not possible.

Note: High barriers to entry = + factors (favorable to industry)

Low barriers to entry = − factors (unfavorable to industry)

Overall rating = strongly unfavorable for the incumbents

2. **Bargaining power of buyers:**
   (to what extent are your customers locked into you?)

	Yes (+)		No (−)	REMARKS
1. Are there a large number of buyers relative to the number of firms in the business?			X	Buyers are numerous. Yet suppliers are numerous too.
2. Do you have a large number of customers, each with relatively small purchases?			X	The customers are the wholesalers and importers. They are powerful.
3. Does the customer face any significant costs in switching suppliers?			X	No switching costs for wholesalers. For the importers who outsource manufacturing, some commercial secrets may be involved.
4. Does the buyer need a lot of important information?			X	They have access to virtually all the information.
5. Is the buyer aware of the need for additional information?			X	They know how and where to get the information.
6. Is there anything that prevents your customer from taking your function in-house?	X			Labor cost, regulation, skills.

	Yes (+)		No (−)	Remarks
7. Your customers are not highly sensitive to price.			X	
8. Your product is unique to some degree or has accepted branding.			X	
9. Your customers' businesses are profitable.	X			
10. You provide incentives to the decision makers.	X			Commission to reps and agents.

Note: Low bargaining power of buyers = + factors (favorable to industry)

High bargaining power of buyers = − factors (unfavorable to industry)

Overall rating   **= unfavorable**

3. Threat of substitutes (some other product or service that performs the same job as yours)

	Yes (+)		No (−)	Remarks
1. Substitutes have performance limitations that do not completely offset their lowest price. Or, their performance is not justified by their higher price.		X		Fireworks as traditional ways of celebrating are hard to replace. Fireworks as promotional means have lots of substitutes.
2. The customer will incur costs in switching to a substitute.		X		Not financially. Maybe emotionally.
3. Your customer has no real substitute.			X	People will come up with substitutes if forced to.
4. Your customer is not likely to substitute.			X	If regulation requires, one has to.

Note: Low threat of substitution = + factors (favorable to industry)

High threat of substitution = − factors (unfavorable to industry)

Overall rating   **= medium**

4. Bargaining power of suppliers:

	Yes (+)		No (−)	Remarks
1. My inputs (materials, labor, supplies, services, etc.) are standard rather than unique or differentiated.	X			Skilled workers are scarce elsewhere, but abundant in Liuyang.
2. I can switch between suppliers quickly and cheaply.	X			The only concern is the quality of the materials.
3. My suppliers would find it difficult to enter my business or my customers would find it difficult to perform my function in-house.		X		A supplier in Liuyang may start making fireworks themselves easily.
4. I can substitute inputs readily.			X	
5. I have many potential suppliers.	X			
6. My business is important to my suppliers.			X	
7. My cost of purchases has no significant influence on my overall costs.		X		Variable costs are the major costs in fireworks. Yet, costs are low.

251

Note: Low bargaining power of suppliers = + factors (favorable to industry)
　　　　High bargaining power of suppliers = – factors (unfavorable to industry)
　　　　Overall rating　　　　　　　　= favorable

5.　Determinants of rivalry among existing competitors:

	Yes (+)		No (–)	Remarks
1. The industry is growing rapidly.			X	
2. The industry is not cyclical with intermittent overcapacity.	X			The seasonality of the demand is somewhat evened out because of the diversity of the cultures.
3. The fixed costs of the business are a relatively low portion of total costs.	X			The fixed costs are very low for small workshops. Medium for large factories.
4. There are significant product differences and brand identities between the competitors.			X	Liuyang fireworks used to enjoy strong name recognition, but price competition has become the game.
5. The competitors are diversified rather than specialized.			X	They tend to be specialized.
6. It would not be hard to get out of this business because there are no specialized skills and facilities or long-term contract commitments, etc.		X		Exit is hard for large SOE factories. Hard for Liuyang because it is the pillar industry. Exit is easy for small workshops.
7. My customers would incur significant costs in switching to a competitor.			X	
8. My product is complex and requires a detailed understanding on the part of my customer.			X	Everyone can find out about how to make fireworks.
9. My competitors are all of approximately the same size as I am.			X	

Note: Lower level of rivalry = + factors (favorable to industry)
　　　　Higher level of rivalry = – factors (unfavorable to industry)
　　　　Overall rating　　　　= very unfavorable

6.　Overall industry rating:

	Favorable	Moderate	Unfavorable	
1. Threat of new entrants.	1	2	9	Barriers to entry are very low in the industry. The incumbents are constantly under the threat.
2. Bargaining power of buyers.	3		7	Buyer power is strong. The buyers are price-sensitive, well-informed, and can switch with ease.
3. Threat of substitutes.		2	2	Substitutes are not a problem if fireworks are viewed as celebrating traditions. Substitutes are a

				threat if fireworks are used as promotional means.
4. Bargaining power of suppliers.	3	2	3	Supplier power is relatively low. The profitability levels are not affected by the suppliers significantly.
5. Intensity of rivalry among competitors.	2	1	6	The competition is cutthroat price rivalry.

A NOTE ON THE CHINESE FIREWORKS INDUSTRY STUDENT HAND-OUT WORKSHEET ON INDUSTRY STRUCTURE

Note to the students:

This worksheet was developed to apply Porter's Five Forces analysis to an industry. For each of the factors listed below, place an "X" in the appropriate column (Yes, No or Moderate). Once you have completed the analysis of the five forces, compute the number of factors for each category, and write down the number for the overall analysis.

1. Threat of entrants:

	Yes (+)		No (−)
1) Do large firms have a cost or performance advantage in your segment of the industry?			
2) Are there any proprietary product differences in your industry?			
3) Are there any established brand identities in your industry?			
4) Do your customers incur any significant cost in switching suppliers?			
5) Is a lot of capital needed to enter your industry?			
6) Is serviceable used equipment expensive?			
7) Does the newcomer to your industry face difficulty in accessing distribution channels?			
8) Does experience help you to continuously lower costs?			
9) Does the newcomer have any problems in obtaining the necessary skilled people, materials or supplies?			
10) Does your product or service have any proprietary features that give you lower costs?			
11) Are there any licenses, insurance or qualifications that are difficult to obtain?			
12) Can the newcomer expect strong retaliation on entering the market?			

+ factors (favorable to industry)

− factors (unfavorable to industry)

Worksheet on Industry Structure

2. Bargaining power of buyers:
(to what extent are your customers locked into you?)

	Yes (+)		No (−)
1) Are there a large number of buyers relative to the number of firms in the business?			
2) Do you have a large number of customers, each with relatively small purchases?			
3) Does the customer face any significant costs in switching suppliers?			
4) Does the buyer need a lot of important information?			
5) Is the buyer aware of the need for additional information?			
6) Is there anything that prevents your customer from taking your function in-house?			
7) Your customers are not highly sensitive to price.			
8) Your product is unique to some degree or has accepted branding.			
9) Your customers' businesses are profitable.			
10) You provide incentives to the decision makers.			

3. Threat of substitutes: (some other product or service that performs the same job as yours)

	Yes (+)		No (−)
1) Substitutes have performance limitations that do not completely offset their lowest price. Or, their performance is not justified by their higher price.			
2) The customer will incur costs in switching to a substitute.			
3) Your customer has no real substitute.			
4) Your customer is not likely to substitute.			

4. Bargaining power of suppliers:

	Yes (+)		No (−)
1) My inputs (materials, labor, supplies, services, etc.) are standard rather than unique or differentiated.			
2) I can switch between suppliers quickly and cheaply.			
3) My suppliers would find it difficult to enter my business or my customers would find it difficult to perform my function in-house.			
4) I can substitute inputs readily.			
5) I have many potential suppliers.			
6) My business is important to my suppliers.			
7) My cost of purchases has no significant influence on my overall costs.			

5. Determinants of rivalry among existing competitors:

	Yes (+)		No (−)
1) The industry is growing rapidly.			
2) The industry is not cyclical with intermittent overcapacity.			
3) The fixed costs of the business are a relatively low portion of total costs.			
4) There are significant product differences and brand identities between the			

competitors.			
5) The competitors are diversified rather than specialized.			
6) It would not be hard to get out of this business because there are no specialized skills and facilities or long-term contract commitments, etc.			
7) My customers would incur significant costs in switching to a competitor.			
8) My product is complex and requires a detailed understanding on the part of my customer.			
9) My competitors are all of approximately the same size as I am.			

Worksheet on Industry Structure (continued)

Overall industry rating:

	Favorable	Moderate	Unfavorable	Remarks
1) Threat of new entrants.				
2) Bargaining power of buyers.				
3) Threat of substitutes.				
4) Bargaining power of suppliers.				
5) Intensity of rivalry among competitors.				

Ruihua Jiang prepared this teaching note under the direction of Professor Paul Beamish as an aid to instructors in the classroom use of the case The Chinese Fireworks Industry, No. 9A99M031. This teaching note should not be used in any way that would prejudice the future use of the case. Ivey Management Services prohibits any form of reproduction, storage or transmittal without its written permission. This material is not covered under authorization from CanCopy or any reproduction rights organization. To order copies or request permission to reproduce materials, contact Ivey Publishing, Ivey Management Services, c/o Richard Ivey School of Business, The University of Western Ontario, London,Ontario, Canada, N6A 3K7; phone (519) 661-3208; fax (519) 661-3882; email: cases@ivey.uwo.ca. Copyright © 1999, Ivey Management Services Version: (A) 1999-10-08

Case: Home Depot's Strategy under Bob Nardelli
Primary Chapter: Chapter 5
Secondary Chapters: Chapters 3, 4, & 11

Introduction: Home Depot was the biggest home improvement retailer in the world in 2004. Set up in the late 1970s to provide low price, warehouse-like products, Home Depot grew rapidly over the 1980s and early 1990s, adding stores at the average annual rate of 20 percent. However, in the late 1990s, the company's comparable store growth rate began declining. It was also experiencing operational difficulties due to its tardiness in developing systems to manage its rapid growth. In this situation, the board brought in Bob Nardelli as the CEO of the company in 2000. Nardelli was responsible for implementing new initiatives that changed Home Depot's culture and strategic direction. The case discusses the changes implemented by Nardelli at Home Depot in the early 2000s. It discusses the measures he took to eliminate inefficiencies from the company and to streamline its processes. The case also talks about the difficulties that Nardelli, who was the first outside CEO of Home Depot, faced in implementing these changes. The case concludes with an analysis of how Home Depot compared with Lowe, its nearest competitor, in the early 2000s and an analysis of the reasons why the company's share price had fallen. The teaching objectives of the case are: (1) to analyze the growth strategy followed by a large home improvement retailer in the US; (2) to study the retailer's attempt to revive growth in the face of market saturation and the steps it took to offset saturation; (3) to understand the impact on a company's strategy of the passing on of leadership from founders to an outsider and first timer in the industry; (4) to examine the difficulties faced by an outsider in bringing about changes in a company; (5) to understand the competitive position between the two top companies in the home improvement market in the US; and (6) to examine the reasons for a company's comparatively low share price despite its improved financial performance.

Strategy Diamond: The case provides opportunity for discussion on the effects of staging. Initially, Home Depot pursued a strategy of rapid speed into new markets and consequently high growth, which ultimately proved unsustainable. Nardelli then staged policy changes. The speed in which he initiated the changes had positive effects on the financial books but deleterious effects on the morale of employees, including top executives.

The Dynamic Nature of Strategy: Examining the policy changes Nardelli initiated (shifting the company's focus to services and exploring new markets) offers an example of successfully altering a strategy in order to adapt to the changing environment.

Formulation/Implementation: A key point in the case is the ability (or inability) of Nardelli to implement strategy. Although the strategy proved financially sound, the case shows the difficulty and challenges arising from the "human" side of implementation.

Strategic Leadership: The main point of the case is the strategic leadership of Bob Nardelli and how his role as an outside CEO affected his role as strategic leader. The case provides detail concerning his interpersonal roles, informational roles and decisional roles. His style of leadership is also under scrutiny in the case as his "do it my way" attitude alienated many in the company. There is also opportunity to discuss the strategy for finding the right CEO. Would a CEO promoted from within the company have faced the same challenges? Or did Home Depot need "fresh blood"?

HOME DEPOT'S STRATEGY UNDER BOB NARDELLI

SUMMARY

Home Depot was the biggest home improvement retailer in the world in 2004. Set up in the late 1970s, to provide low price, warehouse-like products, Home Depot grew rapidly over the 1980s and early 1990s, adding stores at the average annual rate of 20 percent.

However, in the late 1990s, the company's comparable store growth rate began declining. It was also experiencing operational difficulties due to its tardiness in developing systems to manage its rapid growth. In this situation, the board brought in Bob Nardelli as the CEO of the company in 2000. Nardelli was responsible for implementing new initiatives that changed Home Depot's culture and strategic direction.

The case discusses the changes implemented by Nardelli at Home Depot in the early 2000s. It discusses the measures he took to eliminate inefficiencies from the company and to streamline its processes. The case also talks about the difficulties that Nardelli, who was the first outside CEO of Home Depot, faced in implementing these changes. The case concludes with an analysis of how Home Depot compared with Lowe, its nearest competitor, in the early 2000s and an analysis of the reasons why the company's share price had fallen.

TEACHING OBJECTIVES & TARGET AUDIENCE

The teaching objectives of this case are:

- To analyze the growth strategy followed by a large home improvement retailer in the US.
- To study the retailer's attempt to revive growth in the face of market saturation and the steps it took to offset saturation.
- To understand the impact on a company's strategy of the passing on of leadership from founders to an outsider and first timer in the industry.
- To examine the difficulties faced by an outsider in bringing about changes in a company.
- To understand the competitive position between the two top companies in the home improvement To examine the reasons for a company's comparatively low share price despite its improved financial performance.

This case is meant for MBA/PGDBM students and is designed to be a part of their Strategy and General Management curriculum.

TEACHING APPROACH & STRATEGY

The case can be used effectively in classroom discussions as well as distance learning programs. The moderator may initiate the discussion by asking students to comment on Home Depot's initial strategy of fuelling growth through new store openings. Students may discuss the changes made by Nardelli at Home Depot and how these changes improved the company's operations and competitive position. The moderator may then ask students to comment on the difficulties Nardelli faced in implementing changes and the effect that an outsider can have on a company's strategy and culture. The case may conclude with an analysis of the company's competitive position, vis-à-vis Lowe, and the reasons for the company's low share prices despite improved financial performance. The following questions may be used to aid the discussion:

1. Home Depot was the biggest [retailer] of home improvement products in the US. However, the company's performance began declining in the late 1990s. Comment on Home Depot's strategy of supporting growth by opening new stores. Do you think that it is advisable for retailers to open a large number of stores and use them to fuel growth?
2. What were the changes implemented by Nardelli at Home Depot? Comment on the company's exploration of new markets and its shift of focus to services.
3. Nardelli made drastic changes in the strategy of Home Depot. Why was Nardelli's approach criticized? Do you think that the changes he implemented were too drastic? Discuss Home Depot's competitive position vis-à-vis Lowe and comment on the company's paradoxical share price position, despite its improved financial performance.

ANALYSIS

1.

Home Depot was the biggest retailer of home improvement products in the US in the 1990s and 2000s. Set up as a three-store company in 1979 at Atlanta, the company grew rapidly to establish itself in the US, Canada and South America. Most of Home Depot's growth was fuelled by new store openings, on which the company relied heavily to expand its market. Through the rapid opening of new stores (stores were opened at the rate of 20 percent every year), the company became the market leader in the 1990s. By 2004, it had almost 1700 stores across the US.

While Home Depot's strategy of growing through the opening of new stores was correct in a certain context, retail experts felt that it was not right for a company to rely solely on store openings for growth. Opening new stores was important for a retailer, as they were the primary means through which it could tap new markets. However, prudence should be employed in opening new stores. Setting up stores simply to increase market presence, could lead to stores being set up too close together, sometimes cannibalizing each other's customer base.

Besides, it was also important to develop and install suitable systems to sustain the store growth, without which, growth would become haphazard and eventually lead to operational bottlenecks. For instance, Home Depot grew rapidly, but failed to develop suitable systems for inventory management, purchasing and human resources, because of which, the company's growth started tapering off in the late 1990s. Besides, there was also the threat of market saturation, which was very critical in the retail business. Companies that relied solely on store openings risked blocking off their growth when the market was saturated. In addition to this, if the company's dependence was only on new stores, then sales from older stores could fall due to neglect, thus lowering the overall growth rate.

2.

After Nardelli became the CEO of Home Depot in late 2000, he implemented a number of programs that changed the strategic direction of the company and corrected many of its embedded deficiencies.

*   Nardelli realized that growth would not be sustained simply by opening new stores. Therefore, one of the first things that he did on joining Home Depot was to cut down the store openings for 2001 by nine percent. Instead, he focused on improving internal processes.
*   He improved inventory management by adopting automated inventory systems, which replaced the manual logging in of shipments. He also made it a rule that employees restock shelves and supplies at night, so that they could spend more time with customers during business hours. He also asked store managers to improve inventory velocity, so that stores functioned on leaner inventory.

- By eliminating the nine regional purchasing departments of the company, Nardelli centralized Home Depot's purchasing function at its Atlanta headquarters. This helped the company obtain better deals from suppliers and avoid duplicity of orders.
- Nardelli adopted IT, which was implemented in many of Home Depot's processes like inventory, appraisal, etc., and which streamlined the processes. He also set up self check-out kiosks at over 800 stores, which considerably improved customer service by making billing and check-out faster.
- The layout of Home Depot's stores was improved and made more customer-friendly. Displays were set at eye-level, so that customers could examine them better. Stores were also made brighter, cleaner and more welcoming to make customers feel good about shopping in them.
- Nardelli was also responsible for shifting Home Depot's focus to services, from its traditional market of 'do-it-yourselfers'. Services had the potential to increase the company's revenues, when the market for its products peaked.
- Nardelli also began exploring newer potential markets overseas, as well as in urban and metropolitan areas, in a departure from the company's traditional suburban areas. This was also a move to offset market saturation.

Shifting the company's focus to services and exploring new markets was a good strategy on the part of Home Depot, as these were effective means of offsetting saturation that was likely to set in eventually in its traditional suburban markets. By exploring new areas of business, the company was protecting its long-term growth prospects.

3.

Nardelli was criticized for making changes too fast and too drastically at Home Depot. People said that at the rate at which Nardelli was changing the organization, there was a very great chance that he could make a serious mistake, especially considering that he did not have any previous experience in the retail sector. Besides, it was also said that the changes could upset old timers at Home Depot, who derived a lot of pride from their organization and its culture, and could eventually lead to a fall in morale.

Besides, Nardelli's stress on processes and numbers-oriented management did not go down well at Home Depot, where regional heads and store managers valued their autonomy and flexibility. People also feared that some of Nardelli's changes could alienate the company's suppliers and customers. For instance, his changes in the company's benchmark cash return policy, was said to have had a bad effect on many customer groups.

In the late 1990s and early 2000s, Home Depot was facing increased competition from Lowe, the second biggest home improvement retailer in the US. Firstly, Lowe was growing at a much faster pace than Home Depot (around 14 percent at Lowe in the 2000s, as against Home Depot's rate of around 10 percent), and was set to overtake Home Depot in the near future. Secondly, Lowe's stock had tripled in the first three years of the 2000s, as against Home Depot's, which fell by 12 percent. Thirdly, Lowe's profits rose by nearly 40 percent in 2003, while Home Depot's profits were increasing at about 18 percent. In addition to these metrics, Lowe was found to have better products and more appealing stores than Home Depot, and many customers began to prefer to shop at Lowe.

In the early 2000s, Home Depot's share prices were much lower than they were in the late 1990s and early 2000s, when they had traded at around $70. In contrast, the price was around $38 in the first half of 2004. Analysts speculated about the reasons for the lower price, despite the company's improved financial performance. (In the first quarter of 2004, Home Depot's same store sales rose 7.7 percent, which was the highest rate of growth experienced in the last five years. Revenues at $64.8 billion and earnings at $4.3 billion were also higher than those of the past few years). While it was not possible to reach a definite answer, analysts said that it could be because the market did not have complete confidence in Nardelli and his changes. Another reason could be that the share price was unjustifiably inflated in 1999 and 2000, and the current price reflected its true potential.

ADDITIONAL READINGS & REFERENCES

1. Patricia Sellers, **Can Home Depot Fix its Sagging Stock,** Fortune, March 4, 1996.
2. Nicole Harris, **Home Depot: Beyond Do it Yourselfers,** BusinessWeek, June 30, 1997.
3. Jennifer Bresnahan, **Home Depot's Ron Griffin on How IS Benefits from Corporate Values,** CIO Magazine, May 1, 1998.
4. Roy Johnson, **Home Depot Renovates,** Fortune, November 23, 1998.
5. Lawrence Armour, **Home Depot: Now It Can Be Told,** Fortune, May 1, 1999.
6. Katrina Brooker, **E-Rivals Seem To Have Home Depot Awfully Nervous,** Fortune, August 16, 1999.
7. Cora Daniels, **To Hire a Lumber Expert, Click Here,** Fortune, April 3, 2000.
8. Nicholas Stein, **Winning the War to Keep Top Talent,** Fortune, May 29, 2000.
9. Sam Jaffe, **What's hammering Home Depot?** BusinessWeek, October 18, 2000.
10. **Co-founder trades Depot's orange apron for family and community,** www.findarticles.com March 5, 2001.
11. Patricia Sellers, **Exit the Builder, Enter the Repairman,** Fortune, March 19, 2001.
12. Sam Jaffe, **New Tricks in Home Depot's Toolbox?** BusinessWeek, June 5, 2001.
13. Patricia Sellers, **Home Depot's Home Defense,** Fortune, October 15, 2001.
14. Aixa M. Pascual, **Tidying Up at Home Depot,** BusinessWeek, November 26, 2001.
15. Amy Tsao, **How Home Depot and Lowe Measure up,** BusinessWeek, December 5, 2001.
16. Anthony Williams, **What? Now We Have to Make a Profit *and* Be Ethical?** Business 2.0, February 1, 2002.
17. Aixa M. Pascual, **Lowe is Sprucing up its House,** BusinessWeek, June 3, 2002.
18. Amy Tsao, **Reading Home Depot's Fuzzy Blueprint,** BusinessWeek, June 4, 2002.
19. Patricia Sellers, **Something to Prove,** Fortune, June 24, 2002.
20. Dean Foust, **Home Depot's 'Big Disappointment': Sales,** BusinessWeek, January 17, 2003.
21. Dean Foust, **The GE Way isn't working at Home Depot,** BusinessWeek, January 17, 2003.
22. Janice Revell, **Can Home Depot Get Its Groove Back?** Fortune, February 3, 2003.
23. Matthew Maier, **How to Revive Home Depot,** Business 2.0, May 1, 2003.
24. Dean Foust, **Home Depot Still Hasn't Nailed Lowe's,** Business Week, November 20, 2003.
25. Dean Foust, **Home Depot's Remodeling Project,** Business Week, January 9, 2004.
26. Carol Hymowitz, **How One Savvy Executive Led a Winning Revolution,** Career Journal, March 17, 2004.
27. Janice Revell, **More Room for Improvement?** Fortune, March 22, 2004.
28. **Home Depot preparing to expand to China,** The Boston Herald, June 7, 2004.
29. Jyothi Thottam, **Bob The Builder,** Time, June 21, 2004.
30. Rebecca Zicarelli, **Home Depot's Hardware Warriors,** Fast Company, Spetmebr 2004.
31. Chana R. Schoenberger, **House Call,** Forbes, September 6, 2004.
32. Elizabeth Lazarowitz, **Home Depot Goes Urban, Opens First Manhattan Store,** news.yahoo.com, September 9, 2004.
33. Patricia Sellers, Julie Schlosser, **Its His Home Depot Now,** Fortune, September 20, 2004.
34. Kelvin Taylor, **The Windfall of Hurricanes,** www.fool.com, September 20, 2004.
35. Julie Schlosser, **He'll Take Manhattan,** Fortune, September 20, 2004.
36. Karen Jacobs, **Home Depot, Lowe's see strong post-hurricane demand,** about.reuters.com.
37. www.rabble.ca
38. www.sprawl-busters.com

39. www.youareworthmore.org
40. www.hoovers.com
41. ir.homedepot.com
42. www.homedepot.com

Case: Ryanair: The 'Southwest' of European Airlines
Primary Chapter: Chapter 5
Secondary Chapters: Chapters 3, 4 & 12

Introduction: Ryanair is one of the oldest and most successful low cost airlines in Europe. Started in 1985 as an independent Irish airline, Ryanair expanded to become the biggest carrier on the London-Ireland route. By the late 1990s, it was the biggest low cost airline in Europe. However, in 2002, rival easyJet overtook it to the top position. Ryanair's operations were based on the operational model of the most successful discounter of all time - the Dallas-based Southwest Airlines. Ryanair adopted most of the operational policies which made Southwest Airlines so successful. Along with an operational model to support its strategy of cost focus, the airline also made use of extensive, sometimes cheeky publicity, to make its brand more popular. By early 2003, the low cost airlines segment in Europe showed signs of consolidation. Ryanair and easyJet had emerged as the major players in the market. The positioning of the two airlines vis-à-vis each other also forms a part of the case. The teaching objectives of this case are: (1) to analyze the business model and operating strategies adopted by a successful low cost airline in order to emerge as the leader in a highly competitive market; (2) to examine the role of publicity as adopted by the airline and analyze its efficacy in creating higher brand awareness; (3) to analyze the positioning of the airline vis-à-vis competitors operating in the same market segment, and understand the competitive advantages enjoyed by the airline against rivals; and (4) to study the sustainability of the airline's competitive and operational advantages in the long-run in the light of new competition and the stage of evolution of the industry in which it operates.

Strategy Diamond: A key point in the case is Ryanair's commitment to its differentiators and economic logic. Their low-price strategy prompts discussion on a resource-based view of maintaining a strategy as well as developing an operational model to support that strategy.

The Dynamic Nature of Strategy: Ryanair provides a positive example of a company sticking to their strategy despite the changing environment while at the same time avoiding the pitfalls associated with a myopic view which often accompanies a 'stick to the guns' mentality.

Formulation/Implementation: The case provides an in-depth analysis of the implementation of Ryanair's low cost strategy. The link between formulation and implementation is not explicit, but consideration can be given to Ryanair's goal of lowering prices 5% each year for the foreseeable future and how the company would go about implementing and maintaining such a goal.

Strategic Leadership: CEO Michael O'Leary's unusual techniques present a unique case of a strategic leader putting image (both company and personal) on the line to further the strategic goals of an organization.

RYANAIR – THE "SOUTHWEST" OF EUROPEAN AIRLINES

SUMMARY

Ryanair is one of the oldest and most successful low-cost airlines in Europe. Started in 1985 as an independent Irish airline, Ryanair expanded to become the biggest carrier on the London-Ireland route. By the late 1990s, it was the biggest low-cost airline in Europe. However, in 2002, rival easyJet overtook it to the top position. Ryanair's operations were based on the operational model of the most successful discounter of all time – the Dallas-based Southwest airlines. Ryanair adopted most of the operational policies which made Southwest Airlines so successful. Along with an operational model to support its strategy of cost focus, the airline also made use of extensive – sometimes cheeky publicity, to make its brand more popular. By early 2003, the low-cost airlines segment in Europe showed signs of consolidation. Ryanair and easyJet had emerged as the major players in the market. The positioning of the two airlines vis-à-vis each other also forms a part of the case.

TEACHING OBJECTIVES & TARGET AUDIENCE

The teaching objectives of this case are:

- To analyze the business model and operating strategies adopted by a successful low-cost airline in order to emerge as the leader in a highly competitive market.
- To examine the role of publicity as adopted by the airline and analyze its efficacy in creating higher brand awareness.
- To analyze the positioning of the airline vis-à-vis competitors operating in the same market segment, and understand the competitive advantages enjoyed by the airline against rivals.
- To study the sustainability of the airline's competitive and operational advantages in the long run in the light of new competition and the stage of evolution of the industry in which it operates.

The case is meant for MBA/PGDBM students and is intended to be a part of the Strategy and General Management curriculum.

TEACHING APPROACH & STRATEGY

This case can be used effectively in classroom discussions as well as distance learning programs. The moderator can initiate the discussion by asking students to comment on the growth of low-cost airlines which were based on the Southwest model. The students can then discuss the growth of Ryanair from a small Irish upstart to the biggest low-cost airline in Europe. The moderator can ask students to discuss the operational model of Ryanair and how it compared to the model of Southwest Airlines. Students can also discuss the publicity initiatives of Ryanair and how they helped increase brand awareness. The moderator can conclude the discussion by asking the students to comment on the position of Ryanair in the low-cost market and the future prospects of the airline in the light of the stage in the industry's evolution and the threat of new competition.

ANALYSIS

1.

Ryanair is the oldest low-cost airline in Europe. It was one of the first independent airlines to succeed in Ireland. Ryanair was started in 1985 by three brothers – Cathlan, Declan and Shane Ryan – to provide low-cost, no-frills services between Ireland and London. Soon after Ryanair was set up, the governments of Ireland and England entered into an agreement to deregulate air traffic between England and Ireland. Ryanair obtained an early advantage by being granted a license to operate between London and Dublin.

Over the years, the airline continued to grow and added new routes. However, it faced some managerial problems and there were a number of changes in management. The airline also faced heavy losses due to the intense competition that existed between the airline and the national carrier, Aer Lingus. The intensity of the competition was reduced after the Irish Government introduced its two-airline policy and specified different international routes for the two airlines. This reduced the debilitating competition between the two airlines and led to greater profitability for both airlines.

After the deregulation of the European air services market in 1997, Ryanair was able to expand further and increase its routes to continental Europe. It also set up two new bases in Europe. Expansion of routes and increased profitability helped make Ryanair the biggest low-cost airline in Europe by the mid-1990s. Ryanair remained the largest low-cost airline in Europe till 2002. However, easyJet (set up in 1995) overtook Ryanair to the top position in 2002, after it took over Go, the low-cost subsidiary of British Airways. The combined fleet and routes of easyJet and Go were more than those of Ryanair. However, the CEO of Ryanair, Michael O'Leary, declared that Ryanair would soon reclaim its number one position.

2.

Ryanair adopted operational policies that supported its corporate strategy of cost-focus. The operational model adopted by Ryanair allowed the airline to keep costs under control, enabling it to offer low fares. Some of the components of the airline's operational policy were:

- It operated a simple fleet of planes, flying only one type of plane. This allowed it to keep operations simple and inexpensive by allowing transferability of parts, furnishings and crews between planes.
- The airline flew to secondary airports, which gave it better landing terms. They also had the advantage of being less congested than the major airports which allowed the airline to turn around planes faster.
- By turning around planes faster, (in about half the time taken by major airlines), Ryanair was able to fly its planes a larger number of times per day than its competitors, thus increasing the productivity of the aircraft and making the more profitable.
- It also employed fewer numbers of employees than its competitors, and the per-employee productivity was higher.
- Online sales of tickets simplified the ticketing process allowing the airline to save time and money by reducing dependence on travel agents.
- The airline did not serve food on its flights. This helped it save expenses on food. Selling snacks, in fact, became a new source of revenue. In addition to this, the airline charged the passengers for all the additional services it provided (baggage check-in, handling, etc.). This also helped keep costs under control and increased the sources of revenue.
- The airline flew point-to-point flights which helped keep operations simple. It also rented out its planes, and the space in the overhead cabins and behind the seats to other companies for advertising.

These initiatives helped the airline keep its expenses low and allowed it to charge lower fares for its flights.

Ryanair also had a publicity program which was important in creating and increasing awareness of its brand in the market. The airline often released advertisements which were cheeky and controversial. The media coverage on the controversial nature of the advertisements often generated more publicity for the firm than the advertisements themselves.

3.

Ryanair and easyJet were the two major low-cost airlines in Europe. After the shakeout and consolidation in the low-cost airline industry, Ryanair and easyJet emerged as the major players, as they took over smaller airlines operating in similar markets. Ryanair was the biggest player in the market until 2002 when it was overtaken by easyJet.

Price was the primary competitive advantage that Ryanair enjoyed over easyJet. Ryanair offered fares which were approximately 60 percent lower than the fares of easyJet on similar routes. This fact was played up by Ryanair, which claimed it was the 'true' low-cost airline. Ryanair also announced that it would lower fares by five percent every year indicating its long-term commitment to this strategy.

A big advantage that enabled Ryanair to offer lower fares than easyJet was the huge discounts it got on its purchases from Boeing. As it was based in Ireland, where no aircraft were produced, the US government allowed such discounts to be offered. Besides, it also flew an older fleet and did not undertake a great deal of expenditure on new planes unlike easyJet. Flying older planes did not harm the airline as it had an unblemished safety record. Ryanair also had a better breakeven load factor and a higher operating margin than easyJet and all its other competitors.

EasyJet had certain advantages over Ryanair in terms of the convenience of the airports it flew to and its newer fleet of planes, but Ryanair's operational model probably has greater long run sustainability. EasyJet did not hedge its fuel costs; this could prove costly if fuel prices rose. Besides, unlike Ryanair, easyJet also competed head-on with the major carriers, since it flew to the same airports and targeted the same customers. If the major carriers (with more funds and greater governmental support) decided to become more aggressive in defending their turf, easyJet would find the going really tough. However, experts believed that the industry was big enough to sustain both the low-cost airlines, as long as they did not step on each others' toes.

ADDITIONAL READINGS & REFERENCES

1. Kerry Capell, Carlos Tromben, William Echikson, Wendy Zellner, **"Renegade Ryanair"**, *Business Week*, May 14, 2001.
2. **"How Ryanair Keeps the Cost Down"**, *Business Week*, May 14, 2001.
3. **"Ryanair brothers make £33.4m from shares sell-off"**, *The Irish Examiner*, July 06, 2001
4. O'Connell Patricia, **"Full-Service Airlines Are "Basket Cases" "**, *Business Week*, September 12, 2002.
5. Day Julia, **"Ryanair sells 1m seats for less than a tenner"**, *The Guardian Review*, September 24, 2001.
6. Tomlinson Richard, **"Europe's Businessman of the Year"**, *Fortune*, December 9, 2001.
7. **"The pluck of the Irish"**, *The Economist*, January 24, 2002.
8. Peachey Paul, **"Ryanair 'misled' public over flight destinations"**, *The Independent*, March 13, 2002.

9. Eoghan Nolan, "**Good product, bad brand**", *Marketing Magazine*, July 3, 2002.
10. Capell Kerry, "**Ryanair Rising**", *Business Week*, June 2, 2003.
11. Capell Kerry, "**Suddenly, Life Is Hard for easyJet**", *Business Week*, June 2, 2003.
12. Wachman Richard, "**Can Ryanair soar higher?**", *The Observer*, June 8, 2003.
13. Smith.V.Kenneth, "**easyJet leads low fare airline battle in Europe**", www.webtravelnews.com, September 27, 1999.
14. "**Business Profile: High flier who built a fortune on low fares**", www.telegraph.co.uk.
15. Lee James, "**Ryanair: the first ten years**", www.iol.ie
16. www.thetravelinsider.info
17. www.easyprotest.com
18. www.theolivehouse.it
19. www.bbc.co.uk
20. www.legal500.com.
21. www.msnbc.com
22. www.hoovers.com
23. www.rj'anair.com.

Case: Advanced Micro Devices – Life Beyond Intel
Primary Chapter: Chapter 6
Secondary Chapters: Chapters 3, 4 & 8

Introduction: The case discusses the competition between Intel and Advanced Micro Devices Inc (AMD), the number one and two players respectively, in the global semiconductor industry. The war between the two companies in terms of product superiority, technology transfer issues, pricing strategies, marketing campaigns have been explored in detail. The case provides information on AMD's evolution over the years and traces the events that led to the two companies becoming bitter rivals from business partners. The launches of various microprocessor chips by the two companies, and their competitive moves have also been detailed. The case also briefly discusses the future prospects of the two companies, the industry as well as the consumers in the light of this intense competition. The case is developed to enable students to: (1) examine the nature and dynamics of the global semiconductor industry and the role of the leading players Intel and AMD; (2) learn about the strategies adopted by companies to survive in an industry that is primarily controlled by high technological obsolescence, economy of scale, price competition, and intense rivalry; (3) analyze how original equipment manufacturers and end users play an important role in determining the market share of a company functioning in the semiconductor industry; (4) understand the marketing strategies adopted by a challenger to garner market share in a highly competitive market with several players with good brands; and (5) evaluate the direction in which the industry and the two companies are heading and analyze the pros and cons of the competitive moves for all the parties concerned.

Strategy Diamond: Fundamental to this case are the differentors and staging used by both Intel and AMD. The case shows in considerable detail the pricing, imaging, and customization strategies along with the staging of each of these as AMD and Intel compete. The case also prompts discussion on the benefits and challenges of having a first-mover strategy versus a follower strategy in such a dynamic industry.

The Dynamic Nature of Strategy: The semiconductor industry is known for its dynamism. Interesting perspectives are garnered from this case by comparing the strategies of Intel and AMD to the nature of the industry. The case stimulates discussion about the effectiveness of Intel and AMD's strategies in an industry of rapid product obsolescence. Additionally, it demonstrates how competitor's moves influence and affects your own strategy.

Formulation/Implementation: The purpose of the case is not specifically designed to explore the link between formulation and implementation. However, analysis can be undertaken on the formulation and implementation of strategy in such a competitive and dynamic environment.

Strategic Leadership: Strategic leadership is not specifically addressed in this case. However, because both companies have had rather public and dynamic leaders, interesting discussions are easy to motivate on leadership by asking students to do some advanced background work on the leaders of these companies and then integrating that knowledge into discussion about how the personalities of the CEOs shaped the strategic propensities of the firms.

ADVANCED MICRO DEVICES — LIFE BEYOND INTEL TEACHING NOTE

SUMMARY

The case discusses the competition between Intel and AMD, the number one and two players respectively, in the global semiconductor industry. The war between the two companies in terms of product superiority, technology transfer issues, pricing strategies, marketing campaigns have been explored in detail. The case provides information on AMD's evolution over the years and traces the events that led to the two companies becoming bitter rivals from business partners. The launches of various microprocessor chips by the two companies, and their competitive moves have also been detailed. The case also briefly discusses the future prospects of the two companies, the industry as well as the consumers in the light of this intense competition.

TEACHING OBJECTIVES & TARGET AUDIENCE

The case is developed to enable students to:

- Examine the nature and dynamics of the global semiconductor industry and the role of the leading players Intel and AMD.
- Learn about the strategies adopted by companies to survive in an industry that is primarily controlled by high technological obsolescence, economy of scale, price competition, intense rivalry.
- Analyze how OEMs and end users play an important role in determining the market share of a company functioning in the semiconductor industry.
- Understand the marketing strategies adopted by a challenger to gamer market share in a highly competitive market with several players with good brands.
- Evaluate the direction in which the industry and the two companies are heading and analyze the pros and cons of the competitive moves for all the parties concerned.

The case is aimed at MBA/PGDBA students and is intended to be a part of the Strategy and General Management curriculum.

TEACHING APPROACH & STRATEGY

The case can be used both for classroom discussions as well as for written assignments. The moderator can start off by asking the students about the current global PC and microprocessor markets. Students can be divided into groups of five or six and each group can present its analysis to the class. The moderator can introduce (to the students) the following issues:

- Other technology-intensive industries similar to microprocessors and the strategies adopted by players in them.
- The strategies adopted by companies to counter competition, particularly in the microprocessor market.
- The role of marketing (product development, pricing, advertising etc.) in enabling a product gain sustainable competitive advantage in the long run.
- The pros and cons of competition driving industry innovation and strategies in general.

ADDITIONAL READINGS & REFERENCES

1. Blackwood Jonathan, **Bargain Chips**, www.techweb.com, 1998.
2. Lemos Robert, **The Future Looks Bleak For AMD**, www.news.zdnet.co.uk, February 10, 1999.
3. Cringley X Robert, **The Aging of Intel**, www.pbs.org, February 25, 1999.
4. Silverman Dwight, **New Chip Has a Speed Edge Over Intel**, www.dwightsilverman.com, August 26, 1999.
5. Kanellos Michael, Wilcox Joe, **AMD Counters Intel With 800-MHz Athlon Chip**, www.news.com, January 6, 2000.
6. Stanfield Heather, AMD War, www.linux.omnipotent.net, March 6, 2000.
7. Sam Jaffe, **AMD is Still Scratching for Respect**, www.businessweek.com, July 25, 2000.
8. Kanellos Michael, **Intel, AMD Battle For Chip Speed Crown**, www.marketwatchcnet.com, July 28, 2000.
9. Masse Cheryl, **Chip Fight**, www.computeruser.com, October 2000.
10. Connolly Chris, **AMD Duron 800 MHz**, www.gamepc.com, October 10, 2000.
11. Spooner John, **Best Buy Puts Brakes on Pentium 4**, www.znet.com, November 28, 2000.
12. **Intel and AMD Power Up 64-bit Processors**, www.win2000mag.net, December 2000.
13. McDonald Tim, **AMD Trumps Intel in Cheap-Chip Speed Race**, www.newfactor.com, January 8, 2001.
14. Stam Nick, **Athlon vs. P4: Intel Escalates the Rivalry**, www.pcmag.com, January 16, 2001.
15. Kanellos Michael, **AMD Chip Name to Echo Pentium**, www.marketwatch-cnet.com, May 9, 2001.
16. **AMD Unveils New Processors**, www.blonnet.com, June 19, 2001.
17. Gray F Douglas, **AMD Launches Athlon XP Processor**, www.pcworld.com, October 9, 2001.
18. Hagen Eric, **The Future Of the Athlon XP**, www.anandtech.com, October 10, 2001.
19. Neel Dan, **AMD's Athlon XP Snubs Megahertz Ratings**, www.infoworld.com, October 12, 2001.
20. Mainelli Tom, **Does Anybody Understand AMD's New Chip Names?** www.pcworld.com, October 17, 2001.
21. Hoie W Oystein, **AMD's Future Plans**, www.infosatellite.com, November 21, 2001.
22. Port Otis, **The Chip War Moves to Terahertz Terrain**, **www.businessweek.com,** December 17, 2001.
23. **Recovery Heats Up AMD-Intel Rivalry**, www.taipeitimes.com, December 27, 2001.
24. McDonald Tim, **AMD Releases Speedy New Athlon**, www.newsfactor.com, January 7, 2002.
25. McDougall Paul, **Intel, AMD Continue Rivalry With New Superfast Chips**, www.informationweek.com, January 7, 2002.
26. McDonald Tim, **Mobile chip speed wars roll on**, www.wirelessnewsfactor.com, January 28, 2002.
27. Magee Mike, **AMD Outlines Consumer Plans Ahead,** www.theinquirer.com, January 29, 2002.
28. Brown Spencer Ken, **Chip Rivals Intel, AMD Seek Different Niches In 64-bit Bout,** www.sanjose.bizjournals.com, June 7, 2002.
29. McDougall Paul, **Intel, AMD Continue Rivalry With New Superfast Chips**, www.commonweb.com, July 1, 2002.
30. Hughes Rob, **Complaint Develops Against P4 Marketing**, www.geek.com, August 19, 2002.
31. Popovich Ken, **AMD, Intel Release Faster Chips, Cut Prices**, www.eweek.com, August 21, 2002.
32. Osborne Brian, **Intel Slashes Prices Up To 52%,** www.geeg.com, September 4, 2002.
33. **AMD Launches Largest Global, Integrated Branding and Advertising Campaign in Company History**, www.biz.yahoo.com, **September 16, 2002.**
34. Singer Michael, **'AMD me' Unleashed**, www.siliconvalley.internet.com, September 12, 2002.
35. Rao L Prashant, **AMD Plays the x86-64 Card With Opteron and Hammer**, www.express-computer.com
36. **Widowmaker, Intel 'back in the drivers seat', www.tswn.com, October 8, 2002.**

37. Dunn Darell, **AMD and Intel Turn Up the Heat in Handheld Market**, www.ebnonline.com, November 2, 2002.
38. Abreu Elinor Mills, **AMD to Take Charge; Cut Costs, Jobs, www.reuters.com,** November 7, 2002.
39. Sigvartsen Ana Leticia, **AMD, Intel Processors Get Cheaper**, www.infosatellite.com, November 13, 2002.
40. Hodgin C Rick, **AMD Lowers Low-end Prices By Up To 53%, www.geek.com,** November 15, 2002.
41. **Hackman Mark, AMD, Intel Reach Milestone With Debuts of 1-GHz Athlon, Pentium III,** www.ebnonline.com, November 19, 2002.
42. Antonelli Cesca, **Look Who's Winning the Chip Wars**, www.bloomberg.com
43. AMD **Vs Intel**, www.cyberaddicts.net
44. www.intel.com
45. www.dacs.org
46. www.amd.com

FEEDBACK

The case was reviewed by the faculty at the ICFAI Center of Management Research (ICMR), Hyderabad, India. The review revealed that although there wasn't much difference between the products (in terms of performance) of AMD and Intel, Intel had a slight advantage over AMD because of its strong brand image. Faculty also agreed that competition between AMD and Intel was mainly in the areas of technology and price. It was also felt that though the intensive rivalry between AMD and Intel was benefiting the consumers (in terms of low prices for the microprocessors), it might harm both the companies in the long run.

Case: Airbus: From Challenger to Leader
Primary Chapter: Chapter 6
Secondary Chapters: Chapters 3, 4 & 8

Introduction: The case study focuses on the growth of Airbus and it also covers extensively the competition in the aerospace industry. The case provides a detailed account of the structure of the aerospace industry and the nature of competition in the industry. It explains how Airbus achieved a leadership position with market share increasing from 13% in 1995 to 57% in 2002. The case also provides information about the Airbus's A-380 aircraft and how the success of this model could provide a competitive advantage for Airbus. The case is structured as to enable students to: (1) understand the structure and nature of competition in the aerospace industry; (2) understand how innovative product development can lead to competitive advantage, catapulting a company to the No. 1 position; (3) understand the strategies adopted by a challenger to take on the established and entrenched market leader in a highly regulated industry; (4) understand the impact of operational efficiencies on the success of a company; and (5) evaluate the impact of the external environment on the performance of the aerospace industry.

Strategy Diamond: The case focuses on the strategies adopted by a challenger – Airbus, to take on Boeing, the aerospace market leader. Differentiation is the main focus here as the case outlines Airbus's attempts to gain market share by finding the niches left in Boeing's product lines, initiating price discounting strategies and offering more efficient aircraft. The case prompts discussion on whether Airbus's success is due to these initiatives or to the subsidies they received from European Governments.

The Dynamic Nature of Strategy: The case focuses on aspects of competitive interaction that can create dynamism in industries. The aerospace industry has high barriers to entry due to its highly capital-intensive nature, and its subjection to heavy state regulations. Discussed in the case is Airbus's transformation from a consortium focused on providing jobs and safeguarding home-country political and economic interests, to a corporation actually focused on turning a profit. The case also addresses the issues the industry faced during the late 90's economic recession and the ensuing terror attacks of 9/11.

Formulation/Implementation: While not the main focus of the case details are provided about the challenges Airbus faced while trying to implement its strategic goals across a company owned and operated by several different countries.

Strategic Leadership: Aside from quotes from various members of management, strategic leadership is not specifically addressed in this case. This case is better suited for specifics of types of competition (duopoly) and competitive interactions.

AIRBUS – FROM CHALLENGER TO LEADER

SUMMARY

The case study focuses on the growth of Airbus and it also covers extensively the competition in the aerospace industry. The case provides a detail account of the structure of the aerospace industry and the nature of competition in the industry. It explains how Airbus achieved a leadership position in the industry with market share increasing from 13% in 1995 to 57% in 2002. The case also provides information about the Airbus's A-380 aircraft and how the success of this model could provide a competitive advantage for Airbus.

TEACHING OBJECTIVES & STRATEGY

The case is so structured as to enable students to:

- Understand the structure and nature of competition in the Aerospace industry.
- Understand how innovative product development can lead to competitive advantage, catapulting a company to the No. 1 position.
- Understand the strategies adopted by a challenger to take on the established and entrenched market leader in a highly regulated industry.
- Understand the impact of operational efficiencies on the success of a company.
- Evaluate the impact of the external environment on the performance of the aerospace industry.

The case is intended for MBA/PGDBM level students as a part of the Strategy and General Management curriculum.

TEACHING APPROACH & STRATEGY

The case can be used effectively both in classroom discussions and in distance learning programs. The moderator can provide background information on the following topics:

- The characteristics of a duopoly market
- Role of governments in the development of an industry and strategic importance of the aerospace industry
- The impact of the dispute between the US and the EU over government support to Airbus

ANALYSIS

1.

When Airbus was set up, US airplane manufacturers led by Boeing dominated the aerospace industry. Boeing's 747 family of jets was popular with airline companies and Boeing ruled the sky. Though Airbus built airplanes using the latest technology and they cost less than Boeing's planes, still airline companies did not come forward to purchase aircraft from Airbus.

Airbus got its first orders from European state-owned airline companies. To survive in the industry Airbus would have to penetrate the US market, the biggest market for aerospace companies due to the vibrant US airline industry. Initially Airbus faced problems in financing the costs of product development costs. Product development in the aerospace industry is highly capital-intensive and generally the advance amounts received from the airline companies are used in the manufacture the airplanes. With few customers for its planes, Airbus found it difficult to finance its product development initiatives.

In order to increase its market share, Airbus started by offering heavy discounts to the airline companies. Subsequently Airbus received several orders. To overcome its financial difficulties, Airbus approached European governments for financial support. In its initial years, Airbus' consortium partners forwarded huge amounts as loans to Airbus with no obligations regarding the repayment of loans and no fixed interest rates.

2.

In the late 1960s, some European governments came together and set up Airbus to fight the dominance of the US manufacturers. In order to gain market share, Airbus decided that instead of copying Boeing products, it would come up with products that would fill the gaps in Boeing's product line. For instance, initially Airbus launched single-aisle twin-engine jet fliers, exploiting the gap in the Boeing's product line. Airbus products also used better technology than Boeing's planes.

Airbus was able to gain market leadership due to its products and operational efficiencies. Boeing's production operations practices dated back to the Second World War and it had never tried to upgrade its production practices due to the dominance it enjoyed in the industry. Though it faced competition from Lockheed and McDonnell Douglas, both were weak as compared to Boeing. Boeing also had monopoly position in the 400+ jets category and its Boeing 747 was the only product available in that category.

However, incorporating new technological features such as 'fly by wire' in its planes, and using efficient operational production practices, Airbus came up with products that offered low operational costs for the airline companies. Due to its innovative product development, Airbus was able to become the market leader.

Boeing also had host of HR problems that resulted in frequent strikes and shutdowns of its operations. Airbus, on the other hand, was relatively free of HR problems as most of its employees were employed on a contract basis and it had the liberty to employ workers as per its production requirements. Airbus had only 45,000 permanent employees compared to Boeing's 112,000 employees.

With its innovative products, Airbus is likely to continue to differentiate itself from Boeing and sustain itself in the long run.

3.

The aerospace industry has high entry barriers and is also subject to heavy state regulations. The heavy capital high technology requirements of the industry ensure that there are only a few players in the industry. Prior to the Second World War, Britain dominated the aerospace industry; however after the war, the US emerged as the dominant force in the aerospace industry. For a few decades, the US aircraft manufacturers led by Boeing were dominant players and faced very little competition. Though several European countries had high technology and expertise, they were not strong enough to compete with Boeing.

In order to reduce American dominance in the aerospace industry, Germany, Britain and France came together and launched Airbus Industrie. With the entry of Airbus Industrie, Boeing faced a formidable competitor threatening its market dominance, for the first time. In the early 1980s, Lockheed quit the commercial jet market to concentrate on defense contracts, leaving only three players in the commercial jet market.

The industry still experienced heavy state regulation and high competition. Boeing accused Airbus of cutting prices heavily to gain market share and of receiving excessive subsidies from European governments - charges that Airbus refuted. The US government alleged that the EU was providing financial subsidies to Airbus, which according to the US, was against the GATT agreement. The EU countered this, saying that Boeing too received indirect subsidies in form of defense contracts from NASA. The dispute was settled in 1992, with the signing of the Airbus Accord. However both companies continued to compete stiffly for more market share.

In 1997, McDonnell Douglas was taken over by Boeing. This changed the structure of the industry as it was left with only two players – Boeing and Airbus Industrie. With this consolidation, the market structure took the form of a duopoly.

In the early 2000s, Airbus took over as leader in the aviation market, primarily on account of its innovative products and greater operational efficiency. In 2001, the terrorist attacks in the USA contributed to a sharp downturn in the airline and aerospace industries. Most airline companies cancelled orders for new aircraft, resulting in revenue declines for both players.

ADDITIONAL READINGS & REFERENCES

1. Healy Tim, **Competition: Battle for Asia,** www.asiaweek.com, March 29, 1996
2. **Can Airbus Partners Unite?** BusinessWeek, July 22, 1996.
3. Edmondson Gail & Browder Seanna, **Angst at Airbus,** BusinessWeek, December 23, 1996.
4. Edmondson Gail & Browder Seanna, **A Wake Up Call for Airbus,** BusinessWeek, December 30, 1996.
5. **Peace in Our Time,** The Economist, July 24, 1997.
6. Guyon Janet, **The Sole Competitor,** Fortune, January 12, 1998.
7. Henkoff Ronald, **Boeing's Big Problem,** Fortune, January 12, 1998.
8. Edmondson Gail, **Up, Up, and Away at Last for Airbus?,** BusinessWeek, February 9, 1998.
9. **Airbus Highflier Grounded,** BusinessWeek, February 2, 1998.
10. **Hubris at Airbus, Boeing Rebuilds,** The Economist, November 26, 1998.
11. **Boeing Admits it 'Let Clients Down',** www.news.bbc.co.uk, September 8, 1998.
12. **Fearful Boeing,** The Economist, February 25, 1999.
13. Taylor III Alex, **Blue Skies for Airbus,** Fortune, August 2, 1999.
14. Edmondson Gail, **Overhauling Airbus,** BusinessWeek, August 2, 1999.
15. Burgner Norbert, **The Airbus Story,** www.flugrevue.com, February 2000.
16. **Airbus Gets a Boost,** The Economist, April 6, 2000.
17. **Rivals in the Air,** www.news.bbc.co.uk, June 23, 2000.
18. **Airbus Steals Boeing Ground,** www.news.bbc.co.uk, November 30, 2000.
19. Useem Jerry, **Boeing Vs Boeing,** Fortune, October 2, 2000.
20. **Airbus Draws First Blood,** www.news.bbc.co.uk, June 18, 2001.
21. Matlack Carol & Holmes Stanley, **Trouble Ahead for Airbus?,** BusinessWeek, October 1, 2001.
22. **Bettering Boeing,** The Economist, July 18, 2002.
23. Holmes Stanley, **Showdown at 30,000 Feet,** BusinessWeek, July 22, 2002.
24. **Airbus Just May Win This Dogfight,** BusinessWeek, August 5, 2002.
25. **Bashing Boeing,** The Economist, October 17, 2002.
26. Matlack Carol & Holmes Stanley, **Look Out, Boeing,** BusinessWeek, October 28, 2002.
27. **Boeing vs Airbus,** The Economist, April 17, 2003.

28. **Boeing Can Assemble 7E7 in 72 Hours,** The Economic Times, June 6, 2003.
29. www.flugrevue.com
30. www.airwise.com
31. www.aviationnow.com
32. www.seattletimes.com
33. www.news.bbc.co.uk
34. www.airbus.com
35. www.speednews.com
36. www.Boeing.com

RELATED CASES STUDIES

1. Avis – Still Trying Harder
2. Jet Blue Airlines Success Story

FEEDBACK

The case was reviewed by faculty members at the ICFAI Center for Management Research (ICMR), Hyderabad, India. The faculty members are of the opinion that the case is informative and leaves [a] lot of scope for discussion. The case is structured in a logical and well-organized manner. The rise of Airbus covered in the case is interesting.

Case: Moving Tata Consultancy Services into the "Global Top 10"
Primary Chapter: Chapter 7 (Corporate)
Secondary Chapter: Chapter 8 (International)

Introduction: This case examines a critical strategic decision facing India's largest software services firm, Tata Consultancy Services (TCS). Tata provides technology services around the world. Tata Consultancy Services (TCS), formerly a division of textiles and manufacturing conglomerate Tata Group, is a leading provider of consulting and outsourcing services, with operations in more than 30 countries. Tata Group owns more than 80% of the company.

The case is written around TCS's decision to enter the business process outsourcing (BPO) market. TCS pioneered the software services market in India and was the market leader, but it has been a laggard in BPO. TCS sees a need to move up the value chain into BPO because this is where growth is greatest and smaller competitors have already carved out strong positions in this attractive market. The case is organized around three questions: How might TCS move up the software value chain? Should TCS enter the BPO business? If so, Should it do so through acquisition, alliance, or organic growth?

The case is conceptual in nature, but not lacking in data concerning the industry and the company. The case teaching note is comprehensive. An industry note is provided to give the instructor more background.

Finally, most students have experience with BPO from the consumer's point of view. Many will have had first hand experience with calling a firm's customer service line only to realize that they are speaking with someone in India. Indeed, it may have been a TCS employee they were speaking with. The issue of BPO is also one that can generate significant interest because outsourcing has been such a politically hot potato in recent years. The case provides good insight into the issue from the viewpoint of the provider of BPO services.

Strategy Diamond: This case examines TCS's potential move into a seemingly related arena. The issue of which vehicle to use is central to this case. Should TCS move in through organic expansion, or find the needed skills externally through acquisition or alliance? The instructor's teaching note has some additional data and hints on the logic of these alternatives. There is not much focus on economic logic in the case, other than at an intuitive level. Thus, the case does not challenge students quantitatively. Staging is a legitimate issue to discuss, though the case is presented in a way that suggests TCS must move quickly.

Strategic Leadership: The protagonist in this case is S. Ramadorai (Ram), the current CEO of TCE. After a brief introduction, there is not much information on the CEO; the case focuses entirely on the issue he is facing. However, there is data to suggest that moving into BPO requires a set of organizational resources and capabilities that are not entirely consistent with the existing resources and capabilities possessed by TCS. Thus, how Ram can navigate a move like this brings up many issues about implementation levers and leadership tasks.

Formulation/Implementation: As just noted, BPO requires some organizational capabilities that are not currently resident in TCS. If the idea of entering BPO appears appealing, the execution of this plan may require some heavy lifting. Most students, however, may not have sufficient familiarity with labor markets in India to have a sense for whether this would be a difficult move or not. If you have a few students from India, this would be an excellent opportunity for you to use them as a resource.

The Dynamic Nature of Strategy: This case really is about the evolving nature of competition within the software services industry. In addition, while the case is focused on TCS in India, it provides ample data about the global market of software services and the global dynamics driving BPO.

MOVING TATA CONSULTANCY SERVICES INTO THE "GLOBAL TOP 10" TEACHING NOTE

Abstract. This case study examines three strategic questions that India's largest software services firm, Tata Consultancy Services (TCS), faced in 2003. TCS had pioneered the industry and remained the market leader; of late, its lead over domestic rivals had been slipping, even while much larger multinational rivals were establishing large Indian operations. TCS needed a strategy to move up the software value chain. Meanwhile, a new industry was emerging, namely business process outsourcing, growing at 50 percent per year. There seemed to be synergies between BPO and software services, but also differences. TCS's Indian rivals had made major investments in BPO, while TCS had only a small presence. TCS had to quickly settle on its BPO strategy. The questions are: 1. How may TCS move up the software value chain? 2. Should TCS enter the BPO business? If so, 3. Should it make a major acquisition or grow organically?
Keywords: software, business process outsourcing, India, Tata Consultancy Services, value-chain, strategy.

1. CASE SUMMARY

Begun with the formation of TCS in 1974, India's software exporting industry has grown impressively since. In the fiscal year ended March 2003, India's software industry generated $9.98 billion in annual revenue, of which $7.5 billion was export revenue. Almost all this revenue is in software services, particularly the programming of customized applications.

TCS pioneered the industry and remains its market leader, employing over 20,000 persons. Of late, its lead over the competition has been slipping. Meanwhile, since 1999, an export-oriented business process offshoring and outsourcing (BPO) industry has emerged in India and is growing rapidly. BPO has links to TCS's traditional business of software development; however, as of 2003, TCS had only a small presence in this business.

1. What strategy should TCS use to move up the software services value chain?
2. Should TCS enter the BPO business?
3. If you believe TCS should enter the BPO business, then should it make a major acquisition or grow organically?

2. KEY ISSUES, TARGET AUDIENCE AND APPROACH

Key issues for consideration:

1. The software services value-chain, its de-integration and globalization.
2. The growth of India as an important part of the global production of software services, TCS's leading position in the industry and its strengths and weaknesses.
3. The specialization by most Indian firms—including TCS—in the limited segment of applications programming and in only a few industries.
4. The BPO value-chain, its de-integration and globalization.
5. The recent growth of India in the provision of BPO services and TCS's relatively minor position in the industry.
6. Acquisition versus organic growth.

It is recommended that this case be taught to graduate management students. Students should be encouraged to read about the software development cycle and the business process offshoring cycle prior to analyzing the case. The case contains references to these; the Internet is also a good source for such material. Alternatively, the instructor may extract it from the material below.

3. CASE ANSWER

The answer is developed as follows: The first step is to understand the software service development cycle commonly called the "Waterfall Model". Moreover, the Waterfall Model can be extended to Business Process Outsourcing. The second step is to place TCS into the context of Michael Porter's Five Forces model.

The Waterfall Model

The Waterfall Model is a convenient method for understanding the software services development cycle (or value chain). This model illustrated in Table 1 conceptualizes software development as a series of sequential processes, each of which (with one exception) is less skill-intensive than the earlier one. The initial processes typically use less labor, and later ones use more. At its apex is strategic consulting, which includes the starting points of conceptualization, requirement analysis, and architecture and technology determination. Of all stages in the cycle, this work typically requires the highest level of technical expertise, the closest interaction with the client and the deepest domain skills. Downstream follow engineering services (the integration of the technical capabilities of the core product into the program) leading to a system specification and design, and the programming of the resultant system (termed applications programming). The work of engineering services, like consulting, requires domain skills (in product engineering) and close interaction with the client. System specification and design requires fewer domain skills but higher-end software skills than engineering services. Once the system is specified, the program is written; this work primarily requires programming skills. After the program is written, it needs to be finished through testing and debugging code; once finished, it needs maintenance and quality assurance support. With the development of the Internet, offering software as a web service is increasingly being integrated into the earliest stages. Hence, web services (also called e-business or infrastructure services) are spread across the cycle. Finally, the work of systems integration makes the components of software and hardware compatible and interoperable. It requires some domain expertise, though less than engineering services, primarily requiring hardware and software skills.

This is shown below:

Table 1: The waterfall model

Process=>	Strategic consulting	Engineering services and system design	Applications development and maintenance	Systems Integration	Web services and other
Relative advantage of geographical proximity to the client.	H	H	L	M	M
Share of labor hours (%).	10	17	48	15	10

278

Share in global value-chain (%).	31.5	21.8	15.6	27.1	3.9
TCS revenue share (%).	3	0	70	22	5

Notes: 1. H = high, M = medium, L = low, derived from materials in the case.
2. Share of labor hours from Industrial Note.
3. Share in global value-chain derived from Industrial Note, after excluding IT education and training.
4. TCS revenue share obtained from Supplementary Table 2 of the case.
5. Figures are for 2001.

The software services value-chain started to globalize in the mid-1980s with the use of Unix and C as the standard operating system and programming language and the development of workstations (the case has termed this the "U-W standard"). Indian firms till then had mostly been doing conversion work, i.e., converting users' applications to new operating systems and hardware, mainly as a result of IBM's growing market share. The U-W standard enabled some portions of the software development process, notably applications development, to be done remotely from others. TCS began such work in the mid-1980s, developing along the way complex competences such as the remote management of software projects, a capability that it pioneered in the Indian software industry.

TCS currently earns revenue mostly from applications programming (see the table above). Such work receives only 15% of the value of a software project and is at the bottom of the value-chain.

The waterfall model can be applied to the offshoring of a business process as well. At its apex are strategic consulting and reengineering services, followed by process specification and design, process implementation and process migration services (including process integration and quality assurance). The comparison with software services is shown below:

Table 2: Comparison of components of work in BPO and software services.

BPO=>	Strategic consulting	Reengineering Services	Process specification and design	Process implementation	Migration services, including process integration & Quality Assurance
Software services	Concept, technology determination and system architecture	Engineering services	System specification and design	Applications programming and Quality Assurance	System integration
Use of open standards	L	M	M	H	M

The kinds of BPO work being offshored to India are at the lowest end of the value chain, particularly process implementation, while higher end work continues to be done by clients or their consultants. Thus, TCS takes the risk that doing such work will perpetuate its current position as a low-end services provider.

In the case of both software outsourcing and BPO, for TCS there are few important suppliers, because TCS' inputs are standard commodities and there is little opportunity for differentiation on the input side. The four forces that are most problematic are the bargaining power of customers, the threat of new entrants, the threat of substitutes, and the competitive rivalry with existing players. We examine each of these four forces in their turn for both software services outsourcing and BPO.

Table 1 in the context of competitive forces helps to explain why TCS built its business around applications programming: given the problems of distance, and operating from India, this was the easiest component of the business to build. In the early days of the software exporting business, the software vendor market was dominated by a few large global suppliers such as IBM. Indian firms were viewed as too small to matter for obtaining significant business. In addition, they competed actively with each other at the low-end. The result was that TCS and its Indian peers chose components of the business that were relatively low value-added and relatively simple to do.

TCS also faced a client market that was dominated by the large banks and insurance companies. While it actively sought alliances with larger vendors as a competitive strategy, its most successful strategy was to directly approach clients and accept the lower rates that its competitive position necessitated.

Looking ahead, TCS must continue to work to reduce the bargaining power of customers by trying to move the purchase decision away from price. This means that TCS must deliver more than undifferentiated programming by moving up the value chain. Such a movement is difficult in software services because the customers have deep domain expertise and almost invariably wish to retain the tasks grouped under strategic consulting in Table 1. Moreover, customers understand that if they outsource the strategic consulting, then their bargaining power will be reduced. TCS must develop sufficient expertise so as to make outsourcing these tasks a compelling value proposition. Of course, it is exactly in these realms that the multinational outsourcing firms such as IBM, Accenture, and EDS are the most ferocious competitors.

Forging alliances is often viewed as a good strategy to offset clients' bargaining power. However, building alliances with firms working in clients' locations should be discounted as this would further focus TCS in applications' development. On the other hand, the acquisition of a medium-sized American firm with strong client relationships and domain skills could provide an attractive opportunity. Although costs per employee would rise, the rise would be small since labor requirements are lower for higher value-added work (see the table above).

Meanwhile, the threat of new entrants is declining rapidly as the larger firms have rapidly increased their size, market share, and credibility with customers. However, although firms strive to reduce their direct competition through product differentiation, in each market segment there continue to be numerous players.

A key concern for TCS is competition from existing players as it has generated competition for existing business and created significant pricing pressures. Globally, firms such as EDS have positioned themselves as capable of undertaking large, "turnkey" projects in order to differentiate themselves from competitors such as IBM and Accenture that focus on higher value-added work such as consulting. This suggests an organically-driven growth strategy for TCS: that TCS continue to do the same kinds of work that it currently does, but try to capture a greater portion of the value-addition by undertaking larger projects. Though it has already demonstrated a capability in remote project management, it would be required to further increase this capability.

However, there are some risks to this strategy. TCS' large size suggests that it may have already maximized economies to scale in applications development. Adding scope, however, offers the potential for large gains since it necessarily involves higher value-added activities. In the early days, this was difficult, partly due to the technical difficulty in de-integrating the value-chain beyond the modularization of applications programming. Over the past few years, however, engineering services, systems design, and systems integration work have increasingly been outsourced (within the U.S.), suggesting that, if the skills are at hand, such work could be done in India.

Most American providers of such services offer domain and software skills. TCS already has the software skills to move into these areas. But domain skills are a challenge. This is illustrated by TCS's focus on a few industries, notably banking and financial services (Supplementary Table 4 of the case). This reflects a general lack of domain expertise outside the financial services sector in India. Put differently, India does not have global-class, non-technical knowledge in various other industries. As a result it is difficult to offer the full panoply of services a firm would want when it considers outsourcing a software development activity. This may be being rectified as the liberalization of the Indian economy since 1991 has led to the development of a host of new industry capabilities, such as in insurance. This promises an expansion of domain-specific skills in fields outside the traditional industries—but these will develop only gradually.

These facts indicate that it will be difficult for TCS as an organization based and staffed primarily in India to change its revenue mix through organic growth. Acquiring Indian firms doing higher value-added business is a possibility, but there are few such firms in the Indian business environment. Essentially, the constraint that TCS faces is environmental rather than firm specific. In most sectors, Indian business conditions are sufficiently dissimilar to overseas client conditions that local domain expertise is of low relevance.

The threat of substitutes in software services does exist as technology tools to speed coding etc. However, at this time the threat of substitutes seems rather remote.

In summary, the answer to the first question posed is that TCS should grow in software services through (1) Acquisition of a medium-sized American firm with strong client relationships focusing on software-intensive areas complementary to TCS, such as system design and systems integration in financial services; A natural direction is to move first into areas adjacent to applications programming that require more IT-related skills and fewer domain skills, such as system design and systems integration. There are several such firms in the U.S. that could be attractive acquisition targets. However, managerial and cultural issues could also play a significant role. (2) Organic growth through undertaking larger projects; (3) Adding domain capabilities in step with the development of such skills in India. However, it should not consider overseas strategic alliances in allied domains or overseas acquisitions that provide new industry skills.

4. TCS AND BPO

TCS's decision on whether to make a large investment in BPO is analyzed as follows:

1. What is TCS' competitive positive in the BPO industry?

Unlike software services, TCS is a relatively small player in the BPO industry in India. The BPO business is divided into broad segments: call-center work (which includes a large component of IT-intensive technical support work) and back-office work. TCS entered the business much later than its traditional software rivals and initially focused primarily on call-center work. Nevertheless, TCS has some advantages over others in the industry. The first is that it can use its software business to improve its competitive position in the industry. Many of its software clients might become BPO clients due to their familiarity with TCS and its credibility in doing work overseas. On the other hand, the BPO business might affect TCS' software business as well. These linkages are analyzed as follows:

a) Retaining client relationships: BPs, unlike software development, are transaction-oriented rather than project-oriented. Once a software project is completed, it is common for the client to put the next project up for open bidding (despite a satisfactory experience). However, it is less likely that a client will switch its BP provider, as the migration process involves high initial costs and a long migration cycle. Hence, the software division may retain clients better if the firm also provides BP services.

b) Obtaining work linking software and BP: Some BPs, but not all, involve a considerable amount of software work. For example, TCS might automate a client's payroll system (a software project) and then manage payroll processes as well (a BP). Thus, its BP capabilities might allow it to earn higher value for a software project by offering to [fulfill] the service outcome of the project. This is a successful model in the U.S.: large firms such as EDS offer such integrated services.

c) Building domain expertise: Although TCS and other Indian firms currently do low-end, back-office work, over time more high-end work and even transitioning to front-office work might be possible. For example, a stockbroking operation might begin by offshoring post-deal settlement work, but then add automated trading and some of the more routine research functions over time. Over longer periods of time, even more sophisticated work such as sales call updates might be added. The advantage of BPO is that it lends itself to incremental increases in the number of services provided, with small value-added slices being added to the offshored work as the offshored operation gains in capability. This reflects the nature of BPs, that they will typically either be provided by a single outsourced provider or done in-house. This allows for the BP provider to build domain expertise that may then be leveraged to also climb the software value chain. By contrast, a firm that only offers software services will find it difficult to get clients to agree to add incremental work since there typically will already be other firms fulfilling the clients' needs in adjacent fields such as engineering services and systems integration.

2. How will the BPO business be affected by the software business?

a) There are key operational areas in which the impact of software work on BP is low: (1) skills sets needed for BPO at the operational level are different, requiring accountants, sales clerks, telephone operators, and so on, rather than software engineers. (2) The clients, though they might be in the same firm, are likely to be different, especially if the client-finn is large. Software services are normally marketed to the firm's CIO or CTO, while BP services are marketed to the firm's operations departments, such as accounts and HR.

b) There are also areas of synergy. The greatest for TCS is its long-established domain expertise in financial services that could help the firm obtain BPO work in the financial services industry. Further, TCS's credibility in software services should assist in securing BPO business from the same firm. Also, the BP operations can leverage off a similar set of IT-infrastructure management capabilities as are required for software services, such as remote project management and network management.

c) Moving up the BP value-chain: to the extent that TCS has the capability of moving up the software value-chain, this may assist in migrating up the BP value-chain.

3. Should TCS enter BPO and, if so, how?

As noted for software outsourcing, TCS is not affected by the competitive position of suppliers because its inputs are standard commodities with little scope for differentiation. The key challenges remain the bargaining power of customers and the competitive rivalry with existing players, although the threat of new entrants and substitutes is not negligible.

As noted in the case, TCS has hitherto made a few small investments in BPO, one as a joint venture and a small airline-industry related acquisition. An outcome of the above analysis is that, since software operations are to be ICS's core business for several years to come and since moving up the value-chain is a desired goal, entering BPO is advantageous because it could assist TCS in achieving its core goals. There are several disadvantages and TCS will have to develop personnel and marketing teams that are appropriate for BPO. It seems important for TCS to enter the BPO field. Ideally, TCS should build a BPO business that can leverage off the software business, such as managing back-office processes in finance, rather than in less-linked businesses such as call-centers. However, it may be impossible to simply "cherry pick" the most desirable businesses where there are considerable synergies between software and BPO. Still building the business within TCS rather than through alliances is the better strategy.

In the BPO realm there are similar difficulties for firms offering undifferentiated services such as call centers or simple claims processing. Moreover, for many firms, activities such as claims processing, mortgage application screening, data entry, or GIS data entry are only the most routinized activities in a larger business process. Frequently, the entire business process may not be viewed as a core function, and therefore the firms are willing to outsource more of the higher value-added activities in the business process. This willingness could permit the BPO firm to capture a larger portion of the entire process and in the process more deeply enmesh the customer in the relationship. This can serve to reduce the power of the customer AND reduce the threat from rivals and new entrants.

Moreover, unlike the more mature software industry, the configuration of markets and the rivals is changing constantly. For example, IBM, which is TCS' ideal-typical rival (through much larger and more diversified), announced in April 2004 that it was purchasing one of the premier independent Indian BPO firms, Daksh, for approximately $150 million. The implication is that IBM will be a "new entrant" in the BPO business. Thus at this point in the maturation of the BPO industry rivalry is likely to increase as global IT service firms seek to integrate BPO into their overall offerings.

In the case of BPO, substitutes are definitely a possibility. In the case of call centers, voice recognition software is constantly improving and there are products on the markets that can operate effectively in highly defined situations. Though this software will surely improve, at this time it appears as though it will be able to substitute for only some percentage of the total number of calls. In the case of claims processing, mortgage scoring, etc., the use of e-forms and software-driven character recognition systems clearly will decrease the need for routine data entry. However, auditing, monitoring, or editing functions require human judgement, but can also be done in India. So, non-human substitute methods are being developed, but there are opportunities to move further up the value chain where judgement is required.

In fact, interestingly enough, in the apparently low value-added BPO fields, movement up the value chain may be easier than in software. The reasons for this are the complexity of business processes and the fact that firms outsourcing the process may not see the entire process as a core competency. This would make them willing to outsource the entire process, rather than trying to retain the highest value-added portions for themselves. This suggests that TCS should consider making a serious commitment to the BPO field soon.

Overseas acquisitions appeared to be the most appropriate route for TCS to build its software business. The corresponding advantage of this strategy for BPO work is that it would provide TCS with a base of clients. It might allow a more rapid ramp-up to doing higher-end work. However, unlike software, a more cautious approach seems to be in order. TCS needs to first increase its understanding of the business and create a process implementation capability of sufficient scale prior to acquiring value-added overseas capabilities.

A domestic acquisition is an option, its advantage being a quick start and existing clients. However, TCS's existing client-base should make client acquisition relatively easy. Further, it is likely that its established project management skills can be leveraged for rapid ramp-up. This should ameliorate the risk of being left behind. For these reasons, TCS should grow organically rather than through acquisitions, with a focus on those domains (primarily financial services, but also manufacturing and telecommunications) in which it already has skills that have been used in its software services work.

INDUSTRIAL NOTE

1. The Origins of the IT Software Services Industry and Its Development in India. Understanding the Software Services Industry

A fundamental distinction in software is between services and products. Note that India delivers software services, not products. Put differently, Indian firms provide a customer-specific program and not a program for general use such as Microsoft Word, Oracle Enterprise Manager 10, or Quicken TurboTax. Any piece of software may be written in either form, i.e., either as: (1) a product or package, designed to be replicated in its original form across many users, with no or minimal customization needed prior to use, or, (2) a program specifically for a client's needs, i.e., customized. The latter activity is part of a wider group of activities termed software services (see below).

It is generally true that services are more constrained by geography than products that can be shrink-wrapped and transported physically or over the wires. Hence it might seem odd, given the physical distance of India from its clients' locations in developed countries, that India exports services and not products. Indeed, software firms (excluding those from India) mostly export products, not services.

There are three types of software, in descending order of complexity:

1. System level software: programs that control and support the control of the internal operations of the computer, such as operating systems software, driver software, virus scan software and utilities.
2. Tools software: programs that help applications to work better, such as database management software and programmer tools.
3. Applications software: programs that deliver solutions to the end-user, such as word processing software and financial accounting software.

The above list also sorts software by costs, which depends on the complexity of the software. It also sorts software by order of use: system level software is used by tools software, and tools software is used by applications software. In some cases, applications software works directly on systems software.

Cost drives the choice between products and customized programs for most users. Hence, the more complex and costly a program, the more likely is it to be developed as a product. However, the more varied an end-user's needs from another end-user, the more likely is the program to be developed as a customized program. Since variations in need appear most at the stage of applications, most customized software is applications software. This is shown in the following table:

Table Al: Software types and programs used

	Product used by:	**Custom Program used by:**
Operating System	All users	None
Tools	Most users	Some users
Applications	Small and large users	Large users

284

As noted above, custom program development is part of the larger field of software services solutions. Software service solutions is a large field whose full range is as indicated in table A2 below. It includes such work as making sure that the software and hardware work together, and also training on how to use a program. The table below shows how much was spent globally on each component of software services in 2001.

Table A2: Global software services spending by categories of work in the software development cycle, 2001

	Global software services spending ($billion)	Percentage share (%)	Labor hours— share of project (%)
Consulting	103.0	29.5	10
Applications Development/ Outsourcing	51.0	14.6	48
Web Services	12.8	3.7	10
System Integration: Hardware/Software Deployment and Support	88.4	25.4	15
Engineering Services, System Specification and Design	71.0	20.4	17
IT education and training	22.7	6.5	N/A
Total	348.9	100.0	100

Source: Adapted from Nasscom, 2003, p. 35 and TCS documents

Definitions:
Consulting refers to work on IT strategy, system conceptualization and architecture.
Applications Development/Outsourcing refers to work on creating the applications programs.
Web Services refers to services provided over the World Wide Web, such as inventory tracking.
Systems integration refers to the work of making the software and hardware components compatible and interoperable up to the required specifications.
Engineering services refers to the work of integrating the technical capabilities of the core product into the program, leading to the work of creating a system specification and its design.
Note: 1. The figure for applications development and outsourcing above includes only customized work and does not include the spending on developing applications programs as products. However, the other numbers, such as for systems integration, includes work done on making software products work.

The table above lists the work in order of use and is sometimes termed the waterfall model of software development. The work of providing software services for some application usually begins with an IT strategy, following which the software system is conceptualized, with appropriate architecture and technology. This leads to the system's design and specification, after which the operating systems, tools and applications are developed (or purchased as products). It is unlikely that only customized software will be used to deliver a solution to a client. As noted above, the operating system and tools will usually be packages, while the applications programs will be a mix of customized and packaged programs. The exact mix is determined as a result of the system's specification and design. Once the different software components are ready, the job of the systems integrator is to put it all together into a single, working software system, which may include web services.

In practice, software suppliers are specialized by service processes presented in the first column, though some—including successful ones such as EDS—may offer all. This specialization may have happened as a consequence of how the business developed. In the early days, firms that wanted customized software tended to do most of the work in-house, including the writing of code. Over time, some of the components listed above began to be outsourced, starting with the less complex pieces, such as software systems maintenance and, later, the programming of applications and systems integration. More recently, parts of the IT strategy have been outsourced.

The skills needed vary across the different service processes, as does the need to interact with others in the supply chain. An aspect of importance to India is that applications development requires only programming skills and limited interaction. This makes it possible to design and specify an application in one firm and have it developed in another. Thus, a user might contract with a U.S. firm for system specification and with an Indian programming firm for development.

Offshoring of software development was enabled by the introduction, in the mid-1980s, of the workstation, with its sophisticated graphics and numerical computation capabilities. For smaller firms, the workstation's advantage (unlike the PC) was its capacity to run applications (that earlier had to be outsourced to the EDP firms). Hence, smaller firms began to demand software products and services tailored to their businesses. Of equal significance, mainframe applications could also be programmed on workstations.

The widespread adoption of the Unix operating system for workstations and mainframes and the shift to writing programs in high-level languages, such as C, from the mid-1980s onwards was also an important change from when clients' computers operated on a variety of operating systems and applications were written in many languages.

Both the latter two developments, Unix/C and workstations (in short, U-W), greatly improved the economics of software development. A software vendor could now own any manufacturer's workstation, yet program for a mainframe or other workstation. Not surprisingly, there was a gradual and complete shift to the U-W standard for software development for mainframes and workstations.

Table A3: **Work done in the software industry, 1970–2002**

	India
1970–80	MNE system and software product development.
Reason for type of work	Joint ventures between American computer makers and local firms, following upon TCS outsourced work for Burroughs in 1974.
1981–90	MNE conversion work for U.S. markets; some product and custom applications development work.
Reason for type of work	Follower of US-trends in outsourcing; U-W standard and new computer policy and tax breaks in 1984/5.
1991–2002	Customized applications programming by domestic firms.
Reason for type of work	Economic reform in 1991 permitted intensified overseas presence of domestic firms.

2. Business Process Offshoring and Outsourcing in India

The offshoring and outsourcing of business processes to India has emerged only recently, mirroring a global trend to relocate components of back-office services, such as payroll and order fulfillment, and some front-office services, such as customer care, from the U.S. and other developed countries to English-speaking, developing nations especially India, but also other nations such as the Philippines.

The globalization of BPO depends upon a number of factors: The first is the establishment of a high quality telecommunications infrastructure. Second is the increasing digitization of the objects of service work, which increasingly permits changing its geography of provision. When a service activity, such as the processing of an insurance claim, is examined as a totality, then it appears to resist relocation. For example, the assessment of a claim is likely to require at least some contact with a client. In fact, very few service operations can be done only on the computer, since they require some level of face-to-face interactivity, either among co-workers or with persons outside the organizations, such as vendors and clients. However, there are activities within the entire claims settlement process that do not require any in-person interaction. These can often be parsed into components requiring different levels of skill and interactivity. Once this examination and often reengineering of the business process has been completed, certain activities within the entire process, whether skill intensive or not, can be relocated offshore.

BPO to India underwent a dramatic expansion after the telecommunications infrastructure became adequate, something that occurred roughly in parallel with a series of government reforms of the telecommunications system begun in the 1999. These reforms including opening telecommunications provision to the private sector were critical to enabling the timely delivery of services. This combined with earlier successes in providing software services to give overseas clients a level of comfort with moving business activities to India. The earlier experience helped to minimize the natural concerns among firms about the security, continuity, and advantages to be derived relocation offshore.

The cost advantages of BPO in India are large. According to an Indian trade body, Nasscom, the direct cost of an Indian employee in a BPO operation is $10,354 per year compared with American costs of $55,598.[2] Not surprisingly, the business has grown spectacularly. One reason for this is that it is much easier to have rapid ramp-up in services than in manufacturing. In 2002-03, the industry's revenue in India was $2.375 billion compared with $1.475 billion in the previous year.[3]

The activities most commonly offshored are telephone support operations, outbound call centers, benefits administration, and payroll management. There are differences in the skills requirements between call centers, which have a high level of customer contact, and back-office BPOs such as payroll management, which are highly technical and replicable. India's high facility with the English language has certainly been an important factor. The industries that have offshored to India are many, but financial services industries have led the way, perhaps because of India's domain skills in this area. Many foreign banks and finance companies that were already operating in India to serve the local markets opened business process subsidiaries for their parent and its multinational subsidiaries. The pioneers in undertaking services for their global operations were Amex and GE Capital, but multinational BPO firms like Convergys and specialist outsourcers like TeleAtlas, have followed, as have Indian generalists and specialists.

Many Indian IT firms including the three largest, TCS, Wipro, and Infosys have BPO operations, but TCS remains significantly smaller than the other two. The IT firms' believe their advantages include vast experience of interaction with the global economy and adequate internal resources. They expect that this

---

[2] Nasscom (2003)
[3] Nasscom (2003)

prior experience will allow them to develop executive and managerial talent capable of securing overseas contracts, managing the interface with foreign customers, and migrating activities across national and firm boundaries. Another advantage they have is their domain expertise, which can be utilized in providing help desk and other support for IT, financial and telecommunications firms. Finally, they also have skills in process automation that may be attractive to clients seeking to obtain more than just labor cost savings from offshoring the business process to India. This is expected to be especially attractive in IT-intensive fields such as supply-chain management and product development.

However, the IT firms have challenges as well. India's legacy of state-controlled growth until 1991 has created a shortage of skills outside the financial services sector. The sophistication of Indian firm practices in payroll, claims processing and benefits management are limited. In terms of securing BPO contracts, the customer's key decision maker is not the Chief Information Officer or Chief Technical Officer who normally decided on software outsourcing. For BPO the critical decision makers are usually the managers in charge of the various responsible divisions or departments. Moreover, the ultimate approval rests with the Chief Financial Officer or Chief Executive Officer. This means that the Indian IT firms selling BPO services must convince a different set of managers in their prospective customer-firms.

There are also workforce differences between IT outsourcing and BPO. Whereas, in the IT sector the workforce largely consists of engineers, in BPs the workers' degrees are predominantly in commerce and social science. Since BPO work often requires direct interaction with customers, the salient workforce skills are interpersonal, rather than technical. Further, many BPs are undertaken in real time so errors and mistakes have an immediate impact. Moreover, Service Level Agreements are tightly written and monitored in real time so problems are exposed nearly immediately. In contrast, in software, bugs can be rectified later. Also, BPs that require customer interaction can be extremely stressful, putting a premium on skillful workforce management.

The ability of Indian IT firms to enter the business process outsourcing space will be tested. At the moment, the industry is growing so rapidly that a true test of managerial prowess may not come until later when many foresee a shakeout. This means that difficulties may remain hidden until growth slows. However, it is also possible that by that time the Indian firms will have built such close relationships with their customers that exit by the customers may no longer be possible. What is clear is that the BPO business provides a tremendous opportunity for India. But, also, the speed of its growth and evolution means that the competitive landscape will change rapidly with a large number of entrants. Competition on the basis of price, quality, and reliability will be ferocious.

References:

Nasscom, (2003), *The IT Industry in India: Strategic Review 2003*, New Delhi, India: Nasscom

This teaching note has been peer reviewed by the editorial board of the Journal of Strategic Management Education (JSME). For further information on this textbookjournal please visit the Senate Hall Academic Publishing website at www.senatehall.com.
The authors thank Jayashree Rukmani for research assistance, TCS officials for interviews and access to internal documents and Charles Holloway of the Graduate School of Business, Stanford University for comments. We also thank the editor, Peter Neilson, and three anonymous referees for their comments. An Industrial Note, as well as the Teaching Note, is available from Senate Hall Academic Publishing.

Case: McDonald's and The McCafé Coffee Initiative
Primary Chapter: Chapter 7 (Corporate)
Secondary Chapter: Chapter 12 (New Ventures)

Introduction: The setting for this case is a local franchisee of McDonald's in Canada is trying to stop the slide in relative market share in the breakfast hours. He sees that establishments with more (and better) coffee offerings seem to be getting all the growth. On a vacation to Europe he sees that many McDonald's there have a small restaurant within a restaurant that specializes in higher end coffees (McCafé). Upon his return to Canada, he convinces McDonald's that it should try to launch this new concept in Canada. This case provides an opportunity to explore the challenges of product diversification. While the scope of the diversification is rather modest to what might be explored in other cases (say diversifying from auto manufacturing to consumer financing), the principles are similar and in some ways it makes for a nice introduction to the concepts of diversification because the nature of the product diversification is relatively easy to understand. The case teaching note is structured around the logic of the resource-based view, and helps the instructors walk the students through the nature of McDonald's resources and whether they would offer an opportunity to create a position in the breakfast market that creates value.

This case teaching note has some data that is not included in the student case. Depending on the level of your students, you may find it helpful to distribute some of this data before your case discussion (the case writers assume a rather sophisticated level of student, and some undergraduates might have trouble thinking through all of the issues without the data to inform them). For additional background information, you may find it useful to review the Ivey case on Starbucks. In that case you read that Starbucks has been approached many time by McDonald's who would like to form an alliance to allow them to offer Starbuck's coffee. Starbucks declines because they are worried about brand dilution.

Strategy Diamond: This case allows you to examine moving into apparently related arenas (McDonald's already offers coffee on its menu, it is simply moving into the gourmet segment). The vehicle is taken for granted in the case; this in an organic expansion. (While the case is not written around finding alternatives like an acquisition or alliance, the instructor could easily spend a few minutes on this in the discussion. See the note above about McDonald's multiple attempts to form an alliance with Starbucks.) Most of the discussion in this case will probably be centered on differentiators and how McDonald's existing differentiators both constrain options and provide a possible defensible competitive position for expansion into this segment. The instructor's teaching note has some data that also allows for an interesting discussion of the economic logic (e.g., data on the prices charged by McDonald's and competitors for coffees and allied breakfast products).

Strategic Leadership: The protagonist in this case is Ralph Sgro, a local franchisee who owns several McDonald's in Burlington, Ontario, Canada. Thus, the level of leadership complexity is rather modest, yet this facilitates undergraduate students being able to clearly understand the leadership issues. They intuitively understand what it might take to run a McDonald's and how implementation levers might be exercised by an owner.

Formulation/Implementation: As students begin to discuss proposed implementation of the McCafé concept, you may want to spend some time on what levers are necessary for this to be successful. This is frankly not the meat of the case, but the case is simple enough that implementation might actually be fruitfully explored simply because the students will have a better understanding of the organizational contingencies that must be accommodated. What can Sgro do to increase the probability of McCafé being successful? Most students will have clear ideas about this, but you'll want to help them be systematic in their thinking.

The Dynamic Nature of Strategy: This case really focuses on just a cross section of time in the industry, so it may not appear to be a case about dynamic strategy. Yet, when viewed in context of what has been happening in the industry, it is easy to see that we are seeing on franchisee's (and McDonald's as a corporation) attempts to reposition his stores to better fit a changing competitive environment. Thus, while the case is isolated in time, it is the evolving nature of his competition that gets us to this decision point.

TEACHING NOTE
MCDONALD'S AND THE MCCAFÉ COFFEE INITIATIVE

CASE OVERVIEW

While McDonald's breakfast and snack sales had been increasing, they had not kept pace with industry growth. The primary barrier to this sales growth in the Canadian market, according to Ralph Sgro, was the quality of the coffee. McDonald's in Canada had been attempting to build its coffee brand equity for many years now. McDonald's had switched to the Higgins & Burke coffee (Mother Parker's brand), but had little success changing customer's negative perceptions about its coffee. To truly change customer perceptions, McDonald's needed to revolutionize its coffee programs.

McCafé was introduced in response to this coffee issue. McCafé was a full-service coffee bar, located in a McDonald's restaurant as an extension to the front counter or located as a stand-alone restaurant. More than 300 McCafés existed worldwide, in 19 countries including the United States. Ralph Sgro, a franchisee in Burlington Ontario, first visited McCafé in Rome and spearheaded a team to bring McCafé to Canada. While McDonald's would have liked to get a piece of the lucrative coffee market, McCafé's main objective was to eliminate coffee as a barrier to breakfast and snack sales. The question guiding this case study is whether McCafé strong initial sales can be sustained.

TEACHING OBJECTIVES

1. To understand the challenges of working in a mature industry and the convergence of industry barriers that escalates competition
2. To understand the challenges of product diversification
3. To recognize when product diversification can lead to sustainable competitive advantage

Background Readings

Jay Barney, *Gaining and Sustaining Competitive Advantage,* 2nd edition, Pearson Education Inc., Upper Saddle River, New Jersey, 1998, p. 173.

David J. Collis and Cynthia A. Montgomery, "Creating Corporate Advantage," *Harvard Business Review,* May-June 1998, pp. 71–83.

Constantinos C. Markides, "To Diversify or Not To Diversify," *Harvard Business Review,* November-December 1997, pp. 93-99.

Assignment Questions

- Based on initial results, Sgro believed that McCafé appears to have resolved the losses in breakfast sales. Do you agree?
- Will McCafé's results be sustainable in the long run?
- How do you think the industry will react to McCafé?
- In terms of future initiatives, what strategies would you recommend to Sgro?

NOTE TO INSTRUCTOR

The assignment questions have been organized around Barney's VRIO framework. The analysis to address those questions has also relied on the Collis and Montgomery and the Markides articles. You may want to write the students' responses on a blackboard or a whiteboard in such a way so that the answers to each question are covered on a discrete part of the board. At the end of the discussion, you can walk through the question and show the parallel to Barney's framework. Barney's framework argues that a resource or capability provides sustainable competitive advantage if it is valuable, rare, inimitable, and the firm is organized to exploit it. If any one of these conditions is not met, the firm will either not have a competitive advantage or it may not be sustainable. Exhibit TN-1 summarizes Barney's framework and Exhibit TN-2 applies it to the McCafé situation.

While the analysis can go a number of directions, students will probably argue that while McCafé is a good idea initially, it will be readily copied because the quick-service food industry is mature. However, as the instructor probes, it may become more evident to students that McDonald's resources, capabilities and organization best allow it to exploit the McCafé concept. As long as McDonald's is able to provide good quality, fast service, and standardized and relatively inexpensive product, other food service competitors and coffee retailers may not be able to imitate the McCafé formula very easily. To highlight the change in attitudes that students will experience as they analyse the case, you may want to take a vote at the beginning of class as to *whether McCafé will help McDonald's emerge a winner in the coffee industry.*

CLASS DISCUSSION

Based on the initial results, Sgro believed that McCafé has resolved the losses in breakfast sales. Do you agree (i.e. is McCafé's product *Valuable*)?

Initial indications were that McCafé has halted the erosion of sales. As a direct result of the implementation of McCafé, as described in the case, coffee sales increased over 30 per cent in the first six months of operations compared to the previous year.

These sales increases were even more impressive considering that McCafé did not engage in a national advertising campaign. McCafé operated in only one of six Burlington stores and was advertised only on local billboards and in the local newspaper. These revenue indications suggest that customers found McCafé valuable.

Other coffee retailers sell the same products that McCafé offers. Why would McCafé attract customers (i.e. is McCafé *Rare*)?

There are three attributes that made McCafé unique from its competitors. First, McCafé was the only restaurant that offered specialty coffee and a full food menu simultaneously. McCafé customers could order a variety of breakfast meals and also receive a good-quality cup of coffee. None of the other quick-service food restaurants offered specialty coffee. Although several coffee retailers sell muffins, doughnuts, bagels or other pastries, none have been successful at imitating McDonald's food sales, such as the Egg McMuffin, at the same quality and competitive price.

Second, McDonald's was recognized for providing quick uniform service. For example, in the drive-through, McDonald's had a customer throughput goal of 90 seconds or less (including ordering), and most stores attained this goal. In contrast, Tim Hortons drive-through service-time goal was 100 seconds. Starbucks and Second Cup offered good-quality coffee, but the quality of the coffee depended on the skill of the baristas, so the coffee was not always of uniform quality.

Finally, McCafé brewed and specialty coffee was cheaper than its specialty coffee rivals by up to 50 per cent (see Exhibit TN-3). However, although McCafé desserts and treats were significantly less expensive than its "coffee house" competitors, McCafé desserts were 30 per cent to 40 per cent more expensive than rival Tim Hortons. The overall McCafé offering gave customers an affordable luxury—coffee house products and the coffee house quality, without the coffee house prices. While this offering would not appeal to a high-income customer, it would appeal to more value-conscious customers.

How will coffee retailers and fast-food competitors react to McCafé? (i.e. is McDonald's offering of specialty coffee through McCafé *Inimitable*?)

Competitors could react to McCafé by imitating the following:

1. McCafé's low prices
2. McCafé's full food menu

Starbucks and Second Cup would have to reduce their prices significantly, which could erode their brand image as premier suppliers. Tim Hortons, however, could compete on price effectively, but not likely sustain that position or win a price war, as coffee sales represented a much greater share of its overall revenues than they did for McDonald's. Because McDonald's coffee represented only one per cent to two per cent of its total sales, large coffee margins were not required; McDonald's made most of its revenues on its core products, burgers and breakfast sandwiches.

Second, while competitors could attempt to enter the handheld breakfast sandwich market, their lack of expensive equipment or core competency in operations or menu management made a successful entrance unlikely.

Fast-food competitors, on the other hand, would have to duplicate McDonald's standardized operations and breakfast menu. Although this is a legitimate threat, to date, no other fast-food restaurant has successfully acquired these capabilities.

While McDonald's competitors will attempt to copy McCafé, how effective will they be? What sort of organizational structure does McDonald's have that has made the McCafé concept effective (i.e. is McDonald's *Organized* to exploit McCafé)?

McDonald's strategic asset was its corporate standardization formula for both products and services that were adapted to restaurants across the country. Strategic assets are unique and unassailable competitive strengths.[1] Many competitors had attempted to imitate the McDonald's system, yet none had succeeded in

---

[1] *Constantinos C. Markides, "To Diversify or Not To Diversify," <u>Harvard Business Review</u> November-December 1997, pp. 93 to 99.*

duplicating McDonald's entire service offering. McDonald's had organized the entire company around these standardized operations. New products or operations were created at the head office by an expert team, then tested at different locations to perfect the operations (for example, McCafé in Burlington). Finally, an operational standard was outlined on paper, and given to each store manager as the new venture was rolled out. To support these standards, head-office representatives monitored the quality of operations of their region to ensure McDonald's standards were met. In addition, McDonald's invested in management training, at Hamburger University, to develop its managers into leaders. Using this strength of operations, McDonald's could implement new systems, such as McCafé, seamlessly into its operations. Although competitors could imitate the McCafé experience, they had not been able to imitate McDonald's standardization formula.

McDonald's Corporation had standardized its entire service process, creating a system that allowed it to react to market demands, created a service offering that meets these demands and deploy offering throughout the network of restaurants. The following resources support this process:

- Franchisees,
- A strong corporate/franchisee relationship,
- Shared investments between corporate office and franchisees.

First, involving the franchisees in both the local operations of their stores and national initiatives, such as McCafé, gives McDonald's invaluable access to its customers. Because the franchisees work alongside management, crew and customers, they are at the pulse of trends and opportunities. Therefore, involving franchisees instills entrepreneurial spirit and innovation to this large organization.

Second, a strong corporate/franchisee relationship is the cornerstone of the McDonald's philosophy. This strong relationship enables head office to implement new initiatives and assist the franchisees operationally, thus ensuring McDonald's remained competitive in the industry. While many organizations had strong capabilities at their corporate head office, this relationship allowed McDonald's to push these capabilities down to the front lines.

Finally, McDonald's corporation and the franchisee shared in the cost of each restaurant, which allowed them to roll out new concepts more quickly. McDonald's owned the land, or the head lease, and the building, while the franchisee owned the equipment and decor package. Although McCafé was financed by the franchisee, McDonald's corporate provides support and incentive packages to encourage investment. In addition, McDonald's had significant bargaining power in setting prices with suppliers and construction companies to ensure low-cost supplies for its McCafé owners.

By creating an organization prepared to attack a new market opportunity, McDonald's is organized to exploit new opportunities, such as McCafé.

Exhibit TN-1
VRIO FRAMEWORK

	Theoretically	**McCafé**
Valuable	Do a firm's resources and capabilities enable the firm to respond to environmental threats and opportunities?	McCafé's added value is evident in the increased revenue, both in terms of coffee from McCafé and the spin-off effects on other McDonald's food. In addition, it brings value to the brand through the quality associated with McCafé.

Rare	Is a resource currently controlled by only a small number of competing firms?	Although there are many other coffee retailers, none of them can offer McDonald's or the complementary food products or McDonald's standardized operations. This makes McCafé different from its retail coffee competitors.
Inimitable	Do firms without a resource face a cost disadvantage in obtaining or developing it?	While the McCafé or McDonald's concept can be imitated, no one has been able to duplicate McDonald's standardized operations to date. In addition, the value of the McDonald's brand takes a long time to build, and cannot be imitated in the short run.
Organized to Exploit	Are a firm's other policies and procedures organized to support the exploitation of its valuable, rare and costly to imitate resources?	McDonald's entire organizational structure revolves around an expertise in operations. McDonald's also has many existing stores prepared to roll-out McCafé. However, the franchisees, as the decision makers, must be onside for this investment to be approved.

Exhibit TN-2
EVALUATION OF MCCAFÉ
Resources and Capabilities

Valuable?	Rare?	Costly to Imitate?	Exploited by Organization?	Competitive Implications	Economic Performance
YES	YES	YES	YES	Competitive Advantage	Above Average
McCafé's added value is evident in the increased revenue, both in terms of coffcc from McCafé and the spin-off effects on other McDonald's food. In addition, it brings value to the brand through the quality associated with McCafé.	Although there are many other coffee retailers, none of them can offer McDonald's complementary food products or McDonald's standardized operations differentiating McCafé from its competitors.	While the McCafé or McDonald's concept can be imitated, no one has successfully duplicated McDonald's standardized operations, which is critical to the cost/price equation for McCafé. Further, McCafé is able to leverage the McDonald's brand.	McDonald's entire organizational structure revolves around an expertise in operations. McDonald's also has many existing stores prepared to roll out McCafé. However, the franchisees, as decision makers, must be onside for this investment to be approved.	McCafé adds value, and McDonald's is organized to exploit the McCafé opportunity. However, while McCafé is different from the traditional coffee retailers, the value placed on its "rarity" depends on how much value customers place on getting good	The sustainability of any competitive advantage will be determined by the quality of McCafé's launch across Canada; if McCafé can be successfully implemented and operationally maintained in each and every store, it should bring McDonald's success in the quick-service industry.

294

				coffee with McDonald's food. Furthermore, although operations have proved to be inimitable, much inimitability of McCafé depends on the value of McDonald's brand equity.	
NO	–	–	NO	Competitive disadvantage	Below Average
YES	NO	–	NO	Competitive parity	Average
YES	YES	NO	NO	Temporary competitive advantage	Above average
YES	YES	YES	YES	Competitive advantage	Above Average

Source: Jay Barney, Gaining and Sustaining Competitive Advantage, *2nd edition, Pearson Education Inc., Upper Saddle River, New Jersey, 1998, p. 173.*

Beverages	McCafé			Tim Hortons			Starbucks			Second Cup			Williams Coffee Pub		
	SM	MED	LG	SM	MED	LG	SM	MED	LG	SM	MED	LG	SM	MED	LG
Coffee	0.93	1.03	1.19	0.98	1.07	1.21	1.35	1.75	1.95	1.45	1.64	1.82	1.07	1.25	1.40
Tea	0.89	0.89	0.89	0.93	0.93	0.93	1.40	1.40	2.00	1.21	1.21	1.21	1.25	1.25	1.25
Cappuccino	-	1.69	1.89	-	-	-	2.80	3.55	3.95	2.66	3.32	3.83	-	2.05	2.79
Café Latte	-	1.69	1.89	-	-	-	2.80	3.55	3.95	2.66	3.32	3.83	-	2.59	3.37
Carmel Latte	-	2.18	2.38	-	-	-	3.25	4.00	4.40	3.18	3.83	4.26	-	2.99	3.79
Espresso	0.95	0.95	0.95	-	-	-	1.55	2.00	-	1.50	1.92	-	-	1.25	1.55
Hot Chocolate	-	0.99	-	0.92	1.03	1.13	2.60	2.85	3.10	2.51	2.71	3.00	1.25	1.59	1.99
Frothy Coffee	-	1.19	1.35	1.21	1.31	1.54	-	-	-	-	-	-	-	-	-
Iced Cappuccino	1.59	2.19	2.79	1.69	2.29	2.89	3.00	3.55	4.25	3.22	3.83	4.26	1.25	2.99	-
Desserts															
Squares	1.29			1.25			2.55			2.01			1.49		
Cakes/Danishes	1.29			1.25			3.95			2.01			1.49		
Cookies	0.49			0.35			1.50			1.31			0.80		
Doughnuts	-			0.70			-			-			1.49		

Exhibit TN-3 (continued)

MCCAFÉ PRICES AS A PERCENTAGE OF THE COMPETITION'S PRICES

Beverages	Tim Hortons			Starbucks			Second Cup			Williams Coffee Pub		
	SM	MED	LG	SM	MED	LG	SM	MED	LG	SM	MED	LG
Coffee	-5.0%	-3.7%	-1.7%	-31.0%	-41.1%	-39.0%	-36.0%	-37.2%	-34.6%	-13.0%	-17.6%	-15.0%
Tea	-4.0%	-4.3%	-4.3%	-36.0%	-36.4%	-55.5%	-26.0%	-26.4%	-26.4%	-29.0%	-28.8%	-28.8%
Cappuccino	n/a	n/a	n/a	n/a	-52.4%	-52.2%	-49.1%	-49.1%	-50.7%	n/a	-17.6%	-32.3%
Café Latte	n/a	n/a	n/a	n/a	-52.4%	-52.2%	-49.1%	-49.1%	-50.7%	n/a	-34.7%	-43.9%
Carmel Latte	n/a	n/a	n/a	n/a	-45.5%	-45.9%	-43.1%	-43.1%	-44.1%	n/a	-27.1%	-37.2%
Espresso	n/a	n/a	n/a	-39.0%	-52.5%	n/a	-37.0%	-50.5%	n/a	n/a	-24.0%	-38.7%
Hot Chocolate	n/a	-3.9%	n/a	n/a	-65.3%	n/a	-63.5%	-63.5%	n/a	-37.7%	-37.7%	n/a
Frothy Coffee	0.0%	-9.2%	-12.3%	n/a	n/a	n/a	n/a	n/a	n/a	n/a	n/a	n/a
Iced Cappuccino	-6.0%	-4.4%	-3.5%	-47.0%	-38.3%	-34.4%	-42.8%	-42.8%	-34.5%	n/a	-26.8%	n/a
Desserts												
Squares	3.0%			-49.0%			-36.0%			-13.0%		
Cakes	3.0%			-67.0%			-36.0%			-13.0%		
Cookies	40.0%			-67.0%			-63.0%			-39.0%		
Doughnuts	0.0%			n/a			n/a			n/a		

Note: All prices are relevant to the Burlington, Ontario retail coffee industry ONLY.

Case: Coca-Cola's Re-entry and Growth Strategies in China
Primary Chapter: Chapter 8 (International)
Secondary Chapter: Chapter 4 (External environment)

Introduction: The Coca-Cola's Re-entry and Growth Strategies in China case focuses on the challenges and opportunities facing Coca-Cola as it re-enters China following the opening of the market in 1978. This case does not pose a specific decision dilemma, but rather documents the various challenges that Coke faced and the choices they made to accommodate the demands of the national context. The case provides an opportunity to see how one well known company adapted its strategy to the local conditions and customers of China. The case provides sufficient detail to address the issue of global configurations (e.g., International, Global, Multinational, and Transnational). The case suggests that Coke's success in China is facilitated by its adaptation to the local market. However, there is also an opportunity to identify unique resources that are exploited across national boundaries. The degree to which these need to be adapted should provide a lively discussion in the classroom.

Strategy Diamond: This case provides excellent detail on vehicles and staging. The information is sufficient for the instructor to really develop the principles of staging and sequencing different initiatives, as well as the capabilities of strategic partners, in rolling out a comprehensive entry strategy. The case also covers a rather lengthy time period (1978 to 2003) that the dynamics of strategy are also illustrated (Chapter 6). Differentiators: The case covers some image building activities (sponsorship of specific sporting events and teams). In addition, most students will have a feel for Coke's general differentiators and it is possible to discuss how these might translate to China. Economic Logic: not as applicable in this case, no financial data are included in the case, only information about events and their timing.

Strategic Leadership: This case does not directly illustrate any strategic leadership issues. Any discussion of leadership will need to be initiated by the instructor as the case is not built around leaders or decision points.

Formulation/Implementation: The case begins with the premise that Coke wants to re-enter China. Lots of details about their intended strategy is provided. While there is no specific information about implementation levers, as with strategic leadership an instructor wishing to cover this issue can use the case as context to lead students through a discussion of the implementation implications of Coke's formulated strategy.

The Dynamic Nature of Strategy: The case illustrates the dynamic nature of entry and market development over more than two decades. Coke's initial strategy to enter on its own and partner with only government owned firms is modified over time as it teams up with foreign bottlers who sign alliances with Coke and Chinese partners to develop and manage bottling operations. In addition, Coke's normal method of distribution in developed countries must be modified to local conditions and then slowly rationalized through activities which may later bring economies of scale.

COCO-COLA'S RE-ENTRY AND GROWTH STRATEGIES IN CHINA TEACHING NOTE

SUMMARY

Coca-cola has a presence in over 200 countries worldwide and is acknowledged as the most recognized brand in the world. This case explains Coca Cola's entry and growth strategies in China and the reasons for its success in this market. The case discusses its strategy for re-entry into the Chinese market and its long-term localization strategy. The case also looks at how Coke cooperated with the Chinese government in order to soften the impact of the restrictive policies regarding Foreign Direct Investment in China, and how it designed its marketing and promotion strategies to suit the Chinese market.

TEACHING OBJECTIVES & TARGET AUDIENCE

The case is structured to enable students to:

- Understand the re-entry strategy of a multinational beverage company.
- Understand how a multinational company can work with the government in a situation where policies are restrictive of FDI.
- Understand the long-term localization strategy of a multinational company.
- Understand how a multinational company adapts its distribution, marketing and promotion to the new market that it enters.

The case is intended for MBA/PGDBM level students as part of their Strategy and General Management curriculum.

TEACHING APPROACH & STRATEGY

The case can be used effectively both in classroom discussion as well as in distance learning programs. During the course of the discussion the facilitator can introduce the students to the following issues:

1. There are various entry strategies that an MNC can adopt while entering an international market. What strategy did Coke employ to re-enter the Chinese market and how did it co-operate with the Chinese government to develop its production capabilities?
2. The success of an MNC in international markets depends on how well they manage all the activities in the value chain. Describe how in addition to localization of production, Coke also localized the inputs of production and distribution of its final products.
3. MNCs need to localize marketing and promotion strategies to be successful in international markets. How did Coke adapt its marketing and promotions to suit the Chinese market?

ANALYSIS

1.

In 1978, immediately after China opened its doors to foreign investment, Coke initiated discussions with the Chinese government and set its re-entry process in motion. The new economic policies in China were restrictive and foreign investment and production activity was highly regulated. Coke worked closely with the Chinese government in order to overcome the obstacles posed by restrictive policies. In the beginning, Coke only had permission to import Coca-Cola and was only allowed to sell to foreigners in China. Then in 1980, it signed an agreement with COFCO, a state-owned corporation. According to the agreement Coke built a plant in Beijing and in 1981 handed it over to the Chinese government in exchange for permission to expand its distribution and sales in China. Coke built another plant in Guangzhou and handed it over to the Chinese government in 1982. In exchange for the second plant, both plants would pay Coke for the concentrate that it supplied to them. In 1984, a third plant was built in Xiamen and handed over to the Ministry of Light Industry.

It was a smart move on the part of Coke to build these plants and hand them over to the government, as it had many positive repercussions. On the one hand, Coke was receiving payments for the concentrate and on the other, it was building strong relationships with the government and the state-owned corporations. From China's viewpoint, China was acquiring the long-term benefit of owning plants with up-to-date technology and equipment. In addition, it could use the plants to produce domestic beverages as well. Thus, Coke did not own any bottling plants in China during the first few years after its re-entry. Its first jointly owned bottling plant was opened in Zuhai in 1985. This plant was a result of a joint venture agreement signed with the Ministry of Light Industry in 1984. Also in 1984, the Ministry of Light Industry signed a letter of cooperation with Coke to set up more bottling plants in Shanghai, Tianjin and Qingdao. In the same year Coke signed a contractual joint venture agreement with the Ministry of Light Industry and SITCO to jointly build a bottling plant close to a proposed concentrate plant in Shanghai. According to the agreement, the Ministry of Light Industry and SITCO would own the bottling plant and Coke would own the concentrate plant.

All this time Coke had been developing its production capacity even though it did not have approval to sell to Chinese consumers. It was ready to meet the demand for its products when it finally got approval for this in 1985. After receiving the approval of President Jiang Zemin in 1986, Coke completed construction of its concentrate plant in 1988. The construction of the bottling plant in Tianjin was also finished in 1988 and it produced local Chinese brands of soft drinks in addition to Coke's products. By 1993, Coke had set up a total of 14 bottling plants in China and obtained permission from the Ministry of Light Industry and the State Economic and Trade Commission to build 10 more plants. The government stipulated that Coke should encourage development and production of local Chinese beverages at these new plants.

In 1993, Coke also formed bottling alliances with two bottling companies, Kerry and Swire. It made them its key bottlers and acquired a 12.5 percent stake in each of them. Over the years Coke partnered with Kerry and Swire in 10 and 9 joint ventures, respectively. These joint ventures, referred to as bottling enterprises, were usually three way joint ventures involving Coke, one of the key bottlers, a state-owned enterprise or a local Chinese company, or in some cases both. Thus, each bottling enterprise had a Chinese partner localizing the production process.

In 1996, Coke developed and launched a Chinese brand 'Tian Yu Di', to cater to Chinese consumers who preferred non-carbonated beverages with Chinese flavours. Once again in an effort to cater to the tastes of the Chinese consumers, in 1997, Coke also started producing carbonated beverages under the brand name 'Xingmu'. This showed that Coke was fulfilling the government's stipulation of encouraging Chinese brands and at the same time it was fulfilling an existing demand for beverages with traditional Chinese flavors such as jasmine flavored tea and lychee flavored juice.

2.

Coke's dependence on local Chinese companies and state-owned enterprises for inputs required in production and for other services, including distribution services, indicated that the localization of the

Coca-Cola system was not limited to the bottling and production of the beverages. Bottlers only accepted inputs that met Coke's global standards and developed good relationships with the local suppliers who met these standards. Ninety-eight percent of the final product consisted of local inputs such as water, sugar, PET bottles, glass, paper, closures, crowns and other packaging material. The bottlers also relied upon Chinese companies for trucks and lifting machinery. Coke also engaged local firms for business services such as legal services, financial services, repair services, accounting services, advertising, design, travel, construction, etc.

To overcome the challenges of covering a large geographical area and the lack of good infrastructure, Coke had to develop a different kind of distribution network in China. Coke based its distribution network on where the demand was and the outlets where consumers could actually buy a Coke product. Since a method that would work for one part of China might not work for another, Coke had to customize its methods of distribution for each market. It used both wholesalers and the direct store delivery system to distribute its products in China. The Coke bottlers owned and operated direct store delivery systems, but it was not the primary method of distribution. This system accounted for only about 20 percent of its sales while wholesalers accounted for the rest. Therefore, Coke was primarily dependent on the local Chinese distributors to get its products to the final consumer. These distributors were either state-owned companies or Chinese private wholesale companies.

3.

Coke designed its marketing and promotion strategies around things that the Chinese consumers could identify with or were passionate about. Since local managers were expected to relate better to these things, Coke gave them the freedom to make decisions regarding marketing and promotion strategies. The color red and the dragon are very important features of Chinese culture. Coke used both of these in an advertisement aired on television during the 1996 Chinese New Year. In July 2001, the Chinese government announced that it had received the approval to host the 2008 Olympics. To join in the celebration at being given this honor, Coke immediately introduced a commemorative gold Coca-Cola can in the market.

Soccer is one of the sports that the Chinese people are very passionate about. So in January 2001, Coke became the official beverage and a main sponsor of the national Chinese soccer team. From the time the Chinese team started playing the qualifying matches Coke aired different TV commercials and organized other promotions based on the FIFA World Cup, It commissioned a special song sung by eight popular Chinese singers during a live telecast of the Chinese team's first match. During the World Cup Asian Qualifying Matches, Coke aired "The Dream Never Dies" an advertisement that showed the Chinese soccer fans' enormous support for their national team. Then in October 2001, marking the occasion of the Chinese team qualifying for the finals, Coke introduced a commemorative can and a video disc called "The Road to the World Cup". Coke went even further in early 2002 by organizing a road show called "Hero Tours" so that soccer fans all over China could meet with the team. It also got school kids involved by organizing "Finger soccer" tournaments and flag bearer selections. In May 2002, Coke aired an advertisement called "Home Ground Advantage" which showed a Chinese boy giving the players a Coke bottle filled with soil to give them 'home ground advantage' in the World Cup.

In designing promotions, Coke took advantage of the fact that China had millions of mobile users and that the usage of SMS was very popular. In 2002, during the end of summer Coke ran a SMS contest called Coke Cool Summer which was announced through a television advertisement. Whoever guessed the correct highest daily temperature in Beijing and sent it through SMS, won a year's supply of Coke or Siemens cell phones. According to Coke, it received over 4 million messages during the contest which ran for 35 days. In early 2004, Coke introduced 'Modern Tea Workshop' - a new line of tea drinks; it hired Hong Kong movie stars, Tony Leung and Shu Qi to promote it. In order to promote Coca-Cola it hired

Taiwanese pop-stars S.H.E. and Will Pan. Thus, Coke also used movie stars and singers who were popular with the Chinese public to promote its products.

ADDITIONAL READING & REFERENCES

1. **Two reasons why Coke is it: China and Russia,** March 7, 1994, www.businessweek.com.
2. Mark L. Clifford in Hong Kong and Nicole Harris in Atlanta, with Dexter Roberts in Beidaihe and Manjeet Kripalani in Bombay, **Coke pours into Asia,** October 28, 1996, www.businessweek.com.
3. Zeng Min, **Is China the real thing for Coca-Cola?** February 18, 2000, www.chinadaily.com.
4. Anil K Joseph, **Coca Cola to double its China business in five years, says company official,** August 15, 2000, www.financialexpress.com.
5. Drake Weisert, **Coca-Cola in China: Quenching the Thirst of a Billion,** July-August, 2001, www.chinabusinessreview.com.
6. **Coca-Cola Eyes Western China,** September 2, 2002, www.peopledaily.com.cn.
7. Li Heng, **Coca-Cola has over 50 Percent Market Share in China,** September 4, 2002, www.peopledaily.com.cn.
8. **Basketball Player Yao Ming Sues Coca-Cola,** May 26, 2003, www.china.org.cn.
9. **Coca-Cola launches its World Cup marketing initiative "It's Our Turn",** March 25, 2002, www.coca-cola.com.
10. **Coca-Cola's First Chinese Majority-owned Bottling Plant Set up,** April 16, 2000, www.fpeng.peopledaily.com.cn.
11. **China Seen as Coca-Cola's Largest Market in 10 Years,** February 20, 2003, www.peopledaily.com.cn.
12. **Coca-Cola Tops Again,** 2001, www.bjreview.com.
13. **China Recognizes Coca-Cola for its Social, Environmental Contributions,** January 19, 2003, www.peopledaily.com.cn.
14. Jane Tian, **Beverage maker thirsty: Coca-Cola rosy about potentials in China,** November 28, 2000, Shanghai Star.
15. Brian Morrissey, **Coke Judges China SMS Campaign a Success,** October 30, 2002, www.boston.internet.com.
16. **Coca-cola launches new 2008 Beijing Olympic Games commemorative cans**, August 4, 2003, www.coca-cola.com.
17. **First new Chinese Logo for Coca-cola in 24 years marks start of "Year of Coke" in China,** February 18, 2003, www.coca-cola.com.
18. **Cola war rages on as can suppliers cut off supplies,** Feb 11, 2002, Asian Economic News, www.fmdarticles.com.
19. **Investment of Coca-Cola in China Hit US$1.1b,** July 27, 2001, www.fpeng.peopledaily.com.
20. H.F. Allman, formerly Legal Counsel in China for The Coca-Cola Company, **Transliteration of Coca-Cola Trademark to Chinese Characters,** www.tafkac.org.
21. Ann Chen and Vijay Vishwanath, **Be the top pick in China,** January 16, 2004, www.business-times.asial.com.
22. **Coca-Cola.com.cn Debuts in China,** July 26, 2000, www.chicagopride.com.
23. Geoffrey A. Fowler, Shanghai and Ramin Setoodeh, Hong Kong, **A Question of Taste,** August 12, 2004, www.feer.com.
24. **Is Diet Coke drugged?,** September 7, 2004, www.chinadaily.com.
25. Craig Simmons, **Marketing to the masses,** September 4, 2003, www.feer.com.

This teaching note was written by Suchitra Jampani, under the direction of Sanjib Dutta, ICFAI Center for Management Research (ICMR). It was prepared to accompany the case "Coca-Cola's Re-entry and Growth Strategies in China" (reference number 304-629-1). The case was compiled from published sources. ©2004, ICFAI Center for Management Research (ICMR), Hyderabad, India.

Case: Fuji Xerox and the Xerox Corp.: Turning Tables?
Primary Chapter: Chapter 9
Secondary Chapters: Chapters 6, 7 & 11

Introduction: In the early 1960s Fuji-Xerox is formed as a joint venture of two leading US and Japanese firms. Over time the venture acquires increasing autonomy, as its strategic vision, quality improvement expertise, and innovative capabilities render its most active parent, Xerox, increasingly dependent on its success. The case can be used to illustrate issues relating to corporate control of alliances and joint ventures, and in particular when, whether and to what extent to tighten or loosen control is appropriate. It also allows a discussion of the success conditions for local entrepreneurship in multinational companies. The evolution of alliances and joint ventures over time, and the means by which parties on either and both sides may resolve or exacerbate conflicts according to circumstances may also be probed.

Strategy Diamond: A key point in the case is Xerox's decision to use an international joint-venture as a vehicle. The case also provides a unique view of the inefficiencies Xerox encountered by having multiple international subsidiaries developing and selling products in out-of-domestic arenas and how Fuji-Xerox's differentiation caused cannibalization within the parent company.

The Dynamic Nature of Strategy: The case provides a perspective on the challenges that arise from global expansion and technological change in an industry. Xerox finds itself having to alter its strategy to compensate for the changing environment and/or its lack of perspective in previous strategies.

Formulation/Implementation: The case demonstrates a changing relationship between Fuji-Xerox and Xerox Corp. which strangled the ability to effectively implement certain strategies. The case also highlights the difficulty of formulating and translating a strategy across the boundaries of joint-ventures.

Strategic Leadership: Leaders in the company are mentioned, but the intent of the case is not to illustrate the effectiveness or ineffectiveness of leadership decisions.

FUJI XEROX AND XEROX CORP., TURNING TABLES?
TEACHING NOTE

This case examines the creation and growth of the Fuji Xerox Company, a joint venture between Fuji Photo Film and the Xerox Corporation. The case focuses on the evolution of the firm and its changing relationship with Xerox. It chronicles early joint operating arrangements, the growth in R&D and manufacturing capabilities at Fuji Xerox, and the eventual transformation of the relationship from parent-subsidiary to full partnership. These changes are described in the context of changing realities in the nature of global competition during the last half of the twentieth century. The case concludes in 2000 as the chairman of Fuji Xerox is contemplating a shift in the ownership structure of his firm and the challenges such a shift would entail for the relationships between the firm and its two powerful and important owners.

This case is primarily designed for a unit on joint ventures and other cooperative strategies. Secondarily, it offers insight into the challenges associated with strategy implementation, international business, corporate strategy and dynamic business strategies. It attempts to help students to:

- Gain a better understanding of the dynamic nature of cooperative strategies
- Understand the challenges and opportunities inherent in international business ventures
- Define challenges to managing the implementation of a strategic alliance in which one firm is a part owner of another
- Understand how strategies change over a time in a dynamic industry

1. What were the motivations for each partner in the joint venture between Fuji Film and Xerox? How did the motivations for the ongoing operating alliance between Fuji Xerox and Xerox change as the companies evolved?
2. Describe the alliance linkages between Xerox and Fuji Xerox. Which functions or processes in one firm were linked to the other? What goods, services or information was transferred between the firms? How did these specific linkages change over time?
3. How does the evolving competitive threat from Canon, Ricoh and others affect Fuji Xerox's decision to favor one ownership structure over another? How have Xerox and Fuji Xerox attempted to deal with threats from these competitors in the past? How should they approach them going forward?
4. How has the changing nature of global competition affected the alliance between Xerox and Fuji Xerox throughout its life? What aspects of globalization do you expect to be most important for both of these companies in the future? What type of global structure is best suited to Xerox's specific situation?
5. What facets of alliance implementation helped the alliance between Xerox and Fuji Xerox succeed through the years? What aspects of the implementation were the greatest sources of difficulty for the firms?
6. What position should Tony Kobayashi take regarding the potential sale of Xerox's equity in Fuji Xerox to Fuji Film? How might his company benefit from such a sale? What specific risks would Fuji Xerox face in such a scenario?

This case describes events across a 50-year time span. It provides excellent insight into the proposition that business is dynamic over time. For each core issue below, students will benefit from considering the question at multiple points in timeline of the relationship.

1. Motivations for Cooperative Strategies

What were the motivations for each partner in the joint venture between Fuji Film and Xerox? How did the motivations for the ongoing operating alliance between Fuji Xerox and Xerox change as the companies evolved?

The joint venture
Fuji Film joint venture motives:
- Access to xerographic technology – Rank Xerox would not license it but instead offered a joint venture

Xerox joint venture motives:
- Rapid access to the Japanese and other Asian markets
- Access to Fuji Films capabilities in optical mechanics, chemical technology, and manufacturing

The alliance
Evolution of Xerox's motivation for continuing the alliance with Fuji Xerox:

- As the manufacturing capabilities of Fuji Xerox increased, Xerox viewed the alliance as an important source of production knowledge
- As the research and development capabilities of Fuji Xerox increased, Xerox viewed the alliance as an important source of technology for applications in the rest of the world
- By 1994 Xerox seemed to view Fuji Xerox as an essential strategic partner, almost an equal partner, rather than as a subsidiary.

Evolution of Fuji Xerox's motivation for continuing the alliance with Xerox:
- Fuji Xerox shifted from viewing Xerox as a source of parts and technological designs for copiers destined for the Japanese market to seeing them as a co-developer of innovative technology targeted globally
- As Fuji Xerox became more capable and successful in its own right, its executives sought to be seen as equal partners with Xerox

Students should think about these changing motivations in terms of the alliance life cycle discussion found in the text. As a class, you can discuss each of the phases below and the degree to which this alliance passed through them.
- Product performance focus
- Market position focus
- Learning and capabilities focus

Another interesting class activity is to analyze the wisdom of the initial decision in the case. Was the joint venture investment an effective vehicle for Rank Xerox to execute its corporate strategy at the time of the initial deal with Fuji Film?

2. Alliance Implementation and Benefits

Describe the alliance linkages between Xerox and Fuji Xerox. Which functions or processes in one firm were linked to the other? What goods, services or information was transferred between the firms? How did these specific linkages change over time?

There were four separate agreements in the original alliance that governed Fuji Xerox operations. The technical assistance agreement described the fees to be paid to rank Xerox for access to technology. The original agreement specified that Fuji Xerox would not engage in its own R&D. A manufacturing agreement specified Fuji Film as Fuji Xerox's supplier of consumables like toner and paper. The initial deal included these linkages and transactions:

- Xerox provided parts to Fuji Xerox at agreed upon prices
- Fuji film provided consumables to Fuji Xerox at agreed upon prices
- Xerox provided patented technologies to Fuji Xerox for 5% of sales

Over time, the specific linkages between the firms evolved. Specific changes include:

- Manufacturing practices were transferred from Fuji Xerox to Xerox
- Fuji Xerox provided patented technologies to Xerox
- Finished products were produced by Fuji Xerox and distributed by Xerox
- Fuji Xerox provided competitive insight to Xerox through facilitating meeting with leading competitors in Japan

One exercise that is useful for students is to have them identify how the alliance between Xerox and Fuji Xerox created value for each firm in terms of the following categories:

- Joint investment
- Knowledge sharing
- Complementary resources
- Effective management

3. Industry Analysis - Competitive Factors

How does the evolving competitive threat from Canon, Ricoh and others affect Fuji Xerox's decision to favor one ownership structure over another? How have Xerox and Fuji Xerox attempted to deal with threats from these competitors in the past? How should they approach them going forward?

The activities of these competitors encouraged both Fuji Xerox and ultimately Xerox executives to embrace quality principles and incorporate them into their activities.

Fuji Xerox was able to compare their R&D spending and output to these successful rivals and determine that they were not spending enough or creating enough new technology. Such a direct comparison must have helped Fuji Xerox to convince Xerox to drop royalty payments in the early 1990's on the condition that Fuji Xerox invest those payments in R&D instead.

Fuji Xerox's move to compete fully with Canon and Ricoh also seemed to have precipitated the company's move to expand its sales efforts more broadly. The company argued that it needed to sell to a larger market in order to effectively amortize its increased R&D investment.

Eventually, it could be argued that it was the effectiveness of the Japanese competitors that forced Xerox and Fuji Xerox to seek "codestiny" through tighter integration of the two firms' activities. At the conclusion of the case, Fuji Xerox could see that Canon, Ricoh and Konica were moving from the low-end of the copier market into higher end segments that would result in greater-than-ever pressure on Fuji Xerox to improve it operations to remain competitive.

To best understand the nature of this dynamic threat, students should develop strategic group maps of this industry that indicate the resources and capabilities of Fuji Xerox compared to its competitors. Such maps could highlight the most important competitive dimensions on which the company would be likely to compete in the early years of the new millennium.

4. Industry Analysis - Globalization

How has the changing nature of global competition affected the alliance between Xerox and Fuji Xerox throughout its life? What aspects of globalization do you expect to be most important for both of these companies in the future? What type of global structure is best suited to Xerox's specific situation?

Changes in global competition in this industry have had a large effect on Fuji Xerox and Xerox. Students should discuss issues in the case related to:
- Multipoint competition
- Learning and knowledge sharing and its effect on competitiveness
- Opportunities for global efficiencies
- Need for local responsiveness
- Global customers
- Cultural distance between the partners

The globalization structure chosen by Xerox was entry via joint venture in key markets. Creation of an independent entity, Fuji Xerox, resulted in innumerable benefits to Xerox in the fifty years that followed. Ask students to imagine Xerox's prospects in the Eighties and Nineties if they had tried to sell in Japan with a foreign owned subsidiary rather than in a joint venture with a local partner.

5. Assessment

What facets of alliance implementation helped the alliance between Xerox and Fuji Xerox succeed through the years? What aspects of the implementation were the greatest sources of difficulty for the firms?

Simply by surviving for so many years, this alliance is likely to be deemed a success. Specific elements that led to its success include:
- Ability to change the dimensions of the alliance as external needs and internal capabilities of the participants changed
- Ability to change the relationship over time from parent-subsidiary to near-equal strategic partners
- Bi-directional learning
- Exchange programs for key employees
- Complementary resources and capabilities
- Creation of an additional independent entity, Xerox International Partners, when new skills and structures were needed
- Top executive summits to ensure high level communication

Examples of sources of difficulty include:
- Delays in the ability of Fuji Xerox to pursue R&D enabled Canon and others to capture the low end market in Japan
- Lack of clarity at middle management levels about whether the two firms were part of the same firm or competitors

6. Next Steps

What position should Tony Kobayashi take regarding the potential sale of Xerox's equity in Fuji Xerox to Fuji Film? How might his company benefit from such a sale? What specific risks would Fuji Xerox face in such a scenario?

To answer the questions above, ask students consider the following issues:

- Is a shift in ownership control likely to positively or negatively affect Fuji Xerox's R&D, manufacturing or sales capabilities?
- Is a shift likely to decrease the flow of information and technology between Xerox and Fuji Xerox?
- What new capabilities could be gained from Fuji Photo Film?
- Does the direction of technology innovation in the industry make Fuji Photo Film a more desirable majority owner?
- Will the cash infusion from the sale help Xerox maintain its competitiveness through its current difficult period?

Teaching Plan (one 80 minute session)

Students read and prepare case prior to class.

- Motivations for Cooperative Strategies (15 minutes)

- Alliance Implementation and Benefits (20 minutes)

- Industry Analysis (20 minutes)

- Assessment and next steps for Tony Kobayashi (25 minutes)

Case Update

In April, 2001 Xerox sold half of its 50% stake in Fuji Xerox to its 39-year partner Fuji Photo Film. Xerox collected $1.3 billion from the sale at time when it was greatly in need of cash but capital markets were reluctant to provide it. Xerox was able to record a $300 million gain on the sale. Xerox remains a 25% partner in Fuji Xerox and the two companies continue to actively develop and market products together. In October 2005 the two firms introduced the innovative DC 240/250, which took components from the DocuColor 8000. This new machine marries advanced toners and innovative imaging Raster Output Systems that sweep on and off 32 laser beams to form the image. The result was a "real" digital press in a compact footprint (just 72×84") that could suit any location.

With 34,017 employees as of fiscal year 2004, Fuji Xerox continues to experience revenue and profit growth including 2004 sales (mil.) of $9,487.2 and net income (mil.) of $404.8. The competitiveness on cost of its markets has encouraged Fuji Xerox to continue to focus its manufacturing growth in China. The company announced plans to move 90% of manufacturing to China by the end of 2005 in an effort to better serve both global customers and the growing China market. In addition to serving its core territory in the Asia-Pacific region, including Japan, the company has leveraged ties with Xerox Corporation helped drive sales in other areas around the world. One important partnership as of 2005 was its partnership with Dell to help the American computer maker gain a larger brand presence in printers and copiers.

Fuji Xerox Timeline of Major Business Activities 2000-2005

(Source: Fuji Xerox website)

2000   Acquires Sony Tektronix Corporation's printing business and establishes Phaser Printing Japan Co., Ltd.

Acquires China/Hong Kong Operations from Xerox Corporation.

2001   Consolidated to Fuji Photo Film Group with equity increase to 75% owned by Fuji Photo Film and 25% by Xerox Corporation.

Acquires laser printer business from NEC Corporation

2002   Acquires printer systems operations from Fujitsu.

Fuji Photo Film and Fuji Xerox to integrate logistics-related subsidiaries.

Spins off office laser printer business and establishes Fuji Xerox Printing Systems Co., Ltd.

2003   International Business Company's headquarters moves to Shanghai to oversee Asia and Oceania regions.

Concludes a technology-based partnership with Dell Inc. of the United States.

2004   Expands manufacturing in Shanghai to provide the global market with digital copy and multifunction devices.

Case: Neilson International in Mexico (A)
Primary Chapter: Chapter 9 (Alliances)
Secondary Chapter: Chapter 8 (International)

Introduction: Examining a proposed merger alliance with Sabritas, a Mexican subsidiary of PepsiCo Foods. Sabritas proposes contributing its distribution network and expertises, along with a potential umbrella brand while Neilson would contribute the countline candies that it would manufacture in Canada and ship to Sabritas for distribution in Mexico. Neilson must weigh this proposal against alternative alliance partners that have been identified for the purpose of entering Mexico. The case has a "B" component included in the Instructor's Manual which, along with the Teachers Note, has additional information about changing conditions in the Mexican economy which threaten this alliance.

Strategy Diamond: The deals explicitly with entry into Mexico, thus most of the analysis is directed at alternative vehicles and partners to accomplish this objective. However, there are also issues that relate to the Neilson brand name and the staging of entry as well.

Strategic Leadership: While this is a decision situation case for Howard Bateman, the VP of International Operations for Neilson, the leadership issues are secondary in this case.

Formulation/Implementation: The implementation issues relate principally to the speed at which various alternatives can be implemented, and the effect that this has on the attractiveness of the alternatives.

The Dynamic Nature of Strategy: The case focuses on one aspect of change—orchestrating the entry into new markets. The "B" case (in the Instructor's Manual) introduces another element of dynamism. Namely, currency devaluation puts Neilson and Sabritas in positions of possibly needing to change a key differentiator of their joint strategy (the pricing and positioning of Neilson's candies relative other international products).

Some interesting issues relating to the economic terms of the contract result in some surprises for Neilson when the economy turns south. How Neilson and Sabritas resolve these problems are part of the conclusion and debrief. The case provides an excellent opportunity to delve into the decision to (1) enter a foreign market, (2) the vehicle to use, (3) the partner to allay with, and (4) consequences of the decisions when unpredictable events (inevitably) occur.

NEILSON INTERNATIONAL IN MEXICO (A) & (B)
TEACHING NOTE

SYNOPSIS

This two-case series examines a proposed marketing joint venture which would introduce Neilson brand chocolate bars to Mexican consumers. Pepsico Foods' Mexican subsidiary, Sabritas — already servicing 450,000 retail stores — has suggested a joint branding agreement. Alternative distribution arrangements were available which would allow Neilson to maintain greater control over its name, at the cost of slower market access.

POSITION IN THE COURSE/TEACHING OBJECTIVES

We have used this case with good results in a variety of undergraduate and MBA courses and Executive Programs: Strategy, International Management, International Marketing, and Marketing. The case is easy for students to grasp because "everyone is an expert on chocolate bars." Nonetheless, it is rich in issues, to the extent that if the (B) case is used as a handout for in-class discussion, it will be difficult to finish in an 80-minute period.

Because Neilson's entry into Mexico represented their first, **major** international foray, the case may be best positioned early in most courses. This allows students to develop a market entry strategy, which is typically handled in the first sessions in international courses. If used in marketing, the case may best be used in a section dealing with distribution issues.

The case can usefully provide a number of lessons:

Making a channel work — the top guys make the deal, CEO to CEO; the Gayle Duncans have to make it work; "the devil's in the details."

Planning is an absolute requirement — frequently we do a LOT less planning to launch in an international market than at home. Why? Don't understand the new market; put total faith in an intermediary.

We must assume responsibility for the whole channel — not just hand our product off to a distributor. A failure at any stage means failure of the whole channel.

Culture — not just buying behaviour.

In summary, managing international channels takes investment and commitment. It's certainly not just handing off excess capacity.

ASSIGNMENT QUESTIONS (FOR USE WITH (A) CASE)

1. Should Neilson go with Sabritas? Yes, No, If, But?
2. Compared to Canada, what differences in the business environment are we likely to encounter in Mexico? What issues do these raise for Neilson's overall strategy with regard to the Mexican market?

3.   What fundamental strategic options does Neilson have other than Sabritas? What roles should Neilson/Sabritas play? What long-term expectations should Neilson have?

ANALYSIS

1.   Should Neilson go with Sabritas?

At the beginning of class there will typically be a great of enthusiasm for proceeding with Sabritas. In fact, there may be few points raised in the If? But? Categories. This is fine, we don't push it at this point in the class. In fact, one of our eventual teaching points is that we need to think through the contingencies (the Ifs, Buts) prior to entry into international markets if we wish to avoid unanticipated problems. We do return to this board later in class.

Yes	No

• great partner — Pepsico Foods
  – know consumer goods
 	
  – understand us
  – could take us worldwide
  – Sabritas knows Mexico
• greater market penetration than Neilson could gain alone
 	
• use our excess capacity
• they reach 450,000 market outlets
• will spend much more on advertising than Neilson can
• they'll move **fast**
• little Neilson capital requirement
• will maintain quality better than other distributors
	• we're small in relation to Pepsico
	• we lost the Neilson name with Sabritas' approach
	• what do they know about chocolate bars?
	
	• Sabritas will be a (the?) major competitor to Neilson in Mexico given their other snack foods

If	But
• Neilson retains brand control(?)	• we could (1) look at other entry options, or (2) forget about Mexico

2.   Some differences between Canadian/U.S. and Mexican business environments and implications for Neilson's entry.

Variables	Canada/United States	Mexico	Implications for Neilson
(1) Population Age	27% < 19	50% < 19	Prime purchasing years
(2) Distribution Channels	60% of sales through variety stores & other small outlets	70% of sales through tiendas & convenience	Need wide distribution
(3) Currency Stability	Cdn/U.S. dollars tend to move in tandem	Peso currently pegged to U.S. dollar, but historically volatile	Pricing levels at retail in Mexico will affect volume
(4) Quality of market research data	Good	Poor	Making decisions on unreliable information

(5) Transportation	Good	Fair—Poor	Logistics difficult
(6) Communications	Good	Domestic telephone system unreliable	Communication difficult
(7) Consumer tastes	Neilson knows Canada	Mexico is probably different	Product formulations

3(a) Options

Instructors may wish to sketch out on the board Neilson's basic options (see Exhibit TN-1). Each option has significant risks:

Go alone	• slow and costly brand development
	• distribution will take a long time
Grupo Hajj	• access to only a few retail stores
Grupo Corvi	• access to far fewer outlets than Sabritas
	• no experience carrying non-Mexican products

3(b) Roles of Neilson and Sabritas

Partially, in anticipation of the (B) case and what subsequently happened, we use this portion of class to try and precisely define what roles each will play. The more astute students will have made such points as (1) Sabritas doesn't know the chocolate bar business, but they have marketing responsibility for it; (2) Neilson doesn't seem to be planning on having anyone in Mexico: shouldn't they?

The purpose of this point of class is to highlight that neither party has totally thought through the roles they will play. Our intent here is to put some balance to the great enthusiasm which characterized the early part of class.

(B) CASE

Time permitting, this two page case should be distributed for in-class reading, and then discussed. As the case points out, Mexico has been a roller-coaster ride for Neilson. Such highs and lows, while common in international business, were not anticipated. Out intent with the (B) case is to reinforce some of the lessons/case objectives previously noted in regards to commitment.

WHAT HAPPENED? (1995 AND LATER)

The Mexican economy was devastated by the peso devaluation. It had dramatic and direct effects on such things as imported chocolate bar consumption.

As at July, Sabritas had not ordered **any** shipments from Neilson in 1995. Neilson had to write off inventory, stop production of the Mexican branded products, lay off people who had been hired to support the Mexican market expansion, etc.

Sabritas in turn had also absorbed a large financial loss. Because Sabritas' accounts receivable were not due until months after shipment, they eventually received payments in devalued pesos. In addition, while Sabritas eventually raised price to 1.5 pesos, they did not initially raise commissions to the sales force resulting in a reduction in their enthusiasm to rush the product to the trade. Together, this resulted in a dramatic drop in sales.

Neilson and Sabritas remained committed to redeveloping their business in Mexico.

Exhibit TN-1
NEILSON'S INTERNATIONAL STRATEGY: OPTIONS

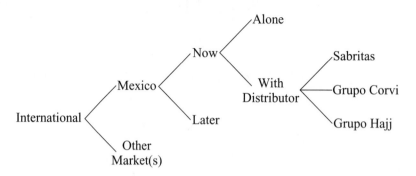

Paul Beamish and C. B. Johnston prepared this teaching note with the assistance of Terry Deutscher as an aid to instructors in the classroom use of the case Nielson International In Mexico (A) and (B), Nos. 9A95G003 and 9A95G004. This teaching note should not be used in any way that would prejudice the future use of the cases.

Case: HP – Compaq Merger
Primary Chapter: Chapter 10
Secondary Chapters: Chapters 6, 7 & 12

Introduction: HP-Compaq merger, one of the largest mergers of the IT industry attracted widespread attention and criticism right from the day the $20 billion merger was announced. Shareholders and members of the founding family opposed the merger as it was planned during the economic slump and integrating such large companies would take at least two years, which would dampen HP's competitive position. But Carleton S Fiorina, HP's CEO, could successfully overcome the opponents and close the deal. Even after closure of the deal, critics and analysts were skeptical about Fiorina's ability to integrate the two companies. However, Fiorina could successfully integrate both the companies. Now, one year after, the merger has started yielding profits for the IT-mammoth.

Strategy Diamond: The case deals with mergers and acquisitions as a vehicle. Examples are given of past failures by HP and Compaq of using acquisitions as a vehicle followed by their subsequent successful merger.

The Dynamic Nature of Strategy: The IT industry is inherently dynamic. The case illustrates how a gridlocked and antiquated strategy can lead to company stagnation and how the corporate culture by-product can become a shield against change.

Formulation/Implementation: The case draws attention to the difficulties of formulating and implementing an effective strategy – in this case a merger. The case illustrates the methods taken by both HP and Compaq to preempt potential problems and resolve existing ones during implementation, including the formation of a "clean team" to help synergize the move.

Strategic Leadership: A major part of the case is the leadership of Fiorina. Specifically, the case highlights Fiorina's role as decision maker and disturbance handler.

Her decisions can be analyzed as she consolidates the company, downsizes the workforce, clears anti-trust regulators, and confronts concerned employees and shareholders as well as a court battle with William Hewlett, a family representative opposed to the merger.

HP – COMPAQ MERGER
TEACHING NOTES

CASE SUMMARY

This case provides an overview of the HP-Compaq merger that occurred in 2002. It introduces both companies, discusses the state of each company at the time of the merger, provides a brief overview of the expected benefits of the merger, and even discusses some dissenting points of view regarding the combination of the firms. While not mentioned in the case, as of September 1, 2001, the $25 billion price tag factored initially in a more than $4 billion premium over Compaq's market cap on Friday, $20.92 billion. But that margin has narrowed along with the price. Even though Compaq's market cap fell to $17.84—its shares fell 14.7 percent—the total deal value fell faster and there is now less than a $2 billion premium for the company.

LEARNING OBJECTIVES

The HP-Compaq Merger case is designed to provide an example where a compelling case could be made either for or against the companies moving forward with the acquisition. Most of the discussion will surround analyzing the companies involved, discussing the reasons for the acquisition, debating whether the acquisition should have occurred, as well as discussing the varying motivations for companies to undertake mergers and acquisitions.

CASE QUESTIONS

1) What problems were HP and Compaq each experiencing? Does the merger represent a solution for these problems?
2) What was each party hoping to gain from the merger?
3) Should this merger have been undertaken?
4) What potential hurdles did the companies need to clear to successfully integrate the companies?
5) What role, if any, did managerial hubris play in this transaction?
6) At this point was the merger successful? Why or why not?

What problems were HP and Compaq each experiencing? Does the merger represent a solution for these problems?

Neither company seemed to be performing well at the time of the merger. While HP had experience strong financial performance from the 1930's into the 1990's, by the Fiorina had taken over in 1999 HP was experiencing disappointing performance. Some of the major difficulties mentioned in the case include:

- Too many brands that confused customers. At the time of the case Fiorina had consolidated these brands and reduced the number of divisions.
- Lack of technology investments. Despite still dominating the printer market, HP was slipping in other markets such as servers and customer service.
- Bloated staffing. For their size, HP employed three times as many marketing people (6,000 vs. 3,000) and its managers supervised significantly less people than their competitors (8.3 vs. 6.3 people).

- HP was also missing trends in markets. In the case it was written that Fiorina realized there was a growing potential for systems build on Linux or Windows NT at a time when its rivals, Dell and Compaq, were already providing these products.

Together these difficulties suggest that HP was drifting and was suffering from mis-management. Fiorina recognized this fact in saying that HP, "was a company with unique assets but untapped potential." She also said that, "we're leaving diamonds in the floor." Despite initiating a campaign that emphasized 'Rules of Garage' and downsizing 6,000 employees, HP's performance under Fiorina continued to be disappointing as evidenced by the fact that, despite the technology boom, HP missed its performance targets for nine consecutive quarters. Also, by mid-2001 HP's market share in the PC industry had dropped by 10.5%.

Compaq's performance was also poor during the time of the merger. Similar to HP, Compaq had enjoyed strong performance in the 1980's into the 1990's. However, by 1999 Compaq had begun to experience its own difficulties. Compaq's CEO, Pfeiffer, was fired in April of 1999 after its failed merger with Digital. At the end of 1999 Compaq promoted Capellas, its acting COO, to the position of CEO.

Capellas immediately initiated a reorganization that cut 8,500 jobs and had Compaq focus on the server market. However, the bursting the technology bubble combined with multiple failed acquisitions seemed to indicate that Compaq was not in good shape heading into this merger.

Overall, the information provided in the case seemed to indicate that each company had been mismanaged in the years leading up the appointment of new CEOs at each company. Also, that each company was in the process of reorganizing and trying to fix the problems that resulted from this mismanagement.

What was each party hoping to gain from the merger?

In this section start by listing what each party hopes to gain from the acquisition and conclude by analyzing whether a mergers was necessary for each company to achieve these savings.

The managers of HP, based on advice from a consulting firm, thought that a number of synergies could be produced if the two firms merged and that by 2004 the combined entity could save an estimated $2.5 billion. Specifically, the logic of the merger relied on synergies resulting from cost savings and competitive synergies. Costs saving were expected to result from:

- Redeploy, and presumably downsize, some of the 145,000 employees.
- Eliminate overlapping product lines. This resulted in cost savings in the form of lower material and warehousing costs.

The process by which the combination would achieve the 'competitive synergies' is slightly less clear. However, there is some discussion of the 'adopt and go' strategy. This involved a series of meetings over four months where managers had to come out with at least one product to eliminate at every meeting. This process helped to both streamline the product mix and also highlight where jobs could be eliminated.

The justification for the merger also seemed rely on a market power justification as well. In trying to sell the deal to the board Fiorina said, "Do you think IT industry needs to consolidate and if so, is it better to be a consolidator or consolidatee?" However, if market power is a reason for the combination, it does not seem certain that this combined company will allow HP-Compaq to dictate pricing or reduce competition in any of the markets in which it competes. This point may cause some debate. While there is not much hard evidence to support either side of the argument in the case, Exhibit 1 seems to indicate that Dell is eroding HP-Compaq's market share even after the firms have combined. This fact may suggest that the market power of the combined firm may not find its way into HP-Compaq's bottom line.

Should this merger have been undertaken?

Start by broadly asking students if they are for or against the merger. Let a few students answer and then move the discussion toward whether a merger was necessary for the savings discussed in the previous question to be realized.

This discuss can be based on the list the savings that were generated in answering the previous question. The instructor can go down the list of synergies and examine whether each synergy would have occurred if: 1) Each company continued to operate independently, 2) The companies entered into an alliance, or 3) Could only be realized through a merger. In discussing the alliance possibility make sure to remind students that Compaq had initially wanted to start this relationship as an alliance and only move forward with the acquisition if the alliance proved to be successful.

What potential hurdles did the companies need to clear to successfully integrate the companies?

A first point to make in this section is that integration is not free, nor are the costs of integration usually mentioned when mergers occur. In this instance, a group called the 'clean team', which consisted of 600 full-time employees, was created to manage the integration process.

The first major issue discussed in the cased was integrating each company's culture. HP's culture was described as was professional and solution driven while Compaq's was described as arrogant and focused more on market share. HP performed what is called cultural due diligence by interviewing numerous senior executives and holding 35 focus groups to talk to employees.

At this point the instructor could turn this into a broader discussion of the role of culture in acquisitions and have the class discuss why understanding the corporate culture of an organization is critical to acquisition success. Or, the instructor could simply discuss cultural integration in terms of one part of acquisition integration and move the discussion forward.

The second major integration issue discussed in the case dealt with the product mix. This was handled through the 'adopt and go' strategy where products were either eliminated or retained based on profitability, market share or brand awareness. The results of the process also significantly influence where headcount was to be reduced. Regarding this revision of product mix, there was no mention of the overarching strategy of the combined company driving this product mix rationalization, the instructor could ask students where deciding which products to keep based on profitability is a good idea and whether there are risks to applying this as a criterion for keeping or dropping a product line.

One last point that could be made in this discussion is regarding the staffing of executive positions. One question that could generate some discussion could be, "How will the fact that the HP CEO was promoted to the CEO position of the combined company affect integration?" This move may signal to employees that HP is acquiring Compaq. This may mean that in uncertain situations, the HP way of doing things may be the default solution. If this is the case, what might the effect be on Compaq employees?

What role, if any, did managerial hubris play in this transaction?

Hubris is defined as exaggerated self-confidence, excessive pride, or arrogance. In the context of mergers and acquisitions hubris may result in managers having unrealistically optimistic expectations about the chances of an acquisitions success.

During the due-diligence phase of this combination there were some potential red flags mentioned in the case in the form of opposition to the merger. Walter Hewlett opposed the deal for a number of reasons, these included:

- The IT industry was not in good shape
- The size of both companies meant that integration would take time and would be complicated.
- This integration would cause HP to further slip in its competitive position. This idea was probably based on the fact that during the years following the merger top management would be focus on integrating these firms rather than its customers and competitors.

Employees of HP opposed the deal as they feared it would endanger their jobs. Further, only 51.14% of shareholders approved the merger after Hewlett led a proxy fight against the merger. While this was enough for the deal to go ahead almost half of all shareholders were against the deal. Also, there was some concern about the blending of corporate culture.

Lastly, as discussed earlier, both firms seem to be having their own difficulties. Each company seemed to be suffering from the sins of either current or past managers. Compaq, in fact, was not in good shape at the time of this merger due to its failure in integrating its acquisition of Digital.

Given these serious concerns and lack of shareholder support, discuss with the class whether the hubris hypothesis is possible.

At this point was the merger successful? Why or why not?

Discuss whether the cost-cutting targets had been met. At the writing of the case, it seems as the cost-cutting targets for the mergers have been met. Again, it may be useful to revisit whether a merger was necessary for the firms to enjoy the cost savings listed in the case.

Some costs savings, such as those generated by eliminating redundant product lines may be unique to the merger, but other reductions may have been possible without the combination. Also, this is an opportunity to discuss the costs associated with the merger. Sources of costs include:

- The acquisition premium paid. Although it is not offered in the case, some premium is always paid by the acquirer.
- The salaries and support for the 'clean team'. With 600 full-time members, the total costs of the clean team could easily be $40-50 million or more.
- Time. The synergies realized from the merger do not happen immediately after the acquisition.

Lastly, discuss whether there were strategic reasons for this merger. Most of the discussion of this merger related to cost savings and little regarding the strategy of the combined companies. Some of the common strategic reasons for mergers to occur include:

- *Reducing Threats*: This rationale applies, for example, when a firm relies on one key supplier and acquires that supplier to eliminate the risk of the firm being 'held up' by this key supplier
- *Increasing Market Power and Access*: Market power is derived when the merger or acquisition allows a firm to influence prices or if price competition is reduced due to the combination significantly reducing rivalry in an industry.
- *Realizing Cost Savings:* Cost savings are the most common synergy and the easiest to estimate. Revenue-enhancement opportunities, such as increasing total sales through cross-selling and enhanced distribution, also represent a significant upside in many M&As.

- *Increasing Financial Strength:* Other synergies can be created by various forms of financial engineering. An acquisition, for instance, can lower the financing costs of the target firm when the two firms' respective credit ratings are markedly different and significant debt is involved.
- *Sharing and Leveraging Capabilities:* Transferring best practices and core competencies can create value. This form of synergy is important in the resource-based view of competitive advantage.

Briefly walk through some or all of these strategic reasons for mergers and ask the class if any of these justifications fit the HP-Compaq merger. Again, based on the reading of the case, there seems to be few strategic reasons for undertaking this merger. Try to see if students can make the case for some of the other synergies listed.

Update

While the initial news regarding the cost savings that resulted from the merger were positive, there is a growing consensus that the merger has failed. In February of 2005 Fiorina was dismissed after "disagreements over strategy at the computer and printer maker." In a statement Fiorina has said: "While I regret the board and I have differences about how to execute HP's strategy, I respect their decision. HP is a great company and I wish all the people of HP much success in the future1." The market seemed to agree that Fiorina was part of the problem in that HP shares surged 11% upon news of her dismissal2.

One of the main reasons for her dismissal was HP-Compaq's decline in the PC market in the years following the merger. From 2000 to 2004 the combined market share for HP-Compaq dipped dramatically. During this four-year period Dell moved from 11.5 to 17.9 percent of the world market, while HP-Compaq (combined sales) dropped from 20.9 to 15.8 percent. With each tenth of a percent worth several tens of millions of dollars in revenues, this change is dramatic and stark. HP and Compaq had collectively almost doubled Dell in 2000, yet now sits firmly in second place as a combined entity3.

Fortunes for HP-Compaq began to decline toward the end of 2003 as investors began shifting their focus examine the firm's strategic position versus its key competitors of IBM and Dell. Analysts and employees seemed to lose confidence in Fiorina around this time. "[Fiorina's] good with marketing; she's a good speaker for the company," says a former HP executive. "But this is a company that doesn't need a statesman. It needs a hands-on operations person4." Going forward analysts are skeptical that this merger will prove to be successful. There are even discussions of HP divesting Compaq.

Teaching Plan
(one 80 minute session)

- What problems were HP and Compaq each experiencing? Does the merger represent a solution for these problems? (10 minutes)
- What was each party hoping to gain from the merger? (10 minutes)
- Should this merger have been undertaken? (20 minutes)
- What potential hurdles did the companies need to clear to successfully integrate the companies? (15 minutes)
- What role, if any, did managerial hubris play in this transaction? (5 minutes)
- At this point was the merger successful? Why or why not? (20 minutes)

APPENDIX

c/Net Article on September 1, 2001

The merger of Hewlett-Packard and Compaq Computer, a major milestone in the corporate history of the two companies, will have little impact on either company's corporate customers for 12 to 18 months, and a moderate impact in the next two to three years.

Organizations should pay careful attention to see how HP and Compaq products they use will be supported and evolved by the combined company.

For the computer industry in general, this consolidation of existing major players reflects a broad trend toward increased technological stability and a somewhat slower pace of innovation. Additional combinations of large global computer companies are possible, as competitors left out of the oligopoly of IBM, HP/Compaq, and Dell Computer attempt to buy their way into the leadership bracket.

Of course, an analysis of the effects of the HP/Compaq combination assumes that this deal will be approved by the U.S. Department of Justice and European regulatory bodies. We believe approval is likely but by no means certain, due in part to the dominant retail-store market share of the new company as well as worries about job cuts. European regulators, in particular, have recently posed obstacles to major mergers (such as GE/Honeywell). Gaining European regulatory approval will probably require some form of job guarantees to France, where HP's commercial PC division is currently headquartered, and possibly to other countries in Europe.

The basic motivation for the HP/Compaq deal seems clear--to transform two companies that have been turning in lackluster results in the PC and server markets into a larger competitor that can leverage massive resources and a substantial customer base. We believe that Compaq's board of directors accepted a relatively low acquisition price (a 19 percent premium over the current Compaq market valuation; about 65 percent of estimated 2002 revenues) because it expects a continuation of disappointing results in upcoming quarters.

This acquisition was driven by three factors: first, the slowing IT marketplace; second, the growing competition from IBM and Dell; and third, the gradual trend toward commodity servers, which is increasingly relegating high-end (and high-margin) Unix and proprietary back-end servers to legacy platform status.

After the acquisition of Compaq, the new Hewlett-Packard would be No. 1 in PCs, No. 1 in servers (in terms of unit sales) and No. 1 in printers, with a large services division. It would be the second-largest computer firm overall, barely trailing IBM--assuming that it can hold on to the current customers of both HP and Compaq. However, severe disruptions in service and product delivery tend to accompany any large merger. It would be reasonable to expect 10 percent to 15 percent of customers to slip away, as both Dell and IBM move aggressively to capitalize on any market confusion or uncertainty.

Savings for the future

The financial rationale behind the deal is that the expected savings generated by the HP/Compaq combination would pay for the consolidation of the companies' product lines and operations, followed by the launch of strong new product offerings and marketing initiatives. In addition to previously announced cuts of about 10 percent of the work force at both HP and Compaq, the combined company would eliminate about 15,000 more jobs, with the exact number depending on how soon the PC and server markets regain their sales momentum.

In its announcement, HP said it expects annual cost savings of $2.5 billion. However, only minimal savings are projected in the near term, and there may even be some revenue loss due to the consolidation.

Furthermore, some revenue may be lost in the longer term as disappointed loyalists refuse to migrate from discontinued legacy products.

We believe that integrating these two competitors will require two to three years of painful restructuring, given the two-plus years that Compaq required to integrate its acquisition of Digital Equipment. HP and Compaq have been fierce competitors in many market segments, with contrasting approaches to product design and marketing, different user bases, and dissimilar organizational cultures. Although this deal will enable significant consolidation of competing offerings, there is little synergy of complementary products.

The great strength of HP is its engineering culture--and its inability to think outside that culture has been a weakness. It remains to be seen how HP's unified culture will mix with Compaq's multiple cultures. Technology issues will not determine the success or failure of this deal. Preserving and enhancing HP's organizational ability to execute will be vital.

Although we expect HP management to move relatively quickly, the sheer number of product lines and channels to be integrated and difficult issues to be resolved is considerably larger than during the Compaq/Digital integration. To HP's credit, it is acknowledging upfront that a long integration phase will be required.

Integrating the sales forces will be particularly difficult, because the sales cultures, incentive programs, and methodologies of the two firms are different. And competition for lower- and middle-management jobs will create distrust that may lead to poor sales and customer support. Additionally, the sheer task of managing such a massive integration will consume significant resources for the next few years.

While HP and Compaq are preoccupied with their marriage, major competitors such as IBM, Dell and Sun Microsystems will have an opportunity to consolidate momentum in the marketplace. In particular, HP/Compaq must protect its current advantage in international sales (vs. U.S.-only sales) compared to Dell. In the near term, this acquisition makes rivals like Sun and Dell look like more focused companies. However, this advantage will be fleeting. In the longer term, the new HP will marginalize Sun as too small and lacking in credible Intel-based offerings.

PCs and servers

In the PC market, we would expect the combined HP/Compaq entity to consolidate its offerings in new product lines within 12 months (one to two product cycles). We believe the HP (and Pavilion) brand name will persist as the marketing focus in the retail PC channel, while Compaq offerings will still be sold to corporate accounts. In the handheld arena, we believe the iPaq product line will be the key offering.

Because the near-term outlook for the PC market remains cloudy--dwindling profits from HP and Compaq PCs were a key driver of this deal--we expect the new HP to focus on slashing costs from its consolidated operations, as it seeks to entrench itself for future PC wars against Dell, IBM and others. The new company's leadership position in the PC sector, now almost a pure commodity business, is negated by diminishing margins. Successful consolidation of the HP and Compaq retail and corporate distribution channels will be at least as important as the melding of their product lines.

In the server market, the combination of HP and Compaq will further complicate an already complex lineup of product lines that has resulted from Compaq's prior acquisitions of Digital and Tandem. The danger is that the new HP will remain preoccupied with resolving differences among legacy product lines while competitors such as IBM and Dell move forward with more coherent offerings for Windows on Intel platforms (Wintel) and eventually Linux on Intel (Lintel).

We believe HP cannot be content with Compaq's profit strategy of milking diverse installed customer bases such as Tandem and Digital. It will need to develop a strategy to drive sales to new server and storage offerings via an orderly migration of current users--as opposed to simply being a "holding company" of diverse legacy product lines.

We expect the HP/Compaq combination to hasten the move to Intel platforms. HP has some near-term technology capabilities (Superdome and N-Class servers are already upgradable to Intel, for instance), but Compaq is developing its own high-end Intel alternative. Both organizations have strong in-house development traditions. We expect Compaq to remain dominant in the Intel midrange, and the combined HP/Compaq will face significant high-end competition only from IBM (with its soon-to-be-announced Summit technology).

We also expect broad Unix (HP-UX and Tru64) integration claims, and both vendors have already committed to Intel ports. However, we believe the result will be about 80 percent HP (trying to leverage HP-UX's stronger support among independent software vendors) and about 20 percent Compaq (including Tru64's best-in-class clustering capabilities). It is difficult to see much near-term impact on OpenVMS, MPE/iX and other legacy platforms. Tandem is well on its way to Intel (having started moving from MIPS to Intel initially, before temporarily trying Alpha).

Both HP and Compaq are investing aggressively and emphasizing the Intel Itanium processor family for their long-term high-end server direction. Even if there are few near-term synergies, in two to three years--when McKinley and higher-end Itanium products emerge--the combined entity should be well positioned to capture a good piece of that market.

The combined HP/Compaq will have a massive list of server customers to which it will be able to upgrade or sell new server and storage products. Users of Compaq legacy server products should expect a quickening pace of efforts to migrate them from these products to new product lines as HP/Compaq strives to move from its past of disparate Unix legacy platforms toward a cohesive lineup focused more on Wintel (and Lintel) offerings.

For corporate customers buying Wintel servers, there will now be three strong players--HP, IBM and Dell. That will still be enough to keep pricing reasonable.

Storage and service

The strongest intersection of the two companies appears to be in storage. Compaq is a leader in the low-end to midrange market, and the HP/HDS offerings at the high end are competitive with those of EMC. The sheer size of the combined user base could make EMC's life more difficult in the long term. Because storage is increasingly driving the entire systems picture, the HP/Compaq's enhanced ability to get a foot in the door with storage offerings will help the companies sell some of their weaker offerings.

(See news story: HP's incredible shrinking deal)

The services dimension, which currently accounts for about 20 percent of both HP and Compaq, is another potential growth area for a combined HP/Compaq, even though at first glance this deal takes HP in a radically different direction compared to its previous (abortive) effort to acquire PricewaterhouseCoopers. Although IBM leads in the services market, a much higher percentage of its services business is integration services, while the majority of the HP service business is break/fix support.

During the past year, both HP and Compaq have reiterated their desires to grow and differentiate their respective businesses around integrated solutions and services, as their core hardware business is increasingly marginalized. Compaq is currently the largest integrator of Microsoft products, while HP is particularly strong in installing and upgrading management systems for Windows 2000 environments. Selling more HP/Compaq services will also facilitate hardware sales.

Although parts of the Compaq services story remain strong (such as systems integration services), we have seen it increasingly fall off in the outsourcing market (usually low-end services such as break/fix). Compaq had ambitions of growing toward the IBM services model, but it never made the hoped-for headway after the acquisition of the Digital services arm. It has been too "Compaq-centric" in its approach to sourcing services and often unwilling to fit into a more heterogeneous scene.

Both companies have had similar visions of "IT as a utility" and "IT delivered as a service" that mesh well. However, we expect HP to streamline the services functions from Compaq to raise revenue per employee, and we should see some internal reorganization focus in an attempt to dispel the interdepartmental rivalry that marked problems in the Digital services absorption into Compaq. Moving to a 30 percent to 40 percent growth model for services (vs. the current 7 percent to 9 percent) will be an impossible goal unless the potentially large and unwieldy services arm is aligned appropriately across company technology sectors and market verticals.

Also on the services side, we expect HP to look for synergies in Compaq Telecom to augment its opportunities in business, operations and enhanced network services. Compaq Telecom offers close to 10,000 telecom architects and consultants and, on the software side, Compaq's TeMIP is a direct competitor to HP's OVC (OpenView Communications) for telecom network management.

If this merger is finalized, we recommend that corporate customers of server and software products from HP and Compaq actively monitor plans for how these products will be supported and evolved. Although the impact on users will be minimal for 12 to 18 months, subsequently there will be more drastic product support changes and disruption. In two to three years, users should expect significant changes in HP/Compaq products and services as the combined entity moves to consolidate operations and merge overlapping offerings.

Meta Group analysts Jack Gold, Mike Gotta, William Zachmann, Dale Kutnick, David Cearley, Steve Kleynhans, David Folger, David Yockelson, Herb VanHook, Nick Gall, Brian Richardson, Rakesh Kumar, Rob Schafer and Louis Boyle contributed to this article.

---

1 i-Technology News Desk. February 9, 2005. Breaking News: "Bye Bye Carly," Says HP. http://java.sys-con.com/read/48147.htm.

2 i-Technology News Desk. February 9, 2005. Breaking News: "Bye Bye Carly," Says HP. http://java.sys-con.com/read/48147.htm.

3 Strukhoff, Roger. January 25, 2005. OPINION: Fiorina Under Fire, HP Underperforming? http://opensource.sys-con.com/read/47910.htm.

4 Elgin, Ben. February 21, 2005. The Inside Story Of Carly's Ouster. Business Week Online. http://www.businessweek.com/magazine/content/05_08/b3921007_mz001.htm

Case: Cisco Systems, Inc.: Acquisition Integration for Manufacturing (A)
Primary Chapter: Chapter 10 (Acquisition)
Secondary Chapter: Chapter 11 (Implementation levers)

Introduction: Cisco is a company that aggressively used acquisitions as both an external source of R&D and as a vehicle for product/market expansion. The case provides rich detail about Cisco's acquisition processes. While the case focuses on a specific transaction that Cisco is contemplating, the background data includes extensive information and Cisco's methods for integrating acquisitions. Thus, the information generalizes well to the broader questions dealing with targeting and integrating acquisitions. The (B) case tells students what happens, and shows Keller leaving on a plane to culminate another acquisition.

Strategy Diamond: The case is focused squarely on acquisitions as a vehicle of corporate strategy. The details are thorough and allow for significant analysis concerning how acquisitions affect and are affected by the other elements of a firm strategy.

Strategic Leadership: Students are presented the case through the eyes of Cisco executive David Keller. The processes used by Cisco include leadership mechanisms used to facilitate effective acquisition integration. For instance, the management buddy system and integration project managers are two mechanisms used by Cisco to smooth integration of new acquisitions.

Formulation/Implementation: This case is perhaps one of the richest available for detailing how the formulation of a strategy that includes acquisitions is dependent on the processes used to implement the acquisition integration. The Cisco method includes key processes designed to make the integration of high-tech acquisition a smooth transition. The case also does a nice job of highlighting the issues which can complicate successful integration (i.e., incompatible incentives, physical location, autonomy) as well as reveal what Cisco has done to overcome these problems.

The Dynamic Nature of Strategy: The network routing industry is an inherently dynamic context. Cisco's strategy needs to not only be flexible to accommodate the industry dynamism, but the case also allows for analysis of how Cisco proactively shapes the environment through continually repositioning itself and changing the target for other firms.

The case does provide information about Cisco's previous successes and failures and provides an opportunity to discuss how Cisco has learned from these experiences to become more consistent in its acquisition success.

CISCO SYSTEMS, INC.: ACQUISITION INTEGRATION FOR MANUFACTURING (A) AND (B) TEACHING NOTE

I. INTRODUCTION AND OVERVIEW

Cisco Systems, a provider of the infrastructure elements needed to create and maintain the Internet as well as individual organizations' Intranets, has sought to develop a leadership position in each of several segments of the market. A key element of that strategy has been a willingness to acquire new products (and their related product development organizations), and to put them into the Cisco system for selling, manufacturing, and delivering products. Given Cisco's rapid growth rate, its strong position in the "new economy," and its track record at successful acquisitions and their subsequent integration, this case provides an excellent vehicle for talking about the elements of their approach, their overall framework, and how it complements their business strategy.

The case itself describes the Cisco approach to capturing the potential value from an acquisition and then details a proposal for one such acquisition. Generally, students would be given the (A) case to prepare in advance of class and the short (B) case would then be used three-quarters of the way through the class. In addition to describing a proposal for a specific acquisition (Summa Four Corporation), the (A) case also raises many of the concerns that a small company like Summa Four would have when being acquired by a much larger company like Cisco Systems. The case provides a good balance of strategy, systems, and processes for acquisitions, as well as people and retention issues following completion of an acquisition. The (B) case describes the first couple of months of Cisco ownership of Summa Four, following completion of the acquisition. It identifies additional questions raised by Summa Four employees concerning the progress towards integration and the implications of anticipated future moves by the new owner, Cisco Systems.

Suggested Assignment Questions for Cisco (A)

1. Have you been involved on either side of an acquisition transaction? Was that acquisition successful in your opinion? Why or why not? (This question is especially appropriate for executive audiences.)
2. Identify what you believe are the most important elements (criteria, processes, specific actions, etc.) of Cisco's approach to selecting and integrating acquisitions. For each of the elements you have identified, describe why it is important (what is its purpose?), and specify whether you would characterize it as typical (conventional practice by companies doing technology acquisitions) or unusual?
3. How would you improve Cisco's acquisition selection and integration process? What is missing? What would you add or modify? Why?
4. What are the specific challenges of the Summa Four acquisition? In your opinion does the Cisco process adequately address these challenges? Why or why not?

Depending on the audience, one also might want to use a background reading along with the (A) case. One possibility for the reading is, "Capturing the Real Value in High-Tech Acquisitions" by Chaudhury and Tabrizi, *Harvard Business Review,* No. 99503, September-October 1999.

II. CASE ANALYSIS

There are several types of analysis that a student might be expected to do in preparing the (A) case. One of the *first* and most important of these involves examining why Cisco does so many acquisitions. This can begin by looking at Cisco's business strategy, which is to use acquired products and product lines as a significant driver for rapid growth and the acquisition of technical talent and know-how. Also, Cisco's desire to have a broad range of products and to serve multiple segments in the Internet and Intranet world requires that as new product lines broaden and deepen and become relevant and applicable, Cisco needs to quickly enter and take a leadership position in those markets. That's often best done by acquiring someone who has come up with a dominant design and has real technical strength. The Cisco business strategy also requires that they continually leverage their sales force and the Cisco brand to feed the "growth model" around which they have built their business.

It should be clear to students that acquisitions are central to the Cisco business strategy. They not only provide products, people, and technology, but they enable the company to evolve its strategy from a product market perspective. Clearly, the fact that Cisco has done so many acquisitions, and thus has so many people who joined the company through an acquisition, has helped create a perspective and environment that is very conducive to a continuation of the strategy.

An aspect of Cisco's business strategy that the most thoughtful students will want to address deals with what changes the role of acquisitions will undergo as Cisco gets larger. Even at the time of the case (late 1998), Cisco is getting large enough that it's beginning to encounter the challenge of speed and agility that are generally present in small companies, but much less common in large companies. However, Cisco is also realizing the benefits of scale, and recognizing that in order to continue its rate of growth it will either have to do more and more acquisitions at a faster pace or do larger acquisitions. How Cisco balances the benefits of size and scale with the attributes of acquired small companies which have ideas, technology, and speed will be a major challenge.

Finally, the most thoughtful students might look at what some of the limits are to the Cisco model and the role of acquisitions in that model. Clearly, one of the things that makes the Cisco model work is the continued increase in the company's valuation and the price of its stock. This makes joining Cisco and giving up one's existing small company stock options for Cisco options, an attractive proposition. Obviously, if the stock were to hit a plateau or fall, things would look very different. Similarly, if the segments in which Cisco competes were to fall upon hard times or their growth rate were to slow dramatically, that too would change the perspective of small companies and their key employees with regard to the attractiveness of being acquired by Cisco.

A *second* major area for analysis has to do with the Cisco process for acquisitions. Here it might be useful to develop a list of key processes or key elements and then to develop a matching list that describes the purposes of those. The table below suggests one such list.

Key Processes/Elements	Purposes
Management buddy system	Providing information and assurance
Apply Cisco Systems (MRP and Autotest)	Quality, speed and control so that the Cisco brand name and image are maintained
Up-front human resource involvement (keep the employee whole)	People focus and achieving a smooth transition without turnover
Waiver of acceleration of options and replacement of options with Cisco options	Aligning financial and human resource incentives

327

Retention incentives	Buy time so acquired employees can get comfortable, and feel at home before they consider leaving
Forecast and business plan (ROI)	Set expectations of "success" and then exceed those
Key roles for acquired managers (for example, integration project lead)	They know the people, they have experience leading those people, and they can help keep them focused and be trusted in the process
Ramping up short-term sales by introducing products to the Cisco sales force	Make the financial results a high payoff and win-win for the organization (this also ensures that employees in the acquired organization are seen as valuable contributors)
Scenario planning without preconceived conclusions	Explore options openly and seek consensus and buy-in for the best decisions

One of the areas of analysis that is particularly important for students to understand is that there are a handful of areas where Cisco insists on certain things happening. For example, Cisco's MRP system, including parts numbering, and Cisco's product testing routines (Autotest), must be implemented within the first 90 days. This enables Cisco to guarantee its customers that Cisco's standards of quality, reliability, and serviceability are being met. It also insures that Cisco can ramp up volume as the Cisco sales force begins selling those products. Finally, it's Cisco's experience that most small companies have much more people-dependent systems than IT-based systems in these important areas, and Cisco needs the control in order to make things scaleable. Another example of something Cisco insists on is that all of the company's offered products are in the Cisco sales list on the day the merger closes. This enables the Cisco sales people to begin selling immediately, but it also gives a sense of momentum and success to those in the acquired organization. The fact that Cisco seems to do so much on-line, including the majority of its order entry and customer order tracking, enables the sales force to take advantage of new products immediately.

A *third* major area of analysis that the thoughtful student will want to address has to do with the Summa Four acquisition itself. A place they might want to start is with the kinds of questions that a Summa Four employee would want to ask if they were about to be acquired by Cisco. Some of the things that one can imagine an employee being concerned about would include:

A. Anxiety about the future of their job, the impact of the Cisco culture, and the financial realities of their pay, benefits, stock options, and bonuses.

B. Uncertainty about where their job might be located and how they will be viewed within this larger organization.

C. Classic concerns about working for a big company versus working for the small company they've become accustomed to.

D. Will Summa Four's concerns and its knowledge of customers, technologies, products, and markets be "heard" within Cisco.

E. Concern for the way in which suppliers, customers, and other employees will be treated following the merger.

F. Possible differences in expectations. (The classic form of the question is, "What haven't they told us yet?")

In addition to identifying these kinds of concerns on the part of Summa Four people, it's also useful to examine some of the specific action plans and possible solutions that Cisco and Summa Four might work out to address those. Particularly important in this is the process by which those get worked out. Will they be decided and discussed by Cisco and then imposed on Summa Four, or will the Summa Four people be a peer in their discussion and resolution. Some of the specific areas and possible ways in which those might be addressed would include the following.

Issues/Challenges	Possible Solutions
Small company/informal processes	Keep current factory and supply chain (but implement Cisco MRP System and Autotest) for now
Many suppliers/many parts	First adopt MRP parts numbering and Autotest before worrying about substituting new suppliers or rationalizing parts lists
Maintaining the customer base	Determine where each product is in the product life cycle and work out plan for the remainder of the product life
Location of manufacturing	Use existing factory for all legacy products until their end of life
Location of engineering	This is a particularly sensitive concern and they probably need to look at alternative scenarios and then make a decision jointly after careful consideration
Longer-term new products plans (Project Alpha)	Install Cisco's new product introduction process and develop a roadmap and time line for Alpha
Longer-term manufacturing plans (for example, for Alpha)	Initiate a task force of Cisco and Summa Four people to begin considering the alternatives and what will be best for the business

III. TEACHING SUGGESTIONS

A teaching approach that has been used very successfully with both MBA students in an elective course on operation strategy and with executives in courses ranging from New Product Development to General Management and Business Strategy, has been to divide the class discussion into five main elements. The *first segment,* which might take 10 minutes or so, can be used to address why Cisco does so many acquisitions. This discussion should get at the nature of the overall Cisco strategy, the role of acquisitions in that strategy, and the way in which Cisco organizes and approaches acquisitions (for example, the criteria used and the pre-acquisition task forces) in order to execute that strategy.

A *second segment* of the teaching plan, particularly important for executives, is to get some data from the participants regarding their experience with acquisitions. Here it's often useful to explain the general results of academic research regarding acquisitions. That research suggests that:

The acquired shareholders usually do very well.

The acquiring shareholders usually do not do very well.

And the acquired employees often leave within the first year.

In this 5 to 10 minute segment of the class discussion, it's useful to let participants express their experience either as part of the acquiring company or as part of the acquired firm with regards to acquisitions. By getting this out early, it then makes it easier for them to focus on Cisco and the Summa Four acquisition for the remainder of the class.

The *third segment* of the class discussion might go as long as 20 or 25 minutes. This third area should focus on the Cisco processes for acquisitions. A useful way to start this discussion is by having the class build a table where the Key Processes/Key Elements are shown on the left-hand side of the table and the

Purposes of each of those are shown on the right. This allows the class to see the breadth, pervasiveness, and depth of the Cisco approach.

It might also be useful towards the end of this part of the discussion to contrast the integration of an acquired firm with that of an organ transplant. In order for an organ transplant to be successful, several things are needed.

A. A healthy organ of the type needed must be identified.
B. That organ has to be kept alive and well up until the transplant occurs.
C. The insertion of the organ into the patient's body has to be carefully planned and executed.
D. The patient who is to receive the organ needs to be prepared and the vital systems connecting that organ to the patient's body must be hooked up immediately.
E. The patient's immune system has to be managed carefully to prevent rejection of the new organ.

In order to conclude this segment on Cisco's process for acquisitions, it's useful to talk about how it might be characterized with such words as "disciplined but flexible," "systematic and process oriented but people count," and "business purpose driven but humanistic." One might also ask the class what they think the limits are of the Cisco approach.

The *fourth segment* of the class discussion can shift on the Summa Four acquisition and what Summa Four employees are likely to be concerned about at this point in time. Developing a list of those concerns is one of the ways in which those students who have experience with acquisitions can bring that experience to bear. If time permits, it's also useful to develop a list of specific issues and challenges and the class' suggestions as to how those might best be addressed.

The *fifth* and final major segment of the class can then turn to the (B) case. This two-page case can be handed out and the class given a chance to read it. Following that reading a 10 or 15 minute discussion of what's now happening, can take place.

Perhaps the best place to start the discussion, following the students' reading of the Cisco (B) case during class, is to ask what has surprised Cisco, and are you surprised at those areas of concern. Clearly the two biggest issues have been the HR issues—those dealing with benefits, the undesirability of moving from Manchester, New Hampshire to Chelmsford, Massachusetts (or anywhere else for that matter, especially in a tight labor market), and the future of the Manchester site. The other big issue has been the complexity and the challenges of bringing the supplier system, manufacturing, and all of the other aspects of the business into the Cisco fold. Following a brief discussion of these two main areas, it's then useful to focus a couple of minutes on what changes the students would recommend to Keller with respect to future acquisitions and with respect to Cisco's acquisition processes. Suggestions likely to be brought up would include additional topics for due diligence, further strengthening the HR approach to pre-empt anticipated Summa Four kinds of issues, and strengthening of the post-acquisition effort and its duration. Finally, it's useful at the close of the class to ask the students for their general evaluation of Cisco's acquisition approach and for what they think of the Summa Four situation.

IV. UPDATE

On a couple of occasions when the Cisco (A) and (B) cases have been taught, David Keller and others from Cisco have sat in on the class. They've made several important points. One is that Summa Four clearly benefited from the fact that some of the earlier acquisitions that Cisco had made had been disasters. Cisco had decided that much more planning and thinking, both before the acquisition and after its completion, would be of great benefit. In essence, Cisco has decided that discipline and systemization are needed to gain freedom and flexibility. One of the things that was clear in the Summa Four acquisition is that both Summa Four and Cisco agreed that if they could exceed the business performance expectations (both in terms of sales and profits), that would provide additional credibility and time for the transition. That is in fact what happened.

Another big issue that the Cisco people focused on in the Summa Four acquisition was making sure that they built trust through personal relationships and processes that were fair and provided "voice" to the Summa Four people. One of the things they did was to recognize the Summa Four people as the voice experts and to get them involved in a number of projects that Cisco had where they needed that kind of expertise. They also asked for help in customer visits and in field support from the Summa Four people. Finally, they tried to avoid arrogance or conveying any sense that Cisco had the answers.

The next big area they focused on was making sure that the head of the integration team was a Summa Four person. They chose the CFO because of his acceptance by the people, his broad background, and his leadership skills. They then built a cross-functional team of Summa Four and Cisco people, and that team focused on the short-term and medium-term integration issues. They quickly built momentum, and that has worked very well. Finally, with regards to the closing of Manchester and the move to Chelmsford, Cisco basically decided that given the growth of the company and given the strength of the Summa Four people and technology, that Cisco might be able to maintain a satellite operation in Manchester for at least two or three years and maybe much longer. The process they used to address that issue is what they refer to as scenario planning, and they've involved the Summa Four people in all of those discussions. Thus, both sides have been focused on what would be best going forward and how can that best be executed.

One of the things that might be useful to show at the end of class is the summary of the key points in the Chaudhury and Tabrizi *Harvard Business Review* article as shown in Exhibit TN-1, and the September '99 assessment of Cisco's 37 acquisitions to date in terms of their degree of success or failure, as shown in Exhibit TN-2. That September 1999 chart is based on an analysis done by a business analyst outside of Cisco and based on a thorough discussion with Cisco people regarding all 37 acquisitions.

Exhibit TN-1   Acquiring Technology

- Chaudhury and Tabrizi, *Harvard Business Review* (Sept-Oct, 1999):
    - don't acquire for products or technologies
    - acquire for capabilities
- Primary capability resides in the people
    - not individuals, but the team
    - retention becomes job 1
- Cisco: structured process, yet some flexibility
    - mandatory processes provide discipline
    - flexible processes provide adaptability
    - not all acquisitions succeed—despite the PR!

Exhibit TN-2 Cisco Acquisition Performance, September 1999, 37 Acquisitions

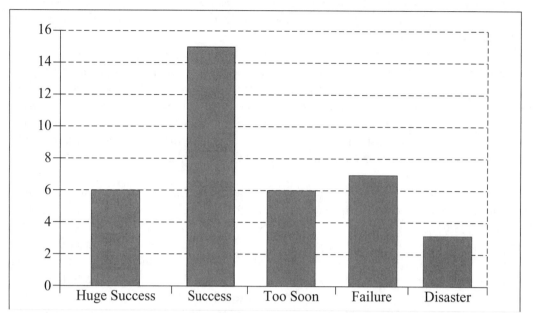

Source: Discussions with Professor Hank Chesbrough, Harvard Business School, Winter 2000

This note was prepared by Professor Steven C. Wheelwright for the sole purpose of aiding classroom instructors in the use of "Cisco Systems, Inc.: Acquisition Integration for Manufacturing," HBS No. (A) 600-015 and (B) No. 600-016. It provides analysis and questions that are intended to present alternative approaches to deepening students' comprehension of business issues and energizing classroom discussion.

Case: Multiplication of Best Practices at Holcim
Primary Chapter: Chapter 11 (Implementation levers)
Secondary Chapter: Chapter 8 (International)

Introduction: Holcim is one of the world's largest cement producers. It has recently acquired a 25% stake in a cement company in Thailand. The local operation is in deep trouble as a result of the recent Asian financial crisis. As one measure to improve the Thai operation, Holcim implements changes to the Thai company's strategy; changing from product focused to customer focused differentiators. As part of this change, the company implements a specific process to assure customer satisfaction and compliance with the strategy. Later, after perfecting the process in the Thai operation, it is then exported to the Viet Nam operation. Thus, the case examines in some detail the implementation of a process aimed at monitoring the implementation of an overall strategy.

Strategy Diamond: The case deals with the implementation of a new management practice designed to make the local unit more customer focused (i.e., to improve its differentiators). After some trial and error, the process is a success. The practice is then exported to Viet Nam. Thus, this implementation lever is rolled out in sequence across new domains. Replication is an issue raised by the case and the sequencing of this replication in new divisions.

Strategic Leadership: The case illustrates top management commitment to the implementation efforts. Specifically, motivation, example, and physical presence are emphasized in aiding the roll out effort.

Formulation/Implementation: The case is more focused on the nuts and bolts of implementing a practice designed to improve differentiation of Holcim's products. Thus, the link between formulation and implementation is implied, but not drawn out explicitly.

The Dynamic Nature of Strategy: The context of the case is the management of operations in Thailand and Viet Nam in the wake of the Asian financial crisis. The case is actually about how to implement a change within an organization and how to then replicate that change across other divisions.

MULTIPLICATION OF BEST PRACTICES AT HOLCIM: A HISTORY OF FIRSTS TEACHING NOTE

CASE SUMMARY

In August 1998, Holcim, one of the world's largest cement [producers], acquired a 25% stake in Thailand's Siam City Cement and decided to move it from a production-focused company to a customer-centric organization. Consequently, a new tool, webSALES, was developed under Holcim's management directives. WebSALES is a web-based platform that allows customers to order their cement via the Internet. It offers a 24-hour delivery service for orders placed via the Internet, enhancing customer's service as well as offering them a high degree of flexibility.

Supported by Holcim managers and external consultants, Siam City Cement experienced the implementation project of this new tool. Finally, after the company's employees and customers had undergone a training program, the first online order of cement was placed on 15 September 2000. It was also the first online cement order in Asia.

The next challenge for Holcim was to implement this webSALES tool at its newly acquired Vietnamese subsidiary. Holcim Vietnam, formerly Morning Star Cement Ltd., is a joint venture by the Holcim Group (with a 65% share) and Ha Tien 1 Cement Company (with a 35% share), a member of the Vietnam Cement Corporation. Holcim decided to adopt a "copy exactly" approach to multiply webSALES from Thailand to Vietnam. Following the same project pattern and training program that had been used to implement webSALES at Siam City Cement, the tool was implemented at Holcim Vietnam and it was rolled-out on 1 December 2001. Certain elements of webSALES such as the software and the project steps, could be copied exactly from Thailand; while other components, such as the motivational techniques and management commitment, demanded local adaptations. Holcim thereafter planned and implemented the best practice in many more group companies, such as those in the Philippines and Indonesia.

TEACHING OBJECTIVES

The purpose of this case is to teach the difficulties and key success factors of the multiplication of a best practice.

We suggest dividing the teaching into two blocks. Block I only deals with the term 'best practices' on a theoretical level and as applied to the Holcim case study. In Block II, however, the *multiplication* of a best practice and its difficulties and key success factors become the focal point of the analysis. Topics such as the transfer of explicit and tacit knowledge, national and organizational culture, the importance of top management commitment and organizational learning can be discussed and analyzed in depth. We propose discussions, with the corresponding estimated duration, on the following questions:

Block I: Best practice		
1. What happened in the Holcim case?	10 min.	10 min.
2. What is a best practice?	10 min.	20 min.
3. What is the Holcim case's best practice?	10 min.	30 min.
4. How does a good practice become a 'best practice'?	10 min.	40 min.

Block II: Multiplying best practice		
1. How did Holcim multiply its best practice?	10 min.	50 min.
2. What were the success factors of the multiplication process?	20 min.	70 min.
3. To what extent can a best practice be multiplied?	20 min.	90 min.

BLOCK I: 'BEST PRACTICES'

1. What happened in the Holcim case?

This question allows the students to summarize the case and get an in-depth understanding of the case.

2. In general, what is a best practice?

The aim of this question is to discuss and describe a best practice in general.

Elicit a "best practice" definition from the students that mentions that it is a practice that has shown to produce superior results; has been selected through a systematic process, and judged as exemplary, good, or successfully demonstrated. This definition should help the students understand the recurrent theme of the case and help them to provide useful answers to the following question.

3. What is the Holcim case's best practice?

The students exchange ideas on Holcim's best practice 'webSALES', which should include references to its customer benefits and success in Thailand and Vietnam. The students are required to discuss the various aspects of the webSALES tool, specifically mentioning the following:

- *Characteristics* of webSALES
- *WebSALES' embeddedness* in a customer-centric organization
- *The success* of webSALES in Thailand and Vietnam (and further countries)

This discussion helps to familiarize students with the characteristics of webSALES. Then elicit a summary of webSALES' most salient points and lead the students to understand that these meet the definition of a best practice. The students should next be challenged to describe the single most important incentive for multiplication – webSALES' great success. The discussion on the reasons for webSALES being a best practice is a useful link to the next question.

4. How does a good practice become a 'best practice'?

First of all, it is useful to have students reflect on what "best" implies in term of a "best" practice. They should be led to develop an understanding that for a good practice to become a "best" practice, it should be adapted to (1) the company's objectives, (2) the market conditions, (3) the corporate culture, (4) the culture within the different groups in the company. In other words, only when a company takes these variables into account, can it create a starting point for its practice to become a best practice.

The next step is to discuss the difficulties involved in measuring "best". It should be underlined that it is extremely difficult, or at least very cost-intensive, to measure the contribution that any one specific procedure or action makes to business success. This makes assessing what is "best" even more difficult.

The question: "How does one ensure that a best practice truly remains best? could follow, developing an understanding that the delineation of "best" practice can only be achieved on an ongoing basis through constant negotiation and re-negotiation of what constitutes "best" on all levels of the company. Hence the rationale for establishing a knowledge marketplace as a forum (Holcim Asia Services) for such "re-negotiation".

Each time the existing best practice is enhanced, it becomes an even-better practice, and so-on.

At this point a connection can be made with the practice, by introducing Holcim Chart

1: From a good practice to best practice.

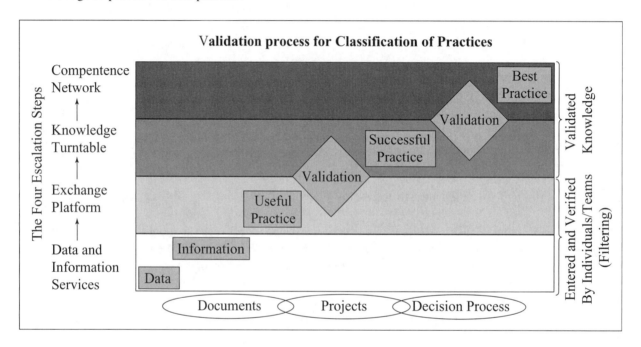

Learning processes in a company

A company achieves a best practice by using the practice, gaining experience with it, and enhancing it, re-using it, gaining new experience and enhancing again. This is the link to Agyris/ Schön's concept of single and double loop learning.

Single loop learning happens when members of the organization respond to changes in the internal and external environments of the organization by detecting errors, which they then correct. There is a single feedback loop to detected outcomes of organizational concepts and initiatives that will be modified. This is organizational learning within existing structures. On the other hand, *double loop learning* means not only the correction of detected outcomes of organizational concepts and initiatives, but also the change in the underlying norms and structures of these concepts and initiatives.

With *reference* to the Holcim case, we want the students to note that the enhancements of webSALES can be described as a single loop learning process. On the other hand, the shift within the Holcim subsidiaries in Thailand and Vietnam, from a production-focused company to a customer-focused company, is a result of a double loop learning process, since underlying norms and structures were changed.

Literature recommendation:

- Argyris, C./ Schön, D. (1978): Organizational Learning: A theory of action perspective, Reading: Addison-Wesley.
- Garvin, D. (1993): Building a learning organization, in: Harvard Business Review, 71:4, p. 78-91.
- Probst, G./ Davenport, T. (2000): Knowledge Management Case Book, Best practices, Munich: Publicis MCD Verlag.
- Probst, G./ Raub, S./ Romhardt, K. (2000): Managing knowledge, Building Blocks for Success, Chichester: Wiley.
- Leibold, M./ Probst, G./ Gibbert, M. (2002): Strategic Management in the Knowledge Society. Erlangen/ London: Wiley.

BLOCK II: 'MULTIPLYING A BEST PRACTICE'

1. How did Holcim multiply the best practice 'webSALES'?

Develop a description of the multiplication process in Vietnam. The aim is to discover that is was a copy *exactly* multiplication process in both, ((1) the *implementation* process of the tool and (2)) the *tool* itself.

(1) The implementation process

Above all, and more important than the discussion about the tool itself, get the students to discuss the different steps of the implementation process in Thailand and Vietnam, in order to realize that Holcim multiplied the implementation process as whole even though there were adaptations in style. While discussing the implementation process, students should be asked about the formation of a project team and the training classes for employees and customers in both Thailand and Vietnam. We want to emphasize that there was an exchange of people within the different teams in which the Thai webSALES experts participated in Vietnam. Overall, the webSALES implementation process was copied-pasted exactly.

(2) WebSALES the tool

On the other hand, Holcim Vietnam modified some webSALES functions. The three modifications (truck number report, delivery update and delivery report) should be briefly discussed.

However, we aim to underline that it was exactly the same webSALES tool as the one implemented in Thailand when the Vietnamese implemented it. Shortly thereafter, the Vietnamese made certain modifications to webSALES. These Vietnamese enhancements were returned to Thailand, where the company also adopted the modifications.

Although the aspect of the feeding back of enhancements has already been discussed, we want to underline that, basically, even if there were some enhancements, the webSALES tool was exactly replicated in Vietnam.

2. What were the success factors of Holcim's multiplication process?

Students have to identify the key success factors and discuss them in class. In addition, encourage students to find key success factors that are not directly specified in the case. The following key success factors are evident:

(1) Top management commitment:

What was the top management's role in the multiplication process?

The initiative to implement webSALES in Thailand and replicate it in Vietnam was clearly taken by the top management. The initial inspiration to launch webSALES in Thailand came from Paul Hugentobler and his team. As this proved to be successful in Thailand, the top management planned to multiply it to Holcim's other Asian companies.

However, when the webSALES initiatives started in Thailand, the top management was already fully convinced of their usefulness and eventual success. Acting from this powerful belief, they could *motivate* their employees, and set an *example*. For any initiative or project to be successful, it is important that it has a sponsor, preferably the top management who is also *physically present* when basic steps in the implementation process are achieved. This makes the whole concept more *credible*. This was exactly the case within Holcim. The top management was physically present, convinced of webSALES' benefits and therefore the employees were motivated and convinced that they were taking part in something special.

It is interesting to note that videos were made of all the events and the most important meetings, all of which bear witness to the top management's commitment.

Strategic and operational management

Strategic and operative management should be mentioned within the teaching process. This case not only illustrates how important commitment is for the success of a project, but also top management's role in the process: making strategic decisions, deciding to implement webSALES, and later to replicate it in Vietnam and (probably) also in other Asian subsidiaries. The employees executed the decision and were, therefore, responsible for the operational management.

(2) People networks, cross-company teams

Description of people networks

Another key success factor of the multiplication process are the people networks that Holcim set up in order to support the exchange of knowledge and experiences from Thailand to Vietnam and vice versa. For a successful multiplication, it was important to link employees who had actually been confronted with the topic in Thailand with employees who were going to implement the best practice in Vietnam.

In a next stage tacit/explicit knowledge and its transfer from both a theoretical as well as a practical point of view, and how this is illustrated by the case, will be dealt with.

Tacit and explicit knowledge

The differences between tacit and explicit knowledge should be clarified and these terms embedded in Schein's iceberg model (1984).

Tacit knowledge is personal, context-specific and hence hard to formalize and communicate. *Explicit* knowledge however, refers to knowledge that can be verbally transmitted as well as captured in a written form. With Schein's iceberg model, students are lead to understand that the top of the iceberg is explicit knowledge and everything that is under the surface refers to tacit knowledge. In general, most of the knowledge in a company is tacit and difficult to identify and transfer to other employees.

With *reference* to the case, explicit knowledge is captured in webSALES' documentation: the description of the templates, and the characterization of the different steps for the implementation. Tacit knowledge resides in the Thai employees' experiences of the implementation process: experiences with the customers, during the training classes, and with colleagues.

Transfer of tacit knowledge

At this stage it is necessary to focus on the difficulties of transferring tacit knowledge. Tacit knowledge can only be transmitted if the relevant employees meet one another face-to-face. Holcim sent experienced employees from Thailand to join the implementation teams in Vietnam. They created people networks in order to contribute valuable knowledge.

In terms of knowledge management theory, it is possible to refer to Nonaka/Takeuchi's (1995: 62) model of knowledge conversion – see Graph below. They discuss the possibilities of transferring tacit to tacit knowledge, tacit to explicit, explicit to tacit and explicit to explicit knowledge.

	Tactic Knowledge *To* Explicit Knowledge	
Tactic Knowledge	**Socialization**	**Externalization**
From Explicit Knowledge	**Internalization**	**Combination**

Recommended literature:

- Nonaka I./ Takeuchi H. (1995): The knowledge creating company. Oxford: Oxford University Press.
- Probst G. / Raub S. / Romhardt K. (2000): Managing knowledge. Building blocks for success. Chichester: John Wiley & Sons Ltd.
- Davenport T. / Prusak L. (1998): Working knowledge. How organization manage what they know. Boston: Harvard Business School Press.

(3) Consideration of different cultures of the subsidiaries

Another key success factor was the consideration of the different cultures in Thailand and Vietnam. In a discussion on this factor, reference should be made to Hofstede's (1983, 1990) study on the influence of national cultures on individuals and therefore on the organizational culture. He analyzed 40 national subsidiaries of a large multinational business corporation (IBM) and revealed four independent dimensions of differences among national value systems: 'power distance' (large vs. small); 'uncertainty avoidance' (strong vs. weak); 'individualism' vs. 'collectivism' and 'masculinity' vs. 'femininity'. The aim of this section is to have students discuss the influence of a national culture on a company. Reference may be made to the potential barriers that the cultures of Thailand and Vietnam could have formed. The discussion should be closed by emphasizing that the national culture has to be taken into consideration when multiplying a best practice.

Recommended literature:

- Hofstede G. (1983): National cultures in four dimensions, International Studies of Management and Organization, 13: 46-74.
- Hofstede G./ Neuijen B./ Ohayv D./ Sanders G. (1990): Measuring organizational cultures: A qualitative and quantitative study across twenty cases, Administrative Science Quarterly, 35: 286-316.
- Schein E. (1999): The Corporate Culture Survival Guide. San Francisco: Jossey Bass Publishers.

(4) The "story"

This part serves to show students that a best practice multiplication has to evolve around a "great story" that management should tell employees in order to motivate them. The "story telling" served as a catalyst for the successful implementation of webSALES in both Siam City Cement Company and Holcim Vietnam.

It should be understood that creating a motivating atmosphere around a central "story" is a pre-requisite to stimulate dynamism in employees as well as being an incentive for change in a company. However, it should be pointed that the same "story" cannot be used everywhere. Creativity is required to keep adapting the story to the corporate and national cultures of the different locations in which the best practice is being multiplied.

For the story to be effective it should point out the benefits and the reflected pride of being part of a revolutionary project; convincing arguments about the best practice should create excitement and build a team spirit amongst employees. WebSALES' "greatness", communicated via a 'national' story in Thailand and Vietnam respectively, was a driving force in leading all the employees towards a common goal.

3. To what extent is it possible to "copy-paste exactly" a best practice?

In this section, students should first reflect upon the idea that a best practice can be deconstructed into different elements, each of them allowing for a certain degree of replication. Some components can be fully replicated, whilst others will be more difficult to replicate, because the location in which the best practice is being multiplied demands specific adaptations. Give the following examples:

(1) Technical dimension: Some elements of the best practice are purely technical (webSALES software of the project steps of webSALES implementation), and can therefore be multiplied according to a "copy-paste exactly" method - which simply means that it can be integrally copied. This can be explained by the fact that it is possible to have full control of technicalities.

(2) Social dimension: Other characteristics such as management commitment, the management's motivational techniques (the "story") and the general level of motivation amongst employees are intrinsically related to the subsidiary in which the best practice is being multiplied. However, these characteristics cannot be multiplied exactly and will have to be adapted to the location, since they depend on variables such as corporate culture and national culture (which cannot be total controlled).

Becoming a faster learning organization

In a last section, discuss the following questions with reference to Holcim becoming a faster learning organization:

- To what extent can Holcim use this case as a showcase to initiate more best practice multiplication within the company?
- In your view, could this case motivate people in other Holcim subsidiaries to multiply their best practices? If so, how?
- How does an approach of multiplying best practices help an organization to become a faster learning organization?

These questions allow the students to think about further perspectives regarding best practice multiplication within Holcim. An analysis of these questions provides an overview of the case and, therefore, a natural conclusion to the discussion.

This teaching note was written by Heidi Armbruster, Stefano Borzillo and Professor Gilbert Probst, University of Geneva, HEC. It was prepared to accompany the case "Multiplication of Best Practices at Holcim" (reference number 403-004-1). The case was made possible by the co-operation of Holcim. © 2003, H Armbruster, S Borzillo and G Probst, University of Geneva, HEC, Switzerland.

Case: Implementation of the Balanced Scorecard as a Means of Corporate Learning: Porsche
Primary Chapter: Chapter 11
Secondary Chapters: Chapters 3, 4 & 6

Introduction: Porsche was able to regain its position as one of the world's most successful sports car manufacturers after a long crisis had been overcome. In order to maintain this top position and to stay ahead of competitors, it was crucial for the small and independent company not to stagnate, but to continuously improve every single element of its business. Striving to find new ways to secure its future, decisions were taken in 2000 to implement a balanced scorecard in the international dealer network to turn it into a learning organization. Knowledge had to be collected from dealerships around the world and turned into a profit for the entire enterprise. The management instrument, here called Porsche Key Performance Indicators, was designed with the assistance of an experienced automotive IT consultancy as well as all levels of the distribution network. In addition, ways had to be found to ensure that it would be used efficiently. By following the idea of the balanced scorecard from the initial decision to its design phase and implementation, this case focuses on its use as a source of corporate learning rather than as a controlling tool.

Strategy Diamond: Students are well familiar with Porsche's products and its differentiators and arenas. The company's strategy is not a central part of the case; it is taken as a given as the firm attempts to implement measures to help it execute that strategy.

The Dynamic Nature of Strategy: The case prompts discussion on the key factors that really matter for continuous improvement in the changing industry. Outlined are some of the steps taken to ensure that Porsche's key performance indicators would not be static but instead adapt to the changes in the business environment which before had undermined some of their core assumptions.

Formulation/Implementation: The case is centered squarely on implementing a balanced scorecard as a means to measure performance and turn the Porsche's dealer network into a learning organization. The case describes the process beginning with the formulation of the goals and ideas to the implementation of the design phase, the development phase and the rollout phase of Porsche's key performance indicators. Additionally, the case incites discussion on potential problems that can arise when implementing a large internal structure change.

Strategic Leadership: Andres Schlegal presents the balanced scorecard initiative. There is opportunity to discuss the method he used of choosing his implementation team as well as his strategy to infuse cooperation within the company.

IMPLEMENTATION OF THE BALANCED SCORECARD AS A MEANS OF CORPORATE LEARNING:THE PORSCHE CASE TEACHING NOTE

I. ABSTRACT

Porsche was able to regain its position as one of the world's most successful sports car manufacturers after a long crisis had been overcome. In order to maintain this top position and to stay ahead of competitors, it was crucial for the small and independent company not to stagnate, but to continuously improve every single element of its business. Striving to find new ways to secure its future, decisions were taken in 2000 to implement a balanced scorecard in the international dealer network to turn it into a learning organization. Knowledge had to be collected from dealerships around the world and turned into a profit for the entire enterprise.

The management instrument, here called Porsche Key Performance Indicators, was designed with the assistance of an experienced automotive IT consultancy as well as all levels of the distribution network. In addition, ways had to be found to ensure that it would be used efficiently.

By following the idea of the balanced scorecard from the initial decision to its design phase and implementation, this case focuses on its use as a source of corporate learning rather than as a controlling tool.

II. PURPOSE AND POSITIONING

The case, accompanied by this teaching note, lays the foundation for a discussion of a broad range of corporate learning issues related to the balanced scorecard's life cycle. When generalized, this case will also help students to learn about the design phase of a project, its deployment and its progress in the context of corporate learning.

Appropriate for second-level undergraduate students, it is also suitable for graduate classes in business sciences. It would also be apt for an executive education program. Basic prerequisite knowledge of the balanced scorecard as introduced by Kaplan and Norton is helpful but not required. For executive education programs the suggested teaching method is to focus more on the practical implementation and to be less theoretical.

In the case, only a small portion of the Porsche Corporation is subject to scrutiny: the international Porsche Sales Organization, i.e., the Sales Operations department at the headquarters, the subsidiaries in the markets and the dealerships. The case follows the balanced scorecard from the initial management decision up to the early life system. Students can therefore explore the possibilities of using the balanced scorecard not only as a controlling tool, but also as a source of corporate learning, consider its limits and understand how projects are managed in a learning environment.

As the case ends with the initialization of the hot phase, students are encouraged – after investigating the project's past and the presented outlook – to think creatively ahead and imagine what else could be accomplished in terms of corporate learning. Further readings are recommended to spur students' creative thinking.

All information given in the teaching note is derived from the case. Everything that goes beyond what is stated in the case is mere speculation by the author - inspired by his own experience.

III. CASE QUESTIONS

This teaching note offers a set of trigger questions with which to initiate the class as well as several assignment questions for group work. The suggested questions will be treated in an overall context in the following discussion plan and supplemented with additional teaching content.

Trigger questions for introduction in class

1. What do you know about Porsche?
2. What do you think are the main problems of such a company?
3. What is a balanced scorecard?
4. What is a learning organization?

Group assignment questions

1. Describe in detail what Porsche expected from the implementation of the balanced scorecard.
2. Does the Porsche Sales Organization comply with the image of a learning organization? Compare with approaches such as Garvin, Senge, Probst et al.
3. Explain the role of the KPI project for (a) the different types of individuals confronted with it at Porsche, (b) the dealerships as a whole, and (c) the Porsche group.
4. Show where the balanced scorecard project worked in favor of Garvin's five main activities and where it worked against them.
5. What hindered learning? What might hinder learning in future? How could these obstacles be mitigated?
6. Presuming that everything went according to Porsche's plans; would more learning have been possible? What could have been done differently or additionally?

IV. DISCUSSION PLAN

The suggested teaching approach begins with a survey of the existing knowledge of Porsche in the class in order to arouse the students' interest and to bring everyone to the same level. After having reached a common understanding of the company, the case could be distributed. Students should then familiarize themselves with the case. Due to the length of the case this is best done at home as a preparation for class. After that, the assignment questions of your choice could be discussed by groups of students. If only a single session is planned for the case, the distribution and preparation should be done in advance. Groups should then present their results in a following class session. The following paragraphs also include some suggestions on where to add further learning content.

Introduction in class

In order to trigger the exchange of prior knowledge of the company, the following questions could be asked. Depending on the available time, the case and the company could be quickly introduced with the information given below. Alternatively, a single student or a group could be asked to prepare a short presentation on Porsche. Sufficient supplementary information is provided on the Porsche website http://www.porsche.com.

Question 1: What do you know about Porsche?

Porsche, based in Stuttgart-Zuffenhausen, Germany, is one of the smallest independent and yet most successful sports car manufacturers. In 2001/02, it generated 4.9 billion € in sales, with only slightly more than 10.000 employees producing and selling over 55 thousand cars (see Exhibit II: Porsche Group Highlights).

Question 2: What do you think are the main problems of such a company?

As a small enterprise in the premium segment, Porsche has to meet many challenges in a highly competitive industry. One of them is certainly the size of the competitors that Porsche faces. Being a multiple of its size, they could enter Porsche's market segment and if they were supported by an unprecedented marketing campaign, Porsche would not be able to counter this attack. Its relative budget restrictions also make it difficult for Porsche to stay on the edge of research and development. For instance, the platform of the sports utility vehicle Cayenne was developed in a joint effort with Volkswagen to minimize risks.

VW then turned it into its Tuareg and profited by selling an SUV with Porsche technology. However, it has to be said that Porsche still has a major focus on R&D and has already developed some of the most thrilling technologies in the automobile sector, such as ceramic brakes. Porsche furthermore possesses its own design and research center that develops everything from elevators to fork lift trucks on demand.

Dependency on a single segment poses manifold dangers as well, the success of the whole enterprise being inextricably bound to the fate of this single segment. Moreover, the targeted segment is small and therefore only few scale effects can be realized during production. This last problem, however, is overcompensated by the high margins that can be achieved in this particular segment.

Now that Porsche has been introduced, it is necessary to ensure that the students are familiar with the balanced scorecard. Depending on when the students last encountered this topic, you could either encourage them to share their knowledge with one another or brief them yourself.

Question 3: What is a balanced scorecard?

The balanced scorecard is an approach to strategic management that was developed in the early 1990s by Robert Kaplan and David Norton. To counter the weaknesses and shortfalls of previous management approaches, the balanced scorecard offers a clear prescription as to what companies should measure in order to balance the previously biased financial perspective in reporting.

> *"The Balanced Scorecard retains traditional financial measures. But financial measures tell the story of past events, an adequate story for industrial age companies for which investments in long-term capabilities and customer relationships were not critical for success. These financial measures are inadequate, however, for guiding and evaluating the journey that information age companies must make to create future value through investment in customers, suppliers, employees, processes, technology, and innovation."*[i]

In this spirit, the balanced scorecard suggests measuring the enterprise from four perspectives as a basis for strategic management:

- Financial Perspective
- Customer Perspective

- Internal Processes Perspective
- Learning and Growth Perspective

Further information on the balanced scorecard, which is not the main topic of this teaching note, can be found in Kaplan and Norton's books (see "References" and "Additionally Recommended Readings").

Before getting to grips with the material, all the students need to have the same understanding of a learning organization. By responding to the following question, students will show what they have retained from previous courses on the subject.

Question 4: What is a learning organization?

Corporate learning was first specifically described in 1990 by Peter M. Senge in his book "The Fifth Discipline"[ii], although traces of learning in organizations and learning organizations can be found in earlier literature. Since his definition of learning is very vague and difficult to implement, many scholars after him have tried to formulate the concept more precisely. Among them was David A. Garvin who offered the following definition:

"A learning organization is an organization skilled at creating, acquiring, and transferring knowledge, and at modifying its behavior to reflect new knowledge and insights."[iii]

See also further definitions by Peter Senge, Gilbert Probst etc.

An interesting link can be made between a learning organization and knowledge management following the Probst/Büchel (1997, p. 15) definition:

"Organizational learning is the process by which the organization's knowledge and value base changes, leading to improved problem-solving ability and capacity for action."

Case work in Groups

With the case at hand, students will be able to reflect on the above definition and discuss to which extent the balanced scorecard helps the Porsche Sales Organization to comply with the definition. The students will see that Porsche is a company that actively manages its learning process to ensure that learning happens on purpose rather than merely by chance.

The following simple introductory assignment forces students to read the case carefully and helps them to return to the story.

Group assignment 1: Describe in detail what Porsche expected from the implementation of the balanced scorecard.

The expectations regarding the Key Performance Indicators were wide-ranged and abundant. Since operational and tactical decisions often sacrifice long-term growth for better short-term results, the balanced scorecard was expected to procure the strategic alignment of dealership managements, which would eventually improve long-term profitability. Furthermore, the standardization of the dealership reporting in all the company's markets was thought to lead to a great saving in administration costs. Moreover, the benchmarking of the dealerships was believed to unveil potential for future improvement.

The acquisition of corporate knowledge was another main expectation. Knowledge was to come from the consultants and from the dealerships themselves, which were thereafter to share it among one another. This knowledge was expected to serve as a basis for the selection of certain dealership characteristics and for their improvement.

Porsche also thought it likely that dealerships could be run more profitably if the dealerships' management could be made aware of the detailed figures that the balanced scorecard could provide. This, furthermore, would significantly change the job of the regional manager, who previously had to do many calculations by hand. Regional managers would obtain a huge store of data on their dealerships, which they could then use in their consultations.

The headquarters also expected to amass comprehensive data on the dealerships and to intensify communication between all levels of the Porsche Sales Organization.

Above all, Porsche wanted to secure its already strong position in the market segment even further.

The learning issues can then be examined by starting off with Garvin's definition and applying it to Porsche.

Group assignment 2: Does the Porsche Sales Organization comply with Garvin's image of a learning organization (for the definition, please see Question 4 above)? Compare with approaches such as Garvin, Senge, Probst etc.

Garvin's definition includes four abilities that have to be mastered by an organization in order for the organization to have learning ascribed to it. These are (a) creating, (b) acquiring, and (c) transferring knowledge as well as (d) being able to change the organizational behavior to reflect this new knowledge and insight.

a) Every day when Porsche employees set out to do their jobs, knowledge is created. There might be a technician who realizes that a certain screw does not have to be loosened in order to change a broken windscreen wiper, or a marketing manager who realizes that decreasing the size of the price tag on cars increases sales. Furthermore, the huge research and development department of the company yields massive knowledge. In fact, all companies comply with this first condition.

b) Knowledge can also be acquired from outside sources, e.g., from consultants. However, since this was the consultancy's first balanced scorecard and since Porsche was their first multi-market project, knowledge transfer possibilities appear to have been limited. External sources could also include competitors that are benchmarked, or a fellow dealership somewhere else. At the same time, however, the latter is a transfer within the entity Porsche Sales Organization.

c) The sum of the bits and pieces of knowledge is essential for the success of the enterprise. All too often, the small advantages remain unrealized as they are offset by some disadvantageous behavior. Porsche seeks to find all its knowledge in order to make it available to all of its dealerships. Thanks to the balanced scorecard, the transfer of knowledge is now largely facilitated as it shows the regional managers the specific weaknesses of certain dealerships and allows them to be matched to the corresponding strengths of others. Due to confidentiality issues only the regional manager can learn directly from the better dealership and, thereafter, teach the weaker one.

d) The potential that arises from knowledge has to be turned into a success factor through change – changing the way things are done, changing the organizational structure, or changing whatever becomes necessary. The case shows a clear intent to change, but proof of change at the level of the dealerships is not provided. While, during the development phase, the headquarters showed that they were able to adapt in respect of previous experiences, it is still to be seen whether the dealerships will act accordingly. Since the headquarters were aware of this potential problem, a major focus of the project management was to convince the dealerships to do so.

By meeting Garvin's four requirements, and having complied satisfyingly in respect of the key Performance Indicator project, the Porsche Sales Organization can be called a learning organization.

Group assignment 3: Explain the role of the KPI project for (a) the different types of individuals confronted with it at Porsche, (b) the dealerships as a whole, and (c) the Porsche group.

a) Five different types of individuals deal with the Key Performance Indicators in one way or another: the dealership accountant, the dealership general manager, the regional manager, the market manager, and the director sales. The latter two are treated as representatives of their departments.

   i. The dealership accountant is responsible for the data collection and entry into the system. He is the linchpin in the creation of the balanced scorecard since he collects the results from the different places in the dealership and submits them for report generation. Based on his data, the dealership will be evaluated and eventually become a best practice or a target of aid. In general, accountants are suitable for this kind of task because they are already responsible for the financial reporting and have acquired a certain experience with reporting tools, as well as in working with computers. The accountant could additionally assist the dealership manager by pointing out urgent and important issues according to the approach suggested in the case.

   ii. The dealership manager or general manager, who is in charge of the dealership, is the one who can best motivate his employees to comply with all requirements of the Key Performance Indicators. He is the one who will make the decision to change or not when the report is evaluated. The manager can furthermore have particular pages of the report distributed within his dealership and determine objectives for the team. This makes him the key player for the possible improvements indicated by the balanced scorecard.

   iii. The regional manager, who is a consultant for the dealerships in his region, provides help wherever possible. The regional manager receives the KPI reports of all his dealerships and has access to the database of raw data, which allows him to analyze dealerships in far more detail and benchmark one to another.

   iv. This information allows him to approach dealerships to inquire why they are performing so well in certain indicators and so weak in others. As he is already trusted by the dealerships, he can become the ideal pivot and thereby spur the learning processes. No one else in the hierarchy has such a bird's-eye view of all the information available at his particular level, since only regional managers have *manageable* groups of dealerships. Above all, the regional manager's work can be regarded as the main pillar for an efficient evaluation of the data acquired through the balanced scorecard and thus for the transfer of knowledge.

   v. The market manager receives the reports but is not as actively involved in the process as the dealerships and regional managers. His main interest is the financial health of all dealerships in his market. He therefore only keeps track of the general issues and is involved in the design and roll-out phase.

   vi. The role of the director sales, i.e., the role of the headquarters, is similar to that of the market manager, but even more limited. As hundreds of dealerships have to be profitable, he cannot get caught up in too many details. He rarely intervenes in other issues, and when he does so, this is generally restricted to the introduction of new tools such as the balanced scorecard, which was primarily introduced by his department. At this stage of the project the headquarters generally monitors the development of all dealerships, chooses the best practice dealerships in consensus with the markets and publishes information that the dealerships require.

348

b) The Key Performance Indicators report is provided for each individual dealership, thereby providing the dealership's management with the best-structured and most detailed information it has ever received. Seeing its results compared to the average of all dealerships and the average of a selected top group, the dealership can determine its strengths and weaknesses. After gaining additional knowledge through a knowledge exchange with other dealerships, e.g., by reading about best practices, a dealership can improve its long-term performance.

c) The Porsche company profits from the improved performance of its dealerships through the use of the balanced scorecard. When more cars are sold and customers are even more satisfied, the group's results are improved and shareholder value rises. Additionally, a mass of information on individual dealerships is accumulated by the headquarters and subsidiaries, which could be used for market research or the like.

Teaching Content

According to Garvin, learning organizations should master five main activities to foster their learning. He calls them the building blocks:

1. Systematic problem solving,
2. Experimentation with new approaches,
3. Learning from their own experience and past history,
4. Learning from the experiences and best practices of others, and
5. Transferring knowledge quickly and efficiently throughout the organization.

Group assignment 4: Show where the Key Performance indicator project worked in favor of Garvin's five main activities (see teaching content above) and where it worked against them.

Additional Teaching Content

Before discussing the answers to this assignment, students should be familiarized with measurement as a basis for learning. Write the following sentence on the blackboard and ask the students to reflect on it in the context of measurement:

When hiking one does not notice the environment changing, unless one opens one's senses and notices the surroundings.

It is hoped that with this sentence students understand the necessity of measurement and, thus, the general business postulate: "If you can't measure it, you can't manage it." Success and failures have to measured, and the development followed for a long period as a basis of learning. Without the knowledge that something that could be learned exists, learning will never occur. In this context, the balanced scorecard is an impressive tool with which to provide a basis for learning, because it monitors thousands of figures and allows benchmarking among dealerships from which best practices or experiences can be derived.

Garvin's first main activity, "systematic problem solving", requires reliance on a scientific method for solving problems rather than on guesswork. Porsche pursued this process of planning, doing, checking and responsive acting, as formulated by Deming, as closely as possible. After the decision to implement a balanced scorecard had been taken, the project team started a comprehensive planning process. Information on the balanced scorecard was acquired from all possible sources, e.g., books, the Harvard Business Review and university papers. They also studied information on the pilot markets and relevant dealerships. The project team also sought to profit from all available knowledge of the deployment of such a tool. This knowledge came mostly from inside the department that had deployed similar applications before as well as from the consultants, who had wide experience of reporting systems for the automotive industry. On this basis, the project team developed the balanced scorecard and soon convened with the markets' representatives to reach a broad understanding.

The introduction into the market was accompanied by a strict evaluation of each step. This evaluation—mostly based on checklists—served as a source for further adaptation of the deployment process. Moreover, Porsche planned to continue this approach of continuously evaluating and adapting the system in a prescribed cycle throughout its lifetime. The resulting Key Performance Indicators is a system that allows decisions to be taken that are based on facts rather than on mere assumptions. This kind of fact-based management is further supported by the new ability to cross-evaluate and benchmark dealerships.

The accuracy and precision of the data are a cornerstone of the system. Dealerships are consequently requested to take all possible steps to ensure the accuracy of their data. Yet, at this point, a further improvement could be easily implemented: Dealerships would be more likely to resubmit corrected data if they were to receive an updated report afterwards. The accuracy and depth of the system allow the underlying causes of problems to be traced in an unprecedented way. Although it will not often be necessary to browse through the whole evidence, Porsche has made a major effort to ensure that any information can be retrieved through a drill-down approach that only requires a few mouse clicks.

Garvin's theory continues with the second main activity, "experimentation with new approaches". This activity is targeted at systematically searching for new knowledge. The Key Performance Indicators system presents an ongoing program in the sense that Garvin meant this, meaning that it aims at incremental improvements with a continuing series of experiments. The dealerships all have a very superficial knowledge of how things are done. With the usage of the KPI System, this superficial knowledge becomes deep understanding. Every employee is enabled to relate to specific indicators that measure his personal contribution and can thus determine his personal emphasis. This is further enforced by the KPI info flyer that Porsche plans to distribute to all dealership employees. Employees are supposed to always keep this paper, which provides general information on the main indicators and the personal emphasis, at hand. Time will tell if this is enough to comply with Garvin's condition. It would certainly be useful if the company were to inform employees in detail of the underlying cause-and-effect relationships as well as of possible exceptions or unforeseeable interferences.

Garvin's third condition, "learning from their own experience and past history", is perhaps the one that profits most from the balanced scorecard project. In order to be able to learn from the past, companies must know what happened; this knowledge is provided by the balanced scorecard's measurements. The Key Performance Indicator report also focuses on long-term development, thus displaying the history of certain figures. By studying the course of these historical values, a dealership is empowered to act. Although the headquarters and all other involved parties may have had the best intentions to do so, the case does not provide any information on whether the mere awareness of the past history really did lead to the creation of new knowledge.

During the development phase of the balanced scorecard, existing experience was used wherever possible, for instance, by drawing on the training department's skill to create the training, renaming the tool to Key Performance Indicators to avoid conflicts, and by predicting that the learning curve would reduce the deployment time from 1.5 days to a single day.

Garvin continues his main activities with "learning from the experiences and best practices of others", which can be reduced to his third condition applied to external sources. This extension of the horizon—looking beyond one's frontiers—often offers a completely new perspective. Many processes are what they are because they have always been that way. Nobody has ever seen the necessity to challenge them, since everyone takes certain habits for granted, as if they were a "law of nature". As soon as external examples with the same or even better results become available, these processes will be questioned, and they and the external examples may even be mutually improved by applying the detailed knowledge that they have gained of one another. The Key Performance Indicator project was planned to trigger exactly this. In order to achieve learning, it is important to study how work is done, rather than simply studying the results. This was the purpose of giving the dealerships the opportunity to learn from best practice dealerships that will be discussed in the circular, or bringing market representatives together on Corporate KPI Conferences.

Another part of the balanced scorecard is the customer perspective. This evaluation of customer satisfaction leads to an amplified communication with customers and informs the dealerships about specific needs, wishes and ideas that stimulate learning, too.

During the development and deployment of the tool, it was possible to retrieve detailed knowledge from the North American subsidiary that had previously created a similar system, but which had only covered financial indicators. A mass of information was also exchanged on the markets' various reporting systems from which Porsche Italia profited especially. Additionally, the project team always kept an open ear during the deployment phase, encouraging dealers to provide feedback in order to learn from them and to improve on the team's own work.

Many dealers had acquired previous experience, some even with competitors' systems, and this they shared—when possible—with their fellow dealers during the workshop sessions.

The last main activity postulated by Garvin as a requirement for a learning organization is the "quick and efficient transfer of knowledge throughout the organization". This transfer of knowledge is largely facilitated by the Internet, which has become increasingly available for learning in recent years. Porsche uses the Internet as a medium through which to transfer detailed written information faster than by surface mail. The oral transfer of knowledge, e.g., by phone, or through site visits, is also encouraged by the KPI project. The communication that this triggers is further extended by the planned training sessions, in the form of workshops, to discuss particular issues that appear to be of major importance, or that seem to offer a high potential for improvement.

Although minor improvements appear to be possible, it can be concluded that the balanced scorecard project mainly complied with Garvin's theory.

Additional Teaching Content

An activity that can also be regarded as essential to successful corporate learning is the continuous storage and management of knowledge. Knowledge originates in the brains of individual employees. This, however, can lead to major problems when employees retire, leave or are dismissed. When this happens, a part of the company's "brain" is removed and it "forgets". If the Key Performance Indicators were accompanied by a knowledge database, selected important knowledge could be stored systematically and updated over time.

These three steps, selection, storage, and updating, ensure the proper continuous storage of valuable knowledge. Despite storage media being very cheap, selection has to occur because the information overflow would render the database dysfunctional. Once stored, this knowledge has to be updated as reality evolves and new facets develop. Porsche could then use the retained knowledge almost indefinitely.

In time, Porsche could certainly create a database containing the collected information and make it accessible to all dealerships. However, considering the bulk of figures, this knowledge base would be difficult to compile, even after the most stringent selection. Even worse, this incredibly huge database would probably lead to immense administration costs.

Their idea of presenting only the main indicators in a manual, shows that Porsche had foreseen the above problem. However, a solution to this problem had not been found at the time the case was written.

Group assignment 5: What has hindered learning? What might hinder learning in future? How could these obstacles be mitigated?

Obstacles not only accompany the implementation of any new tool - the balanced scorecard is no exception - and obstacles can hinder learning in future as well. The process of gradually achieving the ability to circumvent and avoid these obstacles can also be categorized as a way of learning.

The learning processes generated by the Key Performance Indicator project do not start smoothly as, by definition, the balanced scorecard does not inquire into the underlying reasons, but only displays results. Being aware of the possibility to improve by viewing the average results of the selected top group does not yet enforce a learning process. Information on the reasons for successes has to be made available. But the planned regular best practice newsletter will not be able to provide the necessary information on the plethora of topics at the right time. These two systems represent push systems that firmly put the information ball in the dealerships' court, regardless of utility and demand. However, a pull system that allows the dealerships to obtain important data on demand would be of much greater usefulness as it would meet the various needs of the individual dealerships. The regional manager's assistance, which is a pull system, could be supplemented with the knowledge database - another pull system - as described above.

Due to confidentiality issues, dealerships cannot access their fellow dealerships' data and are thus unable to contact a dealership directly to profit from a certain interesting result's background, because they are unaware of this result. A smart way of circumventing this problem would have been to encourage regional managers, who benchmark their dealerships, to put dealerships in contact with each other if a fruitful relationship were envisaged in respect of a particular indicator. After consultation with both dealerships to obtain their consent to waive confidentiality, the regional manager could have the dealerships contact each other to mutually increase their knowledge. While the weak dealership would grow to the level of the teaching dealership, the latter would grow even further by learning from the other's failures and, possibly, from the other's good ideas, too. The sheer mass of figures might overwhelm people when they are introduced to the balanced scorecard. It is said that a company cannot be controlled by more than ten figures, since people are in general incapable of grasping more at a time. If this holds true, the danger of an information overflow through the Key Performance Indicators is immense, although Porsche has tried to prevent this through the drill-down approach and the traffic light system described in the case. Both try to direct attention to the problematic issues, preventing readers from spending too much time on irrelevant figures.

Additional Teaching Content

Learning implies change. Often old ideas have to be erased from people's brains and replaced by new ones. Old habits have been strengthened through the years. Changing them can pose a key obstacle. In one of his remarkable articles on the model of the nature of human beings, Jensen states[iv] that people have a tendency to resist change in the absence of a major crisis. This reluctance to learn is explained by his Pain Avoidance Model, which states that people subconsciously seek to avoid anything that could cause pain or uncertainty. This pain can be of psychological nature, induced by something that threatens to change the lens through which one views reality. It is a self-harming human behavior—Jensen calls it non-rational—that has its roots in evolution and that was ingrained thousands of year ago when man frequently found himself having to make "fight or flight" decisions.

Students' creative spirit can be evoked by letting them draft their own ideas on the issue.

Group assignment 6: Presuming that everything went according to Porsche's plans; would more learning have been possible? What could have been done differently or additionally?

After having analyzed the obstacles to learning, it can be said that more learning would become possible, if these obstacles were overcome. Especially the link between the result figures in the report and the underlying knowledge has to be strengthened. Learning will only prevail if the headquarters and the markets put a strong effort into communicating knowledge between the dealerships. The average Porsche dealership is very small and therefore it cannot afford to send important employees or managers to many seminars. Consequently, personnel rotation programs that are frequently proposed in the context of corporate learning will also fail; a dealership cannot send its sole accountant away for a couple of weeks.

As the knowledge transfer on a personal level is limited, only written transfer remains. The best practice example, which is to be published in the regular circular, will probably not have a huge impact, simply due to its long publication cycles and its narrow focus. A better proposition would be to monitor all dealerships for extreme results in a certain figure. A standard description form to explain the reasons for and causes of their achievements and failures could then be filled in. This data could be published in an online database afterwards, which should consequently be linked to the report. Furthermore, an online forum could be established to allow dealers to discuss certain figures. The approximate 170 dealerships will certainly provide a constant flow of communication to the forum.

From the information provided in the case, it cannot be deduced whether things have been unlearnt – be it on purpose or unplanned. Yet it can be speculated that the potential transfer of knowledge from the roll-outs of previous projects was not fully used, as a clearly documented generic roll-out process is not mentioned in the case. It appears that lessons learned from previous roll-outs were communicated only by word of mouth and this fades in time. The longer the period since antecedent projects have been completed, the less the knowledge that is transferred in this way.

Wrap up and what really happened

After the groups have presented and discussed their results, the students will have heard about various issues in respect of corporate learning at Porsche. They will have understood that the balanced scorecard, which is mainly a strategic management tool, can also serve brilliantly as a basis for generating corporate learning. It is then important to consolidate the lessons learnt at the end of the session. Students should keep in mind that the balanced scorecard alone does not yet turn any enterprise into a learning organization. Finding knowledge is facilitated by the tool itself, but then a subsequent system has to ensure that learning really takes place. Finally, all knowledge ends up with the employees and therefore, what matters most, is the spirit of the people.

Students might also be interested in the subsequent development of the story:

By mid 2003, the Key Performance Indicator System had continued its success story. The system had been implemented in Great Britain, France, Italy, as well as in Australia and while the personal flyer was already distributed in Australia it was ready for print in most other markets. Thus a number of approx. 65

dealerships were connected with plans to connect all of the 86 German dealerships by July 31, 2004. A first Corporate KPI Conference had been scheduled for November 2003 and everyone was looking ahead.

However, the difficulties mentioned in Assignment 6 were hard to overcome. The markets depend solely on the regional manager and the circular as learning media to exchange knowledge. Thus the importance of the regional managers for corporate learning has increased dramatically since the dealerships have to rely almost uniquely on them to acquire ideas and information from which to learn.

V. ADDITIONALLY RECOMMENDED READINGS

In addition to the references at the end of the teaching note, some literature can be recommended:

Gilbert J. B. Probst, Steffen Raub, Kai Romhardt, Managing Knowledge (London: Wiley 1999)

Tom Davenport, Probst, Gilbert, Knowledge Management Case Book (London: Wiley/Publicis, 2000)

Marius Leibold, Gilbert Probst, Michael Gibbert, Strategic Management in the Knowledge Society (London: Wiley/Publicis 2002)

Gilbert Probst, Bettina Büchel, Organizational Learning (London: Prentice Hall, 1996)

Robert S. Kaplan, David P. Norton, *The Strategy-Focused Organization: How Balanced Scorecard Companies Thrive in the New Business Environment* (Boston: Harvard Business School Press, 2000)

> This book is the second book by Kaplan and Norton and provides their latest findings concerning the balanced scorecard. It draws upon their experience during the six years since the publication of their first book.[i]

References

[i] Robert S. Kaplan, David P. Norton, *The Balanced Scorecard: Translating Strategy into Action* (Boston: Harvard Business School Press, 1994)

[ii] Peter M. Senge, *The Fifth Discipline* (New York: Doubleday, 1990)

[iii] David A. Garvin, "Building a Learning Organization," *Harvard Business Review,* July-August 1993

[iv] Michael C. Jensen, "Self-Interest, Altruism, Incentives, and Agency Theory," *Journal of Applied Corporate Finance,* Vol. 7, No. 2 (Summer 1994)

This teaching note was written by Professor Gilbert Probst, HEC, University of Geneva, and Jan Dominik Gunkel, WHU, Otto Beisheim Graduate School of Management. It was prepared to accompany the case "Implementation of the Balanced Scorecard as a Means of Corporate Learning: The Porsche Case" (reference number 903-030-1). The case was made possible by the co-operation of Porsche AG. © 2003, G Probst, HEC, University of Geneva, Switzerland, and JD Gunkel,WHU,Vallendar Germany.

Case: Blue Whale Moving company, Inc.
Primary Chapter: Chapter 12
Secondary Chapters: Chapters 3, 5 & 11

Introduction: This case follows the start-up and evolution of a new venture based in Austin, TX. The two founders had tried a variety of management structures and controls over the preceding years, yet they remained unsure about which was the most effective. While they liked the idea of having a vice-president in charge of day-to-day operations, they wondered whether their direct involvement was essential to the functioning of the firm and were concerned that a vice-president might impede this contact. Everything seemed to go so smoothly when the business was smaller and people were guided solely by the Blue Whale vision of customer service. Now the business was more complicated and control of the business and its employees was much more difficult. Despite the "growing pains," Brad Armstrong and Blake Miller were as excited as ever about the possibilities that lay ahead of them, but they knew one thing for sure, the journey would not be easy. They had to not only get control of their business, but also reach the goal of expansion they set forth in their mission statement. As they planned their discussions regarding the actions to be taken on some of the specific labor issues, they each thought individually about what needed to be done to get the entire business moving in the right direction again. It was important to Blake and Brad that Blue Whale expand in its current markets, as well as in new markets. In the Blue Whale Vision Statement, they established an aggressive goal of opening 100 Blue Affiliates in different cities by the year 2000. As a first step along this path, they made a concerted effort to expand by opening offices in other Texas cities. Although they were optimistic about their plans, they questioned the timing and implementation of their expansion efforts. They also wondered if they could continue to use the management approach that had made their initial efforts so successful.

Strategy Diamond: The case deals with Blue Whale's initial entry strategy into the moving business and describes their proposals for how they would differentiate and 'win' in a highly competitive and crowded moving market. As the company matures Blake and Brad are faced with establishing a plan for their staging and vehicles for their aggressive expansion.

The Dynamic Nature of Strategy: Blue Whale Moving Company finds itself as an industry leader in the region because of its unprecedented strategy. Competitors soon begin copying Blue Whale's strategy and the regional industry goes through a sort of mini paradigm shift. The case provides opportunity for discussion about opportunities and challenges certain strategies can cause in an environment.

Formulation/Implementation: A key point in the case is the behind-the-scenes detail about the formulation and the subsequent implementation of Blue Whale's strategy. A key point is whether their current implementation methods can continue during their future growth.

Strategic Leadership: Brad and Blake face control issues as leaders in the company. As the firm continues to expand geographically, financially and in size of work force, they feel less and less able to determine the direction of the company.

BLUE WHALE MOVING COMPANY, INC. (A) & (B)
TEACHING NOTE

This two-part case examines the founding and early growth of the Blue Whale Moving Company – a firm that opened in Austin, TX in 1988. The case focuses on the process through which the founders, Blake Miller and Brad Armstrong, conceive, develop, implement and grow a unique business concept and operating vision in the Austin moving industry. It chronicles meetings in which Miller and Armstrong conceptualize their new business plan and describes the operating environment in the firm's early days. The (A) case concludes in 1993 as the founders contemplate how to meet their vision for growth by turning their successful local firm into a large multi-site business. The (B) case, which is best discussed in a full separate session, is set in late 1994 and describes the founders' struggles with replicating success in new markets and maintaining success in their original location as they step back from day-to-day operations.

Both cases are designed for a unit on new venture creation. Secondarily, they offer insight into the challenges associated with strategy implementation. They attempt to help students to:

- Learn about the entrepreneurial process
- Gain an understanding of the challenges in translating a strategy into action
- Learn about the difficulty of transferring success in a single site to additional locations

1) Are Miller and Armstrong entrepreneurs? What personal attributes and aspects of their experience with Blue Whale Moving Company are most important to your determination?

2) Describe the steps undertaken by Miller and Armstrong to create this new venture. What did they do well? What steps might they have done differently to improve Blue Whale's chances of success? What were the key resources and capabilities brought to the business by the founders that enabled their business concept to succeed?

3) What was the state of the moving industry in Austin prior to the creation of the Blue Whale Moving Company? Were any macro-economic factors thought to be important for the near future? What competitive forces did an Austin moving company have to consider in 1988? What were the characteristics of a typical competitor's strategy prior to Blue Whale's entry?

4) What about Miller and Armstrong's business concept and/or approach to business were unique and were likely to have provided competitive? As of 1993, what aspects of Blue Whale's performance can be regarded as successes? What aspects of Blue Whale's performance can be seen as lacking?

5) Describe the causes of Blue Whale's failure to grow according to the vision laid out by the founders. Was the strategy flawed? Did the founders fail to develop the needed implementation levers? Or, was the failure mostly attributable to a failure of strategic leadership?

6) What steps could Blue Whale's owners take in late 1994 to improve their performance and get the firm back on [its] early growth trajectory? Is it at all likely that Blue Whale could be restructured to meet the goal of 100 locations in cities worldwide by the year 2000? If not, what would a more appropriate vision for growth look like?

1. Defining Entrepreneurship
Are Miller and Armstrong entrepreneurs? What personal attributes and aspects of their experience with Blue Whale Moving Company are most important to your determination?

In the book, we define entrepreneurship as the consequence of actions based on the identification and exploration of opportunity in the absence of obviously available resources. Miller and Armstrong fit this definition well. In Miller's case, he had ideas about how to better operate a moving company but appeared to have not thought seriously about turning those ideas into a business venture prior to his meetings with Armstrong. Armstrong had financial resources and a general knowledge of sales and business management but did not have an obviously available business idea to pursue until he began discussions with Miller.

A class discussion could begin with students providing elements of their own definition for what makes an entrepreneur. Student ideas could be captured on the board and classified as either; 1.) necessary, 2.) somewhat indicative or 3.) not indicative of entrepreneurship. When a sufficient list has been developed, the class could discuss which attributes of entrepreneurship were exhibited by Miller and Armstrong in the case.

2. The Entrepreneurial Process
Describe the steps undertaken by Miller and Armstrong to create this new venture. What did they do well? What steps might they have done differently to improve Blue Whale's chances of success? What were the key resources and capabilities brought to the business by the founders that enabled their business concept to succeed?

As identified in Exhibit 12.2 of the Carpenter/Sanders text, the entrepreneurial process consists of three important elements, opportunity, resources & capabilities, and the entrepreneurial team.

The discovery of the opportunity seems to have only been possible through a combination of the resources and capabilities of the partners. Miller had ideas about how to better operate a moving company while Armstrong possessed the energy, know-how and money to get the project off the ground. Unlike new ideas from established firms, this story describes a classic case of opportunity arising more from chance than from an underlying assessment of resources and capabilities. When they first met after graduation, Miller was simply looking to make a business contact. While Armstrong hoped to identify a way to work with Miller because of positive past experiences, neither man knew the direction their relationship would go. Through discussions of several possible ways to work together they developed their idea for a different kind of moving company.

It may be useful to discuss with students what was effective and ineffective about the partners' entrepreneurial process.

Effective:
- They seem to have created a division of labor that worked well for the functioning of the firm with Miller running day-to-day operations and Armstrong serving as an evangelist for the company in the community.
- They acted quickly – idea to implementation time was short – so that a great deal of time and money was not spent on conceptualizing.
- They structured the firm to be low-cost and nimble in the early going. This enabled them to test their ideas before they had to manage a large organization.

- They created an early model that had a positive cash flow by keeping overhead low and ensuring sales before hiring more than a single additional mover.

Ineffective:
- Profitability calculations seem to have been sketchy and the costs based on old models of service activities rather than the newly proposed model of hiring employees and paying for performance.
- They may not have properly anticipated what needed to be done to scale up the business from a level where everything could be personally supervised to one in which processes and control systems would have to replace their direct oversight.

3. Industry Analysis

What was the state of the moving industry in Austin prior to the creation of the Blue Whale Moving Company? Were any macro-economic factors thought to be important for the near future? What competitive forces did an Austin moving company have to consider in 1988? What were the characteristics of a typical competitor's strategy prior to Blue Whale's entry?

Performing an industry analysis is a critical step in reaching conclusions about a business case. It allows students to better understand the context in which the decisions and actions in the case take place. The class should consider and discuss the following as a precursor to assessing the business created by Miller and Armstrong.

Macro economic factors to consider
- The Austin moving market was likely to be highly affected by the overall economic conditions in Austin. In this case, growth looked promising for the city and region and such growth would have a very positive impact on the regional moving industry.

Competitive forces to consider
- The most important competitive force was probably the degree of rivalry in the market. In the Austin moving market, the high degree of rivalry was evident in low margins and competition on price dominating relations with customers.
- Another important factor making the industry less attractive to participate in was the low barriers to entry by new firms. Any two strong guys with a rented truck could be a potential competitor. Barriers to exit were also extremely low making the competitive landscape hard to track and manage.
- In favor of participating in the industry, the only real substitute was self-moving which is not an option for many and less likely to be undertaken in the context of growing economic conditions.
- Low customer and supplier power contributed to making the industry more attractive.

Typical competitor strategy
- Non-descript name
- Competition on price
- Use of independent contractors as movers rather than hiring employees
- Rented or leased equipment to keep capital investments low
- Creation of partnerships with complementary businesses such as real estate firms to drive sales leads
- Low concern for mover qualities other than strength
- Little attention to/management of customer satisfaction

4. The Business Model

What about Miller and Armstrong's business concept and/or approach to business were unique and were likely to have provided competitive? As of 1993, what aspects of Blue Whale's performance can be regarded as successes? What aspects of Blue Whale's performance can be seen as lacking?

What was unique about the business model?
- Vision-led management style
- Differentiation on customer service, not price
- Primary emphasis was on meeting a psychological need – stress reduction – rather than on moving goods
- Hiring movers as employees rather than using subcontractors
- Memorable, whimsical branding

Indicators of successful performance as of 1993
- Awards and recognition
- Sales growth
- Customer perceptions as evidenced by high repeat business rate and high referral rate
- Excellent rapport between Miller and the moving employees – he was seen as "one of them"

Indicators of a lack of success as of 1993
- The negative trend in profitability
- Disconnect between employees and Armstrong
- Lack of progress toward the goal of successfully expanding beyond the original location

5. Strategic Implementation and the Failure of the Vision

Describe the causes of Blue Whale's failure to grow according to the vision laid out by the founders. Was the strategy flawed? Did the founders fail to develop the needed implementation levers? Or, was the failure mostly attributable to a failure of strategic leadership?

One approach to analyzing the failure of Blue Whale to grow can be found in Chapter 12's discussion of why organizations fail. This section identifies both internal and external causes of failure that may be applicable to Blue Whale Moving Company. Ask students if any of the following apply to Blue Whale. Discuss which factors were likely the most important for Blue Whale.

Forms of external change – these were probably not the most important factors for Blue Whale
- Economic change
- Competitive change
- Social change
- Technological change

Forms of internal change – consistent with the idea that most businesses fail due to internal causes, one of these may have been Blue Whale's downfall
- Management failure
- Financial failure

Perhaps the failure was not the result of a change at all (either internally or externally). Chapter 11 in the text notes the interdependence of strategy formulation and strategy implementation. Further, it identifies implementation levers and strategic leadership as important components of strategy implementation. If change did not cause failure in this case, maybe there was something fundamentally flawed about Blue Whale's strategy or implementation plan that made the lack of success in growing highly likely by design.

Ask students to consider the causes of the failure growth in terms of these three components of strategy. One approach is to have the students identify strengths and weaknesses of each component and discuss which they believe was most important in the inability of Blue Whale to expand beyond Austin.

Two important sources of failure are clear. First, the strategy itself may have been flawed in terms of its economic logic. It is not clear that that the firm can be profitable given the initial pay system that was a key element of differentiation. Second, there appears to have been a mismatch between the strategy and the strategy implementation. The founder's failed to put implementation levers in place that would enable other individuals to effectively implement core elements of the strategy. It appears that the business model can only function properly when Miller and Armstrong are providing direct leadership. This works well at a single location but is mismatched with the idea of rapid expansion of the concept.

6. Strategic Renewal

What steps could Blue Whale's owners take in late 1994 to improve their performance and get the firm back on it early growth trajectory? Is it at all likely that Blue Whale could be restructured to meet the goal of 100 locations in cities worldwide by the year 2000? If not, what would a more appropriate vision for growth look like?

Possible answers to this question could be far-ranging depending on whether students believe that the goals of the firm should change. If students believe that the original vision is still desirable, significant changes should be recommended in terms of leadership and implementation levers. If students believe that new goals are called for, there are many strategy and implementation possibilities that can be developed and discussed using traditional strategy analysis tools.

Teaching Plan
Session Plan A (one 80 minute session)

Session 1 - Students read and prepare case (A) only for this session case B should be handed out as an update or as part of a homework assignment

- Define entrepreneurship and the entrepreneurship process followed by Miller and Armstrong (15 minutes)

- Conduct an industry analysis at the time of the founding of Blue Whale Moving Company (20 minutes)

- Discuss the Blue Whale Moving Company business model and its potential for achieving a competitive advantage (20 minutes)

- Discuss the successes and failures of Blue Whale as of 1993. Solicit ideas from students about actions the company could take to meet its current challenge to manage its growing pains (25 minutes)

Session Plan B (two 80 minute sessions)

Session 1 - Students read and prepare case (A) only for this session

- Define entrepreneurship and discuss whether Miller and Armstrong are entrepreneurs (15 minutes)

- Discuss Blue Whale's founders' entrepreneurship process (15 minutes)

- Conduct an industry analysis at the time of the founding of Blue Whale Moving Company (15 minutes)

- Discuss the Blue Whale Moving Company business model and its potential for achieving a competitive advantage (15 minutes)

- Discuss the successes and failures of Blue Whale as of 1993. Solicit ideas from students about actions the company could take to meet its current challenge to manage its growing pains (20 minutes)

Session 2 – Students read and prepare case (B) for this session

- Identify causes of organizational failure and determine which were important in Blue Whale's case (20 minutes)

- Ask students to identify the strengths and weaknesses of Blue Whale's strategy, implementation levers and strategic leadership in an effort to identify the source of its failure to achieve its mission (30 minutes)

- Facilitate a planning session for a five year plan for Blue Whale Moving Company. What are realistic goals for the organization? Can they succeed with the existing strategy? Do they need different leadership? Should some current leaders leave? What leadership skills should they seek? Can the students identify specific implementation levers that would be a high priority in the five year plan?

Case Update

As of January 1, 2006, the Blue Whale Moving Company, Inc. continues to operate in the Austin, TX moving market. It still receives high marks for service including recognition as the best moving company in Austin in 2005 by the Austin Chronicle. Some aspects of Blue Whale Moving company remain since the conclusion of the written case in 1994. Blue Whale still uses employee movers rather contractors and still touts its commitment to customer service as its most important competitive advantage. The original vision to grow the firm to 100 locations all over the world seems to have been abandoned as there are no locations other than the original Austin site. While the firm offers some related services like storage and move-related cleaning, they have also not expanded widely in terms of the services they offer.

Management changes since 1994 have been significant as the only member of the original management still involved with the company is Brad Armstrong. He is listed on the company website as "Founder" and is apparently not involved in day-to-day operations. The firm has a new president in charge of operations and a new chief financial officer since the time of the written case. Blake Miller, along with his interior-designer wife, has started a new company called Copper Palm Moving and Interiors. The new firm is aimed at upscale customers and offers to not just move the customer's furniture and décor to a new home, but to artfully decorate the new spaces using a combination of new and moved items.

Case: Reviving Iridium
Primary Chapter: Chapter 12 (Restructuring)
Secondary Chapter: Chapter 11 (Implementation levers)

Introduction: This case fits nicely with Chapter 12 as it follows Iridium from its conceptualization by a few engineers at Motorola, through its founding and launch, through the IPO process, into financial trouble and bankruptcy, and finally through its restructuring and revival.

Strategy Diamond: The case provides sufficient detail to examine the company's original and new strategies and their important differences. The case touches on all five elements of strategy. With hindsight, it is difficult to see how the original strategy had a compelling economic logic. However, the case does provide enough details to discover that the assumptions made in the original planning were likely wildly optimistic. Small differences between planned and actual adoption rates, or small differences between planned subscription prices and actual, would doom the project. In contrast, the restructuring story is just the opposite; the price paid out of bankruptcy court is so low that variance from planned rates would have much less dramatic effects on the success of the venture.

Strategic Leadership: There is little data on the leadership during the original Iridium launch, other than names and tenures. Much more detail is provided on the leadership of Dan Colussy, the entrepreneur who buys Iridium out of bankruptcy.

Formulation/Implementation: A key discussion point in this case deals with whether the problem with Iridium was a poor strategy or poor execution. The case quotes a competitor's as opining that the strategy was fine, but the implementation was flawed. However, this assessment is subject to a self-serving bias. This competitor is following a very similar strategy to that tried by Iridium. This question should generate much debate.

The Dynamic Nature of Strategy: The dynamic nature of this case is a combination of the entire cyclical path of Iridium's life cycle(s) and the unpredictability (and risk) associated with leading edge technological innovations. As quoted in the case: "the brilliance of the technology cannot take precedence over the market case."

REVIVING IRIDIUM

SUMMARY

The case discusses the problems faced by Iridium after the launch of its mobile satellite services. These problems landed the company in deep financial trouble, which led Iridium to file for Chapter 11-bankruptcy protection in the US Bankruptcy Court. The case also talks about Dan Colussy's turnaround strategies that resurrected the company and made it a success.

TEACHING OBJECTIVES & TARGET AUDIENCE

The case is developed to enable students to:

- Examine the consequences and implications of assumptions associated with launching a new product, service and its impact on the survival and success of such ventures.
- Identify the critical success factors in the mobile satellite services industry.
- Apply SWOT analysis as a means to appreciate its impact on the success of a strategy with respect to a new large project with considerable resource commitment.
- Understand the strategy adopted to revive a bankrupt company and ensure its survival and possible success.

The case is aimed at MBA/PGDBA students and is intended to be a part of the Strategy and General Management curriculum.

TEACHING APPROACH & STRATEGY

The case can be used both for classroom discussion as well as for written assignment. The moderator can start off with the technology involved in wireless phones and talk about the problems in the wireless phone services industry in general and Iridium in particular. Students can be divided into groups of five or six and each group can present its analysis to the class.

ANALYSIS

1.

Iridium filed for Chapter 11 bankruptcy to overcome its financial problems. The company had huge outstanding debts to pay. From the very beginning, Iridium had problems with its satellite telephone systems venture. The company conducted a 10-year research before it launched its satellite services. Iridium invested billions of dollars in the project. It had to bear huge recurring costs every year in the form of maintenance of the satellite constellation and other ground infrastructure.

After taking into account the gestation time of the project, initial and recurring costs, Iridium had no option but to recover its high investment by pricing its services on the higher side for the customers. Moreover, commercializing its services was also not an easy task. As a result, Iridium priced its handsets at $3000 each and charged as much as $7 per minute per call. These prices were exorbitant and failed to attract enough buyers and hence the company was not able to build a sizeable customer base.

There were other problems as well. Iridium's target market segment was the high-end business travelers. Such people were always on the move and preferred sleek and easy carry phones. Iridium's handsets were very bulky (each weighing as much as 1 kg) at the time of their launch.

There were many technical glitches in the system and bugs, which had to be fixed because of which the actual launch of the services was postponed by 5 weeks. This kept the customers waiting for Iridium's services.

2.

The factors that determine the success or failure of a satellite telephone services industry are:

- **Competition from other forms of service:** Iridium had many competitors (Globestar, Inmarsat and ICO, etc.) all trying to capture the same market. Iridium faced competition not only from those who MSS service providers but also from cellular phone service providers. These two services were complementary in nature. Iridium's handsets cost $3000 each and service charges were as high as $7/minute. Iridium's closest competitor Globalstar sold its handsets for $750 each and charged .35-.55 cents/minute, which affected [Iridium] badly.
- **Customer demand:** It is one of the critical success factors for any form of satellite telephone services. Demand depends on the customer segments, the price and quality of the services offered. Iridium initially focused on business executives who made frequent foreign trips. However, since the price of the services was high and the quality of services offered were not up to expectations, [Iridium] found only few takers.
- **Cost and financing:** A company operating in the satellite telephone services industry must make efforts to keep project costs on the lower side as well and employ the right means of project financing. For this to happen, it should reduce the time in installing systems and commercializing the services. The means of financing should be such that there is a balance between debt and equity. Too much debt will lead to higher interest on loans without any revenues in the initial years.

Iridium's project cost was very high. The company spent about $5 billion to construct and maintain the 66 LEOs and other ground based-networks whereas Globalstar spent about $2.6 billion to construct and maintain its 48 LEOs and other ground-based networks. Although the idea was good and Iridium managed to procure enough funds, huge investments in R&D and maintenance of the satellite system forced the company to price its services at the higher end, which eventually lead to its failure.

- **Ability of companies to capture different market segments:** The services offered by a company in the mobile satellite services industry should cater to various customer segments of the market failing which there will be very less demand for its services. Through from the case, it seems that Iridium was in a hurry to be the first company to launch satellite telephone services and it did not do enough research on the potential market for its services. When Iridium was launched, it focused only on a single market segment. It was only after Iridium re-launched its services that it started to target different market segments like the government, military, humanitarians, heavy industry, maritime, aviation, and adventure industry.
- **Access to critical foreign markets:** Satellite services are profitable only if they can be used the world over. Organizations operating in this industry should be able to capture not only the domestic market but also international markets. Iridium offered global satellite services and marketed its product in different countries. However, initially when the company offered very bulky handsets, which several customers preferred not to carry during overseas trips.
- **Success of innovative new technologies in the long run:** Pioneering a technology is not enough until it can be used profitably in the long run. It may so happen that many competitors can emerge

and offer improved technology. As the market becomes crowded with competitors, the profits earned by each company may reduce and gradually reach a saturation point wherein the companies would only able to breakeven or they may even incur losses. Therefore, the returns from a new technology are maximum during the initial years of introduction. However, Iridium failed to capitalize on the new technology it introduced.

3.

The Strengths, Weaknesses, Opportunities and Threats (SWOT) analysis for Iridium:

Strengths

- Iridium pioneered the concept of satellite telephone services.
- Iridium had the financial backing of some of the leading companies in the industry.
- The company offered its services through LEO satellites which were technologically superior to GEOs or MEOs since they offered benefits like complete global coverage including all oceans & all land areas (north and south poles also), small handheld pagers and phones instead of laptop size terminals, no significant transmission delays and longer battery life.
- Iridium's satellite services were better than the normal cellular phone services since they could be accessed across the globe.

Weaknesses

- The concept of satellite telephone systems is new and therefore a lot of investment in terms of R&D.
  - Iridium could not be commercialized the concept in the initial years, It ran into losses.

- Iridium did not carry out enough market research to Assess the real needs of the target customers.
- Iridium's handsets were not ergonomically designed.
- Iridium's services were very costly.

Opportunities

- Since Iridium pioneered the concept of satellite telephone systems, the company has the opportunity to make huge profits out of this business.
- Iridium has the opportunity to identify the various areas where satellite telephone services could be put to use profitably.

Threats

- The major threat for Iridium came from competitors who offered superior satellite services at low prices.
- Iridium's services were highly technology oriented. Therefore, the company had to take every care to avoid system failure. Technological obsolescence was another threat the company faced.

The company has every ingredient to be a success in the near future provided it does not repeat the mistakes it had committed earlier. It can cash in from its services by offering them to a wide range of customers. The company can also extend its technology to provide other technological solutions to corporate organizations.

4.

Dan Colussy took several steps to revive the ailing company and relaunch its services to customers. Since the company was acquired at only $25 million, compared to the $5 billion being spent initially, he was not under any cost pressures. The Chapter 11 filing allowed the company to put in place a financial restructuring plan and reduce its debt pressures.

Dan Colussy first entered into a contract with Boeing to keep up and maintain the 66 satellites in orbit. Next he made Iridium's services more affordable to its customers. Iridium adopted many strategies for this. The company charged flat rates of only $1.5/minute as service charges from its customers. Even the price of handsets came down to $1000 and less. The handsets were also made lighter (less than 400 grams) and easier to use.

Initially, Iridium offered only voice communications. After the re-launch, it introduced other services like data services, paging services and SMS. The concept of SIM cards many Internet enabled features were introduced for better user control.

Iridium also expanded its markets and started focussing on different segments like the government, military, humanitarians, heavy industry, maritime, aviation, and adventure that needed satellite communications. These market segments had a more practical use of the satellite telephone systems. Iridium also enhanced its customer services (after-sales also) by setting up a 24/7 customer support call centers.

ADDITIONAL READINGS & REFERENCES

1. Blodgett Mindy, **Delayed Satellite Launch Hampers Global Network,** www.computerworld.com, February 03,1997.
2. Fisher James, **Sprint Telecenters Wins Multi-Million Dollar Contract to Support Global Communications Consortium Iridium LLC,** www3.sprint.com., January 21, 1998.
3. Taylor A Leslie, **Market Demand for Mobile Satellite Services: Satellite Statistics Phillips' Satellites 99,** www.ita.com, February 4, 1999.
4. Farmer Austria Melanie, **Iridium Posts Wider Loss,** www.news.com.com, April 26, 1999.
5. Stewart Fist, **Iridium and the LEOs,** www.electric-words.com., May 1999.
6. Sheridan H John, **Bullish On Iridium,** www.industryweek.com, June 21, 1999.
7. **Telecommunication Will be Wireless,** Government Computerization Newsletter No 13, www.unescap.org, June 1999.
8. **Iridium Files for Bankruptcy Protection,** www.space.com, August 13, 1999.
9. **Iridium Files for Bankruptcy**, www.ustoday.com, August 13, 1999.
10. Goodman S Peter, **Without an Angel Iridium's Sky Will Fall**, www.washingtonpost.com, March 16, 2000.
11. Motta Mary, **Iridium Falls to Earth**, www.space.com, March 17, 2000.
12. **Iridium Announces End of Satellite Telephone Service,** www.floridatoday.com, March 20, 2000.
13. Brown S.P, **Iridium Eradication**, www.splittrader.com., March 22, 2000.
14. Motta Mary, **Analysts Say Iridium's Downfall Has Limited Ripple Effect,** www.space.com, August 29 2000.
15. **Eleventh Hour Bid Rescues Iridium,** www.eham.net, Nov 17, 2000.
16. Weiss R. Todd, **Pentagon Awards $72M Wireless Contract to Iridium**, www.computerworld.com, December 11, 2000.
17. Weiss R. Todd, **Iridium Satellite Launches Service Today**, www.computerworld.com, March 28, 2001.

18. Mathewson James, **Iridium is Staying Alive. This is a Deal for the Ages.**, www.computeruser.com., August 6, 2001.
19. **For the Consumer- How Wireless Works,** www.wow.com., September 11, 2001.
20. **The World's First Global Handset-Iridium Handset – Our Story,** www.iridium.com.
21. **Corporate Eact Sheet,** www.iridium.com.
22. **Falling Prices Hit Operators,** www.specials.ft.com.
23. **Services-Iridium**, www.matrixmaricom.com.
24. Gordon Masson, **Iridium Service Heralds a New Era in Personal Communications.**
25. **IRIDIUM LLC: Company History,** www.iridium.com.
26. **Whatisasimcard**, www.travelbuyarc.com.

FEEDBACK

The case was discussed by a group of research associates and faculty members as part of a faculty development program at the ICFAI Center for Management Research (ICMR), Hyderabad, India.

The group felt that prices of handsets for using Iridium services were exorbitant and failed to attract buyers. It had hampered the company's growth prospects and the building of a sizeable customer base. Initially Iridium targeted the high-end business travelers but Iridium's handsets were bulky and this segment preferred sleek phones, this target segment could not be tapped satisfactorily. The participants also felt that technical problems in the systems also affected the business adversely.

Most of the participants were of the opinion that though Iridium had taken care of many of the above problems while re-launching, it might not be too successful as the customer base for satellite telephones is rather small and the costs involved in the technology are very high.

Case Synopsis
Case: DaimlerChrysler: Corporate Governance Dynamics in a Global Company
Primary Chapter: Chapter 13
Secondary Chapters: Chapter 8, 10 & 11

Introduction: The development of the corporate governance system of DaimlerChrysler is of special interest, because few companies made such an organizational leap to globalization in such a short period of time. At the time of the merger in 1998, Daimler-Benz AG was an export-oriented, predominantly German company, whereas Chrysler Corporation focused almost exclusively on the US market. The $36 billion merger to form DaimlerChrysler AG (DC) was massive by any standard. But what happened afterwards? This case gives a detailed overview of what took place in the five years after the announcement of the deal in 1998. The main purpose of this case is to outline the intricacies DC encountered in the process of merging American and European corporate governance features. DC had to design a governance system, which overcame national differences, regulatory divergence and reflected business developments. Although DC was based in Germany, it was operating globally and had to comply with many rules and regulations. How could DC set up a governance system, which offered on the one hand transparency and accountability while allowing top managers enough time to properly do their day-to-day job?

Strategy Diamond: The case highlights the far-reaching implications mergers have on strategy. DM faces questions such as: What will be our new product mix? Through what combination of channels will we operate? What will be the sequence of our new initiatives?

The Dynamic Nature of Strategy: The case discusses risk exposure inherent in a merger and the need for flexibility in strategy. Specifically the case discusses the changing market, differing business models, and the difficulty of sharing technology and components. All of these give a poignant example for the essential element of agility – even in large corporations.

Formulation/Implementation: A core part of the case is the formulation and implementation of DM's merger strategy as well as their strategy to become a truly global company. The case outlines an overview of the phases beginning with merger and integration and ending with maintaining sustainable success.

Strategic Leadership: The principal focus of the case is the link between strategy and corporate governance as a whole and not the decisions or direction of one particular leader. The case can initiate discussion on the difference between governance and management, and possible power shifts from supervisory boards to executive boards of management in the development of strategy.

DAIMLERCHRYSLER: CORPORATE GOVERNANCE DYNAMICS IN A GLOBAL COMPANY TEACHING NOTE

DEFINITIONS

Corporate governance:	Distribution of power, accountability and responsibility at the helm of a company.
Corporate governance system:	Rules, processes and structural features that make corporate governance work.
Corporate governance structure:	Organizational indicators of the corporate governance system, e.g., number of independent directors.

CASE SYNOPSIS

The development of DaimlerChrysler's corporate governance system is of special interest because few companies have made such an organizational leap to globalization in such a short period. At the time of the merger in 1998, Daimler-Benz AC was an export-oriented, predominantly German company, whereas Chrysler Corporation focused almost exclusively on the US market.

The $36 billion merger to form DaimlerChrysler AG (DC) was massive by any standards. But what happened afterwards? The case gives a detailed overview of events in the five years after the deal was announced in 1998. Its main purpose is to outline the intricate challenges DC faced in the process of merging American and European corporate governance features. DC had to design a governance system that overcame national differences and regulatory divergence and reflected business developments. The case is a useful platform for discussing corporate governance trends in global companies.[1]

Note: This case is not a typical decision case, but rather sketches out the corporate governance developments at DC between 1998 and 2003. The instructor may want to look at three other IMD cases for more details on strategy and the role of the boards during the merger negotiations (*refer to Suggested Reading for instructors*).

DaimlerChrysler: Corporate Governance Dynamics in a Global Company starts by giving a detailed background and timeline of the developments in the first five years of the merged company. The case outlines how DC organized its post-merger integration, its revised strategy of focusing solely on care, trucks and services, and the difficulties the company faced along the way. This timeline, with its five-phase model, facilitates the discussion of the various issues.

Once participants understand the strategic moves and the high level of expectations of DC after the merger, the instructor should lead the discussion to create the link between strategy and corporate governance. Although DC was based in Germany, it operated worldwide and had to comply with many rules and regulations. How could DC set up a governance system that offered, on the one hand, transparency and accountability and, on the other hand, allowed top managers enough time to do their day-to-day job properly?

---

[1] The authors thank President Peter Lorange, Professors Bill George and Fred Neubauer (all of IMD) for their input on this teaching note.

The case creates tension and generates heated debates in the classroom. Participants tend to disagree strongly on strategy (purpose of the merger and risks associated with the partnerships in Asia), leadership issues and various regulations, Moreover, their will be considerable tension regarding the behavior and involvement of the boards.

LEARNING OBJECTIVES

The case highlights how corporations, regardless of country of origin and industry, are struggling with globalizing their corporate governance. It takes participants through the changes at DC and leaves it up to the participants and instructor to interpret the results. This case will force participants to confront the "real issues" of corporate governance in global organizations. These organizations have to navigate through conflicting regulatory issues and find the right internal structure for decision-making and monitoring while keeping an eye on the business.

The authors believe that there is no single best corporate governance practice, but rather that every corporate governance system is the result of four forces in varying degrees (*refer to **Figure 1***).

Figure 1: Four Forces Influencing Corporate Governance Systems[2]

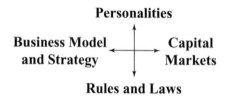

This model is helpful for analyzing corporate governance developments at DC and for structuring the case discussion. Participants will learn:

1. Merging two companies has far-reaching **implications for strategy and management**:
   a. Entering new geographies and/or business segments can be full of surprises and often requires new organizational skills.
   b. Although merging companies have many internal issues to solve (e.g., structure, top management selection), the competition does not.
2. A general **introduction to corporate governance:**
   a. Basic principles of corporate governance include defining roles, responsibilities and processes (management and control).
   b. A good board ensures compliance, selects top management and adds value by advising on strategy and monitoring its implementation.
3. Through M&A, companies can became global players in a short period, but they have to **organize corporate governance systems** accordingly:
   a. Companies have to combine different legal/board systems (e.g., two-tier boards, labor representation, co-determination, salary levels),
   b. Any system has to comply with applicable laws and meet the standards for transparency, while avoiding disproportionate bureaucracy for management.

---

[2] Steger, Ulrich. "Beyond Preventing Crime: Where Does Corporate Governance Really Add Value?" *IMD Perspectives for Mangers,* No. 101, Septembers 2003: 1. Also in: Steger, Ulrich (ed.). *Mastering Global Corporate Governance,* Chichester: Wiley, forthcoming 2004.

4. **Corporate governance** in globalizing companies **evolves**:
   a. The corporate governance system may require several adjustments in order to meet the organizational needs.
   b. In general, the power shifts to the executive/management board.

POTENTIAL USES OF THIS CASE

The case was initially written for executives, but it can also be used with MBAs.

When used with MBAs, the case gives a good introduction to corporate governance in a global company. Although MBAs will generally have only limited exposure to governance issues immediately after graduation, it could be useful for them to understand what makes their top management tick. Participants will deal with basic questions such as what is corporate governance about? How do you assess strategy and risk exposure? To what extent can companies control risk? How do boards function? How are roles and responsibilities split in order to ensure compliance? What are the roles of various committees?

When the case is used with executives, the debate will center on why things evolved the way they did at DC. How did DC overcome differences in business models, personalities and stakeholder orientations? What went well, what did not work out? How can companies manage or prevent risk? Can corporations diversify their risk exposure through globalization? The instructor can broaden the discussion by asking whether corporate governance needs are converging around the globe? Have board structures really globalized? Can labor representatives on the board keep up with the issues of a global company? How much complexity can corporations handle regarding corporate governance?

TEACHING STRATEGY

The authors recommend analyzing the case using the framework in Figure 1 (Four Forces Influencing Corporate Governance Systems). Participants will analyze DC's performance on the four dimensions, evaluate the outcome and recognize the changes in the corporate governance structure. The session should finish with a powerful wrap-up of key learning's for the corporate governance dynamics in large corporations. We have identified three key learning's:

1. **Learn as you go:** With globalization, the mismatch between national legal frameworks and management structures continues to grow. Corporations have to design their own corporate governance structure that reflects the changes in the company and/or the business.
2. **In globalizing companies, the power shifts to the executives:** In a global company, the center of power shifts from the supervisory board towards the executive directors/board of management. They shape strategy and corporate governance!
3. **You cannot be everybody's darling:** The perceptions of different stakeholders are volatile and contradictory. Pleasing all stakeholders is impossible and leads only to additional work and more bureaucracy.

These conclusions may seem counterintuitive at first. The instructor will find a detailed list of conclusions in the wrap-up section of this teaching note.

ASSIGNMENT QUESTIONS

Suggested Student Assignment (prior to class):

	Topic	Assignment Question	In-class Discussion Timing
1	Understanding the goals of corporate governance	Why has corporate governance moved to center stage of management? What is the purpose of corporate governance?	10 min
2	Understanding the strategy	What were the milestones of DC's strategy between 1998 and 2003?	20 min
3	Governance is about behavior	To what extent can the changes in regulations overcome the corporate governance crisis?	10 min
4	Governance structures change over time	Outline the key changes in DC's corporate governance system (rules, processes, structure features) after 1998. What explains the changes?	25 min
5	Key learning's	What global trends in corporate governance do you observe?	15 min

Timing

0–10 minutes: Introduction (*refer* to **Appendix 1** *for the opening statement*).
10–90 minutes: Questions 1 to 5 (including Wrap-Up and Useful Quotes, at the end of the teaching note). When used with executives, Question 1 may be omitted.
Note: References to *exhibits* are to those at the end of the case; *appendices* will be found at the end of this teaching note.

ANSWERING TO ASSIGNMENT QUESTIONS

Question 1: Why has corporate governance moved to center stage of management? What is the purpose of corporate governance?

It is important for the instructor to make clear that corporate governance is very important, but there is no one-size-fits-all corporate governance system. In a nutshell, a good board serves three purposes:

1. It ensures compliance.
2. It selects/evaluates the top management of a company.
3. It adds value in strategy formulation and in monitoring and controlling implementation.

Examples such as Enron, Kmart, Swissair and WorldCom have shown that bankruptcy is a threat when corporate governance fails. The lapses in these companies included management mistakes, accounting scandals and fraud. Recent collapses cannot be blamed solely on corporate governance, but a good corporate governance system would have raised some warning signs early on and would have triggered action.

If participants are inexperienced with corporate governance issues, the instructor may have to explain the principles of governance:

1. The general understanding is that the board is responsible for managing the affairs of a company in the best interests of the shareholders/stakeholders in accordance with the law. For participants, it is important to think about what makes a good board, how board add value and who is the ideal board member? Good board members have to meet demanding requirements (*refer to **Appendix 2** for what makes a good board*).

2. Nowadays, the key question is whether board members understand the strategy and correctly assess the risks taken. The instructor may have to define good strategy/management. According to Fredmund Malik,[3] successful companies can be recognized by their: position in the market, ability to innovate productivity, ability to attract good people, liquidity and profitability. Board members have a multitude of reports/tools available for assessing a firm's strategy and risk exposure (*refer to **Appendix 3** for the director information checklist*). As non-executive board members are not involved on a daily basis, they often struggle with information overload, misrepresentation of figures and situations, and limited time involvement for each company.

   Conflicts between boards and executive managers arise because of their different roles and objectives. In economic terms, this is a typical principal-agent problem. Managers (in this case the agents) need the power to make decisions quickly and to take reasonable risks. However, non-executive board members (principals) are naturally concerned about their responsibility, liability and personal risks and hence they do not want the management to take excessive risks.

Question 2: What were the milestones of DC's strategy between 1998 and 2003?

The case gives a good example of how the leadership changed over time. What was initially a "merger of equals" was forced into a turnaround only two years later. The merged company was facing a crisis at Chrysler and in other places (e.g., Freightliner). To many, these difficulties came as a surprise, but they clearly showed the increasing complexity of running a global company.

Schrempp, who was already under great pressure due to the falling stock price, was able to consolidate his power in the process. It is fair to assume that some members of the supervisory board were also surprised by the magnitude of the problems and told him to "fix" whatever needed to be fixed. As a result, Schrempp made tough decisions. With his decisions, he became stronger in relation to the board, following the "lifecycle model of boards." In this model, the power shifts over time from the board to the CEO.[4]

The timeline in *Exhibit 1* provides a good structure for the systematic analysis of events. We suggest issues are divided according to "strategic issues" and "people issues/personalities."

STRATEGIC ISSUES

- *Daimler and Chrysler had different business models:* The business strategy for manufacturers in the premium sector is very different from those in the mass market. Obvious differences included market orientation (premium vs. mass), technology (modern vs. available), mindset (global vs. NAFTA) or, put differently, DC was about Mercedes-Benz's engineers vs. Chrysler's street fighters!
- *Sharing technology and components in difficult:* On paper (*refer to **Appendix IB***), there was little overlap in products between the companies. This avoided potentially ugly, head-on competition between Mercedes-Benz and Chrysler, but made it more difficult to reap savings. Although the initial savings/synergy target of $1.4 billion (about 1% of sales) was seen as low, the attitude of

---

[3] Malik, Fredmund. *Die Neue Corporate Governance.* Frankfurter Allgemeine Buch, 2002: 153ff.

[4] George, William W. (Bill). *Authentic Leadership: Rediscovering the Secrets to Creating Lasting Value.* San Francisco: Jossey-Bass, 2003.

Mercedes employees was to protect the brand image and profits. Their unwillingness to share platforms ("there will be no platform sharing," page 3) made it very difficult to realize savings in excess of the $1.4 billion.[5] At the same time, participants will understand Mercedes' concerns about amortizing high R&D expenditures or the very limited exclusivity contracts with suppliers. But the instructor may want to question whether Chrysler customers really needed Mercedes' cutting edge technology or was it just a matter of pushing technology over to Chrysler. Were Chrysler customers willing to pay for the technology?

- *Was DC really global?* Observant participants will note that DC was strong in mature markets (Europe, North America). However, DC remained relatively weak in future growth markets such as Asia (*Exhibit 2*). Asia was definitely the missing link in DC's global agenda. Expanding into Asia was a logical step, but did the company have the financial resources and management capacity to do so? The instructor should push participants to recognize that future synergies will originate from Chrysler and DC's Asian partners, rather than Mercedes.

- *Markets can change within a few years:* With increasing competitive pressure on Chrysler's bread-and-butter products (minivans and SUVs), Chrysler was in a "real mess." Chrysler had problems not only with revenues, but also with costs. Its inability to reduce overhead due to union contracts proved disastrous. *Exhibit 4* highlights uncompetitive manufacturing practices, leading to an extremely high breakeven point in 2001, at 113% of plant capacity (page 5). Between 1998 and 2000 Chrysler went from being the darling of the auto industry to being a turnaround candidate.

- *Focusing on core competencies solves some problems but creates others:* Selling off some non-core companies generated cash for DC. The timing was good and DC was able to fetch top prices for divestitures. DC had resources for making far-reaching acquisitions (stakes in Mitsubishi Motors, Hyundai Motors, Detroit Diesel/Western Star, Mitsubishi Trucks); financing the losses at Chrysler; and still paying a dividend—even in the tough year of 2001. At the same time, the portfolio was becoming heavily focused on cars, and DC as a company was more vulnerable to the "profitability desert" in the mass market.

- *Flaws in strategy become very visible during bad times:* Freightliner, with its growing market share, was long seen as *the* success story within the trucking industry. In Freightliner's case, the financial exposure only became apparent after the truck market collapsed. Market values dropping below book values can lead to unforeseen financial exposure.

- *DC hits difficult relations with the capital markets:* In general, capital markets did not like the automotive industry, due to its low growth potential, unfavorable cost structure and high dependency on the economic cycle (industry-specific disadvantage). DC paid much attention to financial analysts and their recommendations, such as focusing on core competencies. However, the efforts were not sufficient to prevent Wall Street from writing off DC (starting in mid-1999, page 3). When DC failed to meet a quarterly earnings goal in 1999, the share price shared its decline. Capital markets have surprises in earnings (company-specific disadvantage, as DC did not deliver the promised earnings). The question arises of whether car companies can really please the capital markets (*Exhibit 12*)?

The instructor should ask participants whether the merger helped to overcome the strategic threats of both companies. The threats included volume, size, cost disadvantages and limited growth opportunities. The instructor may want to prepare a transparency of the merger rationale as seen by Dr. Rüdiger Grube, Chief Strategist of Daimler-Benz, prior to the merger (*refer to Appendix 4*).

---

[5] Economies of scale and synergies explain to a large extent the success of the Renault-Nissan alliance. Both companies were in the the same business segments (small and medium-sized cars)—but on different continents. Renault was strong in Europe and Nissan was strong in Japan and the US. Therefore, they were able to reap huge economies of scale.

PEOPLE ISSUES/PERSONALITIES

In a merged company of this size, it was just a question of time before personality clashes happened, especially with strong characters like Schrempp and Stallkamp:

- Although the initial IRT structure (***Exhibit 3***) has been described as a professional discussion group and lasted for only one year, this set-up had one big advantage—it helped to assess the quality of board members or at least their ability to work together. Each IRT was jointly run by one German and one American board member. The IRTs came to a sudden stop when, in September 1999, Schrempp, announced the end of integration. With the departure of Stallkamp, until then president of Chrysler, it became clear to everyone that problems might lie ahead. Some observers raised the issue of a power struggle within Chrysler. The party was definitely over.
- The instructor may want to ask why Schrempp did not bring in one of his trusted Mercedes managers as early as September 1999? The instructor should try to push participants here. Bringing in one of his associates would not have been in line with the idea of a "merger of equals," and, at the time, Eaton was still co-chairman.
- Behind the scenes a lot more must have gone on, as shown in Phase 3. "Deliver the numbers" implied that Chrysler remained autonomous, but it had to deliver the promised results. Autonomy was necessary for political reasons, as Chrysler's top management would otherwise have blamed operating difficulties on the management in Stuttgart. Nevertheless, Chrysler's top crew knew that they would be in trouble if they did not meet the forecasts. They failed to meet the anticipated profits and a management shake-up was necessary in late 2000. A financial loss of $5 billion in 2001 highlighted to the outside world the scale of the difficulties.
- As the crisis was unfolding at various companies in the group, Schrempp—as some newspapers argued, already concerned about his job—used his common sense. He sent people he knew and trusted to the troubled companies in order to fix them. In addition, DC started a series of internal structural changes (***Exhibit 1*** and Question 4).

The instructor may want to ask whether more former Chrysler management board members would have survived had Chrysler's performance been better? "Deliver the numbers" was also a way to remove managers of non-performing units. From a corporate governance perspective, this was done with a significant number of former Chrysler board members and an American union representative on the supervisory board. The instructor may want to probe whether participants agree with the role and involvement of the (supervisory) board, or should they have been involved earlier on? Did the board accept too many risks? Was the push toward globalization too rapid?

Question 3: To what extent can the changes in regulations overcome the corporate governance crisis?

For global companies, the changes in regulations post-Enron were considerable. It is useful for participants to familiarize themselves with some of the main categories of the new regulations. ***Exhibit 5*** gives an overview of key categories of the German Code. In DC's case, the American and German legislation was contradictory (***Exhibit 6***).

Compliance with the law in necessary, but not sufficient, for high-performing boards. It will *not* distinguish them from the competition. Jeffrey Sonnenfeld argues that good boards figure out how to work together.[6] He offers a few guidelines for creating high-performing boards:

---

[6] Sonnenfeld, Jeffrey A. "What Makes Great Boards Great." *Harvard Business Review,* September 2002: 2–8.

1. A virtuous cycle of respect, trust and candor.
2. A culture of open dissent.
3. Fluid portfolio of roles.
4. Individual accountability
5. Performance evaluation.

High-performing boards also concentrate on the *behavior of boards*. Board members have to set the example and "live the correct behavior." Sonnenfeld's guidelines should also be included in the "do's and don'ts" for boards—the unwritten laws and regulations. These invisible laws can normally not be observed by outsiders, but are very visible to the "inner circle." One example in DC would be how the company deals with union members on the supervisory board. Is there a distinction on the supervisory board between members from the capital side and members from the labor side? Despite very heavy public criticism of DC's strategy, there was no mutiny on either board. Why?

Question 4: Outline the key changes in DC's corporate governance system (rules, processes, structural features) after 1998. What explains the changes?

The instructor may have to explain the basic differences between unitary and two-tier boards. DC was incorporated in Germany (among other reasons, to be able to leverage Daimler-Benz's tax credits) and thus had a German two-tier system (*refer to Exhibit 7 for the management board and Exhibit 10 for the supervisory board*). In this system, the management board made the decisions and was controlled by the supervisory board, which had labor representation. This set-up had some apparent disadvantages:

- The supervisory board had 20 members, and when both boards met, about 40 people were present. With so many people (plus many staff involved in preparing the material), it was difficult to keep important details secret. During Phase 4—when drastic measures were needed—it became apparent that structural changes were necessary. It was just not possible to discuss highly confidential things with so many people around the table. As a result, DC created many new committees.
- "Americans don't trust two-tier board" (page 14). This statement had far-reaching implications. Most efforts to please American shareholders were not successful and their numbers fell sharply over the years. From an equal shareholding between Europeans and Americans at the time of the merger, the majority of DC's shareholders in 2002 came from Germany (57%), with 21% in the rest of Europe, 14% in the US and 8% in the rest of the world (page 14). But the impact of this change could not be detected in the corporate governance dynamics. DC had to behave like a *global* company, regardless of fluctuations in ownership.

At this point, the instructor may want to ask participants how they would have structured the corporate governance efforts.

ORGANIZING DECISION-MAKING AT THE EXECUTIVE LEVEL

Regardless of the abovementioned structural "realities," eventually business developments drove the corporate governance of DC. There was a lot of "learning by doing" involved; however, the real impetus for change came only as a result of various crises within the company and the big shake-up of committees at the end of Phase 4 (*refer to Exhibit 1 for an overview of the events*):

- The Chairmen's Integration Council ceased to exist with the departure of Stallkamp and other leading executives.
- The Automotive Council, set up after the Chairmen's Integration Council, also failed due to the limited synergy potential between Mercedes and Chrysler. Mercedes employees resisted any

exchange of expensive parts such as platforms and engines. Exchanging commodity-type parts was not enough.

- The real savings potential came only when DC bought equity stakes in Mitsubishi and Hyundai. Now a clearly positioned premium brand could deliver new technology (in a controlled, carefully managed approach), whereas the volume brands could save due to large production volumes. With its new partners in Asia, DC was able to standardize components, implement common sourcing and share platforms and reap synergies, e.g., by producing a "world engine" with a planned production rate of 1.5 million units per year.

At HQ, a way had to be found to make the worldwide sharing manageable. DC transferred the decision-making power to the new Executive Automotive Committee (EAC). *Exhibit 9* outlines the far-reaching issues being discussed in the EAC. The presence of Schrempp and Jürgen Hubbert, CEO of Mercedes-Benz, highlights the importance of the EAC. (Note: In some years, the EAC met even more often than the management board.) For legal and cultural reasons, the coordination between Mitsubishi and Hyundai took place in the Alliance Committee, which functioned in a similar way to the EAC. The EAC was also the role model for the truck division. The corporate strategy department organized all the meetings mentioned above and, as a result, became the knowledge and information broker within DC.

ORGANIZING SUPERVISION AND STAKEHOLDERS

The shareholder committee had no formal decision-making power, which rested with the supervisory board, but its mission was to "restrict itself to debate and counseling and (...) to support opinion forming among the shareholder representatives," (CFO Gentz, page 12). Originally it was modeled on the US-style board of directors, with the two chairmen of the management board, all ten shareholder representatives and four outsiders (former Chrysler directors who were not on the DC supervisory board).

It was not uncommon in the German system of co-determination for the two benches—shareholder and labor—to meet separately before meetings of the supervisory board. However, once the DC integration process was routine, the shareholder committee was stopped due to an overlap of issues.

The labor committee continued for another reason: co-determination allowed only German employees to elect their representatives on the supervisory board. US, Canadian and Mexican workers were severely underrepresented, with only one US labor representative serving on the board (in a union seat). The labor committee at least allowed foreign employees to make their voice heard.

The Chairman's Council, chaired by Schrempp, did not replace the shareholder committee, but covered some of the strategic issues in a more focused way. The high-caliber members of this committee, including selected members of the supervisory board (e.g., Hilmar Kopper) and external CEOs and chairmen of international companies, "provided advice to management on global business strategy issues." In fact, elements of American and European corporate governance structures were combined to meet the specific requirements of a truly global company and the interests of the different stakeholders. The role of the Chairman's Council was to provide the "real" input into strategy, while the supervisory board had more of an auditing role. For example, Lord Browne, CEO of BP Amoco left the supervisory board, but joined the Chairman's Council (*refer to Exhibits 10 and 11*).

DC has changed its corporate governance system three times since 1998: initially, it was a consensus-oriented system, which then moved to checks-and-balances, and eventually became a CEO-centered model (*refer to Appendix 5 for descriptions of each model*). Participants should also understand the evolving role of the management board. *Exhibit 8* shows the decreasing number of management board meetings after the EAC was started. The management board was becoming a co-coordinator for different committees (*refer to **Figure 2** below and **Exhibit 8***).

Figure 2: Level of Supervision and Meeting Frequency in 2003

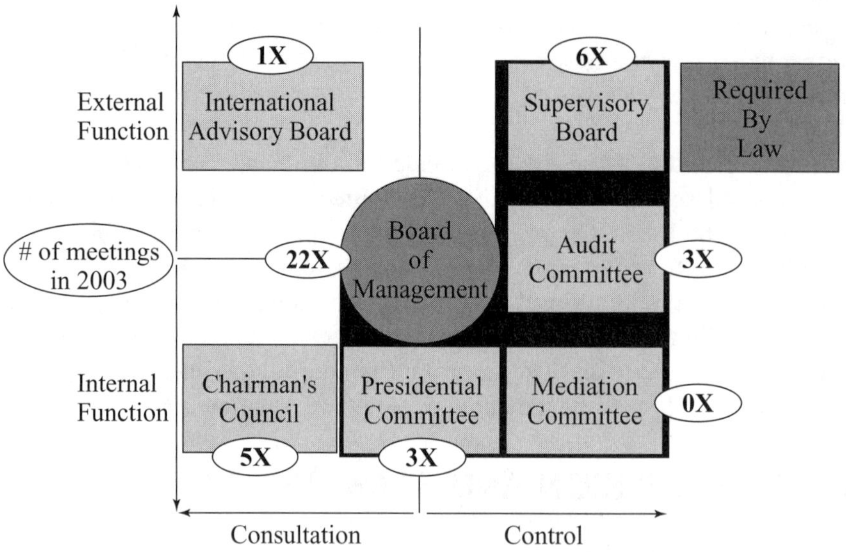

Note: Meetings of the Presidential Committee, Audit Committee and Mediation Committee are for 2002. The Presidential Committee meetings shown here are additional ones, since this committee always meets before meetings of the supervisory board.

Question 5: What global trends in corporate governance do you observe?

This question is intended as a preparation for the wrap-up. Participants should realize trends in corporate governance tend to be global and not company-specific developments. They apply to many companies in various industries.

In DC's case, the merger and the move into Asia started the corporate governance dynamics. In other companies, the corporate governance dynamics may be caused by changing industry structures, or relocation of major activities to a specific region (e.g., moving biotech research to the US).

WRAP-UP
KEY LEARNINGS FROM DC

Lesson 1: Learn as you go

A standardized approach to corporate governance in global corporations does not exist. Already, legal compliance for global companies is difficult because of contradictory national laws (pages 7 to 9 and *Exhibit 6*):

- *Legal configurations of boards differ:* In the US, board members have individual responsibility, as shown by the requirement for the CEO and CFO to certify financial statements. In Germany, members of the management board act collectively as "organs" of a company and have to sign off the books. Different laws lead to different (personal) liability risks.
- *Disclosure requirements* and accounting rules differ widely.

- *The appointment of auditors* is the obligation of the audit committee in the US, whereas the annual general assembly appoints auditors in Germany. In the US, the general assembly has fewer legal rights than in Germany.
- As *directors from the labor side* are not considered independent, a codetermined supervisory board in Germany can *never* have a majority of "independent" directors.

The list goes on, but good corporate governance goes beyond mere compliance with the law. It needs to add value in strategy formulation, monitoring and controlling its implementation, and in selecting/evaluating the leadership. Corporate governance in global companies also has to reflect the complexity of the business lines and organizational structures (e.g., global product lines, regions, key accounts). DC as a pure automotive/trucking company is relatively "simple" compared to more diversified giants such as Nestlé or Shell.

DC dealt with the complexity of global operations by creating various committees and councils. The outcome was a decision-making process that took the preparatory work into legally non-binding committees and the final decision-making into legally binding bodies:

- Supervisory board: In the division of labor between the Chairman's Council and the supervisory board, we assume the former focuses on the strategic discussion and idea contribution, while the latter looks more at compliance and has the final say in selecting members of the management board.
- Management board: Here the work is also shared. The Executive Automotive Council (EAC) details the product strategy (the dominant strategy component in an automobile company), while the full management board covers the functional aspects (e.g., finance, HR).

Although decentralization helps to effectively manage complexity, it also has its drawbacks. Without a strong leader, it can set free many counter-productive forces, leading to internal politics, inconsistency, duplication of efforts, etc. This is why Schrempp positioned himself as a "de facto" CEO after various crises, although without the legal responsibility of a CEO. Schrempp strongly relied on the corporate strategy department for keeping it all together.

For DC to get to the point, where they had a "workable corporate governance setup," it took several adjustments (*Exhibit 1*). This was learning by doing, with the executives of the management board playing an important role.

Lesson 2: In globalizing companies, the power shifts to the executives

Despite the public's high hopes of independent directors on boards, it is natural for power and responsibility in global companies to shift to the (full-time) executives, The risk exposure of companies similar to DC is considerable:

- *Currency risk:* As a result of selling in several dozen markets of varying importance, currency fluctuations or financial crises can easily multiply country risks.
- *Financial services risk:* As DC (among others) learned, the financial services division is a source of profit, but risky if managers are allowed to "buy" market share today at the expense of future earnings when the risk materializes. Leasing contracts can result in heavy losses if market prices fall below residual values in the books. When the contract expires, a loss occurs.
- *Technology risk:* Top management has to select carefully from various technologies. Missing one technology trend could mean suffering for half a decade. Should DC accelerate the fuel-cell technology to replace the combustion engine or not? With which fuel (e.g., natural gas or hydrogen)?

Should DC finance hybrids in the meantime? What about diesel particle filters, fuel efficiency, "drive by wire," lightweight materials, already relevant for tomorrow's cars?

- *Product liability and warranty risk:* The former is a nightmare in the US; the latter is a trade-off between accelerated market introduction and maturity of new technology or designs, such as increasingly complex electronics.
- *Branding risk:* As a result of multiple brands, incorrect product positioning can cause problems.
- *Exit risks:* Due to asset specificity (e.g., high cost of factory closures), it is not easy to change direction.
- *Residual risks:* Those that nobody had even dreamed about before they happened (e.g., the roughly $8 billion Kerkorian lawsuit over the "merger of equals").

The above are just some of the risks board members in the automotive industry have to deal with. Board members—whether on a unitary or a two-tier board—have to make decisions under immense time pressure, with limited resources, sometimes with a lack of knowledge/appropriate data on certain issues and other constraints such as the pressure of a consensus. Given these additional pressures, it is even more important for boards to focus on the procedure and ensuring internal checks-and-balances. In addition, boards have to install countervailing forces at the executive level, e.g., balancing a bold CEO with a strong CFO. For non-executive board members, it is more important to raise pertinent questions than to try to provide answers.

In DC's case, the supervisory board must have agreed to the shift in power to the management board. Otherwise, Kopper would never have accepted being a member of Chairman's Council with Schrempp being the chairman of this board!

Lesson 3: You cannot be everybody's darling

Expectations of corporate governance are high and have become conflicting. Not too long ago, capital markets told companies to "focus only on core businesses." Today, they favor greater risk diversification. Even if companies make commitments to the financial markets and creating shareholder value, they can cause much confusion. Do companies want to please short-term speculators or long-term investors looking to fund their children's education?

Besides the capital markets, considerable pressure comes from the press. When Novartis, widely regarded as an example of best practice in corporate governance, combined the two roles of chairman and CEO (but appointed a lead director), the company got bad press. In the past, however, the common US practice of "job integration" (combining CEO and chairman) had been praised as good for making bold decisions in contrast to the slow decision-making of the European consensus "wimps." Currently DC is criticized for not publishing the individual salaries and benefits of its board members. Given the many stakeholders (or sometimes only commentators), their widely differing interests and perspectives (and sometimes also their short memories), it is impossible for any global company to be everybody's darling—neither in their corporate governance practice nor in any other area. Creating transparency and providing reasons for certain decisions is the best way to limit the current wave of criticism against companies (and its potential impact).

In DC's case, the new supplement on Corporate Governance in the Annual Report can definitely be seen as a way of explaining what DC was trying to do.

KEY LEARNINGS FOR CORPORATE GOVERNANCE IN GENERAL

- When formulating strategy, good boards think through the whole business system rather than simply deciding on a low-cost or differentiation strategy. Board members ask about the segments served, where the company wants to go, at what speed, how to differentiate and what is the economic logic (*refer to* **Appendix 6** *for the strategy framework*).
- Successful boards try to understand the risks taken and make sure no one cuts corners in search of short-term gain.
- Good board members are independent, in the sense of having no personal ties with the management board.
- It is not the board's job to drive up the stock price.
- Board members realize the importance of board evaluations.

USEFUL QUOTES FOR THE WRAP-UP

The enormous potential of our brands, also in the growth markets such as Asia, is obvious. When we talk to the financial community, the strategy itself is not questioned. Instead we hear questions such as: Do you have the people, the financial capabilities and the required time to implement? My answer to these questions is yes.[7]

Jürgen Schrempp, September 2003

The U.S. car-buying public hoped Mercedes would bring a visible quality increase to match Chrysler's innovative designs. Instead, the Germans busied themselves maneuvering Chrysler's top brass out of the picture while doing nothing for the Chrysler line. No way to sell cars.[8]

Letter to the Editor, *Business Week,* October 2003

Unfortunately, in the past far too many CEOs have shown little interest in the balance of power that results from sound governance. As we have witnessed, some of them flagrantly abused the power they had been given. In contrast, authentic leaders know the difference between governance and management, and want the two to be clearly separated so that each can function effectively. They realize strong systems of governance will provide the stability needed when the company faces a crisis.[9]

Bill George, board member of Goldman Sachs and Novartis, 2003

SUGGESTED ADDITIONAL READING

For participants (with the case)

Dayton, Kenneth N. "From the Boardroom." *Harvard Business Review,* January-February 1984: 34–37.

Hambrick, Donald C. and James W. Fredrickson. "Are you sure you have a strategy?" *Academy of Management Executive,* Vol. 15, No. 4 2001: 48–59.

---

[7] "Ein hartes Stück Arbeit." Interview with Jürgen Schrempp. *Der Spiegel,* September 8, 2003: 116 ff.
[8] *Business Week,* October 20, 2003: 10.
[9] George, William W. (Bill). *Authentic Leadership: Rediscovering the Secrets to Creating Lasting Value.* San Francisco: Jossey-Bass, 2003; 155.

Sonnenfeld, Jeffrey A. "What Makes Great Boards Great." *Harvard Business Review,* September 2002: 2–8.

For instructors

Cases

Neubauer, Fred, Ulrich Steger, and George Rädler. *The DaimlerChrysler Merger: The Involvement of the Boards*. Case IMD-3-0771. Lausanne: IMD, 1999. The case gives a detailed background of the different behaviors of the board during the merger negotiations in early 1998. The case can also be found in *Corporate Governance: An International Review,* Vol. 8, No. 4, October 2000: 375.

Steger, Ulrich and George Rädler. *DaimlerChrysler Merger (A): Gaining Global Competitiveness*. Case IMD-3-0834. Lausanne: IMD, 1999. Explains both the situation the two companies faced prior to the merger and the modalities of the deal. The case was also published in Thompson, Arthur A., and A.J. Strickland. *Strategic Management—Concepts and Cases*. 12th edition, Boston: McGraw-Hill Irwin, 2001: C50-C63.

Steger, Ulrich and George Rädler. *DaimlerChrysler Merger (B): Shaping a Transatlantic Company*. Case IMD-3-0835. Lausanne: IMD, 1999. The second case in the series explains in detail the first steps taken to create one company, DaimlerChrysler. The case was also published in Thompson, Arthur A., and A.J. Strickland. *Strategic Management—Concepts and Cases*. 12th edition, Boston: McGraw-Hill Irwin, 2001: C64-C73.

Other material

DaimlerChrysler's website http://www.daimlerchrysler.com provides up-to-date information. Look under Investor Relations and then "Events" for recent presentations or "Reports" for Annual Reports.

DaimlerChrysler. Annual Report 2002. Corporate Governance, pages 150–55.

Carver, John and Caroline Oliver. *Corporate Boards that Create Value: Governing Company Performance from the Boardroom*. San Francisco: Jossey-Bass, 2002.

George, William W. (Bill). *Authentic Leadership: Rediscovering the Secrets to Creating Lasting Value*. San Francisco: Jossey-Bass, 2003.

Monks, Robert A.G. and Nell Minow. *Corporate Governance*. Cambridge, MA and Oxford: Blackwell Business, 1995.

Steger, Ulrich. "Beyond Preventing Crime: Where Does Corporate Governance Really Add Value?" *IMD Perspectives for Managers,* No. 101, September 2003.

Steger, Ulrich (ed.). *Mastering Global Corporate Governance*. Chichester: Wiley, 2004.

Strebel, Paul. "Focus on Corporate Specifics–Not National Clichés: Cross-Border Lessons from the DaimlerChrysler Merger." *IMD Perspectives for Managers,* No. 93, August 2002.

APPENDIX 1
OPENING STATEMENT

Why DaimlerChrysler?

Globalization, liberalization, deregulation and a general focus on core competencies led to strong M&A activity during the 1990s. Not surprisingly, worldwide global M&A activity hit new peaks. Between 1992 and 2001, the number of M&A transactions increased from 7,500 to around 28,800, with an increasing proportion of international mergers.

The car industry is mature, suffers from overcapacity and is rapidly consolidating. For companies unwilling or unable to grow internally, M&A may be the answer.

The DaimlerChrysler case study demonstrates very nicely how the two companies merged. It covers the developments after the deal was signed and continues up to 2003.

To start the class, it maybe useful to show a few slides from the merger negotiations:

Appendix 1A: *Geographic Spread 1997* – Chrysler was strong in North-America (90% of sales) and Daimler-Benz was strong in Europe (63% of sales).

Appendix 1B: *Combined Product Portfolio* – Very little product overlap between the companies.

Appendix 1C: *Timeline of the DaimlerChrysler Merger in 1998* – Shows the very different levels of board involvement during the merger negotiations. Interestingly, the Chrysler board was informed as early as February, whereas the Daimler-Benz management (executive) board found out about the deal only in April and the supervisory board a day before the announcement. This different behavior was caused by stricter disclosure laws in the US and the fear of "information leaks" in the German system.

This case is a real-life example of what happens after a merger (selecting people, making the synergies happen, designing a strategy, meeting growth targets) with a special focus on corporate governance and board issues.

Appendix 1A (continued)
Geographic Spread of Chrysler Corporation and Daimler-Benz AG

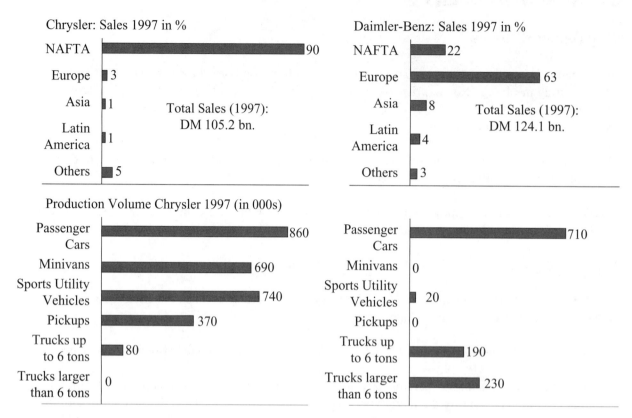

Chrysler: Sales 1997 in %

NAFTA 90
Europe 3
Asia 1
Latin America 1
Others 5

Total Sales (1997): DM 105.2 bn.

Daimler-Benz: Sales 1997 in %

NAFTA 22
Europe 63
Asia 8
Latin America 4
Others 3

Total Sales (1997): DM 124.1 bn.

Production Volume Chrysler 1997 (in 000s)

Passenger Cars 860
Minivans 690
Sports Utility Vehicles 740
Pickups 370
Trucks up to 6 tons 80
Trucks larger than 6 tons 0

Passenger Cars 710
Minivans 0
Sports Utility Vehicles 20
Pickups 0
Trucks up to 6 tons 190
Trucks larger than 6 tons 230

Note: DM = Deutsche Mark, €1 = DM 1.96

Source: DaimlerChrysler AG, as used in Neubauer, Fred, Ulrich Steger, and George Rädler. *The DaimlerChrysler Merger: The Involvement of the Boards*.
Case IMD-3-0771. Lausanne: IMD, 1999: 3.

Appendix 1B (continued)
The Combined Product Portfolio of DaimlerChrysler AG

		Market Segment						
		Compact	Medium	Upper Level	Luxury	Pickup	Minivan	Sport/ Utility
PRICE Level	High	A-Class ⬤	C-Class ⬤	E-Class ⬤	S-Class ⬤		Town & Country ⬤	● / ⬤ Grand Cherokee
	Medium	Neon ⬤	Cirrus/ Stratus ⬤	Intrepid/ Concorde ⬤	LHS/ 300 M ⬤	RAM ⬤	Caravan ⬤	Durango/ Cherokee ⬤
	Low	Neon ⬤	Breeze ⬤			Dakota ⬤	Voyager ⬤	Cherokee/ Wrangler ⬤

⬤ Mercedes-Benz models   ⬤ Chrysler models

Source: DaimlerChrysler AG, as used in Neubauer, Fred, Ulrich Steger, and George Rädler. *The DaimlerChrysler Merger: The Involvement of the Boards.* Case IMD-3-0771. Lausanne: IMD, 1999: 4.

Appendix 1C (continued)
Timeline of the DaimlerChrysler Merger in 1998

MERCEDES-BENZ					
January	**February**	**March**	**April**	**May**	**Fall of 1998**
January 12: Schrempp visits Eaton (17 minutes)	**Early February:** Cordes, Grube are informed	**March 2:** Schrempp, Cordes, Eaton, Valade meet in Switzerland and discuss corporate governance issues	**April 7:** Management Board is informed	**May 3:** Management Board approves	**September 18:** Shareholder Meeting of Daimler-Benz AG Approval rate: 99.89%
	February 12: First Meeting Schrempp, Cordes, Eaton, Valade		**April 16:** Kopper (head of Supervisory Board is informed)	**May 4:** Feuerstein (Works Council) is informed	**October 26:** Share Exchange ends 97% of DB shareholders exchange
	February 13, 14: Cordes, Hubbert, Zetsche meet Ford executives		**April 19:** Detailed Explanation to the Management Board	**May 6:** Supervisory Board is informed	
	February 17, 18: Financial Advisors enter			**May 7:** Merger Announcement	**November 17:** DCX shares are traded
				May 14: Daimler-Benz Supervisory Board approves	

CHRYSLER					
January	**February**	**March**	**April**	**May**	**Fall of 1998**
End of January: Eaton calls Schrempp	**February 5:** Board is informed	**March 5:** Update for Board	**April 7:** Update for Board (with bankers)	**May 5, 6:** Update for Board (with bankers and lawyers)	**September 18:** Shareholder Meeting of Chrysler Corp. Approval rate: 97.5%
		March 23: Update for Board	**April 22:** Update for Board	**May 6:** Unanimous Approval by the Board	**November 17:** DCX shares are traded
			April 29: Update for Board (with bankers)	**May 7:** Merger Announcement	

Source: DaimlerChrysler AG Prospectus, Company Sources, as used in Neubauer, Fred, Ulrich Steger, and George Rädler. *The DaimlerChrysler Merger: The Involvement of the Boards.* Case IMD-3-0771. Lausanne: IMD, 1999: 9.

APPENDIX 2
WHAT MAKES A GOOD BOARD?

Minimum Input from Boards

1. Defining and setting the goals/priorities of a company.
2. Establishing policies on what to do and what not to do.
3. Checking goals.

Value Added by Boards-Roles of Boards[10]

1. Expert advice—expert advisors to management.
2. Safeguards—ensuring proper disclosure of information.
3. Useful connections—contacts across industries, etc.

But who is the ideal board member? Kenneth N. Dayton[11] published a list of 11 criteria for selecting directors. Although the list dates back to 1984, it is still valid:

1. Integrity.
2. Wisdom.
3. Independence.
4. Valid business or professional knowledge and experience that can bear on our problems and deliberations.
5. Proven record of accomplishment with excellent organizations.
6. Understanding and general acceptance of our corporate philosophy.
7. An inquiring mind.
8. Willingness to speak one's mind.
9. Ability to challenge and stimulate management.
10. Orientation to the future.
11. Willingness to commit time and energy.

APPENDIX 3

Director Information Checklist

- Operating statements, balance sheet, statements of cash flow.
- Management comments explaining variances in results.
- Share of market information.
- Minutes of management committee meetings.
- Key media articles on the company and competition.
- Financial analyst reports for the company and major competitors.
- Consumer preference surveys.
- Employee attitude survey.

Source: Monks, Robert A.G. and Nell Minow. *Corporate Governance*. Cambridge, MA and Oxford: Blackwell Business, 1995.

---

[10] Carver, John and Caroline Oliver. *Corporate Boards that Create Value: Governing Company Performance form the Boardroom*. San Francisco: Jossey-Bass, 2002.

[11] Dayton, Kenneth N. "From the Boardroom." *Harvard Business Review,* January-February 1984: 34-37.

APPENDIX 4
MERGER RATIONALE AS SEEN BY DR. RÜDIGER GRUBE, CHIEF STRATEGIST OF DAIMLER-BENZ AG IN 1997

Daimler-Benz AG

Fact		**Associated Threat**
Daimler Benz was only No. 15 globally size wise	→	Volume disadvantage
Consolidation expected to continue	→	Size disadvantage and limited influence
Heavily exposed to mature markets	→	Limited growth potential
Very dependent on the premium market	→	Lack of "balancing mechansim"
Little production volume for amortizing heavy R&D investments	→	Cost disadvantage

Chrysler Corporation

Fact		**Associated Threat**
Chrysler only sixth-largest car manufacture	→	Volume disadvantage
Consolidation expected to continue	→	Potential take-over target
Very dependent on the mature North American market	→	Limited growth opportunities
Vulnerable in the sports-utility and minivan segment	→	Insufficient presence for premium cars
Limited access to premium technology	→	Know-how disadvantage

Source: Grube, Rüdiger and Armin Töpfer. *Post-Merger-Integration*. Stuttgart. Schäffer-Poeschel. Verlag, 2002: 98.

APPENDIX 5
TYPICAL CORPORATE GOVERNANCE MODELS

Name	Description	Advantages	Disadvantages
CEO- centered	This model is very often found in the US and France—where the role is often combined with that of the chairman of the board.	Allows for quick decisions and strategy implementation.	Tends to be a system with few checks and balances.
Checks-and-balances	This model is not only found in Germany in two-tier boards (e.g., executive and supervisory) but also in the UK, where the non-executive chairman and the majority of the independent directors define the boundaries within which the CEO and top management team can operate.	Good for CEO selection and control.	Often lacks strategic input.
Owner-centered	A big shareholder or the owner's family pull the strings.	Focus on owner's interest.	Succession.
Consensus-oriented	This model also looks at other stakeholders such as banks, suppliers and customers.	Close relationships with banks facilitate funding.	Slow decision-making. System is often built on "old-boy-networks."

Source: Steger, Ulrich. "Beyond Preventing Crime: Where Does Corporate Governance Really Add Value?" *IMD Perspectives for Managers,* No. 101, September 2003: 2-3; also published in Steger, Ulrich (ed.). *Mastering Global Corporate Governance.* Chichester: Wiley, 2004.

Appendix 6
Strategy Framework

Where will we be active?
(with how much emphasis?)
- Which product categories?
- Which market segments?
- Which geographic areas?
- Which core technologies?
- Which value-creation stages?

What will be our speed
and sequence of moves?
- Speed of expansion?
- Sequence of initiatives?

What are our values and goals?
What is our business model?
What risks are we taking?
Prerogative of the Board

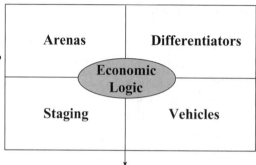

How will we win?
- Image?
- Customization?
- Price?
- Styling?
- Product Reliability?

How will we get there?
- Internal development?
- Joint ventures?
- Licensing/franchising?
- Acquisitions?

How we obtain our returns?
- Lowest costs through scale advantages?
- Lowest cost through scope and replication advantages?
- Premium prices due to unmatchable service?
- Premium prices due to proprietary product features?

Source: Adapted from Hambrick, Donald C. and James W. Fredrickson. "Are you sure you have a strategy?" *Academy of Management Executive,* Vol. 15, No. 4, 2001: 48–59.

Case: Trouble in the "Magic Kingdom"
Primary Chapter: Chapter 13 (Governance)
Secondary Chapter: Chapter 2 (Strategic Leadership)

Introduction: This case fits perfectly with Chapter 13 as it follows the chronicles the accusations of governance lapses at one of the world's most famous (and loved) companies. The case presents evidence of possible problems with the structure of the board, the combination of the CEO and Chairperson of the board, and the compensation of the executives. The case provides an opportunity to explore the relative effectiveness of various governance mechanisms.

Strategy Diamond: While the case is clearly focused on governance, there is ample history provided about Disney's entry into various new arenas and the sequencing of their corporate strategy over multiple decades.

Strategic Leadership: Leadership is the core of this case, as the governance problems are seemingly revealed in questionable leadership practices. Yet, Eisner's track record also has a long period of tremendous success. Some students will be turned off by his autocratic and self protective style. Others will be willing to overlook these stylistic issues because of the tremendous wealth he created for shareholders. But, now that super normal performance as gone away, even many of these students suggest it is time for a change.

Formulation/Implementation: The intent of the case is not really to explore the formulation/implementation linkage. However, like many cases, this is something that can be easily explored. Are Disney's current troubles simply a function of how Eisner implements his ideas? Or, has the entertainment industry passed him (and his strategies) by?

The Dynamic Nature of Strategy: Disney was a possible takeover target just prior to Eisner being brought in to rescue the company. He seems to have taken the firm 360 degrees, as the case ends with rumors about Disney being a target again. In between these crises are years of prosperity, and modest success, battles of personal wills, strategic missteps, and accusations of serious misdeeds. There is little in the way of competitive dynamics built into the case, but that perspective can easily be added by the instructor if that is of interest (perhaps by using other entertainment industry cases during the term).

TROUBLE IN THE "MAGIC KINGDOM" – GOVERNANCE PROBLEMS AT DISNEY

SUMMARY

The case discusses the governance problems at Disney. In late 2003, Roy Disney and Stanley Gold, both of whom were directors at the company resigned from the board in protest against the bad governance practices at Disney. They alleged that CEO Michael Eisner ran the company like a 'personal fiefdom' and that the board was only a rubber stamp to his decisions. The case looks into this allegation and studies a few instances which support the fact that Disney did not conform to the principles of good corporate governance. It also discusses the future of Disney in the context of the allegations of bad governance and the bid by Roy and Gold to oust Eisner from the company and install a new board.

TEACHING OBJECTIVES AND TARGET AUDIENCE

The case is designed to help students to:

- Understand corporate governance practices at a major media conglomerate.
- Appreciate the importance of good governance to maximize shareholder benefit, especially in large companies.
- Analyze the implementation of new governance norms at a large media company and the credibility of these norms.
- Examine the importance of critical issues like succession planning and board independence in large public companies.
- Study some of the important elements of good governance and the problems arising out of bad governance.

The case is meant for MBA/PGDBM students and is intended to be a part of the Ethics and Social Responsibility curriculum.

TEACHING APPROACH AND STRATEGY

This case can be used effectively in classroom discussions as well as distance learning programs. The moderator can initiate the discussion by asking students to comment on the importance of good corporate governance, especially for large public companies. Students can then discuss the governance practices at Disney and their efficacy. They can also discuss whether the new governance norms adopted by the company were credible or designed as an eyewash for analysts.

Students can then proceed to analyze some of the instances of bad governance at Disney. The discussion could conclude with an analysis of the future of the company in the context of the resignations of its directors and the allegations of bad governance.

ANALYSIS

1.

Since the late 1990s, Disney had been featuring regularly on analysts' lists of the worst boards in corporate America. It was generally believed that the Disney board was overly dependent on Eisner and that he could get the members to pass anything he wanted. Things were brought even more sharply into focus with the resignations of two of the company's directors, Roy Disney and Stanley Gold. In their resignation letters, both men had severely criticized Eisner and alleged that he did not run the company in accordance with the principles of good governance. They also planned to launch a public campaign to oust Eisner from office and appoint someone else, who would not run the company like a 'personal fiefdom'.

Disney had been facing several problems in governance. The board was completely overshadowed by Eisner, who also functioned as the chairman of the company. Most of the board appointments were made by Eisner, many from among his personal friends or acquaintances. Because he played an important role in the appointments, most of the board members did not oppose him on any issue and he held sway over them. Besides, many of the board members were not independent, having worked, or currently working at Disney. The question of member independence was also arbitrarily decided by Eisner, who did not always keep to the parameters specified by governance experts.

Eisner's compensation was also against the principles of good governance. Although his initial base salary was a rather low $75, 000, he was amply rewarded by the huge bonuses granted to him and the options that he encashed in the mid-1990s, when Disney stock was trading at around $40. However, even after the company's performance began to decline in the late 1990s to early 2000s, he was rewarded because of his options. His compensation and bonus too were fixed by the board in a rather arbitrary manner, as the compensation committee of the board was composed of mostly his personal friends. Therefore the method of fixing the compensation, as well as the actual compensation was criticized.

One of the issues on which Eisner was criticized the most was his reluctance to employ a system of succession planning. Even after nearly 20 years as the CEO of Disney, Eisner showed no interest in stepping down and had not even identified a possible successor, who would take over in case of an emergency.

Eisner was responsible for the company's problems to a great extent. As he exercised undue influence over the board, he was able to get his own way in most of the issues and was not answerable to anybody at the company. Although the company adopted new corporate governance guidelines in 2002, the resignations and the allegations of Roy and Gold suggested that they were probably just an eyewash meant to silence critics.

2.

Eisner was severely criticized for not identifying a successor at Disney. He had been at the helm of Disney since 1984, but showed no inclination to step down and make way for a younger person. He had never spoken publicly about who would follow him and was said to have the name of a possible successor in a closed envelope in his drawer. This was to be opened in case of an emergency that prevented Eisner from performing his duty. However analysts felt that it was not a good practice to keep the name of the next CEO, a secret from the board.

Analysts also said that, like most autocratic leaders, Eisner showed a disinclination to yield his power and position to another person. He did not want another person to start gaining importance (as the CEO-successor automatically would), while he was still in the organization. However it is always risky for a company not to have a formal succession plan. For instance, if something suddenly happened to the CEO, the company would be left without proper leadership because no one else would be prepared or trained to take up the top job. A lack of effective leadership would be likely to result in a fall in performance and may also attract takeover bids. If a successor is appointed arbitrarily or without a proper plan, the board would not be familiar with the person and it may take some time for normalcy to return. Therefore, experts in corporate governance advocate that all public companies have a formal and well developed succession plan, so that the transition from one CEO to another is smooth and the interests of the company and the shareholders are well protected.

There was also the question of independence of the board at Disney. It was observed that in 2002, out of the 16 board members, half were either former or current employees of Disney and therefore, were not independent. Out of the rest, another four or five members were personal friends of Eisner. Therefore, there were a negligible number of directors who were really independent. Besides, the question of director independence was arbitrarily decided by Eisner. Several people, who would otherwise not qualify as independent, were appointed to important committees. This was against the principles of good governance, which required that as many directors as possible be independent.

3.

Although the board at Disney was recognized as one of the worst boards in corporate America, the corporate governance problems at the company were brought sharply into focus with the resignations of Roy and Gold and their allegations against Eisner.

There were a number of people who believed that it was a mistake for the duo to resign. They believed that Roy and Gold could have accomplished their objectives more effectively as company insiders and members of the board. They would have been able to exercise greater influence over the other board members, if they had been board members themselves. By resigning they had alienated themselves from the company and lost considerable influence.

However, there were others who felt that it was a good move on the part of Roy and Gold to resign. By resigning, they were able to show their opposition more strongly and this would add conviction to their arguments. Besides, their resignations and the tide of publicity that followed, brought immense exposure to their campaign and highlighted the problems at Disney.

In the light of the resignations and the allegations that followed, the future of Disney became the subject of much speculation. It was believed that the threats to remove the CEO and the adverse publicity against the company's governance would expose the company to a number of takeover bids. There were also a number of demands from shareholder groups and investment companies to implement new norms that would improve the governance at the company. Many believed that if Roy and Gold succeeded in their intentions, Disney would reinvent itself as a new company with better governance norms.

ADDITIONAL READINGS & REFERENCES

1. **"Elbow Power",** The Economist, November 19, 1998.
2. **"Attributes of a Good Board",** BusinessWeek, January 24, 2000.
3. **"The Best and Worst Corporate Boards"** BusinessWeek, January 24, 2000.
4. Marc Gunther, **"The Wary World of Disney",** Fortune, October 15, 2001.
5. Marc Gunther **"Has Eisner Lost The Disney Magic",** Fortune, January 7, 2002.
6. **"Disney or Doesn't He?",** The Economist, January 10, 2002.
7. Ronald Grover, **"Eisner's Challenge: Beat the Buzz",** BusinessWeek, August 16, 2002.
8. Frank Ahrens, **"At AOL and Disney, Uneasy Chairs",** Washington Post, September 18, 2002.
9. **"Disney Top Shareholders Urged to Meet",** money.cnn.com, September 11, 2002.
10. Dan Milmo, **"Eisner survives as Disney board backs recovery plan",** The Guardian, September 25, 2002.

11. David Teather, **"Magic kingdom may expel Eisner"**, The Guardian, September 25, 2002.
12. **"Peacemaker to Aid Disney shake-up"**, news.bbc.co.uk, September 25, 2002.
13. **"Disney board backs Eisner's plan for growth"**, www.telegraph.co.uk, September 26, 2002.
14. **"Wobbly Kingdom"**, The Economist, September 26, 2002.
15. **"The Tragic Kingdom"**, The Economist, July 24, 2003.
16. Marc Gunther, **"Boards Beware"**, Fortune, November 10, 2003.
17. Ronald Grover and Gerry Khermouch, **"Renovating This Old Mouse"** BusinessWeek, November 10, 2003.
18. Ronald Grover, **"Stalking a Wily Prey at Disney"**, BusinessWeek, December 2, 2003.
19. Gary Gentile, **"Gold 2nd to Quit Disney Board"**, Newsday, December 2, 2003.
20. **"Wishing Upon a Star"**, The Economist, December 4, 2003.
21. **"A Tale of Two Boards"**, The Economist, December 4, 2003.
22. Ronald Grover, **"Eisner's Very Repressive Regime"**, BusinessWeek, December 4, 2003.
23. Richard Verrier and James Bates, **"No Succession Plan at Disney"**, The Herald, December 10, 2003.
24. **"Succession Planning"**, The Economist, December 11, 2003.
25. Marc Gunther **"Disney's loss is Eisner's gain"**, Fortune, December 22, 2003.
26. Marc Gunther, **"The Directors"**, Fortune, December 27, 2003.
27. Marc Gunter **"Mouse Hunt"**, Fortune, January 12, 2004.
28. **"Corporate Conflict"**, www.cbsnews.com, December 1, 2003.
29. **"Disney Corporate's Mouse Droppings"**, www.cbsnews.com, December 1, 2003.
30. **"Disney Heir Quits; Blasts Eisner"**, www.cbsnews.com, December 1, 2003.
31. finance.yahoo.com
32. www.disney.com

CHARLOTTE BEERS AT OGILVY & MATHER WORLDWIDE (B)

In May 1994, IBM awarded Ogilvy & Mather its entire worldwide advertising account—more than $500 million in annual billings.[1] After years of management turmoil and inconsistent positioning of company products by a multitude of advertising agencies, IBM's image had flagged severely. To consolidate with O&M, IBM resigned its 40 other agencies. The event was unprecedented in advertising history.

The consequences were also unprecedented for Ogilvy & Mather. Accepting IBM's offer required resigning from a $50 million Microsoft account and a $30 million Compaq account to avoid potential conflicts of interest. In response to the announcement, AT&T surprised both Ogilvy and IBM by withdrawing a $100 million account.[2] The IBM win was followed soon after by a $80 million multinational account for Kentucky Fried Chicken.[3]

Winning the IBM account—described by one executive as the greatest brand challenge of all time—created high excitement throughout the agency and drew industry attention to Brand Stewardship. One industry observer noted:

All the major agencies focus on brands. What is amazing is that no one had staked out this territory before. She came up with the term and put all the muscle of the organization behind it. The packaging was brilliant. The timing was brilliant. She preempted other agencies by stating the obvious before anyone else did, and by stating it in a way that resonates well with clients.

Some senior executives felt that, as confidence returned, individual initiative at the regional and WCS levels would grow and carry change forward. Commented Lazarus, "The most critical thing was having something to re-energize and re-ignite our organization." That same confidence worried other members of the senior team. Kelly O'Dea wondered whether the agency, flushed with success, was looking far enough into the future. Rod Wright agreed, noting, "We don't spend enough time looking five and ten years out."

In 1994, Charlotte Beers made several decisions that she believed would facilitate the implementation of Brand Stewardship. She charged each member of the Board of Directors with finding and hiring "one spectacular person—a young David Ogilvy." Beers herself hired a worldwide director for the IBM account; his title—Worldwide Brand Director, IBM—was the first at Ogilvy to include the word *brand*. In April, in recognition of the need for better coordination of North American client accounts, the U.S. and Canadian offices were consolidated into a North American region, headed by Shelly Lazarus. Rod Wright was asked to run O&M Direct North America, while continuing his worldwide roles as executive director of the Chairman's office and chairman, Asia/Pacific. In Europe, Beers appointed Mike Walsh CEO and moved Harry Reid to a new post, that of COO Worldwide. As COO, Reid would focus on administration and operations throughout the Ogilvy network.

Beers announced the creation of an executive committee in April. Members were Lazarus, O'Dea, Reid, Thedens, Wright, and Walsh and two other senior executives—Flavio Correa, president of O&M Latin America, and Steven Goldstein, chief financial officer. Their first major task was to align the firm's executive incentive and compensation system with Brand Stewardship and WCS priorities. Following

---

1. "IBM Combines Ad Accounts in One Agency," *Wall Street Journal,* May 25, 1994.
2. "Ogilvy's Big Bet on Big Blue," *Business Week,* July 4, 1994.
3. "Chicken Wings," *Adweek,* August 22, 1994.

months of what was described as a "heart-wrenching discussion," they reached a decision to link compensation more closely to performance and established their first long-term incentive scheme. More important, discretionary executive bonus funds were redirected from the geographic regions to WCS. In the past, only heads of agencies, countries, and regions had been eligible for bonuses. Now, not only would Brand Directors be eligible, but their allocations would come from a pool reserved previously for the geographic regions.

The regional chairmen of Asia/Pacific, Latin America, and Europe organized Brand Stewardship training conferences for senior account and creative executives. By the end of 1994, Walsh and Wright had completed production of a "Brand Steward's Handbook," outlining for all Ogilvy employees the practical and philosophical roles of each discipline in fulfilling Ogilvy's vision. The handbook provided guidelines for developing brands across borders—ones that were true to local markets, yet were developed in collaboration with the WCS teams.

Beer's theme for 1995 was "Deliver on Promises." Referring to the agency's signature color, she told her top executives to make good on the promises of Brand Stewardship by making Ogilvy's red redder. "Red for fuel, red for fury when necessary, red for urgency, red for passion. Those are the reds we want in our company. In the next year."

Research Associate Nicole Sackley prepared this case under the supervision of Professor Herminia Ibarra as the basis for class discussion rather than to illustrate either effective or ineffective handling of an administrative situation.

NEILSON INTERNATIONAL IN MEXICO (B)

Neilson International proceeded with the venture with Sabritas S.A. de C.V. in Mexico and launched the Milch brands, nationally, in the fall of 1993. By fall of 1994, the portfolio of brands had been expanded to included Jersey Milk, Sweet Marie and Capri (also known as Choclairs). Although research coverage in Mexico was not as detailed in scope as it was in Canada and the United States, the Milch business was estimated to have captured 16 to 20 per cent of the Mexican chocolate confectionery market. In 1994, Neilson sales to Mexico exceeded $23 million. This constituted the largest portion of Neilson's international sales. Additional capacity had to be built in Toronto.

Milch brands were widely accepted by consumers at the one peso price, and competitive activity intensified with many of the local companies launching products at similar retail price points. Other import bars continued to be offered in the range of 1.5 to 3.0 pesos, reinforcing the position that Milch brands offered imported quality chocolates at Mexican prices. In late 1994, Nestlé purchased La Azteca from Quaker, whose Carlos V brand was the market leader in Mexico.

Milch distribution continued to grow with Sabritas' increased effort to add dedicated confectionery routes. Although competition remained intense, Milch bars dominated the shelves in the North and North Western markets of Monterrey, Obregon, and Tijuana—specifically because the culture in these regions was influenced heavily by the United States. Milch's distribution efforts were especially strong in the traditional local retail stores known as "tiendas"; distribution into other channels was also increasing.

The venture was modelled on a true partnership, with both companies benefitting from increasing sales and share growth but independently responsible for their own profitability. Neilson was progressively providing greater input on marketing issues. In fact the Toronto-based Neilson project manager had been visiting Mexico every two weeks. Sabritas meanwhile continued to concentrate on distribution and merchandising. Together, the partners had plans to expand the Milch line throughout Latin America.

In December of 1994, faced with a tremendous deficit in its Current Account, the newly elected president of Mexico, Ernesto Zedillo Ponce de Leon was forced to float the peso freely against the American dollar. The devastating impact was a more that 40 per cent devaluation in the peso. With the economic and social challenges this crisis presented, and both increasing commodity and packaging costs, both partners were suffering from significantly reduced margins. Something had to be done.

Raising the price to the next logical retail price point, 1.5 pesos, would essentially cover the devaluation, but cause a host of other dilemmas. For example, would the change be followed by other confectionery companies? How would consumers, and the trade, respond to a 50 per cent price increase? This latter question raised a more fundamental concern about the overall stability and potential of the Mexican market.

CISCO SYSTEMS, INC.: ACQUISITION INTEGRATION FOR MANUFACTURING (B)

Cisco Systems, Inc.'s (Cisco) acquisition of Summa Four Inc. (Summa Four) officially closed on November 5, 1998. By the beginning of 1999, it had become apparent that the integration would take longer and was going to be more challenging than originally anticipated. While many changes to the manufacturing operations were well under way, the job of integrating the two companies proved to be exceedingly complex. Summa Four had multiple products in different development generations, a manufacturing facility in Manchester, New Hampshire, and 210 employees who were resistant to being "Ciscoized". David Keller, vice president of manufacturing, new product introduction, and technology at Cisco Systems, knew that the remaining issues needed to be resolved quickly if Cisco was going to be able to successfully integrate acquired companies at the same breakneck pace as in recent years.

With the closing of the Summa Four deal, Cisco assessed Summa Four's product lifecycles and began to assign R&D and production to the most appropriate facilities. Cisco initially suggested moving the Summa Four engineering group from Manchester to Cisco's Chelmsford, Massachusetts facility. This would have allowed Cisco to quickly integrate the next generation development effort, Project Alpha—one of the major reasons for the acquisition—into their own development process. Chelmsford, with over 1,000 Cisco employees, provided what appeared to be an ideal location. As it turned out, many of the Summa Four engineers were unwilling to relocate to the new site. After some discussion Cisco allowed them to remain in Manchester with the understanding that the facility would work closely with Chelmsford to implement Cisco's new product introduction processes. Manufacturing on the Alpha would also begin in Manchester, and then be transitioned to Cisco's Silver Creek site for the ramp-up to full production volumes. The production of Summa Four's existing products was also expected to continue at Manchester until they were eventually phased out. Given the strength of sales in early 1999, this would probably not be for another two to three years.

While many of Summa Four's employees saw significant benefits resulting from being a part of Cisco, they did feel that there were some "rough spots" along the human dimension of the integration. One senior Summa Four manager said,

I think the acquisition has been very successful, and Cisco has developed a good science for doing due diligence, evaluating the technical capabilities of a company and determining an appropriate price, but they have done far less with HR. When Cisco first showed up, they announced that the engineering organization would be kept together for one to two years, that manufacturing would disappear within six months, and everyone else could expect their jobs to last less than a year. As it turned out, things now look much longer term. While the future looked quite tenuous initially, that is much less the case now.

One of the areas in which Summa Four's employees felt particularly vulnerable was their benefits and the detailed terms of employment. Gary Wilder, operations manager at Summa Four, echoed much of the sentiment of his employees when he said,

Apparently, at Cisco the answer to every question in HR is "It's on the Web." Being a big, internet-based company, Cisco doesn't expect people to get answers from other people when it comes to everything from their 401K to vacation to sick leave policies. Instead, they expect people to "Look it up on the Web." At Summa Four, as a small company, everything was based on personal contact. In fact, there were lots of manufacturing people at Summa Four who did not have regular access to a terminal and certainly had not dealt previously with these kinds of issues through a web site. Many of our hourly workers thought of the Web as something you encounter in an old barn.

These people needed lots of help, including personal contact. When they didn't get it, people felt hung out and the Summa Four managers had to spend a considerable amount of time with individual employees going through a lot of detailed fundamentals. Basically, Cisco made a lot of Internet-literate assumptions that did not hold.

Despite the rumbling from some Summa Four employees, Cisco's HR department could point to at least one resounding success. Since the acquisition, only one of Summa Four's 210 employees had left, and that individual had not been eligible for the retention incentives because they joined the firm after the acquisition was announced. This statistic was particularly important given that Summa Four had historically experienced significant turnover at all levels due to the hot job market in New England.

Some Summa Four employees felt that the retention incentives were a significant factor in their decision to stay. In addition to the usual stock option package, in this case, Cisco had offered every employee a retention bonus equal to a significant percentage of their salary at the time of the acquisition simply for staying for two years. Additionally, Cisco agreed to honor the Summa Four bonus system for the first six to nine months, before installing the Cisco bonus system for key managers.

As Keller reviewed the Summa Four integration process, he wondered what lessons he should take forward to the next acquisition. How adamant should he be in requiring the acquired company to quickly merge into Cisco's structure? Should he allocate additional HR resources to ease the transitions, or was some grumbling just to be expected? Would Cisco be able to retain the acquired Summa Four employees, or was the retention bonus just buying time before a mass departure? These questions and more raced through Keller's mind as he began to shift his attention to the impending Selsius Systems acquisition in Texas.

BLUE WHALE MOVING COMPANY, INC. (B)

Despite the concerted efforts of Brad Armstrong and Blake Miller, co-founders of Blue Whale Moving Company, Inc., the company was not as profitable as they had hoped and was becoming increasingly difficult to manage. It was now October 1994 and everyone knew that something needed to change. It was becoming evident that Blue Whale's "growing pains"[1] reflected the problems that the fast-growing company had been experiencing since its inception six years earlier. They had tried everything they could think of: a number of different managers, various forms of marketing, and modifications to their management controls, but nothing seemed to work. As the two owners pondered probably the most important decision of the firm's existence, each thought about what could be done to address Blue Whale's constantly changing needs.

Blue Whale Moving Company was co-founded by Brad Armstrong and Blake Miller. Blue Whale had been an extraordinary success for the first few years. From an initial investment of $10,000 in 1988, revenue soared to $1.7 million by 1993. But it was now October 1994 and everyone knew that something needed to be done.

BLUE WHALE MOVING CO.

The local moving business that Armstrong and Miller established was supposed to be different from other moving companies. The two entrepreneurs constantly stressed the importance of customer service in their organization. While the mainstream attempted to undercut their competition in price wars, Blue Whale targeted the large number of customers who felt that a professional, stress-free move had an intangible value for which they would pay a premium.[2] Armstrong and Miller recognized that moving meant a transition for most people, whether good or bad, and that these individuals were particularly sensitive and responsive to the perceived quality of the move.

OPENING BRANCH OFFICES IN HOUSTON AND DALLAS

In April and September of 1991, Blue Whale opened up branch offices in Houston and Dallas, each of which was only about a 4-hour drive by truck from Austin. Armstrong and Miller decided to let two employees that had worked in sales in the Austin office manage the branches. In addition to the standard professional relationships Miller established, he helped the managers hire a team of movers and a support staff for the office. After the initial start-up, he visited the branch offices two days out of every week to further train the managers in the Blue Whale style and support them as they began to make their own managerial decisions. Once both sites were active, this meant that Miller was on the road four days out of the week. Miller was particularly happy about expansion into the Dallas market because he had grown up there and felt a great deal of pride in owning his own business at such a young age. Armstrong saw the move more as an opportunity for revenue growth.

---

[1] "Growing Pains" was how Brad Armstrong referred to the problems Blue Whale experienced in 1993-1994.
[2] "Austin's Gentle Giant: The Blue Whale Moving Company," *Moving and Storage Times*, Vol. 23, No. 24, March 15, 1993.

Over the first few years, neither Houston nor Dallas performed especially well. While Houston provided a great deal of revenue, the large size of the city caused a number of problems. This size meant greater distance moves, which dramatically increased truck maintenance and personnel costs. Additionally, it was difficult to focus marketing on one particular area because there were so many neighborhoods throughout the city. The phone in Houston was constantly ringing, but most of the moves were not very profitable due to the high costs. Dallas, on the other hand, was having trouble drumming up business at all. Since moving crews were frequently idle, the manager and salesmen tried to book any moves they could. This often meant low price apartment moves that the movers found tedious and unprofitable. Not surprisingly, turnover in Dallas was very high.

Despite the concerted efforts of Armstrong and Miller, the Blue Whale branch office in Dallas was losing a lot of money. They had tried a number of different remedies in Dallas: a number of different managers, various forms of marketing, and modifications to their management controls but nothing seemed to work. As the two owners and their Dallas manager prepared to meet for probably the most important decision of the firm's existence, each thought individually about what could be done to make Dallas profitable. Would it mean cutting costs? Increasing revenue? Both? Could the branch become profitable at all?

Many employees felt that the problems that the Dallas office was experiencing now were simply the most obvious symbols of the problems that the fast-growing company had been encountering since its inception in Austin six years earlier. In that sense, Dallas took on even more importance because the situation there posed questions relevant to the entire company. It was becoming clear that as Blue Whale grew, it was increasingly difficult to manage it as if it were still a small company. It seemed that something needed to be done. Armstrong and Miller both understood that their decisions about Dallas could determine the fate of the business as a whole.

"GROWING PAINS" IN AUSTIN

Brad quit his law practice and began working full-time at Blue Whale in late 1991. His marketing expertise was an important aspect of the rapid growth Blue Whale experienced in the 1991-1992 period. In part because Brad was then working full-time, Blake felt confident that he could take time off without hurting Blue Whale. As a result, he decided to take a sabbatical from April, 1992 to April, 1993, during which he rarely checked in on Blue Whale. He had been experiencing tremendous pressures (such as the death of his father and breakup of his marriage) and his marathon hours were no longer sustainable. During Blake's absence the movers came to rely on Jim Traynor, who had not yet been promoted to vice-president, to solve their management problems.

Beginning during Blake's absence and continuing after his return in 1993, a rift began to develop between Blue Whale's movers and its managers. This developed because of the lack of understanding that each "side" had for the other. Movers felt that management was becoming less and less approachable and that the owners and managers would do anything they could to "cheat" the movers out of money. Brad and Blake, on the other hand, felt that the movers were "spoiled" by the already inflated commissions they were receiving and were unsympathetic to the financial problems of the firm.

The feeling among Blue Whale movers was that it was the movers who "made it happen." They felt that the awards and honors being accumulated by Brad and Blake were a direct result of the movers' efforts in the field on a daily basis. Furthermore, they felt that Brad and Blake not only failed to appreciate this, but also tried to lower their pay on a regular basis. The feeling culminated at the end of 1993. When the movers expected, but did not receive, the year-end bonus in 1993 that had been distributed in each of the previous two years, they made their anger known. In addition, a medical insurance plan that Brad and Blake had promised would be in place by mid-1994 never materialized. Throughout the year, morale continued to fall and a number of experienced movers decided to seek other employment opportunities.

Brad and Blake understood the movers' feelings and tried to respond to the issues that were raised. Blake wrote a letter to all Blue Whale employees in December 1993, detailing the reasons for the missed bonus (see Exhibit 1), but it was met with subdued hostility. Additionally, the owners had begun experimenting with ideas on how to adjust the pay scales of its movers downward. Since movers' pay was commission-based, every time Blue Whale increased its prices (about ten percent once a year) the movers effectively got a pay raise. Also, at the end of the year, each mover received a performance-based raise equivalent to one or two percent of the price of a move. Since movers generally received between fifteen and twenty percent of the price of a move, this structure essentially gave movers a pay raise of over 20 percent each year.[3] This labor cost was spiraling out of control and Brad and Blake felt they needed to address it. The owners knew that their movers were making more than the industry norm, but they were not clear on how to communicate the need for these changes and achieve buy-in from each of their employees. They tried weekly company-wide meetings, but those quickly deteriorated into "bitch" sessions, as opposed to being a forum for interactive communication.

When problems with the movers began to arise, Blake stopped "hanging out" with them on a daily basis. He and Brad decided that it blurred the line between management and employee and wanted to make it clear that the two owners had a *business* to run. It was at this time that the owners installed Jim Traynor as vice-president. When Blake retreated into the office, it made the movers even more distrustful of management than they had been before.

Interestingly, Armstrong was not around the office very much during 1993 and 1994. Traynor and Miller referred to Armstrong as their "bombardier," someone who would come in occasionally and drop little bombs all over the office. It seemed that when Armstrong was in the office, employees spent a lot of time putting out "fires" and cleaning up loose ends. Some employees grew resentful of this intrusion. Furthermore, these employees felt that Armstrong was "all talk" and that most of the hype and awards he and the firm had received were "just for show."

HOUSTON AND DALLAS

Neither Houston nor Dallas was proving to be very successful. Dallas had had three managers in the previous year and none were able to achieve the revenue goals for which Armstrong and Miller had hoped. In May, one manager left to start his own moving business, but soon rejoined Blue Whale and was reassigned as the Houston manager. He replaced a Houston manager that Miller had characterized as "a person who couldn't say no." This manager did not do a good job of managing the business in a cost-efficient manner. He wrote checks for everything and costs soon ran out of control. Unfortunately, the manager that moved from Dallas to replace him promptly broke his ankle upon arrival and was unable to assume his job responsibilities for six weeks.

The person that replaced the departing Dallas manager was previously in sales. The problem was that even with Miller's help two days a week, this manager proved totally unable to sell business in the local area. He instead spent his time putting out the operational "fires" that would arise on a daily basis. Armstrong and Miller replaced this manager in September with the administrative person who

---

[3] $((.02 \text{ raise} + .2 \text{ base})(1.1 \text{ increase}))/.2 \text{ base}$

had assisted each of the previous two managers. The young woman had a penchant for details, but had only been with the company, and the industry, for six months. Armstrong and Miller decreased operations to one truck and one moving crew and told the manager to just try to keep the schedule full. They knew their lease agreement and yellow pages advertisement ran until May 1995 and they did not want to renege on any of their commitments.

The Issue of Control

Brad and Blake's control of their managers and their employees had historically been relatively informal. Each put a great deal of time and effort into empowering employees instead of enforcing restrictive control mechanisms. With a background in law, it was important to Brad that this empowerment be done in a non-legalistic manner. He often noted his personal preference for influencing his employees' actions by sharing the values and vision of Blue Whale, rather than applying rules, regulations, or legal documents. Similarly, Blake felt that the best way to inculcate these ideals was through personal interaction with employees on a daily basis. The two owners agreed that the values that were the most important to the success of Blue Whale were best learned in an informal and unobtrusive manner.

In 1994, however, the two owners worried that they had allowed control of the business to slip away from them. They began to establish "interpersonal agreements" with all of their managers (see Exhibit 2 for one agreement). Even though Brad and Blake stressed that these agreements were solely intended to make a manager's responsibilities clear to both parties, the managers generally felt that the agreements were like "contracts."

FUTURE PLANS

Expanding the Business

It was important to Armstrong and Miller that Blue Whale expand in both its current markets, as well as in untapped markets. In order to reach their objective of 100 cities by the year 2000, they would need to make a concentrated effort to expand by any means possible. At question was the timing of the effort, as well as the manner of expansion. Their efforts to compete in the Houston and Dallas markets were not as successful as they had wished and no one was sure exactly what it would take to make this goal a reality.

Future Development

In addition to the growing pains that Blue Whale was experiencing in 1994, there were a number of major goals that Armstrong and Miller set out to accomplish in the near future. These would undoubtedly play an important role in the development of the firm.

New Facility

In 1995, Armstrong and Miller planned to move the administrative office in Austin to a new building two miles away. The building was desirable for many reasons, including ample parking for trucks and trailers, specially designed office space, and a 300,000 cubic foot warehouse that could be used for storage of household items.[4] The lease on the building was much more than in the current location, but Armstrong and Miller both felt that the money could be easily made up by the storage capability. Storage is an important and lucrative aspect of the moving business. It is not uncommon for customers to have a lag between when they must vacate their old premises and move into their new one. Storing their goods in the interim period would increase the profitability of the job significantly. While Blue Whale employees were excited about the new facility, they were still a little hesitant due to the events of the preceding two years.

Franchising

The Blue Whale vision statement had set a goal of doing business in 100 cities by the year 2000. The manner in which Armstrong and Miller planned to fulfill this goal was to franchise the Blue Whale concept in the 100 "most promising" U.S. markets.[5] They hired a franchise consultant to put together a proposal and were currently compiling all of the business information and procedures necessary for a operations manual that would be given to each new franchisee. Armstrong was very excited about franchising, while Miller felt that Dallas and Houston should be straightened out before entering into this mode of expansion.

FOUNDATIONS FOR THE FUTURE

The two founders had tried a variety of management structures and controls over the preceding years, yet they remained unsure about which was the most effective. They liked the idea of having a manager responsible for each Blue Whale city, but at the same time they wondered whether the administrative functions of the branches could be better handled at the main office in Austin. Additionally, they wondered whether a branch manager should be responsible for profit and loss or should their responsibility be only to build sales in the local area. They pondered whether the best person to manage each branch was a mover, as they had historically hired, or maybe just a salesperson with a lot of local contacts. Finally, they questioned whether it might be beneficial for one or both of them to become more involved in the business again.

Everything seemed to go so smoothly when the business was smaller and people were guided solely by the Blue Whale vision of customer service. Now the business was more complicated and the need to formalize many of the managerial issues made control of the business and its employees much more difficult. Despite the "growing pains," Brad Armstrong and Blake Miller were as excited as ever about the possibilities that lay ahead of them. As they planned their discussions about the fate of the Dallas office, each thought separately about what would be necessary to get Dallas, Houston, and the entire business moving in the right direction again.

---

[4] The current location was extremely cramped and dilapidated. There was little room for parking trucks and next to no room for storage.

[5] Blue Whale International, Inc., franchise proposal, 1995.

Exhibit 1. Letter describing missed bonus written by Blake Miller

December 22, 1993

Dear Blue Whaler:

As you all know, there has been a great deal of discussion about bonuses at year end. We regret the confusion, while at the same time feel some anger and resentment about feeling compelled to give a gift. Nobody, not even employers, want to feel like they have to give somebody a present. However, it was always our intention to give all of you substantial Christmas bonuses like we did last year. However, we never intended to lead anyone to believe that Christmas bonuses are a "sure thing," or guaranteed. Likewise, all bonuses, including Christmas bonuses are intended to be unexpected, discretionary, "gifts," from the company to its employees. If you were mislead into thinking that you would be guaranteed extra money at Christmas time, we take full responsibility and apologize to you and your family. The truth of the situation is that the company just doesn't have the extra money, this year, for year-end bonuses.

We, in our good intentioned, but overly optimistic, minds thought that we would be able to give each of you a gift of $50-$100. In order for us to have given each of you this kind of gift we would be required to find $2,500-$5,000 personally and this was not currently acceptable. A gift of $10-$20 was possible but we were afraid that it would be considered an insult. Likewise a gift of a ham or other token gift may have been perceived in poor light.

We are angry at ourselves for creating this situation. In the future, I hope that you will never "count" on receiving anything beyond your normal pay. In this way, when bonuses are given, you will be all the more pleased.

We hope that you will accept this explanation and apology and stick with us into 1994 as we pursue our joint vision of 2000.

Yours Truly,

Blake B. Miller

Brad L. Armstrong

BLUE WHALE MOVING COMPANY, INC.

INTERPERSONAL AGREEMENT - JIM TRAYNOR

<u>DISCLAIMER</u>

IT IS NOT THE INTENT OF THIS DOCUMENT THAT A LEGAL CONTRACT BE CREATED HEREBY. THIS AGREEMENT IS MADE BETWEEN THE UNDERSIGNED EMPLOYEE OF BLUE WHALE MOVING COMPANY, INC. AS A MANAGEMENT TOOL ONLY AND NEITHER BLUE WHALE NOR THE UNDERSIGNED INTEND TO CREATE AN EMPLOYMENT CONTRACT WITH THE USE OF THIS DOCUMENT. THE UNDERSIGNED SHALL FOREVER BE "EMPLOYEES AT WILL," AS THAT TERM IS UNDERSTOOD IN THE STATE OF TEXAS, UNLESS AND UNTIL A DOCUMENT ENTITLED "EMPLOYMENT CONTRACT" IS CREATED AND SIGNED BY THE PRESIDENT AND SECRETARY OF BLUE WHALE MOVING COMPANY, INC.

I. **Parties**. This Up-Front Contract is made between Jim Traynor, and Blake Miller & Brad Armstrong.

II. **Purpose**. This agreement is intended to clarify Blake Miller and Brad Armstrong's expectations of Jim Traynor's job performance and standards, to list and specify with precision what Jim Traynor's job activities include, how Jim Traynor will be evaluated with regard to those activities, what attitudes Jim Traynor will be responsible for demonstrating, what skills he will be required to master and how he will be taught those skills, what resources will be available to Jim Traynor, the tangible personal and corporate results that are expected of Jim Traynor, and the consequences of his performance. It is our intent that Jim Traynor strive to consider all the positive and negative consequences of his decision-making on the company at large in the present and how his decisions will impact on the company of the future.

III. **Expectations**

A. **Activities**

1. **Strokes**. Jim Traynor will give two (2) real strokes daily and will report on those strokes monthly until giving strokes is an integral part of his personality. You have a fabulous opportunity every morning to greet your movers, inspect their equipment, and instill some pride and self-esteem in your work force before they start their work day. You also have an invaluable opportunity to build trust, loyalty and commitment. The Blue Whale culture has always been built during this thirty minute period; use this time effectively and comprehend the value of it.

2. **Monthly Reports**. Jim Traynor will prepare monthly reports in writing for Blake Miller and Brad Armstrong to include information on the following:

Safety/Employee Health	Training Agenda & Syllabus
Equipment Road Worthiness	New Employees
Financial Condition	Outside Sales
Strokes	Customer Satisfaction Rating
Networking Activities	Corporate Culture Development
Publicity Efforts	

3. **Semi-Annual Goal Accomplishment Report**. Jim Traynor will prepare a semi-annual report in writing setting forth every employee's personal goal accomplishment from their list of 5 things or otherwise. This report will then be used to honor and recognize individuals for their goal setting and achievement skills at our Labor Day and Spring parties. These reports must be delivered to Blake Miller & Brad Armstrong no later than two weeks

prior to the scheduled party. It is also important for me to know the names of those individuals who have excelled in representing the Blue Whale ideal, over time, so that they might be recognized in some meaningful way.

4. **Networking**. Jim Traynor will make and attend one (1) meeting per week with new contacts for the purpose of spreading the Blue Whale vision and philosophy and thereby create other personal centers of influence for Jim Traynor and Blue Whale. Specifically, you should contact chambers of commerce, real estate agents/brokers, former and future Entrepreneur of the Year award recipients, Lion's Club, Rotary, Young Men's Business League, etc. It is our intent that these meetings be designed to create outside sales opportunities for commercial accounts.

5. **Teaching**. Jim Traynor will identify, recruit from within, and teach new leaders how to be an officer of Blue Whale and all that it stands for. The goal is for Jim Traynor to replicate himself continuously thereby building the base of Blue Whale's future success by exhibiting and demanding Blue Whale's code of excellence. You must practice what you preach.

6. **Results**.

a. Accomplishment of Blue Whale's vision in its entirety, daily, through recitation of the vision during quotes, before commencement of the move, and during the follow-up call back. Maintain a customer satisfaction rating above 9.0 at all times. The vision, when used consistently and correctly will help you build relationships with your men and through the communication of the Blue Whale culture and work ethic you will discover an immediate reduction in problems such as damages, poor equipment maintenance, customer complaints, poor telephone skills, poor booking skills/practices, poor call-handling practices, theft, trash accumulation and uncooperative employees.

b. An empowered work force who is given the opportunity to change and grow using his or her innate abilities to perform their job and know that the use of their day has out lived their day by creating trust, loyalty and family.

c. Each employee is a "success" because he has decided what he wants to have, do, become and share, and is progressively accomplishing those goals through the accomplishment of Blue Whale's organizational goals.

d. Twelve percent (12%) profit annually.

e. Innovation and cutting-edge leadership in our industries. You must be constantly vigilant about identifying problem areas before they become destructive and tailor solutions to these areas which may aid or benefit the entire organization.

f. Jim's constant and steady growth. Regular trips outside his comfort zone. You are a professional mover and should be proud of that title. Your movers' self-esteem will only be as good as your self-esteem. Decide how you feel about being a "mover." This is not the typical moving company from our past and you must not treat your people the way you have been treated by other moving companies.

g. $2,000,000.00 in gross sales for 1995.

h. Every employee that you have contact with knows that you are **SOMEONE TO BELIEVE IN** because you demonstrate through your attitude, the strokes you give and the up-front contracts that you honor, that you **BELIEVE IN THEM**. You must create a "feeling" among your men such that they will do anything that you ask them to do, not because they are afraid of you, but rather because they respect you and yes, "love you."

i. A well groomed and attired work force, constantly improving their personal habits, behaviors, and attitudes because they can see that they are not "just movers." Specifically, every mover must be clean and clean-shaven, with neat, clean and combed hair, wearing a clean uniform, and be drug and alcohol free.

j. An educated work force capable of teaching the GIRI material. Jim must quickly master all new material so that he can teach it to his subordinates. A work force that has mastered basic communications including reading, writing and standard American English speech and sentence structure.

k. Improve all employee's feelings of professionalism, energy, success, team spirit, and vision. Specifically and immediately, you must begin a communication skills training program.

l. A clean and well policed work environment free from cigarette butts and other debris. Your employees must take pride in themselves and their work. Therefore, you have a duty to keep your work environment clean and neat and free from garbage. Likewise your trailers must be clean and their interiors organized. Trailers must have blinkers, brake lights and brakes in good working order, road worthy, and properly licensed and registered..

m. A minimum sixty percent (60%) referral rate.

n. A smoke-free, tobacco-free, and alcohol-free environment twenty-four (24) hours per day.

o. A work force that knows and believes that you will always make yourself available to hear their complaints, ideas and suggestions.

p. Full compliance with all Blue Whale company policies including but not limited to its theft reporting policy.

q. Develop a relationship with your local NationsBank banker.

r. Learn how to read and understand our financial statements.

s. Learn how to manage your petty cash account, log and moneys. Be able to teach your staff proper money handling procedures and regularly audit and inspect for compliance.

t. A plan of action by 1 December 1994 for a profitable moving supply operation.

u. A plan of action by 1 February 1995 for a profitable records storage operation.

v. An ICC authority, if necessary.

B. **Attitude**

1. Jim will dress appropriately during work hours with an emphasis on role-modeling excellence in his punctuality, appearance, language, grooming, personal behavior, habits, truthfulness, honest, integrity, ethics and morals. Benchmarks for success include wearing a tie daily unless you have to work in the field and a coat and tie on days when you have networking/sales appointments, discontinued use of profanity, moderate use of alcohol, if any, continued role modeling of the importance of the Golden Rule and The Work Ethic, continued attention to the Truth in all dealings, and adherence and enforcement of Blue Whale's tobacco-free and alcohol-free work place policies. Jim will encourage others to excel in these same areas.

2. Every employee of Blue Whale who finds himself handling moneys is instantly in the position of fiduciary and as such accepts the highest responsibility to his employer; Jim must rigidly and relentlessly adhere to and profess the proper procedures for complying with this fiduciary duty.

C. **Skills**

Jim Traynor will be involved in continued training of one kind or another forever. This training may be delivered by in-house trainers, including Blake Miller & Brad Armstrong, or by outside contract trainers and off-site seminars. Jim Traynor will be responsible for recommending plans of action and specific courses and areas of training that he desires to Blake Miller & Brad Armstrong for approval. Blake Miller & Brad Armstrong will be Jim Traynor's direct coaches.

IV. Resources

A. Human

1. Blake Miller & Brad Armstrong are available to Jim Traynor at least two (2) hours per week each for specific skills training and as otherwise needed during the work day and after hours by phone at home.

2. Jim Traynor will have at his disposal every employee of Blue Whale.

3. Jim Traynor may use vendors of services, supplies, equipment and information, including but not limited to, the categories of public relations, printing, aviation, event planning, accounting, insurance, marketing, computers, real estate, advertising, training, etc. It is required that Blake Miller & Brad Armstrong be involved at a decision making level with the selection of the person, company or product that fills each of these categories. You are specifically **NOT** authorized to sign any contract without Blake Miller or Brad Armstrong's prior approval.

B. Organizational

1. The Vision as a tool.

2. Manuals as they become available.

3. Video tape training materials as they become available.

4. Specific skills training and role-models.

5. Corporate culture and all that it entails, including but not limited to our video training tapes, notes, and kadas; written and oral histories of the company; phone quote audio training tapes; public relations press kits; customer reference list.

C. Financial

1. The budget.

2. Authority to hire and fire.

3. Direct access to Accountant & Attorney.

4. Direct access to public relations contact.

5. Monthly corporate financial information.

D. **Technical**. Computers, telephones, fax machines, postage machines, copiers, furniture, trucks, trailers, moving supplies and equipment, office supplies and equipment, and petty cash.

V. **Reviews**. Jim Traynor will receive informal inspections and reviews as deemed desirable by Blake Miller & Brad Armstrong. Jim Traynor will receive formal job performance reviews in writing annually after receiving the year-end financial reports. Additionally, .as the Austin branch manager, Jim receive written inspection reports after every such operational readiness inspection.

VI. **Consequences.**

A. **Positive.** If Jim Traynor substantially performs the contents of this agreement, he will continue to receive his salary and will insure his place in Blue Whale's future. He will have demonstrated his management & leadership skills and will be in line for promotion in terms of salary and responsibility. He will receive regular and deserved continued performance strokes and will be in line for regular raises, bonuses and other perquisites. If Jim Traynor fulfills the requirements of this agreement in its entirety, he will receive an outstanding performance stroke during a special company meeting along with the keys to his company leased 1995 Lexus LS400. The current financial condition of the company makes it difficult to foresee exactly how your future financial increases will be structured. It is currently our intent to integrate a form of incentive bonus based on market performance for market heads. There will be further discussion and decisions on this subject after the company at large reaches profitability.

B. **Negative.** If Jim Traynor fails to substantially perform the contents of this agreement, he will receive counseling and instruction at the first failure in any area. Once instruction has been given and understanding demonstrated, he will receive a negative injunction at the next failure to perform any element of this agreement. At that time he may also suffer a financial penalty which will be deducted from his pay. Subsequent failures could lead to demotion, reassignment, reduction in salary, and/or termination.

BLUE WHALE'S VISION

By 31 December 2000, Blue Whale will have become pre-eminent in the moving and storage industry, with locations in 100 cities worldwide.

Marked by complete commitment and dedication to the highest standards of moral and ethical excellence, Blue Whale will be delivering an exceptional service experience created uniquely for each customer, by radiating positive energy throughout our team, and reflecting that love and respect upon our customers and all those who we serve.

Only then will successful evolution into other markets, products and services be guaranteed.

Dated October ___, 1994.

_____
Jim Traynor

_____
Blake B. Miller

_____
Brad L. Armstrong

Research Associate Adam Friedman and PhD Student Chris Long prepared this case under the supervision of Professors Sim Sitkin and Laura Cardinal as a basis for class discussion rather than to illustrate either an effective or ineffective handling of an administrative situation. Laura Cardinal was at the Fuqua School of Business, Duke University at the time the case was developed. She is currently at the Kenan-Flagler Business School, University of North Carolina at Chapel Hill.